P9-BIE-721

SEATTLE SURVIVAL GUIDE

THE ESSENTIAL HANDBOOK FOR CITY LIVING

THERESA MORROW

SEATTLE SURVIVAL GUIDE

THE ESSENTIAL HANDBOOK FOR CITY LIVING

SASQUATCH BOOKS
SEATTLE, WASHINGTON

Printed in the United States of America

Library of Congress Cataloging-in-Publication Data
Morrow, Theresa. 1949–
The Seattle survival guide : the essential handbook for city living / by Theresa Morrow.
p. cm.
Includes index.
ISBN 0-912365-36-6 : $16.95
1. Seattle (Wash.)—Handbooks, manuals, etc. 2. Seattle (Wash.)—Directories.
3. Seattle (Wash.)—Description—Guide-books.
I. Title.
F899.S43M68 1990 90-9127
979.7'772'0025—dc20 CIP

Design by Kris Morgan
Interior illustrations by Eldon Doty

Sources for Seattle Survival Guide maps:
page 15: City Kites/Michael Aurigemma
page 18: Puget Sound Multiple Listing Association
page 19: Seattle Engineering Department
page 36: Seattle Survival Guide Research
page 41: Washington State Department of Transportation
page 44: Puget Sound Council of Governments
pages 49, 51: Metro
page 53: Seattle Survival Guide Research
pages 55–57: Seattle Engineering Department
page 59: Port of Seattle
page 60: Seattle Survival Guide Research
page 62: Washington State Department of Transportation
page 75: City of Seattle Office of Long Range Planning
page 99: Seattle Survival Guide Research
page 188: David Buerge
pages 213, 216: Seattle Arts Commission
pages 246, 249, 251–52: Seattle Police Department
page 278: Seattle Survival Guide Research
page 282: Boaters Task Force
page 288: Department of Parks and Recreation
pages 301–02: Seattle School District

Sasquatch Books
1931 Second Avenue
Seattle, WA 98101

CONTENTS

INTRODUCTION

When I was in seventh grade, Interstate 5 came blasting through my Capitol Hill classroom, flattening it into parochial-school rubble. I should have known then that someday this city would need a survival guide.

Today it's road warriors on Aurora, coyotes in Ballard, sharks in city hall, falling graupel in Fremont, congestion on Pill Hill, neon elephants on Denny. It's a jungle out there!

This is a guide to meeting the challenges and adventures of urban living, whether they be rubble-inspired or something as mundane as withstanding freeway gridlock. Of course, survival in this most livable city is not the same as survival in New York, Washington, D.C., or even San Francisco. Street smarts here have more to do with the Mercer mess and where to sit at the Opera House than whether the mayor will be in jail tomorrow.

That's why this survival guide is like the city itself. It's fun—filled with inside tips from a web of networking Seattleites. It's serious—full of statistics on who we are and why. It's eclectic—including everything from the best day for a picnic to what the city looks like from the top of the Darth Vader building.

This is *not* a guide book for tourists. It's designed for people who live in and around the city. It's for those of us who know Seattle as home base. You won't find information about which Gray Line tour to take; you *will* find out why your neighborhood park has been closed at night, and who to call about it.

Because this is a complete handbook, we are giving you the unpleasant facts as well as the pleasant. This book is not for the squeamish. Seattle is, after all, a city, and such things as car thefts and child abuse do happen here. Pretending they don't won't help. Take the facts presented here and use them to ask questions and to make decisions as you navigate your way through the urban maze. Nothing would make us happier than if your *Seattle Survival Guide* became dog-eared from being poked at with your irate finger as you ask your local hospital or school, "What about this??!".

To gather the mountain of information which follows, we organized an army of researchers who, armed with notebooks and insatiable curiosity, stormed city departments, cabbies' hangouts, libraries, espresso bars, schools, and just about every file cabinet in town. We interviewed Seattleites in the African-American community, parents facing the school system, stockbrokers after work, activists at The Dog House restaurant, and artists in galleries. We learned how to spell Syttende Mai, where to go to drink coffee with the city's bigwigs, how to talk to panhandlers in Pioneer Square.

Each chapter of the *Seattle Survival Guide* is divided into sections. First comes the basic information, an overview to the main issues facing us today. We know this is risky—issues change—but we want to give you a measuring stick of where the city is and an indication of where it is going.

About the charts and tables: The figures used are the latest available at press time. We rattled a few glass cages to get the most up-to-date information available. Still, incredible as it seems, in 1990 often only 1986 numbers are available.

The Inside Edge items come from astute people in the know. Some express ways to cut through bureaucratic red tape, some give tips for easier living (that best day for a picnic, for example), some are just plain good ideas.

Finally, the resource lists tell you where to go for further help and who to get hold of for more information. As in all books like this, we must warn you that things change. Groups come and go. Call ahead to confirm that a group is still functioning from the same office and at the same hours.

We had exceptional help from city employees in preparing this book. A special acknowledgment goes to the folks at the Seattle Public Library Information Center and to those answering the Citizens' Service Bureau phone lines at city hall. Jim Diers at the Office of Neighborhoods admirably restrained himself from rolling his eyes when he was called by yet another researcher. The people at Allied Arts received their share of phone calls, too. And thanks to the thousands of people who bumped into one of our researchers and ended up being barraged with questions about where they lived, what shortcut they took to work, and what their freeway of choice was.

A special thanks goes to the researchers and contributors themselves: Jayne Askin, Bruce Barcott, Brenda Bell, Lisa Blacher, Carlene Canton, Barry Foy, Rod Franklin, Linda Fullerton, Kim Hill, Stephanie Irving, Mary Miller, Fred Moody, Margarita Overton, Lori Park, Jon Waite, Kate Wolf. They did yeomen's work, especially Kim Hill, who tracked down the more obscure facts herein. And thanks, of course, to those at Sasquatch Books, especially Chad Haight, who can take credit for the original idea and for convincing me to enter the fray, and Anne Depue, whose sharp editorial eye and unflappable demeanor are immensely appreciated.

Despite everyone's best efforts, we have undoubtedly missed some significant facts about Seattle, or failed to list groups and individuals who contribute to the city. Now it's *your* turn to help—at the back of the book we invite you to outline the important issues and organizations you feel should appear in the next edition of this book.

Those who have been impatiently awaiting the *Seattle Survival Guide* sometimes ask what overall impressions I've come away with after looking at Seattle through a magnifying glass. There are several of course, but the most prevailing impression is that Seattleites have great hope for the future of this growing city. That hope comes from an unabashed confidence in each and every resident's ability to effect change. When there's crime, whole neighborhoods rise up and shout it down. (For instance, in Mt. Baker, currently threatened by gangs, residents say, stubbornly and simply, "We'll stay and fight.") When our minority communities feel the pinch, they organize. When they say they'll have blacks in the boardrooms—well, we know they will. And when the woman running the shelter sounds tired and discouraged when asked about the few beds available for teen-agers living on the streets, we know she's still there talking to the kids.

It's this eager sense of empowerment and willingness to help that sticks with me, and it's to those anything-but-apathetic Seattleites that this essential handbook for city living is dedicated.

Theresa Morrow
September 1990

CHAPTER

1

SEATTLE FROM A–Z

BOOKS

GHOSTS

INVENTIONS

PIRATES

TATTOOS

FIRE HYDRANTS

HISTORY

NUNS

STAIRS

UFOS

Seattle has the largest per capita moviegoing population in the country. It has 24,002 stairs to help residents up and down the hills. It favors rose tattoos. So, it seems appropriate to toot the city's horn with a pursuit of such trivia—so here it is, a completely arbitrary list of factoids about Seattle, from A to Z, with a certain amount of liberty taken with the alphabet.

A

Number of clams in an **acre** of clams: 1,568,160

Number of clams Ivar's sells in a year: 200,750

Number of years it takes for Ivar's to sell an acre of clams: 7.81

B

Bookcity. Annual per household expenditure for books in Seattle is $106.91. The nationwide average is $57.

Seattle 1987 book sales (in millions): $77.4

Seattle bookstores per 10,000 households: 1.56

Source: U.S. Dept. of Commerce

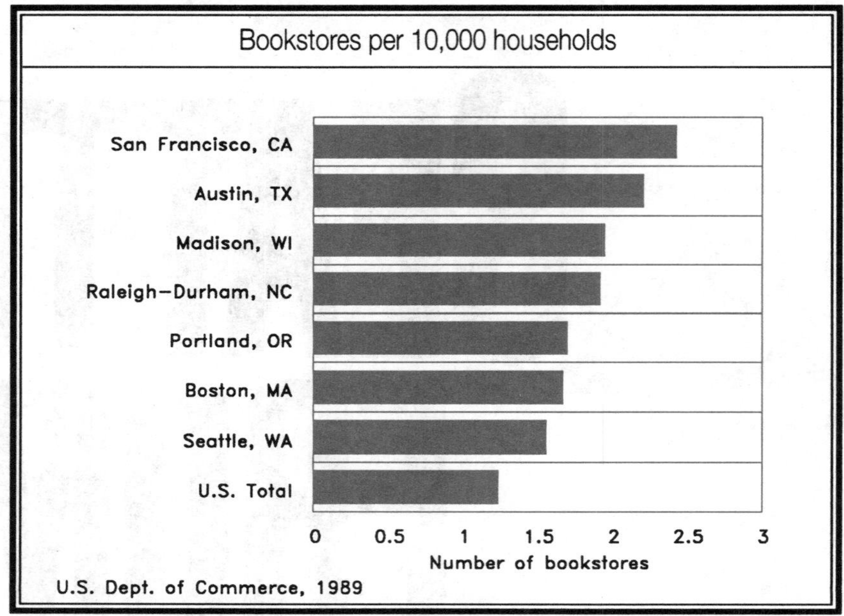

Elliott Bay Book Co.—where tourists stop in their tracks when they see the stacks of books—stocks about 110,000 titles. The all-time Elliott Bay best seller? *If You Want to Write* by Brenda Ueland, a small paperback of essays on creativity.

And the University Book Store is one of the nation's largest booksellers of general-interest books. Number of titles: 79,100

C

The best place to go for **chess**-playing—or Parcheesi or Go, for that matter—is the Last Exit on Brooklyn right near the UW. It's at 3930 Brooklyn Avenue NE. And there's the Seattle Chess Club, founded in 1911 and with an average of 70 checkmating members. 523-1553.

Co-ops: Seattle is Co-op Capital, what with the likes of REI and Group Health. REI, a Seattle native, is the nation's largest co-op and, thereby, also Seattle's largest, followed by Group Health Cooperative of Puget Sound, then Puget Consumer Co-op and People's Memorial Association. Then there are hundreds of smaller co-ops, not to mention agricultural co-ops and credit unions.

Why is Seattle such a co-op happy city? People surmise it's because of the strong Scandinavian community here (co-ops have long been a part of Scandinavian culture), and part of that pioneering spirit that is always looking for alternative ways of getting things accomplished.

Want to start your own co-op? Call Puget Sound Cooperative Federation, 4201 Roosevelt Way NE, Seattle, WA 98105, 632-4559. Carol Bergin is the director.

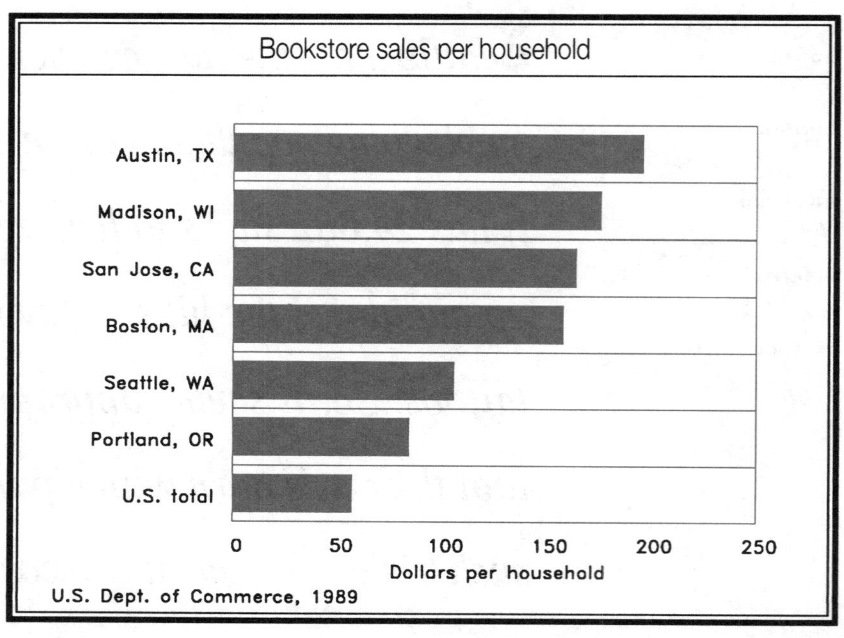

REI or Group Health membership numbers are status things these days; the closer to #1 your card, the more native you are.

The #1 card at Group Health Co-op went to Bill Jordan. The story goes that Jordan was an employee who was sent to get the new membership cards printed. He did—and grabbed the choice one.

Lloyd A. Anderson is #1 at REI and has been since 1938. His status was confirmed when the first REI co-op card was issued in 1951.

D

Whatever happened to the Sunset **Drive-in**? And how about the Sno-King? Ah, well, VCRs haven't totally done away with drive-ins. There's the Midway in Kent, the Valley 6 in Auburn and Puget Park Drive-in in Everett. But in case you're going for old times sake, make sure your AM car radio works—most drive-ins no longer have those speakers that hang on the window, but use an AM broadcast instead. And in case you think nobody goes to drive-ins anymore, think again; at the Valley 6 they warn you to come early on weekends.

For people crazy about **dials**, here are some fine, old-fashioned street clocks to wait for your dates under:

Ben Bridge's Jewelry, Fourth and Pike
Benton's University Jewelers, 3216 NE 45th Street
Carroll's Fine Jewelry, 1427 Fourth Avenue
Century Square, 1529 Fourth Avenue
Elliott Bay Book Co., First Avenue S and S Main Street
Fifth Avenue and Pine Street in front of Jay Jacobs
First Hill, Madison St. between Summit and Minor avenues
Greenwood Jewelers, 129 N 85th Street
The Hongkong & Shanghai Banking Corp., 705 Third Avenue
Lake Union Cafe, 3119 Eastlake Avenue E
Menashe & Sons Jewelry, 4532 California Avenue SW
West Earth Co., 406 Dexter Avenue N

E

That old **Elephant** Car Wash has attained cult status. The original car wash, started in 1951 at 2763 Fourth Avenue S, was not called Elephant Car Wash, but when some enterprising owners decided to find a gimmick in 1956, they held a contest for a new sign and logo. Several sign companies worked on the project and the winning logo was the flashing pink, neon elephant that can now be seen at two locations in Seattle, and in Tacoma, Federal Way, and Puyallup (these last are known as Lil' Elephants). Wouldn't you know—there are also two in California.

The signs are famous. They were featured on the cover of *Car Wash* magazine (oh, did you miss that issue?). And Elephant Car Washes were mentioned in *Cosmopolitan* as a place the '90s woman can still go to meet a nice guy (mostly referring to the young urban professional males that frequent the place for their weekly car washes, although the guys who work at Elephant say it was referring to them).

As if that wasn't enough, a New York ad agency asked permission to use the name and logo on a New York phone book. Ah, the price of fame.

As for local recognition, you can find a miniature elephant logo on the ceiling of Von's, a downtown restaurant on Pine Street. Tourist momentos include stickers, key chains, post cards, and the like.

The Elephant signs are some of the last remaining big flashing neon signs around. Why, even historical preservation types were on their side when talk started a few years ago about reducing the number of large signs around Seattle. One thing's sure: The elephants will never forget their support.

The two Seattle car washes are now owned by Bob Haney.

As for **elevators**, there are 5,000 of them in downtown Seattle buildings (the Columbia Center alone has 46). The fastest elevator in Seattle, at Two Union Square, goes 1,600 fpm (feet per minute). And here's a fact for you: Seattleites get stuck between floors in elevators at the rate of about one per month.

F

There are 2.8 dogs per **fire** hydrant in Seattle.
Number of fire hydrants in Seattle: 17,855
Number of dogs licensed in the city: 50,000

G

Ghosts mostly hang out at the Pike Place Market. Supposedly an Indian woman who glows white walks through walls on the lower level of the Market. Whoever spies her will die an unusual death, so there aren't too many around who can admit to seeing her. Also at the Market is the Fat Lady ghost, a 300-pound woman who fell through a ceiling and landed on a table.

By the Bead Store an Indian ghostman, who never really appears, plays tricks now and then.

In Georgetown, at a turreted house called the Georgetown Castle, a ghost called Sarah is followed around by a portrait of a Sicilian, for some reason.

In the Arctic Building, the ghost of someone who jumped out a window during the market crash in 1929 hangs around. He's probably still looking for his cronies at the old Arctic Club.

At Capitol Hill Methodist Church, the Rev. Daniel Bagley and his wife supposedly haunt the corridors, enveloped in a bluish light.

H

Seattle can **house** 12,835 visitors on any one night in some 65 **hotels** in the city and its suburbs. Average cost? $65 per room. Cheapest area? Near Everett—about $43 per night. Most expensive? Downtown, where the average cost of a room is $75/night.

The city is full of **history**. The Museum of History and Industry, the city's preeminent historical museum, opened in 1951. It's at 2700 24th Avenue E and is open from 10 a.m.–5 p.m. daily.

To join, call 324-1126 for a membership application. Memberships are from $25 for individuals ($15 for seniors) up to $1,000 for Founders.

Most neighborhoods have an historical society—check branch libraries for contacts.

For a list of some other area historical societies, see page 361.

I

Inventiveness, inventions, and inventors—we've got them all. But what's really been invented here? You need to visit the UW Engineering Library patent depository to find out. You can do a patent search there to find out if anyone else has the same idea for that domestic animal toothbrush you've been working on.

But first, a word on that product you know will make you a million bucks: Only 10% of products patented make it to the marketplace. Most patents pending these days are for computer technology and biotech products. (Another factoid is that 45% of all U.S. patents are foreign, and half of those are Japanese.)

Companies like Nintendo, Boeing, and John Fluke hold the majority of Seattle's patents. (Boeing has 3,008 patents from the years 1969 to 1989. In 1944, it patented a car—if that particular idea had taken off, Boeing could have been the Ford of the West.) And there are the patents for Seattle Blues (jeans), the Seattle Foot, and trademarks like the Happy Face (courtesy of David Stern).

But here we list a few patents obtained by inventive locals.

Polyploidy oysters. These oysters don't spawn and therefore can be eaten year round. They are the second animals to be patented in the U.S., and the polyploidy technique was invented by UW professors.

A thumb-supported **reading magnifier**.

Movies that talk back, a talking video that allows you to program your name, and other words, so that the movie characters talk directly to you. Invented by a Seattle man.

A shirt hold-down device. Invented by a Bellevue woman, the device is a piece of cloth that wraps around under your crotch and attaches to shirttails with elastic fasteners. Her husband was undoubtedly thrilled.

Taco plate. This plate has raised molded plastic ridges to hold your taco upright. From the picture in the patent book, it looks as if you could hold about three tacos on the plate—plus vegetables and a dairy product.

Mousetrap. Yes, it's true, a Kent man actually invented one. It's a bucket (or pit) filled with water and covered with a rather tippy bridge. Bait is on one end and the mouse goes after the bait and tumbles off the bridge into the water. Hmmm—no one said it was a *better* mousetrap.

A vehicle message-holder was invented by an Indianola man. The message can be flashed on a sign from one car to another, presumably to tell someone what a lousy driver he or she is—or to ask for a phone number.

A Seattle woman invented **a tray for auto passenger compartments**. Cheese and crackers, anyone?

A wind-powered floating home may sound like a sailboat, but it looks like a windmill set atop a bathtub.

A flashlight/umbrella. A Seattle man invented an umbrella that is also a flashlight—maybe that'll put a stop to those lost umbrellas.

Hat with audio earphones.

A lifting handle for toilet seats.

Article of **wearing apparel with an erasable writing surface**—for those quick memos.

And that **toothbrush for domestic animals** was patented in 1959 by Bird Eyer of Seattle.

Guitar-shaped pasta. Well, that was patented by a guy from Illinois, but we're throwing it in just to show that Seattle isn't the only place to come up with weird patents.

J

Jimi Hendrix's grave. No, he's not under that rock at the zoo, even though the plaque is dedicated to him. Hendrix is buried at the Greenwood Memorial Park Cemetery, 350 Monroe, Renton. The cemetery is open until 7 p.m. daily.

The grave is marked with a flat gravestone, located near the sundial. It's a popular site, especially in summer when the cemetery receives at least 10 calls a day about it. The number is 255-1511.

K

Is the idea of a retractable roof on the **Kingdome** a good one? It might be a good one, but it won't work, according to a study done for King County. A Seattle engineering firm found that putting in a movable roof system would be too expensive, so the idea was dropped. So we have to be happy with the Kingdome's concrete roof, the largest unsupported concrete roof in the world.

We love **kites**. Lots of Seattleites belong to kite clubs. There's a Washington Kite Flyers Association and the American Kite Flyers Association and avid kite flyers are trying to get a Western Kite Flying group started. If you are a member of one of these clubs, you are privy to all the contests during the year. Two big contests are: the Stunt Kite Regional, in June at Long Beach; and the International Kite Festival in late August, also at Long Beach. To join a club, ask for an application at any kite shop.

L

Seattle's been named the Most **Livable** City by so many publications we don't pay attention to it anymore. Fortunately, people keep lists of those mentions.

Seattle's rankings

1990—*Bicycling Magazine*, Best North American City for Bicycling
1990—*Sports Travel*, Fifth Hottest Sports City
1990—*Working Mother* magazine, March issue, Sixth Best U.S. Metropolitan Area for Working Mothers
1989—Conde Nast *Traveler* magazine rates Seattle among the world's top 10 travel destinations
1989—Louis Harris survey, Second Best Place in U.S. to locate a business
1989—*Money Magazine*, #1 City to Live in America
1989—*The New York Times* calls Seattle the nation's espresso capital
1989—Prentice Hall, *Places Rated Almanac,* #1 Most Livable City in U.S.
1989—*Savvy* magazine, Second Best City for Raising Kids (Minneapolis-St. Paul is 1st)
1989—*Town and Country* calls Seattle "a summer resort with it all"
1989—*USA Today*, #1 City of the Future
1989—*Zagat United States Hotel Survey*, City with the Best Hotels in the U.S.

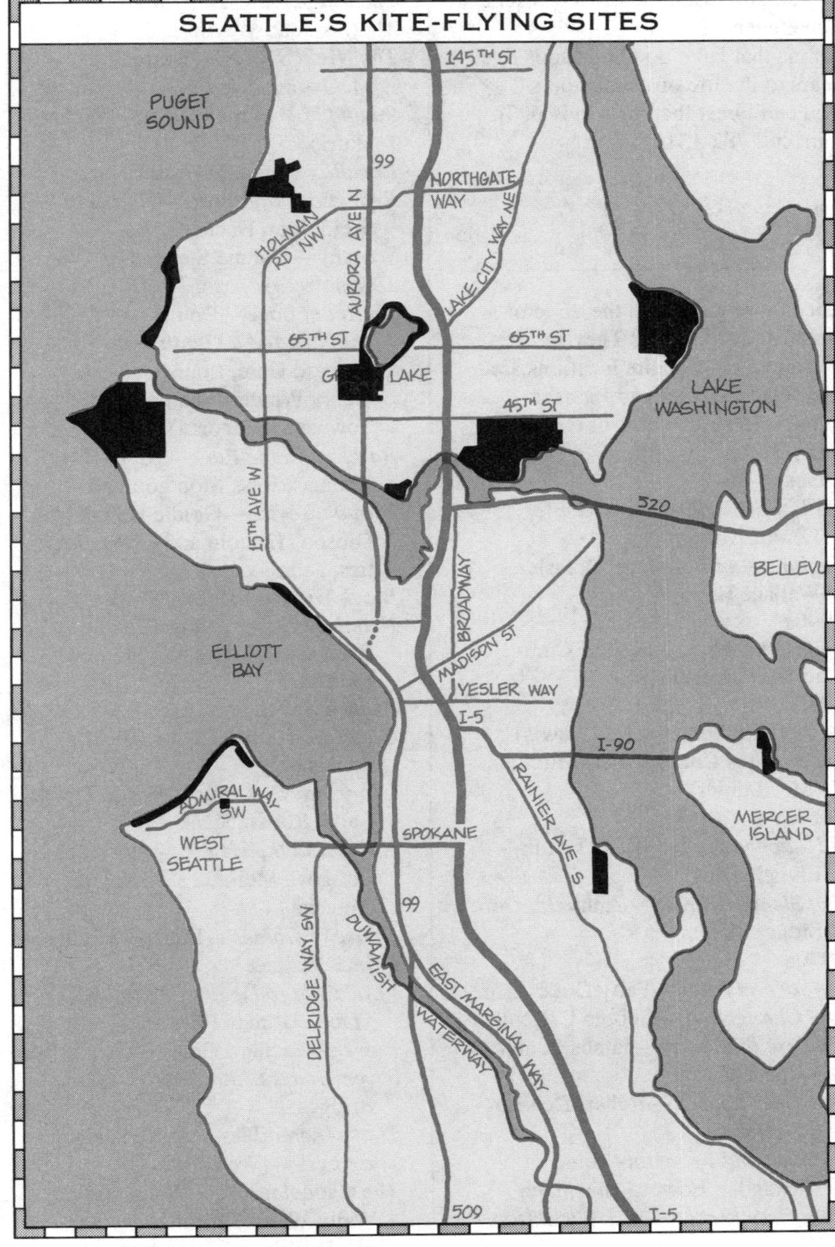

1988—*Money*, 11th best place to live
1988—*Savvy*, nomination for Best City for Women
1986—Rand McNally, *Vacation Places Rated*, #1 Vacation Destination
1986—Partners for Livable Places, Most Livable City
1982–86—Rand McNally, *Places Rated Almanac*, #1 Recreational city
1984, 1975—National Conference of Mayors, Most Livable City
1983—Rand McNally, *Places Rated Almanac*, Fifth Most Livable City
1977—*Family Circle* magazine, Top Ten Best Cities
1977—*New West* magazine, Best City
1975—*Harpers* magazine, Most Livable City
1972—*Town and Country*, "a city for Americans to covet"

Then there are the **lawn** bowlers. The Queen City Lawn Bowling Club claims that lawn bowling "adds five years to the life of its members." You can't beat that for survival. To join, call 782-1515.

M

See those guys with the director's chairs and the lights? They're filming **movies**—favorite locations are Pike Place Market and Pioneer Square. Here are some of the more famous films made here:

1930s

Call of the Wild—Clark Gable, Loretta Young

Tugboat Annie—Marie Dressler, Wallace Beery

1940s

You Came Along—Robert Cummings, Lizabeth Scott

1950s

To Hell and Back—(Fort Lewis)

Track of the Cat—Robert Mitchum (Mt. Rainier)

1960s

It Happened at the World's Fair—Elvis Presley

The Slender Thread—Anne Bancroft, Sidney Poitier

1970s

Before and After—Patty Duke Astin

The Changeling—George C. Scott

Cinderella Liberty—James Caan, Marsha Mason

The Deer Hunter—Robert DeNiro (Mt. Baker)

Eleanor and Franklin—Jane Alexander, Edward Herrmann

Five Easy Pieces—Jack Nicholson (San Juan Islands)

Harry in Your Pocket—James Coburn, Walter Pidgeon

Hit—Richard Pryor, Billy Dee Williams

Idaho Transfer—Peter Fonda (Redmond)

Joyride—Desi Arnaz, Jr.

The Lives of Jenny Dolan—Shirley Jones

MacArthur—Gregory Peck (Bremerton)

The Magician—Bill Bixby

Mc Q—John Wayne

The Night Stalker—Darren McGavin

99 and $^{44}/_{100}$ Percent Dead—Richard Harris

Parallax View—Warren Beatty

Reflections of Murder—Tuesday Weld, Joan Hackett

Scorchy—Connie Stevens

1980s

An Act of Love—Ron Howard

An Officer and a Gentleman—Richard Gere, Louis Gossett, Debra Winger (Seattle, Port Townsend, Tacoma)

Barefoot in the Park—Richard Thomas, Bess Montgomery

Bird on a Wire—Goldie Hawn, Mel Gibson (Lincoln and Grant Counties, aerials only)

Black Widow—Debra Winger

Fabulous Baker Boys—Beau Bridges, Jeff Bridges, Michelle Pfeiffer

Frances—Jessica Lange

Ghost Dad—Bill Cosby (Seattle, aerials only)

Glory Days—George Wendt, Diane Ladd, Robert Stack

Harry and the Hendersons—John Lithgow, Melinda Dillon, Don Ameche

House of Games—Lindsay Crouse, Jack Wallace

I Love You to Death—Kevin Kline, Tracey Ullman (Tacoma)

Power—Richard Gere

Seven Hours to Judgment—Beau Bridges

That's Incredible—John Davidson

The Abyss—(Westport)

The Chocolate War—John Glover, Wally Ward (Kirkland)

Three Fugitives—Nick Nolte, Martin Short (Tacoma)

Twice in a Lifetime—Gene Hackman, Ann-Margret, Ellen Burstyn

War Games—Matthew Broderick, Ally Sheedy

War of the Roses—Michael Douglas, Danny DeVito, Kathleen Turner (Coupeville)

Winds of War—Robert Mitchum

We have some excellent **mummies**; in fact, if you want to be preserved, this is the place.

The mummy at the Burke Museum is no longer on display. However, for those mummy enthusiasts, you might be able to see it if you beg. The mummy was excavated in Fayum, Egypt. It belonged to the Ptolemaic dynasty from 323 B.C. to 30 B.C. It was purchased by M.S. Backus from the Museum of National Antiquities at Gizeh and was given to the Burke Museum in 1902. The mummy case was excavated in Thebes.

And, of course, there are "Sylvester" and "Sylvia" at Ye Olde Curiosity Shop. Sylvester was owned by a true eccentric in California who kept the mummy in a specially built settee.

He would often invite guests over to his home, sit them on the settee and then when they were ready to leave, he'd lift up the lid of the settee and show them what they'd been sitting on. It takes all kinds.

Anyway, Sylvester died of a gunshot wound, still visible in the mummy, in his lower left side just above the pelvic area. His body was found in about 1895 by two cowboys riding in the Gila Bend Desert in central Arizona, and scientists say he was mummified by natural dehydration caused by the hot sands and dry air. If you touch him, say the shop workers, he feels just like leather.

Sylvester's partner for eternity (or for the life of the Ye Olde Curiosity Shop, which was founded in 1899) is Sylvia, a Spanish immigrant found in Central America. She's assumed to have died of tuberculosis contracted during her long sea voyage in the early part of the nineteenth century. She was found with her burial shoes on.

Ye Olde Curiosity Shop acquired her from a man who was just passing through town. He saw Sylvester and asked if they wanted a female to go along with him.

As for the names, the owner, Joe James, thought up both of them.

N

There are 685 **nuns** in Seattle.

See also, **N** is for Nostalgia, page 21.

O

Puget Consumer Co-op sells approximately 17,000 lbs. of **oat** bran every six months.

P

Pirate culture. Lots of people tend to think those rowdies who wield a mean cutlass during Seafair are obnoxious, but the Seafair Pirates think of themselves as "giving our all for goodwill and civilization," according to Dick Alba, head of the group of about 40 men.

The pirates are actually part of the Ale and Quail Society (yes, ale as in beer, quail as in young women) and a throwback to the 1950s. The society was started in 1947 by some guys from the Washington Press Club. When Seafair began, the members tried being clowns, but it just didn't take.

Here's what it takes to be a Seafair Pirate:

- You have to be sponsored by a member in good standing.
- You're on probation for a year and have to do things like polish the existing members' shoes, or go get them drinks (it's no wonder women aren't members—they're too smart).
- You have to take part in such things as raids on bars during Seafair and be willing to sing songs that go like this:

"On a beach on Alki we landed
to take this town by force;
We'll take it singlehanded,
but just the girls of course..."

You have to follow the captain's orders, no matter what, and cannot go off on "private operations."

- You have to be loud and boisterous—just standing around looking big won't cut it.
- You are evaluated four times by the group for your presence in public, and you need to go to meetings. There are business meetings year round every other week and every week during summer. Believe it or not, pirates go to pirate conventions around the world, and staunch members wear pirate rings.
- "If you can't hold your booze, you won't make it through the first year."
- You have to be interested in other people—the pirates entertain at nursing homes, hospitals, etc.
- You get two extra points if you're over 6 feet tall. (Alba, for example, is 6'4", weighs over 200 lbs., has a shaved head and handlebar mustache.)

To join, or to enlist the pirates to entertain, write Seafair Pirates, P.O. Box 30674, Greenwood Station, Seattle, WA 98103.

Just to show they're up on the times (and to get insurance), the pirates do have a designated driver when they go out in their rig, the *Moby Duck.*

Their response to parents' complaints that they scare kids during parades? "Too bad you raised a sissy."

Oooh, those guys are mean.

Q

Quiet! Seattle likes quiet. You can be fined $50 for playing boom boxes, car stereos, or other portable audio equipment loud enough to be heard 50 feet away. Check out the boom box law signs down by Seward Park.

Speaking of quiet, the ambient daytime noise level in Seattle is 55 decibels (the human voice at three feet is 60 decibels). At night it's 10 decibels less. Shhhhh.

R

Seattle isn't a very **religious** city. In fact, the city has one of the country's lowest church memberships. Rev. William Cate of The Church Council of Greater Seattle says only about 30% of those in the region claim a religious affiliation.

Real estate is either sizzling, stabilizing, or in a state of flux around Seattle depending on who you ask at any given moment. There's little doubt that the market shot up dramatically in 1989–90, and though it may have slowed relative to the initial spurt, housing costs remain high and demand is growing no matter how you measure it. Californian immigrants are not entirely to blame, but anyone pointing a finger is usually found facing south.

S

Since we have so many hills, it's only natural that we have so many **stairs**. There's a guy in Seattle who's taken this to the extreme. Don Glickstein is an urban outdoor staircase fanatic; he's gone to the city's engineering department and pawed through card files to come up with a database of all Seattle's outdoor stairways, when they were built, where they are, and what they're made of.

He says if you put the city's stairs together, you'd have a staircase of 24,002 steps and 1,245 landings, rising 2.7 miles—and those are just the ones maintained by the engineering department, not those belonging to the park department or University of Washington.

Here are a few facts pulled from Don's list:

Oldest urban staircases: Second Avenue N and Ward Street, 34 steps of monolith concrete with pipe railings, built in 1906. And on Second Avenue N between Prospect and

Ward, monolith concrete, 75 steps, pipe railings, also 1906.
Longest staircase: Pigeon Hill, from SW Charlestown to Marginal Place SW, 228 steps, five landings, made of prefabricated concrete slabs and with wooden hand railings. (The slabs are from Seattle's defunct trolley system, recycled into stairways.)
Staircase with most landings: On S Lucile Street, connecting 18th Avenue S to 20th S, 28 landings, 169 steps.
Favorite for joggers: On E Blaine, from Lakeview to Broadway, 211 steps, 9 landings, pipe rails.

Where to see a rare wooden staircase: There are seven all-wood staircases, the longest on 20th NE, between NE 100th and NE 98th, 37 steps.
Shortest staircase: On Queen Anne's W Garfield between Ninth Avenue W upper and Ninth W lower, 2 steps.

T

Seattle's favorite **tattoos** seem to be roses, butterflies, and peace symbols, according to an informal poll.

Most unusual tattoos? At Tattoo You on E Pike, they've done a Scrabble Square on someone's back (the tattoo-er wanted to play a whole game, but the tattoo-ee didn't go for it), and a life-size Levi's pocket with a $100 bill sticking out of it on somebody's rounded bottom "so they'd never be broke."

U

In an average year, 90 **UFOs** (Unidentified Flying Objects) are sighted here. These are categorized as daytime sightings of disc-shaped objects which come to a sudden stop, hover, and then fly away.

The UFO Reporting and Information Service actually gets from 100 to 200 reports of these things, but a

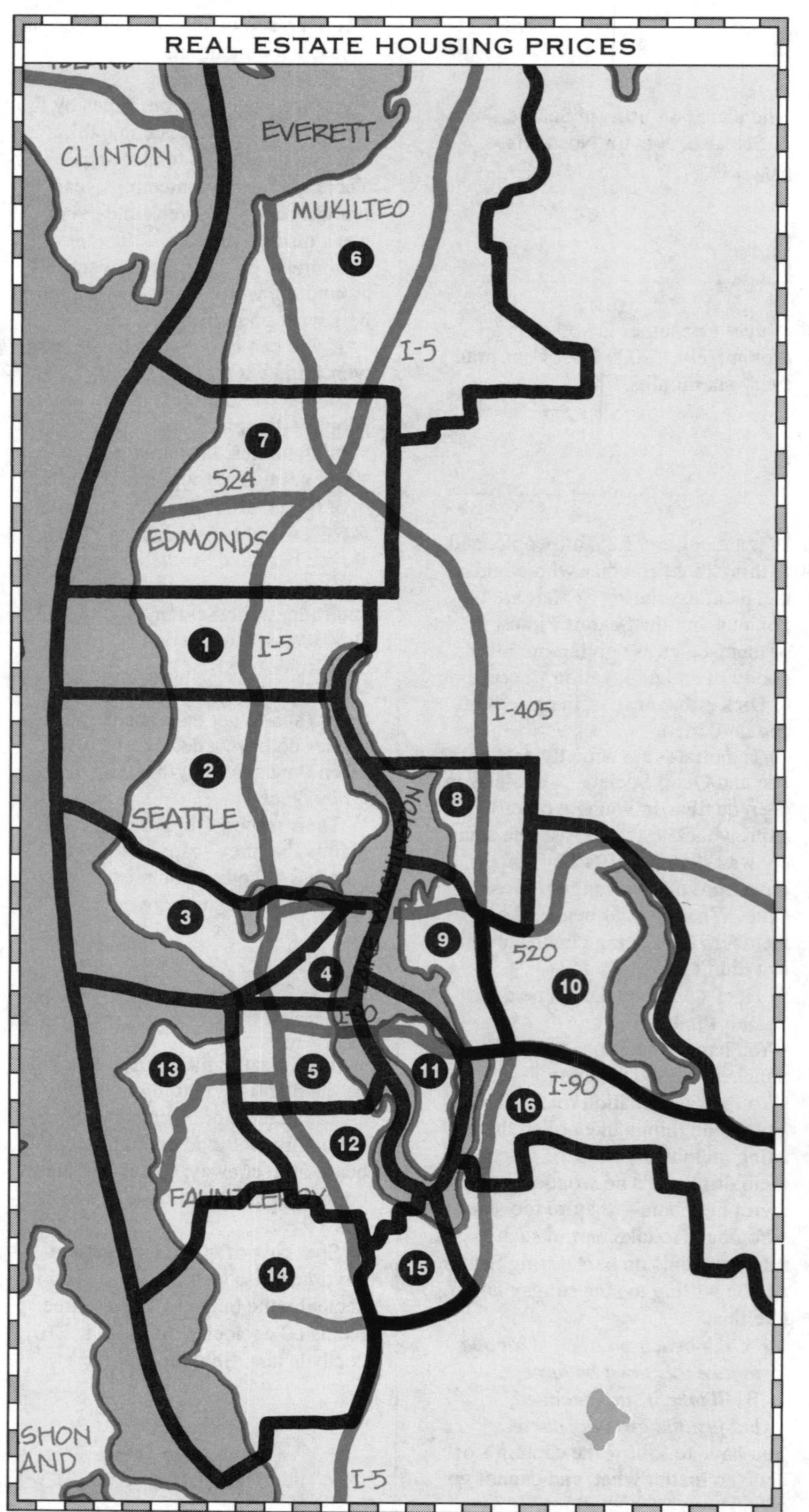

Average prices for houses in Seattle

January to July, 1990

Source: Puget Sound Multiple Listing Assn.

Area	Avg. price sale	Avg. days on market	No. of sales
Area 1	$133,970	23	432
Area 2	$165,360	20	1,399
Area 3	$206,652	31	733
Area 4	$185,935	36	163
Area 5	$130,481	48	48
Area 6	$148,456	65	1,366
Area 7	$143,543	24	943
Area 8	$192,543	48	402
Area 9	$401,417	62	191
Area 10	$170,876	28	586
Area 11	$411,187	64	137
Area12	$ 97,656	51	221
Area 13	$136,697	25	602
Area 14	$111,428	36	544
Area 15	$103,187	46	133
Area 16	$218,093	43	537

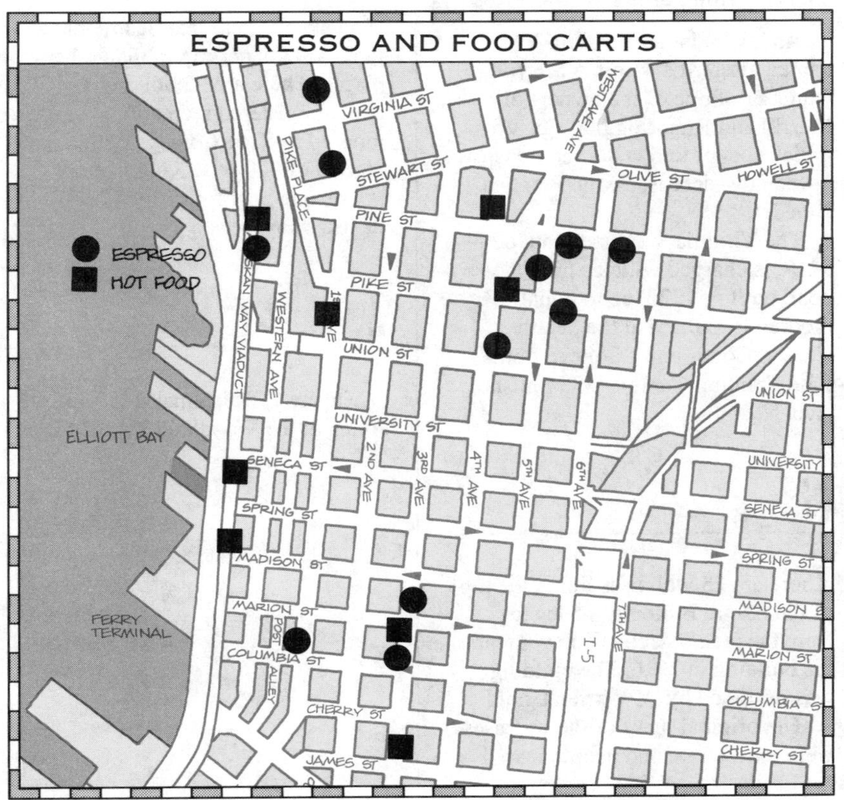

number of these are multiple reports of a single UFO. Nighttime sightings are considered useless, by the way.

Fewer than 5% of all reports are considered remotely authentic.

Though UFO experts are reluctant to talk about it, they admit there have been some abductions of the locals by these UFOs.

Seattle sightings occur mainly around the perimeter of the city, never over the city, and in the outlying areas.

To report a UFO call the UFO Reporting and Information Service, 721-5035.

V

Espresso **vending** is a way of life in Seattle, and now you can swig your java right on the streets thanks to the vendors who are peddling from carts. The city allows carts only for food, non-alcoholic beverages, and flowers. There are about 35 carts out there—some vendors show up more regularly than others.

Here's where they are:

1. 4300 SW Alaska St.—espresso
2. Pike Place Hillclimb at Alaskan Way—hot dogs
3. 1500 Alaskan Way—2 carts: sno-cones and juice
4. 5447 Ballard Ave. NW—flower cart
5. 301 Broadway E—espresso
6. 433 Broadway E—flower carts
7. 612 Broadway E—espresso
8. 2604 California Ave. SW—food
9. Third Ave., north of James St.—food
10. 10 Madison St. (north side of Alaskan Way)—food
11. 20 Mercer St. (Tower Books)—cart and tables, espresso
12. 315 Pike St.—food
13. 500 Pike St. (in front of Coliseum Theater)—espresso
14. 600 Pike St. (by The Locker Room)—popcorn
15. 601 Pine St. (I. Magnin)—espresso

16. 11 Seneca St. on south side at Alaskan Way—food
17. 501 Stewart St.—bottled iced tea
18. 525 Queen Anne Ave. N.—espresso
19. 811 First Ave. (Colman Bldg.)—popcorn
20. 811 First Ave.—espresso
21. 1901 First Ave. (Zebra Club)—espresso
22. 2025 First Ave.—espresso
23. 114 First Ave. S (New Orleans Cafe)—sausages and prawns
24. 1423 First Ave. S—popcorn/hotdogs
25. 1600 First Ave.—popcorn
26. 115 First Ave. S—popcorn/hotdogs
27. The alley between S Washington and S Main, 200 block of First Ave.—bakery
28. 516 Third Ave.—espresso
29. 801 Third Ave.—food and espresso
30. 916 Third Ave.—espresso
31. 1400 Third Ave.—popcorn
32. 1400 Fourth Ave.—espresso
33. 1601 Fourth Ave. (The Bon)—food
34. 1603 Fourth Ave. (monorail)—popcorn
35. Nordstrom, Fifth Ave.—espresso

And, who is the **Virginia V** named after? It's Virginia Merrill, daughter of one of the owners of Merrill and Ring Logging Co. Virginia is better known to Seattleites as the now-deceased Mrs. Prentice Bloedel.

The Virginia V Foundation, 624-9119, is charged with keeping the boat, built in 1922, operational. It's moored in Ballard at the Seattle Central Community College Maritime Training Center, 4455 Shilshole Ave. NW.

W

There are 25 **walruses** lining the top of the Arctic Building—a legacy from the men's Arctic Club who built the building in 1916. The building was designed by A. Warren Gould.

The original tusks of the walruses were terra-cotta, and people feared they'd fall off onto pedestrians below ("Marvin was speared by a falling tusk"). So in the 1950s the tusks were removed, leaving some sad-looking de-tusked walruses. When Stickney-Murphy Architects renovated the building in 1981–82, they replaced the tusks with specially cast epoxy ones.

If you're hanging around the Arctic Building, check out the plaster cornices of fruits and vegetables in the Dome Room off Cherry Street. Originally a ballroom, the room is now used for city events.

X

Approximately 8,000 people become **x-husbands** and **x-wives** in King County each year. (But another 13,700 get married.)

Y

You always hear that Seattle has more **yachts** per capita than other places. There are 72,569 registered and unregistered recreational vessels moored in King County. With a population of 870,651, King County boasts one boat for every 12 residents. Ahoy!

Z

There are 1,215 animals (258 species) living at the Woodland Park **Zoo.**

N IS FOR NOSTALGIA

When it comes to nostalgia, no one has reminiscences quite as varied as Emmett Watson, Seattle's native son curmudgeon. Watson, who pounds out three columns a week for the Seattle Times, *shares herewith some soulful Seattle memories.*

I once knew a great lady in this town, sort of an Everyman's grande dame, great in dignity and compassion, short on any kind of pretense. Her name was Betty Bowen—and I wish Seattle had her back.

Once when a pitiful band of protesters marched against the scarring, brutal freeway wiping out entire downtown neighborhoods, she was too ill to march with them. She hired a surrogate from the Millionair Club to march in her place, carrying her personally hand-lettered sign: "I am divided about sin but I am against cement!"

Betty Bowen despised monstrous things, such as the massive, intimidating skyscrapers that have become Seattle's signature; she abhorred the giant schemes and unshapely developments that have despoiled Seattle. She had a reverence for old neighborhoods, old people, old buildings—the things that form our traditions.

Someone once asked Betty Bowen what might be the single best thing we could do to make Seattle better, to improve it. She waved her long, ivory cigarette holder contemptuously and snapped, "Put it back!"

Would that we could.

Hardly a day passes when one does not wish to put things back—vanished restaurants, obsolete schools, customs and traditions, long-gone people.

Henry Broderick comes to mind. I wish we could bring him back. He was an Establishmentarian, to be sure, but he was an individualist. His real estate office down on Second and Cherry was a town meeting place to discuss ideas, trends, new concepts. He lunched at the Rainier Club or the Harbor Club, but he also consorted with street people and bums.

He never owned a car, always rode in cabs. When he was seriously ill at Providence Hospital, word went out that the old pioneer needed blood. The call filtered into the cabbies' intercom system, and within minutes some 30 taxicabs descended on Providence with drivers ready to give blood.

Sometimes I would meet Henry at Von's at Fourth and Pike. Now, there was a restaurant, kiddies; I wish we had *that* back. It had, at one time, the largest, most varied menu in the world.

For many years it never closed its doors. Von's was home for show people, the sports crowd, publishers, editors, news hawks, sportswriters. At Von's you could savor the world's richest oyster stew; you could mingle with boxers and fight managers, pick up a girl, meet a celebrity, place a wager, or borrow money to pay your check. There is nothing like Von's around today.

I wish we could put Sicks' Stadium back. At one time the finest minor league baseball park in America, Sicks' Stadium housed baseball when the game was more innocent, when players flourished without agents and fans could buy a box seat without taking out a bank loan.

I must have seen a thousand ball games at Sicks' Stadium, featuring the old Seattle Rainiers. Adolph Catalini, of Sullivan Florists, always sat in the box seat nearest home plate. Any Seattle player who hit a home run would get a $10 bill from Adolph, shoved through the wire screen.

Union Street? Put it back! The Union Street of today is a series of clothiers and dress shops, genteel antique places, interior decorating shops, all so upscale and lifeless. Whole blocks of the street have vanished, and the heart of it, between Sixth and Seventh, is now a parking lot for the Sheraton Hotel.

The old Union Street was raffish, low-down, and fun. At the corner of Sixth and Union was the Magic Inn, a basement nightclub that brought in top acts. There was Bob's Chili Parlor, where the fight crowd, the pimps, and their ladies hung out.

Upstairs was the Italian Club, an elegant bar and eatery that never seemed private. The Italian Club used to have slot machines along two walls, going full blast, presided over by Johnny Scali and Louie Rispoli, and bartenders who served a drink that would make a mule walk backward.

On Union Street, too, was the Richelieu Cafe, and across from that, in the old Eagles Auditorium, was housed the Seattle Press Club. It was in the Press Club that I first learned to drink, sipping tentatively at whiskey sours. It was in the Press Club, too, that I heard the great Paul Robeson, one huge hand cupped over his ear, give a concert without musical accompaniment, every note perfectly on pitch.

Where are the great characters that gave Seattle substance and vibrancy? Nobody today can begin to match Dave Beck, the jaunty, bellicose Teamsters union boss who came to rule everything that moved on wheels.

Nobody around anymore like puckish Ivar Haglund or Rudi Becker, he of the Paul Bunyan demeanor, who drove around in his pickup truck with his Scotch and soda in a swinging dashboard glass-holder. Nothing at all like George Vanderveer, the great criminal-law attorney who moved fast, drank hard, and picked fights with truck drivers in Pioneer Square.

No lawyer I know of today is as smart and courtroom wise as Charley Burdell—rumpled, warm, funny, of whom we used to say, "Charley is the only guy in town who can wear a new suit out of Littler's and get picked up for vagrancy two blocks away."

Places, people...gone, all gone. Seattle is, to be sure, more sophisticated and worldly, but those innocent times produced characters that added richness to a remote seaport town.

These are just a few of the things I would like to put back, but of course that is impossible. As Granny Rice, the great versifier and sportswriter once penned, "Not all the wealth that the mines set free can buy you an hour that used to be."

Don't let anybody tell you that Seattle nostalgia ain't up to standard anymore.

Emmett Watson
September 1990

CHAPTER

2

WEATHER AND OTHER DISASTERS

SUN

FREEZES

MYTHS

EARTHQUAKES

UMBRELLAS

RAIN

CLOUDS

LORE

TURTLENECKS

SUNGLASSES

Beware! This chapter could be hazardous to your (mental) health. It's been rumored for so long now that Seattle doesn't really have that much rain—less precipitation than New York, after all—that some Seattleites have come to believe it. But does it

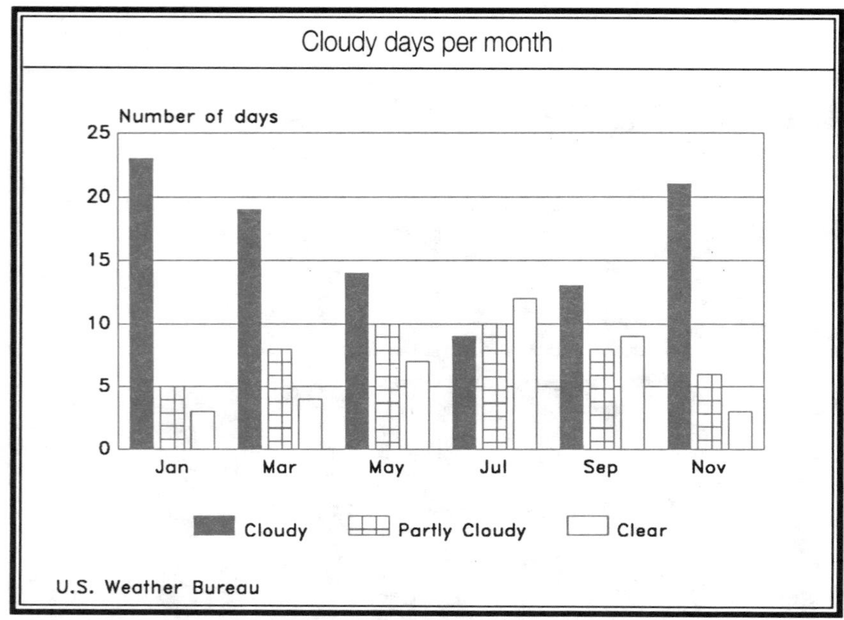

really matter how much it rains when 201 days of the year are cloudy on average, and another 93 are partly cloudy? It's amazing local tots ever learn the word "sun." Annually, Seattle only gets 45% of the maximum sunshine available each day.

Now that we have Emmett Watson (famed Lesser Seattle crusader) actually grinning, here are the dismal facts about Seattle weather.

WHITHER THE WEATHER

Seattle is, on average, 386 feet above sea level. On a globe, look for latitude 47° 36'N, longitude 122° 20' W.

The city averages 34.1 inches of rain a year, and 8.1 inches of snow/sleet. (That's inner city. If you include the county, the average is worse at 39 inches of rain, 15 inches of snow.)

BABY, IT'S COLD OUT THERE!

Average date of first freeze: December 1
Average date of last freeze: February 23
Average freeze-free period: 281 days

SEATTLE'S "CLOUD PEOPLE"

Weather watchers have been tracking Seattle's weather for just about 100 years—a short time when you consider how long weather has been around. But things haven't changed that much: The first entry in the U.S. (Seattle) Weather Bureau says, "May 1, 1893: Cloudy but pleasant with light to fresh southerly winds."

At the University of Washington there is a group referred to as "the cloud people." They are really part of the Department of Atmospheric Sciences, and they usually have an eye on local weather. There has been variability in Seattle's weather lately, the "cloud people" say, but no real trend toward warming or cooling is apparent. They do report that the snowpack has been below normal since the mid-seventies. Part of the problem with spotting trends is that the weather records are relatively recent compared to long-term weather cycles.

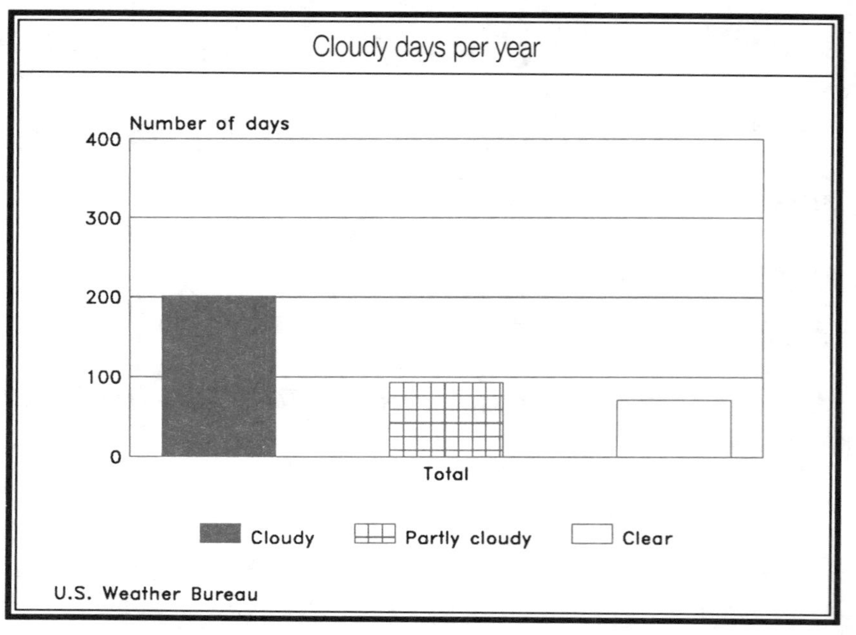

WEATHER TO THE MAX

Seattle's greatest snowstorm: January 6, 1880—40 inches on the ground. The storm was so bad that hundreds of barns collapsed and transportation was halted, but the snow melted pretty quickly.

Seattle's coldest day: January 31, 1893—3°F with 24 inches of snow in downtown Seattle. Green Lake was frozen to a depth of 10 inches near the shore, 8½ inches in the center.

Seattle's hottest day: July 16, 1941—100°F. The same temperature was reached again on June 9, 1955. In 1945 the weather station was moved to Seattle-Tacoma International Airport, and there the record is August 9, 1981—99°F.

TORNADOES, HEAT ISLANDS, AND MORE

Seattle is sheltered from coastal storms by the Olympic Mountains to the west and from inland cold waves and heat waves by the Cascade Mountains to the east.

Downtown Seattle is a "heat island" due to downtown buildings, steam pipes, pavement, autos, and sewers, which retain heat, raising the temperature 1°–3° higher than the surrounding countryside.

The area's warmish winters come from the ever-present rain and clouds that trap the heat energy of condensation and hold it near the ground.

An influx of cold, dry, dense continental polar air can cause a drop in Seattle temperatures, but the Cascades block most of this air. Usually the weather is maritime weather: Sea breezes flow toward the land from the Sound (and even from Lake Washington) during the day; land breezes flow back toward the water at night.

Prevailing winds

	MPH	Direction	Wind chill factor
Jan.	11	SE	16°
Feb.	11	SW	20°
Mar.	12	SW	23°
Apr.	11	SW	27°
May	11	SW	—
June	10	SW	—
July	10	SW	—
Aug.	9	SW	—
Sept.	9	N	—
Oct.	10	S	—
Nov.	10	S	26°
Dec.	11	SSW	20°

Explanation: For instance, on an average day in January the wind blows 11 mph from the southeast. The outside temperature feels like 16° F. Source: U.S. Weather Bureau

Trees help keep the environment temperate, but clear-cutting causes hotspots which are also coldspots in winter. Trees also thrust air upward on the windward side of mountains, and can account for as much as 6% of local rainfall.

Chicken Little, if she were a Seattleite, would be right: The city sky *does* fall—in the form of 257,090,863.98 TONS of rain each year.

Seattle has less thunder and lightning than many parts of the U.S.,

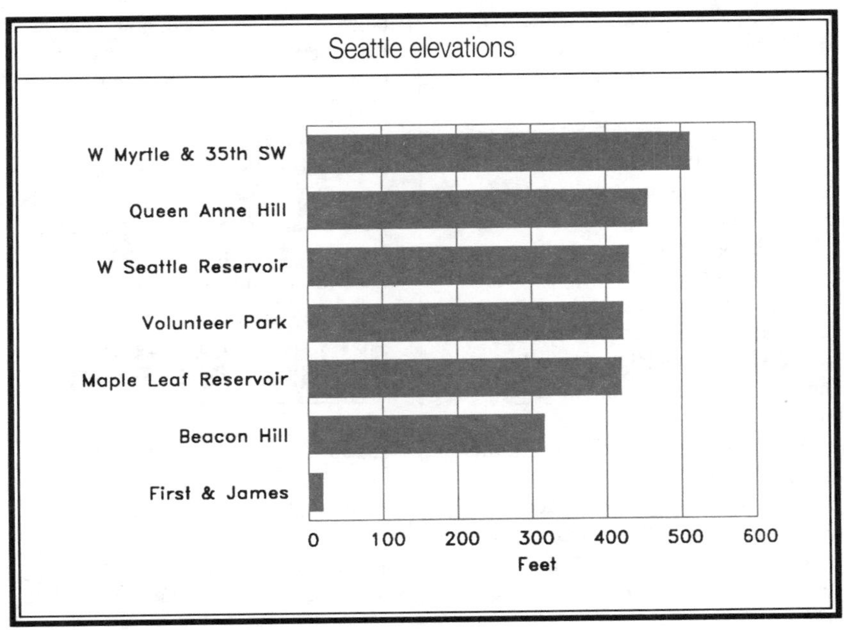

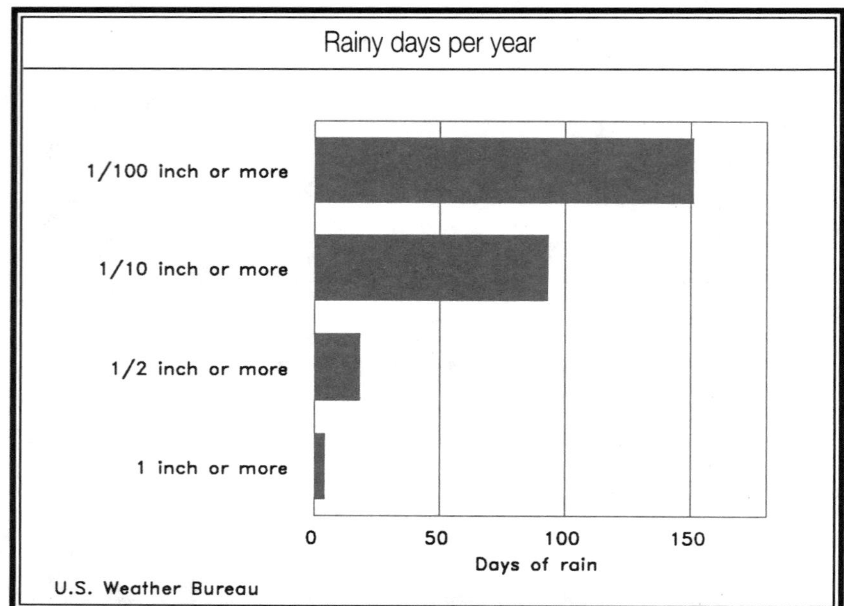

with only six thunderstorms per year. The city also has less risk of damage from hail, since most of the hail here is small, ⅛ to ¼ inch in diameter, and most falls in late winter and early spring before new growth.

Seattle also has "graupel," which looks like a cross between snow and hail, but is really crumbly snow pellets the size of buckshot to small peas. But no local ever says, "Look, it's graupeling outside!"

One of Seattle's worst winter hazards is invisible but you know it when you hit it, either in the car or on foot. Black ice is a transparent film of frozen water that takes on the color of the material on which it forms. Black ice occurs when temperatures hover around the freezing and melting points, as they often do during a Seattle winter. Typically, moisture freezes on a freeway overpass, melts, and then quickly freezes again. Unbeknownst to a traveler, the roadway has become treacherously slick.

Winds are usually mild, but some windstorms do reach 70 mph, and the West Point lighthouse recorded 83 mph winds during the famous Columbus Day storm, October 12, 1962.

Tornadoes are rare, but they have occurred at View Ridge/Sand Point on September 28, 1962 and in South King County on December 12, 1969.

Seattle has fewer bugs than other cities because most bugs need intense heat to thrive. And, though we're Way Out West, we don't have tumbleweed or sagebrush.

Weather does affect the circulatory systems of human beings. Spring Fever, a listlessness brought on by balmy weather, is real, and so is the extra pep we feel during wind and rain. Our bodies respond to the change in temperature, which in turn results in energetic, rainy-day crowds at the shopping malls, a favorite rainy-day sport and the reason malls were created in Seattle to begin with. Northgate, the first covered mall in the U.S., opened in 1950.

DEBUNK THAT MYTH

It's Japanese currency and not the Japanese Current, as many people think, that is affecting the area. According to the National Weather Service, the Japanese Current is very weak near our coastline. The California Current is warmer and stronger. The prevailing westerly air currents cross vast reaches of ocean, acquiring water vapor and a temperature near that of the sea. This effect is from the general currents of the ocean, not from the Japanese Current.

WEATHER LORE (TRUE STUFF)

Heavy rainfall occurs about 30 days after a meteor shower.

• Raindrops are not always round or teardrop shaped. According to a study by General Electric scientists, raindrops can change their form as often as 50 times per second. They can look like jellybeans, pancakes, gourds, peanuts, hot dogs, ducks, footballs, and even human feet.

• When rain is due, ants go into hiding, spiders tighten their webs, and a halo forms around the sun or moon.

• "Big snow, little snow—little snow, big snow" is an Indian saying which refers to the size of snowflakes versus the quantity of snow.

• On a spring or summer day, good weather is likely if dew is on the grass before sunrise.

• Early morning ground fog means the day's weather will be good.

• Water birds fly higher in good weather than bad.

LOCAL WEATHER ADAGES, ODDITIES, AND OBSERVATIONS

"Their land has a blurry beauty (as if the Creator started to erase it but had second thoughts)."

—Tom Robbins, *Another Roadside Attraction*

"A rust-brown smudge ballooned over Seattle, end to end, a thousand feet thick. Mac knew the locals were telling themselves that if they were getting headaches and their eyes were bloodshot and their noses ran, it must be something else. Seattleites had a stunning town, but it grew dirtier by the minute. It was only Northwest vanity that kept people calling it fog."

—Earl W. Emerson, *Black Hearts and Slow Dancing*

"Summers in Seattle are like that—hot one day and chilly the next. What visitors don't understand is that too many days without rain, too many hours of uninterrupted sunshine, cause Seattleites to get crabby."

—J.A. Jance, *Improbable Cause*

"If Mount Rainier is visible in the afternoon, it is a sure sign of good weather for the next 24 hours."

—Anonymous

"The rain it raineth every day
Upon the just and unjust
But mostly upon the just because
The unjust hath the just's umbrella."

—Anonymous

SEATTLE CEMENT?

Yes, our snow really is wetter than elsewhere. Because Seattle's temperatures hover right around the freezing point of 32°F, our snow is warmer and actually contains more water per snowflake. Wet snow occurs at temperatures high enough to bond crystals into large snowflakes and is typical of the maritime borders of continental land masses lying between latitudes 40° and 60°.

One inch of rain near the freezing point is equivalent to about 10 inches of wet, heavy snow. The same inch of rain at temperatures well below freezing would produce 12 inches or more of drier, fluffier snow with very solid crystals. Unlike Seattle snow, this snow is very cold, very light, and is not bonded together. Seattle's wet snow, because it compacts more easily, is ideal for snowballs (if not for skiing!).

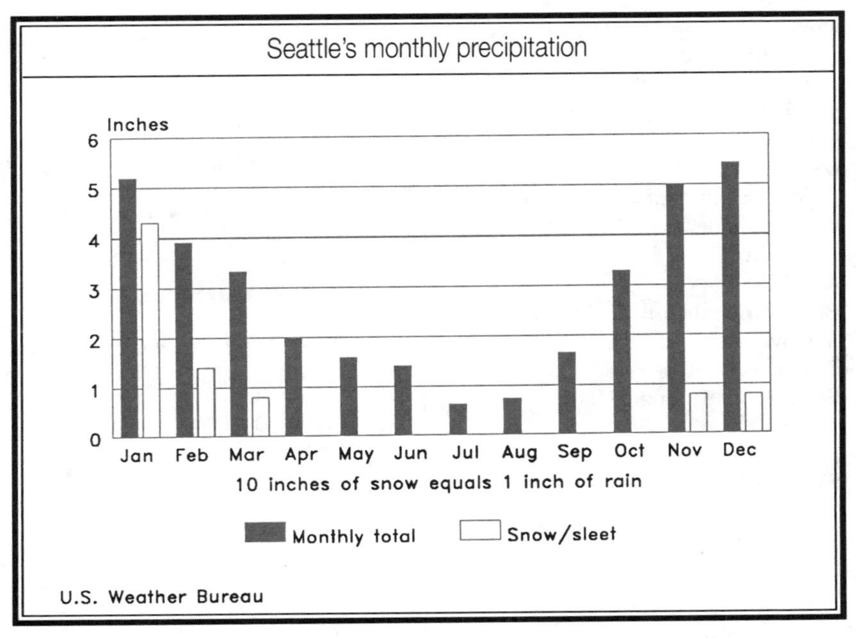

YOUR CONVERGENCE ZONES

Seattle has plenty of mini-climates, mostly due to rain shadows, wind channelling, and convergence zones where cold air from inland masses combines with mild, wet air from the Sound.

The largest rain shadow is created by the Olympic Mountains to the advantage of places like Sequim, on the Olympic Peninsula, where half as much rain falls as in Seattle, which

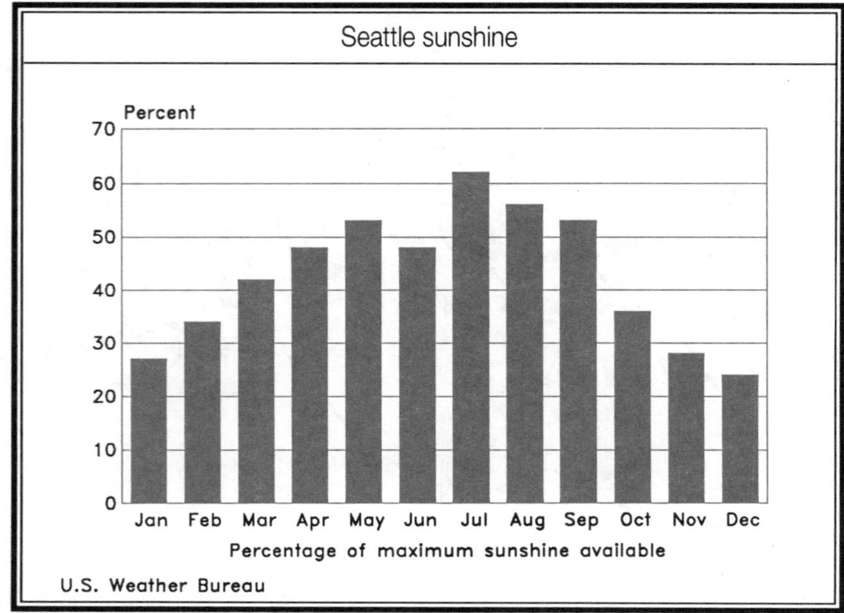

is far enough outside the shadow to get dumped on.

Within the city, the tops of hills are likely to be rainier or snowier than the flats. So yes, it really does snow more on Queen Anne Hill, which is both high and in a convergence zone. Since North Seattle lies closer to the Sound than other areas of the city, the weather there tends to be worse due to several convergence zones.

Tall downtown buildings cast shadows at ground level but generate heat at the same time, and so act as both mini-convergence zones and wind channels. For years considered Seattle's windiest corner by downtown workers, Fourth and Union's title has recently been challenged by the Columbia Center at Fifth and Spring. The curved shape and extreme height of this building (954') generate twister-like winds which can keep almost any form of city debris whirling in the air.

The Safeco Building (308') in the University District is suspected of being windier at the base of the building's east side than anywhere else in the U District (including the Faculty Senate in full debate).

THE SHAKING EARTH

Is there such a thing as earthquake weather? Probably not, though longtime *P-I* weatherman Walt Rue once said in print that it's conceivable air pressure might have a contributing effect if all other conditions were right. Most scientists disagree, however. We do know that animals are sensitive to earthquakes and birds have been known to leave an earthquake area prior to the event. Perhaps the unusual stillness prompts people to notice something different in the air and call it earthquake weather.

Seattle's two greatest quakes occurred under the following conditions:

April 13, 1949
Barometric pressure 30.26 inches
Sky overcast
Temperature 50°F
Wind 4 mph from the North

April 29, 1965
Barometric pressure 30.14 inches
Sky clear
Temperature 47°F
Wind 4 mph from the East Southeast

HIDDEN FAULTS AND UPFRONT ERUPTIONS

Ever since the 1989 San Francisco earthquake, there has been intense interest in knowing when the "big one" will hit Seattle. The truth is that not a great deal is known about earthquakes here, except that we have small quakes daily, have had major ones, and that we can expect more small quakes every day and a major one "someday."

Because Seattle's last major quake was 25 years ago, some people suggest we're overdue for another.

Best days for a picnic: For people who don't like surprises, such as rain during a summer barbecue, there are days to bet on.

Odds favor scheduling an event during the "Dog Days," a period beginning July 26 and lasting four to six weeks, when Sirius the Dog Star rises with the Sun. According to ancient astrologers, this is a time of plagues, madness, and drought. Four of Seattle's eight driest days occur during this stretch.

July 26 is consistently one of Seattle's driest days—good time to go on a picnic; although July 19, historically Seattle's driest day, might be better if you want to avoid the plagues and madness that start the following week.

The reason it's so difficult to predict is that, according to the UW Seismology Lab, Seattle and the rest of Western Washington are covered by deep silt and glacial deposits that cover faults until a quake occurs. Unlike California, where bedrock is often exposed and faults are obvious, Western Washington's bedrock is covered by water, earth, or vegetation, making it almost impossible to detect cracks. According to geologists, the only two areas where bedrock is exposed in the greater Seattle area are in Everett, and on the southern tip of Bainbridge Island. There might be lots of faults around—but they're hidden.

Most seismic activity here is the direct result of major earth plate movement, rather than slippage of faults within a plate as in California. Still, some major faults are known to exist such as the Mt. St. Helens fault zone, which is about 65 miles long. The Mt. St. Helens eruptions in 1980 may have eased pressure along the fault lines and postponed a huge quake.

Mt. Rainier had major rockfalls in 1963 and 1985, though whether this indicates increased volcanic activity is not clear. An ancient eruption of Mt. Rainier sent mudflows all the way to what is now Burien.

Mt. Baker to the north is also an active volcano and typically fault lines lie in the area of volcanoes.

If Mt. Rainier or Mt. Baker blew, the major dangers would be from mudflows and flooding, UW scientists say. A warning system is in place so people could flee the mudflows.

For earthquake preparedness, instruction, and general information, the UW Seismology Lab highly recommends Information Circular 85, *Washington Earthquakes*, published by Washington Department of Natural Resources Publications Dept., Division of Geology, TY-12, Olympia, WA 98504.

WEATHER SURVIVAL, INDOORS AND OUT

Our weather doesn't seem extreme compared to other areas of the country, but it is unpredictable. You can leave home in the morning with wool sweaters, gloves, and L.L. Bean duck boots and be roasting by noon. Dressing to be warm and dry, but not too warm and not too encumbered, can be tricky.

Clothing trends

The myth is that Seattleites dress in what some call the Seattle tux:
Cotton turtleneck T-shirt
Chamois shirt
Ragg wool sweater
Khaki pants
Gore-Tex™ hooded jacket with zippers, pockets, and drawstrings

In truth, the myth is pretty close to reality.

REI sales for 1989:
Cotton turtlenecks: 11,000
Chamois shirts: 3,400
Gore-Tex™ jackets: 5,100

Ask any suited lawyer—he or she has something like this outfit waiting at home. (You don't have to ask computer whizzes, writers, or architects—they're usually wearing some variation of it at the office.) And the future? Well, the data are pretty iffy, but it seems that turtlenecks are on the rise (500 more sold in 1989 than 1988), but chamois shirts are on the way out (REI sold 4,700 in 1988 compared to the 3,400 in 1989).

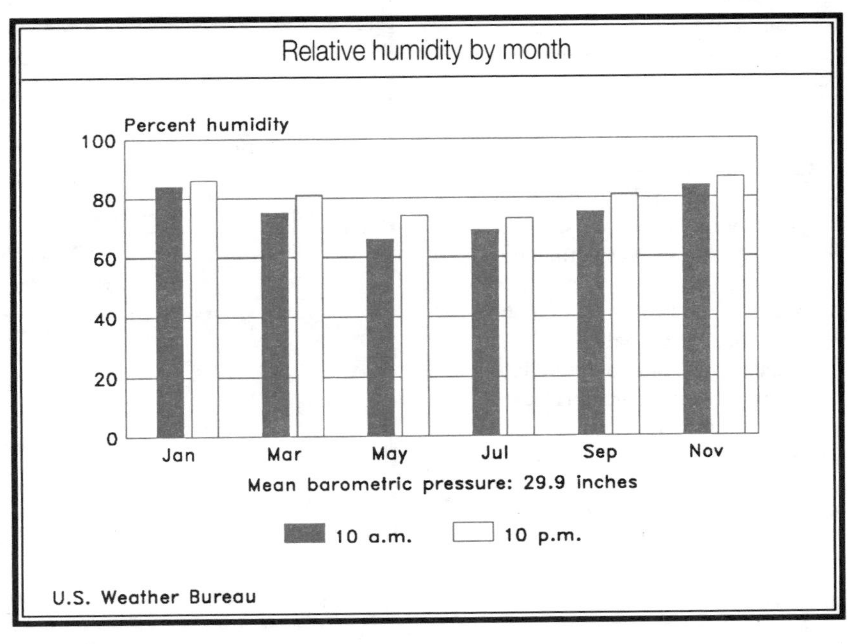

BUMBERSHOOT COUTURE

If layer dressing is a matter of survival, so apparently is an umbrella. This is a change from the old days when true Seattleites looked down their wet noses at anyone carrying an umbrella. It's a rare downtown office that doesn't have a "department umbrella" for those surprise squalls someone wasn't ready for. Some of us still would not be caught dead under one.

The Bon Marche alone estimates it sells over 13,000 umbrellas per year. Multiply this by the numbers sold by Nordstrom, Frederick's, Fred Meyer, Lamont's, Penney's, Pay'n Save, K Mart, and every drugstore, supermarket, and convenience store in the city—and that's a lot of umbrellas. How many? We called ShedRain in Portland, third-largest umbrella company in the world and largest supplier of umbrellas to the West Coast, and they're too busy making umbrellas to count how many they sell, but did say they restock most large Seattle stores four times per year in contrast to other areas of the country, which order once or twice each year.

RUMORS, RUMORS

Seattle's iffy weather has given rise to two odd rumors, both of which we would like to confirm are true (or mostly true).

Rumor 1. It never rains on the Bellevue Arts and Crafts Fair.

According to Nancy Fisher of the Bellevue Arts and Crafts Fair, never in its 18-year history has the event been cancelled or postponed due to rain. It's held the last full weekend in July, and though Fisher would not go so far as to say no stray raindrops have ever fallen, she does say that the Fair is annually besieged by callers wanting to know this year's dates so they can schedule weddings, picnics, barbecues, and other outdoor events the same weekend.

The attending hearsay that the "no rain" condition is insured by Lloyd's of London is not true, but only because the Fair has never called Lloyd's. According to a local Lloyd's representative, Lloyd's will insure virtually anything for a price.

Rumor 2. More sunglasses are sold each year in Seattle than anywhere else in the nation.

David McDonald, local sunglass representative for Ray-Ban, Vuarnet, Serengeti, Lantis, and Gucci, says Seattle is always in the top 5% of shades-selling centers. Top sales months are January through July or August. Why does Seattle, with its scarcity of sun, sell so many sunglasses? Simple, says McDonald.

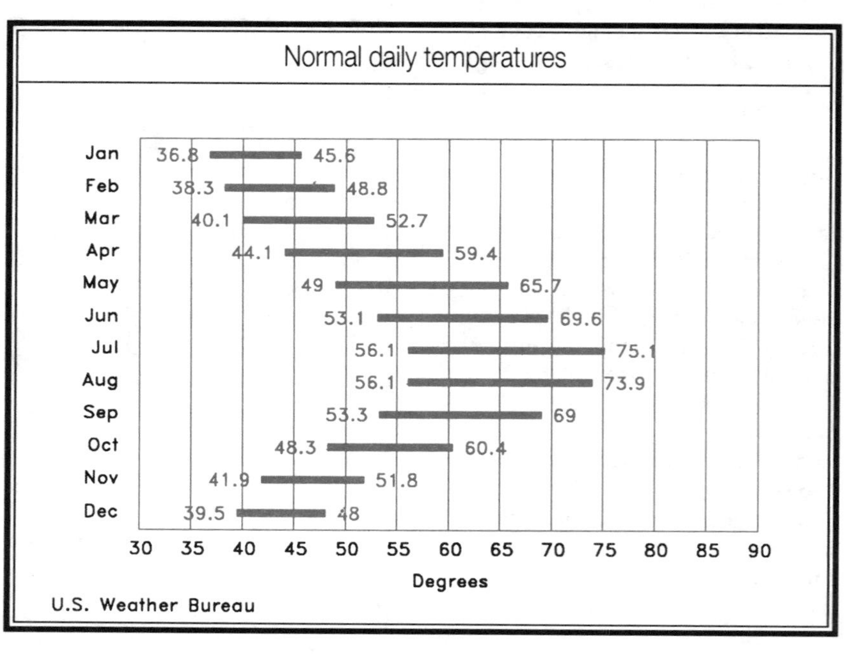

"It's not like LA, where you have to wear your sunglasses every day and you know where they are. People here use their sunglasses so seldom they lose 'em, sit on 'em, don't have 'em when they need 'em. Then they have to buy another pair."

WEATHER INFO

Have pencil and paper handy when calling these phone numbers. You'll get masses of menu numbers, alternate phone numbers, temperatures, windspeeds, and more thrown at you. If you hang up and call back after going for a pencil, you may have to wait through several busy signals as the recording you just hung up on wends its way to the end and rewinds. Ain't technology wonderful?

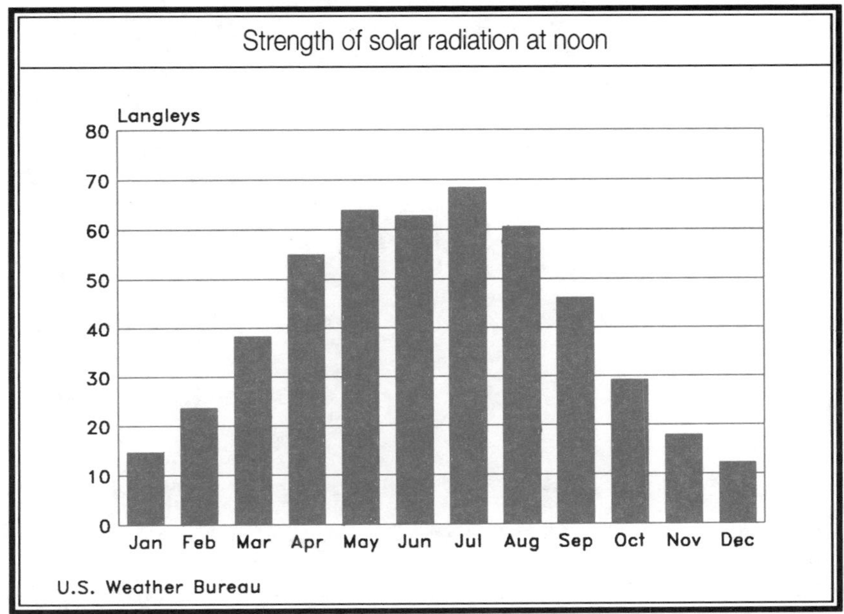

National Weather Service Forecast
526-6087

Pilot One-Call Briefing
767-2726
Menu numbers for local weather conditions and route forecasts for many routes from "Seattle to...."

Seattle Times Infoline
464-2000
Menu numbers: Inland Waters, 9910; Straits and Coast, 9911

Washington State Highway District
1-976-ROAD
Mountain pass reports, October 1 through March 31.

Cascade Ski Report
634-0200

Northwest Ski Report
634-0071

Seattle Times Infoline
464-2000
General Ski Reports, 9011; "Big Three" Ski Report (Alpental, Snoqualmie, Ski Acres), 2443.

Air Pollution Control
296-5100
Air-quality index and burn ban info.

Coast Guard
Emergencies: 286-5400
To report chemical and oil spills: (800) 424-8802

24-hour Emergency Spill Response
867-7000

Marine Weather Radio Broadcasts VHF Weather 1 or Weather 2
NOAA KHB60, 162.55 Megaherz
Or purchase a Marine Weather Radio. Cost? About $25.

Veteran Seattleites won't sit next to a door or up close to large expanses of restaurant windows in the wintertime; unlike their counterparts in the East or Midwest, windows here often aren't double glass and you might have white caps on your soup if you're unlucky enough to be next to one.

Nor do old hands charge up to the edge of the curb to wait out a red light. They stand well back behind the shelter of the building on the corner to avoid the wind and the knee-high splash from the buses. Especially at Fourth and Union; at the Columbia Center, forget it. There's no place to hide.

CHAPTER

3

THE INSIDE TRACK ON TRAFFIC

GRIDLOCK

DRIVING TIMES

BRIDGES

PARKING

CARPOOLING

SHORTCUTS

RUSH HOUR

BOTTLENECKS

TOWING

GAS

Clogged, slowed to a crawl, stopped up, overturned, one lane moving, bridges up—gridlock! Even if you never drive south of Seattle, you know to avoid the S-curves and Kennydale Way like the plague. Copter jockeys and other traffic announcers sound more and more like sports announcers with rapid-fire commentary on the morning and afternoon commutes. And these days, they're listened to more than the Mariners. Traffic is bad out there—and it can only get worse.

As of June 1990, 848,000 cars zoom in and out of Seattle each day. Actually, they don't zoom, they crawl. Average speed during rush hour is 22 mph. And rush hour is actually rush *hours*: from 6 a.m. to 9 a.m. in the morning and from 3:30 p.m. to 6:30 p.m. in the afternoon. What's more, people are rushing from farther away than in the past.

- In 1980 the average trip length in the region was 6.5 miles and took 14 minutes.
- In the year 2000 the average trip will be 7.9 miles and 20 minutes.
- In 2020 the average trip will be 8.3 miles and 26 minutes.

Source: Puget Sound Council of Government

Seattleites buy 1.81 cars per household, up from 1.7 a decade ago. What are they buying? The Honda Civic is Seattle's no. 1 choice, followed by Ford Taurus, followed by almost any 4WD pickup truck—especially those with expanded cabs.

All those new cars—and new people—are making gridlock a way of life. But don't worry, you can find ways to survive the traffic crunch. Consider chucking the car and biking it, busing it, or walking it. (See Chapter 4, page 47, *Getting Around Gridlock.*) Or learn a basic premise: the fastest line between points A and B is often a fullish circle. To put it another way, Seattle shortcutting is an art not to be taken lightly.

UNLOCKING THE GRID

The best shortcutters understand Seattle's logical street layout. With all those hills in the way, the streets might not seem to follow any pattern, but they do.

First of all, downtown lore has engrained the Jesus Christ Made Seattle Under Protest road key in us all (for the uninitiated, the first letter of each word represents a street or two streets of the same letter running south to north; e.g., J is for James, C for Cherry and Columbia, M for Marion and Madison, S for Spring and Seneca, U for University and Union, P for Pike and Pine).

Then you need to know that all arterials are marked with broken yellow lines.

As for street-smarts here's one man's way:

"Draw the lines of the old tic-tac-toe game; then we can name the 'boxes' made by those lines with compass directions. The box at 12 o'clock high is north, the box at 1:30 is northeast, 3 o'clock is east, and so on. Of course, the box in the middle would have no compass direction, and that's exactly as it is in the center of Seattle where the streets are without compass directions. All other streets in the city will have a direction, either before or after the street's name, or number, depending on whether they are technically a street or an avenue.

There are two basic street classifications: arterials and non-arterials. Arterials are protected from cross traffic; that is, the side streets have at least a yield sign and usually a stop sign. And commercial vehicles in excess of 10,000 pounds gross vehicle weight cannot travel on an arterial except when that's the only way to get to a destination. Unless otherwise posted, the speed limit on arterials is 30 mph and 25 mph on non-arterials.

Sage drivers at Yellow Cab depend for their livelihood on the more esoteric cuts. Military Road off Airport Way next to Boeing Field is a great "sneak" under the highway, says one. Ditto that for Albro Place, the Boeing Access Road, and SW 129th Street. An experienced driver calls the Aloha jog west across lower Queen Anne vital to his success.

"Streets run east to west and, unless in the downtown area, will have a compass direction before the name or number. For example: 1502 NE 65th or 4101 SW Manning. And, as you might expect, the avenues run north to south and the compass directions come after the name or number. For example: 4775 Brooklyn Avenue NE, or 5707 47th S. The not-so-common diagonal thoroughfares are often called 'ways' (like Denny Way or Yesler Way), but they may just as often be called roads or drives.

"Now for the good news: there is an easy way to keep all this straight. Remember Brooklyn Avenue NE? First of all, no one ever says 'Avenue Brooklyn.' Avenue always comes after the name or number and so do the compass directions. If you need another mnemonic, then look at this way of spelling 'aveNuE.' It has

an NE in it, so if I hear Brooklyn NE or 35th NE, I think of Brooklyn aveNuE, or 35th aveNuE."
Source: *Seattle Homes* by Jim Stacey

THE ART OF SHORTCUTTING

Look at it as a challenge. It's rush hour, you have to get to the waterfront, and you're up on Broadway. You know it'll take an hour to get through all the lights on Madison. Tootle north on Broadway to Harvard. Zip down Harvard to the Eastlake overpass, cut down Denny to just before Fifth Avenue with the monorail in sight. Turn left on a little zag to Fifth, then quickly dodge cars and pilings under the monorail to get over to Wall. Turn right (quick, get in the righthand lane so you don't get in the 99 entrance crunch), and zip down to Alaskan Way. It's clear sailing from here. And don't you feel smug?

With effort and initiative, you can achieve a sublime level of navigating skill. Success depends on the degree to which you are willing to cut U-turns where permissible, negotiate speed islands, and do some sharp heel-and-toe work. If you have to go through a neighborhood, go slow—you'll still beat the freeway traffic.

Traffic reporter "Avenging Annie" of KISW-FM offers simple advice: "Don't drive during rush hour." For those who can't afford this luxury, the best alternative is to creatively chain together smaller throughways that will run at least 10 blocks in any single direction.

Consider the "forgotten roads" that the wise drive to avoid the No Man's Land of the I-5 corridor. Dexter is one—broad, fast, and usually empty. Another "highway of choice" is Aurora, lights and all.

Annie offers NE 65th and NE 75th streets as examples of forgotten roads in northeast Seattle. Each moves well without subjecting drivers to a prohibitive number of lights, and they can be used in conjunction with other streets—70th is one—to get beyond I-5's mess.

Yet we may forever strive in vain to find the ideal route around the Montlake Bridge gridlock during a Huskies game. The sad fact is that some bottlenecks are not negotiable. Best to cut your losses by finding the forgotten streets in other parts of town. It's bound to be worth the effort, and if you're very lucky, you

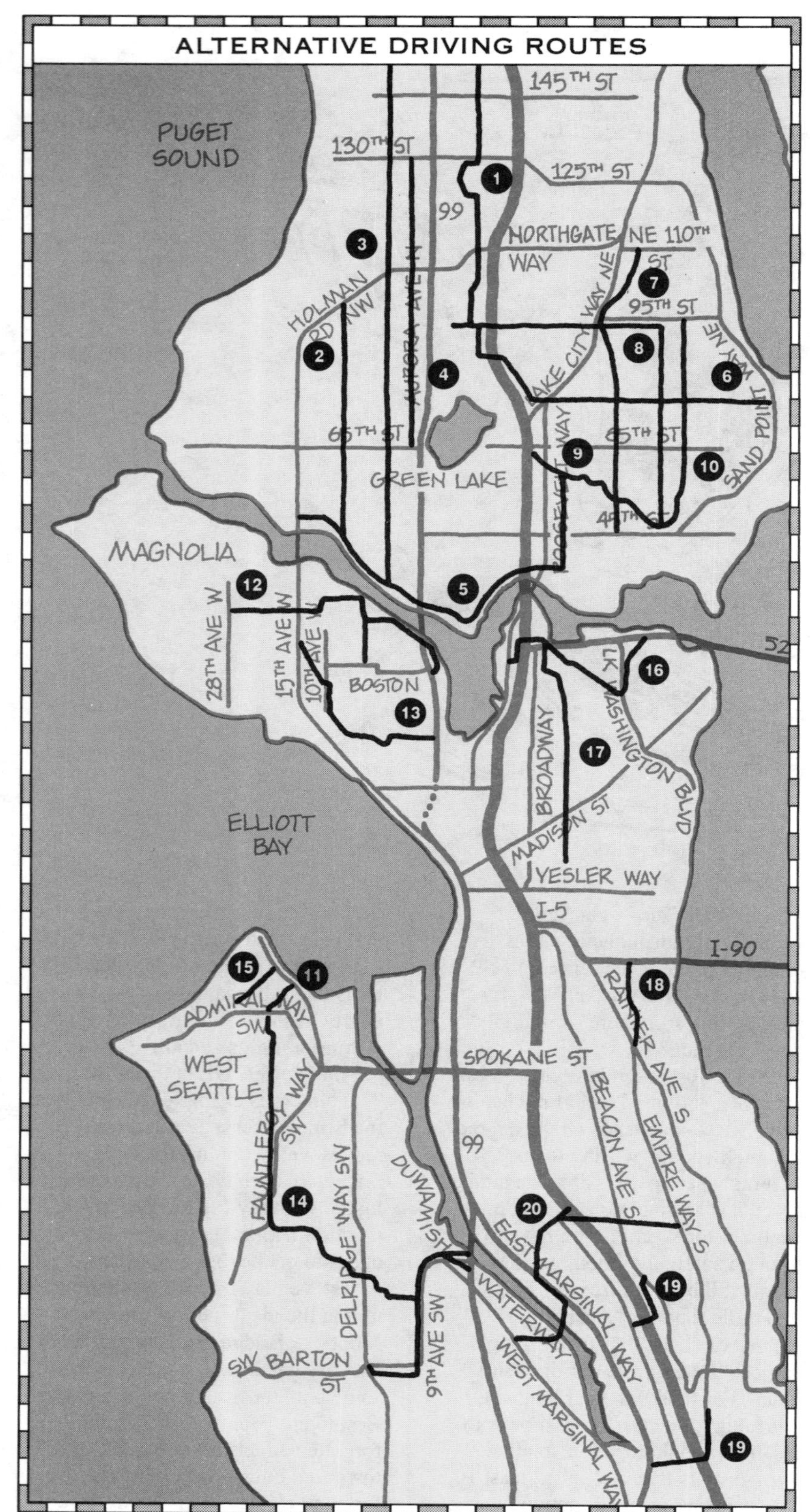

might stumble across one or two that were never really "discovered" in the first place.

20 SHORTCUTS AND SOME STREETS OF ILL REPUTE

We've divided the city into four sections in keeping with its hourglass shape.

Northwest Seattle

Areas to avoid: Intersections NW 85th Street and Aurora, NW 85th Street and 15th Avenue NW, Northgate Way and NW 45th.

Best north/south access: Third Avenue NW, Dayton Avenue N. Open east/west access includes N 130th Street, NW 80th Street, NW 75th Street.

1. To avoid the I-5 crawl around Northgate, **get off at NW 85th Street** and go west to Meridian. Head north to 205th and beyond (with slight detours around North Seattle Community College and Haller Lake).

2. **Eighth Avenue NW:** Good access north/south from Leary Way to Holman Road.

3. **Fremont Avenue N:** Good access from 65th Street NW to 130th Street NW (an alternative to Greenwood or Aurora).

4. **Greenwood Avenue N:** Access from N 36th Street to 145th Street N. Speed islands, residential, go slow.

5. To avoid 45th through Wallingford and Fremont from the U District, take Brooklyn Avenue NE or 15th Avenue NE south to N Pacific Street. Then head west to take N 34th Street to the Fremont Bridge. Go right on Fremont Avenue N to Fremont Place and left to N 36th and Leary Way NW to access Ballard from the south. Better yet, turn right before Fremont—Stone Way to Bridge Way N to Fremont Way and on to Leary is a good alternate route.

Northeast Seattle

Areas to avoid include University Way and 45th (or almost anywhere and 45th), NE Northgate Way, N Lake City Way.

Best north/south access: Sand Point Way NE, 35th, 25th, and 15th avenues. Best east/west access: NE 65th and 75th streets.

6. **NE 75th west to Banner Way** (access just before interstate): Quick way to get from Magnuson Park or View Ridge over I-5 to North Green Lake, Aurora, and Shilshole (via NW 85th Street). Banner Way shortcut works going east if you take 80th instead of 75th.

7. **25th Avenue NE to Ravenna Avenue NE:** Great scenic way for moving from north U District area to Lake City while avoiding Lake City Way NE during the rush. Ravenna begins curving parallel to Lake City Way after crossing 75th Street.

8. **35th Avenue NE north or south to 92nd Street and west to north Green Lake or Aurora:** 92nd is a vital throughway to the west side.

9. **40th Avenue NE to NE 52nd Place**, turn right and this merges into 39th Avenue NE, then to NE Blakely Street. (This winds around, a little narrow.) Go across 25th Avenue NE to Ravenna Park area, where you must take a left and immediate right onto Ravenna Avenue NE to get up to left turn onto NE Ravenna Boulevard and into the U District or Ravenna. This route would allow you to avoid 65th if it's crowded.

10. **40th Avenue NE** has north/south access between 88th Street on its north end and Sand Point Way on the south end; good alternative to Sand Point or the congested area of 35th NE.

Southwest/Central Seattle

Avoid California and Fauntleroy streets.

Good north/south access includes Airport Way S, 35th Avenue SW, 49th Avenue W. In West Seattle, SW Thistle Street provides good east/west access.

11. **Get off hill onto Harbor Way** in West Seattle from Fairmount Avenue SW.

12. **To cut time** getting onto Nickerson Street in Queen Anne from Magnolia, take W Dravus Street east to 11th Avenue W, go left to Bertona Street and right to Nickerson. You can go right on Third Avenue W prior to Nickerson to access the top of Queen Anne. When coming from the east and using Dexter Avenue N as a parallel alternative to Westlake Avenue N, cut a corner to the Third Avenue hill from Florentia Street, just past the Fremont Bridge.

13. **To avoid Mercer Mess**, take Aloha off Queen Anne or Highway 99 and go west to First Avenue, then go left one block to W Olympic Place, which merges into Olympic Way W. This goes to 10th Avenue W, then take a left one block on Howe Street to 11th Avenue W, which turns into Gilman Drive, leading to 15th Avenue W.

14. **Take Highland Park Way exit** from First Avenue S bridge on Duwamish Waterway. Follow it to Holden Street, then turn right to 16th Avenue SW, take a right and immediate left on Austin Street. This merges into Dumar Way SW. Go up Sylvan Way hill, merge into SW Morgan Street. From here, 40th Avenue SW is better than 38th for northern access because it eventually merges into Fairmount Avenue SW. That goes down scenic route to Harbor Avenue SW. Slight righthand jog at SW Hanford Street to stay on 40th. (Marginal Way SW is a much quicker alternative to this northern access if you don't want to access any neighborhoods.)

15. **Ferry Avenue SW** also cuts down from top of hill to Harbor Avenue SW, joining at area of Salty's restaurant.

Southeast Seattle

Avoid 23rd Avenue E and Jackson Street. North/south access includes Beacon Hill Road, Martin Luther King Jr. Way, and Wilson/Seward Park Avenue S. Best east/west access includes Graham, Orcas, and Othello streets.

16. **To access Roanoke Street** on the way to Montlake, take Eastlake Avenue E north, then go right on E Louisa or E Lynn streets, up to Boylston Avenue E, then turn left to Roanoke. An **alternative to the 24th Avenue E** paralysis when getting onto 520 is to take Roanoke to Delmar Drive E to Boyer Avenue E to Lake Washington Boulevard in the Arboretum, then go left up to the more isolated eastbound 520 on-ramp.

17. **15th Avenue E** is a good, if crowded, parallel to Broadway on Capitol Hill. Follow it north until it turns into Boston, then turn right on 11th (or Federal) and wind down to Roanoke, where you can either head down to Montlake or up to the U District. Try 12th Avenue E, too.

18. **Cheasty Street to Beacon Avenue S** or Columbian Way and 15th Avenue S helps dodge broken streets around the Jefferson Park golf course. To access Cheasty Street shortcut, turn right off Martin Luther King Jr. Boulevard onto S Winthrop Street, which merges into Cheasty Boulevard S. No lights, a great scenic shortcut.

19. **Military Road** south of Beacon Hill is a good I-5 crossing. Also the **Boeing Access Road** (south of Boeing Field), which intersects with Martin Luther King Jr. Way for open access north through Madrona.

20. **Graham Street west to Swift Avenue S**, then north to Albro Place, west to Ellis Avenue to E Marginal Way, south on 16th Avenue S, and across the 14th Avenue S bridge to Cloverdale Street, which carries you from the far southeast side to far southwest side.

AND MORE...

That takes care of the four sides of the city. But here are a few general tips:

Express lanes are always the fastest.

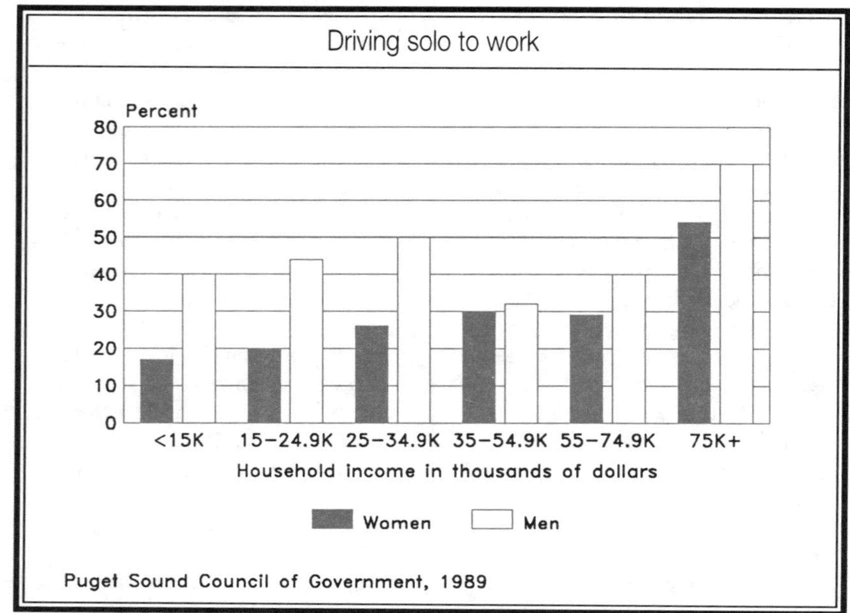

Commuter High-Occupancy-Vehicle **(HOV)** lanes are another good alternative (north and south on I-5, westbound on 520). The three-or-more-persons rule applies here and it is enforced. Fellow commuters have even been known to report violators.

A tip to the daring: Police usually hang out just on the west side of the Mercer Island Lid (tunnel).

It may be ugly and it's definitely not the safest place during an earthquake, but the **Alaskan Way Viaduct/99** is a route that you can always count on to be virtually stopless. Even with the 40-mph speed limit (which is enforced), the route is a good alternative to I-5 at rush hour. However, accessing it can be tricky. Beware of making a U-turn when heading south on First to get to the Royal Brougham Way access ramp—police watch from a nearby parking lot. But that's the best access to 99 from Pioneer Square...

You used to be able to cut through Broadmoor, but, our spies say, no more; the guards will actually call the person you say you're visiting and then you're in trouble.

East/westbound: Between the half-hour of 5:30–6 p.m. there just isn't any good path across the lake. In general, I-90 is going to be less crowded than 520. When the old I-90 bridge reopens (eastbound only), there's no doubt that this will be the faster route. Unfortunately, it's not scheduled to reopen until 1992.

North/South I-405: At rush hour, try to avoid this entirely. Best alternative is, believe it or not, I-5 to I-90.

Some desperate souls do anything to avoid I-405. They choose to go around the lake, up to Mountlake Terrace, and then east, but that's only if I-405 is *really* congested.

If you're heading to the north end of the Lake, **522 (Lake City Way)** can be a decent alternative on some days.

Once on the east side Bellevue Way, which parallels I-405 from I-90 to 520, can often save some time.

Redmond bottleneck: The stoplight at the end of 520 often causes congestion. If you're going into Redmond the best way to avoid this stoppage is to exit at NE 51st Street. Turn right at the ramp to Lake Sammamish Parkway, then north on Redmond Way. This will take you right into town.

Downtown from I-5 avoid the Union Exit, which drops you into the middle of one of the most congested spots in Seattle (partly due to the Convention Center).

That **Convention Center** bottleneck on I-5 can be avoided heading north if you take the Madison Street exit. It eventually becomes an entrance and you're back on I-5—ahead of all those trucks stuck under Freeway Park.

Fastest route to the **Winslow/Bremerton ferry:** Don't follow the signs. Some drivers claim they can get to the ferry in 10 minutes from virtually anywhere—here's the secret: James Street Exit from I-5. Take immediate right (at Columbia) and sail down the hill to Colman Dock. If you need to find parking you might want to allow double that.

Pike Place Market to Pioneer Square: First and Second avenues can be abysmal in the late afternoon. Duck down Post Alley to Western and miss them both.

Pioneer Square to Lake Union: Get onto Western as soon as you can, follow it north to entrance to

Table of transportation statistics for Seattle Central Business District (CBD)

Daily vehicle trips to Seattle CBD: 248,075
Daily person trips to Seattle CBD: 358,100
Morning peak hour vehicle trips into Seattle CBD: 19,200
Morning peak hour person trips into Seattle CBD: 43,400

Source: Seattle Office of Long Range Planning, 1989

Travel time to downtown in minutes

Area of residence	Drive alone	Bus	Carpool
Federal Way/Auburn	43.96	55.33	45.28
Kent/Soos Creek	46.90	67.12	44.45
Burien/Tukwila/Renton	26.07	42.73	29.63
Issaquah East	34.77	52.64	38.82
Bellevue	29.20	46.12	30.59
Redmond/Kirkland	38.45	46.82	40.90
South Seattle	14.50	34.65	20.03
Capitol Hill/Queen Anne	15.25	25.48	15.61
North Seattle	20.49	30.69	17.27
Shoreline	24.09	39.43	36.07
Lynnwood/Edmonds	37.21	46.89	34.34
Mill Creek/Cathcart	39.67	51.61	42.59
Marysville/Snohomish	50.85	75.64	54.0

Source: Puget Sound Council of Governments, 1987

Battery Street tunnel, take your life in your hands merging with 99 traffic, and turn off at the first right, or next right if you miss it, then zip up to Westlake. Buses create a mess on First and Third avenues during rush hour.

How to avoid the Mercer Mess: Stay away from it entirely and backtrack to another freeway entrance—the Olive Street entrance, for example. Get onto Olive from Boren, cross over the freeway, stay in the left lane, and you'll merge with cars coming down Olive to enter the freeway to the north. To go south on I-5, follow Boren north to Howell, turn right, and follow the signs to I-5 south. It's worth the foray into downtown even if you have to go as far as University to approach the dreaded I-5.

Sources: Metro traffic reporters, Seattle Survival Guide research, assorted traffic survivors, and shortcut sleuths.

HOW LONG CAN IT TAKE?

You think you have it bad, take a look above at how long it takes your neighbors to get to work.

WHERE THE CARS MEET

Hear the word "congestion" and what comes to mind? Not something you treat with nose spray but those horrible intersections where one car sneaks through at a time. Sometimes that's because of stoplights, sometimes because of a bottleneck (as in the case of the Montlake Bridge, where 58,900 cars over 24 hours squeeze into a street that has a traffic version of arterial sclerosis).

Most congested intersection and longest light: First prize goes to Greenwood Avenue N and N 145th Street. The light is set at a 150-second cycle length in the afternoon in heavy traffic.

Second prize: California and Alaska streets, where the light is set at a 120-second cycle from 11 a.m. to 7:30 p.m.

Why are some signals faster than others? There are two reasons; first, some signals for large or major intersections (e.g., Greenwood and 145th) are actuated. This means that the signal cycle is activated directly by the presence of a car or pedestrian

For those of you who don't relish the idea of shortcutters using your neighborhood for their backroad driving, here's a tip. The City of Seattle Engineering Department runs a Neighborhood Speed Watch Program that loans out a radar unit free to one person in the neighborhood and trains him or her to use it. Information on speeding vehicles is recorded on a form—make, model, license number, and color. And the residents can clock speeds. Once the Engineering Department receives the forms, it tracks down the culprits via license plate numbers and sends him or her a letter saying the residents are concerned. What does the Department find? That most speeders live in the neighborhood. For information on the Speed Watch Program, call 684-7570.

through the use of underground sensors beneath the asphalt which are pressure-sensitive, and can detect the presence of a car's weight on the road. This, in turn, activates the signal's cycle. Pedestrians, of course, activate the signal by hitting the "walk" button.

Second, the signals at intersections along a straight-shot thoroughfare (e.g., NE 45th and NE 50th streets) are *progressed*. This means that each light's cycle is "progressively" timed and varied throughout the day to cycle in keeping with the flow of the traffic, thus eliminating as much stop-and-go movement as possible. For instance, say there is no traffic on NE 45th heading east. You could travel from the freeway to 15th Avenue NE (UW) through a half-dozen lights without stopping, if you were doing the speed limit. That's because each light is progressively timed; each light cycles to "green" just as you get to it.

The above two methods are the most efficient. A third method would be to just pre-time signals at all-way–walk intersections with the emphasis on pedestrian safety rather than optimum traffic flow (such as near schools, by the Market, etc.).

At non-signalized intersections, there must be five or more accidents in a year before the intersection will be considered for signal installment.

Source: Seattle Engineering Department

WHEN IN A RUSH...

So it seems as if rush hour starts at 2 p.m. on Fridays? Projections show that by the year 2000 peak-period hours of delay on the freeway/expressways will double. Twenty years after that, it'll triple. That doesn't even take into account the clogged arterials.

One other thing about rush hour multiplication: Between 1988 and 2000, roughly $500 million worth of gasoline will be wasted by vehicles sitting on congested roadways in the Central Puget Sound region, according to a study by the Puget Sound Council of Government.

Top 20 accident locations in King County

State Highway	Location	Total Accidents	Milepost
5	SR 405/Southcenter Parkway/SR 518 Interchange (Tukwila)	212	153.90 to 155.04
5	Mercer Street Interchange (Seattle)	209	166.46 to 167.13
520	Evergreen Point Floating Bridge (Seattle and Medina)	157	1.63 to 3.98
5	Lake Washington Ship Canal Bridge (Seattle)	139	168.34 to 169.18
405	SR 167 Interchange (Renton)	138	2.12 to 2.51
5	SR 18 Interchange (Federal Way)	137	141.76 to 142.26
5	Swift-Albro/Corson-Michigan Interchanges (Seattle)	135	160.70 to 161.91
5	SR 520 Interchange (Seattle)	131	167.80 to 168.23
5	Spokane Street/Columbian Way Interchange (Seattle)	107	162.64 to 163.28
520	SR 513/Montlake Boulevard Interchange (Seattle)	106	0.78 to 1.36
5	NE 145th Street Interchange (Seattle)	106	0.78 to 1.36
405	NE 8th Street Interchange (Bellevue)	100	174.31 to 174.76
5	NE 4th Street Interchange (Seattle)	89	169.19 to 169.62
5	NE Northgate Way Interchange	86	172.47 to 173.02
405	SR 520 Interchange (Bellevue)	85	14.40 to 14.93
90	Mercer Island Floating Bridge (Seattle and Mercer Island)	82	4.21 to 5.84
5	NE 175th Street Interchange	75	175.95 to 176.35
99	First Avenue S Bridge (Seattle)	71	26.26 to 26.91
5	SR 516 Interchange (Kent)	68	148.88 to 149.45
5	S 320th Street Interchange (Federal Way)	67	143.57 to 144.03

Source: Washington State Department of Transportation, 1989

AUTOMOBILE ACCIDENTS

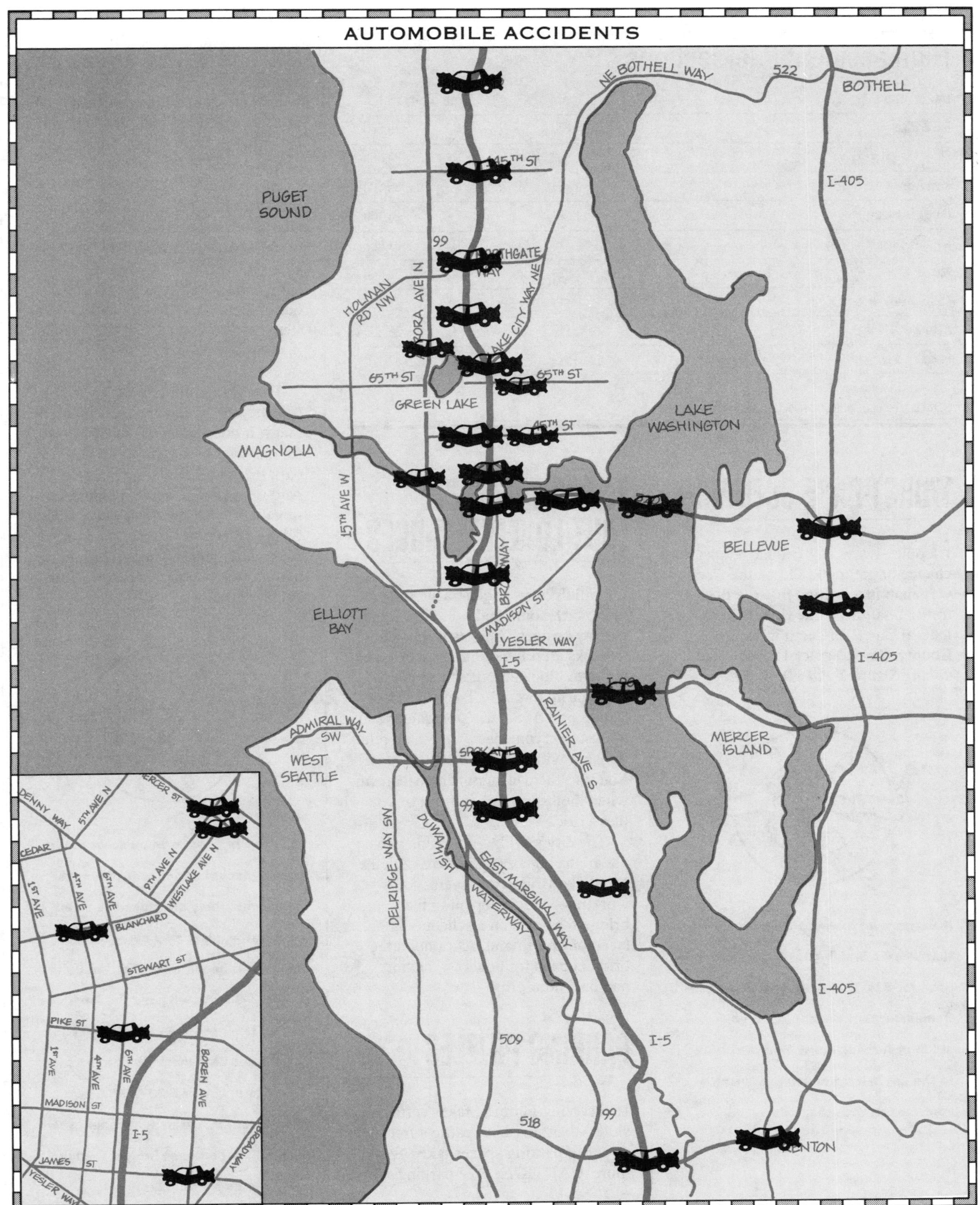

High accident intersections

Intersection	Accidents	Total daily traffic
6th & Pike	23	19,500
9th & Mercer	23	35,500
15th Avenue NE & NE 45th	21	36,300
Boren & James	21	24,100
Martin Luther King Way & S Othello	20	31,600
Mercer & Westlake	20	38,800
15th Avenue NE & NE 65th	19	23,300
Aurora & N 80th	19	38,600
Fremont & N 34th	19	32,100

Source: City of Seattle Engineering Dept., 1988 records

WORST-CASE SCENARIO

People always say you have more chance of getting killed on the freeway than in a jet, and it's true that traffic fatalities come right behind natural causes of death in King County. (See Chapter 15, page 229, *Taking Seattle's Pulse*.)

It seems a lot longer, but the truth is that when a bridge goes up, it's only open for 3 to 3½ minutes on average. Remember that the next time you're stuck at the University Bridge staring at the car in front of you and wishing you were on the other side.

THOSE DAMNABLE (BUT LOVELY) BRIDGES

Seattle's horrendous traffic funnels both north/south and east/west into narrow bridges. And, as if those bottlenecks aren't enough, those bridges go up to block auto traffic and let boat traffic through. They're a frustrating part of Seattle's character and almost everyone has a love-hate relationship with the city's 161 bridges. You love them at sunset and hate them when they spring up in front of you like a brick wall.

The city's bridge-operation people are trying an experiment with the Montlake Bridge that seems to be working—they're opening the bridge for boats on a schedule instead of on demand. After noon the bridge opens for boats on the hour and half-hour only.

PARKING PUZZLES

If surviving in traffic takes certain skills, sleuthing out Seattle's free or cheap parking spaces takes even more. CAUTION: Free parking spaces in Seattle are an endangered species. The ones that existed at the beginning of 1990 have been virtually wiped out by an industrious City of Seattle parking crew. The ones listed below were free last time we saw them.

In general, you're going to find most free parking on the rim of what's normally considered downtown—before 8 a.m. Many times if you get there at 7:55 you'll find a spot, and by 8:05 you may be plum out of luck. (P.S. If you have a good stereo system in your car, don't bother reading any further: Just pay for a safe spot.)

For those willing to play parking roulette, the general rule of thumb is that if it doesn't say NO PARKING (in one way or another) you CAN park there without being ticketed. And if you are ticketed, contest it: Legally you're safe. Read signs carefully—many are free for an hour or four and others say no parking north of sign (which implies that it's free south of sign).

Seattle's bridges open on demand for boats—except during weekday rush hours when they are closed to small-boat traffic. Most ship canal bridges are closed to boats Monday through Friday 7–9 a.m., 4–6 p.m.; the Montlake Bridge is closed 7–9 a.m., 3:30–6 p.m. And on the Duwamish, the First Avenue S Bridge is closed 6:30–8:30 a.m., 3:45–5:45 p.m. Large oceangoing vessels still get an open bridge, though, even during those hours.

The "no parking 30 feet from corner" signs can often be stretched to, say, 15 feet without a meter maid noticing. No guarantees for that tip though.

If you really like to live dangerously, try parking in an alley and putting a note in the window that says, "Just loading" or "My car broke—I'll move it as soon as I can." (No guarantees for that one either—but it has been known to work for brief periods of time.)

South end/waterfront

1. On the west side of First Avenue (between Dearborn and Royal Brougham) there's unlimited free parking. (The east side is one free hour only.)
2. The east side of a little strip along Railroad Way just off First Avenue S (just behind Franglor's Creole Cafe).
3. South of S Jackson Street underneath the Alaskan Way Viaduct and along Alaskan Way: The largest free parking area in Seattle is filled at night with ferry commuters (who usually move their cars by 8 a.m. each morning) and during the day with BC Stena Line patrons. Still, there always seems to be a way to squeeze your car in—especially if you drive far enough south. Careful, though: It's not paved in parts, mammoth potholes and puddles abound, and you may have to chance it over the ruts of the unused railroad tracks.

Lincoln Towing, which has a contract with the city, tows 15 to 20 ticketed cars per day from under the viaduct south of Jackson Street. Reasons for the tickets vary: parking at an angle in parallel parking zone, parking too close to the railroad tracks, parking over 24 hours, and parking in "no parking east of here" zones. It is poorly signed. But if you are lucky, you will find a good, free spot here. (Beware! See "The Toe Truck," page 46.)

We can't surmise that it's because of frustration over a crowded 99, but the Aurora Bridge has long been known as the suicide bridge. An average of three people jump from the bridge per year. 1988: three suicides, one probable suicide. 1989: two suicides, one probable. 1990 thru June 19: three suicides. Source: Seattle/King County Medical Examiner's Office

4. On the east side of Alaskan Way between Main and Jackson streets there's a strip of angle-in parking for about 20 lucky drivers.
5. Fifth Avenue (west side), there's free parking for one block north of Jackson.
6. South Lane Street (the whole street, a small one a few blocks south of Jackson in International District).
7. Maynard south of South Lane.
8. Occidental south of King Street, there's angle-in parking. Watch for loading docks, but as long as you stay clear of ramps, you should be OK. These fill up early.

Also, where Yesler Way crosses I-5, free parking abounds on both sides of the street.

North end/Pike Place Market

1. Heading north, it's a bit tougher to scam a free space. Most of Alaskan Way north of Pike Street is a maximum of three free hours (tourists and Victoria Clipper traffic); however, there are a few spots north of Blanchard Street on the west side (only) of Alaskan Way.

HEARD ON THE STREET

"It's a hard thing for people to hear that the bridges are part of the charm of the city when they're sitting in traffic, but you've got to stop and smell the roses. Try to lower your stress and think about how really lucky we are to live in this part of the country."

Bill Couch, Bridge Maintenance and Operations Manager

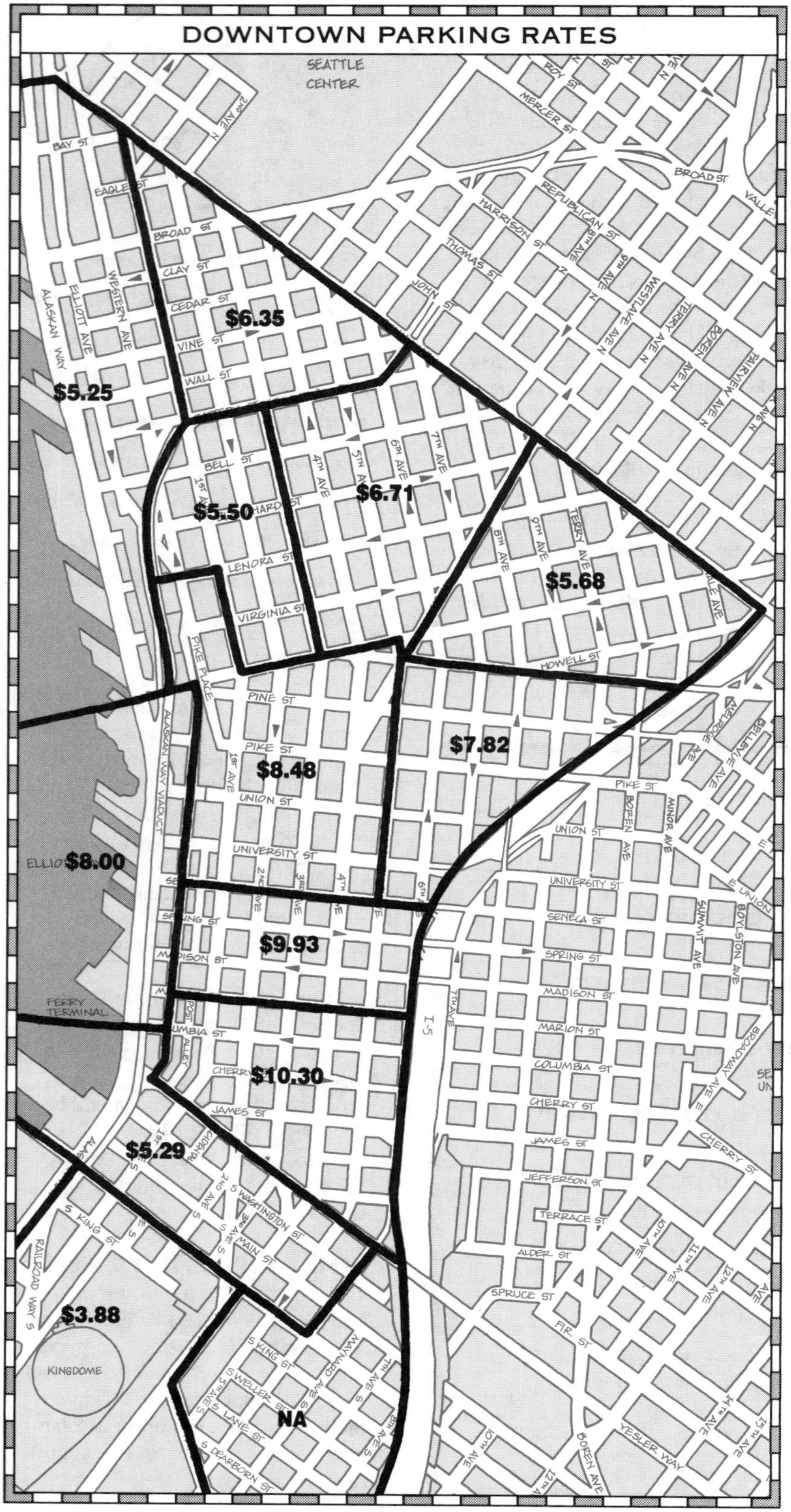

DOWNTOWN PARKING RATES

$6.35 $5.25 $5.50 $6.71 $5.68 $7.82 $8.48 $8.00 $9.93 $10.30 $5.29 $3.88 NA

2. At the southeast corner of Alaskan Way and Broad Street there's a gravel lot that's completely without restrictions.
3. Elliott Avenue (one-way southbound) is virtually a free for all, though it fills early (before 8:30 a.m.) with students from the Art Institute of Seattle.
4. A half-dozen of the cross streets between Elliott Avenue, Western Avenue, and First Avenue allow unlimited parking (north from Battery). A bit of Bell Street (between Western and Elliott) is approachable only from Elliott—but is the closest place to Pike Place Market to scam a space. These spots fill before 8 a.m. almost every day.
5. Finally, on Second Avenue between Denny and Bell you can usually find broken meters and park there for free.

WHEN THERE'S NO CHOICE BUT TO PAY . . .

When in doubt use a privately owned lot. The rationalization here is that if the meter runs out, a city parking ticket will cost you at least $16 and go on your record (and if you don't pay it'll go up...and after only three unpaid tickets the City of

For some people, it just gets to be too much. To report an abandoned vehicle in a public area, call the Seattle police at 684-8763.

Seattle will issue a warrant). Privately owned parking lots (Diamond, Central, United Parking) run anywhere from $1.75 to $9.50 a day. Usually prepayment is required; however, if you forget to prepay and chance upon a ticket, it will run you the equivalent of the lot's daily charge. Lots charging any more than $10 a day should be boycotted.

WHAT IT COSTS

If you pay for parking in commercial lots, chances are if you don't want to walk a ways, you'll pay, on average, $7.45 per day ($93.34/month) downtown; $5.54 ($46.86/month) on First Hill; $3.54 ($35.79/month) on Lower Queen Anne.

A handful of under $3 spaces still exist downtown and there are plenty in the $4–$8 range and some in the $9–$10 range. The $3 lots are usually (but not always) full by 9 a.m. Here's a list of under and about $3 lots:

Dearborn and Royal Brougham
$1.75/day

Western between Bell and Wall
$2.50–$2.75/day

Pine and Alaskan Way
$3/day

One block north of Pine on Alaskan Way
$2/day

Elliott at 99
$2.50/day

First and Bell
$3.25/day

Virginia and Terry
$3.50/day

International District, Jackson Street lot
$3.50/day, $52/month

TRAFFIC FACTOIDS

Number of parking meters in Seattle: 8,600
• Parking tickets issued in 1988: 510,756
• Unpaid parking tickets since 1981: 227,000
• Uncollected ticket amount owed to Seattle since 1981: $9.7 million
• What an overtime parking ticket will cost you: $16
• What happens if you don't pay in 15 days: It doubles to $32.
• How many meters are looted in a year: 1,200 totaled, 2,000 broken
• Parking per hour downtown: $1 (four quarters; nickels not accepted)
• Cost for ticket for parking in truck loading zone: $35
• Most expensive parking ticket: $50 for parking in a space reserved for the handicapped

How to pay a ticket: Go to the cashier's window on the first floor of the Public Safety Building, Third Avenue and James Street. Hours are 8 a.m.–5 p.m. Or mail your check to P.O. Box 34108, Seattle, WA 98124-1108. Include your license plate number on the check.

Tell the magistrate: The city won't say how many parking fines are lessened or forgiven altogether if a case is contested, but if you're really strapped it's a good idea to throw yourself on the magistrate's mercy. He or she will almost always give you a break—and will allow you to pay over time.

Number of vanity licenses in Washington State: 70,000

Source: Seattle Survival Guide research

TROUBLE CALLS

When you see anything wrong with traffic signs or signals in Seattle, call the City of Seattle Engineering Department at 386-1206 or, after business hours, 386-1218.

DOWNTOWN GAS PUMPS

The concrete jungle has few gas stations, and fewer garages where you can get anything repaired. But here are some gas stations close in:
Seattle Center: Arnold's Texaco, 150 Mercer (Mercer and First Avenue N) and at 10 Denny Way (Denny/Queen Anne)
Mid-town: old Seafirst Building Chevron, 1001 Fourth Avenue, in parking garage
Fourth and Columbia Parking (Chevron), 723 Fourth Avenue, at entrance of parking garage
Kingdome Shell, 511 S Dearborn
Raphael Fred Chevron, Ninth and James
Southend: First and Royal Brougham (Texaco)

THE TOE TRUCK

Contrary to popular belief, the little pink "toe truck" at Lincoln Towing is only a little over 10 years old. Though it's not a Seattle old-timer, the truck has found a place (right next to the Elephant Car Wash sign) in Seattle lore. The punsters at Lincoln Towing got the idea for the truck in 1980 and asked Ed Ellison, Seattle body shop expert, to build it. He made it out of a Volkswagen bus, reconstructing the body with fiberglass. A Seattle sculptor molded the five toes on top and the Lincolns put a light inside so the toes would light up.

The truck has been used for parades and promotions—it has starred in three Torchlight Parades. It also visited schools, grabbing the attention of otherwise distracted school kids while the Lincolns talked about auto safety.

The Toe Truck still runs and the boom on the back can even tow small vehicles, but for now it's retired and sits in state at the Mercer Exit, where it can watch potential business come its way.

CARPOOLS—ONE SOLUTION

Everybody's pushing carpools, and with good reason. They're not only good for you, they're good for society as well. And they save money. Seattle Commuter Services (a city group) offers low-cost carpool parking throughout downtown Seattle and surrounding areas.

The parking costs $17/month per carpool and since you have to have three or more people in a car, that's divvied up to make it a really good deal. (Some lots are open to two-person carpools.)

Carpool resources

Seattle Commuter Services, carpool parking
684-5088

Metro Carpool Ridematching
625-4500

Metro Vanpools
625-4500

Traffic resources

City of Seattle Engineering Department
600 Fourth Ave.
Seattle, WA 98101
684-5349

Downtown Seattle construction hotline
464-6897

Puget Sound Council of Governments
216 First Ave. S
Seattle, WA 98104
464-6174

Seattle Police Traffic Section
610 Third Ave.
Seattle, WA 98104
684-8762

Washington State Department of Transportation Information
562-4000

Impounded vehicles on public property
684-5444

Complaints about vehicle impounds and tows
386-1297

Residential parking permits
684-5087

Traffic violations
684-5600

Illegal parking on public property
684-8763

To report trucks over legal requirements
684-5086

Drivers licensing locations

464 12th Avenue
464-7331

320 N 85th Street
545-6755

907 N 135th Street
364-2830

6337 35th Avenue SW
764-4138

CHAPTER

4

GETTING AROUND GRIDLOCK

BUSES

FARES

SHORTCUTS

FERRIES

BIKES

STREETCAR

AIRPORT

PASSPORTS

Over 10,000 workers pedal their way to city offices daily, while another bunch of pencil pushers carpools, zooming down those diamond-studded lanes. About 120,000 trips to and from work are made on Metro buses every day. And each day 17,751 commuters jump on Washington State ferries and float to their jobs. No one is counting those who simply hoof it to the office, but however you cut it, those who leave the car in the garage have an edge over drivers stuck on overpasses.

AHHH, METRO

Metro figures it carries 70 million passengers from stop to stop annually (those aren't all different people—this figure counts how many trips people make and includes free-zone riders). It's easy and cheap, and the folks at Metro have a wonderful customer service department where they tell you just which bus to get for where you want to go.

Here's how it works: Each bus route has a published timetable with a route map, schedule of times, and fare information. The schedule says when the bus will arrive at a bus stop.

You can pick up timetables on the buses and at most public locations around the city (libraries, shopping centers, 7–Eleven stores, and Bartell Drugs). Or you can call Metro's 24-hour number: 447-4800. They'll send you a timetable or tell you when to appear at the bus stop.

New schedules are published three times a year: in February, June, and September.

Metro also offers free, color transit maps at two locations downtown: in the Exchange Building (Second and Marion) and at the Customer Stop (Fourth and Seneca).

CLINKING COINS

Metro drivers don't carry change, so have the right coins in hand. If Metro gets its way, you'll have to come up with a greenback.

A two-zone fare means you've crossed the city limits during the trip; peak times are weekday commuting hours.

Metro fares

(subject to change in 1991)

	1 Zone	2 Zone
Adults	$0.75/peak $0.55/off-peak	$1.25/peak $0.85/off-peak
Youth/student (5–17 yrs.)	$0.75/peak $0.55/off-peak	$0.75/peak $0.55/off-peak
Seniors/disabled (with permit)	$0.25/peak $0.25/off-peak	$0.25/peak $0.25/off-peak

Unless you're in the downtown free zone, pay when you get on the bus if you're coming into town. Going out of town, pay when you get off.

Free zone: The free zone is in effect between 4 a.m. and 9 p.m., and its borders in downtown Seattle are: Jackson Street on the south, Sixth Avenue on the east, Battery Street on the north, and the waterfront on the west.

If you really use the bus a lot, you can buy a monthly, three-month, or annual pass.

Monthly pass: $26 one zone/peak, $42 two zone/peak.

Three-month pass: $72 one zone/peak, $114 two zone/peak.

Annual: $286 one zone/peak, $450 two zone/peak. (Off-peak monthly and annual passes are available too.)

You can buy a pass by mail or from a variety of locations, or call 624-PASS.

A PET PEEVE

You catch the bus and you know where you want to get off, but soon you are reading or daydreaming, and before you know it you are in West Seattle. Why can't Metro bus drivers call out stops? The drivers aren't required to say anything at all, unless they've been asked a question about a route or something. To be fair, many of them do call out the stops—in fact, there's one who rattles off all the buses you can transfer to at a given stop. He's a marvel—and you sure can't daydream with him yelling out a long list of memorized route numbers.

Here's the way to get the word: When you board the bus, ask the driver to call out your stop. When you hear the call, pull the signal cord above the window. And say thanks.

DOGS AND BIKES

Whether or not you can take Fido on the bus depends completely on the bus driver. If he or she is allergic to dogs or doesn't like them, then no, you can't bring your dog along. But if the driver says it's OK, then you

Don't bother swearing at the bus driver for not letting you get on in the middle of the block. And don't bang on the doors of the bus either. Drivers are only allowed to pick up passengers in bus zones—that's why they won't stop for you even if you sprint to catch that bus that's only half a block away from the stop.

can. For anything bigger than a lap dog, you pay the same fare for the dog as you pay for yourself.

As for your bike, it's not allowed *in* the bus. However, many buses have bike racks (see section on bikes below), and on specified routes at specific bus stops you can load your bike for free.

Not all buses can accommodate wheelchairs. But 70% of Metro's fleet is wheelchair accessible and 72% of the routes are. Schedules are marked with an "L" sign (meaning lift-equipped) to indicate accessibility.

BUT IS IT SAFE?

There's been some controversy over whether Metro drivers should be allowed to carry guns. Right now they are not. Crime on the buses is a problem primarily in areas of high population density. Most assaults on operators occur in the Rainier Valley area, downtown, or in the U District.

Metro has instituted programs such as "Youth Team," in which young people chosen by Metro ride on buses that carry school kids and talk to the kids. Within the last year vandalism on the buses has decreased by nearly 75%, partially because of such programs.

Customer conflicts as reported by the driver, from yelling to assault, have only been counted since September 1988. For the first three quarters of 1989 there were 281 such conflicts reported.

THE TUNNEL

The buses that run through the tunnel under downtown serve destinations such as the U District, Southcenter, Sea-Tac Airport, Bellevue, and Northgate.

The advantages of the tunnel can be expressed in mere minutes:

• Length of time it takes a bus to travel through downtown Seattle on

Metro safety statistics

Operator assaults	1988	1989
Non-injury	49	44
Injury	27	18
Spitting	26	36
Total	102	98

In the first half of 1990 injuries to drivers have decreased over the same period in 1989 by 29%.

Source: Metro

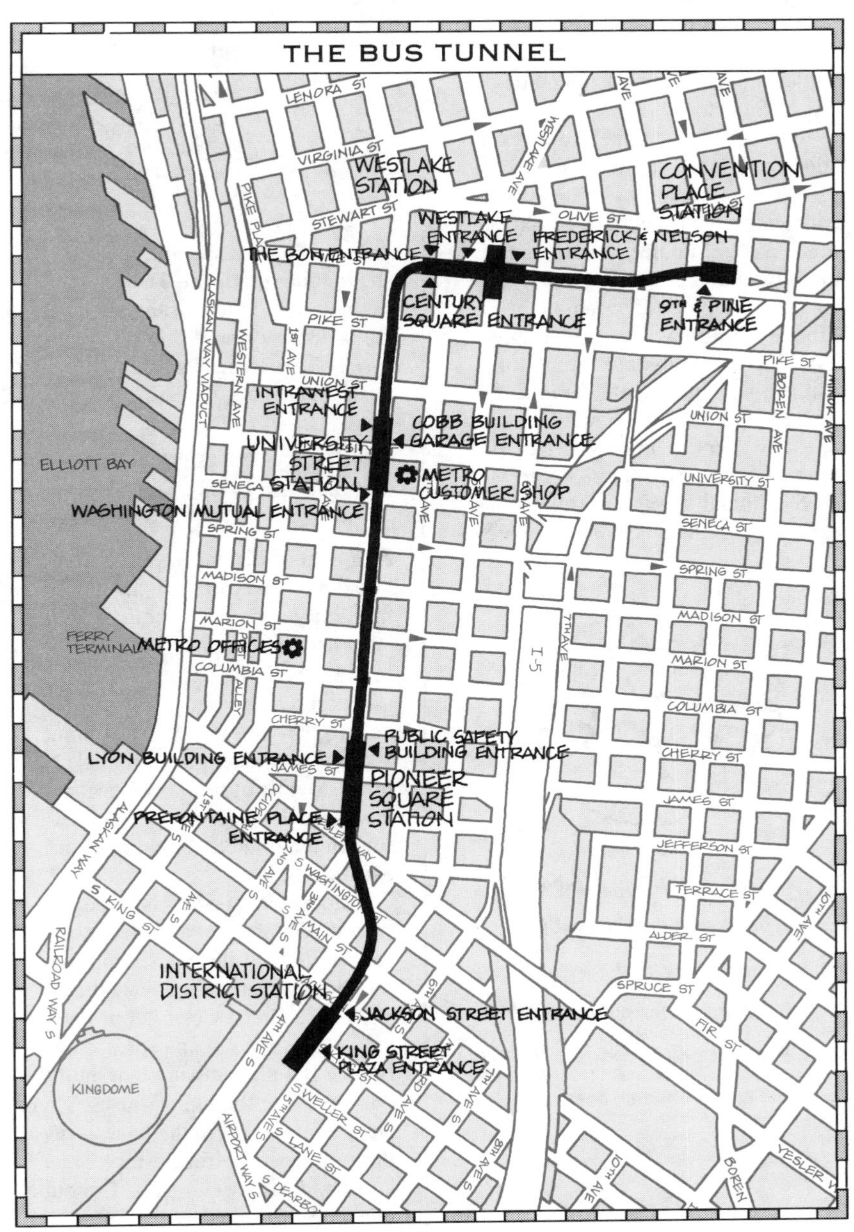

surface streets during rush hour: 20 to 25 minutes.

•Length of time it takes a bus in the tunnel: 8 minutes.

There are still buses on the surface, notably on Third Avenue, where no parking is allowed.

There are five tunnel stations, each designed to reflect the neighborhood it serves. For example, someone thinks the area around Third and University is high-tech oriented, so video and electronic gadgets decorate that station.

The tunnel operates between 5 a.m. and 7 p.m. Monday through Friday and between 10 a.m. and 6 p.m. Saturday.

Two new street routes have been added as a result of the tunnel:

1. The First Avenue circulator connecting the Pike Place Market, First Avenue, Pioneer Square, and the International District. These buses leave every 15 minutes, Monday–Saturday, 9 a.m.–3 p.m.

2. The Third Avenue circulator connecting Third Avenue, Pioneer Square, and downtown retail areas operates every 15 minutes Monday through Saturday, 9 a.m.–3 p.m.

The tunnel works like this: In each station, the bus stops in an area called a bay—a specific space at the loading platform. The bays are labeled with letters of the alphabet. Signs list the routes that stop at each bay, so you'll always catch your bus at the same bay.

Six thousand to 10,000 umbrellas are lost on Metro buses annually. If you lose something on the bus, call 684-1585. Maybe someone turned it in. Most unusual thing turned in to Metro's lost and found? A human heart.

TUNNEL FACTS

Amount of dirt taken out of tunnel: 900,000 cubic yards, or six stories high if piled across a football field.

Where it went: Various landfills (e.g. Federal Way, Paine Field).

Passengers estimated in the tunnel: 18,000 per year. **Cost** of tunnel: $450 million. **Length** of tunnel: 1.3 miles. **Depth** of tunnel: 60 feet below street level. Number of **elevators** in the tunnel: 28. Number of **escalators**: 46.

Another West of Mississippi record: The longest and steepest escalator West of the Mississippi is in the Pioneer Square tunnel station.

What's Breda Costruzioni Ferroviarie? No, it's not an espresso bar. It's the Italian company that built the bus shells for the tunnel buses. There were a few snags in the buses—in the gear systems, for example, but angst and expenses will be forgotten when all the buses are rolling.

BENSON'S STREETCAR

Metro operates the Waterfront Streetcar, but city councilman George Benson is the streetcar guru. He even hands out free passes, so enamored is he of the whole idea (which was his, of course). The streetcar, which came from Australia, is no longer just a tourist attraction; it now serves a real trans-

The singing streetcar operator: Eldo, a guy with a white beard and a hat that says "motorman" on it, drives the streetcar most days from the morning until 3 p.m. Just look for his beard and ask him if he'll sing for you. He sings as he rolls along and/or if there's a request from a rider.

portation purpose since its run was extended from the waterfront up Main Street and into the International District.

The streetcar isn't free downtown; it costs $0.55 to go from the International District to Pier 70, $0.25 for senior citizens and the disabled.

Municipality of Metropolitan Seattle (METRO)
821 Second Ave.
Seattle, WA 98104
447-4800
Transit director's office: 684-1441
Metro director's office: 684-1983
Metro council chambers: 623-8644
Metro tunnel info: 684-1420
Metro rider and bus info: 447-4800 (24 hours) or 684-1739 (TTY/TDD users)
Metro lost and found: 684-1585
Driver commendations and complaints: 447-4824 or 684-2029 (TTY/TDD users)
Metro community relations: 684-1138
Pass information and sales: 624-PASS
Ridematch/Vanpool info: 625-4500
Tunnel: 684-1420

Other bus services

Greyhound Bus Station
811 Stewart St.
624-3456
Greatest number of scheduled bus routes connecting Seattle to other cities. For package service, call 628-5555.

Gray Line of Seattle
720 S Forest St.
624-5077

Charter bus services

Greyhound Travel Services
Eighth and Stewart
628-5534

Cascade Trailways
2209 Pacific Ave.
Tacoma, WA 98402
838-3465

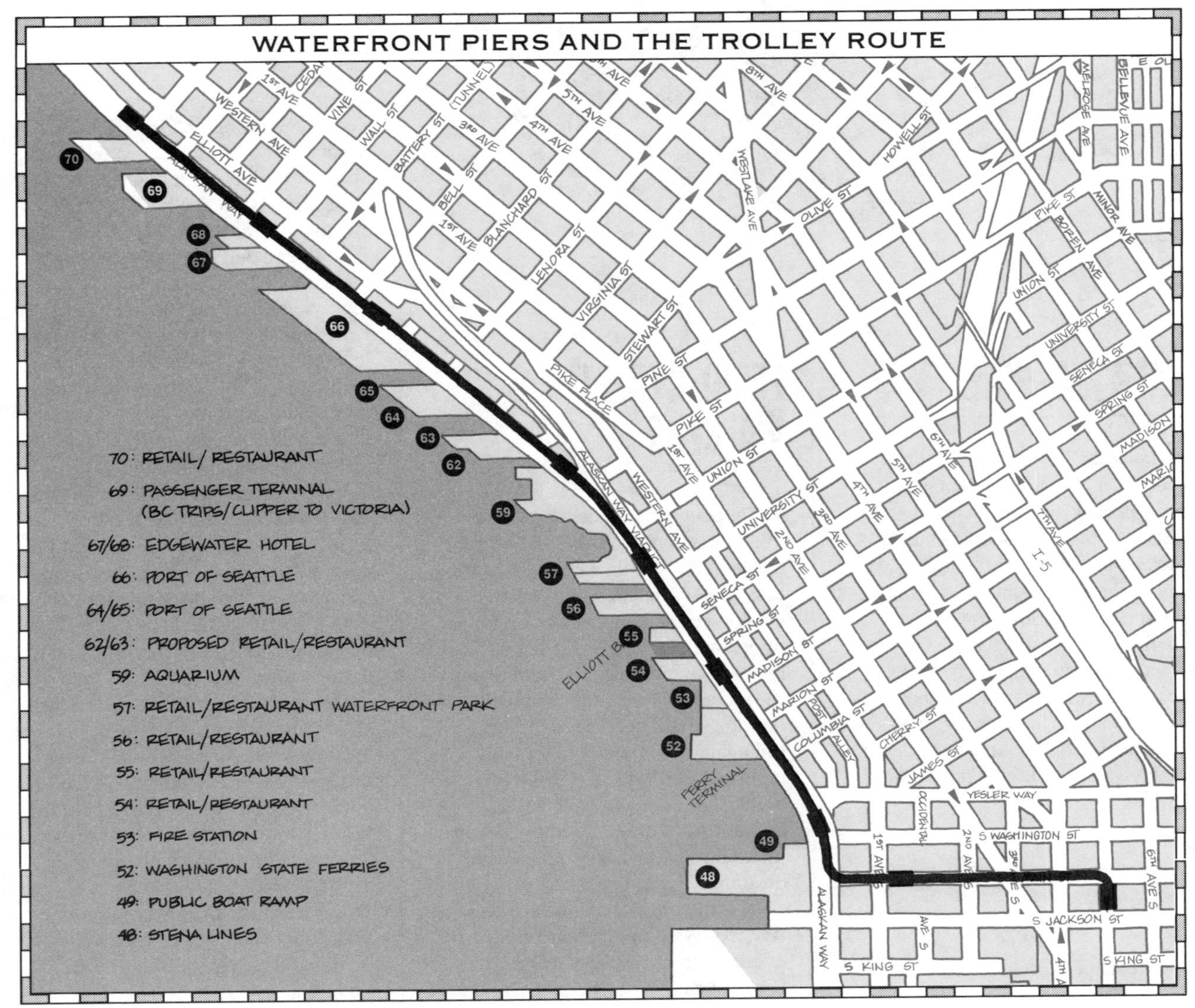

WALK AND BIKE

Using your feet instead of your wheels has the same advantages that using a kayak does over a power boat: You can take advantage of narrow passages and pretty much go the way of the crow—in a straight line.

Especially in downtown Seattle, where one-way streets and massive structures block the way for autos, feet can save the day. That's not to say there aren't hazards: Seattle doesn't have the reputation of being the Jaywalking Ticket Capital for nothing.

LEGAL STREET WALKERS

City planners and developers have finally begun to consider the plight of the pedestrian in a city where it's easy to get drenched by the rain. Almost every new highrise has a tunnel or inside path where you can cut corners and avoid traffic. With the long escalators and elevators inside the buildings, you need never climb a hill again. The trick is to look for highrises that take up a complete block. They usually have access on both sides of the building and an internal route that does not depend on stairs.

1. From the waterfront to Sixth Avenue: Walk up the Marion Street overpass from the ferry terminal to First Avenue, enter the lobby of the Federal Building on First between Madison and Marion. Then take the elevator to the fourth floor to get out at Second Avenue. Cross the street and take the covered escalator up the First Interstate Plaza. Walk through the bank to Third Avenue. (Use the revolving doors or you might get yelled at for letting the wind into the lobby.) Then cross the street to the Seafirst Building, take the escalators up to Fourth Avenue. From there you can either head uptown via the pedestrian bridge that runs across Fourth, or cross the street and take the escalator (or elevator) in the Seattle Public Library from Fourth up to Fifth Avenue. From there you can go one more block uphill by crossing Fifth to the U.S. Courthouse and taking the elevator there up to Sixth.

2. From Second Avenue and University uptown: Thank goodness for the new Washington Mutual Tower. It not only offers a route up the hill, but is pretty inside as well. Enter the WMT from Second, take an escalator or elevator to the main lobby on Third. Cross the street to Seattle Tower and take an elevator to the fifth floor. There is a covered outdoor walkway and a bridge to the Four Seasons Olympic mezzanine.

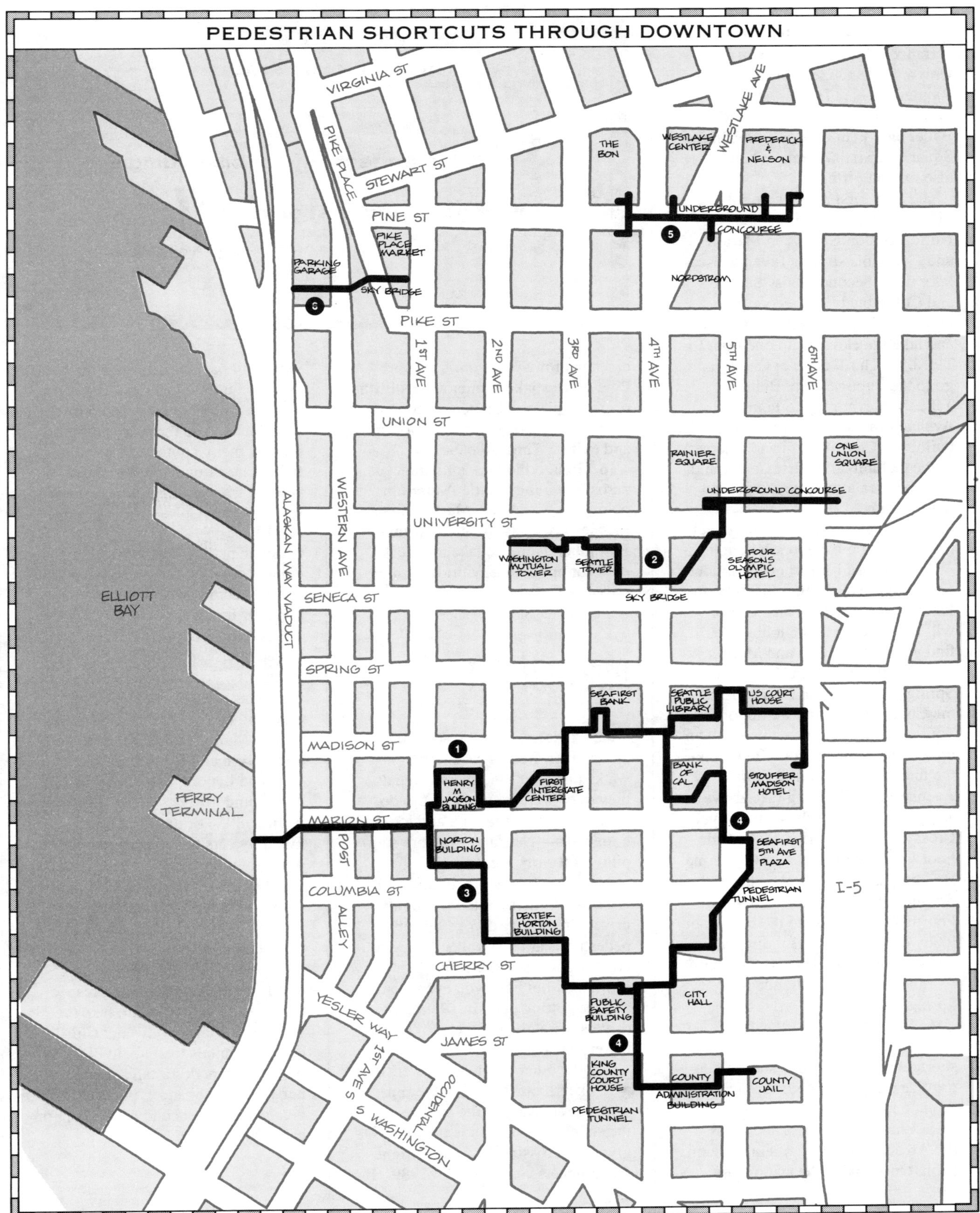
PEDESTRIAN SHORTCUTS THROUGH DOWNTOWN
VIRGINIA ST
WESTLAKE AVE
PIKE PLACE
STEWART ST
THE BON
WESTLAKE CENTER
FREDERICK & NELSON
PINE ST
UNDERGROUND
CONCOURSE
5
PIKE PLACE MARKET
NORDSTROM
PARKING GARAGE
SKY BRIDGE
6
PIKE ST
1ST AVE
2ND AVE
3RD AVE
4TH AVE
5TH AVE
6TH AVE
UNION ST
RAINIER SQUARE
ONE UNION SQUARE
UNDERGROUND CONCOURSE
WESTERN AVE
ALASKAN WAY VIADUCT
UNIVERSITY ST
WASHINGTON MUTUAL TOWER
SEATTLE TOWER
2
FOUR SEASONS OLYMPIC HOTEL
SKY BRIDGE
ELLIOTT BAY
SENECA ST
SPRING ST
SEAFIRST BANK
SEATTLE PUBLIC LIBRARY
US COURT HOUSE
MADISON ST
1
HENRY M JACKSON BUILDING
FIRST INTERSTATE CENTER
BANK OF CAL
STOUFFER MADISON HOTEL
FERRY TERMINAL
MARION ST
4
POST
NORTON BUILDING
SEAFIRST 5TH AVE PLAZA
COLUMBIA ST
3
PEDESTRIAN TUNNEL
I-5
ALLEY
DEXTER HORTON BUILDING
CHERRY ST
YESLER WAY
CITY HALL
PUBLIC SAFETY BUILDING
JAMES ST
4
1ST AVE S
KING COUNTY COURTHOUSE
COUNTY ADMINISTRATION BUILDING
COUNTY JAIL
OCCIDENTAL
S WASHINGTON
PEDESTRIAN TUNNEL

Leave the hotel by the main entrance (where the doorman is, on University) and cross the street to Rainier Square. There's an underground walkway there past Eddie Bauer and on to One or Two Union Square on Sixth Avenue. (You can also exit on Fifth.)

3. From First Avenue uphill to Fifth at Marion: On First enter the Norton Building between Marion and Columbia streets. Take the escalator up to Second. Cross Second and Columbia to the second-floor lobby of the Dexter Horton Building and take the elevator up one floor to Third. At Third, cross at Cherry and go to the Public Safety Building. Take the elevator up to Fourth Avenue (on the fourth floor of the building). Cross Fourth and Cherry to the Columbia Seafirst Center and take the escalator up to the second-floor atrium.

There's a great pedestrian tunnel here—but you have to ask people where because it's somewhat hidden. Follow it to the Seafirst Fifth Avenue Plaza Building where an elevator will take you up to the lobby. You'll find yourself on Fifth and Marion.

4. Northbound from Cherry to Spring, beginning on Fourth: Enter the Columbia Seafirst Center on Fourth and Cherry, take the escalator up to the atrium's second floor. Take the tunnel to the Seafirst Fifth Avenue Plaza Building (see above) and go up to the Fifth Avenue level. Cross Fifth and Marion to the fifth-floor lobby of the Bank of California Building and take the elevator to the first-floor lobby on Fourth. Cross Fourth and Madison to the fifth-floor lobby of the Seafirst Building. Take the escalator or elevator to the Third Avenue lobby and entrance near Spring Street.

5. The concourse at Westlake Center: Definitely not a lengthy shortcut, the new tunnel station does provide a dry way to get from Sixth Avenue to Third. Enter Frederick's on Sixth, go downstairs and cross the Arcade to the station entrance on Fifth. Once inside the station you can head for Nordstrom's across Pine or Westlake Center across Fifth, or past Westlake Center to the Bon where you can take an escalator up and exit on Third Avenue.

6. Go into the parking garage across from the Seattle Aquarium below the Pike Place Market. Take the elevator up to Western Avenue. From there you can take another elevator up to the sky bridge which crosses over to the Market.

Source: Seattle Survival Guide research

HEARD ON THE STREET

"It's the perfect city for bike riding if you're not going east or west."

A city cyclist

ONE FOOT OUT

Cars, it seems, don't respect the city walker. Red lights and crosswalks just aren't the sacred signals they once were, and it's best to do what your mom told you and look both ways—carefully—before stepping off a curb. According to the Harborview Injury Prevention and Research Center, 70 to 90% of all drivers in the city don't stop for pedestrians at crosswalks. (They're eligible for a $47 ticket for that infraction, but have you ever seen anyone getting one? In 1989, 920 drivers were given tickets for violating crosswalks.)

On the other hand, jaywalkers do get tickets, some 3,565 of them per year, for crossing in the middle of the street. If you include the tickets given for crossing against the light, 5,802 tickets were given in 1989. (If you don't pay, the city won't come after you unless you rack up several of these—they're considered mere infractions. And there are no figures on how many contested jaywalking tickets are thrown out, but those who've tried arguing their case say they either get a lesser fine or none at all.)

Some people treat jaywalking as a contest of wills, car vs. body, but the battle becomes serious when you consider how vulnerable pedestrians are. As you'd expect, most pedestrian fatalities happen in the busy areas of the city. For example, in 1989 there was a fatality at Dexter and Roy, and one at Ninth and Seneca, two on Martin Luther King Way S, one at 14th and E John, another at First and Lenora, and others spread out around town.

In 1989, 6 of the 13 pedestrians killed by cars were in crosswalks when they were hit, 4 were jaywalking, 1 was hit by a truck backing up, 1 was hit when crossing in an unmarked intersection, 1 was a little boy playing in the road.

In 1988 and 1989 there were 15 and 13 pedestrian fatalities, respectively. Kids, in particular, take the brunt of it. Harborview and Children's hospitals treat about 80 kids involved in pedestrian/car accidents per year. After cancer, pedestrian accidents are the second most common cause of children's deaths.

WALKING ALTERNATIVE

Feel like getting your exercise by walking but aren't crazy about gas fumes? Try mall walking, the latest fad (especially for senior citizens) at the sprawling shopping malls. At Northgate Mall, for example, walkers pace up and down from 7:30 a.m. until the shops open around 9:30 a.m. The mall is one-quarter mile from one end to the other. Every Wednesday morning from 7 a.m.–9 a.m. there are two nurses and an exercise physiologist on hand to do free blood pressure testing, health checks, and to give out information on walking. Contact number is Northwest Hospital, 365-7587.

Bellevue Square also has a walking program, sponsored by Overlake Hospital. Sea-Tac Mall at Federal Way has a program sponsored by St. Francis Hospital.

WITH WHEELS AND HELMETS

Two percent of the city's commuters ride bikes to get to work. That makes Seattle one of the highest cycling commuter communities of comparable size nationwide. More kids in Seattle wear bicycle helmets than in other cities, but that's still only 5%. In Portland the rate is 1%; in San Francisco it's one-half of 1%.

The most common bike route is to the U District. If you're going there from downtown, it's best to go up Broad, then head north on Dexter. Follow it to the Fremont Bridge, cross it, get onto N Pacific Street and then onto the Burke-Gilman Trail, which leads you straight to the U.

Causes of accidents for kids on bikes: ages 4–5, riding out of driveways without looking; ages 6–7, intersection crossings; ages 8–9, running stop signs. Main cause of accidents for adults: riding against traffic.

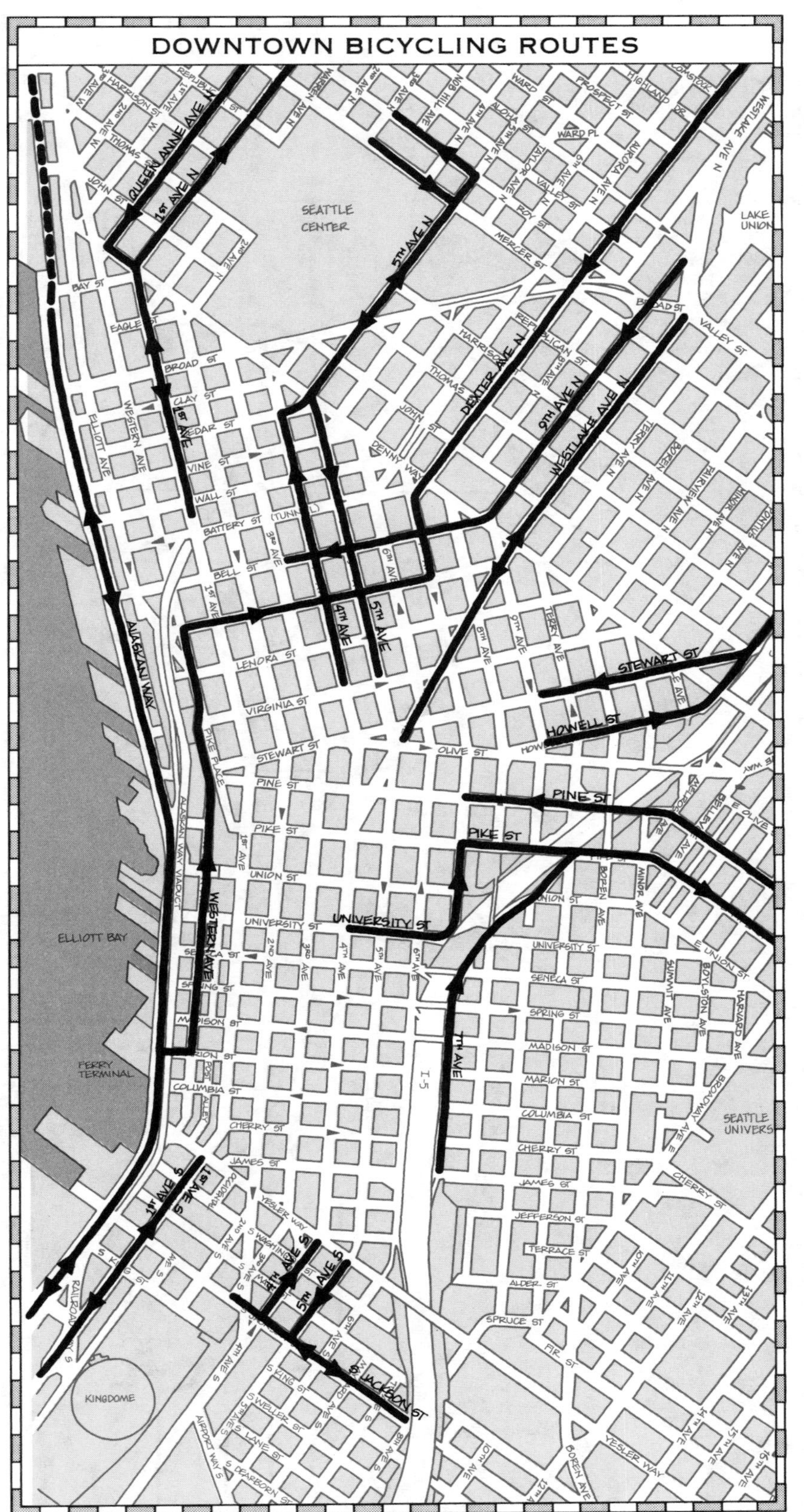

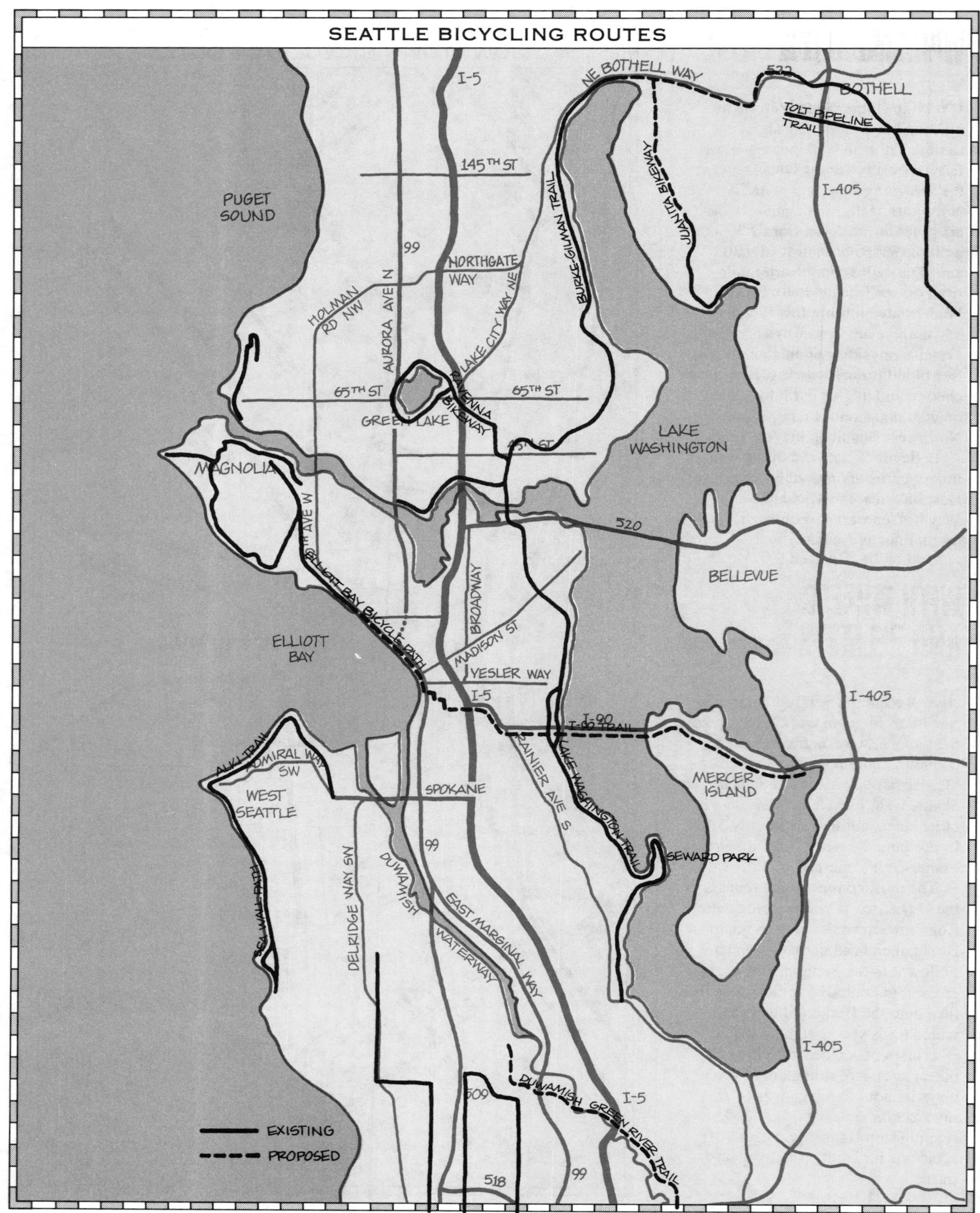
SEATTLE BICYCLING ROUTES
I-5
NE BOTHELL WAY
522
BOTHELL
TOLT PIPELINE TRAIL
145TH ST
PUGET SOUND
BURKE-GILMAN TRAIL
JUANITA BIKEWAY
I-405
99
NORTHGATE WAY
HOLMAN RD NW
AURORA AVE N
LAKE CITY WAY NE
RAVENNA BIKEWAY
65TH ST
65TH ST
GREEN LAKE
45TH ST
LAKE WASHINGTON
MAGNOLIA
15TH AVE W
520
BELLEVUE
ELLIOTT BAY BICYCLE PATH
BROADWAY
ELLIOTT BAY
MADISON ST
YESLER WAY
I-405
I-5
I-90
I-90 TRAIL
ALKI TRAIL
ADMIRAL WAY SW
RAINIER AVE S
LAKE WASHINGTON TRAIL
MERCER ISLAND
WEST SEATTLE
SPOKANE
99
SEWARD PARK
DUWAMISH WATERWAY
EAST MARGINAL WAY
SEA WALL PATH
DELRIDGE WAY SW
I-405
DUWAMISH GREEN RIVER TRAIL
I-5
509
EXISTING
PROPOSED
99
518

BICYCLING Q & A

Q. What traffic laws apply to bicyclists?
A. All.
Q. What position in the lane should a bicyclist use?
A. If you're going at the speed of traffic, use the middle of the lane. If you're slower, ride as near to the right side of the right through-lane as is safe except when preparing to turn, when passing another bicycle or vehicle, or on a one-way street (where it's legal to ride on the left). If the right through-lane is too narrow to permit sharing with cars, and when drain grates or the like prevent riding on the shoulder, bicyclists should ride in the middle of the right lane. You are only required to ride on the shoulder on limited access highways. When five or more vehicles are lined up behind you, you must pull off the road and let them by.
Q. What lane position should a bicyclist use through an intersection?
A. The same as a car, but where the intersection is particularly scary,

City bike riding is a serious thing; one false move and you lose your life or a limb. About 250 bicycle/car accidents are reported each year. There are one or two bicycle fatalities per year. Most bike accidents don't involve cars; 90% are caused by rider error. Where do they happen? At intersections and on suburban streets and—to an overwhelming extent—in the U District.

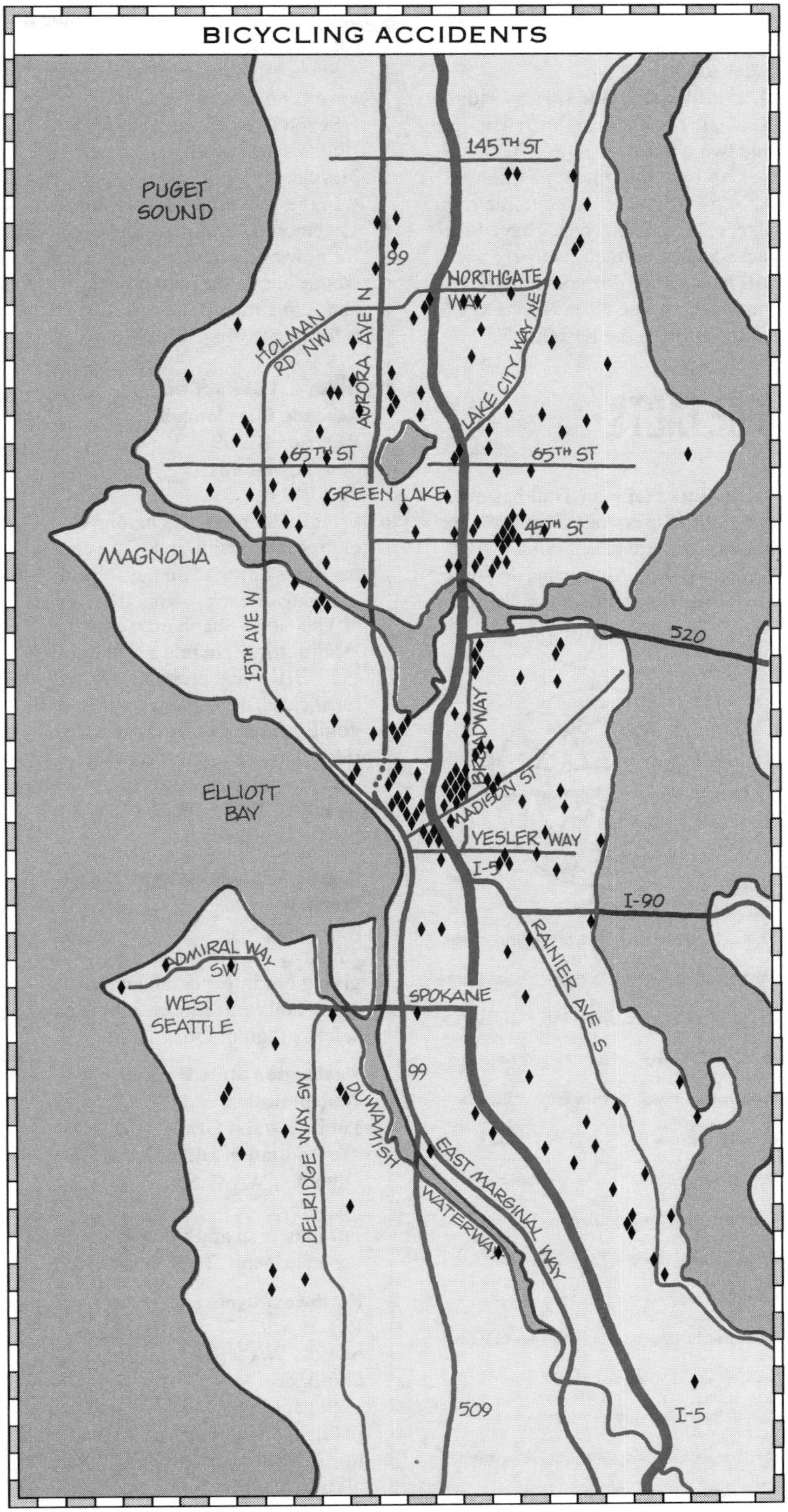

BICYCLING ACCIDENTS

PUGET SOUND
145TH ST
99
NORTHGATE WAY
HOLMAN RD NW
AURORA AVE N
LAKE CITY WAY NE
65TH ST
GREEN LAKE
45TH ST
MAGNOLIA
15TH AVE W
520
BROADWAY
ELLIOTT BAY
MADISON ST
YESLER WAY
I-5
I-90
ADMIRAL WAY SW
RAINIER AVE S
WEST SEATTLE
SPOKANE
DUWAMISH
EAST MARGINAL WAY
WATERWAY
DELRIDGE WAY SW
509

it's a good idea just to dismount and use the crosswalk. (Sometimes it's faster too.)

Q. Is it illegal to ride side-by-side?

A. No, the law allows bicyclists to ride two abreast.

Q. Can I put my bike on a bus?

A. Yep—if you're going to the right place. Some Metro buses have bike racks and using them is free. (You still have to pay for yourself.) Those buses travel nine routes in the system, mainly to the Eastside.

BIKE FACTS

• The Burke Gilman Trail has over one million users per year: 70% are bikers, 30% are pedestrians.

• Over 45% of Americans do some bicycling. It's estimated that well over 50% of Seattleites use a bike to some degree.

• Since 1973 more bikes than cars have been sold in the U.S.

• Seven to eight percent of UW students and faculty commute by bicycle.

• In the I-90 tunnel a complete bike system will be in place by 1992. But for now bikes have their own concourse above the auto tunnel. It's lit and four cameras are installed along it for monitoring.

The city gives out free bicycling maps that specify several urban, scenic bike loops. Call the engineering department at 684-7570. King County puts out a map too in conjunction with REI. The county map is $4 at REI or Metsker Maps. And then there's a book called Touring Seattle by Bicycle by Peter Powers and Renee Travis. It sells for about $10 and has 3-D fold-out maps with contours, points of interest, route profiles, and even a calorie counter. Plus, there are usually two routes for the same area, one challenging and one easier.

Bikers' resources

Cascade Bicycle Club
P.O. Box 31299
Seattle, WA 98103
522-BIKE
Over 2,500 members belong to this club. Membership is $15 a year and meetings are held on the second Tuesday of each month at 7:30 p.m. at The Good Shepherd Center in Wallingford. There's a ride line (522-BIKE and press #2) listing local rides, mileage, type of people going (singles, unemployed, married, etc.), and contact number. The group has several committees, including BATS (Bicycles as Alternative Transportation).

Seattle Engineering Dept. Bicycle Program
684-7570
An advocacy office within the city giving out information and taking complaints and concerns. Has a safety program too.

Washington State Dept. of Transportation
Public Affairs Office
Transportation Bldg., KF-01
Olympia, WA 98504
562-4000
For bike map and freeway guide for the state, send $0.50 to these folks.

Northwest Cyclist
P.O. Box 9272
Seattle, WA 98109
286-8566
Free paper with ride calendar, club listings, tours, maps, news, and features. Nine issues per year. Available all over the place—or try REI.

BY AIR AND BY SEA

If you think the highways are congested, take a look at the seaways and skyways. On a Friday afternoon at Anacortes, the line for those cute little green-and-white ferries goes on forever. But there are ways to maneuver through airports and ferry lines.

GRIDLOCKED SKIES

Seattle-Tacoma International Airport officials freely admit they're in trouble because of the three-fold increase in landings and take-offs since 1959. Capacity at the airport is 400,000 flights per year and the Port of Seattle (which runs the airport) says that will be reached in about 10 years.

The first key to getting in and out of the airport hassle-free is to leave the car behind. Airporters serve communities from as far away as Bellingham. Call 431-5906 for information, departure times, etc. ($6 from downtown).

ShuttleExpress is touted as a major relief in terms of getting to the airport, even if you do have to be ready quite a while ahead of time. It has 24-hour, door-to-door service. Call 622-1424 ($12).

Greyhound has several daily trips to the airport from downtown Seattle and vice versa. Call 624-3456 ($2.50/one-way, $4.75/round-trip). And Metro has three routes that go that way: 447-4800.

Taking a taxi from within the city limits costs $21–$22. Sea-Tac recently arranged for a cooperative cab company to get choice spots at the airport cab stands. The drivers have to wear clean uniforms and have fairly reliable and clean cars. The cars are painted white, and they have a green-and-white logo on the side. The co-op is called STITA (Seattle-Tacoma International Taxi Association), 246-9999.

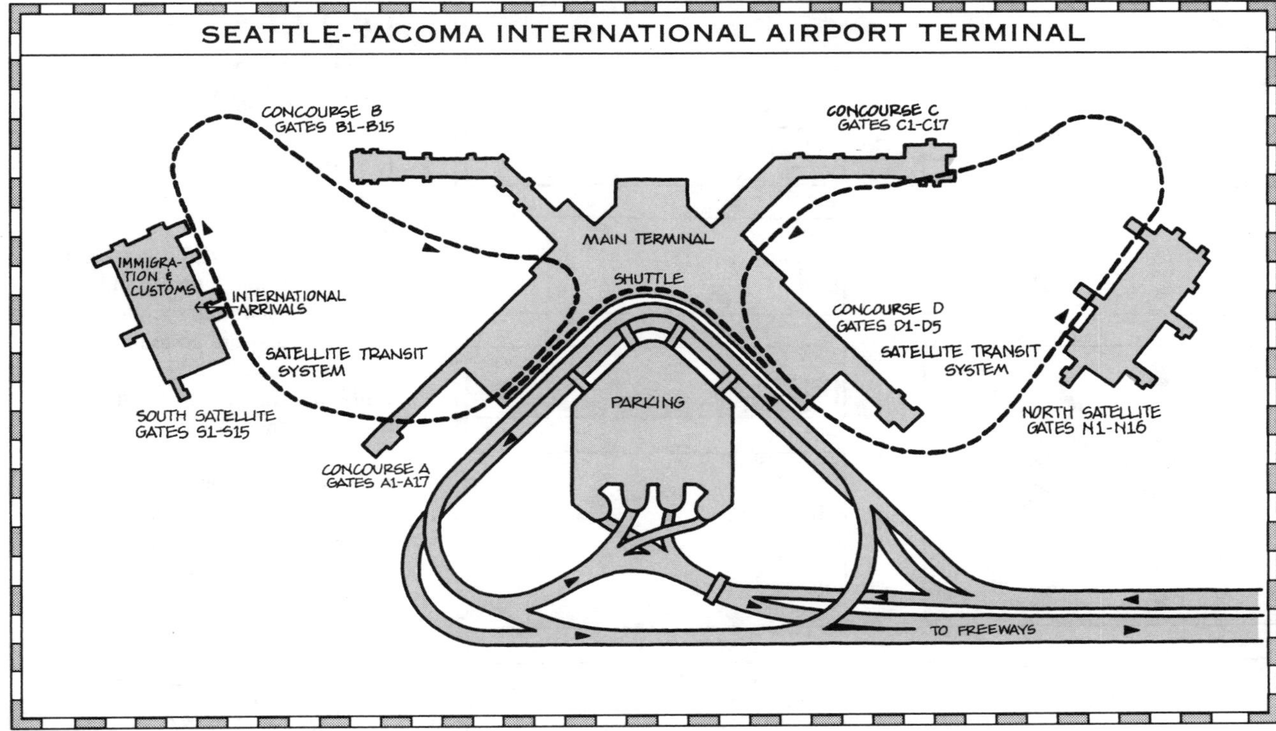

Limousine services run anywhere from $30 to $60 depending on the day and company.

And many hotels provide courtesy car service to and from the airport, as do some of the seaplane companies.

ROUTE OF CHOICE

If you absolutely must drive to the airport, it's best to avoid I-5 altogether. From downtown take Alaskan Way or the viaduct south. That puts you on E Marginal Way. Turn off onto the First Avenue S bridge and follow Highway 509, which is usually fairly open, to the airport. You can also take 99 all the way south to 170th S. Turn right there and right again after going under the overpass. This route has lots of stop lights—509 really is best.

Once you get to the airport, you have to park the ol' buggy. That'll cost you. At the port's own lot, the daily rate is $10 (first 30 minutes free), but you can save by parking a little further away. Lots usually have a free shuttle to the airport. See page 60.

AIRPORT SERVICES

The airport doesn't have a passport center, but Mutual of Omaha runs a foreign exchange and Western Union center, which is open 6 a.m.–9:30 p.m. daily. (Travel insurance is available here in case you get that if-God-had-wanted-people-to-fly-he-would-have-given-them-wings feeling.) You can also pick up tickets from a travel agent at this desk.

Other services include:

- Cash machines. At least four machines, open 24 hours.
- Two US West communication centers, one in the main terminal and one at the north terminal. You can use the copy machines, FAX (outgoing only), and booths with phones and desks. There's a small conference room available on a first-come, first-served basis.
- VIP room that includes a large conference room, kitchen, large lounge, two offices, and two smaller studios for small meetings. But it isn't for riff-raff; it's for Port of Seattle trade or business customers.
- Large rooms that rent out for wedding receptions (quick getaway variety). Call 433-5605 for catering reservations.
- An auditorium for 250 people.
- Tours. If you've always been fascinated with airport workings, this is the ticket. These free tours run three days a week (Tuesday–Thursday) from 9:30 a.m.–11 a.m. You can get special tours at other times for groups, such as senior groups and school kids (youngest is kindergarten). In a six-month period last year 4,500 people took airport tours. Call three weeks in advance, 431-4067.
- Meditation room. For those lonnng waits.
- Barber shop, shower, and shoeshine shop. All in main terminal (a second shoeshine shop is located in the north satellite).

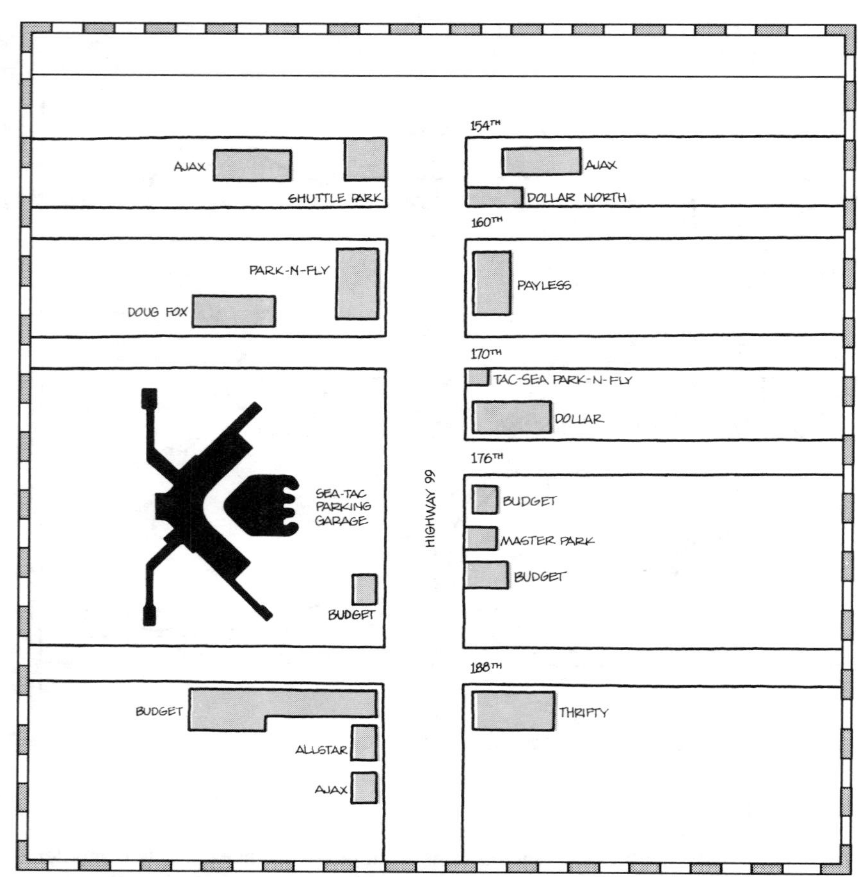

Airport parking rates

Ajax#1, #2and#3	$6.95/day (3rd day free)	
Allstar	4.50/day	$27.00/week
Budget (2 valet lots)	7.25/day	46.00/week
Budget (2 self-parks)	5.00/day	32.00/week
	4.50/day	28.00/week
Doug Fox	7.25/day	45.00/week (7th day free)
Dollar	6.00/day	42.00/week
Dollar#2(unsecured)	4.25/day	
Master Park (valet)	7.00/day	
Master Park (self-park)	5.50/day	
Park & Fly	5.25/day	38.50/week
Payless	4.50/day	27.00/week
Shuttle Park	5.50/day	33.00/week
Tac-Sea Motel	4.35/day	25.00/week
Thrifty	7.25/day	50.75/week

For info, call Sea-Tac's Skyline information number, 431-4444 or toll free, (800) 544-1965.

HOW TO GET A PASSPORT

If you're planning to get out of the country, you need a passport. It's important to apply for it right away—it takes 2½ to 3 weeks to get a new passport, although they'll put a rush on it if you sound desperate. If this is your first passport, go to the Passport Agency, Room 992, Federal Office Building, 915 Second Avenue. Take along evidence of U.S. citizenship and proof of identification, plus two passport photos (go to a passport photo place—there are plenty near the Federal Building and they know the required dimensions of the shot).

The absolute best-kept secret at the airport is Ken's Baggage and Frozen Food Storage. Ignore its limited name: This little gem of a shop will do almost anything for you. It's down on the baggage claim level just under the escalators. Ken's will notarize your letter, unlock your car, lend you jumper cables, make you copies, store everything from skis to computers while you're away, and even sell or store dog kennels. They'll package your bike for shipping, deliver stuff, rent you a baby stroller, and take care of your UPS and Federal Express business. Ken's is privately run. 433-5333.

And take $42 (adults) or $27 (minors). Thirteen-year-olds and up need to apply in person.

If you have had a passport issued in the last 10 years, you don't need to get a new one. And if you have had a passport within the last 12 years, you can reapply for a new one by mail—provided you submit your old passport with the new application.

The office is open Monday through Friday, 8:30 a.m.–4:30 p.m. If you call the agency at 442-7941 or 442-7945, they'll send you a booklet answering questions about visas and passports.

Seattle Passport Agency
Federal Bldg.
915 Second Ave., Room 992
Seattle, WA 98174
For information: 442-7941
Other assistance: 442-7945

Seattle-Tacoma International Airport
P.O. Box 68727
Seattle, WA 98168
433-4645
Airport information: 431-4444

Travelers Aid
433-5288

King County Airport
Boeing Field
296-7380
Reliever airport for Sea-Tac, with smaller planes and no scheduled passenger traffic. Boeing Field is the 11th busiest airport in the nation in terms of landings and take-offs. It has many corporate and private planes (Burlington Northern, Nordstroms, Pay'n Save, for example), private pilots, and flying clubs.

Kenmore Air
6321 NE 175th St.
Seattle, WA 98155
486-8400 or 364-6990
A seaplane solution. Flights to British Columbia, Kitsap Peninsula, San Juan and Whidbey Islands, Semiahoo.

Chrysler Air
1325 Fairview Ave. E
Seattle, WA 98102
329-9638
Another seaplane company with flights to Canada, the San Juans—"anywhere there's water."

Lake Union Air
950 Westlake Ave. N
Seattle, WA 98109
284-0300
Yet another seaplane company. Flights to Victoria, Vancouver, points north in British Columbia, San Juans.

AT SEA LEVEL

Ferries and waiting go together like rain and slugs. The only way to avoid the lines is: 1) walk on, and 2) get there early. The other secret to ferry riding is not to care if you're on time. It makes for the perfect excuse: "The ferry was late" or "the ferry broke down."

There are 25 ferries plying the Sound on 10 routes.

Ferry facts

- There are 1,250 employees in the ferry system.
- There are 20 terminal locations.
- The Washington State ferry system loses money each year. For 1988 revenue was $57.3 million; expenses were $73.7 million.
- In a year the system carries over 8 million vehicles and over 19 million riders.
- The ferries consume 12.8 million gallons of fuel per year.

CRAZY ABOUT FERRIES?

If you just adore the green-and-white double-enders, visit the Mukilteo Maritime-Ferry Museum. It's near the ferry dock, about three blocks behind the community center at Fourth and Lincoln; open Wednesday–Saturday, 10 a.m.–5 p.m.; Sun-

If you have a choice and can travel during off-peak hours, do it. Busiest times for commuter boats (Bainbridge, Bremerton, Vashon, Mukilteo) are mornings from 5 a.m.–9 a.m. and afternoons from 3 p.m.–7 p.m. On weekends, all the boats fill up with travelers. Overloads are less likely before 9 a.m. and the earlier the sailing the less traffic. Heaviest times for weekend boats are 9 a.m. to early afternoon westbound, and from 3 p.m.–7 p.m. eastbound. Increasingly the boats fill up both Fridays and Saturdays, especially to the San Juans, and then again on Sunday evening. The Kingston boat is more crowded than the Winslow on weekends; delays can be from 30 minutes to 3 hours. But the line for the Winslow ferry extending out from Pier 52 can be horrendous. The new dock down there (just in the planning stages) might help, but until it's done there's no way to avoid the bumper-to-bumper wait on Alaskan Way. For the San Juan ferries get in line two hours ahead of time (and pray).

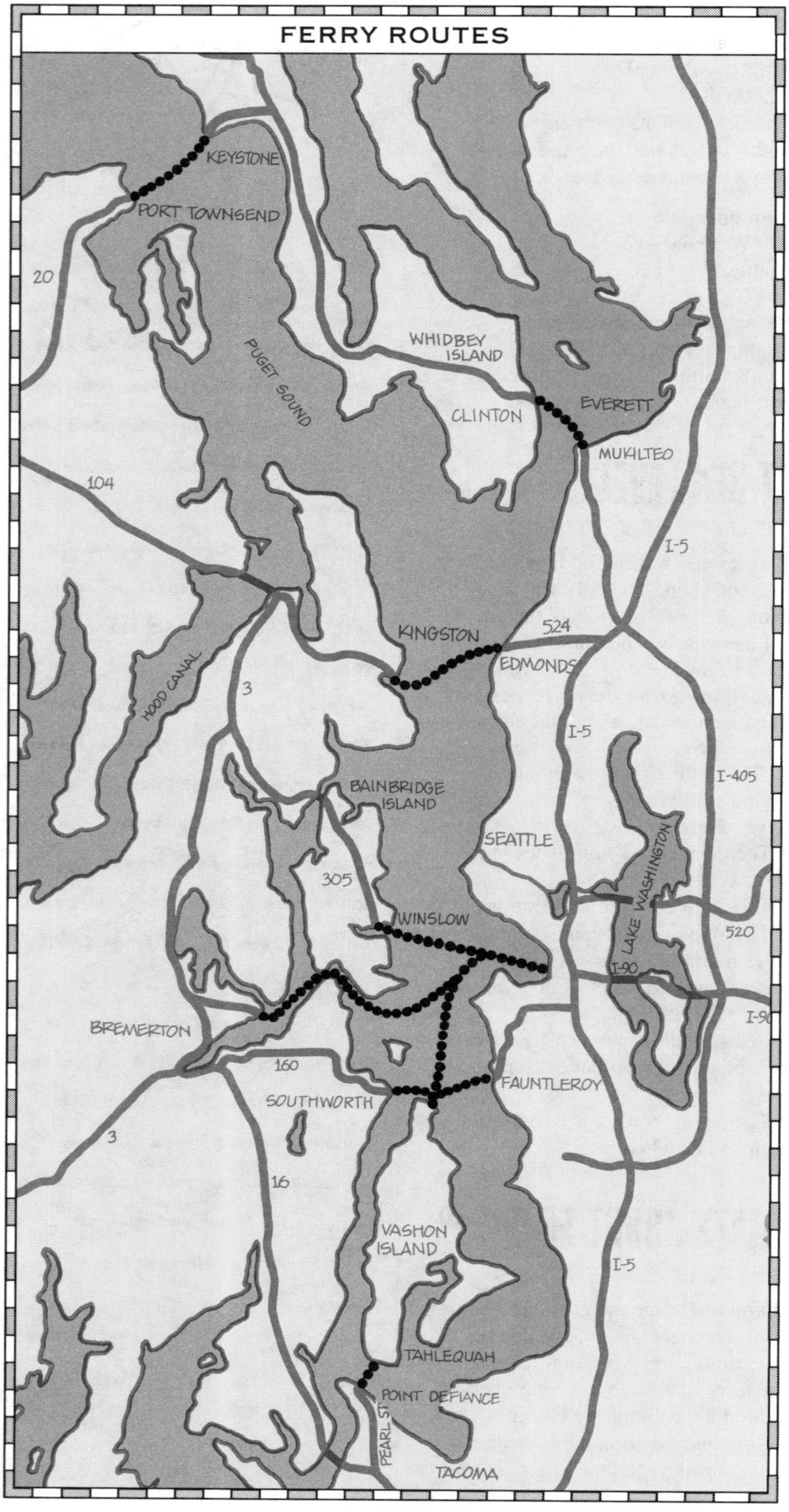

FERRY ROUTES

KEYSTONE
PORT TOWNSEND
20
WHIDBEY ISLAND
PUGET SOUND
CLINTON
EVERETT
MUKILTEO
104
I-5
KINGSTON
524
EDMONDS
HOOD CANAL
3
I-5
I-405
BAINBRIDGE ISLAND
SEATTLE
LAKE WASHINGTON
305
WINSLOW
520
I-90
I-90
BREMERTON
160
FAUNTLEROY
SOUTHWORTH
3
16
VASHON ISLAND
I-5
TAHLEQUAH
POINT DEFIANCE
PEARL ST
TACOMA

day, 1–5 p.m. Call 355-2514 to talk to a curator.

If you are really into ferries, there is a free one run by the state in Eastern Washington across Lake Roosevelt between Wilbur and Republic. The *Martha S.* holds 12 cars and runs between 6 a.m. and 11 p.m.

Here's another bit of ferry trivia: Back in the 1950s one of the hottest ferry controversies concerned the landing signal used by ferries as they approached the dock. The landing signal was described as "a groan and a grunt." After seven years of debate, the issue was resolved when the ferry system reinstated "a warp and two woofs," or what's better known as "one long and two short" blasts. It's a familiar and listened-for signal to regular ferry users; when they hear it from a few blocks away, they know they'd better run for the boat.

WHAT DO THEY MAKE?

Over the years, ferry workers' salaries have become almost a parlor guessing game for riders. You hear that deckhands make $60,000, and ticket takers another good-sized chunk.

Here's the truth:

Ferry personnel salaries, 1989

Ticket takers and terminal attendants: $8.88/hr to start; $13.35/hr experienced. On-dock traffic con-

Note: The ferry system does NOT accept credit cards, but it does accept Washington State checks.

Don't eat on the ferries unless you like to spend a lot of money and don't have active taste buds. For example, a plain hamburger costs $2.19, a soda $0.96, and a cup of beer $2.07.

troller: $12.54/hr. Full-time deck-hands up to Masters: $11–$25/hr.

Captains: $56,000/year (approximately). Ferry system manager: Admiral Harold Parker, $65,000.

Washington State Ferries
Colman Dock
Pier 52
Seattle, WA 98104
Info/schedules/tolls/truck rates:
464-6400
Bremerton-Winslow schedules:
464-6990
Edmonds-Kingston schedules:
464-6960

AMTRAK

The train is a lovely way to travel, if a bit slow and often late, and Amtrak HAS been working on getting real china back in the dining car a la the Orient Express.

The main thing about train travel is that it's relaxed and friendly—Amtrak seems to have a training program for its people that really works. You just have to have enough time to enjoy the trip. You can go on the cheap in the coach car, but if you can, spring for the sleeper rooms; you'll be a lot more comfortable.

Amtrak leaves Seattle for two basic destinations: Los Angeles and Chicago. But it does have several routes. The Coast Starlight, a night-time trip down the coast to L.A., is probably the most popular, and the Empire Builder, through Idaho, Montana, and Wisconsin to Chicago, is a beautiful ride through unspoiled mountain country. The Pioneer route goes to Chicago too, but first drops down to Portland and then runs through mid-America. The Mt. Rainier route is a commuter-type run to Portland with stops at Tacoma, East Olympia, and the like. Amtrak also has bus service to Vancouver from the Seattle station.

Amtrak
King Street Station
Third and Jackson
Reservations or information:
(800) 872-7245
Baggage, lost and found, package express: 382-4128

CHAPTER

5

THE URBAN WILDERNESS

BIRDS

FISH

RATS

CLEAN WATER

OZONE

SEA LIONS

BIG GAME

P-PATCHES

WASTE

RECYCLING

Coyotes in Ballard, raccoons in West Seattle, eagles in Seward Park. Seattle's residents aren't all of the two-legged human variety. Of all the major cities in the U.S., Seattle has perhaps the most abundant wildlife in an urban setting. While we grow used to the call of Canada geese over Lake Union and the sight of orcas in Elliott Bay, most American city dwellers have only pigeons and the occasional rat to liven up their environments. Without packing up the car with tent and camping gear, you can get a taste of the wilds if you just know where to see our exciting native species.

So let's give ourselves a treat. Let's ignore—for the time being—the oil barges plying the Sound and the days when you can't see the skyline through that brown stuff hanging in the air. Let's toast Seattle's urban wildlife and clean waters. (We'll get to the not-so-clean waters later.)

BIRD CITY

Seattle's Puget Sound is resting ground for migrating birds on the Pacific flyway, but also the home of birds who figure this is far enough south (or north) for them and who decide to winter (or summer) here. The city's midway status makes it home to a variety of bird species.

Seattle is one of the lucky western cities in the U.S. where you'll find two endangered species within the city limits. They are:

- **Peregrine Falcons**. They've been spotted in two locations: in the north end of Ballard on the closed-off smokestacks, substitutes for natural snags, where rumor has it that a pair has nested. And in 1989 a pair of Peregrine Falcons was seen in Seattle during the winter months, which means they may be overwintering here. The sighting has led the Department of Wildlife to anchor nesting platforms up on downtown highrises in the hope that if the pair decides to nest, they'll choose a safe spot.

What brings the peregrines to Seattle? A steady diet of their favorite food: pigeons. And the fact that the buildings create walls as steep as the cliffs where they normally dwell.

- **Purple Martins**. Plentiful in Seattle until the 1950s, they have now reached endangered species status. They have been seen nesting on the skybridge next to The Bon, where they've found nesting niches similar to natural tree cavities. The numbers of nighthawks (a member of the Goatsucker family—not really a hawk) have also dwindled in recent years, but they can also still be found in Seattle. They feed on insects at higher altitudes than swallows and swifts do.

AND THEN THE "SEAGULLS"

Not so endangered are the gulls, but guess what? There's no such thing as a "seagull."

You'll find gulls nesting on downtown buildings. We have five or six species: The largest and most common is the Glaucous-winged Gull, also California, Mew, Ring-billed, and Black-headed Gulls—and sometimes Little Gulls.

Downtown, watch for birds of prey such as Red-tailed Hawks, Merlin (also called Pigeonhawk), and kestrels. Redtails have been seen nesting at the King Street train station. Accipiters (Sharp-shinned Hawks and Cooper's Hawks) can also be spotted in the core. These wild-area nesters pass through the city on the lookout for prey—often pigeons on-the-wing or small birds.

BIRD WATCHING

There are three main birding spots in Seattle:

The downtown core
Discovery Park
Montlake Fill

All the above birds are found in the downtown core, but Discovery Park is the "island of habitat" for a variety of bird species. The park offers varied habitat: sandy and rocky beaches; sand cliffs; open meadows facing both north and south; conifer mix, conifer forests, and major deciduous areas; and marshy areas.

Discovery Park provides both nesting habitat and "drop-in" habitat for species passing through on their migration routes. It's also a hangout for birds wintering over. If you want to see one of Seattle's two nesting pairs of Bald Eagles, head to the meadow area and scan the trees behind the maintenance building in the center of the park. The eagles nest in a very large Grand Fir there.

In this sweeping meadow you're likely to spot goldfinches, Red-tailed Hawks, a variety of sparrows, migrating Osprey (if you're lucky), and members of the falcon family: Merlins, peregrines, kestrels, as well as accipiters.

Also in these transition understory/meadow areas, look for Rufous Hummingbirds. It's rumored—but only rumored—that the California Anna's Hummingbird nests in Seattle.

Head for West Point to see seabirds. Here are two miles of wonderful beach habitat—to the north the beach is rocky, to the south sandy. Migrating species pass by West Point because of the narrow passage between the point and Bainbridge Island—about three miles of water allow you a good look at anything flying by.

What's likely to be seen there? A variety of gulls, also Caspian and Common Terns, plus a variety of shorebirds, including Harlequin Ducks in the fall and winter.

Look carefully along the cliffs from the beach area and you'll see a most exciting species, Pigeon Guillemots, which nest in burrows.

Montlake Fill: Once the site of a garbage dump and a fill-dirt dump created from dredging the Montlake Cut, the Montlake Fill is a haven for birds that nest and feed in marshy scrub and wetland. You're likely to see an array of shorebirds, Yellowlegs, Dunlin, Sandpiper, and those species preferring freshwater: Wood Ducks, Gadwall, and teal. This meadow-marsh system—the fill, the Arboretum, and the waterway in between—comprises a complete ecosystem of wetland, scrubby shrubs, and forested swamp land.

The Arboretum also provides tangles of blooming red currant, salmonberry, and blackberry bushes that attract hummingbirds—Rufous and maybe rare glimpses of Anna's Hummingbirds. Coots, Mallards, Great Blue Herons, and other varieties can be seen along marshy shore and waterfront areas. A nature trail runs along this area, where from a wooden walkway you can observe birds feeding and diving. The trail starts at the Museum of History and Industry and winds along the water. Great for kids.

Seward Park: Seattle's second pair of breeding Bald Eagles nests here. Look for tall snags. Veteran Audubon birders claim a third pair may be nesting here soon.

If you enjoy feeding the geese, head down to the south end of Lake Union. You'll be nearly stampeded by herds of Canada Geese. Their numbers in recent years have multiplied to problem proportions.

Like other population boomers, the geese are not native to Seattle. These birds are a Great Basin subspecies from Eastern Washington. A few were released here in the 1930s for a duck club, and they were transplanted here in the 1960s from the Potholes area when a new dam displaced a breeding population and the Department of Wildlife brought the goslings to Lake Washington. Now that generations of them have been comfortably fed by residents, they're here to stay.

The Audubon Society has a species checklist for Discovery Park. Call the park office, 386-4236, or the Audubon Society, 523-4483.

Some of the geese wander within the three-county area of King, Snohomish, and Pierce counties, but they can be considered year-round regional residents, unlike the Aleutian Geese or other species that migrate over the city.

Other areas for birding: Try Magnuson Park and Frink Park and those hidden corners of "greenbelt"—tiny islands of habitat where you're likely to hear or see Olive-sided Flycatchers, Black-headed Grosebeaks, and Western Flycatchers among the Slide Alder, maple, and mixed forests. These greenbelt areas are vital nesting habitats within the city.

Audubon Society
8028 35th Ave. NE
Seattle, WA 98115
523-4483
526-8266 (to report rare bird sightings)
Audubon Society has birding checklists for your sightings covering Seattle parks and other areas. The group also provides birding field trips in Seattle parks and downtown strolls. It also has an ornithologic/nature library and offers classes in bird identification. The Audubon Society has a list of 11 "seed depots" in the city where you can buy bulk wild birdseed. The mix, which is designed especially for birds of the area, includes black oil sunflower seeds, thistle seed, and suet.

Flora and Fauna Books
Natural History Book and Print Specialists
121 First Ave. S
Seattle, WA 98104
A bookstore with a staggering variety of highly specialized birding guide books. Also the hangout for Audubon birders.

PAWS Howl Shelter
743-3845
To report sick or injured birds. Call first.

The Wild Bird Clinic
21234 33rd Ave. S
Seattle, WA 98168
824-6249
Owner: Jonie Butler
Three holding cages outside, and if no one is around they'll be there within 45 minutes after your call. No hawks, eagles, owls, or mammals.

HERSCHEL AND HIS FRUSTRATED FRIENDS

Those sea lions at the locks are actually social and sexual rejects from California.

The name Herschel was given to the first California Sea Lion who became a problem at Hiram Chittenden Locks in the early 1980s. Since then, the collective population of sea lions at the locks has been given the nickname "Herschel," a lovable monicker for mammals who gorge themselves on Steelhead Trout at the locks all winter.

The immature males arrive in Seattle in early November and stay until about mid-May when the steelhead run ends. Too weak sexually or socially to establish their own breeding "turf" in California, the sea lion bachelors' club formed out of sexual frustration.

They've spread their own frustration to the Department of Wildlife, which tries every conceivable scheme to rid the locks of this pack. In 1989, 39 sea lions were deported to Long

Beach, California, and 29 swam the 1,300 miles north back to the Sound.

Herschel consumes 64% of the steelhead run in a year, enough to create a threat to the run's continued existence.

SALMON CULTURE

The two most exciting fish to see in Seattle are salmon and steelhead, and the best place to see them is at the locks (or maybe in the Pike Place Market).

Let's get this straight right off: Salmon and steelhead are two different fish, although both belong to the Salmonidae family—sort of kissing cousins. Some steelhead are wild; some are hatchery fish. Hatchery steelhead have been genetically programmed to migrate earlier than their wild counterparts and there's a limited fishery on them. But wild steelhead are completely protected. The hatchery steelhead begin returning in November and run through January, heading up the Cedar River and Sammamish Slough to spawn. The wild run begins in mid-January and goes through early April. There are about 2,100 wild steelhead B.S. (before sea lions); about 800 after "Herschel" gets his fill. Sea lion migration is tied to the steelhead run—they prefer steelhead to salmon, for some reason.

Four species of salmon migrate through the Seattle area: sockeye, coho, king, and chum. King Salmon are the mature adults, while chinook are the baby kings or "blackmouths."

There is a good-sized salmon run of 30,000 to 50,000 kings up the Duwamish to the Green River.

So who is that fishing out in Lake Union? Most likely Native Americans who have a historic right to the

Know your chums

Type	#s going through the locks	When
Sockeye (reds)	250,000–350,000	Early June–Aug.
Coho (silvers)	60,000	Early Aug.–late Oct. Peak end Sept.
King (chinook)	25,000–30,000 (70% hatchery)	Early June–Sept.
Chum (dogs)	Very small	Late Oct.–Nov.
Steelhead Trout	+/-2,100	Early Nov.–Apr.

Source: Washington State Departments of Fisheries & Wildlife

The best time to see the spectacular sockeye salmon run at the Hiram Chittenden Locks in Ballard is the Fourth of July weekend. Thousands upon thousands of sockeye fight their way into Lake Washington and head for the spawning grounds in the Cedar River and other streams that empty into the lake. You can cheer them on from viewing rooms at the locks or from up above the fish ladders. Another good way to watch the fish is at the Salmon Days Festival in Issaquah the first week of October. Issaquah has a huge run in Sammamish Slough and Issaquah Creek.

fishing grounds there. Fishing for chinook, coho, and sockeye is allowed on Lake Union for the Muckleshoot Tribe, in keeping with their traditional tribal practice. They fish now with fixed gillnets.

CITY WHALE WATCHING

Every once in a while on the ferry between Colman Dock and Winslow someone yells, "Whale!" and all the passengers run to the rail to watch the whales—usually orcas—cavort. Sometimes the whales swim along with the ferry, putting on a show all the way across the Sound. (And sometimes someone yells, "Whale!" only to have someone else point out that the shiny backs are really Dall's porpoises. You can tell them from orcas because the porpoises are smaller and surface more often than the orcas. Sometimes they ride the bow wave of the ferry.)

The ferry is also a great place to see other marine mammals such as Harbor Seals, Harbor Porpoise, and Dall's Porpoise. But it's a bit like the lottery: You take your chances which ferry run will be the lucky one to be followed or led by marine mammals. You can also see whales from the central waterfront, West Seattle, and Discovery Park.

There are three pods of orca in Puget Sound but two—what are called J and K pods—are most likely to pass by downtown Seattle. They travel a 200-mile range north and south, with the San Juan Islands in the center, and come to this part of the Sound as much as once a month, year-round. You might see them more often—about three times a month—in September and October when they're following the salmon runs.

A bit of Seattle trivia: There are two professional fish counters at the locks, stationed in the lower underground area. They count the Sockeye Salmon only. What they do is called taking a "sub sample," meaning they count for 10 minutes every hour for 12 hours, seven days a week when the fish are running. Then they extrapolate the totals.

In the spring the Gray Whales take a detour from their migration route and come into the Sound to feed.

In the summer months the orcas move north to the San Juan Islands. June is the best time to see them in the islands. During the winter L pod moves through the Sound north to the Fraser River in British Columbia to eat salmon headed for spawning.

GOING FISHING?

You see people fishing in Elliott Bay, but should they actually EAT what they catch? No way, say the people at the Seattle/King County health department. Elliott Bay is an estuary system, where the freshwater currents of rivers reach the tides of the bay. Researchers have found tumored, diseased species there, especially pollock, cod, and other bottomfish. Diseased fish with such afflictions as kidney tumors tend to migrate to estuary systems where salinity levels are lower because of incoming fresh water.

This phenomenon of diseased fish migrating to estuary systems has given rise to many theories. One is that saltwater parasites are shed due to the freshwater influx; another is the notion that fresh water may ease the pain and suffering of the diseased and tumor-infested fish. Yum!! Now, let's go fishin'!

SQUID AND OCTOPI

They should make a movie called *The Octopus That Ate Seattle.* One rumor has it that an octopus was found in Puget Sound that weighed 600 pounds! And that there are giant squid 65 feet long!

Most octopi here are much smaller than that (average size: 40 pounds, 8 feet across), but they are plentiful. To see them you need to be a diver (or go to the Aquarium). They like to hang out under piers in Elliott Bay where they are attracted to the concrete rubble of crumbling finger piers. Unfortunately, it's not a great idea to dive in Elliott Bay because the bottom sediment makes visibility so poor. But you can go to the Don Armeni Boatlaunch at Duwamish Head at night to see Benthic Squid and Stubby Squid.

Watery sources

Hiram Chittenden Locks
3015 NW 54th St.
Seattle, WA 98107
783-7059

Marine Animal Resource Center
285-0515
To report stranded seals.

National Oceanic and Atmospheric Administration (NOAA)
526-6341

Ocean Research and Conservation Assn. (ORCA)
827-3015
Educational group; sponsors annual Whalefest.

Seattle Aquarium
1483 Alaskan Way
Seattle, WA 98101-2059
386-4300
Interpretive expert: Buzz Shaw

Whale Hotline
(800) 562-8832
To report whale sightings and strandings in the Sound. Whales have been tracked via the hotline for 14 years.

BIG GAME

Well, OK. There's not a lot of big game right in Seattle, but there's small game that seems like big game when it decides to hide in your attic. And right on the city's doorstep, there's beautiful, somewhat pristine wildlife habitat.

First, our wild neighbors that sometimes seem more like pests than nature's blessings.

Take squirrels, for instance. Those cute little frisky gray squirrels that run along the phone lines are actually non-natives who have aggressively driven away Seattle's native squirrels. Someone thought it would be cute to bring them to the Arboretum from New York 60 years ago, and today they are the dominant force in the city's squirreldom. And they are driving natives and non-natives nuts.

The Eastern Gray Squirrel should not be confused with the Douglas Gray, Red, Flying Squirrel, or chipmunk—all of which are native and now hide out in the forests (squirrel suburbs?) outside the city. The Eastern Grays are prolific because their habitat is not specified; thus, they outnumber the city's natural predators and have few enemies.

They nest in attics, blow up transformers, eat fruit and nut trees, dig holes in yards, eat birdseed from feeders, and can be vicious. They'll bite the hand that feeds them, especially if they've been fed and then the kind feeder stops the handouts.

If a squirrel gets in your attic, try putting mothballs up there. Sometimes they'll leave in disgust. Or try flashing lights or playing transistor radios (set to your teenager's favorite station).

If you have fruit trees be sure the limbs are trimmed away from the house so it's not so easy for the squirrels to get on the roof.

Other than that, the only solution is a rather brutal one. The Department of Wildlife will loan you a trap for the squirrels. Once they're caught, drown the squirrels in a garbage can filled with water.

Why not just move them out to the woods? Because they aren't native and upset the balance so badly. No one wants them to spread any farther.

OTHER CRITTERS

Opossums are pretty common in city yards, especially if you leave your cat- or dogfood out. Same with raccoons. (They're everywhere, but West Seattle takes the prize for most raccoons.)

Opossums are cat-size, with ratlike tails and pointy faces, and usually grayish brown. They have the fur of a cat and the tail of a rat. They like to burrow in woodsheds.

The Department of Wildlife has traps in which you can catch both opossums and raccoons, and then relocate them in the forests outside the city.

People who live near hillsides (and who doesn't in Seattle?) have a chance of seeing Mountain Beavers, or at least of seeing their marks. They like to eat rhododendrons and ferns and otherwise destroy landscaping. They are the size of a cat, brown, and tailless. They develop an extensive trail system underground so that people are led to think several are around, when it's usually just one. They don't leave a mound the way moles do.

The DOW offers traps to catch beavers live. You set the trap right over the hole so the beaver has nowhere to go, and then move the beaver to a forest service road where there's a hillside and let it go.

Every once in a while, someone will see a coyote running down Greenwood Avenue. (They are somewhat common in Bellevue and Redmond and surrounding areas.)

Here's what to do about a rat in your toilet:

1. Put the lid down and pile some heavy books on it (they're strong!).

2. Flush the toilet three or four times.

3. Do NOT try hitting the rat with a broomstick—they're agile and have been known to climb right up the broomstick.

4. If the rat still hasn't gone away, leave the lid shut and wait several hours. Since he's looking for food, he'll probably just go back down into the sewer.

5. Call the health department. If you're really panicky, they'll come help. Otherwise, they'll bait the sewer in a four-block radius around your house and get the nasty rodent that way.

They are mostly nocturnal and will eat cats or small dogs (and they like cat- and dogfood). You can't live-trap coyotes, only fence them out. Keep dogs and cats in at night to protect them. Coyote hotline: 543-7232.

IT'S THE RAT PATROL

"Rat patrols"—teams of 15 to 20 ratcatchers—are a thing of the past, but not because there aren't rats in Seattle. The creepy rodents aren't a health hazard—the last case of bubonic plague was in Tacoma in 1921. Although it seems they're always scrounging for garbage, rats don't need "three squares" to keep alive, only 2–4 ounces of food a day. Unfortunately, their quest for food sometimes leads them up the sewer lines and into toilets where they like to surprise unsuspecting city residents. The health department gets almost 10 "toilet complaints" per month—panicky residents want to know what to do about the rat smiling at them from the toilet bowl. The rats can be as much as 3 inches in diameter—no small mouse, that—but most are long and skinny, not the large Norway rats you sometimes see on the waterfront.

Number of complaints about rats

Seattle only
1988: 1,100 total
1989: 863 total
Rat in toilet complaints
1988: 109
1989: 119
Source: Seattle–King County Department of Public Health

AND STILL MORE CRITTERS

Some people think squirrels are almost as bad as rats, and Seattle does have a healthy population of squirrels. They aren't rabid, although their bites can cause nasty infections.

But wait! Don't forget about bats. There have been cases of rabies reported in bats in the area, so don't fool with friendly bats. Usually they enter your house through the chimney. What to do? Close all doors, open all windows, and get out of there. If they've nested in your attic, close outlets, open vents, and bang on the ceiling to get them out; then cover openings with something they can't chew through.

Average number of complaints about bats in King County: 125/yr.

Direct critter complaints to:
Seattle–King County Department of Public Health
Environmental Health Project
296-4632

ON THE OUTSKIRTS

There is wildlife closer to the city than most people think, or want to believe. Cougar and other big game can be seen 20 minutes from Seattle in a fringe area between the city limits and the last remaining wilderness area nearby. Mt. Si, Tiger Mountain, and Cougar Mountain form an oasis that includes Department of Natural Resources (DNR) state trust and forest management lands.

Mt. Si was purchased by the state in 1977 and has a conservation status. Cougar Mountain Regional Wildland and Squak Mountain are shoulder-to-shoulder with Tiger Mountain State Forest, a multiple use area where visitors can observe wildlife and enjoy other recreational activities. Efforts are being made to preserve an east/west corridor for wildlife by blocking up property around Cougar, Squak, and Tiger mountains—but there is development pressure as Seattle spreads to the East.

What animals can be found there? Deer, elk, Black Bear, cougar, and coyote wander among the trees. Issaquah Creek serves as watering ground for elk, and Tiger Mountain is home to Black Bears.

Wildlife sources

Cougar Mountain Wildland Regional Park
King County Parks
296-4281
Has brochures and info about the area.

Department of Natural Resources
Regional Office
28329 SE 448th St.
Enumclaw, WA 98022
(800) 527-3305

Peak times at the Arboretum: To see the camelias and rhodies in bloom at the Arboretum, go anytime from the end of March to the end of June. Flowering cherries and plums peak in April and May followed by the azaleas.

This office has brochures, maps, and info on Tiger Mountain State Forest and Mt. Si DNR land.

Department of Wildlife
16018 Mill Creek Blvd.
Mill Creek, WA 98012
774-8812

Issaquah Alps Trail Club
328-0480
24-hour hotline listing events and how to participate. This is THE group working on this regional park area.

SEEDY CITY

Whether it's countering the greenhouse effect or just plain love of leaves, Seattleites and seeds go together like lawyers and oil companies.

The Arboretum is the center of flora culture in Seattle, with thousands of plant species maintained by the UW Center for Urban Horticulture but owned by the city's park department.

The best global effort in town is the Seed Exchange at the Arboretum. The volunteers there collect seeds from plants in the gardens and exchange them with other arboretums from around the world. The seeds are mostly cultivars, Norway Maples, and other varieties.

HEARD ON THE STREET

"You don't have to go all the way back to the East Coast to see the fall colors. We have them here."

Volunteer at Arboretum

The fall color display at the Arboretum is spectacular, mostly because Eastern trees such as Sugar Maples have been transplanted here.

Plant sale: Each spring, usually toward the end of April or beginning of May, the Arboretum holds a plant sale at Magnuson Park where they sell cuttings, seeds, plants, grafts, etc. This is a wildly popular (read: crowded) event. The Arboretum gets donations from members' gardens and various greenhouses in the area. The best-selling plants? Rhododendrons (they have a huge variety) and trees.

P-PATCH PROGRAM

Seattle has 24 different P-Patch sites with 1,070 garden plots in all. Each spring 2,500 gardeners plant their hearts out, and each fall they reap the benefits. Seattle's P-Patches are for organic gardening only.

These communal gardens are so popular it's almost impossible to worm your way into one: There's a waiting list of 200 would-be growers. The P-Patch Program monitors the garden plots to make sure they are being used and if they aren't, the program sends out a "weedy letter" to ask the gardener's intentions. The gardener has one week to stick a shovel in the ground and get to work, or the plot is given over to the next person on the waiting list.

Of the sites, 15 belong to the city, and 9 are privately owned.

P-Patch gardeners usually grow vegetables; most grow for their own use, but the produce from the two largest plots goes to a food bank. In 1989 P-Patch gardeners delivered 8.75 tons of vegetables to food banks.

Master Composter Program
Compost Hotline
633-0224
Composting and recycling information sponsored by Seattle Tilth and the Seattle Solid Waste Utility. Call for free map of compost sites and information about guided group tours.

The best time to get to the Arboretum Plant Sale is before it begins. But to do that you have to be a member. Members can get in the day before the sale, from 4:30 to 6:30 p.m. If you aren't a member, you should get there right at the beginning of the sale (usually at 9 a.m. sharp) for best selection. For best prices, go around 4 or 5 p.m. Some prices are lowered as the crowd thins out. To become a member of Arboretum Foundation, call 325-4510.

When you plant your own garden you might want to plant an extra row for someone else. Northwest Harvest, 625-0755, accepts donations of vegetables for food banks throughout the area, thereby supplementing the food banks' usual offerings of canned and dried goods with fresh vegetables.

P-Patch Program
Community Services Division
618 Second Ave.
Seattle, WA 98104-2222
684-0264

Seattle Tilth Association
4649 Sunnyside Ave. N
Seattle, WA 98103
633-0451
Volunteer organization of gardeners interested in ecological food production. An urban chapter of the non-profit Western Washington Tilth Association. Demonstration garden is open to the public and there are tours, lectures, and two annual events: the Edible Landscape Sale and the Fall Harvest Festival.

Washington Park Arboretum
Washington Park
543-8800
The support group for the Arboretum is the Arboretum Foundation. The foundation puts on events, runs school workshops, trains volunteers, and generally raises funds for the gardens. The Foundation number is 325-4510.

WATER, WATER EVERYWHERE...

Puget Sound holds 31 cubic miles of water; 1.5 cubic miles move with each change of the tides. Lake Union and Lake Washington combined have about 25,000 surface acres of water.

Plenty of water, right? But when we start talking about water, we have to talk about water quality, wetlands deterioration, and pollution in the Sound. It's time to get to the not-so-pleasant aspects of our urban environment.

A DROP TO DRINK

Thirsty? Before turning on the tap, consider these facts about Seattle's water:

- The Seattle Water Department supplies nearly 1.1 million people with water.
- On an average day, 166 million gallons of water are used by consumers in the Seattle area.
- Virtually all of Seattle's water comes from the Cedar and Tolt watersheds.
- Demand on the two watersheds isn't just from thirsty people: The Cedar River provides the fresh water needed to keep the level of Lake Washington stable and to keep salt water from entering the lake.
- Residential users consume about 50% of the water supplied by the system. Consumption more than doubles in the summer, when precipitation is at its lowest.
- During summers, about 2% of Seattle's water comes from deep protected wells.
- Treatment of the city's water includes a low level of chlorination for disinfection, fluoridation, and the addition of a small amount of natural minerals.

Need compost? Try ZooDoo Compost from Woodland Park Zoo "where every day is Earth Day" (call 625-POOP). You have to pick it up yourself and it sells out fast, so call early in spring or fall. "Down-to-earth prices": $1 per garbage bag, $40 for a truckload. The zoo offers composting classes, too; info from same number.

For other manure, look in the Yellow Pages and classified ads for dairies and stables with low-cost or free manure.

And don't say the police never did anything for you: You can get horse manure and wood shavings free from the police department (386-4238). Go out to Discovery Park to get the goods.

And the engineering department has leaves, though not for food crops (684-7508, north end; 386-1218, south end).

Since Seattle's such a bean town, you can get coffee chaff from Starbucks by calling their roaster desk (447-1575). The chaff's free but in limited supply, especially in summer. But in the winter they throw it away, so plan ahead.

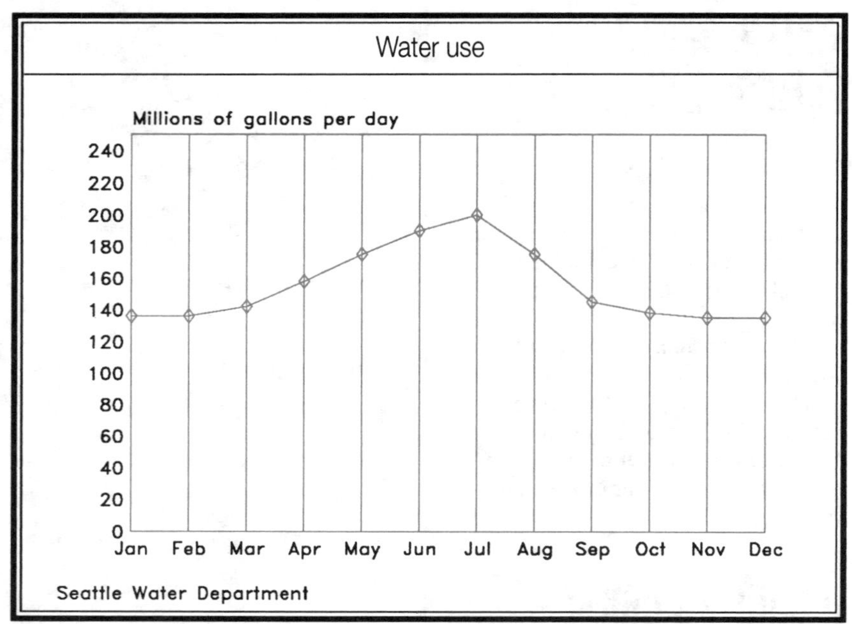

Seattle Water Department
710 Second Ave., 10th Floor
Seattle, WA 98104
Administration: 684-5885
Conservation: 684-5879
Information sheets: 684-5849
Quality info: 684-7404
Information on the water supply system and guide to proper summer lawn care.

WATERSHED CONTROVERSY

There's a huge controversy going on about logging in the Cedar River watershed. It's 80% owned by Seattle, 20% owned by the U.S. Forest Service. The forest service has, in the past, sold old-growth timber from the watershed to private timber companies. At this point, however, there's a moratorium on logging while all the groups involved hammer out a timber management plan.

SOFT OR HARD?

For some reason people are always trying to figure out whether they have soft or hard water—whether their shampoo will lather or just sit there in a slimy mass. Seattle's water is very soft and low in dissolved minerals such as sodium. So lather away.

And about quality, the water contains low levels of compounds called trihalomethanes formed during disinfection, but the levels are within federal and state limits. No synthetic organic compounds indicating industrial or pesticide contamination have been detected.

The water is sampled daily after being collected at representative points in the city.

WAVES OF TROUBLE

We've got trouble, my friends, right here in water city. Those lovely sparkling waters viewed from almost every spot in Seattle are home to fish, aquatic plants—and pollution.

Thanks to an extensive effort beginning in the 1950s, Lake Washington is as clean as it looks, safe for swimming, and free from sewer overflow most of the time. But the city's other bodies of water—including Puget Sound—are depositories for all sorts of things, including bacteria.

Somehow you'd never think that in this high-tech age we would still be discharging raw sewage into waterways, but we are. The city and Metro

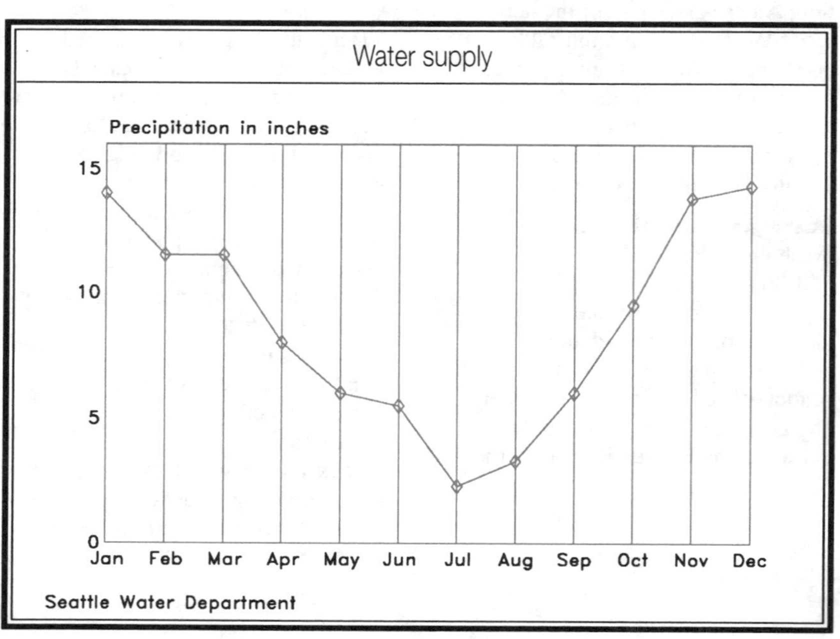

SEWAGE OVERFLOW SPOTS

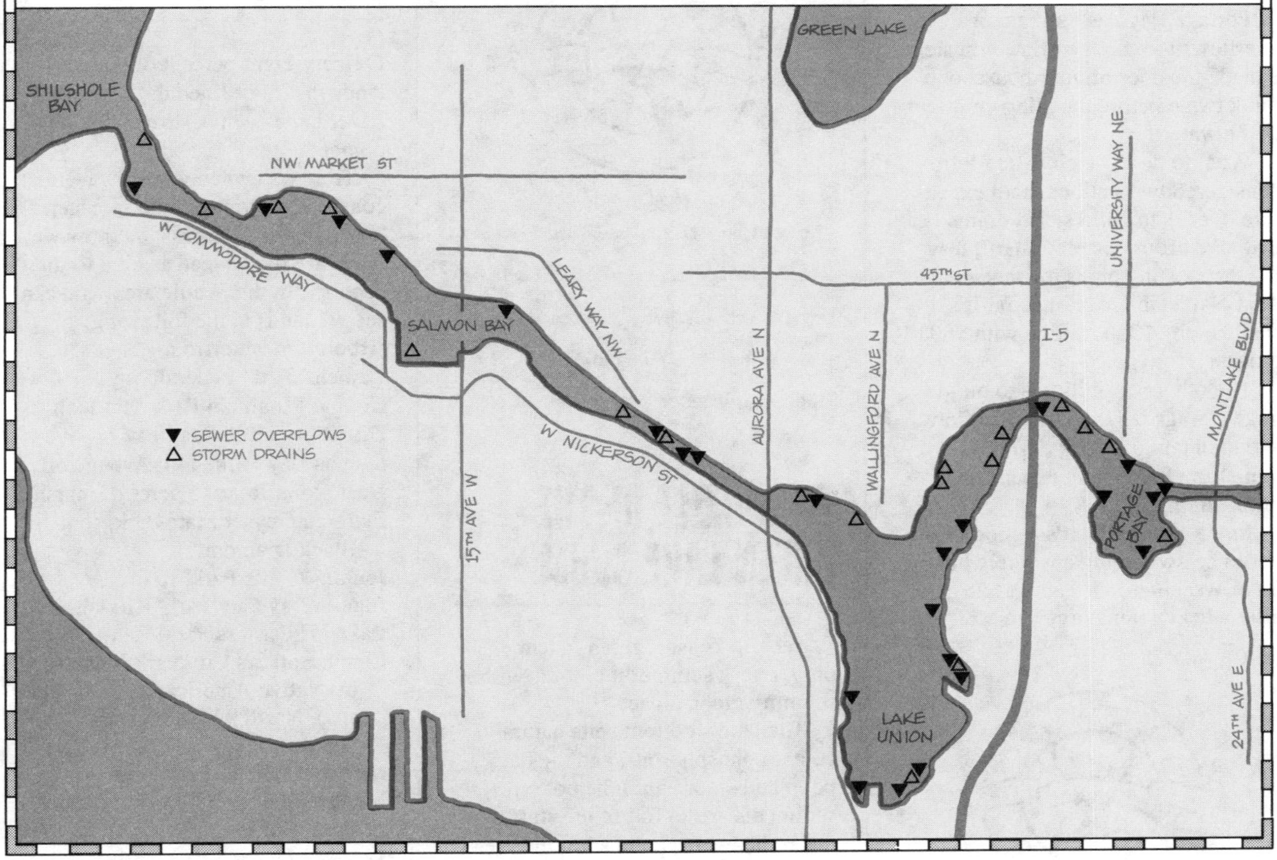

▼ SEWER OVERFLOWS
△ STORM DRAINS

Don't believe that your water quality is so great? Drop a note to the water department and ask for a detailed summary of water sampling results. Water Quality Division, Seattle Water Department, 1509 S Spokane St., Seattle, WA 98144.

are spending buckets of money on decreasing the amount of raw sewage that gets dumped into our water, and hopefully someday storm water will be the only runoff expanding the lakes, rivers, and Sound.

THE RAW TRUTH ABOUT SEWAGE

There are hundreds of overflow pipes all over the city that often spew forth something called Combined Sewer Overflow (CSO). Don't we have sewage treatment plants? We do, but when the heavy rains come the raw sewage is allowed to overflow with storm water into Lake Union, Portage Bay, Elliott Bay, and the Duwamish River. If there weren't overflows, the sewage would back up into houses—an unpleasant thought that makes the overflow system the lesser of two evils.

In Elliott Bay, for example, the Denny Way CSO lets loose as many as 50 times per year. That's discharges of combined runoff and raw sewage. Consequently, Elliott Bay is a toxic hotspot. Metro is capping the contaminated sediments in the bay with sand and will monitor that cap for five years to see if the contaminants can be kept from spreading.

Everyone knows that Elliott Bay is no place to take the kids for a Saturday swim, and you wouldn't swim in the Duwamish River either. But the truth is that Lake Union—which has overflows everywhere dumping combined sewage and storm water into the lake—is worse, as far as polluted sediments are concerned, than either Elliott Bay or the Duwamish.

Portage Bay has its share of overflows too. So next time you step outside the door of your houseboat, think twice before dangling your feet in the water.

What to do? The city and Metro considered two options, both expensive. One is to build storm drains that take off only street runoff, leaving the existing pipes for sewage. That plan is in process; so far it's cost the city $260 million with $80 million left to go.

The other possibility is to build huge storage tanks for the overflow and then pump it back during non-storm hours—an expensive proposition.

In the meantime, it's a good idea not to go swimming anywhere but Lake Washington for about five days after a heavy rainstorm.

If you are really a wetlands fanatic, you can get free copies of "Wetland Walks," a guide to wetlands with public access throughout the state. The state Department of Ecology published it in June 1989. Copies can be ordered by contacting Publications Office, Washington DOE, Mail Stop PV-11, Olympia, WA 98504, 459-6000.

The best time to visit a wetland is near either dawn or dusk when local wildlife is most active. These quiet hours are feeding times for many birds, fish, and animals.

THE PUZZLE OF THE GREEN LAKE SCUM

Green Lake isn't green in name only. Every summer it blooms with a scummy green algae.

The lake's bottom soils naturally contain phosphorous, and the duck poop adds more until the bottom sediments are so full of the stuff that when the warm months hit, the green algae grows like crazy. It's not a health problem; parasites on the ducks, not the algae, cause the swimmers' itch you can occasionally get in the lake. But the algae is pretty unappetizing for swimmers, and if left alone the lake would eventually be covered with it.

The city may flush out the lake with fresh water from Lake Washington periodically, or may end up using alum. Either way, there's someone who doesn't like the solution.

And there's another problem, this one caused by algae removal. As the algae is cleaned out, light penetrates down into the lake and you get bottom weeds plugging up the lake and acting like tentacles grabbing unsuspecting swimmers.

And that's the Green Lake puzzle.

WETLAND WASTE

Ninety-eight percent of the wetlands that once lined the Duwamish River have been destroyed by development.

Time was when wetlands were considered swamps with monsters lurking in the eelgrass, but now wetlands are recognized as vital to the ecology. In the Seattle area, you can see wetlands at the following:

Arboretum waterfront
Camelot Park, Federal Way
Cougar Mountain Park, Issaquah
Discovery Park, Seattle
Dumas Bay Park, 44th Avenue off Dash Point Road (5 acres of marsh)
Flaming Geyser State Park, south of Black Diamond
Jenkins Creek Park, Kent
Juanita Bay City Park, Kirkland
Lake Wilderness Park, Renton
Licton Springs City Park (once used by Native Americans as a health spa), North 97th and Ashworth, Seattle
Marymoor Park, Redmond
Mercer Slough, Bellfields Nature Park, Bellevue
Seattle Aquarium Wetlands Exhibit
Twin Ponds County Park, Seattle
Wallace Swamp Creek Park

THE OIL TRUTH

The chances of an oil spill in Puget Sound are greater than you might think. It's true that tankers can't get this far down into the Sound, but oil barges bunker fuel in and out of the port daily. And they can make a pretty big mess if something goes wrong. Tankers have spilled oil at Anacortes, Grays Harbor, and Port Angeles.

You can't really help with actual clean-up unless you go through Specialized Ocean Training, a 45-hour course that costs $1,000. But you can volunteer to help with bird and

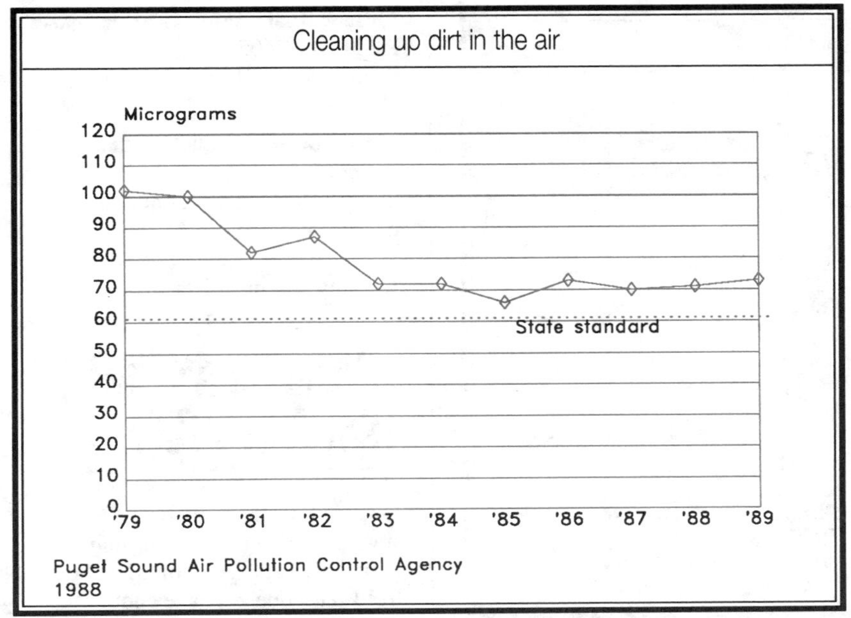

wildlife clean-up by calling the Department of Fish and Wildlife, 774-8812, or the Coast Guard, 286-5540. They will refer you to one of several wildlife organizations that are contacted in such an emergency.

Water resources

Adopt-A-Beach Program
Adopt-A-Stream Program
710 Second Ave.
Seattle, WA 98104
296-6544
Contacts: Betsy Peabody, Ken Pritchard

Adopt-A-Park Program
684-8009

Green Lake Information
684-4960

Puget Sound Water Quality Authority
217 Pine St., Suite 1100
Seattle, WA 98101
464-7320
At this address until Jan. 1, 1991, then Olympia.

Seattle City Light
1015 Third Ave.
Seattle, WA 98104
625-3000

Seattle Drainage and Wastewater Utility
660 Dexter Horton Bldg.
710 Second Ave.
Seattle, WA 98104
684-7774

Seattle Solid Waste Utility
684-7600

Seattle Water Department
710 Second Ave., 10th Floor
Seattle, WA 98104
Conservation: 684-5879

EVERY BREATH YOU TAKE

The Puget Sound Air Pollution Control Agency (PSAPCA) ranks the air in Seattle in three classes: Good, Moderate, and Unhealthful.

Good: Little or no health risk at all.

Moderate: Toxins building up in the air, excessive amounts of carbon monoxide in downtown areas. Haze starts obscuring the outline of the city.

Unhealthful: Carbon monoxide levels downtown rise past federal safety standards. Unhealthful air causes adverse health effects in people in the highest health risk categories (the very young, the very old, pregnant women, those with heart or lung ailments) and respiratory irritation in normally healthy people. You know this is happening when the city outline begins to disappear.

So where do we stand? Seattle is not demonstrably better or worse in terms of air pollution than other cities of its size. One thing the city has going for it is that the sun doesn't shine as much here, which keeps smog levels down. When volatile fumes from gasoline, paint, and solvents mix with oxides and nitrogen from industry and automobiles, and then are exposed to sunlight, a chemical reaction occurs that turns the mixture into smog—what Ken Swigart at PSAPCA calls "bad ozone."

Since the 1970s carbon monoxide pollution in the downtown area has been reduced by more than 90%, mainly as a result of requiring pollution abatement equipment on automobiles and clean-air scrubbers on industrial smokestacks.

In 1972 the city violated the federal standard for clean air on 128 days. Now the city violates the federal standard on average two to six times a year.

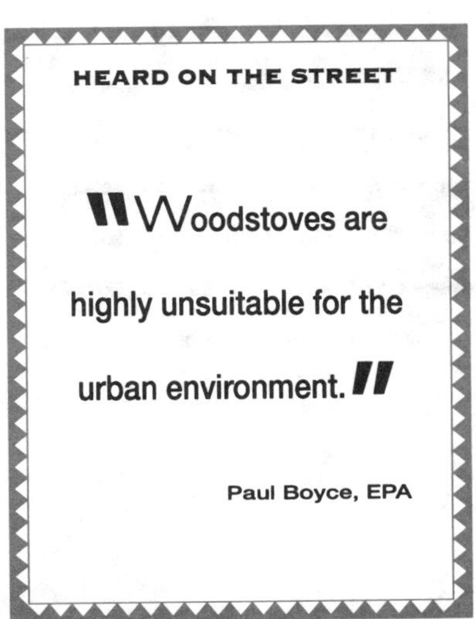

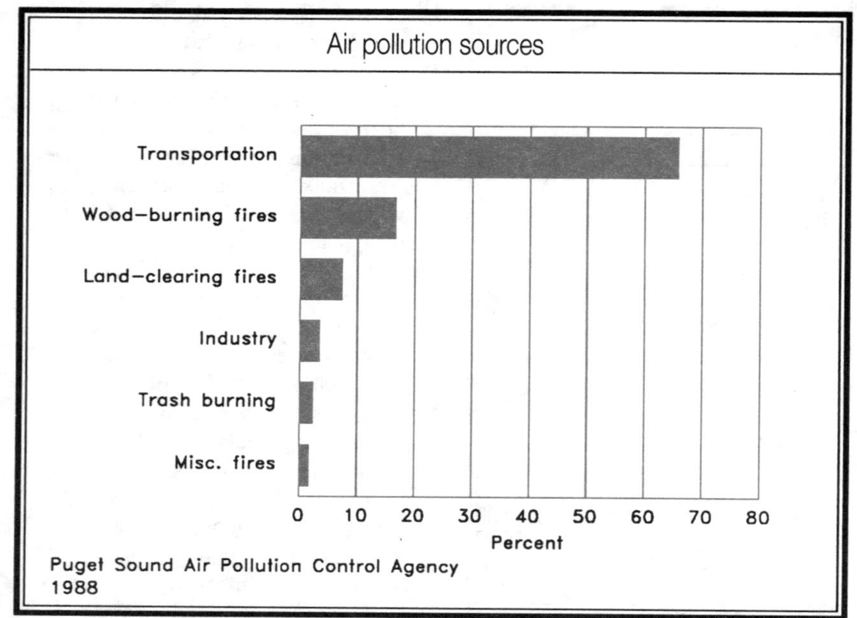

Citizens Against Woodburning Fumes
P.O. Box 27405
Seattle, WA 98125
546-1988

Puget Sound Air Pollution Control Agency
200 W Mercer St., Room 205
Seattle, WA 98119
296-7330
Burning ban info: 296-5100

INVERSION AND ALL THAT AIRY STUFF

The truth is, there are only two smoke cops to enforce burning bans in the city—the Air Pollution Control Board doesn't have enough money to hire more. So you can probably get away with burning on a ban day, but should you? NO. And here's why:

Woodsmoke is a real and growing problem during winter months. Wood stoves and fireplaces contribute respirable particulates into the air. That means that when you say, "Ah, that woodsmoke smell!" and inhale deeply, the smoke particulates enter your lungs, unfiltered,

Since 1983, however, the city hasn't made much progress. In the last seven years "we've been in a holding pattern," says the PSAPCA's Swigart. He predicts that pollution and violations will increase due to sheer growth in the city and county because, he says, "we don't have the resources right now to keep up with it."

When can you breathe easiest? During the rain, believe it or not. Rainy weather is best for air quality because it cleans the air. An informal survey of clean air experts reveals where they do NOT want to live because of poor air quality. They mentioned places downwind of Seattle, such as Issaquah or Kent. "There is a definite pollution plume. And Boeing is the culprit." Toward the west things improve a bit.

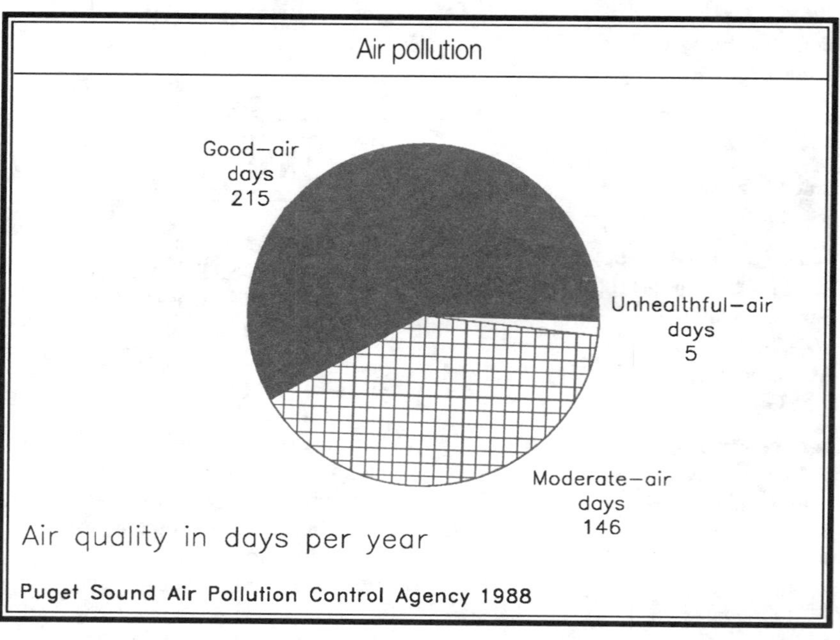

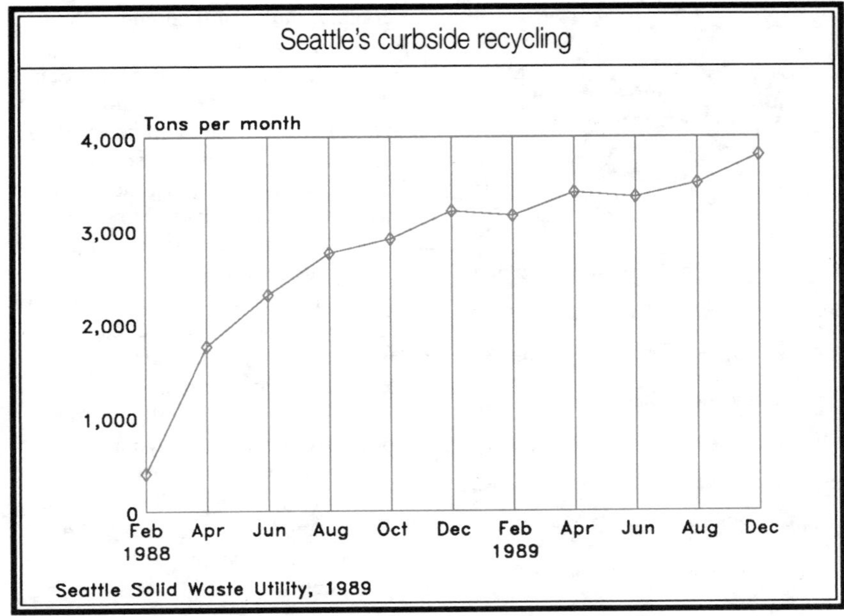

to the deepest (and most sensitive) areas of your respiratory tract.

WHEN TO STAY INSIDE

The absolute worst conditions for pollution are:

In winter: during cold, clear weather when there is little wind and therefore no vertical mixing and no horizontal movement. With wood-stove use, this leads to higher levels of carbon monoxide build-up.

In summer: when we get extended sunny weather and air movement tends to move off land toward water because of high pressure.

THE OZONE PROBLEM

High-level ozone is good, low-level ozone is bad. Up high the ozone protects the earth from ultraviolet rays, but low-level ozone produced by a photochemical reaction with oxides of nitrogen (from auto exhausts and woodsmoke) is a killer. The low-level ozone is produced by a photochemical reaction that requires sunlight, which we don't have much of and so it shouldn't be a problem, right? Wrong. Though we might not have as many days of sun as other places, when we do, we often have an unhealthy level of ozone.

How can you tell? When your eyes feel irritated, there's too much ozone in the air. You're inhaling a potent oxidant into your lungs that, over the long term, can cause respiratory problems, especially in children.

THE BAD NEWS—BARELY HOLDING THE LINE

With a staff of 47 and an annual budget of just $600,000, the state Air Pollution Control Board is worried. The 2010 Report, produced in 1989 by the Washington Air Quality Coalition, cites air pollution as the #1 health risk in the state if we keep on doing what we're doing now. In Washington, 800,000 people are at risk; 600,000 of those in King County. They are primarily young children; the elderly; pregnant women; and those with heart ailments, emphysema, and asthma.

Here's a prediction: The population is supposed to increase by 30% in the next six years. This will be accompanied by a 70% increase in miles driven as more people have to live in outlying areas. And it means more time spent in clogged traffic with engines idling, which means more air pollution.

Source: Washington Air Quality Coalition

Air Pollution Control
296-5100
Provides air quality index and burning ban information.

Environmental Protection Agency
1200 Sixth Ave.
Seattle, WA 98101
442-1567

Puget Sound Air Pollution Control Agency
200 W Mercer St., Room 205
Seattle, WA 98119
296-7330

ALL EYES ON OUR GARBAGE

Seattle virtually bursts its buttons when bragging about its nationally celebrated recycling programs. So New York has barges of garbage

Areas that have exceeded federal carbon monoxide standards: downtown Seattle, the University District, downtown Bellevue, downtown Tacoma, Northgate, and downtown Everett.

looking for a home? Ha—Seattle's got it all figured out: Don't dump that garbage, reuse it.

Seattle has always been recycling-minded: 24% of all residents and commercial businesses recycled in 1987 before the official curbside collection program began in 1988. With that new program, things have taken off.

- The recycling rate for households has grown from 18% in 1987 to a whopping 44% in 1989.
- In 1989 alone, 113,549 households voluntarily signed up for curbside recycling—78% of single-family residences (apartments aren't included in the pick-up program—yet.)
- In 1989 an average of 64 pounds of recyclable material was collected per household per month.
- The program was responsible for taking 20% fewer tons of residential garbage to area landfills.
- The goal is that 40% of all residences and commercial businesses will recycle by 1991, 50% by 1993, and 60% by 1998.

The city's program has won awards and been considered state-of-the-art by other cities for a couple of reasons, including its rate structure.

WHY THE RATE STRUCTURE IS SUCH A BIG DEAL

Most parts of the country charge for garbage service through property taxes or fixed fees for unlimited garbage service. But Seattle uses a volume-based rate structure—the rate goes up for each additional can of garbage as a kind of penalty for not recycling. (It's gently referred to by the Solid Waste Utility as an incentive to recycle instead of a penalty.)

Ever wonder what happens to your yard waste after it's picked up? It goes to Rabanco Recycling Company's Cedar Grove site where it is ground up twice, sifted through a screen, and composted in windrows. Since the program is new, there's no final product yet, but eventually it will be sold for compost.

THE CUTTING EDGE IN THE WORLD OF GARBAGE

There's a new pilot program under way in the Solid Waste Utility. The EPA has given it a grant to field-test a pilot program whereby garbage would be treated just as electricity is. While electricity is billed by the unit, garbage would be charged by the pound. This garbage by-the-pound would create even more incentive to recycle.

HOW TO RECYCLE

Want to get some of those recycling containers but don't know how? Just call the city at 684-7600. Then you have to listen to a long menu of instructions about which number to punch next, but hold on and eventually you can get a Real Person on the phone.

You are eligible for recycling pick-up if you live in a single-family home or multifamily home with up to four dwellings.

If you live north of the Ship Canal three plastic bins will be delivered to your home and then will be emptied once a week. If you live south of the Ship Canal, a 60 or 90 gallon cart on wheels will be delivered to your home and emptied once a month.

If your containers haven't been picked up when they were supposed to be, call 684-HELP and leave a message. The message line is on 24 hours a day, seven days a week. Either your problem will be solved or someone will return your call.

If you have to talk to someone and don't have any of the problems on the taped menu, call the Solid Waste Utility switchboard at 684-7666.

All this talk of recycling and the fact is that the mailbox is full of junk mail—made from trees DBA paper. To stop junk mail, or at least reduce it by 75%, write a postcard to Direct Marketing Association, the central clearinghouse for mailing lists. Tell them to remove your name from their list. Send the card to: Mail Preference Service, Direct Marketing Association, 6 East 43rd Street, New York, NY 10017-4610. Or send it directly to companies that send you unwanted mail—using their pre-paid envelope.

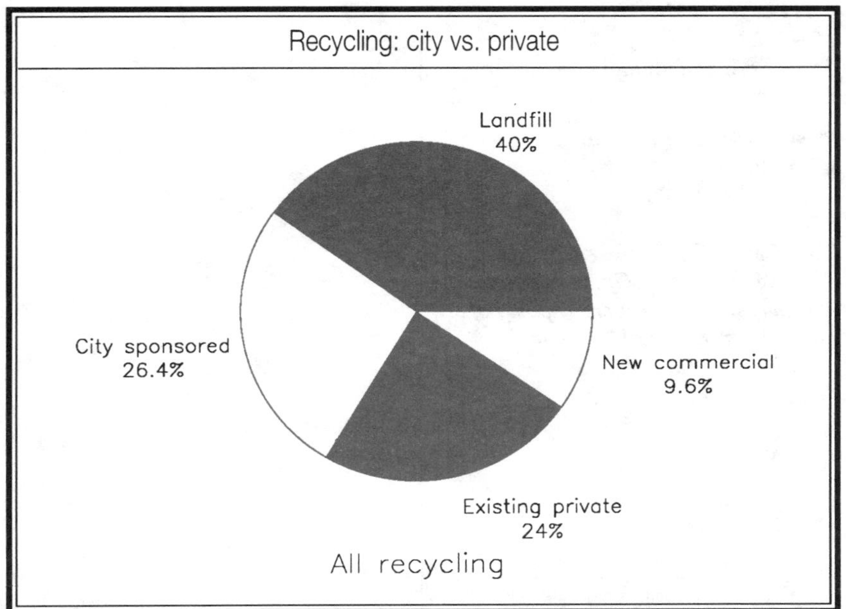

THE PROGRAM

The curb/alley recycling collection program accepts glass, tin, or aluminum, PET plastic soda pop and liquor bottles, milk and juice jugs, soap and detergent bottles, shampoo and lotion bottles. (This program is pretty unusual; once recycled, the plastic is used to make carpet fiber, drainpipes, distributor caps, egg cartons, and polyester fiberfill for ski jackets.) Also accepted are newspaper, mixed waste paper (magazines, advertising mail, cardboard, etc.).

There's also a yard waste program. For $2 a month, the city will pick up grass, leaves, small branches, weeds, sod, brush, or twigs.

The city won't pick up hazardous waste, or large rocks and branches over 4 inches in diameter.

Put your yard waste in an old garbage can, a cardboard box, or a tied bundle and leave it at the curb or alley by 7 a.m. on your assigned day, and voila! It disappears. North of Yesler Way, pick-up is weekly on the same day as your garbage collection. South of Yesler Way it's every other week from March to October, and once a month November to February.

Sixty-two percent of all city residents have signed up for the yard waste program.

Apartment dwellers are on their own where recycling is concerned, at least for now. The city plans to start up services for apartment buildings, but until it does, apartment residents have to take recycling to drop boxes at transfer stations, take the items to private companies, or talk to their building manager about contracting with a private company for pick-up. To find out which private recyclers are nearby, call (800) RECYCLE, a Department of Ecology hotline.

The city offers these other recycling opportunities too:

Recycled paint. Paint that ends up at the hazardous waste site is bulked and made into new paint. You can have it tinted your favorite color. You can get it at:
Preservatives Paint, 12012 Aurora Ave. N
Bailey Paint, 3525 Stone Way N
Parker Paints, 5500 14th NW
Southend Paints, 2924 Fourth Ave. S
Preservatives, 5410 Airport Way S

Diaper education program. New mothers are given information on disposable vs. cloth diapers.
Mattresses and lawn mowers. Private companies pick up old mattresses and lawn mowers from the transfer sites and refurbish them.
Compost program. The city gives away design sheets for portable wood and wire bins for composting.
Grocery bag reuse promotion in cooperation with grocery stores.

THE HAZARDS OF LIFE

That takes care of the not-too-smelly stuff. But what about truly hazardous wastes? You have to take motor oil and car batteries to either the North or South Transfer Station, but any other hazardous wastes (old paint, unidentified chemicals, etc.) must go to the South Transfer Station.

King County also has a Wastemobile stationed in different areas outside the city limits where people can take their hazardous wastes.

And old tires, which never seem to go away, can be taken to:

Casing Supply
Kent
872-2255
You get there by taking I-5 to exit 152, Orilla Road. Go down the hill and Orilla turns into 212th. At the second stop light (at 84th) take a left, go ¼ mile, and turn right behind a large sign. And there you are.

Dumping garbage and hazardous wastes

Solid Waste Utility
Collection, complaints, and billing info: 684-7600 or 684-HELP
Information on how to control your garbage bills: 684-8877

Trash disposal sites

Household hazardous wastes must go to the South Transfer Station during limited hours. Call the Hazardous Waste Hotline below for hours and wastes accepted.

North Transfer Station
1350 N 34th St.
(34th Street and Carr Place)
Mon.–Fri., 8 a.m.–5:30 p.m.; Sat., 8 a.m.–7 p.m.; Sun., 9 a.m.–6 p.m.

South Transfer Station
2800 Second Ave. S
(Second Ave. S and S Kenyon St.)
Mon.–Thurs., 8 a.m.–8 p.m.; Fri.–Sat., 8 a.m.–6 p.m.
$5 per car, regular rates. Additional $5 for chemicals.

Composting Hotline
633-0224
Weeds, hazardous overgrowth on private property: 684-7899

Hazardous Waste Hotline
296-4692
Disposal of liquids/tires/hazardous wastes, disposal of asbestos, referral for health information for removal of asbestos and radon.

Cedar Hills Landfill
296-4490
Accepts hazardous wastes; call ahead.

Indoor Air Pollution Resources
American Lung Association: 441-5100
Environmental Protection Agency: 442-2589
League of Women Voters: 329-4848

Seattle Solid Waste Utility
710 Second Ave.
684-7600
684-HELP (message phone)

Wastemobile
Seattle/King County Department of Public Health
Hazards Line: 296-4692

Where to donate household items for recycling:

St. Vincent de Paul: 623-1492
NW Center for the Retarded: 285-5441
Salvation Army: 624-0200
Vision Services: 633-0160

Drop boxes for donations:

Goodwill Industries: 329-1000
Salvation Army: 624-0200
St. Vincent de Paul: 623-1492

Spill Response Line
867-7229
To report illegal dumping into storm drains or gutters.

Washington Toxics Coalition
4516 University Way NE
Seattle, WA 98105
632-1545
They have a free guide available: *Turning the Tide: A Guide to Safer Alternatives and Proper Disposal of Hazardous Household Products.*

CHAPTER

6

ROOFS AND LADDERS

PERMITS

ARCHITECTS

CONTRACTORS

SOLAR POWER

TREES

ZONING

INSPECTORS

ASBESTOS

WOOD STOVES

TOOLS

"Weekend warriors." That's how contractors and architects snidely refer to the do-it-yourselfers who don't listen to the experts. But urban weekend warriors thrive here, where 70% of the city's land is zoned for single-family residences. In 1988 the Seattle

Building Department issued 1,866 permits for additions and alterations to old homesteads—and that figure doesn't include those who ran the saw out of earshot of city inspectors.

What contractors know is how to avoid standing in city permit lines when they're aching to hit the plumb lines. First of all, a particular weekend project may not even need a permit. To find out if yours does, call the Express Information Station at the city's Department of Land Use Planning. The rule of thumb is that if there is no structural change, and if access and ventilation are not reduced, you probably don't need a permit. You always need a permit to add plumbing and wiring.

The city doesn't list the remodeling projects that require a permit, so before you pound in a nail you should check. But take heart—such things as constructing oil derricks are exempt from the permit process. And the city trusts you to paint and put up wallpaper all by yourself.

NAILS AND GLUE

What you can hammer without city hall looking over your shoulder:

- Tool sheds and other sheds under 120 square feet and under 12 feet in height
- Playhouses less than 120 square feet
- Playground equipment
- Sculptures
- Fences under 6 feet in height
- Movable counters and partitions under 5 feet 9 inches
- Retaining walls not over 4 feet high
- Water tanks holding less than 5,000 gallons
- Walkways and driveways not more than 30 inches above grade and not over any basement or lower story
- Temporary motion picture, television, and theater stage sets and scenery
- Window awnings that don't extend more than 54 inches from exterior walls
- Prefabricated swimming pools not exceeding 5,000 gallons
- Hot tubs
- Minor repairs or alterations that cost less than $2,500 and do not require structural changes.

If your project isn't exempt, pull out your checkbook. For starters, Seattle's Department of Construction and Land Use (DCLU) wants $71 to begin a permit process that can take up to six weeks just to get the application appointment.

CITY SINGLE-FAMILY ZONING REGS

Lot coverage. You can only cover 35% or 1,750 square feet of your lot, whichever is greater, including house, garage, and any other buildings. This does not include decks under 18 inches high or below-ground swimming pools. You can cover your whole lot with playground equipment, as far as the city is concerned.

Height limits. Maximum permitted height for any residential structure is 30 feet, with some exceptions for things like peaked roofs, solar collectors, and chimneys. Maximum height for garages and sheds is 12 feet.

View corridors. Despite Seattle's hilly neighborhoods and incredible views, view regulations only apply to the downtown and shoreline areas. Anywhere else neighbors are left to squabble in court over who's blocking what view. On the shoreline, views are protected for motorists and pedestrians first. Regulations vary per zone; e.g., in some areas, if you live on the water, you can't build on more than 35% of the width of your property.

Yards. A minimum-size front, side, and back yard is required of every single-family lot in Seattle. There must be at least 20 feet from the property line to the house for the front yard, or the average of the two adjoining neighbors' front yard sizes, whichever is less. The back yard must be a minimum of 25 feet from the rear lot line to the foundation, and side yards must be at least 5 feet in width. If you build a chicken coop or whatever in the back yard, you can't cover more than 40% of the total back yard space.

If you get to the point where you want to give up and tear the whole darn thing down, wait! You have to have a permit to demolish anything that required a building permit in the first place. For this privilege you pay from $71 to $213, based on square footage.

City of Seattle
Department of Construction and Land Use (DCLU)
684-8850

DOWN ON THE (CITY) FARM

Urban farmers should cry foul on Seattle's hog discrimination. The only animal you absolutely, no exceptions, can't keep in your yard is the poor, unfairly maligned swine.

There's no reason for the prohibition, city folks say—it's just historic bias. It could have something to do with a pig's love of mud. Take one Seattle pig, one Seattle yard, and one Seattle winter and—well, would you want to live next door?

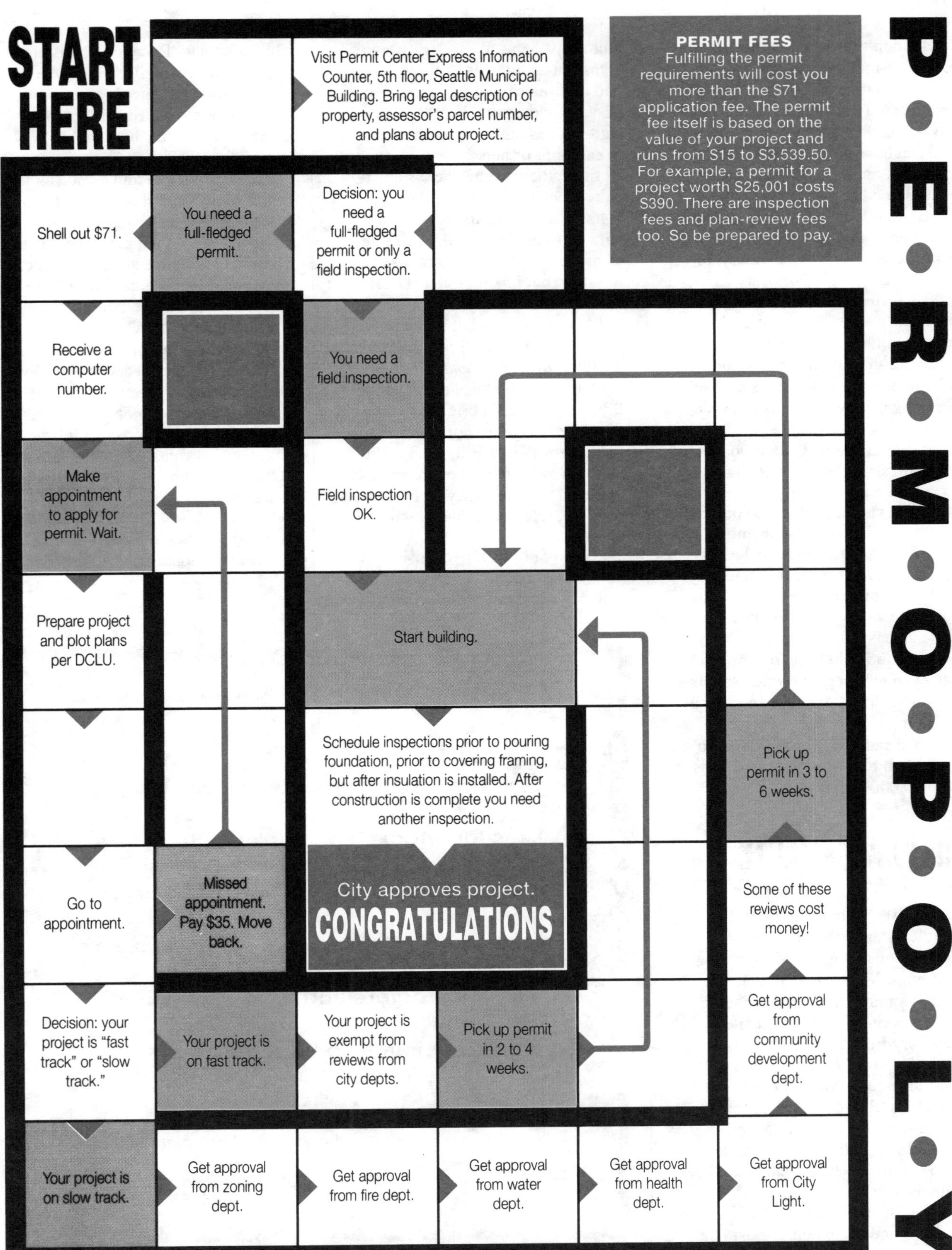
START HERE
Visit Permit Center Express Information Counter, 5th floor, Seattle Municipal Building. Bring legal description of property, assessor's parcel number, and plans about project.
Decision: you need a full-fledged permit or only a field inspection.
You need a full-fledged permit.
Shell out $71.
Receive a computer number.
Make appointment to apply for permit. Wait.
Prepare project and plot plans per DCLU.
Go to appointment.
Missed appointment. Pay $35. Move back.
Decision: your project is "fast track" or "slow track."
Your project is on slow track.
Get approval from zoning dept.
Get approval from fire dept.
Get approval from water dept.
Get approval from health dept.
Get approval from City Light.
Get approval from community development dept.
Some of these reviews cost money!
Pick up permit in 3 to 6 weeks.
Your project is on fast track.
Your project is exempt from reviews from city depts.
Pick up permit in 2 to 4 weeks.
You need a field inspection.
Field inspection OK.
Start building.
Schedule inspections prior to pouring foundation, prior to covering framing, but after insulation is installed. After construction is complete you need another inspection.
City approves project.
CONGRATULATIONS
PERMIT FEES
Fulfilling the permit requirements will cost you more than the $71 application fee. The permit fee itself is based on the value of your project and runs from $15 to $3,539.50. For example, a permit for a project worth $25,001 costs $390. There are inspection fees and plan-review fees too. So be prepared to pay.
P•E•R•M•O•P•O•L•Y

But don't throw away those overalls yet. Right there in Wallingford, or any other neighborhood zoned for single-family residences, you can have a chicken coop. In most cases you can have no more than three chickens, but if you have an especially large lot, you can have more. Single-family zones are designated by minimum lot size in square feet for different zones: S.F. 9600, S.F. 7200, or S.F. 5000. For every extra 1,000 square feet of lot area, you can have one extra chicken (or duck—it's the same for all domestic fowl).

As for the lady down the street with three dozen cats, she's probably breaking the law. The city allows up to three small animals per house in a single-family zone. Only if you have a 20,000 square-foot lot can you have four small animals.

Cows, sheep, horses, and other farm animals (except, remember, pigs) are only permitted on lots of at least 20,000 square feet, and only at the rate of one per every 10,000 square feet of lot area. Barns have to be at least 50 feet from property lines. With 20,000 square feet you can even have a goat (which smells a lot worse than a pig, with or without the mud).

Go ahead and keep bees, but no more than four hives on lots of less than 10,000 square feet.

HELP! ARCHITECTS

Only 10% of home builders in Seattle actually use an architect to draw up plans for remodels or new buildings. Most use a builder, contractor, or architectural designer, primarily because of cost. Architects' fees vary from $9 to $65 an hour depending on the firm and the project. In general you can figure on spending 10% to 15% of the cost of construction on an architect.

Architects simply hate people who call themselves architectural designers. Designers charge less than architects; and, some have good reputations and some don't—just like architects themselves. The difference is that an architect is licensed, has had five years of college, and has passed architectural boards. A designer is basically anyone choosing to call him- or herself that.

In Seattle it seems there's an architect behind every tree. There are 1,400 members of the American Institute of Architects (AIA), Seattle Chapter. The AIA does not make referrals, but its office at 1911 First Avenue has a great photo exhibit of local work and a small space for visitors to peruse portfolios. The "Firm ProFile," available at AIA for $12.50, is a roster of 350 local architectural firms. It includes a brief description of the firm, type of work, and its history. Portfolios of individual architects are available for reference only in the AIA office. They include resumes, references, and photos of work.

The big problem in choosing an architect is in making the best "fit." You want someone you feel comfortable talking to. Remember, this pro is going to be hanging around the house a lot; you don't have to wonder if he or she squeezes the toothpaste tube from the bottom, but almost.

The best way to find a good architect is by word of mouth. Ask owners whose houses you admire who designed them, then get a client list from the respective architect. Get on the phone and ask questions of those clients. And don't be intimidated by the vocabulary: "Arch-speak" can rival the chatter of doctors at lunch.

Be sure an architect can develop plans tailored to specific clients; if all his or her work looks the same, you can bet the architect isn't listening to the individual needs of the client. (Of course, if you like the style, there is a certain security in knowing that what you see is what you'll get.) Ask first, architects should give free initial consultations. If they don't, walk.

HEARD ON THE STREET

"The rough carpenter moves fast, likes loud tools, and thinks a chain saw is a precision tool. The finish carpenter hates noise, likes to work alone, washes his hands before and after eating, and dreams of joints so tight they can't be seen."

Jim Stacey, *Washington Homes*

You can look at a pamphlet of outstanding work by local architects who were selected by a professional jury at the First Avenue AIA office. The pamphlet, from the Honors Award Program, includes photos of projects, along with the address of the house or structure, and the name of the contractor and consultant. Good for leads on whom to hire.

HELP! CONTRACTORS

It's not enough to drive a pickup to call yourself a contractor in Seattle. You're a carpenter or builder or simply a pickup driver unless you are licensed and bonded.

The AIA provides something called a "contractor's qualification statement" for evaluating the expertise of contractors. It asks questions about experience, where the contractor is licensed to do business, trade references, financial assets, and other potentially embarrassing questions.

There are organizations, such as Seattle Master Builders, where you can get referrals. The trouble is that the group recommends members, and all you have to do to be a member is pay dues. Only 10% of all Seattle contractors belong to the Master Builders.

TIPS FOR CHOOSING YOUR CONTRACTOR

Check with Department of Labor and Industry (800-647-0982) for the credentials or record of a contractor.

Call the city building department to check the contractor's license number.

Ask for references, call them, and try to see the work. If a contractor balks at giving references, find another.

If you have the time and money, get a second opinion on the advice or bid a contractor is giving you from a disinterested designer or inspector.

Names to know

Architects of some distinction in the world of Seattle residential architecture, chosen for awards won, work featured in glossy upscale mags, and recognition by peers:

Jim Olson
Tom Bosworth
Arne Bystrom
Stuart Silk
Jim Cutler
Mark Millett
Ralph Anderson
Miller Hull Partnership

Where, one might ask, are the women? There are only 144 women members of the local AIA (10% of total membership).

INSPECT YOUR INSPECTOR

There was a time when somebody at the city issued a policy statement declaring that inspectors must be professional engineers. Slap! A lawsuit. The policy was retracted.

Building inspectors now come in all shapes and sizes, competencies, and lack thereof. Private inspectors don't need to have ANY qualifications—they *give* themselves qualifications in order to get work. (The law outlines some qualifications, but they're so vague as to be virtually unenforceable.) There are 60 or so inspection agencies around, but only five are registered with the engineering department.

Private inspectors can be found at their own private inspection companies. You can close your eyes and take a stab in the Yellow Pages, or you can ask for a reference from the American Society of Home Inspectors, (202) 842-3096. They at least test their members for basic competence. For a pre-purchase real estate inspection, either the buyer or seller hires an inspector to assess the overall structural integrity of a house, determine how it was built and maintained, and generally check out all conditions that might invite problems, such as the dreaded soil/wood contact. The going rate for a general pre-purchase inspection is about $250. Some inspectors also act as "owner representatives," looking at proposals from contractors to determine whether things are on the up and up.

THE SEATTLE HOUSE: BUGS, MOSS, AND ROT

The dreaded mildew and rot.
Causes: Weather from outside seeping in through leaks, especially in basements that aren't sealed, and moisture generated from inside that can't get out.
Signs of impending doom: Blistering paint, mildew or dampness on walls, and sweaty windows. If you aren't sure if you have rot, push an ice pick into suspect wood and see if it goes in too easily.
Solution: You need ventilation, especially in the attic, kitchen, bathroom, and in crawl spaces. Try fans in the living areas, and vents in the crawl space and attic. And get that basement sealed. Also, cut back on houseplant watering and aquariums in the winter.

INSIDE EDGE

Beware of trigger-happy pest inspectors who are eager to treat the symptom (the bugs) rather than the causes of infestation. Be leery of insecticides, especially a suspect method called "tenting" where plastic is literally draped over the entire home and then the place is fumigated to death. Rebuilding portions of the house that invited pests, like damp wood, should take care of the problem, maybe with the help of a little localized, low-key pest control.

BUGS, PESTS, AND CRITTERS

If the thought of mildew makes you sick, take heart. While mildew loves this climate, termites generally prefer a warmer clime. But that doesn't mean there aren't pest problems. The lowly powderpost beetle, for example, and carpenter ants love mold.
Cause: Moldy basements, damp wood.
Signs: Little sawdust piles at the base of wood studs. Powderpost beetles are usually found in older homes.
Solution: Call a pest control company and repair structural damage the little critters caused.

Seattle dream homes

Source: Dept. of Construction and Land Use

Year	New construction no. permits	Value	Remodel permits
1983	5,041	$417,796,431	3,379
1984	5,080	392,166,029	3,409
1985	5,328	595,765,937	3,693
1986	5,467	719,905,894	3,863
1987	6,010	832,832,097	4,425
1988	5,796	787,223,323	4,285

ASBESTOS ANGST

Your furnace and ducts may be insulated with materials containing asbestos; and siding and sprayed ceilings applied before 1978 may also contain the deadly stuff. Don't touch it—have an inspector look at it. Not all asbestos has to be removed.

MOSS ON THE ROOF

Roofs in shaded areas should have a zinc strip installed at the ridge to reduce damage from moss.

HIP, HIP, HOORAY—FOR CITY LOANS

The City of Seattle, along with Seattle Housing Authority (SHA) and Security Pacific Bank Housing Rehabilitation Center, provide home improvement loans at low interest rates to low-income residents. The program is called HIP (for Home Improvement Program, of course). The loans vary, but 20-year, 6% loans are available.

Income limits under HIP are:
1 person household: $22,300
2 person household: $25,500
3 person household: $28,650
4 person household: $31,850
5 person household: $33,850
6 person household: $35,850
Contact SHA, 443-4441, for more info.

YOUR YURT OR MINE?

Yurts and other eccentric structures are allowed, and thrive, in Seattle, but check with the city building department before you build or draw up plans to make sure you comply with local codes. The "builder's bible," as it is called, the *Uniform Building Code*, is available at bookstores for $54.95, or can be found in the architectural library at the UW's Gould Hall (though you can only read it there for two-hour stints).

The most popular alternative home in the city is the houseboat, more correctly known as a floating home. About 480 floating homes are docked in Seattle, divided among 50 docks on Portage Bay and Lake Union. They are so popular that the prices are soaring: $60,000 for a small, rundown houseboat; $1.5 million for a designer one. Since no new moorage is to be found, people are buying old houseboats, tearing them down, and building new ones.

Want one? The Floating Homes Association recommends several ways to find one:

- Visit a realtor.
- Walk around the docks to get a feel for the different areas and to look for For Rent or For Sale signs.
- Put up a "Want to Buy" sign at Pete's Grocery on Fairview Avenue near Lake Union and at Canal Market on Fuhrman Avenue E, Portage Bay. Floating homers frequent both places.

A couple things you should know: Banks considering loans do not always categorize a houseboat as real estate, but as personal property. This makes for financing problems.

Insurance is tough too. Some insurance companies consider houseboats a bad risk, and either charge an arm and a leg or don't offer coverage at all.

If you're thinking of building a houseboat, find someone who's experienced with the idiosyncracies of plumbing and electrical matters at sea.

The city has from time to time tried to do away with houseboats altogether, but floating home aficionados organized the Floating Homes Association to fend off such threats.

There are two ways to own a houseboat: either lease space on a dock or join a cooperative that owns the dock. Some houseboats do not comply with city shoreline law and are only floating because of their historic (or grandfathered) use.

The big houseboat issue today is that houseboats appear to be as upwardly mobile as their owners. As most of the one-story homes are becoming two-story, they grow in value. The city recently raised the height limit for grandfathered houseboats from 16 feet to 18 feet, so second stories are blossoming along the water. (Height limit for conforming houseboats is 21 feet.) This growth means that views and light are being cut, and there's even a tunnel effect between some docks where the little one-story jobs were jammed in years ago.

Another houseboat owners' gripe is that the seaplanes on Lake Union are noisy and so popular that they take off constantly. The seaplane companies have compromised somewhat and the planes no longer take off at the crack of dawn.

Live-aboards are not people who live on houseboats, but people who live on boats. The distinction is that the boats are not on floats, as houseboats are. Over 250 people at Shilshole Marina live aboard. Aside from mold in shoes and fighting with marinas over rates and sewage, people love the life on board and develop small communities within the marinas. Property taxes, nonexistent of course, are a pleasure to talk about. Not all marinas allow live-aboards, and there are strict health restrictions for the boats.

THE SUNSET OF SOLAR POWER

A few years back solar power companies were on every city corner, but there aren't many left now. Perhaps someone decided this isn't the greatest part of the country for solar power, but the most probable reason for their absence is that the federal tax credit for solar anything was abolished by the Reagan Administration.

When financial incentives went, businesses went too. Some people still heat hot water with solar water heaters, however. In 1988, the last year that records are available, 0.4% of residences in the city got their hot water hot by using solar energy.

There are two ways to get hot water from the sun, active and passive. Most solar water systems in Seattle are active says the Washington State Energy Extension. The most common is an active system of rooftop panels that use black metal with glass glazing for collector areas. A small electronic pump circulates water between the panels and the hot water tank.

Washington's latitude is about 48° N. Since latitude affects both the intensity of solar energy and the amount of time it's available, looking at a sun path chart for our latitude helps you choose the best site and angle for solar panels. Climate affects the amount of solar radiation delivered to a site too, of course.

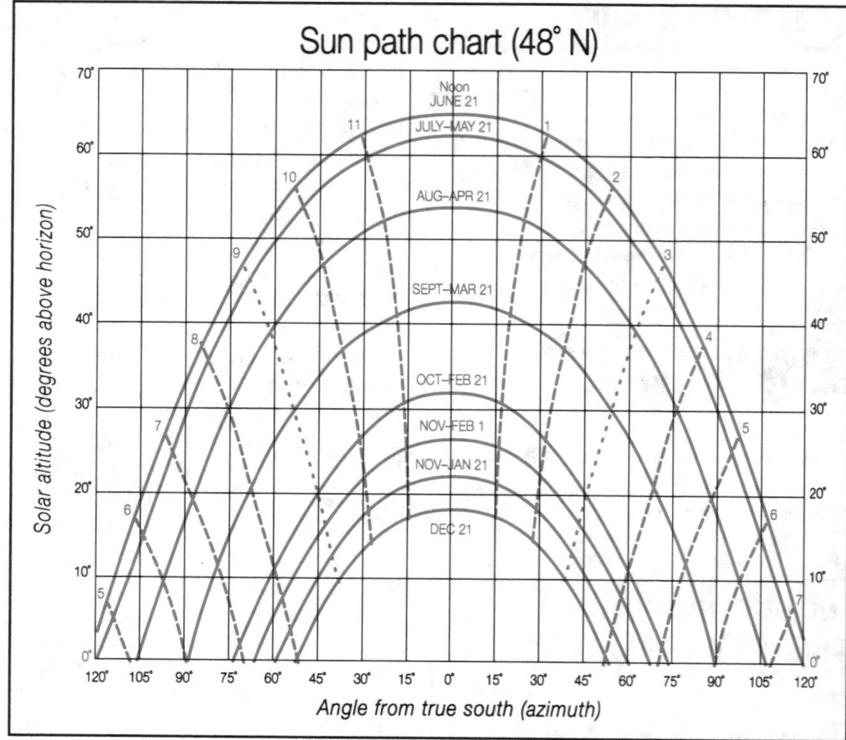

Source: Washington State Energy Extension

Very few contractors in Seattle are qualified to install active solar panels for heating water. Check with the Energy Extension Service for what you need to know about installation and then carefully assess dealers and installers. Ask how long the company's been in business, if they can provide references, and what sort of warranty they provide.

THE HAZARDOUS HEARTH

Statewide 1.12 million households burn wood; half with fireplace only. In some residential areas, it's estimated that wood burning accounts for as much as 85% of air pollution.

In 1981 the city began requiring that all wood stoves have a permit from the building department. The permit costs about $40, and although the ordinance is virtually unenforceable, most major home insurers are making sure homeowners have a permit for their stoves. After you pay the fee, a building inspector comes to your home to inspect the stove and its installation and, for newer stoves, you must show a certificate guaranteeing that it meets emission standards.

As smog from wood stoves has settled over the city in recent years, air emission regulations have been tightened; 1990 opacity (smoke density) restrictions are stricter than ever, and state-trained smoke readers wander the city looking for violations. They use "a visual observation technique" (in other words, they look at the smoke coming from your chimney) and can fine you if your smoke is too dense. (Too dense is anything over 20% opacity—the extent to which an object viewed through the smoke is obscured.)

Usually, dense smoke means you are using wet or green wood, or that your fire needs more air.

In Seattle burning is banned about eight days a year, usually in December and January. Ban announcements are made on radio and TV, or you can call Puget Sound Air Pollution Control for info, 296-5100. The burn-ban season is October–March; April–September you're usually welcome to burn. If wood heat is your only source of heat, you can burn even when a ban is in effect.

STREET-TREE WISE

There's a guy who works for the City of Seattle named Jerry Clark, who practically wears leaves in his hair. As city arborist he is a kind of social worker for trees, calling himself a "spokesperson for good tree policy." Clark is developing an urban forest which he hopes will number 200,000 street trees.

A city arborist has been around in one form or another for 50 years. After a landscape beautification effort by Mia Mann and Victor Steinbrueck, among others, the arborist's office was officially established in 1968. Since then 23,000 trees have been planted in planting strips—the area between the sidewalk and the curb. The most popular trees are maples and ash.

You may not know it, but you own up to 30 feet out into the 60-foot right-of-way of the street in front of your house. But, though you own it, the city manages the right-of-way for the general public. So you have to obtain permits to repair your sidewalk or to plant on the strip. There's no fee for a planting permit, but you'll receive advice from Clark about the proper tree selection to minimize conflicts with such things as utility poles. And you'll learn how to locate trees properly and how to maintain them. The city did a survey of historic urban trees—mostly maple, horse chestnut, ash, cedars, and poplars—and tries to match new trees to them to preserve the character of the streets.

There are few ancient trees left in Seattle, because Henry Yesler and his crew stripped the land when they got here. Some of the oldest are in Schmitz Park and older graveyards.

Seattle City Light will answer your questions about home weatherization and insulation, hot water heaters, energy consumption of discount appliances, alternative energy sources, and available discount loan or grant programs. Call 684-3800, 8 a.m.–5 p.m., Monday through Friday.

Why not offer a City Light employee coffee when he or she comes to do a free energy audit at your house and tell you how to reduce energy usage (and bills)? You must have an electrically heated house to be eligible for the visit. Free water heater insulation blankets may be installed during the check. Call the hotline above and ask about other City Light programs.

URBAN RE-LEAF

People plant lots of things in planting strips, including vegetable gardens. The only time that's a problem is if corn or hay or something limits visibility. Vegetation under 2½ feet is officially allowed.

The city has an "Urban Re-leaf Program," enabling property owners to buy trees at a discount at certain nurseries. The city looks for private donations to subsidize up to three trees for each Seattle resident signing up for the program, and gives a discount certificate to residents good for 50% off trees, up to a maximum value of $20. A list of participating nurseries is available from Clark's office.

Before the tree program, the city handed out 50 to 75 permits per year for trees; in 1989 550 to 600 permits were issued.

TO THROW YOUR OWN NEIGHBORHOOD PLANTING PARTY

1. Call Jerry Clark at the Engineering Department, 648-5040. He'll come talk to your group.
2. Find money, either through the Re-leaf Program or neighborhood matching funds. The Re-leaf Program is quicker.
3. Get a permit and choose type of trees, with Clark's help.
4. Trees can only be planted along city streets when there is a curbed roadway and the planting strip is at least 5 feet wide.
5. Only choose small-scale street trees when planting underneath power lines.
6. Call (800) 424-5555 to locate all underground utilities.
7. Plant small-scale trees between 15 and 25 feet apart. Plant all medium-size trees between 25 and 35 feet apart. Do not plant a tree any closer

Your planting strip along the street is the only sunny place in your yard? Go ahead and plant your vegetable garden there. The city won't care unless your corn grows so high it blocks visibility. And then they only care if someone complains. Whatever you do, don't pave the strip—that's verboten under the city's new push to combat the greenhouse effect by creating an urban forest.

than 5 feet to any utility line or power pole, 10 feet from a driveway, and 20 feet from a streetlight or existing trees.

8. Don't plant between June and September when water is at a premium. The arborist recommends drought-tolerant trees, but even those need water, usually about five gallons once or twice a week.

TREES SUITED TO A SEATTLE URBAN FOREST

Big shade trees: Oaks and ash are generally drought resistant and grow well. Maple is not recommended because it suffers from drought.

Medium shade trees: Flame Ash (35–40 feet, classic look fruitless). View them along 35th Ave. NE, north of NE 85th St.

Pyramidal European Hornbeam (30–35 feet, pyramidal shape, slow grower). See along 19th Ave. E, north of Madison.

Ruby Red Horse Chestnut (30 feet, red flowers in spring, nearly fruitless). See at Hiram Chittenden Locks to west of walkway.

Crimean Linden (45–50 feet, bright green, small foliage). See at 35th Ave. SW between SW Snoqualmie and SW Morgan streets.

Karsura (40 feet, light and dainty branch structure, fall color, needs moisture). See near 35th Ave. E and E Mercer St.

Cleveland Norway Maple (40–50 feet, yellow fall color, smaller than Norway Maple). See along Fifth Ave. downtown.

Red Maple (40–45 feet, fall color, requires most water). For narrow streets, columnar variety of Red Maple is best. See columnar along Madison St., near Boren.

Sweetgum (50–60 feet, semi-evergreen, fall color). See along Fourth Ave. downtown.

Zelkova (40-50 feet, fine-textured, slightly serrated leaf, use as substitute for American Elm). See along 24th Ave. NW, north of Market St.

Small-scale shade trees: Flowering ash (good tree with fragrant flower, dark green foliage, round head, grow in minimum 8-foot strip).

Flowering Cherry: Prunus serrulata (blooms April and May, full sun, moist soil). Selections include Shirofugen (25 feet), Shirotae (20 feet), Akebono (25 feet).

Other flowering cherries include: Yoshino (40 feet, 30 foot spread), Sargent (40 feet, 30 foot spread), Kwanzan (30 feet, 20 foot spread).

Flowering Crabapple: Select only those resistant to scab, cedar apple rust, mildew, and fireblight. Most grow 18 to 20 feet high. Recommended are: Baccat Jackii, Donald Wyman, Doubloons, Red Baron, Floribunda, Snowdrift, Veitch's Crab.

Goldenrain Tree (35 feet, intense sulphur-yellow flower, blooms late spring into summer, fruit until fall. Drought tolerant).

Hawthorn: Recommended are Lavalle Hawthorn (30 feet, shining green foliage, white flowers, and coral-colored berries); Washington Hawthorn (25 feet, white flowers, orange fruits, tolerant of pollution and extreme urban conditions).

Flowering Plum: Recommended are Krauter's Vesuvius Plum (35 feet, 25 foot spread); Thundercloud Plum (25 feet, same spread).

Flowering Pear: Recommended are Chanticleer (upright, 30 feet high, 15 foot spread, fall color); Aristocrat (very upright, 30 to 35 feet, 20–25 foot spread, fall color); Redspire (upright, pyramidal, 35 feet, 25 foot spread, fall color).

Source: City Arborist

SEATTLE'S BIG TREES

As far as size is concerned, Seattle's largest and by far our tallest trees are Douglas Firs, containing more wood per individual tree than any others do. Although a very few cedars and Grand Firs may presently be 200' tall in the city, only Douglas Firs are definitely known to be that tall, with a few even over 250'!

The tallest exotics measured in Seattle during 1987 or 1988 were as follows:

141' Coast Redwood
139' Lombardy (Black) Poplar
122' American Elm
120' European Beech
118' Tulip Tree
115' Certines Poplar
114' Deodar Cedar

Get a permit for a remodel? "Well, you could go that route...," says one builder we know. Only the incredibly naive think the city's building permit stats reflect how many building projects there are in the city. City officials estimate only half the projects that should have a permit have one. If you get caught without one, usually by tattle-tale neighbors, you have to pay up for an "investigation fee." So should you take your chances? Maybe, if you know what you're doing and are only building a deck. But insurance companies are sticklers on knowing that things are up to code and inspected. If your house burns down because of your makeshift wiring, you might be in trouble. And real estate agents sometimes question whether remodels are up to code. There's a safety factor too, so remodeling without a permit is a calculated risk.

114' 'Eugenei' Hybrid Poplar
113' English Elm
112' Sierra Redwood
112' Pin Oak
112' Ghost (Black) Poplar
109' 'Regenerata' Hybrid Poplar
107' Turkish Oak
103' Shingle Oak
102' Simon Weeping Poplar
102' Bolleana White Poplar
102' English Oak
101' Bigcone Pine
101' Smoothleaf Elm
101' Eastern White Pine
101' Red Oak
100' 'Marilandica' Hybrid Poplar
Source: Arthur Lee Jacobson, *Trees of Seattle*

Homeowner resource list

AA Rentals
12558 Lake City Way NE
Seattle, WA 98125
362-5544
Thirteen locations all over the city. Rent all kinds of building equipment, large to small: paint sprayers, loaders, jackhammers, saws, floodlights, etc. Most rent by the day, but some by the hour.

City Arborist
Jerry D. Clark
Seattle Engineering Dept.
Municipal Bldg.
600 Fourth Ave., Room 606
Seattle, WA 98104-1879
684-5040
Hours 7 a.m.–3:30 p.m. (Best time to get Clark is early morning.)

Dept. of Construction and Land Use
4th and 5th floors of Municipal Bldg.
600 Fourth Ave.
Seattle, WA 98101
684-8850 (application, permit info)
Express Information Station open 8 a.m.–5 p.m. Mon., Wed., Thurs., Fri. and 10a.m.–5p.m. on Tues.

Floating Homes Association
2329 Fairview Ave. E
Seattle, WA 98102
325-1132
President: Bill Keasler

40 Rentals
430 SW 153rd
Burien, WA 98166
244-1655
Four locations. Large and small equipment rental.

Handy Andy Rent-a-Tool
10711 Aurora Ave. N
Seattle, WA 98133
367-5050
NE 45th and First NE
Seattle, WA 98105
632-0404

Home Owners Club
1202 Harrison St.
Seattle, WA 98109
622-3500
Membership organization of about 2,000. Dues are $30 per year. Provides referrals for plumbing, electrical, TV repair, contractors, etc. Will even dispatch someone to your home to assess damage.

Madison Tool Rental
2023A E Madison Ave.
Seattle, WA 98122
328-1415

Some private building inspectors have a business on the side setting the "wrongs" they discover "right." For example, a pest inspector might be able to exterminate imaginary critters that were never a problem until he diagnosed them. The inspection might be cheap, but wait until you get the bill for the treatment. Ask inspectors if they have a repair business and if they do, find someone who doesn't.

Mostly smaller equipment but everything for the do-it-yourselfer except large earth-moving machines.

Phinney Neighborhood Association
Phinney Neighborhood Center
6532 Phinney Ave. N
Seattle, WA 98103
783-2244
Classes on home repair, wiring, etc.; a tool bank from which they loan tools, $10 for non-members, $5 for members.

American Institute of Architects/ Seattle Chapter
1911 First Ave.
Seattle, WA 98101
448-4938
Executive director: Marga Rose Hancock

Seattle City Light Consumer Advisory Service
Billing, general info: 625-3000
Wiring info: Residents north of Mercer Street, 684-4990
Wiring info: Residents south of Mercer, 386-1600
Advice on new or upgraded electrical service.

Seattle Master Builders
2155 112th Ave. NE
Bellevue, WA 98004
622-7766

Seattle–King County Dept. of Public Health
Smith Tower, Room 201
506 Second Ave.
Seattle, WA 98101
296-4732 or 296-4727
For plumbing inspection. Call between 7:30 and 8:30 a.m. to talk to inspector, or bring your plans in during the same hours, no appointment necessary.

Washington Energy Extension Service
914 E Jefferson St., Suite 300
Seattle, WA 98122
296-5640 or (800) 962-9731
Answer any and all questions on energy conservation. Have 50 publications on energy conservation available.

CHAPTER

7

THE POWERS THAT BE

THE MAYOR

CITY COUNCIL

VOTING

PROPERTY TAX

PORT OF SEATTLE

CITY HALL

COMMITTEES

COURTS

METRO

NEIGHBORHOODS

Where to go, how to get there, whom to talk to: Life in the web of bureaucracy can be daunting, whether the question is which elevator to take to which office or how to REALLY get someone to listen to you. But in a city the size of Seattle there is still a chance you'll run into the mayor on the street, or a chance you can track a councilman to lunch at Rick's Tower Grill. (This can work both ways: It's not such a treat when lunching at Bakeman's to run into the municipal court judge who just slapped you with the Big Fine.)

HIZZONOR AND FRIENDS

Seattle mayor Norm Rice began his $87,419 per year, four-year job at the beginning of 1990.

Like all city officials, the mayor is elected at-large in a non-partisan election. His duties include: preparing the city budget; giving an annual "State of the City" address in June to the city council; vetoing legislation (the mayor can veto an ordinance passed by the council, but the council can override the veto by a two-thirds vote of all members); appointing heads of city departments, including chief of police, fire chief, director of community development, and others.

The mayor's office is on the 12th floor of city hall, but to reach him you have to go through staff people and squeeze into a tight schedule of meetings, speeches, and handshaking events. The best way to get in touch with the mayor is through one of his staff.

A DAY IN THE LIFE OF THE MAYOR

Mayor Norm Rice's itinerary for May 3, 1990, Thursday:
7:45–8 a.m. Briefing, mayor's office, with Deputy Mayor Bob Watt regarding cabinet meeting.
8–9 a.m. Conference Room, cabinet meeting with 30 department directors, senior staff.
9–10 a.m. Press conference preparation, mayor's office, kick around issues with Mark Murray, press secretary.

Cities, mayors, money and more

City	Population	Council member salary	Mayor salary
Seattle	485,200	$58,457	$87,419
Boston	573,600	42,500	100,000
Minneapolis	356,870	46,500	63,000
San Francisco	749,000	23,928	111,656
Portland	387,870	56,668	67,288

	City Attorney salary	Police Chief salary	City employees per 1,000 population
Seattle	$72,161	$57,900	22.20
Boston	65,000	58,900	35.42
Minneapolis	79,631	71,618	14.80
San Francisco	99,624	94,821	31.19
Portland	64,896	61,235	11.78

Source: *City and State Magazine*, 1989 figures

INSIDE EDGE

You can't always get what you want, as the song says, but the way to get satisfaction from the city is to use the Citizens Service Bureau number, 684-8811. About 500 people per week call this number and sound off about one thing or another to six staffers. They'll answer your questions about garbage pick-up, seaplane noise, and other practical matters, and they'll also explain the mayor's position on an issue to you. They'll take your comments on an issue as well. They send a weekly report to the mayor stating how many people call on a given issue and what their positions are—including whatever colorful quotes seem appropriate.

The other number to remember is City Department Information, 386-1234. That switchboard will get you to the department you're after.

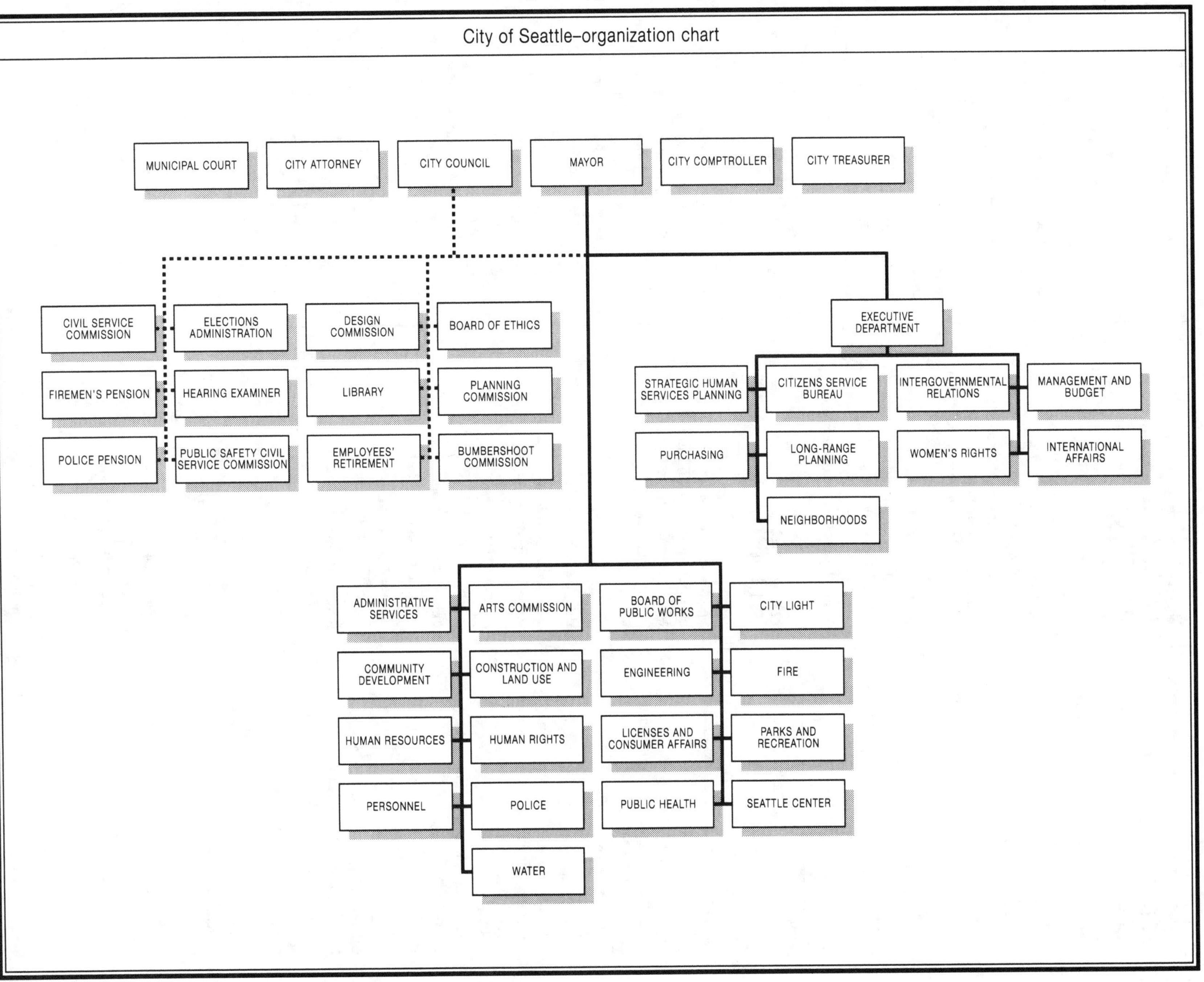
City of Seattle–organization chart
MUNICIPAL COURT
CITY ATTORNEY
CITY COUNCIL
MAYOR
CITY COMPTROLLER
CITY TREASURER
CIVIL SERVICE COMMISSION
ELECTIONS ADMINISTRATION
DESIGN COMMISSION
BOARD OF ETHICS
FIREMEN'S PENSION
HEARING EXAMINER
LIBRARY
PLANNING COMMISSION
POLICE PENSION
PUBLIC SAFETY CIVIL SERVICE COMMISSION
EMPLOYEES' RETIREMENT
BUMBERSHOOT COMMISSION
EXECUTIVE DEPARTMENT
STRATEGIC HUMAN SERVICES PLANNING
CITIZENS SERVICE BUREAU
INTERGOVERNMENTAL RELATIONS
MANAGEMENT AND BUDGET
PURCHASING
LONG-RANGE PLANNING
WOMEN'S RIGHTS
INTERNATIONAL AFFAIRS
NEIGHBORHOODS
ADMINISTRATIVE SERVICES
ARTS COMMISSION
BOARD OF PUBLIC WORKS
CITY LIGHT
COMMUNITY DEVELOPMENT
CONSTRUCTION AND LAND USE
ENGINEERING
FIRE
HUMAN RESOURCES
HUMAN RIGHTS
LICENSES AND CONSUMER AFFAIRS
PARKS AND RECREATION
PERSONNEL
POLICE
PUBLIC HEALTH
SEATTLE CENTER
WATER

Top ten mayoral salaries

City	Salary
1. New York	$130,000
2. Detroit	125,350
3. San Francisco	111,656
4. Houston	104,979
5. Boston	100,000
6. Los Angeles	97,654
7. Seattle	**87,419**
8. Jacksonville, Fla	86,991
9. St. Louis	82,680
10. Memphis	82,500

Source: *City and State Magazine*

South Park Community Center re basketball program for youth called "Shooting the Stars."
3–4 p.m. Back to Metro Council meeting.
4–4:30 p.m. Mayor's office, courtesy call by Dennis Okamoto, newly appointed director of Department of Revenue re tax reform assessment.
4:30–6 p.m. Historical Room, stop by to welcome Education Task Force of National League of Cities.
6–6:40 p.m. Sheraton, Grand Ballroom, Educational Opportunity Program banquet.
6:50–8:10 p.m. Annual meeting, Seattle Trade Center (Court Atrium), Red Cross Annual Meeting, keynote speech.
8:30–9 p.m. Drop by Young Life Banquet at Mt. Zion Baptist Church; brief remarks re at-risk and special education kids.
Source: Mayor's Office, City of Seattle

LOCAL EXECUTIVE SALARIES

Zeger van Asch van Wijck, Port of Seattle executive director: $126,684 (appointed).
Tim Hill, King County executive: $103,000 (elected).
Booth Gardner, governor: $99,600 (elected).
Richard Sandaas, Metro director: $95,000 (appointed).
Norm Rice, mayor: $87,419 (elected).
Source: Seattle Survival Guide research

CITY HALL

Seattle Mayor's Office
600 Fourth Ave., 12th Floor
Mayor Norm Rice: 684-4000
24-hour answering service: 524-2707

Deputy Mayor
Bob Watt: 684-4000

Deputy Chief of Staff
Anne Levinson: 684-4000

Deputy Chief of Staff
Charles Rolland: 684-4000

Deputy Chief of Staff
Tom Tierney: 684-4000

Deputy Chief of Staff
Robert Tovar: 684-4000

Communications Director
Mark Murray: 684-8126

Office Manager
Julia Laranang: 684-4000

Executive departments

Citizens Service Bureau
Director: Elmer J. Dixon, 684-8811

Human Services Strategic Planning Office
Director: Bonnie Snedeker, 684-8057

Office of Intergovernmental Relations
Director: William Stafford, 684-8055

Office of International Affairs
386-1511

Office for Long Range Planning
Director: Richard Yukubousky, 684-8056

Office of Management and Budget
Director: Andrew Lofton, 684-8080

Office of Neighborhoods
Director: Jim Diers, 684-0464

Office for Women's Rights
Director: Linda E. Taylor, 684-0390

Purchasing
Purchasing agent: T.H. Terao, 684-0444

CITY COUNCIL

Every Monday at 2 p.m., nine city council members sit down and hammer out city policies and/or ordinances. They pass laws on zoning codes, traffic regulations, housing codes, and criminal laws. Their posts are sought after and fought for on an at-large basis—meaning that everyone in the city votes for all council members. They serve for four years, in staggered terms so that campaign signs don't simply take over the city at any one time.

It always helps to know someone, even if it's the person holding down

Full city council meetings are held each Monday at 2 p.m. in Room 1101, Seattle Municipal Building, 600 Fourth Avenue. A hearings calendar listing all meetings is published weekly. To get on the mailing list, call 684-8888.

If you really want to be an effective influence on city government, take a staff member to lunch. Develop a solid working relationship with a couple of the council members, and don't forget their underlings. If you're non-confrontational, secretaries and staff people will go out of their way to help you.

the front desk. Begin by asking friendly questions, but don't waste their time.

There's a reason why some lobbyists in Olympia spend thousands of dollars on presents for the legislative secretaries. Their knowledge and powers are too often underestimated.

Seattle City Council
1106 Municipal Bldg.
600 Fourth Ave.
Seattle, WA 98104
Information: 684-8888

Executive Director
Paul Matsuoka, 684-8888

City Council Clerk
Theresa Dunbar, 684-8888

George E. Benson
Council member, 684-8801
Chair: Transportation Committee
Aides: Grace Chien, Benita Staadecker
Term ends Dec. 31, 1993

Cheryl Chow
Council member, 684-8804
Chair: Parks and Public Grounds Committee
Aides: Phil Fujii, Jan Waggoner
Term ends Dec. 31, 1993

Susan Donaldson
Council member, 684-8806
Chair: Land Use Committee
Aides: Janice O'Mahoney, Lucy Steers
Term ends Nov. 1990 (She was appointed to fill Norm Rice's position when he was elected mayor.)

Paul Kraabel
Council president, 684-8807
Chair: Labor Policy Committee
Aides: Beverly Barnett, Jada Berteaux
Term ends Dec. 31, 1991

Jane Noland
Council member, 684-8803
Chair: Public Safety and Environment Committee
Aides: Heather Worthley, Mamie Rockafellar
Term ends Dec. 31, 1993

Dolores Sibonga
Council member, 684-8802
Chair: Finance, Budget, and Management Committee
Aides: Art Ceniza, Eva Murphy
Term ends Dec. 31, 1991

Key to downtown buildings

1. Library
2. City Light Building
3. City Credit Union Building
4. Arctic Building
5. Dexter Horton Building
6. Municipal Building
7. Public Safety Building
8. Alaska Building
9. Prefontaine Building
10. Third and Main Building
11. King County Jail
12. King County Administration Building
13. King County Courthouse
14. King County Garage
15. Federal Courthouse
16. Federal Building

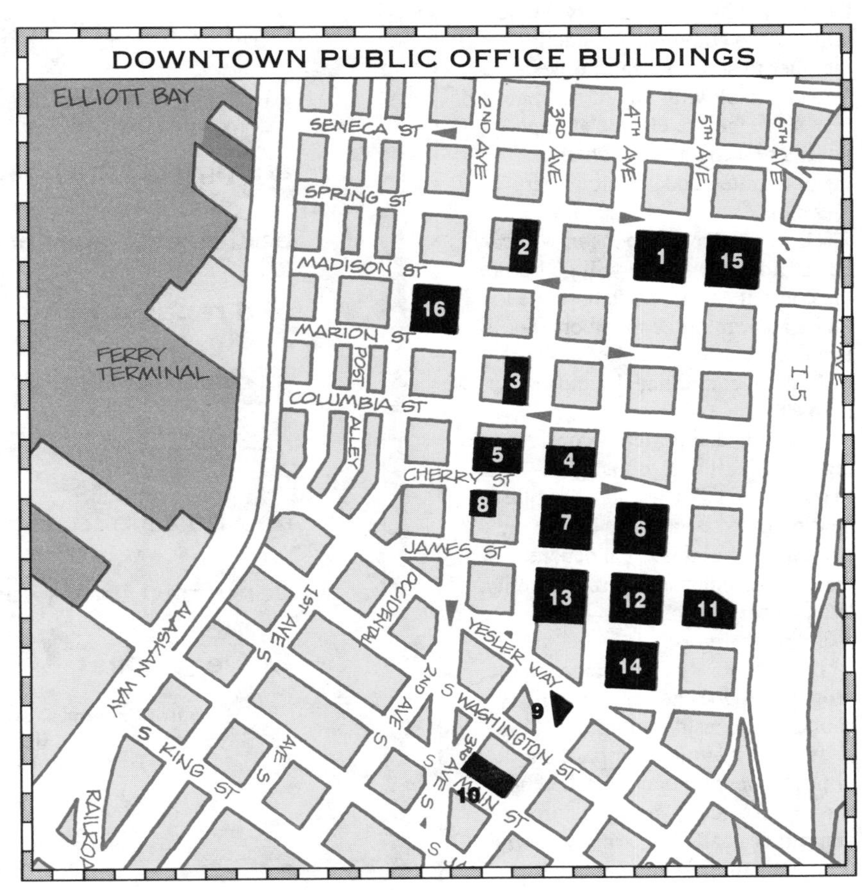

Sam Smith
Council member, 684-8800
Chair: Utilities Committee
Aides: Eleanor Knott, Rose Rapoza, Karen Winston
Term ends Dec. 31, 1991

Jim Street
Council member, 684-8808
Chair: Growth Policies and Regional Affairs Committee
Aides: Darlene Flynn, Frank Kirk
Term ends Dec. 31, 1991

Tom Weeks
Council member, 684-8805
Chair: Housing, Human Services, and Education
Aides: Mary Bourguinon, Julie Davis
Term ends Dec. 31, 1993

FROM IDEA TO BILL

If you have an idea for a bill you'd like to get passed by the city council, you have to convince a council member to sponsor your proposal. You can work with any of the members since they're elected at large, but it's best to go to the chair of the committee under which your idea falls.

Once you have a sponsor, you can be confident your idea will go before the committee, so now's the time to lobby all committee members. Set up appointments with them by calling the committee director (684-8888).

Once the committee is considering the idea, it will probably ask you to come and talk about it. A public hearing may be arranged before the committee, but this often depends on the level of interest—citizen activity, letters received, calls, etc.—surrounding the proposal.

If the committee recommends the proposal, it goes before the full city council for consideration.

If there is enough support, another public hearing may be called before the council. (The chairs of the committees call all hearings, so winning their support helps move the process along to passage by the full council.)

Don't forget the mayor. You need to make sure he's on your side so he doesn't veto the whole thing even if the council approves it.

WHO'S ON WHAT COMMITTEE

Since most of the council work is done in committee, it's important to know who's who and when the committees meet.

Finance, Budget, and Management: Dolores Sibonga (chair), Sam Smith (vice-chair), Tom Weeks, Jim Street (alternates). Meets first and third Wednesdays, mornings. Budget, taxes, fees, personnel, audits, economic development, human rights, etc.

Growth Policies and Regional Affairs: Jim Street (chair), Tom Weeks (vice-chair), Dolores Sibonga, Cheryl Chow (alternates). Meets first and third Tuesdays, afternoons. Growth planning, area plans, neighborhood planning, regional growth strategies, port, FAA, aircraft noise, etc.

HEARD ON THE STREET

"The overall feeling is that our money is not being spent in the right places, that we are not spending enough on the basics. Folks saw those basics as including police protection and repair and maintenance of our streets, sidewalks, and parks. It was very clear they wanted to take back and be able to use their streets and parks and they wanted to fix what we've got first."

Margaret Freeman, chairperson, Budget Committee
of the City Neighborhood Council
Report to Mayor Charles Royer, June 1989

There are copy centers in city buildings where you may copy public records and documents. They are in Room 608, Municipal Building; Room 223, Public Safety Building; Fifth Floor, 400 Yesler Building. The convenience is nice, but it ain't cheap. It costs $0.25 for the first page of each document or book and $0.10 for each additional page or copies, plus tax.

Housing, Human Services, and Education: Tom Weeks (chair), Jane Noland (vice-chair), Cheryl Chow, Jim Street, Dolores Sibonga (alternates). Meets second and fourth Tuesdays, afternoons. Housing, public health, human services, Block Grant, library, education.

Labor Policy: Paul Kraabel (chair), Dolores Sibonga (vice-chair), Jane Noland, Sam Smith, Tom Weeks, George Benson (alternates). Meets second Wednesday, afternoon. Collective bargaining, salaries, hours and conditions of employment.

Land Use: Susan Donaldson (chair), George Benson (vice-chair), Paul Kraabel, Jane Noland (alternates). Meets second and fourth Wednesdays, mornings. Multi-family mapping, code revisions, parking, apartment zoning, environmentally sensitive areas, landmark designations, etc.

Parks and Public Grounds: Cheryl Chow (chair), Susan Donaldson (vice-chair), George Benson, Sam Smith (alternates). Meets first and third Thursdays, mornings. Parks and recreation programs, public lands, property management, open space, and Seattle Center.

Public Safety and Environment: Jane Noland (chair), Cheryl Chow (vice-chair), Sam Smith, Susan Donaldson (alternates). Meets second and fourth Tuesdays, mornings. Crime, fire prevention, law enforcement, justice, corrections, consumer protection, animal and noise control, environmental issues.

Transportation: George Benson (chair), Jim Street (vice-chair), Jane Noland, Susan Donaldson, Paul Kraabel (alternates). Meets first and third Tuesdays, mornings. Transportation planning, construction, traffic control, parking policies, pedestrian safety, coordination with Metro, Puget Sound Council of Governments (PSCOG), and Department of Transportation (DOT).

Utilities: Sam Smith (chair), Paul Kraabel (vice-chair), Dolores Sibonga, Tom Weeks (alternates). Meets first and third Wednesdays, afternoons. Energy, City Light, power planning, cable television, water, drainage, waste water, and solid waste.

YOUR TAX DOLLARS

In October the city budget goes from the mayor to the council in draft form. The city's fiscal year follows the calendar year, so the annual budget goes into effect in January.

City property tax revenue

$ per capita

Seattle	$130
Boston	802
San Francisco	510
Portland	199
Minneapolis	170

Source: *City and State Magazine*, 1989

The city's official newspaper — the one in which all legal notices can be found —is the Daily Journal of Commerce. If you're hoping to bid for consulting jobs or public works projects, keep one eye on the DJC.

For the year 1990 the city budget revenues equal $1.15 billion. About $302 million of that comes from taxes. The largest chunk of city revenue is from the utilities—about $541 million, or 46.8% of the total.

Where it's spent is something else again.

1990 expenditures

Utilities and transportation — $653 million.

Public safety (fire, police, municipal court) — $176 million.

Health and human services (including parks) — $129 million.

General government (executive, law, etc.) — $96.5 million.

Physical development (construction and land use, hearing examiner) — $19.5 million.

Other (neighborhood matching fund, bonds debt service, etc.) — $83 million.

OTHER CITY FACTS

The City has 11,178 employees. Seattle's sales tax is 8.1%. Seattle's average property tax is $1,263. Average monthly City Light bill is $33.99.

VOTING INFORMATION

The city's elections are the responsibility of the King County Superintendent of Elections. For registration information, call 296-1600 or 296-1565.

VITAL STATS

Many people don't darken the door of the city hall unless they need copies of birth or death certificates. To get a copy of a birth certificate, you need to write to Vital Statistics/ Health Department, 11th Floor, Public Safety Building, Seattle, WA 98104, 296-4769. You need to know the person's name, birth date, parents' names (including mother's maiden name), and the city in King County where the birth occurred. Send along $3. For a death certificate, write the above section giving the name, date of death, and city in King County where the death occurred. And send $3. If you want to get a birth or death certificate from outside King County, call the Vital Statistics section at 753-5936. They'll tell you where to write.

Want to be a street vendor and sell espresso or popcorn from a cart? A city permit will cost you $42 a year. But that's not the tricky part; you have to get permission from the business adjacent to your chosen sidewalk spot before you can acquire a permit. And you must have a $1 million insurance policy (so the city isn't liable). Carts cost around $10,000–$20,000. You can vend food, non-alcoholic beverages, and flowers—NO T-SHIRTS (that's what most permit requests are for, though). For information on a permit, call 684-5267.

The Office of Neighborhoods puts out a nifty little pamphlet, "The Whole City Catalog," a guide to speakers for Seattle's community organizations. The booklet lists people in city government who will come and talk to your group about such things as fundraising, long-term care for the elderly, the P-Patch program, and other topics. Call 684-0264.

Other city resources

Comptroller and City Clerk
Norward J. Brooks
Municipal Bldg., Room 101
684-8383
City's bookkeeper, accountant, and auditor rolled into one. Elected position, next election 1991.

Treasurer
Lloyd F. Hara
Municipal Bldg., Room 103
684-5212
Elected position, next election 1991.

City Attorney
Mark Sidran
Municipal Bldg., 10th Floor
684-8200
Elected position, next election 1993.

Community Service Centers
2309 NW Market St.: 684-4060
12707 30th Ave. NE: 684-7526
208 N 85th St.: 684-4096
5214 University Way NE: 684-7542
1825 S Jackson St.: 684-4767
4859 Rainier Ave. S: 386-1931
9407 16th Ave. SW: 684-7416
708 N 34th St.: 684-4054
8201 10th Ave. S: 767-3650
506 19th Ave. E: 684-4574
3054 15th Ave. W: 386-4207
5034 California Ave. SW: 684-7495
Services include information/referral, city utility payments, senior citizen discount, voter registration, and assistance to neighborhoods.

Business and tax information
684-8484

City jobs, Personnel Department
684-7999

Conservation tips and weatherization
684-3800

County jobs
296-5209

Federal jobs
442-4365

State jobs
1-753-5368

Fire Department
Chief: Claude Harris, 386-1401

Human Rights Department
Seattle: 684-4500

Licenses and Consumer Affairs
684-8444

Marriage licenses
403 King County Administration Bldg.
296-3933

Parks and Recreation
684-4075

Police Department
Chief: Patrick Fitzsimons, 684-5577
Police, internal investigations: 684-8797

Senior Citizens
Mayor's Office: 684-0500

Senior Support
Division on Aging: 684-0660

DISTRICT AND MUNI COURTS

Municipal court (see also, Chapter 16, "Cops and Robbers") is where you go when you've violated a city ordinance—and God help you, at least until the city straightens out its court mess; sometimes there are 150 jury trials scheduled in municipal court in a week.

You have to appear in court for serious offenses, such as driving while intoxicated (DWI) or reckless driving. Otherwise, for such things as parking violations and some traffic violations, you tell it to the magistrate. Magistrates are attorneys who have been appointed judges *pro tempore.* Your hearing takes place in the magistrate's office. The magistrate has a copy of the citation (the officer who gave it to you isn't there) and will talk with you about it. You can appeal his or her decision to a municipal court judge, but usually magistrates are kind enough to compromise and lessen your fine or help you find a way to pay it back.

If you want to contest a citation or arrest, you have to go before a judge, one of nine elected to four-year terms. Seattle's municipal judges are Barbara T. Yanick (presiding judge), Helen Halpert, George W. Holifield, Ronald Kessler, Nicole MacInnes, Barbara Madsen, Ron Mamiya, and Stephen Schaefer. One judgeship was open at press time.

Municipal Court
1100 Public Safety Bldg.
684-5600
Judges: 684-8709

Magistrate Hearing Dept.
106 Public Safety Bldg.
684-8704

KING COUNTY

King County is governed by nine council members. They meet Mondays at 9:30 a.m. at 402 King County Courthouse, Third and James. Like the city council, county council members are elected to four-year terms, with elections held in odd-numbered years. The executive is elected too—Tim Hill's term ends in 1993.

General county council information
296-1000
FAX: 296-0198
Council administrator: Gerald Peterson, 296-1020
King County executive: Tim Hill, 296-4040
Deputy King County executive: Rollin Fatland, 296-4040
FAX: 296-0194
King County prosecuting attorney: Norm Maleng, 296-9000 (next election, 1990)

King County Council and Districts

District 1
Audrey Gruger: 296-1001

District 2
Cynthia Sullivan: 296-1002

District 3
Brian Derdowski: 296-1003

District 4
Lois North: 296-1004

District 5
Ron Sims: 296-1005

District 6
Bruce Laing: 296-3457

District 7
Paul Barden: 296-7777

District 8
Greg Nickels: 296-1008

District 9
Kent Pullen: 296-1009

Committees

County committees change around the first of every year.

Comprehensive Plan Update
First and third Tuesday (on call); Cynthia Sullivan, chair; Brian Derdowski, vice-chair; Bruce Laing, Paul Barden, Kent Pullen.

Growth Management, Community and Environment
2 p.m., second and fourth Tuesdays; Brian Derdowski, chair; Paul Barden, vice-chair; Ron Sims, Bruce Laing, Kent Pullen, Cynthia Sullivan.

Health, Housing, and Human Services
2 p.m., second and fourth Wednesdays; Audrey Gruger, chair; Cynthia Sullivan, vice-chair; Lois North, Ron Sims, Greg Nickels.

Law and Justice
9:30 a.m., second and fourth Tuesdays; Kent Pullen, chair; Audrey Gruger, vice-chair; Lois North, Greg Nickels.

Open Spaces, Parks, and Natural Resources
9:30 a.m., first and third Wednesdays; Greg Nickels, chair; Ron Sims, vice-chair; Cynthia Sullivan, Brian Derdowski, Bruce Laing.

Operation and Administration Services
9:30 a.m., first and third Tuesdays; Ron Sims, chair; Kent Pullen, vice-chair; Audrey Gruger, Paul Barden.

Regional Affairs and Governance
2 p.m., first and third Wednesdays; Paul Barden, chair; Bruce Laing, vice-chair; Audrey Gruger, Cynthia Sullivan, Lois North.

Transportation and Public Works
9:30 a.m., second and fourth Wednesdays; Bruce Laing, chair; Greg Nickels, vice-chair; Brian Derdowski, Lois North, Paul Barden.

THE INEVITABLE PROPERTY TAX

Jog on up to the seventh floor of the King County Administration Building, 500 Fourth Avenue, and sit down at the computer terminals in the Public Information Unit. You can call up a bunch of information on houses and property (yours or someone else's) including: property characteristics; property assessed value history (up to five years); property folio number and map location; taxpayers' names and addresses; and a history of local and state appeals since 1984.

Out of 600,000 pieces of property in King County, tax assessments on roughly 20,000 are appealed every other year. Reductions are granted in about two out of three cases. Here's how to appeal:

Review your property data at the Public Information Unit, seventh floor of King County Administration Building. If you still aren't satisfied, get forms from the Board of Appeals/Equalization: 296-3496. You must appeal within 30 days of your valuation notice or July 1, whichever is later. You need a comparative value estimate from realtors or publications. And you can look at every home in the county in the computer databank at the assessor's office, if you want.

The board will then hold a hearing on your case, though you might have to wait 6–12 months for it. If the board decides you're right, the members will recommend a new assessment. If they say you're wrong, you can appeal the decision to the State Board of Appeals. You don't need an attorney to appeal, but you'd better be prepared to put in some time proving you couldn't sell your house for the amount it's assessed. The state pays most attention to other sales in the area.

That's a great service provided by the King County Assessor's Office; it may not offset your property tax payments, but it's nice anyhow.

About those payments, just how does a property's value get set? The assessor determines the value of your house or property by one or more of three methods:

1. Market. This is based on the sales of similar properties—it's the primary method used for residences.

2. Replacement cost. This determines what it would cost to replace the existing structure. Usually used for new construction.

3. Income. This is used only for business property valuation, and measures the income expected from a managed property.

Every two years the assessor comes calling to revalue your house. He or she looks at other houses in the area and recent sales to get the "true and fair value" of your property.

Legally, you don't have to let the assessor into your house when he or she comes around. But psychologically, it's probably a good idea. If you refuse, you might be suspected of hiding an expensive remodeling project, and the inspector's imagination could get carried away. "It's to your advantage" to let the assessor look around, say those in the department.

GOING BACK . . .

If you want to see your house's tax history, you can see the records for 1984 to present on the computer (above), records for 1973–83 on microfiche at the Assessor's Public Information Unit, and for 1860–1972 at the Washington State Regional Archives. The oldest information is limited to name, legal description, assessed value, and taxes, but most of the time there is a photo attached and it's fun to see what the house looked like when it was new. Call the archives, 764-4276.

King County Assessor's Office
296-7300
Assessor: Ruthe Ridder, 296-5195

Office of Tax Advisor
296-5202

County Board of Appeals/Equalization
296-3496

State Board of Appeals
1-753-5446

POWERS THAT BE AT METRO

A 40-member Metropolitan Council governs Metro, a municipal corporation. The council is made up of a federation of local governments with responsibility for water pollution control and public transportation in King County. Council members represent King County, the cities of Auburn, Bellevue, Kent, Kirkland, Mercer Island, Redmond, Renton, Seattle, and other cities and county areas.

The Metro Council meets on the first and third Thursdays of each month at 3 p.m. on the 17th floor of the Pacific Building, 720 Third Avenue near Columbia Street.

Metro has an operating budget of $37 million for 1990, and employs 3,508 people.

Metro names

Chairman of Metro Council: Penny Peabody
Executive director: Richard Sandaas, 684-1983
Clerk of the council (agendas, meetings, committees): 684-1014

Standing committee chairs
Finance/Personnel: Greg Nickels
Rules and Organization: Penny Peabody
Transit Committee: Fred Jarrett
Water Quality: Dolores Sibonga

Metro Staff Offices
Exchange Bldg.
821 Second Ave.
Seattle, WA 98104-1598
General administration: 684-2100
Community Relations: 684-1138
Customer Assistance (transit): 447-4824
Finance, Budget and Administration Dept.: 684-1616
Technical Services Dept.: 684-1724
Transit Dept.: 684-1441
Water Pollution Control Dept.: 684-1233
Directory Information: 684-2100

PORT OF SEATTLE

The Port of Seattle keeps those terminals on the waterfront open and operates the Seattle-Tacoma International Airport. It operates on a $178 million annual budget and collects $29 million in taxes.

If the Port has had its stormy times or troubled waters, as headline writers like to say, it's also had some of the city's most colorful commissioners. There were Ivar Haglund and Paul Friedlander, lawyer Henry Aronson, who caused a big flap, and Jim Wright, whom everyone liked to refer to as a maverick.

Wright tells this story about his days on the commission: It seems that once at the end of a meeting Ivar had his employees from down the street at the restaurant bring in vats of clam chowder for the commission and members of the audience. Paul

How to find out what's really happening inside the port: Call Portwatch, a watchdog group that monitors every meeting (283-0555). Its members are outraged at the way the port spends public money.

Friedlander, of Friedlander jewelry fame, took one look at the free chowder and said, "Next week I'm bringing diamonds."

The days of characters at the port may be over as competition for airlines and container terminals demands more of commissioners. The port also runs Shilshole Marina and Fisherman's Terminal. And it's in the midst of a scheme to bring hotel/residential uses to the waterfront near Pier 66 as well as a transient marina and some open space. The port plans a cruise ship terminal too —if only a pesky federal law called the Jones Act would disappear.

The port commission has five members who meet the second and fourth Tuesdays at noon (they meet in executive session first—no public allowed—and then the regular public meeting gets going at 1 p.m.) at Pier 66, 2201 Alaskan Way. They have work sessions open to the public at the same time on the first and third Thursdays.

To get onto the commission agenda, call 728-3210.

Port commissioners serve six-year terms. Here are their names and when their terms expire:

Patricia Davis, president (Dec. 31, 1991)
Jack Block (Dec. 31, 1991)
Paige Miller (Dec. 31, 1993)
Gary Grant (Dec. 31, 1995)
Paul Schell (Dec. 31, 1995)

Airport Director
Andrea Riniker, 433-5387

Executive Director
Zeger van Asch van Wijck, 728-3201

Marine Division Director
Frank Clark, 728-3374

Port Commission Secretary
728-3199

Port Commissioners
728-3034

Miscellaneous government resources

Washington State Department of Transportation
1-753-6054

Environmental Protection Agency
442-1200

Federal Aviation Administration
241-7912

Federal Communications Commission
764-3324

Federal Emergency Management Agency
487-4600

Health and Human Services
442-0566

Puget Sound Council of Governments
464-7090

DOG HOUSE ACTIVISM

Neighborhood organizations seeking clout in city hall have been spawned in various ways, the most common of which seems to be reaction to change. Whether because of concern about an influx of apartment buildings in single-family neighborhoods or in reaction to industrial pollution, neighbors in need find ways of getting together to be heard by city officials and council members.

The Seattle Neighborhood Coalition (SNC) is a classic example of an institution that has drawn together a diverse group of neighborhood activists: artists, poets, city employees,

HEARD ON THE STREET

"The boundaries are really a guessing game. Seattle's character is extremely diverse and growing more so each year. The city has more or less resolved itself to the differences that make it so unique."

Jim Diers, director, Office of Neighborhoods

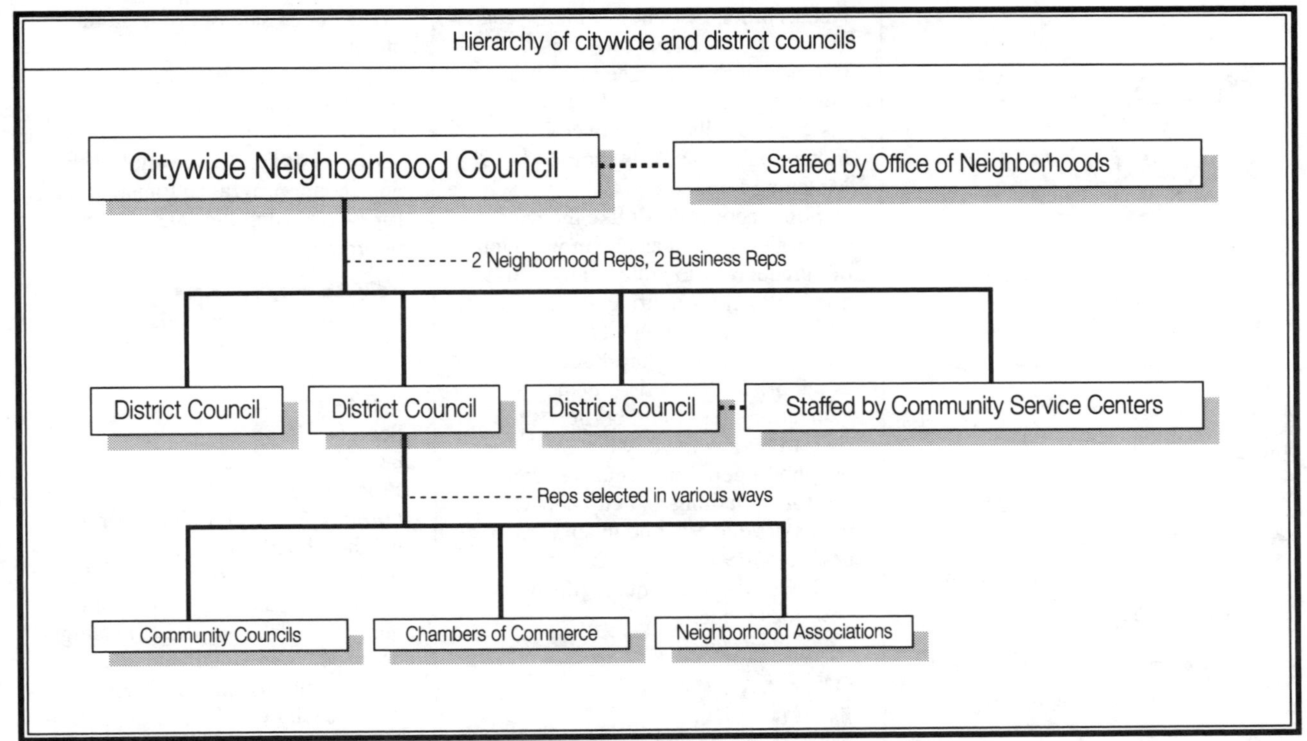

small-business owners, and other professionals. SNC meets on the first Saturday morning of each month at The Dog House restaurant on Seventh Avenue just south of Denny Way, a befitting backdrop for this group of urban Bohemians who sip black coffee and debate the course of Seattle's neighborhoods. Activists from neighborhoods around the city regularly attend these informal Dog House events that are often standing-room-only.

SNC's finest moment came in the mid-1980s, when it took a stand against intrusion of multi-family housing into single-family-residence neighborhoods throughout the city. The fact that then-Mayor Charles Royer won elections twice on a "neighborhoods platform" was like rubbing salt in a wound. SNC objected to increases in multi-family housing, but as the rhetoric heated up, single-family houses were going the way of the dinosaur, especially in Ballard and Fremont. Finally, though, SNC got the ear of the city council, and a scheme was devised to bring together development and neighborhood interests and "downzone" many neighborhoods.

ENTER VISION SEATTLE

In the midst of these neighborhood growing pains, members of the SNC gradually realized the only way to gain clout with city hall was to become political. Vision Seattle was born from the loose ranks of SNC and, in a climate of citizen frustration, produced a slate of candidates to represent neighborhood interests in the election of 1988. These unlikely candidates for city council posts lost by a wide margin, but the message to the city government couldn't have been more clear.

Council members took heed, passing zoning legislation and comprehensive plans for individual neighborhoods that restrict new construction and encourage growth where it can best be managed. Not all the neighborhoods' plans are intact; the planning battle is still under way in many areas, but the city's neighborhoods have at least regained some say in their own development.

NEIGHBORHOOD BUREAUCRACY

One of the results of the city's neighborhood studies has been the establishment of an Office of Neighborhoods as a separate department within city government. The OFN divides Seattle into 13 separate district councils, each made up of businesspeople, and community council and neighborhood association representatives. The councils meet on a monthly basis, tackling such issues as growth, crime, and traffic. Each council is served by the neighborhood's "Little City Hall" or Community Service Center.

Each district council selects two residential and two business representatives to attend the Citywide

Got graffiti on your neighborhood walls? Don't give up. Call the city's anti-graffiti coordinator, Sue Honaker, 684-5004. She organizes community groups to paint out graffiti. She has a paint bank of 2,000 gallons in colors from purple to pukey green. And she has instructions for what treatment to use on all surfaces.

Before you paint over anything, she'll come out and read the graffiti. The city tracks gang hot spots by graffiti. (A current graffiti hot spot is at Second and Pine.) It also tracks such things as hate graffiti, so be sure to record whatever is written before you do away with it.

If a wall is repeatedly hit, the city will organize the painting of a mural there. Murals are generally free from vandalism, probably because would-be graffitti artists recognize them as belonging to somebody.

All you have to do, says Honaker, is pick up a paintbrush and continue to paint out graffiti. "You can't let a vandal condition you to say, 'Why bother?' You have to condition the vandal to say that." Usually it takes only two attempts and they give up.

Neighborhood Council, which meets bimonthly at various locations throughout the city. The OFN provides staff services and helps the district councils haggle over grant money: the city's Neighborhood Matching Fund.

Some people don't like the new setup—they see it as one more layer of bureaucracy to deflect neighborhood influence on city government. Others—like some in city government—see the neighborhood unity as a thorn in their side. The new organization gives neighborhoods the right to review the city budget. Neighborhood representatives can ask for something and city departments have to respond in some manner. In the 1990 budget, the city acted on 209 of the 432 requests the neighborhoods made.

WHAT THE NEIGHBORHOODS WANT

Requests from the Citywide Neighborhood Council of items to be included in City of Seattle 1990 budget:
• Engineering department, 248 requests
—58% of requests for repair and cleanup: Requests include fixing potholes, alleys, and sidewalks; street sweeping; litter and trash removal.
—37% traffic concerns: crosswalks, signage, traffic lights, street lights.
Parks department, 72 requests
—82% for repair, maintenance, or installation of equipment in existing parks; restroom repair; playground equipment and general upkeep; police security patrols.
—11% for youth programs.
—10 requests for open space acquisition.
• Police department, 47 requests
—84% for foot patrols, bus-stop security, park security, and increases in police funding; more police protection, drug enforcement because of "the open sale of drugs on the streets."
—Parking enforcement.
• Homeless/shelters/low-income housing, 18 requests
—Requests for detox van; housing and shelter programs; transients, runaways, latch-key, and day-care programs.

Neighborhood resources
Office of Neighborhoods
Director: Jim Diers
Arctic Bldg., Room 410
700 Third Ave.
Seattle, WA 98104
684-0464
Produces the monthly *Seattle Neighborhood News*, as well as helping neighborhood organizations, managing the matching fund, establishing neighborhoods involvement in city budget, and staffing the City Neighborhood Council. OFN also has a resource library and produces the "Whole City Catalog," a guide to speakers for community groups.

City Office of Long Range Planning
600 Fourth Ave., 2nd Floor
Seattle, WA 98104
684-8056
Plans revisions, downzones, etc.

Seattle Neighborhood Coalition
731 N 87th St.
Seattle, WA 98103
784-7217
Group of activists organized around neighborhood issues.

Vision Seattle
340 15th Ave. E, Suite 350
Seattle, WA 98112
325-8817
Political action group involved with neighborhood issues.

Neighborhood Crime & Justice Center
500 Wall St., Suite 315
Seattle, WA 98121
728-0903
Assists communities in organizing crime prevention councils.

EFFECTIVE POLITICS

Here are some suggestions from various neighborhood council members on how to get things done:

- Be willing to persevere.
- Get educated on the issues.
- Be creative.
- Be willing to step into the larger policy realm; get laws changed and elect officials who will give you improved laws. If you don't get the larger policy changed, you'll just fight the same battles over and over.
- Get involved with the entire community council—you can't carry issues by yourself. And considering different perspectives is healthy.
- Get plugged in with the people who make things move.
- Be willing to work your way around problem people you encounter. Don't be reluctant to hold people in government responsible. If the person you're dealing with isn't giving the service you think is your due, ask to speak to a superior.
- Be open and willing to contact strangers. Be a networking person.
- One community council has a huge roster of officers—25 to 30. Thus it involves as many people as possible and addresses a lot of issues.
- Neighborhood groups need to have a clear sense of their boundaries and identities and to work within those boundaries to solve problems. Only then can they deal with regional problems.

CHAPTER

8

MANNING THE BARRICADES

POLITICAL GROUPS

GOVERNMENT WATCHDOGS

ENVIRONMENTAL GROUPS

AIDS GROUPS

ORGANIZING

CONGRESSIONAL REPS

PEACE ACTIVISTS

SOCIAL SERVICES

WOMEN'S GROUPS

PETITIONS

It's an almost exclusively Seattle thing that whenever two or more city-ites get together, they call themselves a community action group. When there's an issue, at least two groups immediately organize around it. Some are Friends of Something, others use acronyms like WashPIRG or NARAL, some string the cause out, like "Citizens Alliance to Keep the Pike Place Market Public."

In addition to citizens groups, there are boards and commissions beyond belief. But if you want to get involved in those, you have a lot of competition—especially for the prestigious jobs.

Steady cuts during the Reagan years to federally funded social programs have spawned a rising tide of nonprofit organizations providing desperately needed services and education in Seattle. In fact, a struggle over the Seattle funding base is emerging among peace-and-justice groups, environmental organizations, and the human-needs/homeless service providers. There's only so much money to go around—and who fills the gaps? Volunteers.

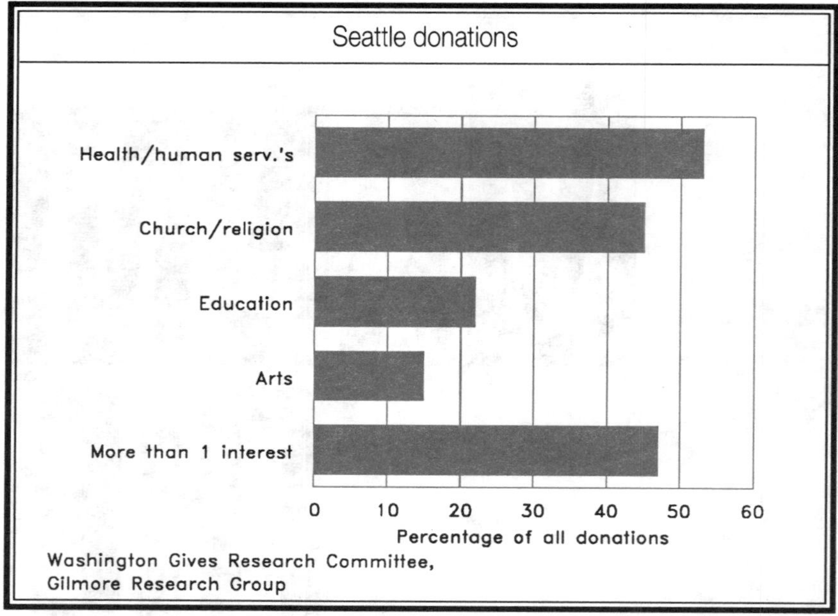

SEATTLE'S RADICALS: POLITICAL GROUPS

If politics is your thing, here's how to start out the establishment way.

Democratic Central Committee of King County
616 First Ave., Suite 340
Seattle, WA 98104
622-9157
Executive director: Kelly McMurray

Democratic facts

As of fall 1990 all state legislators from Seattle were Democrats.

In 1988 Dukakis carried King County, the first time in 20 years a Democrat carried the county in a presidential election. Washington State also carried for Dukakis.

Democratic State Central Committee of Washington
506 Second Ave. (Smith Tower)
Room 1701
Seattle, WA 98104
583-0664
Executive director: Jeff Smith
Chairperson: Karen Marchioro

Radical Women
5018 Rainier Ave. S
Seattle, WA 98118
722-6057
A political group that's part of the Freedom Socialist Party.

The Republican Party
1305 Republican
Seattle, WA 98109
467-1990
Executive director: Kevin Jenne

Republican State Committee of Washington
9 Lake Bellevue Dr., Suite 203
Bellevue, WA 98005
682-8123 (in Seattle)

Revolutionary Communist Party of America
5519 University Way NE
Seattle, WA 98105
527-8558
Meets at Revolutionary Books.

Socialist Party
P.O. Box 31021
Wallingford Station
Seattle, WA 98103
632-5098

Socialist Workers Party
1405 E Madison
Seattle, WA 98122
323-1755

Washington State Rainbow Coalition
P.O. Box 22856
Seattle, WA 98122
726-8928
President: Larry Gossett

You too can be an elected representative of the people. Precinct committee officers are elected every two years by the people who live within the city's voting precincts. All you have to do is file with the King County Office of Elections, pay a $1 fee, and campaign your heart out.

How to get involved in the party of your choice? Call the local central committee office and they'll refer you to your legislative district organization, which meets monthly. There are 16 legislative districts in King County.

UNRELENTING PRESSURE

Congressional reps and how to reach them:

U.S. House of Representatives

First District
John Miller (R)
1406 Longworth Bldg.
Washington, D.C. 20515
(202)225-6311 (Washington, D.C.)
(206)672-4224 (Edmonds)
Committees: Foreign Affairs, Merchant Marine, Fisheries

Second District
Al Swift (D)
1502 Longworth Bldg.
Washington, D.C. 20515
(202)225-2605 (Washington, D.C.)
(206)252-3188 (Everett)
Committees: Energy & Commerce, House Administration

Third District
Jolene Unsoeld (D)
1508 Longworth Bldg.
Washington, D.C. 20515
(202)225-3536 (Washington, D.C.)
(206)753-9528 (Olympia)
Committees: Education & Labor, Merchant Marine, Fisheries

Fourth District
Sid Morrison (R)
1434 Longworth Bldg.
Washington, D.C. 20515
(202)225-5816 (Washington D.C.)
(509)575-5891 (Yakima)
Committees: Agriculture, Science, Space & Technology, Select Hunger

Fifth District
Tom Foley (D)
1201 Longworth Bldg.
Washington, D.C. 20515
(202)225-2006 (Washington, D.C.)
(509)353-2155 (Spokane)
Speaker of the House

Sixth District
Norm Dicks (D)
2429 Rayburn Bldg.
Washington, D.C. 20515
(202)225-5916 (Washington, D.C.)
(206)593-6536 (Tacoma)
Committees: Appropriations

Seventh District
Jim McDermott (D)
1529 Longworth Bldg.
Washington, D.C. 20515
(202)225-3106 (Washington, D.C.)
(206)442-7170 (Seattle)
Committees: Banking, Finance & Urban Affairs, Interior & Insular Affairs

Eighth District
Rod Chandler (R)
223 Cannon Bldg.
Washington, D.C. 20510
(202)225-7761 (Washington, D.C.)
(206)442-0116 (Bellevue)
Committees: Post Office & Civil Service, Ways & Means

U.S. Senate

Brock Adams (D)
513 Hart Bldg.
Washington, D.C. 20510
(202)224-2621 (Washington, D.C.)
(206)442-5545 (Seattle)
Committees: Appropriations, Labor & Human Resources, Rules & Administration

Slade Gorton (R)
730 Hart Bldg.
Washington, D.C. 20510
(202)224-3441 (Washington, D.C.)
(206)442-0350 (Seattle)
Committees: Agriculture, Nutrition, Forestry, Armed Services, Commerce, Science & Transportation

GOVERNMENT WATCHDOGS

Watchdog groups are as much a part of local politics as are candidates shaking hands. Almost every political body has a watchdog group tracking its steps. The groups can be effective at some times, dormant at others. One thing's for sure: They're listened to, no matter how aggravating politicians think they are.

Citizens for Clean Industry
P.O. Box 803
LaConner, WA 98257
324-2217
Contact: Darlene Madenwald
Turf: Anacortes-based group formed to watchdog the industries in the Puget Sound region.
Dues: $10/year
Membership: 100

Citizens to Save Puget Sound
P.O. Box 420
Seahurst, WA 98062
431-0444
President: Vivian Matthews
Turf: Formed to stop Metro from putting sewage plant on the beach at West Point; now monitors Metro. Lobbies in Olympia on water quality issues, and testifies at other local public hearings.
Dues: $10/year
Membership: 70–100

Common Cause
509 E 12th Ave., Suite 11
Olympia, WA 98501
352-4446
Executive director: Chuck Sauvage
Chairman Seattle chapter: Norman Turrill
Turf: Nonpartisan citizens group lobbying for good government. Issues include public disclosure and keeping the process of government open,

accessible, and accountable. Watchdog group focuses on state government, but works on federal, county, and local government, too.
Dues: $20/year. Includes national membership, magazine, and newsletter.
Membership: 4,000 in Seattle area; 8,000+ statewide.

League of Women Voters of Seattle
1402 Third Ave.
Seattle, WA 98101
622-8961
President: Mary Coltrane
Turf: The league is well respected for its research papers and doggedness in following issues. Publishes a free yearly directory of public officials in King County. Send a self-addressed stamped envelope to get one. The league is well known for its LWV's Voter's Pamphlet, a review of key issues and candidates, produced for Seattle citizens prior to elections (the LWV endorses no candidates). The organization also has a Voter Service Committee, a Speakers Bureau, and a variety of active subcommittees.
Dues: $40/year
Membership: 200–600; mailing list of 700. Open to men as well as women.

Metropolitan Democratic Club
3007 66th Ave. SW
Seattle, WA 98116
937-5088
Chair: Nick Licata
Turf: MDC was established in the early 1950s as a liberal alternative to the mainstream party apparatus. Since then it has remained an independent, progressive organization. "Although outside the Democratic Party structure, the members are part of the progressive Democratic Party tradition." MDC sponsors debates, speakers, and forums on topics of concern to Seattleites. Endorses candidates at election time. Events are held downtown and are open to the public.
Dues: $20/year
Membership: About 350. Conservatives need not apply.

Municipal League of King County
414 Central Bldg.
810 Third Ave.
Seattle, WA 98104
622-8333
Director: Cynthia Curreri
Turf: The 80-year-old Muni League is affectionately known as "a good government watchdog." Nonpartisan, nonprofit in nature, it researches the knowledge, character, experience, and effectiveness of candidates. Also researches such issues as transportation, land use, and King County ballot measures (CAP and open space are two examples). The league proposes alternatives to legislators, but is probably most listened to (and most feared) for its ratings of candidates at election time.
Dues: From $25 to $50 for a large corporate membership.
Membership: About 2,000. The group generates *Issue Watch*, a monthly publication.

Portwatch
2573 28th Ave. W
Seattle, WA 98199
283-0555
Contacts: Diana and Martin Swain
Turf: Port of Seattle. Portwatch works to involve the public in port processes. The group monitors the port's marine division decision making with a focus on financial accountability, how property tax levies are spent, port capital expansion, and the budget process. Steering committee meets as activity requires, with annual general membership meetings.
Dues: $5–$15/year
Membership: 180–200

Vision Seattle
340 15th Ave. E, Suite 350
Seattle, WA 98112
325-8817
Contact: Pat Strosahl (political issues committee)

Turf: Very active during the Citizen Alternative Plan (CAP) campaign in 1989, this group took a bath in the 1989 city council election. But it plans to continue to put up candidates for future elections. Issues are growth management, accountable city government, affordable housing, education, public safety, neighborhood empowerment.
Dues: $8 low-income; $15 individual; $30 family; $60 donor; $120 patron.
Membership: 1,200+. Volunteers needed to monitor city council meetings, work in office.

PEACE AND JUSTICE

Peace activists here have only one problem: deciding which group gets their time and money. Many of the groups cluster around "Peace Alley" (45th and University Way NE). Some groups don't have offices but instead have regional representatives who handle the organizational end of things. We don't pretend to be naming them all, but here are some of the main peace and justice groups.

American Civil Liberties Union
1720 Smith Tower
506 Second Ave.
Seattle, WA 98104
624-2180
Contact: Nate Johnson
Turf: Works to protect the civil liberties of all Americans through public education, legislative advocacy, and litigation. Issues include reproductive freedom, privacy, due process, freedom of speech, and all other First Amendment rights.
Dues: $20/year individual or $30/year group.
Membership: 10,000 locally; 260,000 nationwide. Volunteers work in the office doing such things as record keeping and newspaper clipping.

Central American Peace Campaign
4556 University Way NE
Seattle, WA 98105
547-3977
Turf: Washington State group working for a U.S. foreign policy based on international law and the principles of self-determination, human rights, economic justice, and peaceful conflict resolution. Has an education resource center, speakers bureau, and seminars. Also monthly legislative updates, quarterly newsletters, and workshops on effective lobbying techniques.
Dues: $15/year for newsletter; $25/year+ for monthly legislative and action update; $100 enables curriculum support; $350 pays for one trip to Washington, D.C. to meet with Congress members.
Membership: 15,000 statewide; members sign statement of support and agree to pay dues based on ability to contribute.

CISPES (Committee in Solidarity with the People of El Salvador)
P.O. Box 20091
Seattle, WA 98102
325-5494
Contact: Tom Leonard or Lynne Jensen
Turf: Works with Salvadoran people for peace and social justice and against U.S. intervention there.
Membership: About 3,000. Welcomes anyone committed to achieving the goals of the group with any amount of money or time.

Citizens International Center
Council of International Organizations
615 Second Ave., Suite 110
Seattle, WA 98104
623-6008
Contact: Kay Bullitt
Turf: Networking body to help out smaller nonprofit organizations with international focus. Facility is for group use with meeting room available, computers for rent, fax machine, resource center/database, bibliographies, and World Peace Through Law library.
Dues: $35/year
Membership: 150

Conscience and Military Tax Campaign
4534½ University Way NE
Suite 204
Seattle, WA 98105
547-0952
Coordinator: Vivien Sharples
Turf: Provides information and counseling on war tax resistance and redirection. It administers the largest Escrow Account of refused military taxes in the U.S. and redirects refused telephone taxes to humanitarian projects in Central America. Leads workshops, publishes a newsletter, organizes political action, and supports the Peace Tax Fund Bill. Also monthly support group for war tax resisters.
Dues: No dues, but subscriptions to *Conscience* newsletter are $5.
Membership: 600 Escrow Account holders nationwide and 300 subscribers to *Conscience* in the Seattle area (3,000 nationwide). Volunteers

Activist organizations are eager to have both your time and money. If you let them, the fundraising brochures (not to mention the phone calls) can stack up. The best solution is when you sit down with the checkbook to pay the mortgage, choose one group for that month and give something to it. Some people choose the one handling THE hot issue of the moment, others choose a longtime favorite. And if you want to be taken off a mailing list or phone tree, say so—loudly, if necessary.

are needed to do office work, write articles and help with newsletter production, do outreach, help organize public protests, and act as resistance counselors.

Engineers for Social Responsibility
P.O. Box 1012
Seattle, WA 98101
Northwest representative: Richard Horner
Contact: Mike Froebe, 783-2924
Turf: National group that maintains that the responsibility of engineers is to use their skill and knowledge to enhance human welfare. Issues are economic conversion, global warming, etc. on the national level; what to do about Herschel and the steelhead run on the local level.
Dues: $20/$15 student
Membership: 40

Evergreen State Peace Mission
225 N 70th St.
Seattle, WA 98103
789-5565
Turf: Central America, nuclear proliferation, and foreign policy are major issues. Umbrella group that coordinates lobbying on a range of issues. Representatives from its 20 member organizations are briefed on issues and trained for lobbying trips to D.C., where pressure is applied to state delegations before votes are made. Helps activists prepare for trips, provides materials and debriefing sessions in Seattle on return. The Peace Mission is compiling a computer database on state delegation members: voting patterns, details of foreign visits, and policy positions.
Membership: 50,000 Washington State (mainly Seattle and Western Washington).

OXFAM
4534½ University Way NE
Seattle, WA 98105
523-6926
Chairperson: Teri McKenzie
Turf: The active Seattle chapter of OXFAM does world hunger relief work including self-help development projects and disaster relief in poor countries.
Dues: No dues, contributions only.
Membership: No members, but volunteers are welcome to help in the local office.

Peace Corps Recruitment
2001 Sixth Ave., Room 1776
Seattle, WA 98121
442-5490; (800)424-1022
UW campus representative: Jackson School of International Studies, 543-5258
Approximately 6,300 Peace Corps volunteers serve in 70 countries worldwide—including Eastern Europe, a recent addition. Since 1961 there have been 130,000 volunteers nationwide, 5,500 from Washington State. Currently 237 volunteers from the state are overseas.

The University of Washington has been one of the top five schools in the nation for producing Peace Corps volunteers: 2,400 UW grads have served.

Skills most sought after: backgrounds and/or degrees (degrees are preferable) in agriculture, forestry, freshwater fisheries, math, science, education, secondary education, industrial arts, nursing, health, and nutrition. If you have a background in linguistics or experience teaching English as a foreign language, you can put your skills to work teaching secondary-level English. Ninety percent of volunteers have four-year degrees. And the other 10% have strong experience in construction skills and agriculture.

Average age is 31, compared with 23 in the first five years of Peace Corps existence. There's no upper age limit; just good health. The PC doesn't take families with dependent children. The application process takes 4–12 months.

How many get in? Well, the Peace Corps receives 125,000 inquiries nationally in a year, and 20,000 applications. Of those, it sends about 3,500 volunteers overseas. Former Peace Corps volunteers have organized a group called Returned Action Volunteers of the Northwest (RAVN).

Physicians for Social Responsibility
4534½ University Way NE
Seattle, WA 98105
547-2630
Director: Beverly Isenson
Turf: Nonprofit, nonpartisan group doing educational work with issues related to the arms race, nuclear war, and military spending.
Dues: $70/year for physicians; $50/year general public.
Membership: Open membership, 60–70% physicians. Western Washington members total around 1,600.

Pledge of Resistance
225 N 70th St.
Seattle, WA 98103
789-5565
Program of FOR (below) seeking intervention in Central America through lobbying and education rather than violent methods. Advocates nonviolent civil disobedience. The Pledge has 1,530 on its mailing list.

Ploughshares
509 10th Ave. E
Seattle, WA 98102
328-8813
Turf: Citizen diplomacy, international exchange for peace. The group is best known for establishing the Seattle/Tashkent Peace Park, the U.S.– Soviet Partners Project, and the Million Cranes Project (the cranes were a part of the Goodwill Games welcoming ceremony).
Membership: Returned Peace Corps volunteers.

Washington State SANE/Freeze
5516 Roosevelt Way NE
Seattle, WA 98105
527-8050
Turf: A national organization mobilizing citizens through legislative and educational activity. Issues include ceasing nuclear weapons and plutonium production, abolishing apartheid, and promoting economic diversification of military-based economy. Rapid Response Network gives status of legislative actions and tells whom to target with lobbying.
Dues: $10 or more includes one-year

subscription to SANE/Freeze Citizen. Tax deductible.
Membership: 24,000 statewide

Western Washington Fellowship of Reconciliation (FOR)
225 N 70th St.
Seattle, WA 98103
789-5565
Turf: Pacifist group educating people and promoting nonviolent actions to create peace and social justice. Annual conference at Seabeck every Fourth of July weekend draws over 200 people from the Northwest.
Dues: Tax deductible contribution. Subscription to FOR's national *Fellowship* magazine is $15.
Membership: 1,950 on mailing list

Women's International League for Peace and Freedom
2524 16th Ave. S
Seattle, WA 98144
329-3666
Chair: Dorothy Anthony
Turf: 75-year-old peace and justice organization concerned about issues such as comprehensive test ban, undoing racism, ending arms race by year 2000, and opposing intervention of U.S. into affairs of other nations. World headquarters is in Geneva.
Membership: 250 women and men locally.

ENVIRONMENTAL GROUPS

(See also: Chapter 5, page 65, *The Urban Wilderness*)

Adopt-A-Beach
710 Second Ave., Suite 730
Seattle, WA 98104
296-6544
Contact: Betsy Peabody and Ken Pritchard
Turf: Nonprofit group that recruits and trains citizens to monitor and rehabilitate beaches. Works with people who live near beaches to do their own shellfish monitoring and beach surveys.

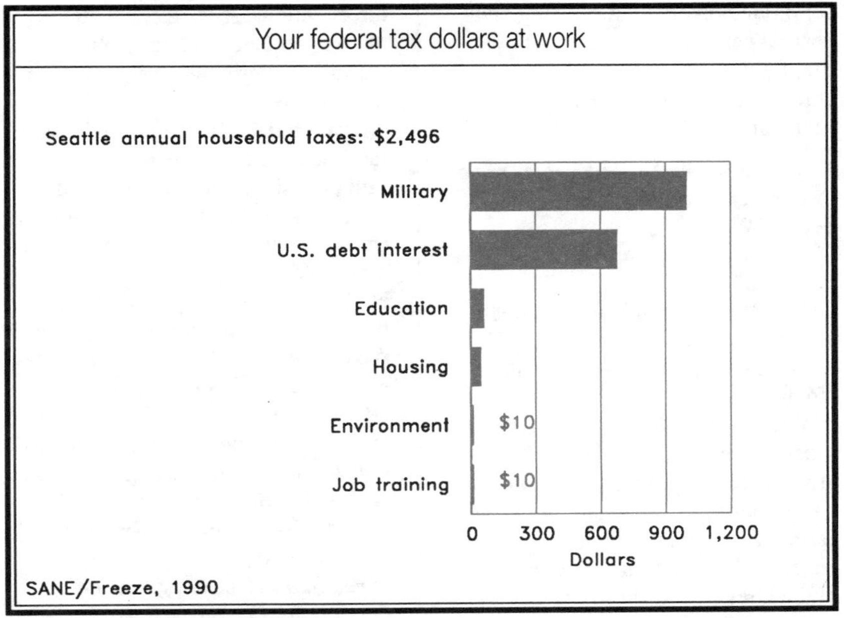

Adopt-A-Park
Seattle Parks and Recreation
210 Municipal Bldg.
Seattle, WA 98104
684-8009
Contact: Parks Coordinator
Turf: Adopt-a-Park was developed in 1982 to enable citizens to participate in the maintenance of their own neighborhood parks. The coordinator sets up individual projects as needed in the parks, such as litter pick-up, weeding, planting flowers.
Dues: None
Membership: Over 500 members including 39 community groups and 12 schools.

Alpine Lakes Protection Society
Route 1, Box 890
Ellensburg, WA 98926
774-5047
President: Jim Chapman
Turf: Alpine Lakes Wilderness and surrounding unit. Works with the Forest Service on management of the 393,000 wilderness acres near Snoqualmie Pass. This is basically a Forest Service watchdog group.
Dues: $15–$100
Membership: 300 volunteers, primarily from the Seattle area, work on advisory committees on such things as timber sales and trails.

Citizens Against Woodstove Fumes (CAWF)
P.O. Box 1442
Bellevue, WA 98009-1442
546-1988
President: Donna Larson
Turf: Nonprofit group educating public about health effects of wood smoke pollution.
Dues: Donation only; $15 recommended.
Membership: 2,000 on mailing list. Volunteers needed to contact legislators, call on phone banks, write letters, work on specific projects.

Clean Air Coalition
American Lung Association of Washington
2625 Third Ave.
Seattle, WA 98121
441-5100
Contact: Janet Chalupnik
Turf: Coordinates lobbying activities, public education through media.

Friends of Discovery Park
3801 W Government Way
Seattle, WA 98199
725-7170
Contact: Elizabeth Berggren
Turf: Protects Discovery Park as an urban wilderness. Includes ecology

committee involved in planting and general park maintenance, work parties, field trips.
Dues: $10/$5 low-income
Membership: 340

Friends of the Earth, Northwest Office
4512 University Way NE
Seattle, WA 98105
633-1661
FAX #633-1935
On EcoNet electronic bulletin board, user name "foewase"; and on MCI electronic bulletin board, user name "foewa."
NW representative: David E. Ortman
Turf: An environmental lobbying group with the goals of restoration, preservation, and rational use of the earth. Issues include Elwha River watershed restoration, preservation of the Oregon and Washington coasts from offshore oil drilling, wetlands preservation, water conservation in Eastern Washington, and investigation of pollution at military bases in Washington.
Dues: $25–$1,000
Membership: 4,000 members in Northwest.

Friends of Union Bay
5026 22nd Ave. NE, Suite 2
Seattle, WA 98105
525-0716
Coordinator: John Huskinson
Turf: To create a management umbrella for Union Bay and its shorelines, including Foster Island. Includes a program for wildlife enhancement and maintenance of open space. The group is fighting two major construction projects: the proposed expansion of the Burke–Gilman Trail through a wetland, and a pipeline from Union Bay to Green Lake.
Dues: None
Membership: 30

Greenpeace
4649 Sunnyside Ave. N
Seattle, WA 98103
632-4326
Executive director: Flye Nui Sumida
Turf: Greenpeace is an international organization that divides its time between lobbying, education, and direct action. Issues include atmospheric (ozone depletion, global warming, alternative energy production); nuclear (nuclear-free seas, nuclear materials, Hanford, production facilities); toxics (paper-and-pulp mill pollution, mud-only incinerators, waterways, etc.); ocean ecology (international driftnets, marine mammal protection, dolphins, whales, etc.). The main group is nonprofit; the sister organization, Greenpeace Action, does not have nonprofit status because it's more political, attacking environmental destruction through grassroots lobbying and direct actions (such as using inflatable craft to interfere with whalers, plugging discharge pipes of chemical polluters, etc.).
Dues: $20/$15 seniors; tax deductible for Greenpeace, not for Greenpeace Action; includes bimonthly magazine.
Membership: 2.1 millon nationwide

Lighthawk: "The Wings of Conservation"
4515 16th NE
Seattle, WA 98105
522-7515
Contact: Marcia Rutan
Turf: Uses volunteer and staff pilots to fly small aircraft over national forests so people can see graphically what's going on with national forest and old growth timber.
Dues: Contribution
Membership: Based in Santa Fe. Volunteers needed for office duties, and pilots with certain standards.
Membership: Coalition of representatives of other groups, such as Sierra Club, Audubon, etc.

The Mountaineers
300 Third Ave. W
Seattle, WA 98119
281-8509
Executive director: Virginia Felton
Turf: When first formed in 1906, the group's original purpose was to "explore, study, preserve, and enjoy the natural beauty of the Northwest," and that remains the purpose today. The Mountaineers are now the third largest outdoor club in the nation. Includes a 3,000 volume library specializing in outdoor topics and a publishing division of over 150 titles. The club offers companionship and the opportunity to try activities such as hiking, sailing, folkdance, bicycling, photography, and many other pursuits. Publishes a monthly magazine of articles and a schedule of activities.
Dues: $61 individual; $17 spouse; $41 seniors; $7 senior spouse; $31 Jr./Student; $42 out of state.
Membership: 11,000+

The Nature Conservancy
Washington Field Office
1601 Second Ave., Suite 910
Seattle, WA 98101
728-9696
State director: Elliot Marks
Turf: TNC is an international organization committed to the global preservation of natural diversity. It identifies lands that shelter natural communities and species, determining what is truly rare. Then it protects habitats through acquisition, and assists government and other conservation organizations in land preservation efforts. TNC manages more than 1,000 preserves.
Dues: $15 or more
Membership: 21,222 statewide; 576,797 nationally.

Northwest Conservation Act Coalition
3429 Fremont Pl. N
Seattle, WA 98103
547-6910
President: K.C. Golden
Turf: Working for clean, low-cost regional energy planning. Promoting widespread consumer involvement in NW Power Planning Council's regional power plan. Membership includes quarterly publication.
Dues: $20 individual; $200 nonprofit organization; business rates subject to negotiation.
Membership: 50 member groups; 200+ individual members.

Northwest Rivers Council
4516 University Way NE
Seattle, WA 98105
547-7886

Executive director: Sandy Nelson
Turf: Started five years ago as Friends of White Water to oppose damming and river pollution. Today the group focuses on protection and sound management for free-flowing rivers in the Northwest. Besides educational and advocacy work, the group takes legislators and other leaders on river-running trips. And it publishes a bimonthly newsletter.
Dues: $15/$25
Membership: Volunteers are needed for office and outside work.

PlantAmnesty
906 NW 87th St.
Seattle, WA 98117
783-9813
President: Cass Turnbull
Turf: To end senseless torture and mutilation of trees and shrubs caused by mal-pruning by educating the public about what constitutes bad pruning, to create a vision of beautiful yards and to nurture respect for photosynthesizers.
Dues: $10, includes newsletter
Membership: 400 in 14 states

Puget Sound Alliance
4516 University Way NE
Seattle, WA 98105
548-9343
President: Kathy Callison
Turf: Formed in 1989, a nonprofit network of organizations and individuals concerned about the future of Puget Sound. The group has two major programs: Wetlands Watch, to preserve the remaining wetlands of the Puget Sound Basin; and Soundkeeper, a full-time environmental ombudsperson who addresses citizen complaints, observations, and concerns. Based on programs on Long Island Sound, San Francisco Bay, and the Hudson River.
Dues: $10 student/fixed income; $15 individual; $25 family.
Membership: 550

Pure Sound Society
P.O. Box 526
Vashon Island, WA 98070
463-5607
Contacts: Doug Dolstad, Brad Wetmore
Turf: Pure Sound's main focus is marine habitat and shoreline restoration work on the Sound. Also has educational programs for teenagers and adults. The restoration programs have included planting 75,000 native wetland species to restore a wetland site on Commencement Bay in Tacoma. Also is monitoring eelgrass beds with the DNR in the South Sound. The mainstay of the programs is the water learning experiences aboard two historic longboat replicas, *Discovery* and *Porpoise*.
Dues: $20 individual; $30 family; $50 associate; $100 sponsor; $250 patron; $500 founder.

Seattle Audubon Society
8028 35th Ave. NE
Seattle, WA 98115
523-4483
President: Jerry Adams
Turf: Formed to enjoy and conserve nature, and educate people about the natural world.
Dues: $20 introductory; then various levels.
Membership: 5,000

Sierra Club
Cascade Chapter
1516 Melrose
Seattle, WA 98122
621-1696
Chair: Andrew Lewis
Turf: Grassroots environmental organization involved in conservation activities, especially lobbying for environmental legislation at federal and local levels. Also sponsors outings.
Dues: $33/year individual
Membership: 13,000 members in Cascade Chapter, which includes most of Washington State. All sorts of volunteers needed, from mailers to people to read forest plans and environmental impact statements, to people to look at and map places, to those with knowledge about air and water quality issues. "We are looking for people with enthusiasm, not necessarily with technical backgrounds. We'll find something for them to do and help them be effective."

The Trust for Public Lands
Northwest Regional Office
Smith Tower, Suite 1510
506 Second Ave.
Seattle, WA 98104
587-2447
Contact: Celia Barry
Turf: A private, nonprofit organization established in 1973 for the purpose of conserving land as a living resource for present and future generations. Uses privately raised funds to acquire and hold land or interests in lands that have been identified as important for public open spaces. Lands are then conveyed to public agencies or other nonprofit land stewards, such as land trusts. The group provides technical assistance to community groups for land trust formation and land acquisition.
Dues: Gifts from $25 up to $250 or more.
Membership: Assisted more than 150 land trusts nationwide.

Urban Wildlife Coalition
935 Kirkland Ave.
Kirkland, WA 98033
622-5260
Contact: Charles Anderson
Turf: The group promotes wildlife with wildlife-watching trips, adopt-a-stream programs, and teaching homeowners how to landscape to bring in wildlife. Also works with city parks and some developments. Members receive monthly info about wildlife trips and inexpensive gardening techniques that improve the environment. Publishes a newspaper with articles on the environment and current efforts to protect it.
Dues: $25 individual; $35 family; $50 supporting; $100 benefactor; $200 lifetime.
Membership: 100

Volunteers for Outdoor Washington
4516 University Way NE
Seattle, WA 98105
545-4868
President: Jan Milligan
Turf: Provides trail and building maintenance; cleans up outdoor recreation areas, such as city, state,

and national parks, and state and national forests.
Dues: $25 adult; $35 family; $15 students/seniors; $50 associate; up to $1,000 for major benefactor. $5 for just the newsletter.

Volunteers in Parks
83 S King St., Suite 212
Seattle, WA 98104
442-5201
President: Vanessa Gilder
Turf: Program funded by Congress to assist the National Park Service when funding cuts reduced the number of staff who maintain parks. Volunteers can select parks and send in an application; they'll be notified when they're needed. The jobs vary depending on the park. Volunteers are reimbursed for most expenses.
Membership: 1,828 volunteers in 1989.

Washington Citizens for Recyling
216 First Ave. S, Suite 360
Seattle, WA 98104
343-5171
Executive director: Babs Baker
Turf: Working to reduce waste and conserve natural resources. Formed in the wake of the unsuccessful "bottle bill" of 1979. Programs include packaging awards/endorsement program for companies and packaging that is "earth friendly," and educational programs in schools. Quarterly newsletter.
Dues: $100 patron; $50 contributor; $30 household; $20 individual.
Membership: 2,700

Washington Environmental Council
4516 University Way NE
Seattle, WA 98105
547-2738
Executive director: Theodore Pankowski
Turf: Provides information, policy, and advocacy on environmental issues in the state. WEC is an umbrella group for about 90 environmental organizations.
Dues: $25
Membership: About 2,000 individuals statewide. Volunteers are needed to work on issues such as growth, air quality, wetlands, forestry, and toxics. Could do a variety of things, including collecting signatures, writing for the newsletter, or serving on research committees.

Washington Trails Association
1305 Fourth Ave., Room 512
Seattle, WA 98101
625-1367
Director: Susan Anderson
Turf: Dedicated to preserving and enhancing trail recreation in the state. The group publishes a monthly magazine about trails, where to go, and safety. In 1989 it published a trail guide called *25 Centennial Trails.* Also protests against logging and new roads near and on trails. "You can't take trails for granted. We've lost hundreds of trails from misuse."
Dues: $35/year; includes subscription to monthly magazine.
Membership: 3,000

Washington Wilderness Coalition
P.O. Box 45187
Seattle, WA 98145
633-1992
Administrative director: Jan Glick
Turf: Working to protect the wilderness in Washington and the natural splendor of public lands, including forests, rivers, and wilderness areas. Empowers, encourages, and needs volunteers.
Dues: $20/year
Membership: 1,000+

WashPIRG (Washington Public Interest Research Group)
340 15th Ave. E, Suite 350
Seattle, WA 98112
322-9064
Director: Rick Bunch
Turf: WashPIRG is student-based and researches and lobbies issues such as pesticide use reduction and consumer education. It is tied to a national Association of State PIRGs, with an office hub in D.C. Trained and paid canvassers visit houses in the area asking for financial and moral support.
Dues: $15/year, with students paying per academic quarter.
Membership: State membership of 30,000+, including members on the UW and Evergreen State College campuses. Non-students can join.

Western Washington Toxics Coalition
4516 University Way NE
Seattle, WA 98105
632-1545
Coordinator: Cha Smith
Turf: The Toxics Coalition has been working since 1981 to reduce society's reliance on toxic chemicals. Issues include pesticides reform, waste management, and toxic household products. Provides technical information, strategies, and alternative management policies to communities. Locally, important issues are groundwater protection, household toxics, and METRO sludge. The Home Safe Home program identifies and promotes safe alternatives to toxic household products; WTC publishes a booklet and series of fact sheets on this issue for a nominal charge.
Dues:$15–$200+
Membership: Over 1,000 statewide. Membership includes *WTC News*, a quarterly newsletter.

Wetlands Watch
4516 University Way NE
Seattle, WA 98105
548-9343
Turf: Formed to preserve the remaining wetlands of the Puget Sound Basin (part of Puget Sound Alliance).
Dues: $10 student/fixed income; $15 individual; $25 family.
Membership: 550

Wilderness Society
1424 Fourth Ave., Suite 816
Seattle, WA 98101
624-6430
Turf: Protecting federal lands (national parks, forests, wildlife refuges, etc.).
Dues: $15 introductory; $30 individual; $15 senior/student/fixed income.
Membership: 400,000 nationwide

Zero Population Growth
4426 Burke Ave. N
Seattle, WA 98103
633-4750
President: Nancy Skinner

Turf: To combat population explosion in the U.S. and worldwide. The group is trying to get population back down to a point where the earth can support it safely.
Dues: Donations
Membership: 600

SOCIAL SERVICES

(See also: Chapter 14, page 217, *Seattle: A City in Need*)

American Red Cross
1900 25th Ave. S
Seattle, WA 98144
323-2345
Turf: Striving to improve the quality of human life; to enhance self-reliance and concern for others; and to help people avoid, prepare for, and cope with emergencies. Services are governed by volunteers. A lot of what the Red Cross does is educating people about health and safety, babysitting, teaching infant CPR, and providing community services such as HOPE (Homeless Outreach Program for the Eastside). Services include disaster preparedness, youth services, and language bank.
Dues: Donations vary according to need.
Membership: NA

Common Ground
107 Cherry St., Suite 410
Seattle, WA 98104-2214
461-4500
Executive director: Steve Clagett
Turf: Common Ground pulls together sponsors, buildings, and funds for low-income housing. It negotiates agreements, arranges repairs, and develops new ways of financing. The group works primarily with churches, community groups, agencies, and nonprofit organizations.

Court Appointed Special Advocates (CASA)
Family Court of King County
King County Superior Court
Third and James, Room C205
Seattle, WA 98104
296-9320
Turf: Represents the interests of children in divorce court proceedings. Training is provided. Call for information packet in order to volunteer.

Crisis Clinic
1515 Dexter Ave. N, Suite 300
Seattle, WA 98109
461-3200 or 461-3210
Turf: Crisis intervention services, information and referral services, and community resources available by telephone. One goal is to make trained volunteers accessible to people in crisis.
Volunteers: Phone lines are staffed by volunteers. Each volunteer is required to participate in an extensive crisis intervention training program involving about 40 hours of classroom work, human problem-solving skills, independent study using the computer system, and practice in a simulated phone room. A one-year commitment is required, and volunteers usually spend four and a half hours per week on the phones.

Displacement Coalition
4759 15th Ave. NE
Seattle, WA 98105
523-2569
Contact: John Fox
Turf: Group organized to protest demolition of low-cost housing in the city.

Easter Seal Society
521 Second Ave. W
Seattle, WA 98119
281-5700
Contact: Nabel Dilley
Turf: Aims to increase the independent living skills of people with disabilities. Programs include camping, therapy, access modification, counseling, education, etc.

Operation Homestead
723-7333
Contact: Ben Vactory
Turf: Organizes people to reopen closed buildings downtown and puts pressure on downtown politicos to prevent illegal abandonment of buildings. Works to stop illegal evictions and to get enforcement of housing code and building maintenance. Recently worked to save the McKay Apartments and Gatewood Hotel.
Membership: 150 activists on all levels, but rallies have attracted as many as 300–400. (Sixty-two were arrested at the McKay rally.)

Plymouth Housing Group
1217 Sixth Ave.
Seattle, WA 98101
343-5427
Contact: Gretchen Reade, 343-7838
Turf: Established in 1980 by members of Plymouth Congregational Church, Plymouth relies on volunteer involvement as part of building rehab—painting, moving furniture, etc.—and on donations of furnishings for units. (PCC picks up in Seattle.) The group is dedicated to preserving and enhancing low-income housing in downtown Seattle. As of March 1988 PHG owned and/or managed over 300 low-cost units of housing in six downtown buildings. Call to volunteer time, furnishings, or money.

Seattle Habitat for Humanity
P.O. Box 99669
Seattle, WA 98199
324-7351
Executive directors: Brian Ritts, Brian Lloid
Turf: Part of a nationwide ecumenical organization that builds and refurbishes homes for sale to low-income families at no profit.
Dues: $25 a month provides a square foot of decent housing for a family, the group says. Larger contributions welcome.

Seattle Tenants Union
3902 S Ferdinand St.
Seattle, WA 98118
723-0500
Director: Dave Pardone
Turf: The union offers organizing services and runs a hotline for landlord/tenant questions. The hotline receives 25,000 calls per year. STU will send people out to organize tenants at housing projects and apartment buildings, and inform them

about their collective bargaining rights. And STU lobbies for such things as mandatory inspections—an issue it finally got through the Seattle City Council recently—enforcement of building code, eviction provisions, and improved tenants' rights laws.
Membership: 700 members

Seattle Urban League
105 14th Ave.
Seattle, WA 98122
461-3792
President: Dr. Roz Woodhouse
Turf: Community service agency founded in 1930 to eliminate racism and secure equal opportunities for ethnic minorities. SUL has an active housing department that counsels and trains families and individuals on how to avoid foreclosure, wise home buying, rental searches, delinquency, and fair housing.
Dues: $25–$100 (corporate)

United Way Volunteer Center
107 Cherry St.
Seattle, WA 98104
461-3765
Contact: Kris Kero
Turf: A free community service provided by United Way, the Volunteer Center maintains a database of people interested in volunteering and connects them with 400–450 organizations in need of volunteers. Also does training in volunteer management for corporations.
Membership: During a United Way campaign, there are 2,000–3,000 active volunteers. United Way receives 3,500 calls from would-be volunteers in a year. Volunteers are needed for a variety of things, but issues are more health and human services related than other agencies. There are some arts, environmental, and local school volunteer opportunities through UW too.

Washington Coalition of Citizens with Disabilities
3530 Stone Way N
Seattle, WA 98103
461-4550
Executive director: Kerry Klockner
Turf: A coalition of groups for people with disabilities, the WCCD offers self-empowering programs, information, self-advocacy training, peer counseling, a job club, a support group for people trying to break into the job market, consultant service, access reviews, and support for independent living. Sends a newsletter to 3,000 people quarterly.
Dues: $15/year; services are free.
Volunteers: SCCD counts on volunteers, with and without disabilities. All that's required is "a sunny face and a sense of humor."

Washington Gives
1305 Fourth Ave., Suite 214
Seattle, WA 98101
343-9631
Chair: Mary Gates
Turf: This is the group with the "Give Five" slogan. It encourages Washingtonians to volunteer and donate to causes they care about. As a guideline, the group suggests giving five hours per week and 5% of your income to the cause of your choice.
Membership: Washington Gives has 150 volunteers of its own who get

the message out, both in the workplace and to individuals. And it has referral lists of organizations needing volunteers that it will send out to anyone interested. Just call the Give Five hotline: (800) 65-GIVE5.

AIDS GROUPS

(See also: Chapter 15, page 229, *Taking Seattle's Pulse*)

ACT UP (AIDS Coalition to Unleash Power)
1206 E Pike St., Suite 814
Seattle, WA 98122
726-1678
Turf: Grassroots organization committed to direct action to end the AIDS crisis. Methods are direct nonviolent protest, and pressure on government and public institutions and individuals impeding appropriate response to the epidemic.
Dues: None
Membership: Several hundred in Seattle area. Open membership. To join, come to a meeting Mondays, 7:30 p.m., Rm. D-624, Group Health Hospital, 15th and John.

AIDS Housing of Washington
93 Pike St., Suite 312
Seattle, WA 98101
623-8292
Executive director: Betsy Lieberman
Turf: Developing housing for people living with AIDS.

Chicken Soup Brigade
818 E Pike St.
Seattle, WA 98102
328-8979
Executive director: Carol Sterling
Turf: Meals, transportation, and other day-to-day services for people with AIDS. Not as much emotional support as Shanti or other groups.
Dues: No fee for clients or volunteers.
Membership: 350–400 volunteers serving 150–200 clients. Especially needs non-biased people who have daytime hours available and can make a four-hour commitment per week for six months. Retired people welcome.

Northwest AIDS Foundation
127 Broadway E
Seattle, WA 98102
329-6923 (info and referral line)
Director: Nancy Campbell
Turf: Social work and case management for people with AIDS. Also advocacy, referrals, emergency housing, and helping AIDS victims get into permanent low-income housing. NW AIDS Foundation is responsible for several education programs in the county, including condom programs and safe sex workshops. Funding: Over half of what the foundation brings in is from private sources.
Membership: Over 600 volunteers help out with fundraisers, mailings, publications, phonelines, safe sex workshops, and speakers bureau. Training is offered.

Shanti
P.O. Box 20698
Seattle, WA 98102
322-0279
Turf: Emotional support and training for individuals and loved ones facing AIDS.
Dues: $50 donation for training; scholarships available.
Membership: Have about 99 volunteers. Volunteers need to apply and go through an interview and a two-weekend training session. Shanti especially looks for good listeners, people who are non-judgmental, who are in touch with feelings without being overwhelmed, and who can take feelings back to a support group rather than put them on the clients. In addition to three hours per week with a client, volunteers are expected to spend two hours with a support group. Shanti asks for a one-year commitment. Also some office volunteers needed.

HEARD ON THE STREET

"A feeling for humanity is more paramount in Seattle than in most other cities. Being human comes first as opposed to lifestyles."

John Rowe, longtime Seattle activist involved in the AIDS effort

ANIMAL RIGHTS GROUPS

Northwest Animal Rights Network
1704 E Galer St.
Seattle, WA 98112
323-7301
Contact: Jerry Esterly
Turf: Grassroots animal rights organization involved in issues dealing with everything from vivisection to vegetarianism to banning fur materials. Focus is on Northwest issues but does not exclude national issues, e.g.

National Meatout and Day for Lab Animals. Philosophy is to speak for those who cannot speak for themselves. Monthly newsletter.
Dues: $25/year
Membership: 300

Progressive Animal Welfare Society (PAWS)
15305 44th Ave. W
Lynnwood, WA 98037
743-3845
Executive director: Tim Greyhavens
Turf: Began in 1967 as an animal welfare and rights organization. PAWS has an animal shelter serving 10,000 abandoned or orphaned animals, and a wildlife hospital serving 5,000 animals. Also has an education program for animal rights.
Dues: $20 individual and up
Membership: 10,000; volunteers are needed and welcome.

Zoo Volunteer Programs
5500 Phinney Ave. N
Seattle, WA 98103
684-4885
Turf: Not truly an activist group, but volunteers are needed for such things as assisting with veterinary records, special events, and docent tours. Docents get a training course that lasts from September to March, four hours a week, and are asked for a two-year commitment. They have to pass a test too. Interns serve in departments and offices and actually care for some of the animals, though they have to have a sponsoring school. And for the kids, pony leaders age 12 to 16 help care for the ponies and operate the pony ring. Riding instruction provided.

POLITICS 'N' ARTS

(See also: Chapter 13, page 199, *Canvases and Curtain Calls*)

Allied Arts
107 S Main St.
Seattle, WA 98104
624-0432
President: Mia McEldowney
Director: Richard Mann
Turf: A volunteer advocacy group for historic preservation, urban design, and arts legislation, all to preserve and augment Seattle's general livability and to create a desirable working atmosphere for artists in the community. Committees and a board provide avenues for citizen participation. The committees include Historic Preservation, Arts Education, Artist Housing, and Downtown and Metropolitan Arts. Allied Arts has forced setbacks, preserved alley corridors (in the Stimson Building), and helped with design preservation in Pioneer Square and the Market. Allied Arts has assisted the King County Arts Commission in formulating guidelines for the use of the new Hotel/Motel Tax revenues allocated to the arts, and continues to lead the fight to save the Spafford murals in Olympia and the historic downtown theaters.
Dues: Yearly membership is $35–$100+
Membership: About 700

CHEMICAL DEPENDENCY GROUPS

Mothers Against Drunk Driving (MADD)
1511 Third Ave., Suite 911
Seattle, WA 98101
624-6903
Turf: Victims' advocates. MADD monitors courts and enforcement policies, and is active in government relations and education.
Dues: Free for victims/families; $20 individuals; $10 seniors/students; $150 businesses/organizations; $40 family.
Membership: 30,000. Volunteers are needed.

Washington State Substance Abuse Coalition
14700 Main St.
Bellevue, WA 98007
747-9111
President: Barbara Daugherty
Turf: Fights substance abuse by maintaining a clearinghouse of drug- and alcohol-related information for the public; forming task forces on college campuses, with other students and in low-income communities; and sponsoring events and influencing legislation.
Dues: $15–$500
Membership: Includes reduced rates at conferences and training workshops, training for community groups, and bimonthly newsletter.

DOMESTIC VIOLENCE

(See also Chapter 14, page 217, *Seattle: A City in Need*)

DAWN: Domestic Abuse Women's Network
854-7867 (hotline)
852-5529 (to volunteer)
Turf: Network of women helping other women, giving them information so they can help themselves.
Volunteers: Women needed who want to help. DAWN asks for a year's commitment, four hours per week and four hours one weekend per month.

King County Domestic Violence Coalition
(800) 562-6025
Volunteers needed for local domestic violence programs.

King County Sexual Assault Resource Center
226-5062
Volunteers needed to staff crisis line and to be advocates. Training offered.

ASSORTED OTHER GROUPS

American Friends Service Committee
814 NE 40th
Seattle, WA 98105
632-0500
Executive secretary: Sylvia Ramariz
Turf: Belief in the dignity and worth

of each person, and faith in the power of love and nonviolence to bring about change. Activities include Yakima Valley Immigration, Seattle/ Portland Gay/Lesbian program, Seattle/Portland Peace Program, Seattle Indian program, Seattle/ Portland South Africa program, etc.
Dues: Contributions. Work is supported financially by people of different persuasions who care about service development, justice, and peace.

Citizens Education Center Northwest
105 S Main St.
Seattle, WA 98104
624-9955
Executive director: Nancy Bagley
Turf: Excellence in public education for all children, including empowering parents to improve education; informing citizens, politicos, and educators about current issues; advocating effective schools; and building alliances.
Dues: $25 individual to $300 corporate; $30 for new members; includes four current publications by the group.

CityClub
1111 Third Ave. Bldg.
Seattle, WA 98101
682-7395
Executive director: Thea Singer
Turf: The must-belong club for the city's leaders, the CityClub bills itself as the place where people and ideas meet in Seattle. The group brings newsmakers to forums to talk, debate, and answer questions on current issues. And the facility is open to members for meetings, use of a private library, and space to read or work downtown.
Dues: $60–$120 individual ($30–$60 spouses); $200–$500 Benefactor and Gold Key; $230–$1,000 corporate.
Membership: About 1,100

Heart of America Northwest
1305 Fourth Ave.
Cobb Bldg., Suite 208
Seattle, WA 98101
382-1014
Executive director: Gerald Pollet
Administrative director: Donna Bernstein
Turf: Dedicated to advancing the region's quality of life. Heart of America was active in preventing local phone service deregulation, reducing a City Light rate increase, and preventing Hanford from becoming the nation's high-level nuclear waste dump. The group has pushed to create a Nuclear Waste Cleanup Trust Fund. It also opposes expansion of Metro's West Point Secondary Sewage Treatment Plant at Discovery Park for environmental reasons. Growth issues embraced.
Dues: $25/year; includes quarterly newsletter and monthly update to interested members.
Membership: 16,800 statewide

National Abortion Rights Action League (NARAL)
105 S Main St., Suite 326
Seattle, WA 98104
624-1990
Director: Esther Herst
Turf: Dedicated to protecting a woman's constitutional right to choose a safe, legal abortion. NARAL lobbies legislators and researches candidates for pro-choice stances before endorsing.
Dues: Donations accepted
Membership: 4,000 statewide. About five volunteers a day help out in NARAL's office. (About 50% of the volunteers are senior citizens.) Just call and they'll rope you in.

National Organization for Women, Seattle Chapter
4057A Roosevelt Way NE
Seattle, WA 98105
632-8547
Executive director: Norleen Koponen
Turf: NOW is the largest multi-issue feminist group in the nation. Twenty years old, it works nationally for equal rights on all levels. Since the recent anti-abortion threats, NOW has been inundated with new members—many of them men. In addition to choice issues, the state NOW organization lobbies for economic and education equity, quality affordable child care, elimination of violence against women, lesbian rights, child support, women's health care, early childhood development programs, etc. Local chapter gives out referral numbers.
Dues: $20–$35; includes local, state, and national newsletter.
Membership: About 1,000 Seattle chapter; 6,000 statewide. Volunteers are needed for office work, community actions, mailings, and special projects. Open to both men and women.

Northwest Women's Law Center
119 S Main St., Suite 330
Seattle, WA 98104
621-7691 (legal referral service)
682-9552 (office)
Executive director: Berta Delman
Turf: Specializes in legal issues and legal action to advance women's rights. NWLC has a litigation program (representing classes of women or individual women whose cases affect overall women's rights); a lobbying program; an education focus (offering free family law seminars, sexual harassment response training, continuing education for attorneys, domestic violence information, and books and video tapes, including a new family law book in Spanish); and an information and referral service where NWLC gives free legal information, but not advice, and refers callers to appropriate attorneys.
Dues: $35/year; less if you can't afford it.
Membership: 500–1,000. Open to all who support women's rights. Volunteers with legal background are especially needed, but anyone interested should call.

Seattle Benefit Gang
3201 Fremont Ave. N, Suite 202
Seattle, WA 98103
632-4987
Executive director: Brock Mansfield
Turf: Volunteer recruitment, training, and placement for Seattle's young adults, ages 21–30. The group organized because that's an age group traditionally uninvolved with the

social service community as volunteers. SBG contracts with nonprofit groups in the city, primarily children's charities, to provide volunteers for them. The volunteer positions are usually about two to four hours per week. SBG will send out a catalog to potential volunteers so they can pick the position they want.
Dues: $10/year
Membership: About 600

Washington Fair Share
P.O. Box 22540
1205 E Pike St.
Seattle, WA 98122
329-9764
Contacts: Michael Powers, David Silas
Turf: Health care issues, public health care akin to Canadian model. Works through Citizen's Action toward national health care. Also works on education issues—the group has several ties to school boards—and toxics, with a possible project on Puget Sound water quality.
Dues: $15/year; $12/year seniors, students.
Membership: About 40,000; 80,000 on mailing list.

Washington State Women's Political Caucus
P.O. Box 9634
Seattle, WA 98109
624-4125
State chair: Melissa Thompson
Turf: WPC is the political arm of the feminist movement. Its main focus is on electoral politics and public policy roles. A bipartisan group, WPC considers itself pragmatic, focusing on getting women into elective and appointive offices for more balanced representation. It endorses candidates locally and nationally. "We are a political organization as opposed to an issue organization."
Dues:$40 in King County; $35 elsewhere.
Membership: 1,500 statewide.
"We're a small group. We deal with people; issues are safer." Needs volunteers for campaign work with endorsed candidates and to chair committees, lead task forces, etc.

NOT-QUITE-GUERRILLA TRAINING

Many activist organizations will train you to acquire a variety of skills, including canvassing, fundraising, computer and office work, and leadership skills. Some of the organizations, such as SANE, train and pay for canvassing. Then there are those who train for nonviolent action protests:

Seattle Nonviolent Action Group (SNAG)
P.O. Box 85541
Seattle, WA 98145
329-7946
Turf: Organizes nonviolence training, or what it calls "creative, nonhierarchical, empowering action for peace with social and economic justice." Protests use street theater, nonviolent civil disobedience, marches, rallies, speaking tours, and the building of positive alternatives. Workshops are offered in meeting facilitation, consensus process, grassroots organizing, anti-sexism, anti-racism, and nonviolent direct action/civil disobedience. SNAG is an affiliate of Mobilization for Survival.
Dues: None
Membership: About 20 activists currently involved; mailing list of 400. SNAG meets twice a month and welcomes new people.

The Western States Center (WSC)
100 S King St.
Seattle, WA 98104
292-9734
Turf: WSC is a Portland-based organization that provides skills training and support services to activists in the Northwest. Staffed by organizers from East Coast citizen action experience, Western States holds workshops and retreats for organizations in Seattle, Tacoma, Boise, Portland, and Salt Lake City. WSC is developing an activist network for participating organizations.

COMMISSIONS AND BOARDS

If radicalism isn't your thing, perhaps working within the city structure is. There are over 90 boards and commissions that recruit volunteers (or sometimes lowly paid people) from the community—all within the city government framework. Here are some:

Aging, Seattle–King County Advisory Council on
Alcoholism and Substance Abuse Administrative Board, King County
Animal Control Commission
Apprenticeship Committee, Joint Advisory
Arboretum and Botanical Garden Committee
Arts Commission
Ballard Avenue Landmark District Board
Bicycle Advisory Board
Block Grant Review Board
Bond Oversight Committee Seattle 1-2-3
Bumbershoot Festival Commission
Citizens Cable Communications Advisory Board
Civil Service Commission
COH-70th and Sand Point Site Committee
Commission on Children and Youth
Conservation Committee (City Light)
Convention and Trade Center, Neighborhood Advisory Committee for Washington State
Design Commission
Downtown Housing Advisory Task Force
Downtown Human Services Advisory Task Force
Downtown Plan Revisions Advisory Committee
Downtown Project Review Panel
Drainage and Wastewater Utility Citizens Advisory Committee
DWI Task Force, Seattle
Economic Development Commission
Education, Joint Advisory Commission on
Environmental Endowment Fund Commission, Skagit

Fair Campaign Practices (Ethics) Commission, Board of
Housing Authority Board of Commissioners
Housing Levy Oversight Committee
Human Rights Commission
Industrial Development Corporation Board of Directors
International Special Review District Board
Kubota Gardens Oversight Committee
Landmarks Preservation Board
Lesbian/Gay Task Force
Library Board of Trustees
Museum Financial Oversight Committee
Northgate Area Comprehensive Plan Citizens Advisory Committee
Park Commissioners, Board of
Park and Recreation Plan Advisory Committee
Pike Place Market Historical Commission
Pioneer Square Preservation Board
Planning Commission
Public Safety Civil Service Commission
Rates Advisory Committee (City Light)
Resources Advisory Committee (City Light)
Sand Point Community Liaison Committee
School Traffic Safety Committee
Seattle Center Advisory Commission
Small Business Task Force
Solid Waste Advisory Committee
Street People and the Homeless, Task Force on
Taxi Commission, Regional
University District Study Citizens Advisory Committee
Veterans' Affairs, Committee on
Water Advisory Commission, Executive
Water Rate Advisory Committee
Water Supply Plan Update Policy Advisory Committee
Women's Commission
Zoo Development Oversight Committee

PUBLIC CORPORATION BOARDS

Burke–Gilman Place Public Development Authority Board
Capitol Hill Housing Improvement Program Council
Central Area Public Development Authority Council
Chinatown–International District Preservation and Development Authority Council, Seattle
Historic Seattle Preservation and Development Authority Council
Indian Services Commission Council
Museum Development Authority Council
Pacific Hospital Preservation and Development Authority Council
Pike Place Market Preservation and Development Authority Council

SISTER CITIES

Another way to get involved is to sign up for the Sister City Committees. Seattle has 14 of those, one for each of these sister cities:

Beer Sheva, Israel
Bergen, Norway
Chongqing, China
Christchurch, New Zealand
Galway, Ireland
Kobe, Japan
Limbe, Cameroon (West Africa)
Managua, Nicaragua
Mazatlan, Mexico
Mombasa, Kenya
Nantes, France
Reykjavik, Iceland
Tashkent, Soviet Union
Taejon, South Korea

For those committees, call the Office of International Affairs, 386-1511.

And if that's not enough, you can also sign up for commissions and boards in other jurisdictions.

So how do you get on one of these boards? Take someone in the mayor's office to lunch. Well, maybe it's not that bad, but it does help to know someone—depending on the prestige of the board position.

Here's how it works: The mayor usually sends out a press release about the opening. Then someone in city hall interviews the potential candidates. Usually the person picked represents a particular neighborhood or group affected by the issue or has expertise in a certain area.

Most competitive of city boards: Arts Commission. If a position opens up, there are as many as 50 volunteer candidates for it. Reason: lots of money, and the Arts Commission makes direct decisions about where it goes.

Least competitive of city boards: Animal Control Commission. The city actually goes out looking for volunteers for that one.

For information on commission positions, call the mayor's office, 684-5030.

Contact: Ned Dunn

Office of the Governor
Assistant for Boards and Commissions
Legislative Bldg., AS-13
Olympia, WA 98504-0413
753-6780

Office of King County Executive
400 King County Courthouse
Seattle, WA 98104
344-4040

METRO
Community Relations Section
821 Second Ave.
Seattle, WA 98104
684-1138
Metro has a 45-member citizens advisory group on transit and a 25-member group on elderly transit. Also has an advisory group on water quality and may have site-specific advisory committees for different projects when necessary.

PETITION CITY: HOW TO FILE AN INITIATIVE

There have been 36 initiatives filed with the city of Seattle since 1973, when the city started counting. Some died before they began because of lack of signatures; others were defeated at the voter's booth. Of the 36, eight passed and became city law.

How to file an initiative

1. File the proposed initiative with the city clerk's office, 101 Municipal Building.
2. The proposal is sent to the city attorney's office, where legal types review its language for legal problems. If there's no problem, they give it a ballot title.
3. Then you have 180 days to collect signatures supporting the petition. The number of signatures necessary to get it on the ballot is 10% of the total votes cast in the latest mayoral election.
4. When you have the signatures, send them in to the elections department. If there aren't enough signatures of registered voters, you have another 20 days to get them.
5. When there are enough verified signatures, they are sent to the city council, which can adopt the initiative outright, or place it on the ballot.

HOW TO TWIST THE ARMS OF THE POWERS THAT BE

Seattle is a clean town, but not devoid of wheeling and dealing. The financial community uses its power in traditional ways, trading support for something it wants—a bus tunnel, for example.

Citizen groups also wield power, but some methods of getting attention work, and others don't. Here's what one activist says works.

Lobby each council or committee member several times, meeting with them individually. (This can work, but didn't in the case of Citizen Alternative Plan—CAP—where advocates ran into a solid wall.)

Filing an initiative is one of the most effective ways to get what you want, if you have lots of support. (The Pike Place Market was saved by an initiative.)

Petitions are a waste of time. They're dropped in the laps of councils with no noticeable effect. A lot of work and little payoff.

Have a central theme. Characterize the problem in some form. The CAP campaign floundered initially because there was no central theme until the month before the election.

Get assistance from a public relations firm. In the case of CAP, campaigners were advised to focus the message. The message was that the character and integrity of Seattle were at stake, just as they had been at the Market. Then it was effective. Professional help is good if you can get it.

Letters to the editor are easy and effective. Just use good sense and be truthful; the truth is always the best course and is hard to deny.

Working the media: The establishment usually gets the coverage, but there are ways you can get heard. Meet with the editorial boards of newspapers, for example. Develop a relationship with court reporters and give them tips. But don't lie to them.

If you can get a 10-minute interview on radio talk shows, do it; it's all part of shaping public opinion and people listen to those. Don't forget radio.

Graphic demonstrations can backfire. The media might think your stunt is silly; if you insult them, it can hurt. But sometimes it's the only way to get heard. For TV, stunts are useful.

Coalition-building between groups is a way to show that others believe in what you're doing. Sometimes it takes a little bit of smoke and mirrors to exaggerate support.

Advertising is expensive; you can do a lot without it. Use volunteer resources instead.

If you are a small minority, without direct connection to numbers of votes, popular appeal, or money, constant pressure is one of the only ways you can be effective.

Get someone in the legal community on your side. The law is a great way to drive a wedge into the system. Lawyers here are very willing to help free of charge; many firms have pro bono accounts, so ask.

Source: Peter Steinbrueck, protector of Pike Place Market and other causes and resident thorn-in-the-side of local politicians.

CHAPTER

9

LIFE IN A GOLDFISH BOWL

NEWS

DAILIES

MAGAZINES

TELEVISION

REPORTERS

WEEKLIES

RADIO

MEDIA

Reporters, says one local attorney, are like alley cats. They're always nosing around for a bowl of milk to lap up. And the thing that's mother's milk to them is anything that smacks of news. The other image of reporters is that they are like Superman protecting the public from unscrupulous characters. They're bursting through walls and opening up meetings. They're uncovering secret wheelings and dealings or pointing to conflicts between a politician's public life and his or her private one.

Not everyone subscribes to a newspaper here, and in fact newspaper circulation here as elsewhere is sinking like a rock in Elliott Bay. But everyone has either an opinion about the local media or gossip about media personalities. (Jean Enersen's hair length, for example, garners about as much interest as who breaks the story on the latest political scandal.

HEARD ON THE STREET

"Seattle is a sleepy town. The newspapers aren't terribly aggressive. I don't know why."

Don Pember, University of Washington Communications Dept.

THE SOURCE: WHERE WE GET OUR NEWS

Seattle boasts two main daily newspapers, *The Seattle Times* (a.k.a. Fairview Fanny) and the *Seattle Post-Intelligencer* (a.k.a. the Pig-I). The city has seven primary TV stations, with the three major network affiliates (KING, KOMO, KIRO) vying for the lead. A slew of radio stations captures the listening public, partially because of the phenomenon of road congestion—a captive audience of disgruntled commuters.

Where Seattle gets its news:

Martin Selig, developer: *The New York Times.*
Jeff Smulyan, owner of the Mariners: The *P-I*, *Seattle Times*, and *USA Today*.
Speight Jenkins, Seattle Opera: *The New York Times* for most news; looks at the *P-I* and the *Times* and *Seattle Weekly*—mostly for music reviews.
Mary Coltrane, president, League of Women Voters of Seattle: National news from NPR's "All Things Considered" and "MacNeil/Lehrer"; local from the *Times* and *P-I*, "Seattle Afternoon" talk show on KUOW-FM, *Seattle Weekly,* and KING-TV.
David Sabey, Sabey Corporation: KIRO-AM "Newsradio" on the way to work; the *Times* and the *P-I, Journal-American* at home, *Wall Street Journal, Forbes/Fortune.*
Paul Schell, developer and port commissioner: *Seattle Weekly*, CNN, the *Times* and the *P-I*, *Puget Sound Business Journal, The New York Times,* and *Wall Street Journal.*
Laurie Gulbransen, owner of The Dog House restaurant: "We have all the news here."

Source: Seattle Survival Guide research

SWEETENING THE MILK

There are ways to talk to reporters, whether they're from newspapers, radio, or TV, and it pays not to be naive. The first rule is to remember that reporters are people, not sharks. But they are people whose job is to question anyone about anything—and their bosses buy their ink in a barrel (or their broadcast tape by the yard).

RULES OF THE REPORTORIAL ROAD

- Don't talk about "managing the news." Any reporter worth half a day's paycheck will bristle at those words, and the news will end up managing you.
- Only call a reporter with a tip if it's really a story. Ask yourself who cares about what you're about to spill, is it important, is it new?
- If you do give a reporter a story, obey the unwritten rule of news etiquette: Don't immediately call the reporter's competitor and give him or her the same story. Everybody wants a scoop, and it's to your advantage to be the source of that Big Story.
- The media learn who is quotable and call on them for comments on breaking news all the time. Good quotes are short, especially for TV and radio. They can be a little longer for newsprint, but if you want to be quoted accurately, keep it brief.
- Any time you speak with a reporter, it's on the record (can be printed). If a conversation is being taped, the reporter has to tell you and get your consent.

• If you agree to talk "off the record" (cannot be used for publication or broadcast), get that agreement from the reporter *before* you speak. And be clear about what's off the record and what's on. Beware of reporters who go back and forth between off the record and on—they (and you) might have trouble later distinguishing what was on and what was off.
• If you tell a reporter something off the record, he or she will most likely call you back and try to get you to say it on the record, hoping you'll change your mind. (That's one reason reporters let you talk off the record in the first place—that and the hope they can get the information confirmed elsewhere.)
• If you give background information, it can be used but not attributed to you. It can be attributed to "a spokesperson" or "an informed source"; if that's the case, expect the people close to you to know who that obscure source is.
• At the end of the interview, after the camera is off and the notebook is closed, remember you are still on the record. Reporters often get their best quotes when the subject is relaxed.
• If a story is wrong, don't hesitate to call the reporter. You're likely to get a better response that way than going over his or her head to the editor. After all, alienating a reporter doesn't get you far. But, if all else fails, call an editor.
• Good reporters don't read a story to a source before it's published; don't bother to ask.

How you can tell when one newspaper is "chasing" another on a story: In the case of the Times, if the P-I breaks a story, the Times' early morning reporters scramble to get it in their second or third editions. So if a P-I story doesn't appear in the Times' first edition and does in the second or third, it's been chased. (Another way to tell is if you are a news source and you get calls from the Times at 6:30 a.m. That means you should run right out and buy a P-I.)

If the P-I is chasing a Times story, it has all the time in the world, from noon, when the Times' last edition is out, to about 9 p.m.

Both papers will usually bury a story in back sections if the other paper has broken it—sometimes to an absurd degree.

FAIRVIEW FANNY, THE PIG-I, AND BEYOND

Seattle's print media have the reputation of being like the Northwest itself: laid-back and relaxed.

The *Seattle Times* and the *Post-Intelligencer* are both dailies, but the resemblance ends there, or so the folks at each will tell you, despite their 1983 Joint Operating Agreement. JOAs are decried as part of a pernicious national trend to concentrate newspaper ownership in fewer and fewer hands. (Now 28 corporations nationally control over 50% of all news media.)

Under the JOA, ads, circulation, and production are done for both papers by the *Times*. In exchange, the *P-I* remains the morning paper, the *Times* the afternoon one, at least for the time being. Nationally, morning papers are the most successful as far as circulation goes. One result of the JOA that makes folks at the *P-I* sad is that the *P-I* has basically lost its presence in the Sunday paper, a joint publication. There is a *P-I* section and it usually features an analytical piece that's worth looking for, but that's just it: You have to look.

There truly is competition between news staffs (despite the fact that reporters at one paper are often married to or living with someone from the other paper). "The competition," says former *Times* ombudsman Frank Wetzel, "is a matter of ego."

The *P-I* does a good job of breaking news stories and is much more the "newspaper of record" than the larger *Times*. For years the sentiment in the city was that if you wanted to find out what was happening locally, you had to read the *P-I*. But in recent years the *Times* has made an effort to cover more local news with metro and suburban zoned pages. Now the *P-I* has two zones, north and south.

The *P-I* is still the fast read, and is, after all, there in the morning. But it has trouble holding on to reporters. The *Times* is more inbred,

Want to get your event covered? Slow news days at the Times are Saturdays and Sundays. Reporters on duty clean their desks on those days, especially in the summer when everyone else is out having a good time. Give them a call on a Saturday morning.

At the P-I, slow news day is Sunday—they have lots of room in the Monday paper.

If you want someone's head to roll, call these reporters. If they call you, say "no comment."

Investigative reporters: Dick Clever (P-I investigative editor), Tomas Guillen (Times), Peter Lewis (Times), Eric Nalder (Times), Carlton Smith (Times), James Wallace (P-I), Larry Werner (P-I), Duff Wilson (Times).

with decisions made by committee, and a little slower off the mark. But the *Times* is strong in investigative reporting and big on full-blown features illustrated by lots of graphics. The *Times* won a deserved Pulitzer for its 1989 Exxon Valdez oil spill coverage.

If you want to stage an event in the morning and have it appear the same day in the *Times*, hold it before 11 a.m. Even at that you'll miss the first couple of editions. But if you want an event to be covered first in the *P-I*, don't hold it 'til 2 p.m.

The *Times* is at an advantage when it comes to national news that happens on the East Coast because of the time difference; but it's at a disadvantage when it comes to final stock market readings. You can get the final stock quotes from the *Times* if you get the night final, which you can only buy in newsstands. The stock quote hotline of the *Times* Infoline, 464-2000, is category 9800; for instructions on how to use it, call category 9801.

Deadlines

At the Times:
First edition: 8:30 a.m.
Second edition: 10:30 a.m.
Third edition: 11:15 a.m.
Night final: 12:30 p.m.
Times final Sunday edition deadline: Saturday at about 5 p.m. Most Sunday editions are on the streets by Friday though.

At the P-I:
First edition: 9 p.m.
Second edition: 11 p.m.–midnight
(A second edition *P-I* can be recognized by a little star under the name —remakes of the second have an additional star.)
The *P-I* is basically closed on Saturday since it disappears from the Sunday paper.

THEY GET LETTERS . . .

The *Times* publishes about 20% of the letters to the editor it receives. The ones that get published are those responding to news, editorials, or columns, and those that are well-written and brief. The *Times* gets from 30–75 letters in a day—the number of letters dwindles when the weather is good or during the holidays. If your letter has been chosen, the *Times* will call to verify your name, address, and phone number.

If you're moved by an event to write, pull out the typewriter and hammer away immediately. Letters about stale news are considered stale themselves. It's OK to respond to someone else's letter in the paper; dialogs between letter writers are sometimes the most interesting part of the paper. Oh, and out-of-town letters don't stand much chance.

Your letter to the editor is more likely to get published if it is short and timely. How short is short? About 300 words, or one page double spaced.

The *P-I* publishes about 13% of its letters, or about 5 of the 30 or 40 it receives in a day. Those that get published have legible signatures, phone numbers, and addresses, and are well-written and succinct—the shorter the better.

Some people write letters to the editor every day or every week—it drives editors crazy and, if you ever want to get published, isn't a good idea. Save your letter for that one irresistible issue, and don't keep calling about when it will be published.

At the *P-I*, the letters editor will verify a letter for possible publication in approximately a week. If you don't hear by then, your letter's probably been round filed. And if you do get a call saying your letter is being considered, that doesn't guarantee publication. Something better may come in and bump yours, but at least you've gotten to first base.

PERENNIAL LETTER WRITING SUBJECTS

These subjects draw the most letters:
Abortion
Gun control
Sea lions
Californians
Flag burning
Euthanasia

The Seattle Post-Intelligencer
Letters to the Editor
P.O. Box 1909
Seattle, WA 98111-1909

The Seattle Times
Letters to the Editor
Editorial Page
P.O. Box 70
Seattle, WA 98111

NEWS RESOURCES

Circulation figures given below are from the 1990 *Gales Directory of Publications and Broadcast Media*.

The Seattle Post-Intelligencer
101 Elliott Ave. W
Seattle, WA 98119
Mailing: P.O. Box 1909
Seattle, WA 98111
448-8000
Newsroom: 448-8350
Circulation: 206,155 Mon.–Fri., 175,554 Sat.
Publisher: Virgil Fassio
Executive editor: J.D. Alexander
Owner: The Hearst Corporation
Editorial page editor: Charles Dunsire, 448-8387
Reader representative: 448-8051
Notable columnists: Jean Godden leads the list here with her local items column, full of juicy tidbits and some downright investigative stuff too. John Hahn does people features, Carol Smith-Monkman is the only local general business columnist, Art Thiel has a large following in sports, Neil Modie does a political column.
North and South bureaus: 448-8033

The Seattle Times
1120 John St.
(Fairview Ave. N and John St.)
Seattle, WA 98109
Mailing: P.O. Box 70
Seattle, WA 98111
464-2111
Newsroom: 464-2200
Circulation: 231,207 Mon.–Fri., 226,707 Sat.
Publisher: Frank Blethen
Executive editor: Michael Fancher
Owner: The Blethen family, with a minority interest held by Knight-Ridder Corporation.
Editorial page editor: Mindy Cameron, 464-2773
Reader representative: 464-8979
Notable columnists: Emmett Watson (native son stuff), Eric Lacitis (news-based, cynical comments), Rick Anderson (rough-and-tough Seattle), John Hinterberger (fluffy stuff, food).
The *Times* has three zoned editions, a new ploy to attract the waning reader population. It's working to some extent, at least to the degree that local news is finally being given its due.
East News Bureau: 453-2130
North News Bureau: 745-7800
South News Bureau: 464-2475
West News Bureau: Oops—apparently those folks don't do anything important yet. No bureau across the water.

And the *Times* has a lot of other goodies too:
InfoLine: Free service with variety of topics from health to local deaths, pass conditions to mortgage rates. Call 464-2000.
TV columnist: Reviews shows and points you in the right direction for your viewing pleasure, 464-2313.
Neighborhood calendar: 464-2296.
Going Places: Blurby events calendar, 464-2391.
Business Monday: Weekly biz section with main feature, profiles, and strategy pieces, sprinkled with inside

Nothing gets people as upset as a change in their favorite section: the comics. Gripe about it by calling the Times, 464-2440, or the P-I, 448-8051. Or actually, maybe we do get upset about other things. Top three complaints aimed at the Times' ombudsman are: ink rubbing off, delivery problems, grammar/spelling.

"memos" about local companies, 464-2266.
Food section: One of the paper's most popular sections (the *Times* still has a test kitchen, a phenomenon among modern papers), 464-2300.
Sports at a Glance: Events in the back of the Sports Section, 464-2275.

AND THE REST OF THE FIELD

The *Times* and the *P-I* aren't the only two papers in the race for readers. Running on their heels are the *Morning News Tribune* (formerly the *Tacoma News Tribune*) and the *Journal-American*. Up north *The Herald* and to the west *The Sun* (Bremerton) hold forth; south in Olympia, *The Olympian* publishes daily, and the *Valley Daily News* publishes in Kent, Auburn, and Renton. The *Daily Journal of Commerce* comes out daily except Sunday.

Another daily, *The Daily*, is published at the University of Washington, and isn't a bad paper at that.

These smaller dailies often do a great job in local news (the *Morning News Tribune* is touted by many newsies as the best paper around). They jab the big guys and needle them with turf wars, especially over the south Seattle/north Tacoma area.

Daily Journal of Commerce
Box 11050
Seattle, WA 98111
622-8272
Circulation: 6,445 (statewide)
Publisher: M.E. and D.O. Brown

The Herald
P.O. Box 930
Everett, WA 98206
624-2499
Circulation: 56,000 daily; 64,000 Sunday.
Owner: *Washington Post*

Journal-American
1705 132nd Ave. NE
Bellevue, WA 98005
455-2222
City desk: 453-4230
Circulation: 27,282 daily; 27,689 Sunday
Owner: Northwest Media, Inc., a wholly owned subsidiary of Persis Corp., which recently made a sweep through the Northwest and now owns the *Peninsula Daily News* in Port Angeles and the three Mercer Island, Bothell, and Woodinville weeklies. Also picked up the *Valley Daily News* in south Seattle. The *J-A* is a bible to Eastsiders; good local sports coverage.

The Morning News Tribune
1950 S State St.
Tacoma, WA 98405
City desk: 597-8511
Editorial page: 597-8638
Seattle bureau: 467-9836
Circulation: 117,703
Owner: McClatchy Newspapers

The Olympian
P.O. Box 407
Olympia, WA 98507
City editor: 754-5420
Owner: Gannett Corporation

The Sun
545 Fifth St.
Bremerton, WA 98310
377-3711
Circulation: 41,630
Owner: John Scripps
Columnist Adele Ferguson is probably the most famous person on this daily. She's covered Olympia so long, she's more of a legislator than the legislators—and when she speaks, they listen.

Valley Daily News
P.O. Box 130
Renton, WA 98035
872-6660
Circulation: 28,213
Owner: Northwest Media, Persis Corp.

ONCE A WEEK

Seattle Weekly
1931 Second Ave.
Seattle, WA 98101
441-5555
Circulation: 31,000
Publisher: David Brewster,
Seattle Weekly is Seattle's answer to the *Village Voice*—a sophisticated, alternative weekly that's been variously described as scrappy, liberal, conservative, a social calendar, an iconoclast, a gossip sheet. One thing that's sure is that the *Seattle Weekly* is just about the only local paper with any urban vision for the city.

"Weekly Wash" features pithy comments from publisher David Brewster and his minions; the "Goings On" calendar is the only way to find out everything happening in the city; and the Arts and Leisure section has the best arts coverage hands down—even the arts community thinks so, although they like to disagree with what the paper says. And the personal classifieds are, well, personal. *Seattle Weekly* comes out every Wednesday.

Puget Sound Business Journal
101 Yesler Way, Suite 200
Seattle, WA 98104
583-0701
Circulation: 14,516
Publisher: Mike Flynn
The *Puget Sound Business Journal* gets its fair share of stories that the bigger papers miss. This lively weekly has a biz bent and puts out excellent annual supplement sections on such things as leasing rates and the top companies and executives in the area. Its *Book of Lists* is a must-have for local businesses.

NEIGHBORHOOD PAPERS

As the city grows, local papers have become more important than ever. They're the only place you can find out well in advance what kind of apartment building is planned for your block, or when the old hardware store owner on the corner retires.

Unfortunately, most community papers are run on a shoestring and some are much better run than others. Those that have been basically gutted and turned into shoppers with a few press-release promo pieces on the front page aren't even worth picking up, but the rest can be invaluable.

Ballard News Tribune
2208 NW Market St., Room 202
Seattle, WA 98107
783-1244
Published weekly by Arnold Wallstron, edited by Don Glockner.

Flaherty Newspapers/Pacific Media, Inc.
2720 S Hanford St.
Seattle, WA 98144
723-1300
Publishes *Beacon Hill News, South District Journal, Capitol Hill Times, University Herald, Madison Park Times, North Central Outlook, Mercer Islander.*

Jack Underwood Publications
P.O. Box 977
Lynnwood, WA 98046
775-7521
Publishes papers in North Seattle, such as *Shoreline, Highlands,* and *Lake City Enterprise, North City, Lake Forest Park Enterprise, Wallingford Enterprise.*

Market News
85 Pike St., Room 407
Seattle, WA 98101
682-7453
The Pike Place Market has had a hard time keeping its own newspaper going, but this newest form looks good. Clayton Park of Fremont fame has taken it on, with back-up from the Pike Place Market Business Association.

Murray Publishing/Pacific Media, Inc.
225 W Galer St.
Seattle, WA 98109
282-0900
Puts out the *Magnolia News* and *Queen Anne News.*

North Seattle Press
4128 Fremont Ave. N
Seattle, WA 98103
547-9660
Terry Dento and Elizabeth White are publishers of this Fremont paper; editor is Clayton Park.

Robinson Newspapers
P.O. Box 16069
Seattle, WA 98116
932-0300
Publishes *Federal Way News, West Seattle Herald, White Center News, Highline Times, Des Moines News.*

AFRICAN AMERICAN AND ETHNIC PAPERS

African American and ethnic papers abound in Seattle, but the most prominent are *The Facts* and *The Medium*, competing African American community newspapers. *The Facts* promotes "good news" about the community and prints mostly press releases. You can buy space for your comments on the front page, too. To know what events are happening, read *The Facts*. *The Medium* is more newsy, but they complement each other. And there's a new one—The *Seattle Skanner*—challenging them both.

Ethnic papers can usually be picked up in community groceries and libraries, or at community centers. Here's a sampling; more are in Chapter 12, page 175, *Ethnicity: Diversity at Work*.

Chinese Daily News
610 Maynard Ave. S
Seattle, WA 98104
223-0802

El Amanecer Hispano
611 20th Ave. S
Seattle, WA 98144
324-7100

The Facts
P.O. Box 22015
2765 E Cherry St.
Seattle, WA 98122
324-0552
Fitzgerald Beaver, Jr. is editor of this long-time African American community newspaper, more opinion piece than news vehicle.

Filipino-American Bulletin
3814 NE 75th St., Suite 4
Seattle, WA 98115
323-6545 days; 526-0423 eves.
Meant to be a more contemporary newspaper for Filipino Americans than the *Herald.*

Filipino-American Herald
P.O. Box 14240
9508 Maynard Ave. S
Seattle, WA 98114
725-6606
Community newspaper since 1942. Paid circulation of about 10,000; free circulation about 7,000.

Hispanic News
2318 Second Ave.
Seattle, WA 98121
768-0421
Weekly bilingual newspaper.

International Examiner
318 Sixth Ave. S, Room 127
Seattle, WA 98104
624-3925

Korea Times
430 Yale Ave. N
Seattle, WA 98109
622-2229

La Voz
157 Yesler Way, Suite 400
Seattle, WA 98104
447-4891
Published by Concilio for the Spanish-speaking of King County.

The Medium
2600 Jackson St.
Seattle, WA 98144
323-3070
Chris Bennett runs this African American community paper. He owns some radio stations and newspapers in other cities too.

North American Post
661½ S Jackson St.
Seattle, WA 98104
623-0100
The region's only Japanese-language newspaper, established in 1946. (Henry T. Kubota was publisher for 30 years. He died in November, 1989, on the day Congress approved reparation payments to West Coast Japanese. He arrived in Seattle from Japan in the early twenties at age 21.)

Northwest Ethnic News
3123 Eastlake Ave. E
Seattle, WA 98102
726-0357
Put out by Ethnic Heritage Council. Calendars from local ethnic communities and profiles of ethnic businesses or individuals. An extensive listing on ethnic art.

NW Nikkei
662½ S Jackson St.
Seattle, WA 98104
623-0100
English-language paper for Japanese community.

Seattle Chinese Post
414 Eighth Ave. S
Seattle, WA 98104
223-0623
Publisher Assunta Ng knows all about the International District. The *Post* is the only Asian legal newspaper in Washington; also the only bilingual Asian paper in the state.

Seattle Skanner
1326 Fifth Ave., Suite 825
Seattle, WA 98102
233-9888
Upstart African American paper, with more of a business focus than the other two.

Western Viking
2040 NW Market St.
Seattle, WA 98107
784-4617
Norwegian-language newspaper, weekly, established in 1889.

COLLEGE PAPERS

Sometimes the college papers have a better grasp of contemporary culture, as lived by 20-year-olds, than anybody else. Pick them up where they're left thrown around campus.

City Collegian
Seattle Central Community College
1701 Broadway
Seattle, WA 98122
587-6959

The Daily
University of Washington
144 Communications Bldg., DS-20
Seattle, WA 98195
543-2670
UW newspaper published just when it says, daily except weekends; weekly in summer. *The Daily* is not only a darned good paper, but fun to read as well.

Ebbtide
Shoreline Community College
16101 Greenwood Ave.
Seattle, WA 98133
546-4101

Spectator
Seattle University
Broadway and Madison
Seattle, WA 98122
296-6470

SPU Falcon
Seattle Pacific University
3215 Third Ave. W
Seattle, WA 98119
281-2104

TRADE PUBLICATIONS

Aero Mechanic
9125 15th Pl. S
Seattle, WA 98108
763-1300
A trade journal for aero mechanics.

Auto and Flat Glass Journal
P.O. Box 12099
Seattle, WA 98102
322-5120
National magazine for auto glass replacement industry.

Computing Resources for the Professional
Computing Information Center
University of Washington ACC, HG-45
Seattle, WA 98195
543-5970
Established 1981; bimonthly.

Condominium News: Condominium Owners & Community Associations League
2620 Alki Ave. SW
Seattle, WA 98116
932-6010
News releases for press and general public.

Grange News
521 Union Ave. SE
Olympia, WA 98502
943-9911
Mailing: P.O. Box 1186
Olympia, WA 98507
Tabloid for farm organizations and cooperatives; established 1912.

High Rise Connection
200 W Mercer St., Suite 201
Seattle, WA 98119
285-8073
Weekly.

Insurance Week
1001 Fourth Ave., Suite 3029
Seattle, WA 98154
624-6965

Marine Digest
1201 First Ave. S, Suite 305
Seattle, WA 98134
682-3607
Magazine established in 1922 for maritime industry.

Marple's Business Newsletter
911 Western Ave., Suite 509
Seattle, WA 98104
622-0155
Michael Parks does a great job with this insiders' look at biz.

Masonic Tribune
225 W Galer St.
Seattle, WA 98119
285-1505

Northwest Construction News
Vernon Publications, Inc.
3000 Northup Way
Bellevue, WA 98004
827-9900
Daily construction bids and awards. Vernon also produces *Pacific Builder and Engineer*, a semimonthly construction magazine, and *Pacific Banker*, a monthly for bank and savings and loan executives in 10 western states.

Professional Agenda
2314 Third Ave.
Seattle, WA 98121
448-5629
Monthly tabloid for professional community.

Puget Sound Consumer
4201 Roosevelt Way NE
Seattle, WA 98105
525-0033

Stocks & Commodities
Technical Analysis, Inc.
3517 SW Alaska St.
Seattle, WA 98126-2791
938-0570
Monthly magazine covering computerized investing, charting, brokerage and advising services. Purpose is to explain methods of trading publicly held stocks and bonds, mutuals, etc.

Washington CEO
2505 Second Ave., Suite 602
Seattle, WA 98121
441-8415
Business magazine for CEOs.

Washington Teamster
553 John St.
Seattle, WA 98109
441-7470
Union publication.

ARTS PUBLICATIONS

ArtsFocus
1514 Western Ave.
Seattle, WA 98101
624-6113
Performing arts magazine.

Backlash
4128 Fremont Ave. N
Seattle, WA 98103
547-9660
Local music.

Earshot Jazz
3429 Fremont Pl. N, Suite 303
Seattle, WA 98103
547-6763
Local jazz scene rag.

Encore
87 Wall St., Suite 315
Seattle, WA 98121
443-0445
Opera house programs for individual groups (PNW Ballet, Seattle Symphony, Seattle Opera).

LCQ (Literary Center Quarterly)
Box 85116
Seattle 98145
874-4034
Local literary arts publication.

Reflex Magazine
117 Yale Ave. N
Seattle, WA 98109
682-7688
Contemporary art and art politics, published in association with 911 Contemporary Arts/Media Center.

Rocket
2028 Fifth Ave.
Seattle, WA 98121
728-7625
Rock 'n' roll.

Seattle Arts
305 Harrison St.
Seattle, WA 98109
684-7171
Monthly arts newsletter published by the Seattle Arts Commission.

RELIGIOUS PUBLICATIONS

Jewish Transcript
2031 Third Ave.
Seattle, WA 98121
441-4553
Weekly published by Jewish Federation and Council of Greater Seattle.

The Progress
910 Marion St.
Seattle, WA 98104
382-4850
Weekly Catholic paper established in 1897. Publisher is Archbishop Raymond Hunthausen.

SENIOR NEWS

Grey Panther News
4649 Sunnyside Ave. N
Seattle, WA 98103
632-4759
Senior citizen politics and events.

Parsley, Sage & Time
Pike Market Senior Center
1931 First Ave.
Seattle, WA 98101
728-2773
Monthly newsletter.

Prime Times
10829 NE 68th St.
Kirkland, WA 98033
827-9737

MISCELLANEOUS SPECIAL INTEREST PUBLICATIONS

Active Singles Life
3450 Sixth Ave. S
Seattle, WA 98134
223-5537

Issue Watch
Municipal League of Seattle
604 Central Bldg.
810 Third Ave.
Seattle, WA 98104-1651
622-8333
10 times/year non-partisan tabloid on city/county/state government. Established in 1911.

Northwest Skier
903 NE 45th St.
Seattle, WA 98105
547-6229
Monthly sports magazine.

The Northwest Technocrat
Technocracy, Inc.
7513 Greenwood Ave. N
Seattle, WA 98103
784-2111
Quarterly science publication "aimed at preparing the people of this continent for social change." Established in 1939.

The Permaculture Activist
Permaculture Institute of North America
4649 Sunnyside Ave. N
Seattle, WA 98103
221-3979
Quarterly newsletter on small-scale appropriate technology for self-reliant food production, etc.

Seattle Gay News
704 E Pike St.
Seattle, WA 98122
324-4297
Weekly gay and lesbian news magazine; circulation about 20,000.

Waves
Northwest Passage, Inc.
1017-B E Pike St.
Seattle, WA 98122
325-8037
A monthly alternative/underground/anarchist newspaper. Edited by the Staff Collective.

SEATTLE'S MAGAZINE GRAVEYARD

It's long been a puzzle why Seattle can't sustain its own metro magazine the way other cities do. In the 1960s, *Seattle* magazine was one of the first local attempts at a polished slick, but it wasn't financially successful. That failure cast a pall on the medium in general; to this day advertisers are leery of supporting local magazines.

Metro magazines differ from state or regional magazines in that they tend to be more political and sophisticated, aimed at the hot tub and brie crowd. State magazines are more pictorial and full of good news extolling the beauty of the area.

Pacific Northwest started as *Pacific Search*, the brain child of Harriet Bullitt, an ardent environmentalist. It tried—with some success—to become the *Audubon* magazine of the Northwest, with a focus on wildlife and the environment. Gradually the focus broadened until the name changed and *Pacific Northwest* emerged. In response to *Washington* magazine (which ceased publication in the summer of 1990), *PNW* became softer. Micromedia, a New Jersey company, bought *PNW* a couple of years ago and heads have rolled since. The magazine is now mostly lifestyle stuff, and it has a *Seattle Home and Garden* offshoot. Circulation is at 81,382.

LOCAL MAGAZINES

Alaska Airlines Magazine
2701 First Ave., Suite 250
Seattle, WA 98121
441-5871
In-flight magazine.

Always Jukin'
221 Yesler Way
Seattle, WA 98104
524-5111
Monthly magazine for jukebox owners and collectors.

Back Nine
1710 S Norman St.
Seattle, WA 98144
324-5619
Northwest golfing magazine.

Bellowing Ark
P.O. Box 45637
Seattle, WA 98145
545-8302
Magazine of modern poetry.

Canoe Magazine
10526 NE 68th St., Suite 5
Kirkland, WA 98033
827-6363
Canoeing.

Fishermen's News
West Wall Bldg., Room 110
Fisherman's Terminal
Seattle, WA 98119
282-7545
A monthly established in 1945 reporting on commercial fishing on the Pacific coast.

Fishing & Hunting News Outdoor Empire
511 Eastlake Ave. E
Seattle, WA 98109
624-3845
Fishing & Hunting News, which prints editions for other states, has a gigantic circulation of 131,394.

Freedom Socialist
Freedom Socialist Party
5018 Rainier Ave. S
Seattle, WA 98118
722-2453
Quarterly socialist/feminist magazine, established in 1966. Circulation of about 10,000.

Golden American
2142 Eighth Ave. N, Suite 205
Seattle, WA 98109
284-1139

Guide Magazine
One in Ten Publishing Co.
1535 11th Ave., Suite 200
Seattle, WA 98102
323-7374
Magazine for and about Pacific Northwest gays.

Inside the Seahawks
5729 Lakeview Dr. NE
Kirkland, WA 98033
828-6538
Weekly during the football season, monthly otherwise.

The New Times
Silver Owl Publications
P.O. Box 51186
Seattle, WA 98115
524-9071
New Age paper.

The New Pacific
1201 Third Ave., Suite 4521
Seattle, WA 98101-3099
583-8566
Quarterly journal of public and cultural affairs for the Pacific Northwest and British Columbia.

Landmarks
835 Securities Bldg.
Seattle, WA 98101
622-3538
Quarterly on Northwest history.

Northwest Yachting
5206 Ballard Ave. NW
Seattle, WA 98107
789-8116
Boating news and features.

Nor'Westing Magazine
P.O. Box 1027
180 W Dayton St.
Edmonds, WA 98020
776-3138
Pleasure boating mag.

Pacific Northwest
222 Dexter Ave. N
Seattle, WA 98109
682-2704
Regional magazine, published 11 times a year by Micromedia.

Pacific Northwest Executive
UW Grad School Business Administration
306 Lewis Hall, DJ-10
Seattle, WA 98195
543-1806

Pacific Northwest Quarterly
4045 Brooklyn Ave. NE, JA-15
Seattle, WA 98105
543-2992
University of Washington history journal on the Pacific Northwest, Western Canada, and Alaska. Established in 1906.

Peninsula Magazine
P.O. Box 2259
Sequim, WA 98382
683-5421
Slick quarterly magazine about Olympic Peninsula.

Seattle's Child
P.O. Box 22578
Seattle, WA 98122
322-2594
Parents' magazine; includes calendar essential to the Seattle child.

Signpost
Washington Trails Association
1305 Fourth Ave., Suite 518
Seattle, WA 98101
625-1367
Monthly magazine on backpacking, hiking, and the outdoors, established in 1966.

Sports Northwest
4556 University Way NE, Suite 203
Seattle, WA 98105
547-9709
Monthly magazine about regional sports; circulation about 25,000.

Washington Fishing Holes Magazine
P.O. Box 32
Sedro Woolley, WA 98284
855-1641
Washington fishing with local maps of best holes.

Other press contacts

Associated Press
P.O. Box 2144
Seattle, WA 98111
682-1812

Knight-Ridder Newspapers
810 Third Ave., Suite 352
Seattle, WA 98104
340-1211

The New York Times
P.O. Box 18375
Seattle, WA 98118
725-3175
Seattle correspondent: Timothy Egan

United Press International
101 Elliott W, Suite 110
Seattle, WA 98119
283-3262

The Monthly (Northwest Edition)
603 Stewart St., Suite 1020
Seattle, WA 98101
682-3565
Monthly tabloid covering regional news of the media professions.

Newsstands

Bulldog News
401 Broadway E
4208 University Way NE
328-2881

Steve's Broadway News
204 Broadway E
324-READ
International newspapers and magazines.

Ynot Magazines and News
2016 S 320th St.

Read All About It International Newsstand
98 Pike St. (in the Market)
624-0140

BROADCAST MEDIA

If you want to reach an audience, don't forget radio. Many people listen all day long, and those who aren't glued to their radios are sometimes glued to the driver's seat of the car, where they're most likely punching the dial in complete boredom.

If you tune in to the AM band, you're likely to meet the most profitable programming around, religious or inspirational programs.

Radio stations come and go, but there are some that hang in there, such as KING, KIRO, KOMO, and KVI. Seattleites listen to whatever is their pleasure—music, sports, or talk —but informal polls show KIRO-AM coming in first for on-the-spot news coverage (it's on day and night at any newsroom city desk worth its salt). KIRO's Jim French is a smooth-talker whose ad delivery is every bit as personal and friendly as his interviews—no wonder advertisers love him. And Dave Ross's Chip Talk is an unusual idea appealing to the computer addicts among us.

KIRO is so successful that it's been one of the top-rated stations for almost 10 years. Its average cost for commercials ranks up there nationally; Don Pember of the UW Communications School says, "Joe Abel even has the plants in the lobby for sale."

KING-AM used to be the radio of record, but has gone more toward talk shows than news lately. Its newest find is Mike Siegel, a shoot-from-the-hip host who doesn't mind alienating everyone in Seattle. He's a bit abusive—some say to get ratings, which he does—and definitely your advocacy journalism type. Fun to listen to, but the word is when his ratings go, so will he.

The other favorite in this city of newshounds is National Public Radio (NPR). KUOW (94.9-FM), the UW-affiliated station, is based in Seattle, and KPLU (88.5-FM), of Pacific Lutheran University, is in Tacoma. They are in a head-to-head battle for listeners in this relatively limited area, with KPLU making an aggressive move to capture Seattle out from under KUOW's nose. KPLU actually covers more breaking Seattle stories than the local station and gets more stories on NPR. KUOW, however, has an afternoon talk show, "Seattle Afternoon," with host Ross Reynolds, that is must listening for anyone interested in what's happening locally. Both stations carry the NPR news shows "Morning Edition" and "All Things Considered."

KUOW has been grappling with its identity as a classical music station recently; KPLU is unabashedly jazz.

HEARD IT ON THE RADIO

Rock

KISW (100-FM): rock 'n' roll.
KXRX (96.5-FM): adult rock. Disc jockey Robin Erickson voted "most radio active" in *Seattle Weekly*'s "Best of Seattle" poll.
KZOK (102.5-FM): classic rock 'n' roll.

Pop and top-40, old and new

KBSG (1210-AM, 97.3-FM): "K-Best," Pops of '50s,'60s, and '70s.
KIXI (880-AM, 107.7-FM): AM is '40s/'50s/'60s hits; FM is adult contemporary of '80s.
KJR (950-AM), classic hits.
KOMO (1000-AM): news, adult contemporary.

KVI (570-AM), oldies.
KZOK (1590-AM): oldies.
KBRD-FM (103.7): easy listening.
KIXI (880-AM, 107.7-FM): AM is '40s/'50s/'60s hits; FM is adult contemporary of '80s.
KLTX (95.7-FM): "K-Lite," soft contemporary.
KNHC (89.5-FM): contemporary hit radio run by Seattle School District.
KNUA (106.9-FM): new adult contemporary.
KPLZ (101.5-FM): personality, entertainment, oldies music, sports, traffic.
KSEA (101-FM): adult contemporary.
KUBE (93.3-FM): contemporary hit music.

News/talk

KEZX (1150-AM): business talk/news.
KING (1090-AM): talk radio. Jim Althoff show from 9 a.m.–noon; Chris Brecher, noon–3 p.m.; Mike Siegel, 3–7 p.m.; Sally Jessy Raphael Show, 7–9 p.m.; Larry King, 9 p.m.–midnight (open phones); Tom Snyder, midnight–4 a.m.
KIRO (71-AM): adult programming, news, information, sports, special events—the Mariners' station. Jim French, Dave Ross, KIRO Sportsline with Wayne Cody.

Jazz, rhythm & blues:

KEZX (98.9-FM): soft rock, jazz, folk and reggae.
KKFX (1250-AM): "K-Fox," rhythm & blues.
KPLU (88.5-FM): jazz and news. Public radio.

African-American/soul

KRIZ (1420-AM): urban, contemporary music; rhythm & blues; jazz; gospel. Community Potpourri, Mon., Wed., Fri., 7:05–7:45 a.m.

Classical

KING (98.1-FM): 24-hour classical music.
KUOW (94.5-FM): classical music, news, specialized music (folk, ethnic, swing). Public radio. "Seattle Afternoon" talk show with Ross Reynolds features local issues/personalities.

Religious

KBLE (1050-AM)
KCIS (630-AM): religious music, information; some interviews and counseling.
KCMS (105.3-AM): contemporary Christian.
KGNW (820-AM): traditional Christian.

Other

KCMU (90.3-FM): new music/alternative from UW. "Audioasis" on Wednesdays at 6 p.m. features live musicians; "Muse" on Sundays at 3 p.m. features women's music and news.
KMPS (1300-AM, 94.1-FM): country.

TV TOWN

Seattle is unusual in that there isn't strong viewer loyalty to one station or another. The three majors run neck-and-neck as far as top-rated news shows are concerned, taking turns at being the much-touted front-runner. Competition means good news coverage—better than elsewhere in the country.

People watch the local stations not only for the news about the city, but also to see the news about the news station. Can Jean Enersen get along with the new folks at KING? Does Aaron Brown sound better at KIRO than he did at KING? And what about KOMO—will it hold its lead in the triad competition? Is KIRO becoming less conservative? And who has the biggest-name commentator these days anyhow?

The city is also unusual in that it has two pioneer family–owned TV stations: KOMO, owned by the Fisher family of Fisher flour fame, and KING, owned by the Bullitts. (KIRO is owned by Bonneville International Corporation.)

That community base may be crumbling, however; the Bullitts recently announced that they would sell KING Broadcasting, 44 years after it was bought by former family matriarch, Dorothy Bullitt.

Seattle's favorite news anchor: Jean Enersen, who's been a reporter in town for 21 years.

All three stations organize a considerable number of public service projects—a result, possibly, of the strong local ties.

KOMO-TV, Channel 4 (ABC)
100 Fourth Ave. N
Seattle, WA 98109
Assignment desk: 443-4141
Public service director: 443-4157
KOMO Job Line: 443-6444

KING-TV, Channel 5 (NBC)
333 Dexter Ave. N
Seattle, WA 98109
Assignment desk: 448-3850
Public service director: 448-3693
Employment Opportunities Line: 448-3915
Public service announcements: 448-3790

KIRO-TV, Channel 7 (CBS)
2807 Third Ave.
Seattle, WA 98121
Assignment desk: 728-8307
Public service director: 728-8203

KIRO-TV Eastside Bureau
13010 Northup Way, Suite 2 C-3
Bellevue, WA 98005

KCTS-TV, Channel 9 (PBS)
401 Mercer St.
Seattle, WA 98109
Assignment editor: 728-6463
Program information: 443-6677

KSTW-TV, Channel 11 (Independent)
2036 Sixth Ave.
Seattle, WA 98121
682-7763
THE source for 10 p.m. news.

KCPQ-TV, Channel 13 (Independent)
P.O. Box 98828
Tacoma, WA 98499
Public service director: 625-1313

KTZZ-TV, Channel 22 (Independent)
P.O. Box 2022
Seattle, WA 98111
282-2202

YOU'RE THE STAR: LOCAL TV TALK SHOWS

Tired of watching everyone else be interviewed? Get yourself on a local talk show—or get some tickets and applaud on command as part of the audience.

"Seattle Today" on KING airs weekdays from 9–10 a.m.—lots of discussion and variety based on local happenings. For tickets and scheduled programs, call 448-3781.

KING also has the Emmy-winning "Almost Live," hosted by John Keister. "Almost Live" pokes fun at Seattle's sacred cows and, appropriately enough, airs just before "Saturday Night Live" at 11:30 p.m. Saturdays. For tickets, call 448-3795.

KOMO takes care of the afternoon with "Northwest Afternoon," 3–4 p.m. weekdays, a panel show with audience. For tickets, call 443-8333.

"Town Meeting," also on KOMO, likes to get the crowd stirred up and arguing. The purpose of this show is to tackle very current and controversial issues and present both sides. It's a bit contrived and sensational, but does hit good topics. It airs 6–7 p.m. Sundays, with repeat episodes Sundays at 6 a.m. For tickets, call 443-4186.

"Seattle Week in Review," on KCTS, channel 9, Fridays at 7:30 p.m. and repeat Sunday at 2 p.m., features producer/host Barry Mitzman and a panel of local reporters talking about the week's news. No audience.

CHAPTER

10

UP, DOWN, AROUND DOWNTOWN

HIGHRISES

DOWNTOWN PARKS

WHAT'S UP TOP

EVENTS

HOTELS

PUBLIC RESTROOMS

THE MARKET

STREET MUSIC

Remember when grandma used to get all dressed up—jet black, beaded necklaces, hat, and all—and "go downtown" on a shopping spree? She'd come home smelling of the trolley and ready to hand out the little plastic horses from Kress's toy department. It was a ceremony, this going downtown, one that all little girls couldn't wait to be old enough to take part in.

Malls don't do it—it's just not the same as going from block to block, breathing all those smells, listening to the street musicians and proselytizers on the corners. Of course, when grandma was around, the Smith Tower was still the tallest building in town, Ivar was still the proverbial patriarch, and the prostitutes stayed put on First Avenue. Life was simpler. Grandma wouldn't recognize Seattle's downtown core today.

HIGHRISE NICKNAMES

Washington Mutual Tower: The Phillips-head screwdriver building.
Fourth and Blanchard Building: The Darth Vader building.
First Interstate Building: Vacuum cleaner tube building.
Old Seafirst Building (now 1001 Fourth): Box for the Space Needle.
Rainier Tower (OK, so its name is now Security Pacific Tower, but have you ever heard anyone call it that?): Golf tee.
Century Square: Ban Roll-on building.
AT&T Gateway Tower: Hmmmm —well, consider it from the waterfront and you won't let your kids look until they're of age.

DOWNTOWN DETAIL

The truth is, grandma probably wouldn't go downtown today. A city survey in 1990 shows that people over 65, and people who have lived in Seattle for more than 30 years, don't use downtown much.

With office buildings springing up like zucchini in the summertime, the character of downtown is changing; some people absolutely hate that change, others relish it.

Changes in downtown housing

Income levels	Rent Levels	1987	1989	% of Total
Very low	to $348	5,852	5,877	65
Low	349-557	973	1,280	14
Middle	558-1,045	649	874	10
Upper	1,046 & up	801	997	11

(based on one-person households)

Source: City of Seattle, Department of Community Development, 1989 housing inventory

What 400 people surveyed in 1989 used the downtown area for in a one-month period: 51% for entertainment; 46% to shop; 30% for non-work-related appointment; 30% for work.

What people like best about downtown:
36% specific sites, like the Pike Place Market (16%)
35% shopping and entertainment
What they like least:
34% traffic congestion
24% lack of parking
16% homeless/panhandlers
14% cost of parking

What they think of recent downtown growth and development, compared to six or seven years ago:
39% said they like downtown Seattle better now
34% liked it better before
20% said their opinion hasn't changed
49% said downtown Seattle is growing too fast
39% thought it is growing at about the right rate
5% felt the growth rate is too slow

What they think of the new office buildings downtown:
56% believed that Seattle is better off, on the whole, because of the new buildings
26% felt it was worse off
5% said the buildings made no difference

Of those surveyed, 91 were infrequent downtown users and hadn't been there in the month of the survey.
Source: Stuart Elway, Inc.

WHERE IS DOWNTOWN ANYWAY?

The absolute center of downtown is the University of Washington tract, where the Four Seasons Olympic and Rainier Security Pacific Tower are—at Fourth and University. From there it fans out, down to the Kingdome and International District to

Downtown growth

Office space absorption	
1987	995,760 square ft.
1988	1.4 million square ft.
1989	1.48 million square ft.

Downtown employment	
1980	161,000
1985	175,000
1989	183,000

Retail sales growth (60 firms tracked)	
1987	+1.20%
1988	+2.10%
1989	+10.36%

Source: Downtown Seattle Assn., Retail Core BIA Marketing Program Analysis, 1990

THE place to stay in Seattle for that really special night is the penthouse suite at the Sorrento Hotel. Amenities? Baby grand piano, library, fireplace, deck with hot tub, kitchen, canopy bed in master suite, sitting room. All for only $700 per night.

the south, and up through the Denny Regrade to the Seattle Center and Mercer Street to the north. It's bound on the west by Elliott Bay and the central waterfront, and on the east by I-5, though most maps show downtown as including Pill Hill, up to Broadway. Downtown has:

A financial district. Well, sort of. There's no formal financial district, but the banks do tend to cluster in one area due to the common sharing of services. Several securities companies are near the First Interstate Building at Third and Marion, but several are scattered throughout the city. So one could say the financial district roughly is between Third and Fifth avenues, from Marion to Union.

A shopping district. Definitely. It's centered at Fifth and Pine, where Nordstrom, Westlake Center, Frederick's, and The Bon are. The area is bounded by Third Avenue, Olive Way, Seventh Avenue, and Pike Street, but is expanding to include Pacific First Centre at Fifth and Union.

The central business district shopping area takes up 4 million square feet of the 7.7 million square feet that make up all of downtown—more space than in any of the seven suburban malls on the outskirts. Until recently that didn't worry the malls—they outshone downtown. But with the new New York-y stores (Ann Taylor, Gucci, etc.) arriving on the scene—and the growing downtown work force—downtown has again come into its own.

- Downtown office space: 21.7 million sq. ft.
- Downtown office vacancies: 12%
- Downtown retail space: 4 million sq. ft.

A theater district. This is a matter of debate, though it's difficult to see how anyone could say there is a theater district, since the performing houses are spread around. But there is that strip of movie theaters on Fourth Avenue up to Sixth near Blanchard. But the old theaters that once made up the theater district are disappearing.

Downtown parks.

- Waterfront Park on Alaskan Way
- Freeway Park between University and Seneca streets over I-5
- Westlake Plaza next to Nordstrom on Westlake and Fourth Avenue
- Occidental Park on First and Washington
- Waterfall Gardens on Main and Second
- Victor Steinbrueck Park at the Pike Place Market
- Pioneer Square Park at Pioneer Square
- Denny Park on Denny and Eighth

Downtown sales volume

1987	$861 million
1988	934 million
1989	990 million (estimated)

Source: City of Seattle, Department of Community Development

Hotels. Seattle has 7,230 hotel rooms in 43 hotels and motels. That includes the venerable Four Seasons Olympic as the leader in luxury hotels, and boutique hotels such as the Sorrento, Alexis, and Inn at the Market. Those command similar rates, an average daily rate in 1988 of $115 per night. Other "first tier hotels" bring in $45 less per night on average. Occupancy rate in 1988 was estimated at nearly 73%.

A waterfront. It's a bit seedy, somewhat tacky, and at a loss for direction, but it's downtown's shoreline.

Conventions. All those people with name badges on come from the more than 320 conventions per year that come to the city.

Neighborhoods.

- Pioneer Square: 20 blocks of historic mixed use.
- Denny Regrade/Belltown: Mixed use, including auto dealers, office

Source: Seattle Downtown Business Assn.

Downtown Seattle's ten largest hotels

Seattle Sheraton Hotel and Towers	880 rooms
The Westin Hotel	865 rooms
Stouffer Madison	554 rooms
Four Seasons Olympic Hotel	450 rooms
Crowne Plaza	415 rooms
Edgewater Inn	240 rooms
Seattle Downtown Hilton	237 rooms
The Warwick Hotel	230 rooms
Mayflower Park Hotel	187 rooms
Sixth Avenue Inn	166 rooms

Don't ever, ever, try driving down Alaskan Way on a Friday afternoon. The waterfront traffic piles up for miles with people waiting to get on the ferry —or simply caught in the ferry line and desperately trying to get out.

buildings, hotel, commercial, and residential.
• International District: Center of Asian cultures, business, and housing.

THOSE SKYSCRAPERS, HIGHRISES, AND TOWERS

What constitutes, exactly, a highrise? Everyone knows that the Columbia Center scrapes the sky, no matter what its height. But what about the Dexter Horton Building? And what about the Norton Building? Those can seem pretty high, especially when the fire alarm rings and you have to walk down from the top floor to the bottom.

But true highrises are those, we've decided, that are taller than the Smith Tower, for 48 years the tallest building west of the Mississippi at about 500 feet. (It took the 605-foot Space Needle to break its record, but most say the record was officially broken by the old Seafirst Building, now 1001 Fourth Avenue Building, which opened in 1969.) Seattle now has several skyscrapers that look down on Ivar's salmon flag waving atop the Smith Tower. Their height varies depending on where you measure from.

Columbia Seafirst Center, 76 stories, 954 feet
Two Union Square, 56 stories, 886 feet
Washington Mutual Tower, 55 stories, 730 feet (above Third Avenue)
Security Pacific Tower, 40 stories, 667 feet
One Union Square, 36 stories, 631 feet
AT&T Gateway Tower, 62 stories, 620 feet
First Interstate Center, 48 stories, 605 feet
Pacific First Centre, 44 stories, 584 feet
Bank of California, 41 stories, 570 feet
Seafirst Fifth Avenue Plaza, 42 stories, 543 feet
1001 Fourth Avenue Building, 50 stories, 500+ feet
Key Tower, 40 stories, 500 feet

Two that qualify for highrise status but are under 500 feet in elevation: **Century Square** at 354.71 feet and **Fourth and Blanchard Building**, 440 feet.

HIGHRISE ROLLERS

Who's behind Seattle's highrises? Martin Selig, a very short man, has a penchant for very tall buildings. But he's not the only highrise developer in the city. The big names, highrise-wise (they all own shorter buildings too) are:
Wright Runstad & Co. (First Interstate Center, Washington Mutual Tower).
Martin Selig (built Columbia Center —later sold to Seafirst—Key Tower, Metropolitan Park Building, Fourth and Blanchard Building, Fourth and Battery Building, and is planning a new skyscraper just short of the Columbia Center building at the Seattle Trust site).
Unico (Security Pacific Bank Tower, Two Union Square, One Union Square).
Prescott (built Pacific First Centre and sold to Seafirst, Century Square).

And the Smith Tower? It's run by the **Smith Tower Limited Partnership**, a San Francisco investment partnership formed after Ivar Haglund tried to sell it to the city for $1. The city said a polite "No thanks."

You can't have a conversation about highrises without having a conversation about the CAP flap. So FYI, here's a definition of CAP (Citizen Alternative Plan): In May of 1989, citizens passed the CAP initiative, which changed the city Land Use Code to set an annual limit on the square footage of usable new office space for which permits can be issued downtown. The annual limit under CAP is 500,000 square feet through 1994, and 1 million square feet for 1995 through 1999. Projects with less than 50,000 square feet of office space are exempt from CAP. And 85,000 square feet of the yearly limit is set aside per year for projects between 50,000 and 85,000 square feet in size. For projects larger than 85,000 square feet, a design review panel decides which ones receive the CAP allocation.

WHAT'S IN IT FOR YOU?

So they're tall. So they create wind tunnels that make you freeze and clutch your latte ever closer. But, unless you're working at Bogle & Gates or a clone of it, what's in those highrises for you?

It used to be that in order to get a bonus of more space or height, developers had to provide such amenities as space for nonprofit groups, human services, parks, or cinemas. These amenities now compete with "pretty," so the public might also get an atrium, overhead weather protection, or a plaza. Cushy chairs are open to everyone in some lobbies; art shows are a bonus.

Next to public space, the most fascinating part of a highrise is the top, those sought-after, statusy office spaces usually occupied by law firms or investment companies. It's not quite fair to say who's in the high spot, since musical office space is the name of downtown Seattle's game, but, at least it gives you an idea of who's likely to be there. (They might not be really on top; most buildings have their engineering equipment somewhere at the top.) If you act like you own the place and zoom up in an elevator, here's what you'll find.

Highrise public and not-so-public spaces

AT&T Gateway Tower

700 Fifth Ave.

What's in it for you: A glass-enclosed 84-foot atrium makes up the main lobby at Fifth and Columbia. The space might be rented for parties at some point. There's a plaza area, outdoor seating, and restaurants. The tower is tied into the tunnel system that connects with Seafirst Fifth Avenue Plaza and the Columbia Seafirst Center underground. There is a health club on the 14th floor run by The Seattle Club, and a 700-car parking garage for tenants and visitors. Suppose the express lane through the base of the building could be considered public space...

What's up top: Offices not full at press time, but there will be five stories of office space inside this glass-walled arch. The offices will have 10-foot-high finished ceilings. Also at the top will be a helicopter rescue pad.

Bank of California

900 Fourth Ave.

What's in it for you: There's an art show in the lobby on the Fourth Avenue side of the building three times a year. In the bank itself you can see continuing exhibits of exquisite pieces of china and dinnerware. On the Fifth Avenue side, there's a hidden plaza, usually empty, where people sit in the sun. The parking garage offers carpooling to tenants and non-tenants. Carpools receive a 35% discount.

What's up top: 41st floor is home to law, law, and more law. Upon leaving the elevators you'll find a directory of several offices and a tiny window to the north. All of the offices are stretched along the southern corridor. They include Burton & Burton, law offices; Lewis White et al., law offices; Arbitration Forums, Inc.; Graham Fitch (law offices); John H. Ludwich (law offices).

Century Square

1501 Fourth Ave.

What's in it for you: Three floors of retail; music and art exhibits in the lobby from time to time. Not really a place to sit down.

What's up top: This building has 5,000 square feet in several vaulted glass arches that could all be considered up top. On the 13th floor, in the southern glass arch, is Sullivan Payne, a re-insurance firm.

They made the best spot a company lunchroom and meeting place, deciding, one would suppose, that since the view is so great and the atmosphere so nice, why not give it to the employees to enjoy. The room has a sweeping view of south Seattle and plenty of glass up top to let the sun shine through.

On the 26th floor, in another vaulted area, is Davis Wright Tremaine, law firm. It occupies more than one floor in Century Square and uses this skylit room for the boardroom, law library, and lunchroom. The view is tremendous. There is something about the northern dome which seems relaxing, soothing almost. With Seattle stretching off to the north and Puget Sound to your left and the afternoon sun creeping up over the top of the glass sky... A good place for employees to take the pack off, but definitely not the place to get any work done.

In the third vaulted area, on the 28th floor, Freeman Welwood & Co., securities brokerage, leases the space, with panoramic view and all, for the president's office. Unless you are close friends of Freeman or Welwood, you can't get in.

Columbia Seafirst Center

701 Fifth Ave.

What's in it for you: There's a dark multi-level mall of stores at the base of the 76-story building and a central seating and eating area. Noisy and dismal in appearance, it's usually full of people on their lunch hour or break. They'll probably hurry back to work, since this isn't a place to linger. But there are also some soft chairs scattered around on the main level and a plaza outside. You can ride the elevator up to the 73rd floor where there's an observation deck—and a charge of $3.50 for adults, $1.75 for children, for the privilege.

What's up top: Way up top there's the Columbia Tower Club and the famous restrooms-with-a-view, but don't try to get in unless you have credentials.

First Interstate Bank

999 Third Ave.

What's in it for you: Restaurant, some retail, and a plaza at the base —and the vacuum cleaner escalator, the best public space in the building. Taking the escalator up and walking through the lobby is a great way to get from Second and Marion to Third and Madison.

What's up top: The 47th floor is used for First Interstate's own executive offices, law division, boardroom, and executive dining room. As you come out of the elevators and turn to the west you are hit with a smiling face and a great view. Behind the receptionist, you'll see an expanse of windows overlooking the Sound; those whose offices are here have obviously done something important for First Interstate. The decor is warm and comfortable in dark wood and granite, and could definitely be described as plush. To the east of the elevators there are double glass doors leading to the boardroom and executive dining room. Windows surround the entire floor, but the view to the west over Puget Sound is a stunner.

Fourth and Blanchard Building
Fourth and Blanchard
What's in it for you: There's a park outside of this building and a small lobby inside.
What's up top: You have to take two elevators to venture to the top of the triangle and, once there, you may question whether it was worth it or not. Exiting the elevator into the dark at the top is a bit eerie. That's partially because, with the angle of the slanted ceiling, you can't really see down to the city toward the west (Elliott Bay), at least not directly. And because the windows are tinted, in the afternoon the whole place sort of glows (when the sun's out at least) or gets really dark (when it's cloudy, which is most of the time). The view is better to the south, north, and east.

One and Two Union Square
600 University and Sixth and Union, respectively
What's in it for you: The best thing about Two Union Square, as far as the public is concerned, is the outdoor plaza with a three-story waterfall. The upper plaza is a garden with umbrella tables. There's an art show in both buildings (usually) and some plush chairs in number Two. The two are connected by a fireplace lobby—good place to warm your hands—and more plazas where there's summertime entertainment at lunch time. Next best thing about the building is that you can wend from here to Freeway Park, or go underground in a tunnel to the Hilton Hotel or Rainier Square.
What's up top: Two Union Square's 56th floor houses GNA, securities firm. By far the most spectacular view of all hits you as you exit onto the 56th floor and look north. There's a huge, huge expanse of windows from floor to ceiling—ominous and breathtaking, as you are all those feet above the freeway. This office space is definitely a child of the '90s; with Seattle the outside view, the inside is cream and pale lime green.

There is a large waiting area, very open and bright with two large boardrooms off to your left and right. These are glass cages that look off to the west and east.

Bogle & Gates, the bigtime law firm, is on the 51st floor, and there is a conference room with catering facilities on the 55th floor.

At One Union Square, Stoel Rives Boley Jones & Grey, law firm, has the 36th floor, an expanse of light that comes from the view and the pale shades of yellow and cream with black iron sculptures placed around the reception area. Three-quarters of the lobby is surrounded by windows that look out to the north, east, and south. The view of the Sound is the property of the western office space. To the east is the boardroom.

1001 Fourth Avenue Building
1001 Fourth Ave.
What's in it for you: If you've been around for any time at all, you know this as the old Seafirst Building. This building has the best free observation area in town. Ride up to the 46th floor and look out the big windows just outside the Mirabeau Restaurant. In the lobby, there's a concierge who helps tenants with taxis and info, and, if asked, he might help out non-tenants too. Art shows are in the lobby and there's a courtyard with seats. Of course, Henry Moore's vertebrae sculpture is still out front. In the Third Avenue arcade, there's a post office and two travel agents. The parking garage has a Chevron service station, a rarity in downtown Seattle.
What's up top: There are actually 50 floors to this building, but, as with most highrises, the top few floors are taken up with the guts of the building's engineering systems. The 43rd to 46th floors are currently home to Riddell Williams Bullitt & Walkinshaw, law firm. Up top, this building will remind you of the days when parquet was the craze; it's very 1970s, wood touched with gold, brown, and cream. This office takes up two floors, a sort of split level reached by a stairway built into the reception area. To the left is a boardroom. The view from the 45th floor reception area is mainly to the south.

Also on the 46th floor is the Mirabeau, which has by far the best view, reaching south, west, and north. To the southwest, from the bar, you can watch the Port of Seattle terminals with the container-carrying trucks moving in and out like little Matchbox toys.

Pacific First Centre
1420 Fifth Ave.
What's in it for you: Three-story retail area of glitzy New York–style shops, public restrooms on the third floor, restaurants, movie theater, and a day care facility. The entire 60-foot atrium is open and there's a wonderful permanent display of Pilchuck glass throughout. Wander around: There are several comfortable plum-colored plush chairs where you can put your feet up, read the paper, and get a respite from the rush outside.
What's up top: Badgley Phelps & Bell investment/brokerage firm has the 44th floor. As for decor, this office has many of the others beat. The waiting area is dark wood, with expansive flower arrangements and a number of plants placed strategically about. Upon entering the reception area you'll see a boardroom and a

view to the east showing off downtown and First Hill. The view of the Sound belongs to Badgley Phelps & Bell.

Security Pacific Tower
(formerly Rainier Bank Tower)
1301 Fifth Ave.
What's in it for you: A well-kept secret is the garden deck above Fourth Avenue, away from retail shops and the lobby piano. You have to go to the third level of the shopping area and head west. Snoop around, you'll find it—tables with umbrellas mark the spot. As for the huge grand piano, anyone can bring music, sit down, and play. This lobby is a perfect meeting spot. The bank's corporate art collection—one of the best in town—can be seen during Artstorm.
What's up top: The 40th floor office belongs to the treasurer of Security Pacific Bank. It will help if you have an invitation or know whom you want to see if you take the elevator up. As the doors open you'll see three or four smiling faces ready to help you, serve you, or convince you you're in the wrong place. This floor is dedicated to conference rooms, carefully guarded by men with wires sticking to their ears and walkie-talkies strapped to their belts. As for the look of the place, the view is panoramic and breathtaking. The decor is a little outdated, mostly orange and cream with a lot of glass/mirror paneling around.

Try counting the 42 stories of the Smith Tower. Even including the basement, you won't find them all. For some reason, the builders fudged on how many stories high the building was. But everyone still says the Smith Tower is 42 stories.

Smith Tower
506 Second Ave.
What's in it for you: Way back in 1914 when the building opened, people rode the elevator up to the observation deck to see the view. Of course, then it was the tallest building west of the Mississippi with its 42 stories, and it cost a quarter to get up there. Today it costs $2 for adults, $1 for seniors and children. The deck is on the 35th floor and gives you a more human look at the city than do its modern-day counterparts. The Chinese Room, also on the 35th floor, is decorated in imported Blackwood furniture. Something called the Wishing Chair is supposed to have been a gift from the Empress of China. The room is for rent for parties. On the main floor is a restaurant, art gallery, and Seattle's oldest cigar store; on the 2nd floor is a child care center; on the 11th floor is the King County Art Museum. Everybody's favorite ride is the elevator, the only manually operated (not just with a real operator, but one that actually pushes the levers) on the West Coast.
What's up top: Ivar's salmon flag is hung from what they call a "bubble" on top of the building. (Every once in a while, in a high wind, the flag rips off and tumbles down Third Avenue.) The bubble was once a large light directing ships into the harbor. Under the bubble is the building's water supply, then, still in the triangular peak, a small private residence where an employee of the tower lives. Under that is the Chinese Room and the observation deck.

Washington Mutual Tower
1201 Third Ave.
What's in it for you: Wander into the atrium on Second Avenue level —not only is the wood-lined room lovely, but there are comfortable chairs and tables where you can bring your lunch. Three times a week a piano player tinkles the ivories. Outdoor seating available for sunny days, and there is a little secret sideroom off the atrium where you can get as much peace and quiet as you want. The atrium (and adjacent plazas) is for rent for parties. At the Third Avenue level are retail shops and, of course, the bank lobby.
What's up top: On the 54th floor is Bateman Eichler Hill Richards, Inc., brokerage firm. This office is a bit of a surprise: In the downstairs lobby of the building you're surrounded by warm, dark wood and the rich smell of espresso. Stepping into the elevators you can't help but feel pampered in the plush habitat. As you proceed to the 54th floor you imagine offices decked out in inviting shades of dark brown and red, emerald green and burgundy. Instead you'll find yourself blinking as your eyes try to adjust to the stark white walls and black-and-white checkered floors leading off to the offices which keep the views of Puget Sound to themselves.

URBAN POCKETS

The Seattle Design Commission presents annual awards for "Urban Designs Which Work." The criterion is whether people used and felt comfortable in the space. And the downtown winners, in 1988, were:

First Interstate Plaza
Nordstrom Espresso Bar, Fifth Avenue
The Norton Building, Second Avenue entrance
Post Alley from Seneca to Madison
Seattle Trust Court

WHERE TO GO WHEN YOU HAVE TO GO

Some call it the toilet-tissue issue. Others the burning issue of public restrooms. When it comes to glamour, the restroom-with-a-view in the

Columbia Seafirst Center wins pants down, so to speak. But it's hardly public, and we're talking survival here. A person could wander up and down Spring, Marion, and beyond in search of a place to go. The issue is so critical that there's a person in the city doing a master's thesis in architecture on public restrooms in downtown Seattle.

Truly public restrooms in downtown Seattle

The **main fire station** in Pioneer Square on Main Street. **Westlake Center**, on the second floor back in the corner, with no signs pointing to it until you're on top of it. (Undoubtedly designed, says one merchant, by someone without kids.) Two in the **Pike Place Market**. But if you don't want to use them (and a lot of people don't), ask a merchant for a key to the merchants' restroom. PPM merchants are incredibly accommodating. **The public library**, on level A, third floor, and fourth floor. **The King County Administration Building**, Fifth and James, all floors. **The King County Courthouse**, Third and James, on all floors, near the interior stairwells. **Seattle Municipal Building**, Fourth and James, the **Public Safety Building**, Fourth and Cherry, and the **Federal Building**, Second and Marion. **The ferry terminal**, Colman Dock, both at street level and upstairs. And don't forget the **Aquarium**. Quasi-public restrooms at the **bus depot** and **train station**, **Pier 70**, and **The Bon** parking garage.

Other quasi-public restrooms can be found in **highrises**; just wander through the lobby areas and look for out-of-the-way doors, sometimes not even marked. And **hotels** are great resources; they almost always have a restroom off the lobby.

In Seattle/King County, restaurants, theaters, auditoriums, and meeting halls are required by county code to have public restrooms—public meaning customers. But the truth is, if you walk in and ask, they'll let you use them; if they don't, look pained. Or put on your customer look and march on through the restaurant to the restroom without saying a word. Fast-food places, like McDonald's, are easiest. Department stores, such as Frederick's, often have not only restrooms, but lounges as well.

LITTLE-KNOWN RESTROOM FACTOIDS

The new Metro tunnel stations have no restrooms.

- The health department gets two complaints per day regarding public urination or defecation downtown.
- 32% of downtown businesses let people use restrooms (that includes Denny Regrade, International District, downtown core, and Pioneer Square).
- 60% of businesses say they have problems with public urination.
- 58% of downtown businesses clean up urine or feces on the sidewalk in front of their doors daily.
- Number of businesses willing to let a public restroom be located within a distance of three blocks: 68% yes, 21% maybe.
- Number of businesses willing to let a public restroom be located within a distance of one block: 55% yes, 21% maybe.

Source: Downtown Human Services Council

THE GREAT PISSING MATCH

Underneath Pioneer Square, right smack in the triangular center of the square under the pergola, is a hidden secret: an expansive, marble restroom, Seattle's first public restroom. Built in 1908 and opened in 1909 by the parks department, the bathroom extends underground throughout the entire triangle. Original access to it was at each end of the pergola; today the only access is through a manhole.

When it opened, it was something to be proud of, the only restroom on the West Coast built in an open area, not hidden away in some municipal building.

It was beautiful: The stalls were made of 1⅝-inch Alaskan marble dividers; there was a shoeshine and concession area where you could buy newspapers, a stand for wet towels, and a lobby area with benches. The little square-block skylights that still exist in much of Pioneer Square provided light, and upstairs the square's totems and trees were there specifically to dress up the bathroom entrance.

But beautiful or not, the restroom was a questionable amenity from the beginning. Its construction was the obsession of one politician who, amidst the grumbles of his city cohorts, twisted the arms of the park board until they took on the project. The city later grudgingly bought the site. But there were plumbing problems—high tide, for example, created some drainage difficulties—and the bathroom closed down in 1939.

In the 1970s, there was a move to get the city to open the bathrooms again. The city met the outcry with a shake of the bureaucratic head and the announcement that the walls were weak. Engineers set about constructing crude braces down there. "It's just an excuse," screamed bathroom proponents, who figured the city simply didn't want to deal with the dark side of public restrooms.

Some say the city sneaked around and dumped sand down there. In fact, rumor has it that one man took some work-study students down there to try to take the mess of sand away bucket by bucket.

The bathrooms are still there, though they're ankle deep in slimy dirt and other debris. The toilets are there, the urinals on the floor, the marble intact. The city has flushed any idea of opening the restroom for the time being.

Source: Son Voung, UW architecture student and author of "Public Restrooms for Seattle," a thesis.

DOWNTOWN STUFF TO DO

The Downtown Seattle Association sponsors events downtown, obviously to attract you and your pocketbook. The events are fun—and mostly free.

Artstorm: Corporate art collections are part of tours, as are Seattle's buildings and architecture. Usually held in February or March.

Easy Streets: A parking program by DSA, Easy Streets works like this: Spend $20 at a downtown store with a special decal and you get a token for parking discount or free ride on Metro.

Holidays in the Heart of the City: DSA brings an antique carousel to Westlake Park, has horse-drawn carriages going up and down the street, and sponsors caroling contests.

Maritime Week: Two weeks of festival including music, tours, and events on the waterfront. Usually in May.

Out to Lunch, summer concert series: Free concerts all summer in parks and plazas throughout downtown. Pick up location brochures at the public library and downtown buildings.

Downtown Seattle Association
500 Union St., Suite 325
Seattle, WA 98101
623-0340
Housing, business, and activities.

Downtown Human Services Council
107 Cherry St.
Seattle, WA 98104
461-3865
Private nonprofit, advocacy for low-income population in downtown area.

THE PIKE PLACE MARKET

Despite the outrage and hoopla about New York interlopers laying claim to the Pike Place Market, ask anyone who the owner of the Market is and they'll tell you it belongs to everyone in Seattle. It's *our* tiles and *our* clock after all, and we're proud of almost everything that happens in the Market. Just let someone try to take it away and—well, the lawsuits and tempers fly and flare.

Best time to shop at the Market depends on what you're there for. For ambience, best time is about 7 a.m., when the farmers are setting up and the dew is still on the sweet peas. For fresh goods, best time is 8 a.m.–11 a.m., before the lunch crowds get there.
For bargains, best time is late afternoon. If the farmers have had a good day, sometimes the prices drop. If they've turned the cash register off, sometimes you can get things gratis.

If you become a regular at certain Market stands, the merchants will save things for you. And the merchants are experts. Tell them whether you want peaches to eat now or save for later. And ask how to cook that fish.

The Market works almost like any other business. In 1973, Pike Place Market Preservation and Development was formed to act as landlord and manager for 80% of the buildings in the Market Historic District. Everybody got mad at the PDA because it leased buildings to the New York investors without a word to the public, but aside from that debacle, the PDA does such things as hand out discount coupons to the Market's low-income residents, manage low-income housing and parking lots, and do promotion.

The Market is as exciting for merchants as for customers. For example, every morning at 9 a.m. the craftspeople assemble at the north end of the Market for roll call. The Market Master (Millie Padua has been doing this for years) calls out names in order of seniority and each chooses the table he or she will sell on that day. Artists must sell two days a week to stay on the seniority list and must sell two weekdays to sell on a Saturday. There's a long waiting list—as many as 400—of artisans who want space at the Market tables.

As for the farmers, they have first pick of the stalls. But as Seattle

Be assertive with Market merchants. Go ahead and pick the vegetable you want from the display—never allow the farmer to pick one out for you, no matter how much you get yelled at.

grows, the distance farmers have to come grows too. And the number of farmers drops. Because of increased promotion, though, the number of farmers seems to have stabilized at around 100.

The number of farmers selling at the Market

1907: Market opens with 6 farmers
1937: 600+ farmers
1942: Japanese internment cut farmer-sellers by half: 300 farmers
1960: 60 farmers
1976: 40 farmers
1987: 99 farmers
1989: 105 farmers
Source: PPM Preservation and Development Authority

Know those stallers

Market terms revolve around selling-stalls. Lowstalls (sometimes called wet tables) are the daystalls rented to Market farmers, those who grow their own. Most of those are on the right side of Pike Place. Highstalls are rented to agents of farmers, those who buy wholesale.

Market facts

105 farmers sell at the Market, a decrease from 114 in 1988. 223 daystalls are on the Market's Main and North arcades. 36 farmers travel more than 100 miles each way to sell at the Market. 400 different products are sold by Market farmers in a year. 220 craftspeople sell at the Market. More than half have been there five years or more. 2,000 daffodil bulbs are planted in rooftop flower boxes in the Market each year. 300,000 pounds of cardboard and 36,000 pounds of newsprint are recycled in the Market each year.
Source: PPM Preservation and Development Authority Annual Reports

INSIDERS' TOUR OF THE MARKET

We all know how DeLaurenti's wonderful smells can drag you right in off the street. And we've heard the yelling from City Fish, listened to the hawkers teasing tourists, and gawked at the parrots at Parrot Market. But there are some things that even natives might miss at the Market. So, just for fun, we tagged along with Michael Yaeger, Market pillar and activist, who, with his wife, artist Sarah Clementson, runs Studio Solstone in the Economy Market Building. We're *not* mentioning places like the Three Girls deli; this is a list of places you might miss—and shouldn't.

1st stop: It's a big decision: Will it be World Class Chili in the Atrium or cioppino at Jack's Fish Spot in the Sanitary Market? Cioppino wins. Jack's has a few stools stuffed in behind the fish market and if you ask

Want to go where the stallers go? You can usually find some on the second floor of Lowell's (Main Arcade) or at SBC coffee (Post Alley).

Craftspeople get into the Market based on seniority, so those with the longest ties choose the best days, namely weekends. If you want to see the regulars, shop weekends; if you want to see the newest crafts, come Monday. Everything has to be made by the craftsperson himself or herself.

for fish 'n' chips he'll whack the fresh fish up right there in front of you. If you don't get a receipt, you get a free meal. But don't worry—they never forget.

2nd stop: Pike Place Creamery, right behind Jack's. This is a stop for just one reason (aside from the real milk with cream on top and farm-fresh eggs you can get here): to meet the owner, who actually introduces herself as Nancy Nipples.

3rd stop: Best rummage sale in town is just outside the Post Alley Market (sign says simply "Rummage sale"). A circle of tables is filled with jewelry, junk, and junque. There's even a rack of clothes. Early in the morning you can get best pick here, where things are usually from estate sales.

4th stop: Up Post Alley, across Pine, past Inn at the Market to the Gravity Bar, hardly the kind of place the founding farmers could have imagined in 1907. Have 'em set up a shot glass of wheat grass, with water chaser, and wait for the rush. Gives you an idea what cows taste when they're chewing their cud. Don't mix with coffee, says the waitress.

5th stop: Staton Hills Winery on Upper Post Alley. Staton Hills has what it takes to get the taste of wheat grass out of your mouth: free wine. Step up to the bar and ask for whatever Yakima wine they're serving today, and you can have a taste. (The merlot is good.)

6th stop: Upper Post Alley, past Stewart House, a Market residence. Stewart House used to be an Alaskan bunkhouse and there's a birdhouse somewhere in the courtyard here that's a replica of the original.

7th stop: The Pike Place Ministry and Clinic. "See, we're a real community."

8th stop: Soames Dunn Building, where the Saigon Restaurant is pronounced best Vietnamese eatery in Seattle by the guide. Inhale. And on to Cucina Fresca. Inhale again.

9th stop: Eagle Park Slim is getting ready to play in the North Arcade, right at the end of Pine Street—a favorite place for musicians (under the clock is too crowded except for somebody like Johnny Hahn, who wheels his piano in there).

10th stop: Downstairs ("First Floor Down Under") to the Hands of the World to see jewelry from all over the place. And on to Old Seattle Paperworks, where everyone paws through old postcards. Past Market Coins (no interest in baseball cards),

Instead of heading down First Avenue when you need to get someplace south on foot, duck through the Market. How to avoid the crowds on the Main Arcade? Go downstairs to the second level where it's relatively calm, or stay in the center of Pike Place (the street) and ignore the yells from drivers.

If you park in the new parking garage, Market merchants will validate your parking ticket and you can park free. There are 32 merchants participating. A list is available in the garage.

and on to taste the real root beer at Pike Place Natural Foods.

11th stop: Lela from Lela's Needlenook, also down under, says she guarantees her work, though it might take awhile and don't be impatient about it.

12th stop: Golden Age Collectibles. Dick Tracy seems to be the rage here, but the other comics tweak at the memory.

13th stop: Market Magic Shop. There's usually a show going on here by the Amazing Beckman or Sheila the Magic Lady, actually Darrel Beckman and Sheila Lyon, owners of the shop. Ask what some trick is all about and you'll get a demonstration. (And ask about the ghost they swear is in the Arctic Building.)

14th stop: Speaking of ghosts, supposedly the ghost of an old Indian chief hangs around down here in the Second Floor Down Under.

15th stop: Shane's Restaurant, to look out the window at what used to be a view and is now the congregate care facility above the new parking garage. We're here to taste the real soft ice cream.

16th stop: Up to Post Alley passage at the south end of the Market where the bridge above is Seattle's Bridge of Sighs. The story goes that Post Alley was all bars and the sailors used to hit them all as they walked down the alley and into Pioneer Square, where they could board the ships and get out of town. From the bridge, they were watched by the sighing wenches they'd left behind.

17th stop: Market Spice in the Economy Market. Free Market tea in a little cauldron in the corner.

18th stop: Don & Joe's Meat Market, for the best secret yet. They sell a tri-tip steak (an East coast cut, says a guy ordering some) for $3.59/ lb. Tastes like filet mignon.

19th stop: Tenzing Momo, Tibetan and tantalizing. You might run into Mae West, Market regular who wears her button collection. Ask her to open her button-laden coat to show you the dirty buttons she keeps inside on her vest. Now that's a collection.

20th stop: The Atrium, to touch the Richard Beyer sasquatch statue in there. There's one particular part of his body that's been rubbed until it shines. Must be for luck.

21st stop: Back at Studio Solstone. Sarah paints and paints; the favorite paintings are still the crab or fish wrapped in the newspaper of your choice. Enter any newspaper office and you'll find one of these paintings customized with the newspaper's name on it.

Market tours are offered on a daily basis except Sundays. They last about an hour and begin at the information booth at 11 a.m. Mon.–Fri. and 10 a.m. Sat. Cost is $3.50 for adults, $2.50 for children and seniors. Children under 6 are free.

STREET MUSIC

Market musicians play in 13 different spots for $10 per year, or $3 per quarter. They can play in one spot, but if someone is waiting, then they have to cut it off in one hour. The Market issued 295 performer permits in 1989, and there are some who play there but aren't registered. The best say they can make up to $100 per day; many don't cover the price of a beer. The two favorite spots are under the clock and at the foot of Pine Street. Larger groups go down to the entrance to the hillclimb in front of the musicians' mural.

Names to know

Market musicians often go on to fame: Baby Gramps hardly ever graces the Market anymore; Artis the Spoonman has been on "David Letterman." Those who are still around include: Johnny Hahn, everybody's favorite, who wheels his piano in and plays his own compositions; Jeanne Towne, the blind lady with the guitar; Eagle Park Slim, blues guitarist, who says he's played with Chuck Berry and B.B. King; Howlin' Hobbit, acoustic blues; Whamdiddle, hammer dulcimer players; Pike Place Trio, classical music; Lee Dehin, acoustic guitar, old-time folk tunes, in front of Starbucks; Gumbo Jazz, vaudeville tunes in 1920s costumes, tap dances too; Robert Crowley, recorder, baroque pieces; and Willie Herbert Williams and Roosevelt Franklin, a capella performers, blues, gospel, and soul.

Pike Place Market News
85 Pike St., Suite 407
Seattle, WA 98101
587-0351
The "community rag you can't live without." Published by the Pike Place Merchants Association and full of news about the Market.

PPM Preservation and Development Authority
85 Pike St., Room 500
Seattle, WA 98101
682-7453

Pike Place Merchants Association
85 Pike Street
Seattle, WA 98101
587-0351

CHAPTER

11

TOP OF THE BOTTOM LINE

TOP EXECS

DIRECTORS

BOSSES

BOEING

SAFECO

SALARIES

STIPENDS

STOCK

MICROSOFT

UNIVAR

Seattle's gone from being a one-horse town, with Boeing as the steed in harness, to a city with a diverse economy, especially in global trade. Computer companies large and small have turned the area east of the city upside down, and medical technology

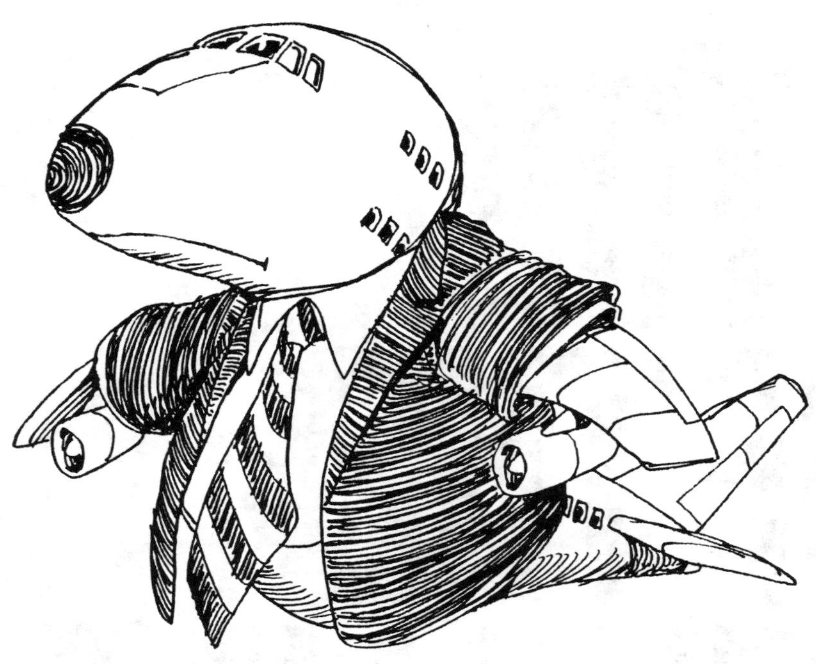

firms are sprouting up in all the burgeoning suburbs. In the city itself the business of transportation, communication, finance, insurance, and real estate keeps those new buildings perking. International trade—especially with the Pacific Rim—is spawning international trade centers and pushing Seattle–Tacoma International Airport to its limits.

Seattle's economy has been dubbed the nation's fastest-growing for a metropolitan area, with 58,000 new jobs estimated for 1990.

The ins and outs of Seattle Big Biz are hidden in annual reports, boards of directors, and stock profiles. At least, they are hidden until you look at the names and companies and find that they are, for the most part, incestuous. Most big-business board members serve on many boards —in fact, looking at the list below, it's hard to imagine that some do anything *but* go to board meetings.

So here it is, a primer of Seattle's Bigtimers. Companies are ranked by annual revenue. For CEOs, we give a rundown of the TOTAL salary (what they made in compensation, stock options, and benefits); for everyone else there are just straight salary figures, which in some cases include bonus or incentive pay. They're rounded to the nearest $1,000.

The "Stock" category for CEOs under "1989 Take-Home Pay" includes the value, in shares or cash, derived from the execution of stock options (or stock appreciation rights, as they are sometimes called) during the year.

The "Benefits" category includes payments made by the company for things such as profit sharing, matching funds for investment plans, supplemental benefit plans, company-paid insurance, company cars, etc. Also note: In all cases, company executives do *not* receive a director's stipend or expenses.

The sources for this information, including the ages given for board members, are 1989 annual reports.

THE TOP FIVE

1. The Boeing Company

7755 E Marginal Way
Seattle, WA 98108
655-2121

The Big Daddy of the Northwest. When Boeing catches cold, the entire city sneezes. The company employs 105,000 workers in the Puget Sound area, which is roughly three times the population of Olympia. Boeing doesn't dominate as it once did (1 in 5 regional jobs were connected to Boeing in 1969; now it's 1 in 10), but still has no peer in the Northwest.

How powerful is Boeing? A few years ago when T. Boone Pickens threatened to take over the company, the state legislature called a special session to thwart the Texan's bid. And in the words of one state senator, "If Boeing doesn't want a new tax, it doesn't get passed. Period."

Employees: 105,000 in Seattle area (nationwide: 163,000)
1989 Revenue: $20.276 billion
1989 Profits: $675 million
NYSE symbol: BA

Who's the boss

Frank Shrontz, Chairman and CEO. This Boise, Idaho native nabbed a law degree from University of Idaho (1954) before studying 'neath the ivy at Harvard (MBA, 1958). Employed by Boeing since 1958, except for stints in government (1973–76 as Asst. Secretary of Air Force and Asst. Secretary of Defense). Took over reins in 1986 from legendary CEO T.A. Wilson, who ran Boeing for 17 years. The company paid Wilson $150,000 in consulting fees in 1989, in addition to his pension and director's stipend.

D.D. Thornton, President of Boeing Commercial Airplanes and Sr. Vice President of Boeing.

B.D. Pinick, President of Boeing Defense and Space Group.

Boyd E. Givan (pronounced Guy-van), Chief Financial Officer.

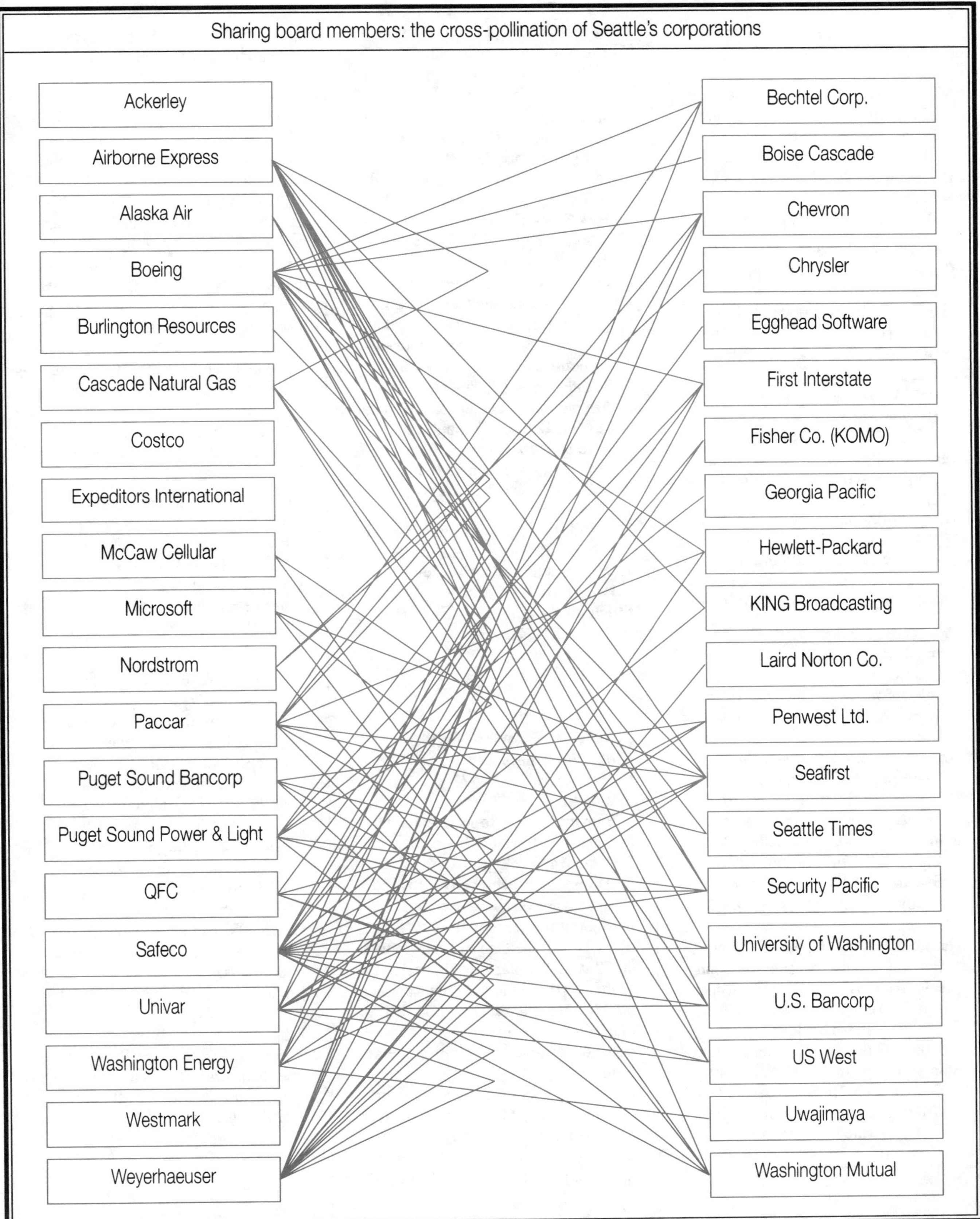
Sharing board members: the cross-pollination of Seattle's corporations
Ackerley
Airborne Express
Alaska Air
Boeing
Burlington Resources
Cascade Natural Gas
Costco
Expeditors International
McCaw Cellular
Microsoft
Nordstrom
Paccar
Puget Sound Bancorp
Puget Sound Power & Light
QFC
Safeco
Univar
Washington Energy
Westmark
Weyerhaeuser
Bechtel Corp.
Boise Cascade
Chevron
Chrysler
Egghead Software
First Interstate
Fisher Co. (KOMO)
Georgia Pacific
Hewlett-Packard
KING Broadcasting
Laird Norton Co.
Penwest Ltd.
Seafirst
Seattle Times
Security Pacific
University of Washington
U.S. Bancorp
US West
Uwajimaya
Washington Mutual

Succeeded longtime CFO and boardmember Harold W. Haynes in April 1990.
Malcolm T. Stamper, Vice Chairman of the Board; President of Boeing from 1972–1985. Retiring mid-1990.
D.P. Beighle, Sr. Vice President and Secretary.
L.D. Alford, Sr. Vice President.

1989 Take-home pay

Frank Shrontz: $910,250 salary, $225,549 stock*, $30,867 benefits, $1,167,000 total
T.A. Wilson: $250,000–$450,000 pension*, $150,000 consulting fee, $43,000 director's fees
Harold W. Haynes: $642,000 (Haynes retired 1990; CFO now Boyd Givan)
Malcolm Stamper: $642,000 (Stamper retiring mid-1990; no replacement as of press time)
D.D. Thornton: $502,000
D.P. Beighle: $403,000
L.D. Alford: $384,000 (1988)
* Estimate based on 1989 Boeing Annual Pension Payable chart.

The board of directors

Annual stipend: $26,000 plus $2,000/meeting plus expenses.
Frank Shrontz, 58, Chairman of the Board. See also Citicorp, Boise Cascade.
Robert A. Beck, 64. Connection: The Prudential Insurance Co. (Chairman Emeritus). See also: Texaco, Xerox, Campbell Soup Co.
John B. Fery, 60. Connection: Boise Cascade (Chairman and CEO). See also: Hewlett-Packard, Union Pacific, Albertson's, West One Bancorp.
Harold J. Haynes, 64. Connection: Bechtel Group, Inc. (Senior Counselor), Chevron (retired Chairman and CEO). See also: Weyerhaeuser, Paccar, Carter Hawley Hale Stores, Citicorp, SRI International.
Stanley Hiller, Jr., 65. Connection: Levelor Corp. (Chairman), and Hiller Investment Co. (Senior Partner), a private investment firm.
George M. Keller, 66. Connection: Chevron (retired Chairman). See also: SRI International, First Interstate Bancorp, Metropolitan Life Insurance, McKesson Corp.
Leo L. Morgan, 70. Connection: Caterpillar Inc. (Director and Retired Chairman). See also: Mobil, 3M, Waste Management Inc., New York Stock Exchange.
Charles M. Pigott, 60. Connection: Paccar (Chairman and CEO). See also: Chevron, *Seattle Times*.
George P. Shultz, 69. Connection: Reagan Administration (Secretary of State 1982–89). Now teaches economics at Stanford. See also: Bechtel Corp. (President, 1975–80); on boards of Chevron, General Motors, Tandem Computers.
George H. Weyerhaeuser, 63. Connection: Weyerhaeuser (Chairman and CEO). See also: Safeco, Chevron.
T.A. Wilson, 69. Connection: Boeing (Chairman Emeritus). See also: Weyerhaeuser, Paccar, Hewlett-Packard, USX Corp.
Stock analysts: Peter Musser at Ragen MacKenzie.

2. Weyerhaeuser Company

33663 Weyerhaeuser Way S
Federal Way, WA 98477
682-6640
(Company's grass-topped headquarters is located just off Interstate 5 in Federal Way.)

Though not technically a Seattle company, Weyerhaeuser wields prodigious influence in the city. It owns 11% of the land in King County, and 2.9 million acres of timberland in the Northwest alone; that's about 3.5 billion cubic feet of wood. It's a mammoth company that has managed to stay somewhat within the family.

Chairman George Weyerhaeuser, now in his early 60s, recently stepped down from the presidency but still retains the CEO's seat, and is one of the most powerful men in the city. A member of the national Business Roundtable, he helped create the Washington Roundtable and King County 2000.

George's two sons are in the business: George Jr. is a VP in the paper company, David is in the hardwood division. The Weyerhaeuser family still holds family reunions, and it's a safe bet they aren't munching beans and wienies: 250 members share a fortune worth over $900 million and control 12% of the company's stock.

The company's political connections are not slight. In 1984 Booth Gardner, then a Weyerhaeuser executive and heir to the family dough, stepped down to tackle the state's problems as governor. Here's the rub: Weyerhaeuser heavily backed his opponent, Republican incumbent John Spellman.

Employees: 10,000 in Washington State
1989 Revenue: $10.1 billion
1989 Profits: $601 million
NYSE symbol: WY
Investor relations: Lowell Moholt, 924-2058

Who's the boss

George H. Weyerhaeuser, Chairman and CEO. Great-grandson of founder Frederick Weyerhaeuser. Yale grad ('49); 42 years with the company, 23 as CEO, probably will retire in next few years.
John W. "Jack" Creighton, Jr., President. Appointed in April 1988 after running the company's successful real estate subsidiary. Expected to take over the CEO's seat when George W. retires.
Charles W. Bingham, Exec. Vice President, Timberland and Forest Products.
Robert L. Schuyler, Exec. Vice President and CFO.
John H. Waechter, Exec. Vice President, Pulp and Paper Products.
Fred R. Fosmire, Sr. Vice President, Human Resources, Technology and Engineering.

1989 Take-home pay

George Weyerhaeuser: $1.06 million salary, $430,528 stock, $7,764 benefits, $1.498 million total.
Jack Creighton: $610,000
Charles Bingham: $450,000
Robert Schuyler: $450,000
Fred Fosmire: $305,000

The board of directors

Annual stipend: $20,000 plus $1,200/meeting plus expenses.

George Weyerhaeuser, 63, Chairman of the Board. See also: Boeing, Safeco, Chevron.

Jack Creighton, 57. See also: QFC, Puget Sound Bancorp, Mortgage Investments Plus.

William Clapp, 48. Connection: Matthew G. Norton Co. (Chairman and President). See also: Alaska Air Group, McDonald Industries, Laird Norton Co.

W. John Driscoll, 60. Connection: Rock Island Co. (private investment company). See also: Comshare Inc., Northern States Power, The St. Paul Companies, Mortgage Investments Plus, Inc.

Don Frisbee, 66. Connection: PacifiCorp, formerly Pacific Power and Light (Chairman). See also: First Interstate Bancorp, Reed College, Precision Castparts Corp.

Phillip Hawley, 64. Connection: Carter Hawley Hale Stores (Chairman, CEO, and middle-namesake). See also: AT&T, ARCO, BankAmerica, Johnson and Johnson, *The Economist*.

Harold J. Haynes, 64. Connection: Bechtel Group, Inc. (Senior Counselor), Chevron (retired Chairman and CEO). See also: Boeing, Paccar, Carter Hawley Hale Stores, Citicorp, SRI International.

E. Bronson Ingram, 58. Connection: Ingram Industries Inc. See also: Inroads Inc., Vanderbilt University.

John Kieckhefer, 45. Connection: Took over for father, Robert, who retired from the board at age 71 in 1989. President of Kieckhefer Associates Inc. (investment and trust management) of Prescott, Arizona.

William Ruckelshaus, 57. Connection: Browning-Ferris Industries (Chairman and CEO) and government background. Ruckelshaus was head of the Environmental Protection Agency under Reagan and served in the Nixon Administration before being axed in the Watergate "Saturday Night Massacre." An attorney to be reckoned with: Local top-drawer law firm Perkins Coie turns to him for legal advice. Was Sr. Vice President of Weyerhaeuser, 1976–83. See also: Nordstrom, Monsanto, Cummins Engine, Texas Commerce Bancshares Inc, Insituform of North America.

T.A. Wilson, 69. Connection: Boeing (retired Chairman and CEO). See also: Hewlett-Packard, Paccar, USX.

Stock analysts: George Haloulakos at Dain Bosworth, Dan Nelson at Ragen MacKenzie.

3. Paccar Inc.

777 106th Ave. NE
Bellevue, WA 98004
455-7400
Fax: 453-4900

The largest producer of class-8 heavy trucks in North America, Paccar builds the 18-wheelers that log the long miles in the U.S. (under the Kenworth and Peterbilt brands) and U.K. (under the Foden brand). Paccar passed Navistar in 1989 as the nation's leading truck manufacturer and now holds nearly one-quarter of the market. Over 500 Paccar dealers sell the trucks in the U.S., Canada, U.K., and Australia. The company also owns Al's Auto Supply, Grand Auto, and an oil equipment subsidiary.

Employees: 3,500 (Washington State)
1989 Revenue: $3.3 billion
1989 Profits: $241.9 million
NASDAQ symbol: PCAR

Who's the boss

Charles M. Pigott, Chairman and CEO. (Pronounced with a hard g, as in picket.) Seattle-born, Stanford-educated grandson of Paccar founder, Chuck Pigott has been CEO longer than some of his employees have been alive (since 1967). His influence in Seattle doesn't live up to the size of his company (but that doesn't necessarily apply to his influence in business—he's on the boards of Boeing, Chevron, and the *Seattle Times*); a few years ago the *Seattle Times* described him as being "notably absent from the councils of power." His favorite philanthropy is the Boy Scouts, they noted.

Joseph M. Dunn, President. Joined Paccar after serving as Vice President at Seafirst (1979–86).

William E. Boisvert, Exec. Vice President and CFO.

David J. Hovind, Exec. Vice President.

Leonard A. Haba, Sr. Vice President.

Mark C. Pigott, Sr. Vice President.

1989 Take-home pay

Charles Pigott: $585,835 salary, $371,000 bonus, $0 stock, $24,723 benefits, $981,558 total.
Joseph Dunn: $650,000 ($415K salary, $235K bonus).
William Boisvert: $282,000 ($247K salary, $35K bonus).
David Hovind: $425,000 ($286K salary, $139K bonus).
Leonard Haba: $319,000 ($233K salary, $86K bonus).

The board of directors

Annual stipend: $25,000 plus $3,000/meeting

Charles Pigott, 60, Chairman of the Board. See also: Boeing, Chevron, *Seattle Times*.

Joseph Dunn, 63. See also: Seafirst.

John M. Fluke, 47. Connection: John Fluke Manufacturing (Chairman). Runs an Everett company, but highly visible in Seattle. See also: U.S. Bank of Washington.

Harold J. Haynes, 64. Connection: Bechtel Group, Inc. (Senior Counselor), Chevron (retired Chairman and CEO). See also: Boeing, Weyerhaeuser, Carter Hawley Hale Stores, Citicorp, SRI International.

James C. Pigott, 53. Connection: Familial (brother of Charles). James has been President of Pigott Enterprises Inc., a private investment firm, since 1983. Also President of Management Reports and Services, a business reports franchising firm. See also: Americold Corp., Northern Life Insurance.

John W. Pitts, 63. Connection: MacDonald, Dettwiler and Associates Ltd. (President and CEO), a high-tech manufacturing company. See also: British Columbia Sugar Refinery Ltd., British Columbia Telephone Co., Canada Trust, Microtel Pacific Research Ltd., Royfund Income Trust.

James H. Wiborg, 65. Connection: Univar Corp. and VWR Corp. (Chairman and Chief Strategist for both). See also: Paccar, Seafirst, Penwest Ltd.

T.A. Wilson, 69. Connection: Boeing (Chairman Emeritus). The grand old man of Seattle industry. See also: Weyerhaeuser, Boeing, Hewlett-Packard, USX Corp.

Stock analyst: Craig Hart at Ragen MacKenzie.

4. Costco Wholesale Corporation

10809 120th Ave. NE
Kirkland, WA 98033
828-8100

Jeff Brotman and Jim Sinegal founded Costco in 1983, jumping into the cut-rate warehouse retailing business just as the industry was taking off. Last year they saw nearly $3 billion in revenue come in from 56 stores, which are football-field large, charge a slight cut (about 10%, compared to retail's 25%) above wholesale, and exact an annual fee from 2 million members. In terms of presence and power in the Seattle area, Costco isn't much of a player (but then again, it's only seven years old).

Costco grew at a ferocious pace in the mid-80s, opening 22 and 20 stores in 1986 and '87, respectively, but expanded too rapidly and had to pull some stores out of the Midwest in 1988. Came back strong in 1989, with nearly a 50% gain in revenue and over 100% gain in profits. Management opened 13 stores in '89 and plans 6 more for 1990, bringing the total to 63. Not a bad place to work, either: Costco store workers are among the highest paid in the industry. Note: 19% of the company's stock is owned by Carrefour Nederland B.V., an international retailing concern.

Employees: 1,640 in Seattle, 10,500 company-wide
1989 Revenue: $2.94 billion
1989 Profits: $27 million
NASDAQ symbol: COST

Who's the boss

Jeffrey H. Brotman, Chairman of the Board. UW grad ('64), also attended law school there ('67). Before creating Costco, worked for an oil exploration company. Also co-founded The Brotman Group, which operates a chain of 30 men's and women's apparel shops. Ran Costco until 1988, when he let Sinegal take over the CEO's chair.

James D. Sinegal, President, CEO, COO. Worked in retail for decades (Fed-Mart, Builders Emporium, The Price Co.) before teaming up with Brotman.

Richard D. DiCerchio, Exec. Vice President, Merchandising, and Director.

Anthony J. Swies, Sr. Vice President, Southeast Operations.

Franz E. Lazarus, Sr. Vice President, Northeast Operations.

Stanley J. McMurray, Sr. Vice President, Merchandising.

1989 Take-home pay

Jeff Brotman: $339,217 salary, $152,500 stock, $81,487 benefits (mostly life insurance), $573,204 total.
Jim Sinegal: $346,000
Richard DiCerchio: $209,000
Anthony Swies: $161,000
Franz E. Lazarus: $163,000

The board of directors

Annual stipend: None. ($1,000/meeting plus expenses.)

Jeffrey Brotman, 47, Chairman of the Board. See also: Sun Sportswear, Carrefour U.S.

James Sinegal, 53. See also: Carrefour U.S.

Richard DiCerchio, 46.

Denis L. Defforey, 64. Connection: Carrefour S.A. (Chairman and CEO).

Hamilton E. James, 38. Connection: Donaldson, Lufkin and Jenrette Securities (Managing Director—James oversees DLJ's mergers and acquisitions and merchant banking activities).

DLJ, along with Merrill Lynch, took Costco public in 1985. See also: Gulfstream Housing, TW Holdings Inc., Vons Companies.

John W. Meisenbach, 53. Connection: Meisenbach, Cashman and Martin Inc. (a financial services company he founded and currently presides over). See also: Pioneer Federal Savings.

Frederick O. Paulsell, Jr., 50. Connection: Foster Paulsell & Baker, an investment banking firm (President). Former Exec. Vice President of Foster and Marshall and American Express.

David Pulver, 48. Connection: Children's Place (co-founder of the apparel chain; also CEO until it was sold in 1982). Currently a private investor.

Ralph R. Shaw, 51. Connection: Shaw Management Co., an investment advisory firm (President). See also: Star Technologies, Riedel Environmental Technologies.

5. Safeco Corporation

Safeco Plaza
Seattle, WA 98185
545-5000

Financial company that operates a number of insurance/finance arms. Trades mostly in business, property, and life and health insurance. Also has credit, investment, and property subsidiaries (the Winmar Co., an arm of Safeco Properties, is developing the region's next big mall in Redmond, to open in 1993).

Employees: 2,500
1989 Revenue: $2.93 billion
1989 Profits: $300 million
NASDAQ symbol: SAFC

Who's the boss

Bruce Maines, CEO and Chairman. Safeco's corporate headquarters in the U District keeps the Tacoma native close to his alma mater—he's UW '48 and UW Law '49 (one year!)—and to Safeco director William Gerberding, who also happens to be President of the University.

Roger H. Eigsti, President and COO.

James W. Cannon, Exec. Vice President of Safeco Corp., President of Property and Casualty Insurance Companies.

Boh A. Dickey, CFO, Secretary, and Sr. Vice President.

Richard W. Hubbard, Treasurer and Sr. Vice President.

Richard Zunker, President, Life and Health Insurance.

L.W. Wells, President, Safeco Properties.

William F. Meany, President, Safeco Credit.

1989 Take-home pay

Bruce Maines: $529,664 salary, $29,299 stock, $92,044 benefits, $651,007 total.

Roger Eigsti: $291,000
James Cannon: $315,000
Boh Dickey: $228,000
Richard Hubbard: $181,000

The board of directors

Annual stipend: $16,000 plus $1,200/meeting plus expenses.

Bruce Maines, 63, Chairman of the Board and CEO. See also: Seafirst, US West Communications.

Roland M. Trafton, 70, retired Chairman of the Board. Connection: Safeco (CEO from 1979–85). See also: First Interstate Bank of Washington.

Roger H. Eigsti, 47. See also: Security Pacific Bancorp. Northwest, Capital Guaranty Corp.

James W. Cannon, 62.

John Ellis, 61. Connection: Puget Sound Power and Light (Chairman and CEO). See also: Washington Mutual Savings Bank, FlowMole Corp., Associated Electric and Gas Insurance Services Inc.

William P. Gerberding, 60. Connection: University of Washington (President). See also: US West Communications, Washington Mutual Savings Bank.

Donald G. Graham, Jr., 66. Connection: Fisher Companies Inc. (President and CEO). Note: Fisher Companies owns KOMO-TV and holds significant amounts of Safeco and Weyerhaeuser stock.

Joshua (Jay) Green III, 53. Connection: U.S. Bancorp (Vice Chairman) and U.S. Bank of Washington (CEO). Grandson of People's Bank founder, and chairman of same until it was taken over by U.S. Bank. Former Chairman (1989) of the Downtown Seattle Association.

Harold W. Haynes, 67. Connection: Boeing (recently retired CFO and board member). See also: First Interstate Bank of Washington, Itel Corp.

William M. Jenkins, 70. Connection: Seafirst Bank (retired Chairman). See also: UAL Inc., United Airlines, Scott Paper Co.

Calvert Knudsen, 66. Connection: MacMillan Bloedel Ltd., a B.C. forest products company (Vice-Chairman). See also: Cascade Corp., Penwest Ltd., Portland General, Security Pacific Corp., Bank of Washington, West Fraser Timber.

William G. Reed, Jr., 51. Connection: Simpson Investment Co. (formerly Simpson Timber) (Chairman). See also: Seafirst, Washington Mutual Savings Bank, Microsoft Corp.

Toni Rembe, 53. Connection: Pillsbury, Madison and Sutro (San Francisco law firm, Partner). See also: Potlatch Corp.

Judith M. Runstad, 45. Connection: Foster, Pepper and Shefelman (Co-Managing Partner in the Seattle law firm retained by Safeco). See also: Seattle Branch of Federal Reserve Bank of San Francisco, developer/UW regent Jon Runstad (husband). The Runstads are often given the informal title of most powerful couple in Seattle.

Henry T. Segerstrom, 66. Connection: C.J. Segerstrom (Managing Partner in the Costa Mesa, Calif. real estate firm). See also: Security Pacific (Corp. and National Bank), Southern California Edison.

Paul W. Skinner, 42. Connection: Skinner Corp. (President of the Seattle investment company). Skinner took over the director's seat when his father, legendary Seattle businessman and philanthropist David E. "Ned" Skinner, died in 1988. See also: Seafirst, KING-TV (married to local news anchor Jean Enersen).

George H. Weyerhaeuser, 63. Connection: Weyerhaeuser (Chairman and CEO). See also: Boeing, Chevron.

Stock analysts: Daniel Nelson at Ragen MacKenzie, Leslie Childress at Harper, McLean.

THE NEXT FIVE

6. Nordstrom Inc.

1501 Fifth Ave.
Seattle, WA 98101
628-2111

The area's top retailer, if not in volume then certainly in prestige and polish. The company prides itself on the best service and highest quality merchandise. The secret's been getting out in the last few years: The company has stores in California and Washington, D.C., and the national press has taken notice, branding Nordstrom the retailing success story of the late 1980s.

Lately the company has been taking its licks, however. A *Wall Street*

Journal article about its labor problems was the talk of the town in spring 1989, and prompted the "60 Minutes" crew to pay a visit. Through it all the store's shoppers stayed, for the most part, fiercely loyal—the company reaps millions in free advertising with its license plate frames "I'd rather be shopping at Nordstrom" pasted on every BMW in Bellevue.

Employees: 6,400 in Puget Sound region, 32,000 nationwide
1989 Revenue: $2.67 billion
1989 Profits: $114.9 million
NASDAQ symbol: NOBE

Who's the boss

Nordstrom is run on a management-by-five-man-junta basis. Five directors run the show, but Bruce Nordstrom is generally acknowledged to be the head of the company.

Bruce A. Nordstrom, Co-Chairman of the Board.
James F. Nordstrom, Co-Chairman of the Board.
John N. Nordstrom, Co-Chairman of the Board.
John A. McMillan, President and Director.
Robert E. Bender, Sr. Vice President and Director.

1989 Take-home pay

Bruce Nordstrom: $300,000 salary (down from $454,000 in 1988), $0 stock, $58,431 benefits, $358,431 total.
Jim Nordstrom: Virtually same as Bruce.
John Nordstrom: Same, except John realized an extra $777,217 by exercising stock options.
John McMillan: $300,000
Robert Bender: $265,000

The board of directors

Annual stipend: $15,000 plus $1,000/meeting.
Bruce Nordstrom, 56, Co-Chairman.
James Nordstrom, 50, Co-Chairman.
John Nordstrom, 53, Co-Chairman.
John McMillan, 58.
Robert Bender, 53.
Barbara Hackman Franklin, 50. Connection: Washington, D.C., consulting firm Franklin Associates (President). Former Director at Wharton School of Business (U. of Pennsylvania).
D. Wayne Gittinger, 57. Connection: Law firm of Lane Powell Moss and Miller (Partner). The Seattle firm handles legal matters for Nordstrom.
John F. Harrigan, 64. Connection: Union Bank (Retired Chairman).
Charles A. Lynch, 62. Connection: Market Value Partners, a Menlo Park, Calif., investing firm. Levelor Corp. (President and CEO). Former CEO of DHL Airways and Saga Corp.
Alfred E. Osborne, Jr., 45. Connection: UCLA. Osborne is a Director and Associate Professor of Business Economics at the UCLA Graduate School of Management.
William Ruckelshaus, 57. Connection: Browning-Ferris Industries (Chairman and CEO) and government (see Weyerhaeuser, board of directors). See also: Weyerhaeuser, Monsanto, Cummins Engine, Insituform of North America, Nordstrom, Texas Commerce Bancshares Inc.
Malcolm T. Stamper, 65. Connection: Boeing (retired Vice-Chairman). See also: Chrysler, Travelers Corp.
Elizabeth C. Vaughan, 61. Connection: North Pacific Studies Center, Oregon Historical Society (Executive Director).
Stock analysts: Marcia Raley at Dain Bosworth, Lesa Sroufe at Ragen MacKenzie.

7. Burlington Resources Inc.

First Interstate Center
999 Third Ave., Suite 4500
Seattle, WA 98104-4097
467-3838

Burlington Northern Inc. (BNI) spun off its natural-resource division in 1988, creating Burlington Resources. The former has returned to its railroad roots and operates out of Ft. Worth, Texas, while Burlington Resources concentrates on energy markets and continues to divest its non-energy subsidiaries. The company keeps its hands in a wide range of energy markets via its subsidiaries: Meridian Oil (oil and gas), El Paso Natural Gas (natural gas pipeline), and Meridian Minerals (precious metals, minerals, and coal). Its Plum Creek Timber unit was spun off in June 1988, and Burlington was looking for a buyer for its Glacier Park Co. real estate subsidiary in mid-1990.

Employees: 100 in Seattle area; most of the company's 5,000 or so employees are in other cities (Meridian Minerals in Denver, El Paso Natural Gas in Texas, etc.).
1989 Revenue: $1.72 billion
1989 Profits: $485 million
NYSE symbol: BR

Who's the boss

Richard M. Bressler, Chairman. Chairman and CEO of Burlington Northern Inc. before the 1988 break-up. Ran Burlington Resources before letting O'Leary take over President and CEO spots in January 1989. Still Chairman of the Board for Burlington Northern.
Thomas H. O'Leary, President and CEO. New York City native, Wharton (U of Penn) MBA. Also on board of Burlington Northern Inc.
Travis H. Petty, BR Vice Chairman and CEO of El Paso Natural Gas subsidiary. Former (1983–88) Vice–Chairman of Burlington Northern Inc.
D.W. Clayton, President and CEO of Meridian Oil.
W.A. Wise, President and CEO of El Paso Natural Gas.
C.T. Bayley, Sr. Vice President, Corporate Affairs, and President and CEO of Glacier Park Co.

1989 Take-home pay

Thomas O'Leary: $525,000 salary, $525,000 bonus, $698,400 stock (not exercised), $8,925 benefits, $1.757 million total.
Travis Petty: $950,000 ($475K salary, $475K bonus).

D.W. Clayton: $600,000 ($300K salary, $300K bonus).
W.A. Wise: $382,000 ($213K salary, $169K bonus).
C.T. Bayley: $400,000 ($200K salary, $200K bonus).

The board of directors

Annual stipend: $30,000 plus $1000/meeting.
Richard M. Bressler, 59, Chairman of the Board. See also: Burlington Northern Inc. (BNI), General Mills, Baker Hughes Inc., Rockwell International, H.F. Ahmanson and Co., Plum Creek Management Co.
Thomas O'Leary, 55. See also: BNI, B.F. Goodrich, Interco, The Kroger Co., Plum Creek Management Co.
Travis Petty, 61. See also: Texas Commerce Bancshares, Texas Commerce Bank. Former Vice-Chairman (1983–88) of BNI.
John V. Byrne, 61. Connection: Oregon State University (President). See also: Benjamin Franklin Savings and Loan, Plum Creek Management Co.
John C. Cushman, III, 49. Connection: Cushman Realty Corp., Los Angeles (President and CEO). See also: Coast Savings and Loan, Coast Savings Financial Inc.
Gerald Grinstein, 57. Connection: BNI (President and CEO). See also: Seafirst, Delta Airlines, Browning-Ferris Industries. Former head of Western Airlines.
Ray L. Hunt, 46. Connection: Hunt Consolidated Inc., Dallas, Texas (President and CEO). Also Chairman of Hunt Oil Co. and Southwest Media Corp. See also: Dresser Industries, NCNB Texas National Bank, Chili's Inc.
James F. McDonald, 49. Connection: Prime Computer Inc., Natick, Massachusetts (Vice-Chairman and CEO). See also: United Telecommunications, DR Holdings Inc.
Walter Scott, Jr., 57. Connection: Peter Kiewit Sons Inc. (Chairman and President of the Omaha, Nebraska, construction and mining company). See also: Berkshire Hathaway, Canadian Imperial Bank of Commerce, Con Agra, FirsTier Financial, Schmalbach-Lubeca AG, Valmont Industries, Plum Creek Management Co.
Stock analysts: Leslie Childress at Harper, McLean, John Rogers at Ragen MacKenzie.

8. Univar Corporation

1600 Norton Bldg.
801 Second Ave.
Seattle, WA 98104
447-5911

Univar is an industrial chemical distributor that operates through two subsidiaries, Van Waters and Rogers Inc. (United States) and Van Waters and Rogers Ltd. (Canada). That business includes everything from domestic distribution of pest-control chemicals to training firemen in Phoenix how to deal with chlorine spills. The company operates offices in cities all across the U.S. and Canada.

Univar's board is sprinkled with representatives of Pakhoed Holding N.V., a shipping concern based in The Netherlands, with which it entered a stock exchange agreement in 1986. Univar is also well represented on the board of VWR Corp., the distribution company formerly based in Bellevue. VWR was a former subsidiary of Univar; the company broke itself up into two new entities, VWR and Momentum Distribution, in early 1990. VWR is now based in the eastern U.S. and Momentum stayed in Bellevue.

Employees: 200 in Seattle
1989 Revenue: $1.3 billion
1989 Profits: $19.97 million
NYSE symbol: UVX

Who's the boss

James H. Wiborg, Chairman and Chief Strategist. Was CEO of Univar 1983–86.
James W. Bernard, President and CEO.
N. Stewart Rogers, Sr. Vice President, Finance.
Nicolaas Samson, Vice President, Administration.
Albert C. McNeight, Vice President; President of Van Waters and Rogers Ltd. (Canada).
Bevan A. Cates, Regional Vice President, Western Region of Van Waters and Rogers Inc. (U.S.).

1989 Take-home pay

James Bernard: $762,000 total (all salary).
James Wiborg: $269,000 plus retirement benefits.
N. Stewart Rogers: $320,000
Nicolaas Samson: $311,000
Albert McNeight: $290,000
Bevan Cates: $238,000

The board of directors

Annual stipend: $10,000 plus $1,000–$3,000/meeting.
James Wiborg, 65. See also: VWR Corp., Paccar, Seafirst, Penwest Ltd.
James Bernard, 53. See also: VWR Corp.
H.P.H. Crijns, 59. Connection: Pakhoed Holding N.V. (Chairman of the Managing Board).
Richard E. Engebrecht, 63. Connection: VWR Corp. (President and CEO). See also: Penwest Ltd., Eldec, Puget Sound Bancorp.
Mark W. Hooper, 43. Connection: Pakhoed Development Inc. (President).
Curtis P. Lindley, 65. Connection: Penwest Ltd. (Chairman and CEO), Univar (former Exec. Vice President). See also: VWR Corp.
Robert S. Rogers, 66. Connection: Familial. Brother of N. Stewart Rogers (Univar Sr. Vice President), brother-in-law of James Wiborg (Chairman). President of Lands-West Inc. See also: VWR Corp.
Andrew V. Smith, 65. Connection: US West Communications (Exec. Vice President). See also: VWR Corp., Airborne Express, Aldus, Cascade Natural Gas, ISC Systems, US Bancorp, Unigard Insurance Group.
William K. Street, 60. Connection: The Ostrom Co. (President). Ostrom grows and distributes mushrooms, and was in Chapter 11

Bankruptcy from 1982–88. See also: VWR Corp., Penwest Ltd.
Nico van der Vorm, 62. Connection: HAL Holding N.V. (Chairman of the Executive Board).
G. Verhagen, 60. Connection: Pakhoed Holding N.V. (Member of Managing Board).
Lowry Wyatt, 72. Connection: Weyerhaeuser (Retired Sr. Vice President and Consultant). See also: VWR Corp., Penwest Ltd., Agri-Northwest, Snavely Forest Products Co. (Pittsburgh).
Stock analyst: Craig Hart at Ragen MacKenzie.

9. Microsoft Corporation

One Microsoft Way
Redmond, WA 98052-6399
936-8080

The Northwest success story of the 1980s. Bill Gates dropped out of Harvard at 19 and teamed up with high school buddy Paul Allen in 1975 to create what would become the most dominant software company in the computer industry and spawn a high-tech culture in the Northwest. In the process Gates and Allen became very rich—Gates is the youngest self-made billionaire in history. Allen left a few years ago to start another business (Asymetrix Corp. in Bellevue), but still retains 17% of Microsoft's stock, worth around $1 billion, and rejoined the board of directors in 1990. Gates himself doesn't see his big money in annual salary—his $208,000 doesn't even put him among the top-50 highest paid Northwest execs—but then he doesn't have to. He controls 37% of the company's stock, worth $1.75 billion.

Microsoft has been described as a velvet sweatshop, a great place to work if high-tech is your life. In theory there are no clocks, you wear what you want, and set your own hours—but they are expected to be long. Gates himself is often in the office late into the night and on weekends. It's an intensely creative atmosphere and has few corporate trappings; the Redmond headquarters is referred to as a "campus."

Employees: 2,500 in Seattle area, over 3,800 total
1990 Revenue: $1.18 billion (fiscal 1990 ended June 30)
1990 Profits: $279.2 million
NASDAQ symbol: MSFT

Who's the boss

William H. Gates, Chairman and CEO. Variously described as technological wunderkind, billionaire workaholic, and World's Most Eligible Bachelor (some employees at Microsoft wear T-shirts that say, "Marry Me, Bill"). Scored perfect 800 on Math SAT; mother, Mary Gates, is on UW Board of Regents.
Steven A. Ballmer, Sr. Vice President, Systems Software. (Controls 7.5% of Microsoft stock.)
Jeremy Butler, Sr. Vice President, International and OEM.
Francis J. (Frank) Gaudette, Sr. Vice President and CFO.
Scott D. Oki, Sr. Vice President, U.S. Sales/Marketing.
Michael J. Maples, Vice President, Applications Software.

1989 Take-home pay

William H. Gates: $207,628 total (salary plus bonus).
Steven Ballmer: $190,000 salary plus $95,000 bonus.
Frank Gaudette: $173,000 salary plus $69,000 bonus plus $618,000 stock conversion.
Michael Maples: $262,000 salary plus $33,000 bonus.

The board of directors

Annual stipend: Nothing, except Robert O'Brien and William Reed, who are paid $8,000/year plus $1,000/meeting.
William H. Gates, 34, Chairman of the Board.
Jon Shirley. Shirley retired as Chief Operating Officer in 1990, but is still on the board. He was replaced by Michael Hallman, former president of Boeing Computer Services. See also: Mentor Graphics Corp.

Paul Allen, 34. Connection: Original founder of Microsoft (with Gates); now heads Asymetrix Corp. See also: Portland Trailblazers basketball team (owner).
David F. Marquardt, 40. Connection: TVI Management (General Partner), a venture-capital limited partnership.
Robert D. O'Brien, 75. Connection: Paccar (Chairman, 1965–78) and Univar (Chairman 1974–83). See also: Intermec Corp., Jay Jacobs.
William G. Reed, Jr., 50. Connection: Simpson Investment Co. (Chairman), parent of Simpson Timber. See also: Seafirst, Safeco, VWR, Washington Mutual Savings Bank.
Stock analyst: Scott McAdams at Ragen MacKenzie.

10. Airborne Freight Corporation

3101 Western Ave.
Seattle, WA 98111
285-4600

Airborne Express (the company differentiates between the service, Express, and the parent company, Freight) delivered 45.9 million documents in the U.S. in 1989, 1.5 million overseas via a fleet of 42 airplanes. Impressive numbers—that manage to compete with Federal Express, the giant of the industry. Airborne's headquarters are in Seattle but its heart is in the Midwest. Like Federal, Airborne operates a centralized hub (in Wilmington, Ohio) through which all packages must pass before delivery.

Employees: 1,100 in the Seattle area, 10,000 company-wide.
1989 Revenue: $949.8 million
1989 Profits: $19 million
NYSE symbol: ABE

Who's the boss

Robert S. Cline, Chairman and CEO. Took over in 1984 from Holt Webster after serving as CFO since 1978.
Robert G. Brazier, President and COO.
Roy C. Liljebeck, Exec. Vice President and CFO.
John J. Cella, Exec. Vice President, International Division.
Kent W. Freudenberger, Exec. Vice President, Marketing.
Raymond T. Van Bruwaene, Exec. Vice President, Field Services.
Graham E. Dorland, Chairman of ABX Air subsidiary.

1989 Take-home pay

Robert Cline: $484,439 salary, $85,369 stock, $11,324 benefits, $581,132 total.
Robert Brazier: $424,000
Roy Liljebeck: $257,000
John Cella: $255,000
Kent Freudenberger: $257,000
Ray Van Bruwaene: $256,000
Graham Dorland: $256,000

The board of directors

Annual stipend: $15,000 plus $1,000/meeting.
Robert Cline, 52, Chairman of the Board. See also: Security Pacific Bank of Washington, N.C. Machinery Co.
Holt Webster, 70. Webster was Chairman and CEO of Airborne from 1968–84. Thereafter he served as a consultant to the company (paid $100,000 per year for his services), until June 1989. See also: Puget Power, Washington Mutual Savings Bank.
Robert Brazier, 52.
James E. Carey, 57. Connection: The Berkshire Bank, N.Y. (President and CEO). Former (1976–85) Exec. Vice President of Chase Manhattan Bank. See also: The Midland Co., Standby Reserve Fund, Standby Tax-Exempt Reserve Fund (both money market funds), Cowen Income and Growth Fund, Cowen Opportunity Fund (mutual funds).
James E. Gary, 69. Connection: Pacific Resources Inc. (Chairman Emeritus), an oil refinery, shipping, and gas utility holding company. Now an international business and energy consultant. See also: Washington Energy Co., Washington Natural Gas, Bancorp Hawaii, Castle and Cooke Inc.
Carroll M. Martenson, 68. Connection: Esterline Corp. (Chairman), a factory automation equipment concern. Former chairman of Criton Technologies Inc., an aerospace and electronics firm. See also: Washington Mutual Savings Bank, Precision Castparts Inc.
Harold M. Messmer, Jr., 44. Connection: Robert Half International Inc. (Chairman, CEO and President), a temporary personnel company. See also: North Carolina National Bank, Health Care Property Investors Inc.
Hiroshi Ohara, 63. Connection: Mitsui and Co., Ltd. (Exec. Managing Director), a global trading company. Airborne entered into an agreement with Mitsui in early 1990 to establish a joint venture company in Japan, to be called Airborne Express Japan.
Ancil H. Payne, 68. Connection: KING Broadcasting (Retired President and CEO). Payne led the five-state broadcasting company from 1974–87 and could turn a fine end-of-newscast editorial in his time. He now heads his own business consulting firm, Ancil H. Payne and Associates.
Richard M. Rosenberg, 59. Connection: Bank of America (President and Vice-Chairman). Former (1986–87) President and COO of Seafirst.
Andrew V. Smith, 65. Connection: US West (Exec. Vice President); was President of Pacific Northwest Bell before PNB was swallowed by US West). See also: VWR, Univar, Tektronix, U.S. Bancorp, Aldus, ISC Systems, Cascade Natural Gas, Unigard Security Insurance Co., Unigard Insurance Co. Also member of UW Board of Regents.
Stock analyst: Daniel Nelson at Ragen MacKenzie.

TEN BIG ONES

11. Alaska Air Group Inc.

19300 Pacific Highway S
Seattle, WA 98188
433-3200

Alaska has survived the post-deregulation airline wars through stealth and cunning. It keeps turning a profit (every year since 1973), dodges the takeover bids its competitors launch at each other, and quietly introduces a few more new routes every year. The Air Group includes Alaska Air Lines and Horizon Air, a small regional carrier the company bought in 1986. Alaska's reputation for service is outstanding; the Seahawks charter Alaska planes for all away games.

Employees: 6,661 (company total)
1989 Revenue: $916.5 million
1989 Profits: $42.9 million
NYSE symbol: ALK

Who's the boss

Bruce R. Kennedy. Educated at University of Alaska–Fairbanks. Took over Alaska in early 1970s from Charles "Uncle Charlie" Willis, the pioneer of the company who had nearly run it into the ground. Since then Alaska has consistently mined the West Coast air corridor for profits. Kennedy's very religious—would like to leave Alaska in next few years to try something else, possibly overseas missionary work.

Raymond J. Vecci, Exec. Vice President and CFO. (Raymond Vecci was promoted to President and CEO in September 1990.)

John F. Kelly, President and CEO of Horizon Air Industries subsidiary.

J. Ray Vingo, Vice President, Finance, CFO and Treasurer.

Steven G. Hamilton, Vice President, Legal and General Counsel, Alaska Air Group.

Marjorie E. Laws, Vice President, Corporate Affairs, Alaska Air Group.

Paul T. Nishimura, Comptroller, Alaska Air Group.

1989 Take-home pay

Bruce Kennedy: $469,000 total (all salary and incentive compensation).
Ray Vecci: $284,000
John Kelly: $184,000
J. Ray Vingo: $209,000

The board of directors

Annual stipend: $9,000 plus $750/meeting.

Bruce Kennedy, 51. Chairman of the Board. See also: Federal Reserve Board of San Francisco (Seattle Branch).

J. Ray Vingo, 51.

Raymond J. Vecci, 47.

John F. Kelly, 45.

O.F. Benecke, 71. Connection: Alaska Federal Savings and Loan (Chairman Emeritus). Former President of Alaska Airlines Inc.

William H. Clapp, 48. Connection: Matthew G. Norton Co. (President), an investment/holding company. See also: Horizon Air, Weyerhaeuser, Laird Norton Co.

Ronald F. Cosgrave, 58, Chairman Emeritus. Connection: Alaska Northwest Properties (Chairman and President). Retired Chairman and CEO of Alaska Airlines Inc.

Mary Jane Fate, 56. Connection: Baan o yeel kon Corp. (President and Exec. Director, 1981–89), an Alaska Native village corporation. Also general manager of family dental business.

Byron I. Mallott, 46. Connection: Sealaska Corp. (CEO), a regional Alaska Native corporation. See also: Alaska Permanent Fund Corp., Security Pacific Bank of Washington.

Robert L. Parker Jr., 41. Connection: Parker Drilling Co. (President and COO), a Tulsa, Oklahoma, oil and gas drilling contractor. See also: International Assoc. of Drilling Contractors, University of Texas Engineering Foundation.

Frank G. Turpin, 67. Connection: Alaska Railroad Corp. (President and CEO), a state-owned railroad. Former president (1978–85) of Alyeska Pipeline Co.; director of Exxon's research and engineering company from 1971–78.

Richard A. Wien, 54. Connection: Florcraft Inc. (Chairman and CEO), an Alaskan retail flooring company. See also: National Bank of Alaska.

Stock analysts: Peter Musser at Ragen MacKenzie, Leslie Childress at Harper, McLean and Co.

12. Puget Sound Power and Light

Puget Power Bldg.
Bellevue, WA 98009
454-6363

Puget Power is the state's largest private utility and, mainly because of the civic activity of Chairman John Ellis, is also one of the companies that make things happen—for better or worse—in Seattle. John Ellis, a 61-year-old businessman, activist, and musician (he's been known to jam with a pick-up band now and then), is one-half of the most powerful pair of brothers in the city. The other 50% is 68-year-old Jim, who was responsible for the creation of Metro, led the fight for Forward Thrust (a bond issue that led, among other things, to the building of the Kingdome), bridged I-5 with Freeway Park, and headed up the committee that built the convention center. City leaders have called Jim "the Mayor Daley of Seattle" and "the most significant man in this community ever." John is no slouch himself, having led campaigns for causes ranging from nuclear power to Bellevue parks.

Puget Power serves over 1.5 million people within a 4,500-square-mile service area that includes most of Puget Sound and part of Kittitas County.

Employees: 2,414 in the company
1989 Revenue: $887.8 million
1989 Profits: $117.7 million
NYSE symbol: PSD
Shareholder services: 462-3898
Manager shareholder services:
W.J. Fritz, 462-3208

Who's the boss

John W. Ellis, Chairman and CEO. 20 years with Puget Power, 14 as CEO.

Richard R. Sonstelie, President and CFO.

Neil L. McReynolds, Sr. Vice President, Corporate Relations.

Robert V. Myers, Sr. Vice President, Operations.

Melvyn M. Ryan, Sr. Vice President, Administration and Subsidiaries.

1989 Take-home pay

John Ellis: $371,000 total ($285K salary, $86K bonus).

Richard Sonstelie: $204,000 ($162K salary, $42K bonus).

Robert Myers: $148,000 ($121K salary, $27K bonus).

Melvyn Ryan: $134,000 ($111K salary, $23K bonus).

Neil McReynolds: $128,000 ($103K salary, $25K bonus).

The board of directors

Annual stipend: $10,000 plus $700/meeting.

John Ellis, 61, Chairman of the Board. See also: Safeco, Washington Mutual Savings Bank, Flow-Mole Corp., Associated Electric and Gas Insurance Services.

Richard R. Sonstelie, 44. See also: First Interstate Bank of Washington.

Douglas P. Beighle, 57. Connection: Boeing (Sr. Vice President and Secretary). See also: Washington Mutual Savings Bank, Peabody Holding Co.

Charles W. Bingham, 56. Connection: Weyerhaeuser (Exec. Vice President).

John H. Dunkak III, 67. Connection: Georgia Pacific (former Sr. Vice President, Western Division, 1982–87). See also: Horizon Bank (Bellingham, Wash.).

John D. Durbin, 54. Connection: Hostar Inc., a hotel equipment company (President and CEO). Also General Partner of John Durbin and Associates, an industrial real estate concern.

Daniel J. (Dan) Evans, 64. Connection: politics. U.S. Senator (1983–89), Washington State Governor (1965–77), and President of the Evergreen State College (1977–83). Retired from Senate in 1989 (Slade Gorton won his seat); now mainly visible as commentator for KIRO. See also: Washington Mutual Savings Bank; McCaw Cellular Communications; Kaiser Family Foundation; Carnegie Commission on Science, Technology, and Government.

Nancy L. Jacob, 47. Connection: Academia and investing. Ms. Jacob is a finance and business professor at UW (served as Dean of UW graduate business school 1981–88) and is managing director of Capital Trust Co. See also: Security Pacific Bank Washington.

Holt W. Webster, 70. Connection: Airborne Freight Corp. (former Chairman and CEO, now a member of the board of directors). See also: Washington Mutual Savings Bank.

R. Kirk Wilson, 51. Connection: Thrifty Foods Inc. (President and CEO). See also: Valley Bank (Mount Vernon, Wash.).

Stock analyst: Lesa Sroufe at Ragen MacKenzie.

13. McCaw Cellular Communications Inc.

5400 Carillon Point
Kirkland, WA 98033
827-4500

How do you amass a fortune that lands you and your brothers in the Forbes 400 while operating a company that has yet to turn a profit? Ask Craig McCaw—he's the genius behind McCaw Cellular, the nation's largest cellular phone company that realized a loss of $163 million on revenues of $504 million in 1989. The answer seems to lie in soothing your stock- and bondholders, who are holding onto their shares and swallowing the red ink (mostly huge investments in cellular equipment and systems) in the hope of cashing in when the company really booms years down the road. Or by not waiting at all—Craig McCaw was the highest paid corporate executive in America last year, but only because he exercised stock options worth $53.6 million, which the company had paid him between 1983 and 1986. His actual "salary" was only $289,000.

Craig and his three brothers (John Jr., Bruce, and Keith—all directors of McCaw Cellular) began with the small communications company their father John E. left them when he died in 1969. Craig took over the company and ran it while still an undergrad at Stanford. McCaw Cellular was worth $27 million in 1980; in 1990 it was worth $4.6 billion. McCaw himself now owns $400 million (9.8%) of the company's stock. The other three split $825 million worth.

Employees: About 100 in Seattle area
1989 Revenue: $504.1 million
1989 Profits: –$163.3 million (loss)
NASDAQ symbol: MCAWA

Who's the boss

Craig O. McCaw, Chairman and CEO. Intensely private, as are his brothers. Quoted in *Forbes*: "We are not public figures, and we don't intend to be."

Wayne M. Perry, Vice-Chairman.

John W. Stanton, Vice-Chairman.

Paul H. Stolz, Vice-Chairman, Regulatory Affairs. Former Ernst and Young consultant, Stoltz came aboard in early 1990 to run LIN Broadcasting, which McCaw acquired after a protracted takeover battle.

Harold S. Eastman, President.

John H. Chapple, Exec. Vice President, Operations.

Mark R. Hamilton, Exec. Vice President and Secretary.

John E. McCaw, Jr., Exec. Vice President, Acquisitions.

Rufus W. Lumry, Exec. Vice President and CFO. Was a Sr. Vice President at Seafirst prior to joining McCaw in 1982.

1989 Take-home pay

Craig McCaw: $288,756 salary, $53,655,000 stock, $0 benefits, $53.944 million total.
Wayne Perry: $274,000
Harold S. Eastman: $731,000 ($331K salary, $400K signing bonus).
Rufus Lumry: $272,000
John McCaw Jr.: $283,000

The board of directors

Annual stipend: $30,000 (raised from $2,000/meeting in 1988).
Craig McCaw, 40. Chairman of the Board. See also: President's National Security Telecommunications Advisory Committee.
John W. Stanton, 34, Vice-Chairman of the Board. Former Exec. Vice President (1983–88) with McCaw. Now Chairman of Stanton Communications Inc. See also: Interpoint Corp.
Wayne M. Perry, 40.
Harold S. Eastman, 51.
Rufus Lumry, 43.
John McCaw Jr., 39. See also: Cellular Telecommunications Industry Association.
Harold W. Andersen, 66. Connection: *Omaha World-Herald* (Publisher, Chairman and CEO). See also: *Raleigh News and Observer*, The Williams Companies, Great Lake Forest Products, Morrison Knudsen Corp.
Malcolm Argent, 54. Connection: British Telecommunications (BT) (Secretary). BT purchased a 20% interest in McCaw in early 1989.
Bruce Bond, 43. Connection: British Telecommunications (Strategist). Prior to joining BT in 1990, Bond was head of strategic planning for US West.
David Dey, 52. Connection: British Telecommunications (BT). BT eased some of McCaw Cellular's debt burden in 1989 by purchasing 20% of the company. Dey formerly worked (1960–85) in senior management at IBM.
Daniel J. (Dan) Evans, 64. Connection: Politics. U.S. Senator (1983–89), Washington State Governor (1965–77), and President of the Evergreen State College (1977–83). Retired from Senate in 1989 (Slade Gorton won his seat); now mainly visible as commentator for KIRO. See also: Puget Power, Washington Mutual Savings Bank; Carnegie Commission on Government, Science, and Technology; Kaiser Family Foundation.
John P. Giuggio, 59. Connection: Affiliated Publications Inc. (API) (President and COO).
Robert A. Lawrence, 63. Connection: Saltonstall and Co. (Partner), a private investment firm. See also: Affiliated Publications Inc. (API), various mutual funds operated under MetLife.
John C. Malone, 48. Connection: Tele-Communications Inc. (President and CEO). See also: Turner Broadcasting Systems, Black Entertainment Television (BET), Bank of New York, United Artists, WestMarc Communications, National Cable Television Association, Tele-Communications Inc.
Bruce R. McCaw, 43. Connection: Familial, and Forbes Westar Inc. (Chairman). Has held various positions with the family business since 1969.
Keith W. McCaw, 36. Connection: Familial. Has held various positions with the family business since 1969.
Barry D. Romeril, 46. Connection: British Telecommunications (Group Finance Director).
William O. Taylor, 57. Connection: Affiliated Publications Inc. (API) and Globe Newspaper Co. (Chairman and CEO of both), an API subsidiary. Publisher of the *Boston Globe*.

14. Puget Sound Bancorp

1119 Pacific Ave.
P.O. Box 11500
Tacoma, WA 98411-5500
593-3600

It's not a Seattle-based company and it's not even among the top three Puget Sound banks in terms of assets, but it is the only remaining major independent bank in town (as they are mighty quick to remind you in their advertisements). Bank of America bought Seafirst, Security Pacific took over Rainier Bank, and U.S. Bancorp swallowed up People's Bank. That leaves William Philip's Puget Sound Bancorp as the largest independent bank in the state, though staying single hasn't been easy. So far Philips has held off the charging California banks that ate up his competition, but nobody knows how long he'll be able to hold out.

The company operates Puget Sound Bank's 82 branches in the state, and also does business as Bellingham National Bank (12 branches) and San Juan County Bank (3 branches).

Employees: 2,456 (statewide)
1989 Revenue: $458 million
1989 Profits: $27.9 million
NASDAQ symbol: PSNB

Who's the boss

William Warren Philip, Chairman and CEO. Former truck driver who now runs a bank and collects Western art. Born in Tacoma, attended University of Washington. 39 years with the company, 18 as CEO.
Roy A. Henderson, President and COO
Richard B. Odlin, Sr. Vice President, Secretary and Director
Don G. Vandenheuvel, Exec. Vice President and CFO
Lazarus S. Politakis, Exec. Vice President
Gary C. Lange, Exec. Vice President
W. Ray Highsmith Jr., Exec. Vice President

1989 Take-home pay

W.W. Philip: $425,000 salary, $36,000 stock, $16,169 benefits, $477,169 total.
Roy Henderson: $285,000
Don Vandenheuvel: $210,000
Lazarus Politakis: $210,000

Gary Lange: $185,000
W. Ray Highsmith Jr.: $125,000 (1988).

The board of directors

Annual stipend: $12,000 plus $750/meeting.
W.W. Philip, 63, Chairman of the Board.
Roy A. Henderson, 47.
Richard B. Odlin, 55.
Robert E. Bayley, 63. Connection: Robert E. Bayley Construction (Chairman).
Richard J. Boyle, 55. Connection: Honeywell (Vice President, Marketing and Business Development).
Samuel H. Brown, 71. Personal investor.
John W. Creighton Jr., 57. Connection: Weyerhaeuser (President). See also: Mortgage Investments Plus, Quality Food Centers.
John C. Dimmer, 61. Connection: First Management Corp. (President), an investment firm.
Richard E. Engebrecht, 63. Connection: VWR (President and CEO). See also: Univar, Penwest Ltd., Eldec Corp.
Frederick M. Goldberg, 50. Connection: Goldberg Investment (Managing Partner). Prior to 1987, President of Goldberg Furniture Co.
Charles R. Hogan, 52. Connection: Puget Sound Marketing Co. (Exec. Vice President).
George H. Hutchings, 67. Personal investor.
Charles H. Hyde III, 37. Connection: Nawamucks Inc. retail grocery (President).
John C. Long, 69. Personal investor. See also: American Savings Financial Corp.
Robert B. McMillen, 54. Connection: Totem Ocean Trailer Express (President and CEO), a maritime transport company.
W.H. Meadowcraft, 61. Connection: Weyerhaeuser (Assistant to CEO George Weyerhaeuser).
Frank J. Roberts, 71. Connection: Jones and Roberts Co. (President), general contractors.
Fred C. Shanaman, Jr., 56. Connection: Rainier Management and Marketing Corp. (President).
Rex M. Walker, 60. Attorney/Orchardist.
Donald K. Weaver, Jr., 60. Connection: Crescent Manufacturing Co. (Former President and CEO).

15. Westmark International Inc.

Columbia Center, Suite 6800
701 Fifth Ave.
Seattle, WA 98104-7001
682-6800

A medical technology manufacturer that keeps a low profile in Seattle. The company was originally a subsidiary of the Squibb Corporation; Squibb spun off Westmark in 1986. The company operates two businesses, SpaceLabs and Advanced Technology Laboratories (ATL). SpaceLabs is a patient monitoring and clinical information company; their main product line is the PCMS (Patient Care Management System). A typical piece of PCMS equipment is the screen that records a patient's heartbeat as pulsing lines and blips. ATL manufactures diagnostic ultrasound products.

Employees: 3,227 company total
1989 Revenue: $438.8 million
1989 Profits: $19.7 million
NASDAQ symbol: WMRK

Who's the boss

Dennis C. Fill, Chairman, CEO and President. A loyal subject of the Queen by birth, Fill attended Ealing College, the Institute of Export and Borough Polytechnic, and served in the Royal Air Force. He is a lifetime Squibb man who joined the company through its overseas arm, Olin Mathieson Chemical Corp., in London in 1958. Fill was President and COO of the pharmaceutical giant from 1978 until Westmark was sent on its own way in 1986.
Carl A. Lombardi, Group Vice President of Westmark and President of SpaceLabs.
Allen W. Guisinger, Group Vice President of Westmark and President of ATL.
Julie A. Brooks, Vice President, Secretary and General Counsel.
Robert T. deGavre, CFO, Treasurer and Sr. Vice President.

1989 Take-home pay

Dennis Fill: $818,426 salary, $0 stock, $905,664 benefits (includes $100,000 apartment and $800,000 performance award), $1.724 million total.
Carl Lombardi: $405,000
Eugene Larson*: $377,000
Julie Brooks: $180,000
Robert deGavre: $338,000
* Larson resigned at end of 1989; he was replaced by Allen Guisinger.

The board of directors

Annual stipend: $20,000 plus $500/meeting.
Dennis Fill, 60. Chairman of the Board. See also: Morton International (formerly Morton Thiokol), Household International Inc.
Carl Lombardi, 46. See also: First Medical Devices Corp., Phamis Inc., Loredan Biomedical Inc., Scribner Kidney Center.
Allen Guisinger, 46. See also: Info-Systems Inc.
Ralph M. Barford, 60. Connection: Valleydene Corp. Ltd. (President), an investment company. Also Chairman of GSW Inc., a manufacturer of consumer products, and Camco Inc., an appliance manufacturer. See also: Bank of Montreal, Bell Canada Enterprises, Hollinger Inc., Molson Companies Ltd., Morton International, Union Enterprises Ltd., Canadian-American Committee, Toronto Hospital, Canadian Institute for Advanced Research.
Harvey Feigenbaum, M.D., 56. Connection: Indiana University Medical Center (Distinguished Professor). Also editor of the *Journal of American Society of Echocardiography*. See also: Editorial boards of *American Heart Journal, American Journal*

of Cardiology, American Journal of Medicine.

Frank J. Pizzitola, 66. Connection: Lazard Freres and Co. (General Partner), a New York–based investment bank. See also: General Waterworks, Lyonnaise des Eaux (Paris), Aqua-Chem, Sipex, GWC Corp.

Harry Woolf, Ph.D., 66. Connection: Professor and former Director of The Institute for Advanced Study (Princeton, New Jersey), Trustee of the Rockefeller Foundation. See also: Alexander Brown Mutual Funds, Merrill Lynch Open-End Investment Funds—Cluster C, Inference Corp., I-STAT Inc.

Stock analyst: Peter Musser at Ragen MacKenzie.

16. Washington Energy Company

815 Mercer St.
Seattle, WA 98109
622-6767

Washington Energy is better known through its largest subsidiary, Washington Natural Gas, which supplies 61 cities and 324,000 customers in the Puget Sound region with gas energy. The parent corporation is also involved in other energy ventures, including Thermal Exploration Inc., an oil and gas exploration and production company operating since 1974. Also Thermal Efficiency Inc., which markets energy conservation and alternative-energy products, and Thermal (yes, they do seem to be fond of that term) Energy Inc., which holds leases and other rights to mine low-sulphur coal in eastern Montana.

Employees: 1,200
1989 Revenue: $366.5 million
1989 Profits: $23.6 million
NASDAQ symbol: WECO

Who's the boss

James A. Thorpe, Chairman and CEO since 1980.

Robert R. Golliver, President and COO since 1980.

Robert J. Tomlinson, Sr. Vice President, Legal, and Secretary.

Paul A. Hoglund, Sr. Vice President, Operations.

*James W. Gustafson, Sr. Vice President.

Charles H. Petek, Sr. Vice President, Finance.

**H.B. Simpson, Vice President, Chief Accounting Officer.

**James P. Torgerson, Sr. Vice President, Planning and Development.

*Gustafson was scheduled to become Sr. Vice President, Operations upon Paul Hoglund's retirement in August 1990.

**Simpson and Torgerson split the duties of Sr. Vice President, Finance upon Charles Petek's retirement in 1990.

1989 Take-home pay

James Thorpe: $399,320 salary, $351 stock, $26,550 benefits, $426,221 total.
Robert Golliver: $231,000
Paul Hoglund: $143,000
Charles Petek: $130,000
Robert Tomlinson: $126,000

The board of directors

Annual stipend: $8,000 plus $600/meeting.

James Thorpe, 60. Chairman of the Board. See also: Seafirst.

Robert Golliver, 54.

Robert F. Bailey, 57. Connection: Alta Energy Co. (President and Chairman), a Midland, Texas, oil and gas drilling and production company. See also: United Bank.

Donald J. Covey, 61. Connection: Unico Properties Inc. (President and CEO), which manages several major office buildings in downtown Seattle.

James E. Gary, 68, Chairman Emeritus. Connection: Pacific Resources Inc. (Former Chairman), a diversified energy company. See also: Airborne Freight, Bancorp Hawaii, Castle and Cooke.

Stanley M. Little, Jr., 68. Connection: Boeing. Little was Vice President of Industrial and Public Relations for Boeing from 1972–87. Little was also a director of Westside Federal Savings and Loan for 11 years until the Seattle S&L was effectively closed down in 1985 by a Cease and Desist Order from the Federal Home Loan Bank Board resulting from, as the proxy puts it, "certain lending activities and capital requirements."

Tomio Moriguchi, 53. Connection: Uwajimaya Inc. (President), a Seattle-based import-export company. See also: Seafirst.

Sally G. Narodick, 44. Connection: Edmark Corp. (Chairman and CEO), a Bellevue-based publisher of print and software educational materials. Founder and partner in Narodick, Ross and Associates consulting firm (1987–89). Previously Sr. Vice President of retail services at Seafirst.

Peggy Locke Newman, 65. Connection: Fisher Properties Inc. (Vice President), real estate investment. See also: Fisher Companies Inc. (Note: Fisher Broadcasting, a subsidiary, has owned KOMO-TV and radio since 1982.)

17. Quality Food Centers (QFC)

10112 NE 10th St.
Bellevue, WA 98004
455-3761

The largest independent supermarket chain in the state, QFC operates 25 stores in the Seattle/King County area. The 34-year-old business has a reputation for great service in the grocery game. Lately it's been going after the upscale shopper, upgrading its departments to compete with competitors like the yuppified Larry's Market. The only major supermarket to avoid labor strife in 1989, QFC settled with the union and attracted flocks of new customers who wouldn't cross the picket lines at Safeway and Albertson's.

QFC was founded in 1955 by L.H. (Vern) Fortin and remained in the Fortin family until 1986, when a private investment firm (Sloan Adkins and Co.) headed by now-Chairman Stuart Sloan bought the company.

Employees: 1,800
1989 Revenue: $318.7 million
1989 Profits: $12.9 million
NASDAQ symbol: QFCI

Who's the boss

Stuart M. Sloan, Chairman. Half of the Sloan Adkins and Co. that bought QFC in 1986. Prior to that, served as President of Schuck's Auto Supply. Let Jack Croco take over the CEO's spot in 1987. Sloan's latest venture is with Egghead Discount Software, where he was President and CEO before taking over as Chairman of the troubled company in January 1990. Currently owns 59% of QFC's stock.

Jack Croco, Chairman and CEO. Been in the grocery game all his life, starting with Albertson's in 1942 as a student-employee. Joined QFC in 1960, been with them ever since.

Dan Kourkoumelis, President and COO.

Marc W. Evanger, Vice President, CFO and Secretary-Treasurer.

1989 Take-home pay

Jack Croco: $520,000 salary, $0 stock, $38,796 benefits, $558,796 total.

Stuart Sloan: $0 (Sloan receives no salary; however, Sloan Capital Co., controlled by Sloan, receives a management fee of not greater than 0.2% of QFC's revenues. That equalled $463,000 in 1988, $637,000 in 1989.)

Dan Kourkoumelis: $281,000

Marc Evanger: $196,000

The board of directors

Annual stipend: $5,000 plus $500/meeting.

Stuart Sloan, 46, Chairman of the Board. See also: Egghead, Security Pacific Bank of Washington.

Jack Croco, 64. See also: Western Association of Food Chains.

John W. Creighton, Jr., 57. Connection: Weyerhaeuser (President). See also: Puget Sound Bancorp, Mortgage Investments Plus, Washington Energy Co.

Fred B. McLaren, 55. Connection: Hughes Markets Inc. (President), a Los Angeles–based supermarket chain. See also: Western Association of Food Chains, Food Marketing Institute.

Ronald A. Weinstein, 48. Connection: Sloan Capital Companies (a principal with the firm); also Exec. Vice President of Egghead Inc. and Chairman of B&B Auto Parts. See also: Egghead, Triple A Specialties, Movietel Inc.

HEARD ON THE STREET

"In reference to Seattle's growth and investment potential: "We analogize this to a car beginning to accelerate down an empty boulevard as the lights ahead synchronously turn green. The driver knows that eventually the lights will turn back to red, but there is plenty of ground to cover until then."

Seattle Real Estate Market, Salomon Brothers report by Robert E. Hopkins, Jill S. Krutick, Sandon J. Goldberg

18. Expeditors International

19119 16th Ave. S
Seattle, WA 98188
246-3711

Expeditors is in the international trade game; the company transports merchandise between countries as an airfreight forwarder and consolidator and customhouse broker. It's not a package delivery service: Need a 20-lb. delivery to Omaha, see Airborne. Need a 20-ton cargo load shipped to Hong Kong, see Expeditors.

Employees: 300
1989 Revenue: $193.6 million
1989 Profits: $9.3 million
NASDAQ symbol: EXPD

Who's the boss

Peter J. Rose, President and CEO.

Kevin M. Walsh, Sr. Vice President.

Gary E. Fowler, CFO, Secretary and Treasurer.

Robert J. Chiarito, Vice President, National Accounts.

Glenn M. Alger, Vice President and Regional Manager.

James L.K. Wang, Far East Regional Manager.

1989 Take-home pay

Peter Rose: $390,251 salary, $0 stock, $750 plus company car and other benefits, $391,001 total.

Kevin Walsh: $377,000

Robert Chiarito: $258,000

Glenn Alger: $199,000
Gary Fowler: $199,000

The board of directors
Annual stipend: $5,000 plus $500/meeting.
Peter Rose, 47.
Kevin Walsh, 39.
James Wang, 41.
James J. Casey, 57. Connection: Avia Group International (Exec. Vice President 1987–89). Avia, a sportswear retailer, is a subsidiary of Reebok. Formerly (1978–85) with Eddie Bauer Inc.
Dr. John B. Cheung, 46. Connection: FlowDril Corp. and Flow Research Inc. (President of both), research and development firms.
David L. Mitchell, 55. Connection: Match Inc. (Chairman and CEO), an import/export consulting firm. Former (1987–88) Chairman and CEO of National 60-Minute Tune Inc.
Jack R. Peterson, 47. Connection: Business Environments Inc. (President and CEO), an interior design company. Former (1981–86) President and COO of a local Anheuser Busch distributor (Bay Distributors).
Stock analyst: Daniel Nelson at Ragen MacKenzie.

19. Cascade Natural Gas Corporation

222 Fairview Ave. N
Seattle, WA 98109
624-3900

Cascade Natural Gas supplies gas energy to 99,000 customers in 86 communities in Washington and Oregon. Comparable figures for competitor Washington Natural Gas, the company with the big blue neon flame atop its building: 305,000 customers in 61 cities. Washington Natural Gas focuses on the most populous areas (Snohomish, King, Thurston, and Pierce counties), while Cascade focuses on the outer regions, places like Bellingham, Bremerton, Wenatchee, and the Tri-Cities.

Employees: 443 company total
1989 Revenues: $174.5 million
1989 Profits: $8.5 million
NYSE symbol: CGL

Who's the boss
Melvin C. Clapp, Chairman and CEO. Took over the top spot in late 1988 from O. Marshall Jones, who had run the company since 1958. Served as Exec. Vice President, 1981–88.
W. Brian Matsuyama, President. UW and Harvard Law School grad, served as counsel to Cascade (through firm of Jones Grey and Bayley) for 11 years prior to joining company in 1987.
Donald E. Bennett, Exec. Vice President and CFO.
Jon T. Stoltz, Vice President, Gas Supply, Rates and Special Studies.
Ralph E. Boyd, Vice President and COO.

1989 Take-home pay
Melvin Clapp: $151,254 salary, $0 stock, $5,000 benefits (director's fee), $156,254 total.
Brian Matsuyama: $123,000
Donald Bennett: $105,000
Jon Stoltz: $87,000
Ralph Boyd: $86,000

The board of directors
Annual stipend: $5,000 plus $500/meeting.
Melvin Clapp, 56, Chairman of the Board.
Brian Matsuyama, 43.
Donald Bennett, 57.
Carl Burnham Jr., 50. Connection: Law firm of Yturri, Rose, Burnham, Ebert and Bentz of Ontario, Oregon (Partner), Counsel for the corporation.
Richard B. Hooper, 73. Connection: R.B. Hooper and Co. (President), investment advisors. Retired Counsel to law firm Stoel Rives Boley Jones & Grey. See also: John Fluke Manufacturing Co.
Howard L. Hubbard, 57. Connection: Washington Federal Savings Bank (President) in Hillsboro, Oregon.
Brooks G. Ragen, 56. Connection: Ragen MacKenzie Inc. (President and CEO), a Seattle-based investment bank.
Andrew V. Smith, 65. Connection: US West (Exec. Vice President). See also: Univar, VWR, Airborne Freight, U.S. Bancorp, Aldus, Tektronix Inc.
Mary A. Williams, 55. Connection: Consultant to the company since 1983. Prior to that she was Vice President of Seattle Trust and Savings Bank.

The Corporate Bigtimers used to hang out at the Four-10, but since its demise it's been difficult for them to find a new watering hole. But just in the nick of time, Vic and Mick's Nine-10 came along (under the First Interstate offices) and once more the suit-set has a place to call home—except that the word is it's a little too open and not private enough for the big deals.
Stockbrokers don't mingle—they're mostly to be found at the Metropolitan Grill.
The big change: Heavy drinking is no longer cool—the baby boomers are on diets and on the wagon. After all, they're now going home to babies of their own.

20. Ackerley Communications Inc.

800 Fifth Ave., Suite 3770
Seattle, WA 98104
624-2888

Barry Ackerley is one of the shrewdest, most successful businessmen in town. In 1990 he became one of the most loathed (or admired, depending on your bent), mainly because of his plan to have the taxpayers—at least partially—build his Seattle SuperSonics basketball team a new arena. If the taxpayers wouldn't play, he said, he'd take his marbles—er, ah, team—and leave town. Ackerley's communications empire includes the Sonics, billboards across the country, and 11 television and radio stations including, locally, KVOS-TV in Bellingham and KJR-radio in Seattle. Ackerley's strategy: to synergize the business by promoting the Sonics on his billboards and broadcasting their games on KJR. The empire is a family affair: wife Ginger heads the company's corporate-giving department, and kids Bill (29) and Kim (26) work full-time for the company.

Employees: 1,000
1989 Revenue: $153.5 million
1989 Profits: –$7.37 million (loss)*
*Ackerley usually posts a loss every year because his profits are pumped back into the company via new acquisitions and debt service.

Who's the boss

Barry A. Ackerley, Chairman and CEO. Iowa native, parents victims of the Depression, pulled self up by bootstraps, and commands $300 million empire. Ackerley started as an ad salesman for *Better Homes and Gardens*, eventually began collecting billboard companies, and grew and grew and grew.
Donald E. Carter, President and COO.
Denis M. Curley, Sr. Vice President and CFO.

1989 Take-home pay

Barry Ackerley: $308,000 total
Donald Carter: $215,000
Denis Curley: $155,000

The board of directors

Annual stipend: Expenses only.
Barry Ackerley, 56.
John A. Canning, Jr., 45. Connection: First Chicago Investment Corp. and First Capital Corp. of Chicago (President), venture capital firms. Over the last three years Ackerley Communications has borrowed $72.6 million from First National Bank of Chicago, a sister company of Canning's First Chicago Investment Corp. See also: Bayou Steel Corp., All Star Inns.
Michel C. Thielen, 55. Connection: Mike Thielen and Associates (President), an advertising agency. See also: Airport Wings Inc. (an airport operations company).

RESOURCE LIST

Daily Journal of Commerce
Box 11050
Seattle, WA 98111
622-8272

Marple's Business Newsletter
911 Western Ave., Suite 509
Seattle, WA 98104
622-0155
Michael Parks does a great job with this insiders' look at biz.

Pacific Northwest Executive
132 Mackenzie Hall
University of Washington
Seattle, WA 98195
543-1819
The quarterly mag is funded by Seafirst Bank for the Business Administration School at UW.

Puget Sound Business Journal
101 Yesler Way
Seattle, WA 98104
583-0701
This business weekly puts out an annual *Book of Lists*, ranking the "biggest, richest, fastest-growing players on the local business scene."

Seattle Public Library
Securities and Company Information Desk
Downtown Library, Second Floor
1000 Fourth Ave.
Seattle, WA 98104
386-4650
Mon.– Fri., 1–5 p.m.
The Seattle Public Library has a special Securities and Company Information Desk where you can get stock and bond quotations, find out about government securities, get info on particular companies, see annual reports, get the latest foreign exchange rate, and more.

Washington CEO
2505 Second Ave., Suite 602
Seattle, WA 98121-1426
441-8325
Business magazine for CEOs.

CHAPTER

12

ETHNICITY: DIVERSITY AT WORK

COMMUNITIES

NAMES TO KNOW

LANGUAGES

ORGANIZATIONS

SEGREGATION

ISSUES

ETHNIC EVENTS

CHURCHES

RESOURCES

HARMONY

Ever heard of the city's Eritrean community? Or know where they're from? (Extra points if you can name the correct hemisphere. The Eritreans are from northern Africa.) Or how about Seattle's Gypsy community—did you know there's even a Gypsy school in the Seattle School District? It's difficult to count the ethnic communities in Seattle; there are almost as many as there are countries of the world, and getting to know them makes for an excellent firsthand geography lesson.

The Ethnic Heritage Council has 320 member organizations, primarily based in the Seattle area, and most of them have at least one annual celebration to which the rest of the city is invited. Some groups have museums—the Nordic Heritage Museum and Wing Luke Memorial Museum, for example—and all have individuals who have made their presence felt in politics, the arts, or social services.

With all that going for it, you'd think Seattle would be among the most progressive cities in accommodating ethnic cultures, but it is actually one of the most segregated cities in the nation in terms of housing distribution for its communities of color. Consider this:

The Central Area and southeast Seattle still house 72% of the city's African American population.

While the city's total unemployment rate is 4.1%, unemployment in the black community is approximately 6%. (Statewide, African American unemployment is 9.5%.)

In the American Indian community, unemployment is even higher: 8%.

Seattle's ethnic diversity includes minorities of color—African Americans, American Indians, and Asians—as well as residents who have held on to the culture of their ancestors—the "Ya, y'betcha" Scandinavians of Ballard or the British who belong to Society of Rusting Tardis, for example.

The best resource for anything ethnic is the Ethnic Heritage Council. The council has a directory, called *Contact*, of 1,500 ethnic organizations in Washington and publishes a monthly newspaper, *Northwest Ethnic News*, which includes a detailed calendar of events plus newsy items about people and social services in Seattle's different communities. The council sponsors events (WorldFest, Fourth of July Naturalization Ceremony), scholarships, and awards.

Ethnic Heritage Council
3123 Eastlake Ave. E
Seattle, WA 98102
726-0357
Council board president: Alma Plancich
Executive director: Sandy Bradley

For resettlement help, start with the International Rescue Committee, the local office of a worldwide organization originally founded to help people escape the Nazis. The committee has resettled thousands of refugees from Southeast Asia, Central America, and Eastern Europe in the U.S. The group offers temporary housing assistance and other aid.

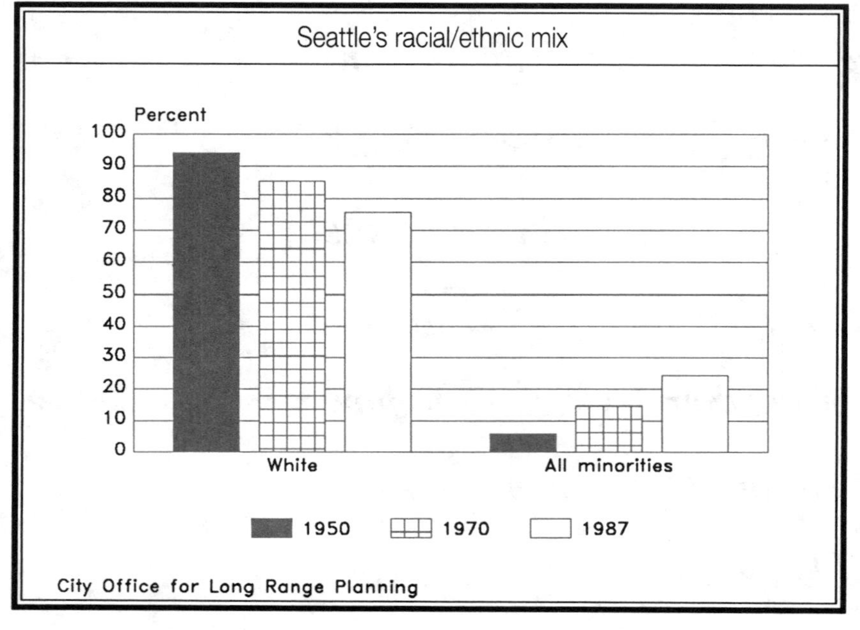

International Rescue Committee
318 First Ave. S, Room 210
Seattle, WA 98104
623-2105

The Ethnic Mix (1987)

Total city population: 491,302
African American: 49,101
Asian/Pacific Islander: 45,132
Latino/Chicano/Mexicano: 16,978
American Indian: 6,775

Unemployment (1987)

Total unemployment in city: 18,006
White: 12,281
African American: 2,891
Asian/Pacific Islander: 1,421
Latino/Chicano/Mexicano: 895
American Indian: 518
Source: Seattle Human Rights Dept.

THE AFRICAN AMERICAN COMMUNITY

There's a movement afoot in Seattle's heretofore mellow African American community aimed at putting blacks in the boardrooms, shaking up the city's biggest corporations, integrating, as one community leader puts it, "the suites."

Economic injustice is the issue of the 1990s. It was no accident that the African American community gave Boeing the Bull Connor Anti–African American Community Service Award early in 1990. The "award" was bestowed because Boeing sold planes to South Africa and because historically there have been no blacks on its board of directors.

Boeing is the first target; Seattle's black community is gathering data on other corporations and their records of promoting blacks.

Why all the activity in a city that has never experienced the kind of riots and radical movements known elsewhere? Because black leaders would like to make Seattle a model of economic development for the rest of the nation. If there is to be true integration of African Americans in society, they say, it will happen first in Seattle, a literate city with a population open to the idea of inclusion. After all, affirmative action began in Washington State and Seattle recently elected a black mayor. Then too, there's an openness within the black community here to develop new strategies—an openness that doesn't exist elsewhere.

That's not to say that Seattle is integrated. The black population in Seattle is small compared with other cities, and it's not unusual to find white Seattleites who don't know any blacks. The first thing a black visitor to the city wants to know is where the blacks are.

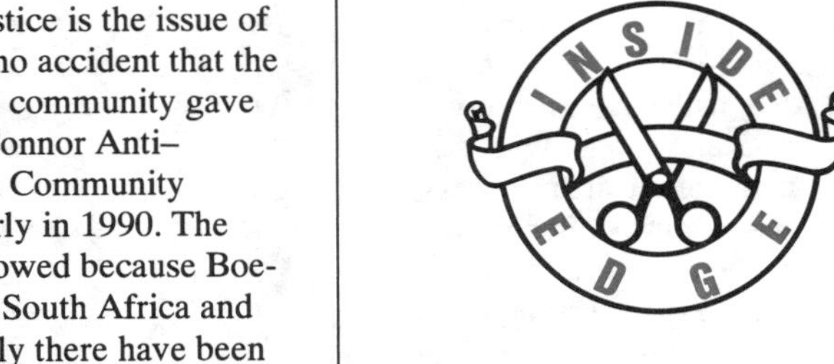

African American community leaders say blacks in Seattle should rely less on government institutions for help, and should go to groups that empower them so they won't become dependent on the system.

Neither side is going out of its way to get to know the other. (Some are, though. No one's counting, but some in the city's black community say there are more interracial relationships in Seattle than in most other cities.) There's not necessarily discrimination on a one-to-one basis; it's in the institutions where it's prevalent. Private schools have low minority populations whereas public schools have high ones.

And boardrooms, well, they're white (and mostly male).

African American leaders also predict the 1990s will be a time of self-criticism and self-help for the black community, but self-help combined with demands for less discrimination in the city's institutions. A potential gang confrontation in the late eighties, for example, resulted in the formation of a role model group for black male youths. And the low scholastic achievement of black kids resulted in the formation of a black coalition that demanded that the school district do more to increase the test scores.

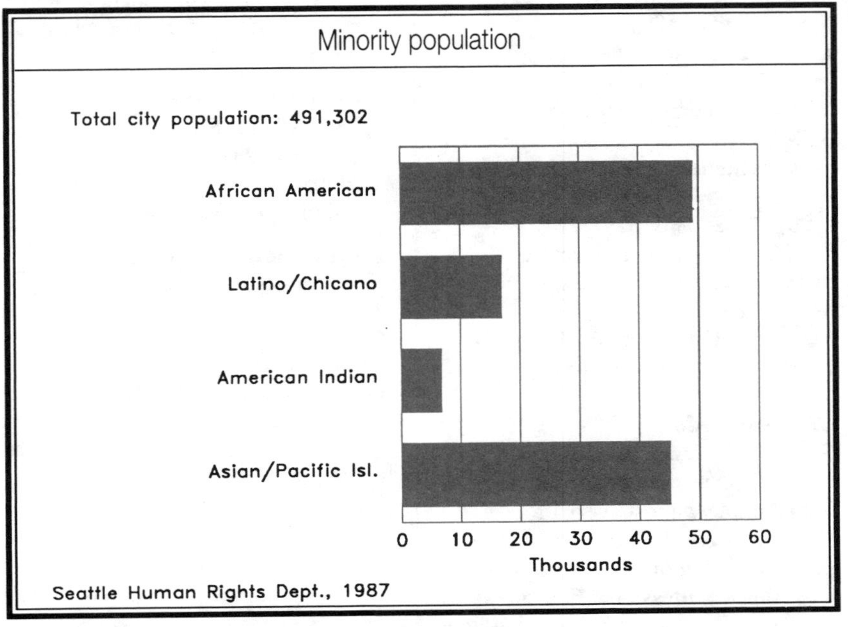

Another push is to develop a sense of community again in the Central Area, which has been ravaged by drugs and gangs. With the high crime rate of the area, successful African Americans often move out, leaving the poorer residents behind. Blacks expect a resurgence of commitment between the middle-class blacks and the lower-class blacks. That commitment calls for families to stick it out in the community, supporting local businesses, providing role models, and becoming involved in African American issues.

For survival, jobs are the key. At the Central Area Motivation Program (CAMP) employment experts assess job seekers' skills and find out what kinds of jobs they'd like—and they often recommend training or schooling. CAMP works with 125 companies who want black applicants. At any one time, CAMP has a pool of 50 to 100 applicants for jobs.

True success will go to African Americans who own their own businesses or become managers or entrepreneurs, says one Seattle community leader.

HEARD ON THE STREET

"There is a lot of discontent in the black community. People say Seattle is the most liveable city, but it's not the most liveable to blacks. They are too poor."

Reverend Zachary Bruce, CAMP

Names to know

Dee Anderson, director, Operation Emergency Center, 725-2100.
Kikora Dorsey, director, Head Start for Seattle Public Schools, activist, 281-6890.
George Fleming, Washington State Senator, 721-4095.
Larry Gossett, executive director, Central Area Motivation Program and president, Washington State Rainbow Coalition, 329-4111.
Reverend Robert Jeffrey, organizer, Black Dollar Days Task Force, 323-4212.
James Kelly, member, Black Community Coalition and State Commission on African American Affairs, 721-4176.
Reverend Dr. Samuel McKinney, pastor, Mt. Zion Baptist Church and community leader, 322-6500.
Michael Preston, Seattle School Board (also executive director, Central Area Youth Association), 322-6640.
Norm Rice, mayor of Seattle, 684-4000 (office).
Millie Russell, community activist/educator, NA.
Eddie Rye Jr., community activist, 722-0726.
Ron Sims, King County Council member, 722-3923.
Sam Smith, Seattle City Council member, 684-8800.
Lacy Steele, executive director, NAACP, 324-6600.
Jeri Ware, community activist, 322-7902.
Jesse Wineberry, State Representative, Forty-third Dist., 786-7944, (800) 321-2808 or 329-7722.
Dr. Roz Woodhouse, executive director, Seattle Urban League, 447-3792.
Pat Wright, director, Total Experience Gospel Choir, 682-4824.

Organizations

Seattle's black community is rich in terms of supporting organizations. For example, almost every profession has its own association, such as the Association of Black Accountants, Black Professional Educators, and the Conference of Black Officials. And then there are social service groups, mainly centered in the Central Area and south Seattle. Business-types network through four fraternities and four sororities, carrying on that college relationship much longer than those of other ethnic groups. Several groups say they are putting together a comprehensive list of organizations. Until then, here's a smattering of key African American community organizations:

Atlantic Street Center
2103 S Atlantic St.
Seattle, WA 98144
329-2050
Parenting and youth issues.

Black Achievers Program
East Madison YMCA
1700 23rd Ave.
Seattle, WA 98122
322-6969
Provides mentors for teen-age participants.

Black Community Coalition
Dept. of Social and Health Services (DSHS)
2809 26th Ave. S, N56-1
Seattle, WA 98144
721-4176
Spokesperson: James Kelly

Black Dollar Days Task Force
124 21st Ave. S
Seattle, WA 98122
323-4212
President: Reverend Robert Jeffrey
The task force distributes an annual *African American Business & Service Directory*. Also organizes Black Dollar Days in February—an effort to encourage patronage of African American businesses.

Black Family Center
Catholic Community Services
P.O. Box 22608
Seattle, WA 98122
328-5773

Black Heritage Society of the State of Washington
P.O. Box 22565
Seattle, WA 98122
Contact: Esther H. Mumford
The group organized in 1977 to bring together people interested in the history, culture, and contribution of African Americans. Exhibits, speakers, photographs, slide/tape features, travel info, index to oral history interviews, ethnic crafts, archives, educational programs, genealogical materials, etc.

Blacks in Government
P.O. Box 94144
Terminal Station
Seattle, WA 98124
726-5976
Civil rights advocacy group for government employees. Includes city, county, state, and federal employees.

Carolyn Downs Clinic
1422 34th Ave.
Seattle, WA 98122
461-4587
Medical center for low-income people.

Central Area Motivation Program (CAMP)
722 18th Ave.
Seattle, WA 98122
329-4111
Executive director: Larry Gossett
Anti-poverty organization: housing, emergency services, employment assistance, energy assistance, minor home repair, outreach program for at-risk youth, rental space for meetings.

Central Area Senior Center
500 30th Ave. S
Seattle, WA 98144
461-7816

Central Area Youth Association (CAYA)
119 23rd Ave.
Seattle, WA 98122
322-6640
Executive director: Michael Preston

East Cherry YWCA
2820 E Cherry St.
Seattle, WA 98122
461-8480
Director: Patricia Hayden

NAACP
P.O. Box 22148
Seattle, WA 98122
324-6600
President: Lacy Steele

Odessa Brown Clinic
2101 E Yesler Way
Seattle, WA 98122
329-7870
Health care for children from low-income families.

Role Models Unlimited
P.O. Box 256
Mercer Island, WA 98040
(800) R-Models
Group targeting black male youth in need of role models. Recruiting men 18 and older for members.

Seattle Urban League
105 14th Ave.
Seattle, WA 98122
447-3792
Executive director: Dr. Roz Woodhouse

Total Experience Gospel Choir
P.O. Box 22776
Seattle, WA 98122
722-4876
Director: Pat Wright
Fifty inner-city youth, ages 6–19, singing spirituals and traditional and modern gospel tunes with piano accompaniment. The choir, which has toured extensively, has been around for 10 years and is a major success.

Washington State Commission on African American Affairs
1011 10th Ave. SE
MS EM-14
Olympia, WA 98504
753-0127
Contact: James Kelly

Washington State Rainbow Coalition
P.O. Box 22856
Seattle, WA 98122
284-9124

Events

Martin Luther King Day Rally, January 15.
Festival Sandiata, Seattle Center. Takes place during February, Black History Month.
Black History Month programs: throughout the city during February.
Soul Festival. Mid-July, Rainier Playfield in Genesee, sponsored by *The Medium* newspaper. African American King and Queen are crowned on Memorial Day to reign over the three-day festival—they are selected as part of a scholarship pageant (as opposed to a beauty pageant). The festival includes Martin Luther King, Jr. Unity Parade, sports events, food, and live entertainment. Gospelrama held Sunday. Purpose is to raise funds for scholarships for African American youths.
The Black Community Festival. The oldest cultural event in Seattle's African American community; three days of carnival rides, concession booths, and candidate handshaking at Judkins Park; includes a Mardi Gras Parade the last Saturday of July. Takes place during Seafair; some say it was the precursor to Seafair.

ROOTS picnic. Annual picnic for pioneer families of the black community. ROOTS (Relatives of Old-Timers) picnic held at Gas Works Park, usually in September.
Annual coat drive. *The Medium* and KRIZ sponsor a coat drive in October, just before the cold weather. One year 4,000 coats were donated to the city's needy.
KRIZ also sponsors a Thanksgiving food drive.
Kwanzaa, celebration of African Christmas, from December 26–31. Held at various locations in the Central Area.

Media

Three newspapers serve the black community: *The Facts*, which has been around since 1961; *The Medium*, begun in 1970; and the upstart *Seattle Skanner*, a brand-new business paper. The two old-time papers enjoy a semi-friendly competition; word is that if you get an announcement of your event in one paper, the other paper won't run it. *The Facts* has historically been read by everybody, *The Medium* by those who want objective, more professionally written news stories.

Seattle Times editorial writer Don Williamson, a new voice for the black community in a mainstream newspaper, is viewed as both an arrogant newcomer and a welcome addition to the establishment scene. Many are withholding judgment, watching whether he follows the rile-up school of journalism: He attacked one of the hub churches in a column when he first came—for attention, black residents say.

The Facts
2765 E Cherry St.
Seattle, WA 98122
324-0552
Editor: Fitzgerald Beaver
"If you want to reach the black community, you have to use *The Facts*," says one activist. *The Facts*, founded in 1961, is known for running opinion pieces written by community members, but its editor insists it's just a "weekly community newspaper." It includes a listing of community happenings. Anything goes —radical to conservative opinions— but if you want something on the front page, you'll have to pay.

HEARD ON THE STREET

"Ignorance is more prevalent than racism. It's more a matter of neither one knowing what's going on. That's more Seattle's problem—on both sides."

George Griffin, African American journalist

The Medium
2600 Jackson St.
Seattle, WA 98144
323-3070
Owner: Chris Bennett
The Medium is more of a straight, objective newspaper, with breaking news and features, than *The Facts*. But community leaders say you have to know somebody to get your issue or event covered. Bennett is a leader in the community and is nationally active in African American media affairs. *The Medium*'s sister publications, also owned by Bennett, are the *Tacoma True Citizen* in Tacoma and *Soul Town Review* in Portland.

Seattle Skanner
1326 Fifth Ave., Suite 825
Seattle, WA 98101
233-9888
Editor: Charlie James
Publisher: Bernie Foster
James says this new paper plans to be around as long as Seattle is. The *Skanner* has more of a business and professional emphasis than the others.

Radio stations

KRIZ 1420-AM Seattle
KZIZ 1516-AM Tacoma
KBMS 1480-AM Portland

The only black-owned radio station in Seattle, KRIZ is an "urban station," offering soul music, news, and features about the African American community. Every Monday, Tuesday, and Wednesday morning from 7:07 to 8:45 there's a community talk show with guests, and Sunday is all-day Gospel programming.

THE ASIAN COMMUNITY

San Francisco's Chinatown doesn't hold a candle to Seattle's ID (International District), at least according to the ID's leaders. The reason? Our

Want to get to know the black community? Go to church. The community heart lies in the very active Mt. Zion Baptist Church, the African Methodist Episcopal Church (both founded in the 1800s), the New Hope Missionary Baptist Church, and the Tabernacle Missionary Baptist Church.

ID is politically savvy, involved, and plugged in to the powers that be in the city. The ID is a cohesive force with representatives in all leadership groups in the city and state.

The result is good health clinics, nutrition programs, child care centers, and the ownership of the Bush Hotel and other buildings by the International District Preservation and Development Authority.

Elected representatives

Cheryl Chow, city councilwoman, 684-8804.
Lloyd Hara, city treasurer, 684-5215.
Gary Locke, representative, Washington State Legislature, District 37, 722-7478.
Dolores Sibonga, Seattle City Council member, 684-8802.
Al Sugiyama, Seattle School Board member, 723-2286.
Art Wang, state representative, 752-1714 (Tacoma).

Organizations

Asian American Journalist Association (Seattle Chapter)
333 Dexter Ave. N, (KING-TV)
Seattle, WA 98109
448-3853
Contact: Lori Matsukawa
Encourages Asian Americans to enter journalism and promotes affirmative action hiring internships.

Asian Counseling and Referral Service
1032 S Jackson St., Suite 200
Seattle, WA 98104
461-3606

Asian Pacific Directors Coalition
4726 Rainier Ave.
Seattle, WA 98118
725-8200
Contact: Reed Yamamoto
The goal is to advocate for human service needs of the Asian Pacific Community, share information, resources, and expertise.

Asian Pacific Women's Caucus
112 Fifth Ave. N
Seattle, WA 98109
722-3339
Contact: Vera Ing
Community organization founded in 1977 to deal with issues affecting Asian women.

Chinatown Chamber of Commerce
508½ Seventh Ave. S
Seattle, WA 98104
623-8171
President: Al Yuen

Chinatown International District Preservation and Development Authority
621 S Jackson St.
Seattle, WA 98104
624-8929
Director: Bob Santos

Chinatown Tours
624-6342, 624-8801

Commission on Asian American Affairs
110 Prefontaine Pl. S, Suite 202
Seattle, WA 98104
464-5820
State agency that advises the governor's office on Asian issues such as bilingual education and affirmative action.

InterIm
409 Maynard Ave. S
Seattle, WA 98104
624-1802

International Examiner
318 Sixth Ave. S
Seattle, WA 98104
624-3925

Kin On Nursing Home
1700 24th Ave. S
Seattle, WA 98144
322-0080

Northwest Asian-American Theatre
409 Seventh Ave. S
Seattle, WA 98104
587-3851
Artistic director: Bea Kiyohara

Wing Luke Asian Museum
407 Seventh Ave. S
Seattle, WA 98104
623-5124

THE CHINESE COMMUNITY

The Chinese came to the West Coast in 1849 for the gold, then to the Northwest for that gold measured in board feet: logs. Seattle's original Chinese community was on the tideflats south of Yesler.

When the 1882 Chinese Exclusion Act was passed to stop Chinese immigration, a group called the "Home Guard" fought to stop the Chinese from being forced out of the city. It was a bloody battle, but today the Chinese community in the Seattle area is large—about 35,000—and very active.

For years the community was quietly taking care of its own, but with population growth and second-, third-, and fourth-generation Chinese Americans coming along, it has achieved more of a presence in the mainstream—especially in the political and business arenas. There was a time 20–30 years ago when Chinese could only get jobs in the laundry, grocery, or restaurant businesses; today there are Chinese American professional business organizations. But there are still few partners in law firms from the Chinese community, and fewer still Chinese politicians on the national level. As the younger generation learns to be more aggressive than its ancestors, that situation should change, community leaders say.

Family associations, benevolent societies, and tongs (social clubs) are still important elements in Seattle's Chinatown. The family associations, based on surname and ancestral origins, used to be a sort of city council of the community, but they no longer have the same influence. The tongs are primarily social. The benevolent societies are traditionally strong community support associations. Younger people are active in these groups to some extent, but they also have formed their own groups that are more geared to the world outside the immediate community.

Organizations

Chinatown Chamber of Commerce
508½ Seventh Ave. S
Seattle, WA 98104
623-8171
President: Al Yuen (721-4901)

Chinatown International District Preservation and Development Authority
621 S Jackson St.
Seattle, WA 98104
624-8929
Director: Bob Santos

Chinese Information and Service Center
409 Maynard Ave. S, Second Floor
Seattle, WA 98104
624-4062
Provides language, advocacy, and other social services to the Asian elderly and new immigrants. Outreach group.

Chong Wa Benevolent Association
522 Seventh Ave. S
Seattle, WA 98104
623-2527
Provides service to the Chinese community.

International District Drop-in Center
409 Maynard Ave. S
Seattle, WA 98104
587-3735

Taiwanese American Citizens League
1826 Allegro Dr.
Olympia, WA 98501
753-2040
Contact: Peter Lin

Media

Chinese Daily News
610 Maynard Ave. S
Seattle, WA 98104
223-0802

Chinese Post
414 Eighth Ave. S
Seattle, WA 98104
223-0623
Publisher: Assunta Ng
Editor: Susan Cassidy

Events

Chinese New Year: Based on the lunar calendar, celebrated by a parade and dinner, both open to the public. Family associations have their own New Year's dinners.

Interim, a community service organization, sponsors a street fair, usually in mid-July, in the International District between Maynard and King; and, of course, there's the Seafair Parade in Chinatown.

THE JAPANESE COMMUNITY

Early on Japanese Americans operated many small farms in what is now Seattle and its suburbs; for years Japanese truck farmers were one of the largest groups of vendors at the Pike Place Market.

During World War II Seattle's Japanese were sent to internment camps, primarily in California and Idaho, and many lost their land and assets. When they returned after the war, things were different. Where there had once been an identifiable "Japan town" cluster of shops and offices along Main Street and north of Jackson, there were now non-Japanese businesses. And there was no welcome home for the internees; they weren't wanted in the central city.

Many Japanese Americans settled on Beacon Hill and in the Rainier Valley, but they never established a central neighborhood again. Today many of Seattle's Japanese are moving out of the city and into the suburbs for education and job opportunities. There are about 20,000 Japanese Americans living in Seattle itself. If there is a hub to the community, it's probably Uwajimaya, and if there is a nominal leader, it's Tomio Moriguchi, president of that incredibly successful Asian department store.

There are two main issues for the city's Japanese Americans today. The first is making sure that those eligible for redress from the government for internment receive their money. The second has to do with Japan bashing because of the trade imbalance between that country and the U.S. In a familiar refrain, says one community member, the white community is having a hard time distinguishing Japanese Americans from "Japan Japanese," and is blaming the Nisei and Sansei here for taking over businesses in the U.S. even though many have never even been to Japan.

HEARD ON THE STREET

"I envision a time in Seattle [when], if people don't wake up...we'll have massive job walk-offs and marches in the streets. If corporations get on board now, they can become models—or else they will become casualties."

Reverend Robert Jeffrey,
Black Dollar Days Task Force

Old-timers remember the huge dragon that wound through the International District during that neighborhood's Seafair parade. But the dragon sadly slipped into the cave of a damp building and deteriorated over the years. Cost of a new one: $15,000. The Chinatown Chamber of Commerce is hoping to raise enough money for a new dragon through its Youth Lions group, which represents the community at different events.

Organizations

Bush-Asia Community Center
Bush Hotel
621 S Jackson St.
Seattle, WA 98104
623-8079

Japan Shumy and Culture Society Dance Group
1724 S Hanford St.
Seattle, WA 98144
329-8769
Contact: Sayoko Boole
Adults perform Japanese folkdances in costume for cultural shows.

Japanese American Citizens League
District Office
671 S Jackson St., Suite 206
Seattle, WA 98104
623-5088
NW district governor: Bob Sato

Japanese American Citizens League (JACL)
Seattle Chapter
316 Maynard Ave. S
Seattle, WA 98104
621-7923
Director: Vicky Toyohara-Mukai
JACL is considered the most active civil rights organization for Asians in the country, and the Seattle chapter is no slouch when it comes to radical moves. The movement for redress for interned Japanese Americans began in Seattle, as did the move to give aliens the right to own property and the move to rescind Executive Order 9066 (the internment order). Redress—making sure those eligible for funds get them—is still an issue for JACL. Civil rights and leadership concerns are also issues for the group. Seattle's JACL includes Doshi, a group of young Sanseis, ages 25–45, who are beginning to get involved, and Tomono Kai, a social support group of widows and widowers. The chapter has 650 members.

Japanese Community Service
1414 S Weller St.
Seattle, WA 98144
323-0250

Japanese Garden Society
1819 129th Pl. SE
Bellevue, WA 98005
684-4743
Preserves and promotes the Japanese Tea Garden in the Arboretum.

Japanese Language School
1414 S Weller St.
Seattle, WA 98144
323-0250
Saturday schooling in culture and language for anyone interested.

Nikkei Concerns
1601 E Yesler Way
Seattle, WA 98122
323-7100
Umbrella organization that runs Seattle Keiro and Kokoro-Kai, an adult day program for Japanese elders at the Japanese Presbyterian Church.

Nisei Veteran Committee
1212 S King St.
Seattle, WA 98144
322-1122
Nutrition and social services for vets. Also, Meiji Kai, a senior citizen center for Japanese, is located here. This is affectionately called "vets' hall."

Seattle Japanese School
643-1661
Eastside school for children of Japanese businessmen living in Seattle temporarily. A way for the children to maintain ties to Japan's culture and education.

What's in a name? Plenty, if you're one of Seattle's Japanese American community. You can hardly talk about the community without using the terms for different generations.

Issei: first-generation Japanese, born in Japan, now in the U.S.

Kibei: born in Japan, living in the U.S., but returned to Japan at some point for education

Nisei: U.S.-born children of Issei

Sansei: children of Nisei

Yonsei: fourth-generation children

Gosei: fifth-generation children

Seattle Keiro Nursing Home
1601 E Yesler Way
Seattle, WA 98122
323-7100
Built by the Seattle Japanese community for care of its elderly.

Events

The Cherry Blossom Festival is held in May. Bon Odori is a festival of folk dances and foods, traditional costumes, and parades. It happens in July or August during Seafair week, and is sponsored by the Seattle Buddhist Church.

Media

North American Post
662½ S Jackson St.
Seattle, WA 98104
623-0100
Japanese newspaper, in Japanese.

NW Nikkei
662½ S Jackson St.
Seattle, WA 98104
623-0100
Editor: Leslie Mano
A monthly newspaper started in 1989, owned by the *North American Post*, written in English for Japanese Americans.

THE FILIPINO COMMUNITY

The first Filipino in the state came to work at a sawmill on Bainbridge Island in 1883. Today the Filipino community constitutes the largest ethnic group among Asian/Pacific Americans in the nation. The term Pinoy refers to Filipino American males; Pinay to women (in the Philippines, it is sometimes used derogatorily). In 1980 there were 27,000 Filipinos in King County; since then the immigrant Filipino population has grown at the rate of about 800 per year, and is bolstered by the traditionally high birth rate of long-time Filipino residents.

The Filipino community was once centered near the old Immaculate

Conception Catholic Church on 18th Avenue. Everybody knew everybody else and the power base was easy to trace. But with the high rate of immigration during the Marcos years, the old power base exists no longer.

The main issue for the local community is the animosity between the recent immigrants and the old-time community. One problem is that the newcomers speak one of the several dialects of the Philippines, and there are biases against those who speak a different dialect. There's even more bias against those old-timers who have been in the U.S. for at least one generation who don't speak any of the dialects. For the community as a whole, English has become the common language, like it or not.

The newcomers see themselves as bringing progressive thinking to the community; the old-timers see the newcomers as snobbish and as rejecting their culture as soon as they get here in favor of materialistic values.

These subcultures within the community have made it divisive, but attempts are being made to hold seminars with representatives from all the groups to talk about unity and political assertion.

While factionalism is the main issue, a secondary and equally important issue is education. The Filipino youth dropout rate reached 12% during the 1980s in Seattle, and of those who graduate, few plan to go on to college. "The kids," sighs one Filipino leader, "want immediate gratification."

Filipino gangs were a problem in the 1970s; there are still "barcadas" (social groups of young people), but they aren't as violent as they once were. However, it's a tentative—and potentially volatile—peace.

Organizations

You really need only know one address to track Filipino affairs: 810 18th Ave. In the old Immaculate School building there are more activities being juggled than there are commands for the famed Khordobah drill team. (It's not a big leap for the people working there; quite a few were students there in the old days and simply traded their student desks for business furniture. The blackboards are still there, as are the statues in the hallway.)

Cabataan Folk Dancers
810 18th Ave.
Seattle, WA 98122
461-4870
A folk dance troupe of 2–19-year-olds. Performs throughout Seattle.

Demonstration Project for Asian Americans
810 18th Ave.
Seattle, WA 98122
322-0203
Contact: Dorothy Cordova
Interpreters; demographic information on Asian Americans in Seattle and King County.

Filipino American Citizens League
361-1836
Contact: Tony Espejo, 296-4210 (work)

Filipino American National Historical Society
810 18th Ave.
Seattle, WA 98122
324-9011
Contacts: Fred and Dorothy Cordova

Filipino American Political Action Group of Washington (FAPAGOW)
4726 Rainier Ave. S
Seattle, WA 98118
725-8200 or 235-8447
Contact: Johnny Corsilles

Filipino Community of Seattle
5740 Martin Luther King Way S
Seattle, WA 98118
722-9372
President: Camillo de Guzman

Filipino Youth Activities (FYA)
810 18th Ave.
Seattle, WA 98122
323-6545
Director: John Ragudos
Provides outreach, job assistance, legal assistance, crisis intervention, liaison with school districts, and recreational activities for young people. Also houses an extensive Filipino library.

International Drop-In Center
405 Maynard Ave. S
Seattle, WA 98104
587-3735
Director: Agustin Salgada
Recreation for senior Filipinos and Asians and other ethnic groups. Social service information center.

Khordobah Drill Team
810 18th Ave.
Seattle, WA 98122
323-6545
The Filipino Youth Activities agency sponsors this well-known drill team for children 9–19 years old. The team keeps from 65 to 125 kids busy practicing, traveling, and performing. They practice four hours every Saturday and perform in ethnic dress. Commands are given in one of twelve dialects.

Events

Pista Sa Nayon ("Feast in Town") was initiated recently by Ron Sims, King County Councilman, as a way to involve the Filipino community in Seafair. Sixty organizations from the community are involved and there is a Street Fair at Rainier Playfield including arts and crafts, food, and folk dancing.

Media

Filipino-American Bulletin
3814 NE 75th St., Suite 4
Seattle, WA 98115
323-6545 days; 526-0423 eves.
Editor: Conrado "Sluggo" Rigor

Filipino-American Herald
2824 S Brandon St.
Seattle, WA 98108
725-6606
Editor: Emiliano Francisco
Oldest Filipino paper in the city.

THE KOREAN COMMUNITY

The Korean Association of Washington estimates there are 30,000 Koreans living in King, Snohomish, and Pierce counties. About one-third of the Koreans live in the Federal Way area. Assimilation has been swift, considering that Koreans only began immigrating here in large numbers following the Korean War. The Koreans have been very successful in small businesses such as the prototypical mom-and-pop grocery store and dry cleaning. (Grocers and dry cleaners have the largest representation in the Washington State Korean Chamber of Commerce.)

The Korean community in Seattle retains a strong sense of identity, fostered in the Korean schools (where schoolchildren take weekend classes in Korean culture, history, language, and manners) and in the churches.

Organizations

Korean Association of Washington State, Seattle Branch
1200 S Angelo St.
Seattle, WA 98108
767-8071
Executive director: Dong Sik Chang
Umbrella organization representing Koreans. It also sponsors the Seattle Korean School. Publishes a hefty phone directory listing Korean individuals and Korean-oriented agencies. The association hopes to become more politically active by registering voters and getting out the vote in the Korean community. The statewide Korean Chamber of Commerce is also headquartered here.

Korean Counseling Center
302 N 78th St.
Seattle, WA 98103
784-5691
A nonprofit organization at the Woodland Park United Methodist Church providing translation services for places (such as hospitals) with Korean-speaking clientele.

Korean Identity Development Society
503 N 190th St.
Seattle, WA 98133
542-8646
President: Sandi Mehl
This group promotes cultural awareness in American families who have adopted Korean children. They have an educational program for kids and their parents and a summer camp. About 600 families are members.

Media

Korea Central Daily News, Northwest edition
13749 Midvale Ave. N
Seattle, WA 98133
365-4000
Published daily.

Korea Times, Northwest Edition
430 Yale Ave. N
Seattle, WA 98109
622-2229
Published daily. Also publishes a directory of Korean businesses.

Korean Journal
33310 Pacific Hwy S, Bldg. 4, Suite 401
Federal Way, WA 98003
661-1767
Published weekly.

THE SAMOAN COMMUNITY

One of the area's largest ethnic populations, the Samoan community numbers about 6,000 in the city; combined with Tacoma and Ft. Lewis, it's closer to 10,000.

The older Samoans were born in the Pacific Islands and grew up in a culture where families formed the basic societal unit. The head of the family was king. Since that philosophy is not so prevalent in the U.S., some Samoans are having a hard time here. The dropout rate among Samoan youth is close to 50%.

The Seattle School District and a nonprofit group called Islander Children and Youth Services provide an intervention program including tutoring, counseling, and after-school activities for at-risk Samoan students. Samoans and other Pacific Islander students number about 1,500 in the Seattle schools.

HEARD ON THE STREET

"Seattle is very segregated, not only in the community, but it nurtures this division in the hearts."

Reverend Zachary Bruce, employment director, Central Area Motivation Program (CAMP)

There's been a lot of press about Samoan gangs, but Samoan spokesman A'emalo Moliga disputes it. He explains that Samoan youth live in extended families and hang out together, but "gangs are not in our blood, not in our culture.... When the media and police start labeling those kids as a gang, the kids might start thinking they are."

Names to know

Paul and Betty Patu, Samoan community leaders, 281-6712.

Organizations

Atlantic Street Center
2103 S Atlantic St.
Seattle, WA 98144
329-2050
A multi-cultural agency providing support services, particularly counseling, to Samoans and other ethnic groups.

Samoan National Chiefs Council of Washington
4859 Rainier Ave. S
Seattle, WA 98118
722-2045

Formerly called the Samoan/Pacific Islander Association, the group shares office space with the city's Southeast Community Service Center. The "chief" is the head of the family (traditionally a man, but sometimes a woman these days), who is entitled to represent the extended family on the council. That's how things were run back in the old villages. Paul Patu, a Samoan who works for the Seattle School District, calls this a "macho-macho" outfit. The group sponsors the Islander Children and Youth Services.
Other Services: There are meals programs in Seattle for Samoan senior citizens at the Delridge Community Center, 4555 Delridge Way SW, and at the Polynesian Senior Center, 2910 S Warsaw, and for Tongan oldsters at the South Park Community Center, 8319 Eighth Ave. S.

Events

Samoan Flag Day, in August, commemorates the signing of the treaty between the U.S. and Samoa in 1900.

THE SOUTHEAST ASIAN COMMUNITY

A flood of refugees from Southeast Asia came to the Seattle area between 1975 and 1980, most entering the country through the sponsorship of local churches. It's difficult to determine population; figures for King County vary from 40,000 to 170,000 Laotians, Cambodians, and Vietnamese. Families joining the original refugees have boosted the population.

The Laotians include the lowland Lao people as well as members of the highland tribes, Hmong, Mien, and Khmu. They all speak different languages. The Hmong people are accomplished textile artisans and have a stall in the Pike Place Market. It's estimated there are from 10,000 to 12,000 Laotians in the Seattle/King County area.

The Cambodians (Khmer) number 8,000 to 10,000.

The Vietnamese are the largest group of Southeast Asians; the unofficial population estimate is 20,000.

Organizations

Asian Counseling and Referral Service
1032 S Jackson St., Suite 200
Seattle, WA 98104
461-3606
This United Way agency administers all kinds of social services to elderly and mentally ill Southeast Asians, Samoans, and Pacific Islanders.

Cambodian Studies Center
19835 25th Ave. NE
Seattle, WA 98155
362-2441
President: Kan You
Organization to preserve and study Cambodian culture.

Council of Vietnamese Associations
P.O. Box 12394
Seattle, WA 98111
296-7884
Secretary: Van Hong
New umbrella group.

Indochinese Refugee Association
410 Seventh Ave. S
Seattle, WA 98104
625-9955

Refugee Federation Service Center
2200 Rainier Ave. S
Seattle, WA 98144
323-9365
Founded in 1982 for Southeast Asian refugees, the service center now helps refugees from everywhere. A million languages are spoken here, and the center provides all kinds of services (resettlement, housing, youth programs, etc.). Various Laotian, Cambodian, and Vietnamese organizations can be reached through the service center.

Southeast Asian Women's Alliance
3004 S Alaska St.
Seattle, WA 98108
721-0243
Director: Judy DeBarros
Group established in 1985 to help Southeast Asian refugee women establish self-sufficiency here. It has since widened its outreach to all refugee women, including those from Eastern Europe. Sponsors classes in ESL, parenting, self-esteem, literacy, and employment awareness. Provides on-site child care. Also counsels residents of Rainier Vista housing project, helping them deal with family conflicts, violence, health problems, etc.

Vietnamese Buddhist Association of Washington
1651 S King St.
Seattle, WA 98144
323-2269

Vietnamese Catholic Community Archdiocese of Seattle
1230 E Fir St.
Seattle, WA 98122
325-5626

Vietnamese Friendship Association of Seattle
2117 S Atlantic St.
Seattle, WA 98134
329-1229 or through Refugee Federation Service Center
President: Kim Long
A social organization that enables Vietnamese to meet and help each other, and encourages cultural awareness.

THE NATIVE AMERICAN COMMUNITY

Seattle's first inhabitants thought this was a liveable place long before the white settlers arrived in the 1850s. They had large, cedar longhouses along the waterfront, ate berries, grains, and the gifts from the sea: clams, salmon, and other fish. The Northwest Indians were distinguished by their highly developed woodworking skills, an orientation toward the water, and an attention to wealth and status. These Seattle natives were basically pacifist. There

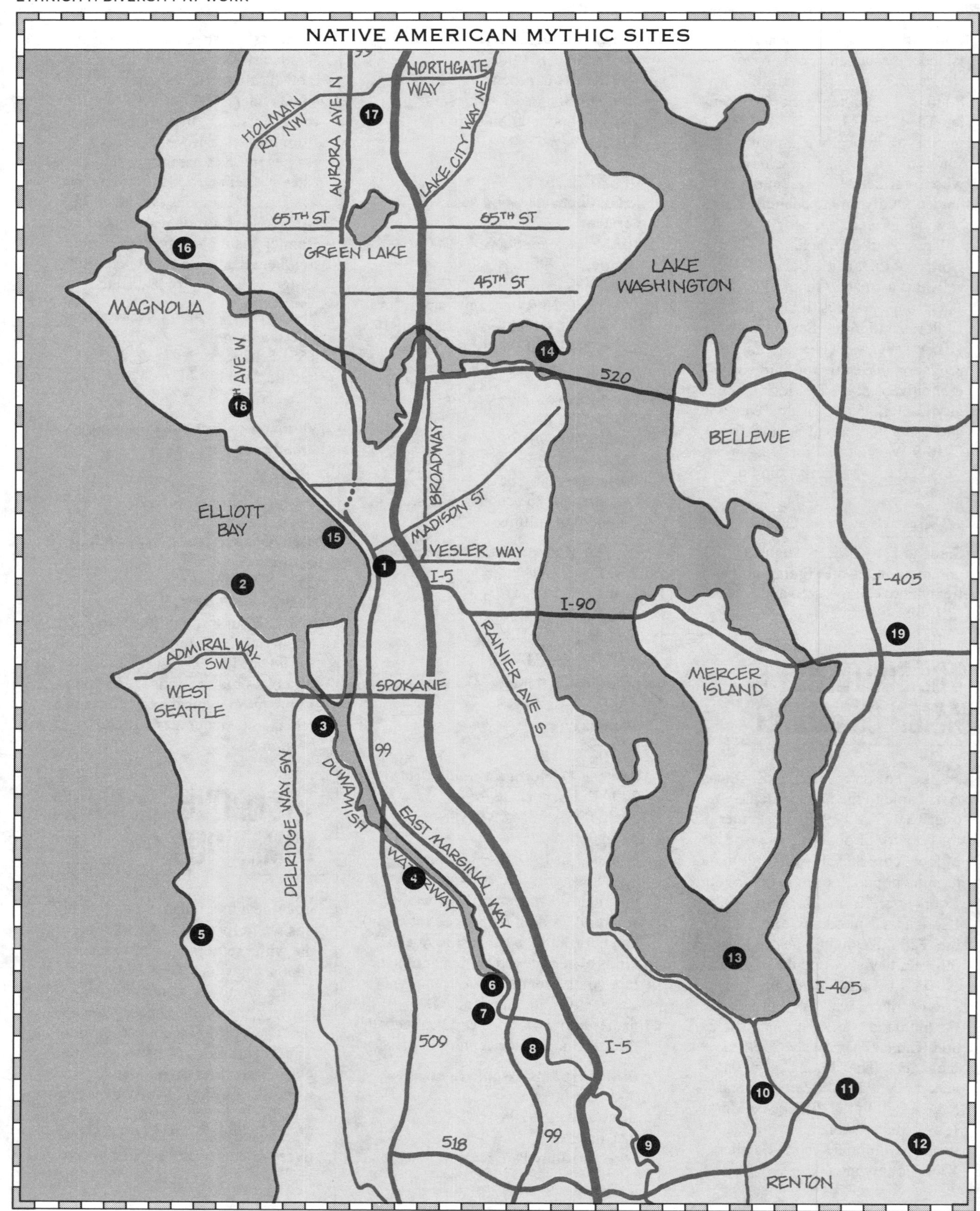
NATIVE AMERICAN MYTHIC SITES
NORTHGATE WAY
AURORA AVE N
HOLMAN RD NW
LAKE CITY WAY NE
65TH ST
65TH ST
GREEN LAKE
45TH ST
LAKE WASHINGTON
MAGNOLIA
520
BELLEVUE
BROADWAY
ELLIOTT BAY
MADISON ST
YESLER WAY
I-5
I-405
I-90
RAINIER AVE S
ADMIRAL WAY SW
WEST SEATTLE
SPOKANE
MERCER ISLAND
99
DELRIDGE WAY SW
DUWAMISH WATERWAY
EAST MARGINAL WAY
I-405
509
I-5
518
99
RENTON
1
2
3
4
5
6
7
8
9
10
11
12
13
14
15
16
17
18
19

Map key to notable Native American sites

Traces of Native American history can still be found in Seattle today, though many sacred sites have been paved over or otherwise used by the white newcomers for their own benefit.

1. Jijila'lich, "little crossing place." A native village existed at the current site of Pioneer Square, or, to be more precise, 20 feet below the current streets. A bust of Chief Seattle is, appropriately enough, prominent in the Square today.

2. Skwuduks, "below the point." At an Indian clamming beach and campsite just east of Duwamish Head, near the West Seattle boat ramp, Seattle's pioneers first met Chief Seattle in 1851.

3. Tola'ltu, "herring's house." Another native village site and the location of a large potlatch house. Part of the village site has been recently excavated by archaeologists.

4. Hucha'chee, "hand cut in two." A potent supernatural site on the Duwamish River near the South Park district. Legends tell of mutilated hands that rose from the river here and terrified passers-by, and of fighting giants who were turned into trees at the end of the mythic age, but who persisted in hurling fire at one another.

5. Psaiya'hus, "where there is an aya'hos." A supernatural site on the beach at Fauntleroy Cove south of the Vashon ferry dock, where a reddish beach was once thought to be an aya'hos, a horn-headed serpent believed to cause earthquakes and avalanches. The place may be the site of a buried village similar to Ozette on the Olympic Peninsula.

6. Kula'had, "the barrier." On the Duwamish River, near where the bridge crosses the river next to the old Duwamish Drive-in Theatre. In Puget Salish myth, it was the site of the climactic struggle between the icy wind of the north and the warm, wet wind from the south that announced the return of the salmon. The stone remains of a mythic ice fish weir can still be seen on the east bank.

7. Sbabade'el, "the little mountain." The center of the world, a rocky hill on the west bank of the Duwamish, just south of the kula'had. This is where the drama of creation, described in Duwamish mythology, was played out.

8. Skwoo'lach, "dirty face." Hill that was the weeping face of the Grandmother at Riverton. Maiden, Mother, and Hag are manifestations of the fertile earth in Puget Salish folklore, and the hill at Riverton was one of the more remarkable images of the nurturing Mother/Grandmother. Here, Duwamish Indians performed rituals designed to hurry the warm rains of spring.

9. Swawatee'htud, "earth beings." A race of supernatural dwarfs were believed to inhabit this hill near Longacres. Site of an extraordinary melange of myths and legends.

10. Skate'lbsh, "where Skaitaw is." The lair of a powerful supernatural wealth-giving being that lived in a hole in the bottom of the now-vanished Black River in Renton.

11. The Mount Olivet Pioneer Cemetery. Here is the grave of William, the great chief of the Duwamish, and of Henry Moses, the last of a noble lineage of the Duwamish and relative of Chief Seattle.

12. Su-whee'-whee-wud, "whistling place." The community of Eliot on the Cedar River, two miles east of Renton. The site of an important trade mart where people from as far away as British Columbia and Alaska traded slaves and copper for foodstuffs from the Columbia Plateau east of the Cascades.

13. Ha'chu, "the lake." In myth, Lake Washington appears as a great swallowing monster that consumes Mercer Island, its heart, each night and yields it up each morning to daylight.

14. Stetee'chee, "little island." Foster Island, at the north end of the Arboretum, was used as a burial ground for the people of Union Bay, the most powerful and numerous group on Lake Washington. The dead were placed in boxes that were hoisted into the trees.

15. Sh-chapau, "subterranean passage." On the shore of Elliott Bay beneath the present Seattle Aquarium was a mythical entryway to an underground stream that allowed whales to enter Lake Union.

16. Bitida'k, "spirit-canoe power." This supernatural being, which enabled shamans to undertake the journey to the land of the dead, was believed to haunt a small stream in Ballard. A dance house was located there, just east of the village of Du Shi'l Shol, at the site of the Hiram M. Chittenden Locks.

17. Liu'ktid, "colored." Reddish ooze still flows from Licton Springs in north Seattle, at about N 97th St. and Ashworth Ave. N, where shamans gathered mud for pigment to paint their paraphernalia.

18. Interbay. At two points on the slopes of Magnolia Bluff and Queen Anne Hill above Interbay, shell middens were found, denoting camps in which people hid to escape slaving parties coming down from Vancouver Island.

19. Sa'tsakal, "head of the slough." A village site near the modern community of Factoria, along 18th Ave. SE just west of the Factoria Interchange, was where hostile forces gathered to attack the fledgling community of Seattle in January of 1856.

Source: David Buerge

were variations among the tribes, especially in language.

The Duwamish tribe lived where Seattle is now. The Suquamish were their neighbors to the north and west, and Chief Sealth, Seattle's namesake, was a leader of both tribes. The Indians welcomed the white settlers initially, and eventually were coerced into selling about 2 million acres of land, reservation sites, and the right to hunt and fish in their traditional sites for $150,000. Seattle-area Indians moved to Pierce and Kitsap counties. After a long, drawn-out treaty dispute, U.S. courts ruled in the 1970s that Indians may take half the yearly salmon catch in Northwest waters.

Once a depressed and disenfranchised people, Seattle Indians have in the last two decades revived pride in their culture. They have started schools and health care programs consistent with their culture, demanded treaty rights, and started to solve economic problems resulting from discrimination. The Seattle Indian community has a reputation for being creative and innovative in developing unique service delivery systems (such as the Department of Social and Health Services Indian Unit, and the Indian Health Board).

According to U.S. Census Bureau estimates, there are about 20,145 American Indians living in the King County/Snohomish area. People in agencies working with this population say it's actually much higher than that.

Names to know

Letoy Eike, UW Office of Minority Affairs and president of the American Indian Women's Service League.
Adeline Garcia, member of the Seattle Indian Health Board.
Jackie Swanson, manager of Southeast Community Service Center.
Bernie Whitebear, director of United Indians of All Tribes.

Organizations

American Indian Heritage Program (Seattle School District)
315 22nd Ave. S
Seattle, WA 98144
High school program:
Bob Eaglestaff, 286-4590
Elementary and middle school program:
Dick Basch, 298-7945
This unusual commitment on the part of the school district includes an alternative school for Native American students.

American Indian Women's Service League
113 Cherry St.
Seattle, WA 98104
621-0655
An old-time group that used to be very active and influential on behalf of American Indians. Getting the Indian Center started was one of its major achievements. Today the league's main activity is running its arts and crafts co-op gallery in the old Broderick Building at Second and Cherry.

Duwamish Tribe
15616 First Ave. S
Seattle, WA 98148
Tribal chairwoman: Cecile Makwell, 244-0606
Governor's office, Indian advisor: Michelle Aguilar, 753-2411

Muckleshoot Group Home
39015 172nd Ave. SE
Auburn, WA 98002
939-3311
Director: Marie Starr

Public Health Service
Indian Health Service, Puget Sound Unit
2201 Sixth Ave.
Seattle, WA 98121
442-4932
Administrator: Larry Jordan

Seattle Indian Center
Leschi Center
611 12th Ave. S, Suite 300
Seattle, WA 98144
329-8700
Director: Ralph Foquero
Main provider of social services to the American Indian population. There is low-income housing for Indian elders adjacent to the center.

Seattle Indian Health Board
Leschi Center
611 12th Ave. S, Suite 300
Seattle, WA 98144
324-9360
A full-fledged clinic, said to be the largest off-reservation health care facility for Native Americans in the country. The Health Board also operates the Thunderbird Alcohol/Drug Treatment Center, 9236 Renton S, 722-7152.

United Indians of All Tribes (UIAT)
Administrative office
Daybreak Star Arts and Cultural Center
Discovery Park
P.O. Box 99100
Seattle, WA 98199
285-4425
Pioneer Square office
102 Prefontaine Pl. S
Seattle, WA 98104
343-3111
Lake Union office
1945 Yale Pl. E
Seattle, WA 98102
325-0700
Director: Bernie Whitebear
Youth program director: Woody Verzola
Provides educational, cultural, heritage, and some social service programs for Native Americans. Head Start preschool and kindergarten classes are housed at Daybreak Star. So is the Sacred Circle art gallery.

At its Pioneer Square office, UIAT runs an outreach program for Native American dropouts, street kids, and kids involved in the juvenile court system. It has a substance abuse and prevention program, tutoring, psychological evaluations, and counseling.

At the Lake Union office, the *Daybreak Star Reader*, a monthly publication for Native American youth, is published. It also has employment and family counseling services and a GED program.

Washington Indian Child Welfare Action Committee
284-1650
Contact: Faye LaPointe

Events

The UW and the American Indian Student Union have a big **pow-wow** every spring and the UIAT hosts a summer pow-wow during Seafair Days in July.

Chief Seattle Days, Suquamish. Across the water, the Suquamish Tribe puts on a weekend fest of canoe races, dances, and great food. It's usually held in mid-August. Call the tribe at 598-3311 for information.

Media

Daybreak Star Reader
1945 Yale Pl. E
Seattle, WA 98102
Monthly publication for Native American youth.

THE LATINO, CHICANO, AND MEXICANO COMMUNITIES

What's in a name? Plenty when you speak Spanish and live in Seattle. Here's a dictionary:
Latinos: from Central and South America
Mexicanos: first-generation Mexican Americans
Chicanos: second-generation Mexican Americans
Hispanic: a word no longer favored.

There are several different factions within the Latino community. Though the Spanish-speaking population in the Seattle area is estimated at 49,000, it does not have the cohesiveness and sense of identity that make well-established Chicano groups in the Southwest potent political forces. Recently there's been an effort to pull the various elements together in a new political coalition representing Chicano/Latino interests. The hope, according to some, is to "be as well organized as the black community" in Seattle.

Names to know

Jorge Chacon, director of Consejo Counseling and Referral Service.
Roberto Maestas, longtime respected executive director of El Centro de la Raza.
Yolanda Martinez, runs the city's neighborhood office at Lake City.

Organizations

Concilio for the Spanish Speaking of King County
157 Yesler Way, Suite 209
Seattle, WA 98104
461-4891
Umbrella organization founded in the 1970s as an advocate for Spanish-speaking groups. Was very political, now less effective. Publishes *La Voz.*

Consejo Counseling and Referral Service
3808 S Angeline St.
Seattle, WA 98118
461-4880
Director: Jorge Chacon
The only mental health agency in Western Washington specifically for the Spanish-speaking population. Has contract with King County to provide mental health services; also receives United Way funding. Has treatment programs for chemical dependency. Consejo treats about 200 clients of all ages each month. Main office is in Rainier Valley; satellite office is at the Sea-Mar Community Health Clinic (see below).

El Centro de la Raza
2524 16th Ave. S
Seattle, WA 98144
329-9442
Contact: Diane Passmore
Director: Roberto Maestas
Founded in 1972 to serve Spanish-speaking people, it's now reaching out to other poor ethnic minorities as well, developing a sort of all-purpose Third World "rainbow" look. Still highly political, it has an international relations department, and takes stands on Central American and international issues. It operates many programs: educational (ESL classes), cultural, day care (Jose Marti Child Development Center), food bank, housing, meals and other social services, as well as an art gallery.

Sea-Mar Community Health Clinic
8720 14th Ave. S
Seattle, WA 98108
762-3730
Director: Rogelio Rojas
The major primary health care clinic for the Spanish-speaking population.

Events

The big one here is the **Fiesta de la Sixth de Septiembre**, celebrating Mexico's independence from Spain. The lesser holiday (but big to Mexican restaurants) is **Cinco de Mayo**, celebrating the defeat of the French occupation in Mexico. There is an Hispanic Seafair in July at Seattle Center, sponsored by the Concilio for the Spanish Speaking.

Media

Hispanic News
2318 Second Ave.
Seattle, WA 98121
768-0421
Weekly bilingual newspaper, begun in 1984. Publisher is Pedro Cavazos.

Also *La Voz*, monthly bilingual newspaper published by Concilio for the Spanish Speaking of King County. (See above.)

THE NORDIC COMMUNITY

So who doesn't know Stan Boreson? Who doesn't know a few Ballard jokes? Seattle without Scandinavians would be like codfish without salt, lutefisk without aquavit.

Insulting as it might be to lump the Scandinavian groups together, it's often done. They include Danes, Swedes, Finns, Norwegians, and, of course, the Icelanders, the smallest Nordic community in Seattle. They had a small colony in Ballard around the turn of the century and their own church, which is now called Calvary Lutheran Church. Then there are the Swede-Finns (Finns who speak Swedish).

Scandinavians from Norway and Sweden make up one of Seattle's largest ethnic communities. Norway ranks second only to Canada as the country of origin of Seattle's first- and second-generation immigrants here today. Sweden ranks fourth after Germany. And that doesn't even include the Finns, Danes, and Icelanders who live here.

In case you're wondering why those immigrants flocked to Seattle, look around, especially at Puget Sound. Scandinavians already knew how to fish, log, build boats, and work in the shipping trade. The land and the resources were familiar and the mild climate was an improvement over the homeland.

The Nordic immigrants settled primarily in Ballard, where many remain today, but their children and grandchildren can be found throughout the city. Over 600,000 Washington residents claimed Scandinavian descent in 1980—most of them are in or near Seattle.

The Nordic Heritage Museum in Ballard (the only museum in the U.S. that includes all five Scandinavian countries) helps keep Seattle's Nordic culture alive. The museum offers classes in Danish, Norwegian, Swedish, and other Scandinavian handicrafts; it also has activities for children, and sponsors films, concerts, art, and historical exhibits.

Nordic Heritage Museum
3014 NW 67th St.
Seattle, WA 98117
789-5707
Director: Marianne Forssblad
Hours: 10 a.m.–4 p.m. Tues.–Sat.; noon–4 p.m. Sun. The museum publishes a booklet that lists all Nordic resources in the Northwest (Washington, Oregon, Idaho)—organizations, arts and crafts, speakers, university experts, consul staff, library holdings, etc.

Names to know

Several Scandinavians have become captains of industry, business, and politics here:

Former and now deceased Senators **Warren Magnuson** and **Henry "Scoop" Jackson**.
Ole Bardahl (Bardahl Manufacturing Corp.)
Eddie Carlson (civic leader and former chief of United Airlines, now deceased).
The Nordstroms

Fourteen members of the state legislature are Scandies, including Seattle area legislators **Joan Brekke, Ken Jacobsen, Dick Nelson, Gary Nelson,** and **Al Williams**.

The Viking crowd also founded some of Seattle's most venerable charitable organizations, such as the Millionair Club and the Lutheran Compass Mission.

THE DANISH COMMUNITY

Bien
1527 W Magnolia Blvd.
Burbank, CA 91506
(818) 845-7300
A weekly Danish newspaper available here.

Northwest Danish Foundation
1833 N 105th St., Suite 204
Seattle, WA 98133
523-DANE
Publishes the *Little Mermaid* newsletter.

THE SWEDISH COMMUNITY

Swedish Club
1920 Dexter Ave. N
Seattle, WA 98109
283-1090
Seattle's premier Swedish organization. There's a restaurant at the club and, before the highrises started renting out their atriums and ballrooms, many a prom was danced away there. Meeting rooms too.

THE FINNISH COMMUNITY

Finlandia Foundation
P.O. Box 342
Seattle, WA 98111
659-2934
President: Aini Messmer
The Seattle chapter of this group is the largest in the U.S. It is mainly a social organization but does charitable and cultural work as well. Regular newsletter.

Finnish American Chamber of Commerce
P.O. Box 40598
Bellevue, WA 98004
451-3983
Small group that promotes business ties between Finland and the Pacific Northwest.

THE NORWEGIAN COMMUNITY

Norwegian Commercial Club
Leif Erikson Lodge
2245 NW 57th St.
Seattle, WA 98107
783-1274
President: John Dahl
Local businesspeople (fishing and shipping are big) of Norwegian descent. Meets twice monthly.

Sons of Norway
Leif Erikson Lodge
2245 NW 57th St.
Seattle, WA 98107
783-1274
THE major Norwegian organization in Seattle, with about 2,000 members. The Ballard lodge is also the main gathering place for the Norwegian community.

Who gets the credit for inventing slimy lutefisk? The Norwegians (no one else wants it). According to a completely unofficial estimate, about 90,000 people of Norwegian descent live in Seattle and the surrounding region—and they all eat lutefisk.

Western Viking
2040 NW Market St.
Seattle, WA 98107
784-4617
Weekly Norwegian-language newspaper published in Ballard. Includes listing of all local Norwegian groups and officers. Henning Boe is publisher and editor.

THE ICELANDIC COMMUNITY

Icelandic Club of Greater Seattle
10045 15th Ave. NW
Seattle, WA 98177
President: Dr. Ed Palmason, 782-3262
The major group. They have a newsletter and social events celebrating major holidays such as Thorrablot (an ancient Icelandic winter festival) and Icelandic Independence Day in July.

THE BRITISH COMMUNITY

About 100,000 Britons live in the Seattle area, mostly maple-leafers from the North; about 60,000 Canadians have settled here.

Organizations

Anglicon
P.O. Box 8207
Kirkland, WA 98034-8207
367-7060
Contact: D.J. Driscoll
Sponsors annual British-American media convention, complete with English video stars.

Caledonian and St. Andrew's Society
543-8947
President: Rick Murchie

Club Britannia
1021 NE 123rd St.
Seattle, WA 98125
363-1094
President: Albert Sanger

Daughters of British Empire
862-6599
Contact: Marie Collins

English Speaking Union of USA
526-2633
Contact: Col. Frank Webster

The Society of Rusting Tardis
524-3696
Contact: Ryan K. Johnson
British media enthusiasts; meet second and fourth Wednesdays of the month.

THE GREEK COMMUNITY

The Greek Orthodox Church is the center of social life in Seattle's Greek community. The two main churches are St. Demetrios (2100 Boyer Ave. E) and the Church of the Assumption (1804 13th St.). Each has an annual festival featuring Greek food, dance, and music that lasts several days; St. Demetrios Festival is in October and the Church of the Assumption in May. By unofficial (and probably high) estimate, there are 10,000 people of Greek descent in the Seattle area.

Organizations

Daughters of Penelope
3704 Belvidere Ave. SW
Seattle, WA 98126
935-4688
Contact: Anna Rakus
The women's auxiliary to the Order of AHEPA. For high-school-age youth, there are two groups: Maids of Athena and Sons of Pericles.

Order of AHEPA
American Hellenic Educational Progressive Association
District governor: George Paul, 827-2059
A nationwide men's group that promotes Hellenic culture and social ideals. In Seattle this is the main organization outside the church. You don't have to be Greek to join but most are.

THE IRISH COMMUNITY

The Irish were a major presence in the early days of Seattle. John Keane, president of the Irish Heritage Club, cites old land claim records dating from 1852 that indicate that 1 in 12 settlers here were originally from Ireland. Like good Irish everywhere, they were natural politicians. Their descendants include U.S. Representative Jim McDermott; John Spellman, former governor; and Brian Boyle, state land commissioner. Tom Foley doesn't count—he's from Spokane.

Organizations

Irish Heritage Club
17043 Northup Rd.
Bellevue, WA 98008
865-9134
Of the seven different Irish-type organizations in the Seattle area, this

is the most important. The club has 300 members and a newsletter called *The Seanachie.*

Society of the Friendly Sons of St. Patrick
123 Third Ave. S
Seattle, WA 98104
623-5311
A men-only fraternal organization. The Seattle group is relatively new, but George Washington was one of the original founders of the Society in this country. The society's primary function here is to put on a big St. Patrick's Day banquet, which is the only time the Society meets.

Other groups: There are a number of Irish dancing and bagpiping groups; contact Heritage Club for information.

And ... Ciaran O'Mahony (781-2665) from County Cork teaches classes in Gaelic, still the everyday language for many Irish citizens.

If you are the type of person who thinks of pubs and a pint of Guinness when you think of Ireland, here's the true Irishman's view of Seattle's sources of Irish libations, taken by unofficial poll: Murphy's Pub (2110 N 45th) is supposedly the most genuine Irish pub in Seattle. F.X. McRory's Steak Chop & Oyster House in Pioneer Square (419 Occidental S), Jake O'Shaughnessey's (100 Mercer), and Kells (in the Market) are also popular.

Events

Irish Week Festival, complete with St. Patrick's Day parade downtown and the laying of the John Doyle Bishop memorial green stripe along Fourth Avenue. Also an **annual summer picnic**, where the Gaelic football team competes against teams in California and Canada. (Gaelic football is similar to soccer and was banned in Ireland by the English in the 1500s because it was so very ... Irish.)

THE ITALIAN COMMUNITY

Italian labor helped rebuild Seattle after the city burned down in 1889. Some early-day Italian immigrants were contractors; others were the bricklayers, masons, and skilled and unskilled laborers who built the streets, highways, and water and sewer systems of the city. They also worked on the railroads and in the mines.

In the early 1900s many Italians had truck farms in south Seattle, the area from Spokane Street to the Kent Valley. Until the Filipinos came along in 1929, the Italians were the major greengrocers at the Pike Place Market.

Organizations

Dante Alighierri Society
309 S Cloverdale St.
Seattle, WA 98108
762-6092 or 643-0938
The local branch of a worldwide organization formed to promulgate Italian culture, the society has a language school and a Montessori school for children. It meets twice a month for Italian programs, films, music, etc.

Sons of Italy Grand Lodge of the Northwest
8201 Third Ave. NW
Seattle, WA 98117
782-0824 or 783-1772
State president: William Oakes

Here's a little Seattle lore to throw out at next year's Folklife Festival: Once upon a time so many Italian families lived in Rainier Valley that the neighborhood around Our Lady of Mount Virgin Church (where Mass was said in Italian) was called Garlic Gulch. There are no figures on how many people of Italian descent are in Seattle, but there are 106,000 in the state. However, the Sons of Italy has about 900 members in the city.

This is the headquarters for the statewide group as well as the Seattle lodge; there is also a lodge in Bellevue. The Sons sponsor lots of social events and an annual Wine Festival.

Events

Festa Italia at Seattle Center is held near Columbus Day. In 1992, 500 years after what's-his-name sailed the ocean blue, this will be a big blowout. It's usually a week-long celebration with events at the Center and a bike race around Seward Park.

THE LATVIAN AND LITHUANIAN COMMUNITIES

Numerically these are minute ethnic groups in Seattle, but their sense of community is very strong, heightened no doubt by the drives for independence in their Baltic homelands.

Most Lithuanians are Roman Catholic; many non-Russian Latvians are Lutherans.

There are approximately 100 Lithuanian families in Seattle, 70% of whom were born in the U.S., and an estimated 700 Latvian families in the Seattle/Tacoma area. The Latvians have their own hotline (365-0155) for the latest news from the homeland.

Organizations

Latvian Association of Washington State
P.O. Box 75081
Seattle, WA 98125-0081
363-7794
President: Talis Jaundalderis
Doubles as state and local headquarters.

Latvian Community Center
11710 Third Ave. NE
Seattle, WA
362-9894
Also the location of the Latvian Evangelical Lutheran Church. All important social, cultural, religious, and educational activities for the Latvian community take place here. There's a Saturday school for kids (culture, history, etc.), and a Latvian choir and dance group.

Lithuanian American Community, Inc.
3883 45th Ave. NE
Seattle, WA 98105
Seattle branch president: Ina Bertulyte Bray
The Seattle chapter of a national group involved in political as well as cultural and social activities.

THE WELSH COMMUNITY

Puget Sound Welsh Association
P.O. Box 19344
Seattle, WA 98109
282-5680
With about 1,000 on the mailing list, this group coordinates Welsh cultural activities. Made up of Welsh

At the hub of the Welsh community: The Seattle Welsh Choir sings a few impromptu hymns in the bar at Le Fleur, the Sand Point restaurant, on Wednesday nights after rehearsal.

Women's Club, Welsh Language Learners, and Seattle Welsh Choir.

THE HUNGARIAN COMMUNITY

Hungarian American Assn. of Washington
P.O. Box 17280
Seattle, WA 98107-0908
232-6575
The group of approximately 1,500 Hungarians has a language and folk-dance school for children and adults, plus picnics and celebrations throughout the year.

THE GERMANS FROM RUSSIA COMMUNITY

American Historical Society of Germans from Russia, Greater Seattle Chapter
17767 14th Ave. NW
Seattle, WA 98177
542-8049
Group founded in 1968 to actively research the history of all Germans from Russia in the Seattle area. Now has about 200 members.

FOREIGN LANGUAGE CHURCH SERVICES

Multilingual

Ballard Free Methodist Church
(Chinese and Japanese), 784-6111

First Slavic Full Gospel Church, Inc.
(Ukrainian, Russian, and Polish), 783-0866

Gold Summit Buddhist Monastery
(English, Mandarin, Cantonese, Vietnamese), 340-0569

Japanese Baptist Church
(Nichigo and Japanese), 622-7351

Seward Park Seventh-Day Adventist Church
(Japanese and Samoan), 725-5253

Specific languages

Arabic
Islamic Center, 363-3013

Cambodian (or Khmer)
Crystal Springs Congregation, 481-1177
First Baptist Church of Martha Lake, 743-0771

Chinese
Chinese Assembly of God, 322-4409
Chinese Baptist Church (American Baptist), 725-6363
Chinese Mission (Southern Baptist), 525-5646
Grace Chinese Lutheran Church, 839-0344
Holy Trinity Lutheran Church, 232-3270
St. James of Jerusalem Episcopal Church, 624-2644

Coptic
St. Mary's Coptic Orthodox Church, 774-3499

Danish
St. John's Lutheran, 784-1040

Dutch
Assumption Roman Catholic Church, 364-9646

Filipino
Cornerstone Bible (Baptist General Conference), 248-3340
Iglesia Ni Christo, 723-0346
Rainier Avenue Free Methodist Church, 722-5616
Ronald United Methodist Church, 542-2484
Seattle Filipino-American Baptist Church, 722-0201
Volunteer Park Seventh-Day Adventist, 325-5544

Finnish
Bethel Lutheran, 789-0864

German
German United Church of Christ, 325-7664

Greek
Assumption Greek Orthodox Church, 323-8557
St. Demetrios Greek Orthodox Church, 325-4347

Japanese
Apostolic Bible Church of Jesus Christ, 246-3115
Blaine Memorial United Methodist Church, 723-1536
Faith Bible Church, 322-8044
Japanese Baptist Church, 622-7351
Japanese Congregational Church, 325-4566
Japanese Presbyterian Church, 323-5990
Konkokyo Church of Seattle, 325-4498
Nichiren Buddhist Church, 323-2252
St. Peter's Episcopal, 323-5250
Seattle Buddhist Church, 329-0800
Seattle Koyasan Church, 325-8811

Hebrew
Bikur Cholim Hchzikay Hadeth, 723-0970
Congregation Ezra Bessaroth, 722-5500
Emmanuel Congregation, 522-6246
Sephardic Bikur Holim, 723-3028

Korean
Korean Community of Seattle, 624-0644
Korean Student Mission, 523-1511
Korean United Presbyterian Church, 367-5858
Westminster Korean Assembly of God, 364-5200

Latvian
Latvian Evangelical Lutheran Church, 362-9894

Norwegian
Ballard First Lutheran Church, 784-1418
Denny Park Lutheran Church, 623-7447
Rock of Ages Lutheran, 783-4161

Polynesian
Polynesian Baptist Church, Renton, 255-3273

Portuguese
Ballard Church of the Nazarene, 784-1418

Russian
St. Nicholas Russian Orthodox, 322-9387

Samoan
Faith Samoan Church of Seattle, 725-4460
Highpoint Samoan Assembly of God, 762-7287
Ola Fou United Church of Christ, 2706 31st Ave. S
Samoan Christian Church, 433-1709
Samoan Community of Seattle, 762-2357

Spanish
Assumption Roman Catholic Church, 364-9646
Blessed Sacrament Catholic, 547-3020
Christ the King Catholic, 362-1545
Evangelic Spanish Baptist Church, 783-7604
Holy Family Roman Catholic Church, 767-6220
Inglesia Ni Crista, 723-0346
Primera Iglesia Bautista Hispana, 241-8079
St. Mary's Catholic Church, 324-7100

Tongan
Rainier Beach United Methodist, 723-9700

Ukrainian
Ukrainian Orthodox Church, 524-3496

Vietnamese
First Baptist Church of Beverly Park, 243-5970
Immaculate Conception Roman Catholic, 322-5970
North Seattle Alliance Street, 363-7570

Source: The Church Council of Greater Seattle, "Directory of Churches, Ministers and Agencies"

ENGLISH AS A SECOND LANGUAGE (ESL)

Classes available at:

Chinese Information/Service Center
409 Maynard Ave. S, Second Floor
Seattle, WA 98104
624-5633
ESL: Beginning-level individual and small-group tutoring at the student's home or at the center. For all Asian groups.

El Centro de la Raza
2524 16th Ave. S
Seattle, WA 98144
323-6484
ESL: Beginning-level classroom instruction and individual tutoring for King County residents of color.

St. James Refugee Program
804 Ninth Ave.
Seattle, WA 98104
682-4311
ESL: Beginning-level small-group instruction and citizenship classes. Primarily for Hmong and Laotian refugees.

University of Washington
103 Lewis Hall
Seattle, WA 98195
543-6242
ESL: Individual on- or off-campus tutoring and campus classes for international students preparing to enter American colleges. Also for non-native speakers wishing to improve English skills. Fee required.

Washington Association of Churches
233 Sixth Ave. N, Suite 110
Seattle, WA 98109
443-9219
ESL: Intermediate and advanced-level classroom and individual instruction for newly legalized immigrants; citizenship classes.

All three Seattle Community Colleges offer ESL classroom instruction and individualized tutoring. (See Chapter 21: "Ivy League, Seattle Style.")

Translation help

Language Bank—American Red Cross
1900 25th Ave. S
Seattle, WA 98144
323-2345
24-hour volunteer emergency service. Offers written and oral interpretation in 70 languages.

Seattle Translation Center
3123 Eastlake Ave. E
Seattle, WA 98102
324-7696
Offers translations of official documents or personal letters. Fee is between 15 and 25 cents per word. Also offers voice-overs and interpretations.

Travelers Aid Society
909 Fourth Ave.
Seattle, WA 98104
461-3888
Group set up to help those away from home—lost travelers' checks, need for accommodations, etc.

CONSULATES

Consulates represent their countries, but they also offer services to Americans. For example, if you're planning a visit to a foreign country, the consul will have tourist information.

For foreigners, of course, the consulate is invaluable. That's where you get passports or a visa, take problems facing you as a visitor, find out where to get in touch with others in your situation. If the consuls can't help, they can direct you elsewhere.

Austrian Consulate
4131 11th Ave. NE
Seattle, WA 98105
633-3606

British Consulate
First Interstate Center
999 Third Ave., Suite 820
Seattle, WA 98104
622-9253

Canadian Consulate General
Plaza 600, Suite 412
Sixth Ave. & Stewart St.
Seattle, WA 98101-1286
443-1777
Immigration: 443-1372

Consulado de Chile
Joshua Green Bldg.
1025 Fourth Ave., Suite 408
Seattle, WA 98101
624-3772 or 624-3780

Consulate of Belgium
2516 42nd Ave. W
Seattle, WA 98199
623-5005

For those lost souls who don't know their genealogy, there's hope. The Pacific Northwest Regional Archives, a branch of the U.S. National Archives, 6125 Sand Point Way NE, 526-6347, has thousands of microfilms of census records for the years 1790–1910 for all states. The archives also has Revolutionary War rolls, military pension records, land records, tract books, entries of settlers, and U.S. District Court records. The other thing that collects in the archives is crowds: there's a full house of ancestor-seekers daily. For that reason, it's best to make an appointment to do your research, though walk-ins are welcome. Volunteers and staff people are on hand to guide you through your own history.

Consulate of Costa Rica
227 Eighth Ave. W
Kirkland, WA 98033
822-3054

Consulate of Denmark
1809 Seventh Ave.
Seattle, WA 98101
682-6101

Consulate of Finland
P.O. Box 40598
Bellevue, WA 98004
451-3983

Consulate of France
400 E Pine St., Suite 210
Seattle, WA 98122
323-6870

Consulate of Guatemala
2100 Fifth Ave.
Seattle, WA 98121
728-5920

Consulate of Honduras
1402 Third Ave., Suite 1019
Seattle, WA 98101
623-6485

Consulate of Iceland
5610 20th Ave. NW
Seattle, WA 98107
783-4100

Consulate of Mexico
2132 Third Ave.
Seattle, WA 98121
448-3526

Consulate of Panama
(Mobile service)
949-4647

Consulate of Republic of Bolivia
15215 52nd Ave. S
Seattle, WA 98188
244-6696

Consulate of Switzerland
P.O. Box 81003
Seattle, WA 98108
762-1223

Consulate General of the Federal Republic of Germany
1617 IBM Bldg.
1200 Fifth Ave.
Seattle, WA 98101
682-4312

Consulate General of Japan
1301 Fifth Ave., Suite 3110
Seattle, WA 98101
682-9107

Consulate General of Peru
7209 NE 149th Pl.
Bothell, WA 98011
488-4705

Consulate General of the Philippines
2033 Sixth Ave., Suite 801
Seattle, WA 98121
441-1640

Consulate General, Republic of Korea
2033 Sixth Ave., Suite 1125
Seattle, WA 98121
441-1011

Coordination Council for North American Affairs—Republic of China in Taiwan
Westin Bldg.
2001 Sixth Ave.
Seattle, WA 98121
441-4586

Norwegian Consulate
Joseph Vance Bldg.
1402 Third Ave.
Seattle, WA 98101-2169
623-3957

Swedish Consulate
Joseph Vance Bldg.
1402 Third Ave.
Seattle, WA 98101-2169
622-5640

THE FOLKLIFE FESTIVAL

Seattle's ethnic showcase is the annual Folklife Festival held Memorial Day weekend at Seattle Center. The people wearing patchouli oil and camping in the parking lot in VWs will propel you back into the 1960s, and the music, dancing, food, and crafts from more than 100 countries are great.

The Folklife Festival folks do more than put on that event: They are a resource for schools and community groups who would like to stage an ethnic event of their own. They help year-round with such programs and have resource lists of what's available and what's needed in the way of space, stage, equipment, etc. The office also conducts multicultural teacher training classes.

Northwest Folklife Festival
305 Harrison St.
Seattle, WA 98109
684-7300
Executive director: Scott Nagel

CHAPTER

13

CANVASES AND CURTAIN CALLS

ONE PERCENT

ARTS COMMISSION

TUNNEL ART

GALLERIES

THE STAGE

TICKETS

ARTS ORGANIZATIONS

ALLIED ARTS

CORPORATE ART

MUSEUMS

BEST SEATS

RESOURCES

Seattle doesn't have one arts scene, it has several. There's no central gathering place for painters, sculptors, musicians, actors. Sure, students from the Arts Institute hang out at the Cyclops, and a smattering of poets can be found at the Still Life in Fremont.

Pioneer Square is home to galleries and even a jazz record shop. But there's no Greenwich Village and, while Seattleites like to take advantage of the arts, they are not very supportive of them when it comes to parting with dollars.

DEBUNK THAT MYTH

Seattle is reputed to be active and involved with the arts, with more live theaters and artists per capita than any other major city in the nation except New York. But per capita support of the arts in Seattle, beyond the sale of tickets, is below the national average. That means arts organizations are sometimes floundering to the point of disaster; in a 1988 report, the League of Women Voters revealed that 12 of the city's 14 arts organizations were in fragile financial condition.

Ticket sales, while high, only cover 50% to 75% of the groups' incomes. So how can a city be so arts-oriented and yet not financially support its arts groups? Perhaps Seattle is blessed with too many good things. Here the arts compete with the outdoors (and arts groups compete with each other). When it's a choice between a donation to the symphony and buying a new pair of skis, well, the skis have it.

MAJOR ARTS ORGANIZATIONS, 1987

Ranked on the basis of combined liquid and endowment assets as a percentage of operating budget.

1. Seattle Art Museum
2. Seattle Repertory Theatre
3. Seattle Opera
4. Bathhouse Theatre
5. Pioneer Square Theater (no longer in existence)
6. On The Boards
7. Pacific Northwest Ballet
8. A Contemporary Theatre (ACT)
9. Group Theatre
10. Empty Space Theatre
11. Seattle Children's Theatre
12. Intiman Theatre
13. Seattle Symphony
14. Northwest Chamber Orchestra

Source: League of Women Voters

IS ONE PERCENT ENOUGH?

Here's what the city's law says: One percent of certain capital improvement program funds must go to the purchase and installation of artworks on city property. To date the results of the 1% ruling include bronze dance steps on Broadway, spinning whirligigs at a City Light electrical substation, decorated manhole covers, and a variety of other art treasures dotting the city.

The amount spent on public art in a year depends on how much is spent by the city on capital improvements. For example, the new Seattle Art Museum will cost $26.7 million, so $267,000 will go to public art from that project alone. The 1% directed toward public art from a capital project is sometimes paid out over several years. The average amount per year of the public art fund over the past 5 to 10 years is around $500,000.

How to really get public arts money: No matter how depoliticized bureaucrats say the process is, getting funding (as well as getting into a gallery) depends on whom you know. "The term networking," says one arts administrator, "was invented in Seattle." Grab onto the coattails of successful artists, use them for references, or have them put in a good word for you. Get to know arts administrators and curators. Opportunities mysteriously come up when you know somebody. Of course, your work has to be good too.

In 1988 approximately 80% of the program's funds came from Seattle City Light. City Light also maintains a "Portable Works Collection," comprising two- and three-dimensional artworks that are rotated on an 18-month schedule among city office buildings, for which it commissions works by local, regional, and international artists.

ART BY COMMITTEE

Guidelines for the 1% program stipulate that at least half the money expended over a five-year period go to artists residing in the Pacific Northwest. The majority of 1% projects are based on an open call for applications; however, in some cases a limited number of artists are invited to apply, and in some cases artists or completed works are chosen directly by the panel.

An evaluation panel for each project is appointed by the Arts in Public Places Committee. Panels of three or more include at least one artist; remaining members may include museum professionals, arts educators, critics, and patrons. Project selections are made by majority vote of the panel. The panel also has the option of declining selection altogether if no artist, work, or proposal can be agreed upon.

The panel selection is finalized by formal vote of the full Arts Commission.

HOW TO GET SOME OF THAT 1%

Getting public funding for your artwork is a highly competitive thing. Artists compete with other artists, minority artists complain they don't get a fair share, and the Medusa of arts politics raises its head. Until recently, the Seattle Arts Commission was under heavy attack for being an insiders' circle, "a closed loop," as one artist put it, with the same artists and their friends getting all the work. But that circle seems to be widening—the Arts Commission's selection of artists for "In Public: Seattle 1991"—an $850,000 public art project in conjunction with the Seattle Art Museum's downtown opening—was given grudging approval by local artists who felt the process more fair than in the past.

The public art process begins with the placement of an ad in the 1% for Art column in *Seattle Arts* and announcements to other media. Artists can then request a prospectus on the project from the Seattle Arts Commission.

HEARD ON THE STREET

"One observation after six months of interviews with members of the arts community is that a prime prerequisite for serving on an arts board is wealth. The resulting board may not be very representative of the community at large."

League of Women Voters report

WHO'S ON THE ARTS COMMISSION, ANYWAY?

The Arts Commission began in 1971 and consists of 15 volunteers appointed by the mayor. At least half of the commissioners are active in the arts or arts administration. There's a paid staff of 15 located in the Center House at Seattle Center. Members of the commission come and go, but as of 1990—and short a few members—they are:

Director: T. Ellen Sollod
Sandy Bradley (traditional folk arts)
Jan Brousseau (dance)
Rita Chavese (visual)
Carl T. Chew (visual)
Bruce Firestone (literary arts)
Marie McCaffrey (visual/graphic arts)
Michael J. Malone (theater and music)
Ben Moore (theater)
Julian Priester (jazz)
David Rutherford (visual)
Charles Rynd (visual/photography)
John Vadino (dance)

Seattle Arts Commission
305 Harrison St.
Seattle, WA 98109
684-7171

One way to obtain a larger foundation or government arts grant when you aren't (yet) well known is to work through an umbrella arts organization. And if you think you're ready for a foundation or government grant but need a nonprofit sponsor, the Allied Arts Foundation may help.

For grant and sponsorship applications, call the Foundation at 624-0432.

HELP FROM ALLIED ARTS

Allied Arts of Seattle has been around since 1954. In the early days it worked on such things as billboard removal, street tree plantings, and public funding for art; currently, it is involved with downtown architecture, historic preservation, and issues affecting small arts organizations and individual artists.

Allied Arts has five committees: Arts Education, Metropolitan Arts Committee, Downtown, Historic Preservation, and Housing.

The well-respected organization also publishes *Access, A Guide to the Visual Arts in Washington State.*

Allied Arts of Seattle
107 S Main St., Suite 207
Seattle, WA 98104
624-0432

What an artist in Seattle needs to survive is pretty much what an artist in New York needs: a job, an affinity for hanging out in laundromats, a love of brown rice and potatoes, and the information that at the Bagel Bakery you can get six day-olds for $1. (But you have to get up early to get them before they're gone—or try just before closing.)

The Allied Arts Foundation gives small grants to unproven artists—seed money for projects where large foundation or government program funding isn't likely. The grants are awarded three times a year.

WHERE TO GAWK

Almost everywhere you go in Seattle you'll stumble upon a piece of public art (sometimes literally, as in the case of manhole covers designed by artists or the duck footprints on First Avenue). The Arts Commission puts out a marvelous free pamphlet showing where the more than 1,000 public art projects are in Seattle. Call 684-7171.

AND, IN THE TUNNEL...

Metro Transit's public art program has resulted in a mile-long art gallery —all inside the new bus tunnel. Artists Jack Mackie, Vicki Scuri, and Sonya Ishii of Seattle, and Kate Ericson and Alice Adams of New York worked with architects on the project from the tunnel's conception. The artwork is in three areas: in the tunnel itself, in the five stations, and at street level at Third and Pine.

In the tunnel the artwork is aimed at helping riders orient themselves to their locations underground with reflective stripes, telephone markers, exit signs, zone indicators, and street guide signs.

Convention Center Station: A waterfall on the south retaining wall, two stylized white pipe marquees with glass and neon inserts, utility poles painted in patterns of green, white, and safety orange.

Westlake Station: Three porcelain enamel murals at platform level, each with a retail theme and reflecting the character of downtown display windows; multicolored terra-cotta tiles with raised patterns of leaves, vines, and flowers; wall tiles impressed with 40 different fabric-like patterns.

University Street Station: High-tech white, black, and red granite in patterns on walls and floors; light-work sculptures on mezzanine level; 23 wall-mounted light-sticks flashing to create images; 14 screens of more than 100 animated symbols and faces.

Pioneer Square Station: Red and gray granite pergola similar to the one in Pioneer Square, six-panel gate including human figures mounted on steel grillwork. Large clocks fashioned from masonry remnants and mounted at each end of the station's mezzanine; tile mural lining one wall with images of Seattle's history; granite pieces arranged as if they are in motion.

International District Station: Steel trellis walkways on plaza level; two poems etched on stainless steel plates and placed on the crossbeams of the trellis walkway. Steel panels embellished with origami designs; 12 symbols of the Chinese calendar built from cut-and-colored bricks set into the station plaza floor; heavy timber and stone performance platform.

On the street at Third and Pine each station entrance has an eight-foot marker in the silhouette of a Northwest personality. The figure corresponds to a quote sandblasted into the stairs leading from the mezzanine to the street level of each station; five-foot metal tree grates for the five species of trees in the program; and two artist-designed street clocks.

Allied Arts of Seattle lobbies against destruction of low-cost housing for artists and also has a list of what housing is available to artists in the city. Call 624-0432.

Metro Downtown Project
M.S. 131
821 Second Ave.
Seattle, WA 98104-1598
684-2100
Arts coordinator: Carol Valenta

A PEEK INTO THE CORPORATE WORLD

Somewhere between publicly funded art and private or commercial collections lie corporate art collections.Though some collections, such as Microsoft's, are displayed entirely in work spaces not accessible to the public, several collections—or at least portions of them—are on public view. Some of the notable ones are:

University of Washington Medical Center, UW campus: An entire program that includes not only artworks (about 120 pieces) but also performing arts and artists in residence. For information, call 548-6308.

Safeco Insurance Company, 45th at Brooklyn in the University District: A collection of over 600 works by Northwest artists (including 50 pieces of Pilchuck glass), exhibited in the mezzanine, lobby, and various other locations in the building. The main exhibition changes six times a year. For information and tours, call 545-6100.

The Prescott Collection of Pilchuck Glass, Pacific First Center, 1420 Fifth Avenue: A permanent collection of works by 36 artists from the international glassmaking community, all formerly or currently affiliated with the Stanwood glass school. For information, call 623-7385.

Sheraton Hotel and Towers, 1400 Sixth Avenue: Over 2,000 pieces of art, some of which are always on display in the hotel's public areas, others in the rooms themselves. For information, call 621-9000.

Unico Properties, One Union Square, 600 University Street: Exhibitions change quarterly; on display in the main lobby.

The best way to see corporate art is during Artstorm, a week-long arts festival produced by the Downtown Seattle Association. Art and architecture tours are part of the event—in many cases it's the only way you can get into, for example, the Security Pacific collection your banker is privy to. Artstorm, usually in February, includes tours, lectures, readings, storytelling, cinema, exhibitions, and music and dance performances all over downtown. A lot happening in a rather short time. Artstorm Hotline: 625-9940.

VISUAL ARTS VENUE

A well-established Seattle arts (and social) tradition is First Thursday in Pioneer Square. The art galleries have simultaneous openings the first Thursday evening of every month, with wine and nibbles at some galleries. The idea was born about 1982 when several gallery owners downtown, noting that something along the same lines was taking place in the University District, decided that combined openings would attract the largest crowds.

They were right; the crowds pour in. As at most openings, the point is much more to see and be seen than to examine the art, especially since crowding is not conducive to art appreciation anyway. But they do buy. Gallery owners love First Thursday; so do the aficionados. First Thursday maps available at most Pioneer Square galleries.

SECRETS OF GALLERY SURVIVAL

New galleries in Seattle come and go with the seasons; no one wants to guess at the average lifespan of a gallery, but all agree that new ones are up against it in this city. The reason? The same reason the music groups have an uphill battle. People primarily come to Seattle not for art, but for the great outdoors; the pull to the mountains and Puget Sound is greater than to the galleries. Another problem is that artists move from gallery to gallery without sticking with one long enough to get themselves—or the gallery—established.

The secret, according to successful gallery owners, is to find a niche where you have a following, or to diversify to the point of having something for everyone.

WHERE THE ARTISTS ARE

Seattle's arts community is no longer centered on Capitol Hill, where art students from Cornish used to frequent the taverns and coffee shops. The artists—as much as they gather anywhere—have moved downtown. You'll find groups of them at the Cafe Counter Intelligence in the Market, Septieme in Belltown, the Two Bells Tavern (also in Belltown), the Frontier Room on First (a mix of alcoholic pensioners, gays, black leather scenemakers, and artists), and the OK Hotel under the viaduct off Main Street.

SAM AND BEYOND

Seattle's museums have free days and memberships.

Bellevue Art Museum
Bellevue Square
Tuesdays free. Open every day.
454-3322

Burke Memorial Washington State Museum
UW campus
Always free except for special shows. Open every day.
543-5590

Frye Art Museum
704 Terry Ave.
Always free. Open every day.
622-9250

Henry Art Gallery
UW campus
Free to UW students and faculty.
Closed Mon.
543-2280

Seattle Art Museum
Volunteer Park
Free Thurs. year-round; Sun., Memorial Day to Labor Day.
Closed Mon.
625-8901

Wing Luke Asian Museum
417 Seventh Ave. S
Free on Thurs. Closed Mon.
623-5124

PLAY IT AGAIN, SAM

In November 1991, the Seattle Art Museum plans to open a new building on Second and University designed by Robert Venturi.

New SAM facts

- The new museum will be 155,000 square feet.
- It will cost $60.1 million.
- The old Volunteer Park Museum will become home to SAM's Asian holdings.
- Three galleries will be devoted to Katherine White's African art collection: one to garments and household items, a second to masks and costumed characters, and a third to sculpture originally seen in shrines.
- Two galleries will be dedicated to work of Northwest artists: Graves, Tobey, Tsutakawa, Callahan, and others.

SAM names to know

Director: Jay Gates
Associate Director, Arts and Exhibitions, and Curator, Modern Art: Patterson Sims
Curator, Asian Art: Bill Rathbun

The thing to do the week after First Thursday is to trot on down to Italia on Second Thursday, where restaurateur David Holt sponsors a discussion series. The topics include individual artist's works, funding, and performing arts. It's free, except for the desserts, wine, and lattes. Italia Restaurant, 1010 Western Ave., 623-1917.

The Center on Contemporary Art (COCA) is a mecca for artists new to Seattle's visual arts scene. It is, undiscovered artists say, truly open to new people, unlike the galleries that have their own stable of artists. COCA's Northwest Annual Competition is open to every city artist. COCA, 1305 First Ave., 682-4568.

ALL THE CITY'S A STAGE

It's always being bantered about that Seattle has the largest theatergoing population of any city outside of New York. True? Possibly—you'll certainly find enough actors to supply several plays per night with casts. In the past couple of years, actors and actresses have flocked to Seattle, and as the available jobs have become glutted, they've created their own. Seattle now has a booming fringe theater scene: Over 35 off-Broadway–type groups present cutting-edge drama.

The Actors Equity Guild here has about 350 members and is growing; another 500 or more non-union actors and actresses are out there too.

A new free referral service for non-union actors is Contact Seattle, run by Jonathan Harris. Theater reps and others looking for actors will call and run down the list of actors and actresses—even the BBC has used the list. Good for those breaking into the theatrical arts world here. Contact Seattle, 323-5826.

FRINGE THEATERS

The fringe theaters have formed the League of Fringe Theaters (LOFT) to promote themselves and to create a clearinghouse of non-union audition and show announcements. The great thing about these theaters is that they are cheap—tickets are often as little as $5. The groups have names like Annex Theatre, Cabar-Eggs, Kings' Elephant Theatre, Playwrights in Progress, Women in Theatre, Unidentified Moving Objects—you get the idea.

And LOFT has a 24-hour hotline providing info on performances, auditions, and workshops. LOFT hotline: 637-7373.

THEATER ON THE CHEAP

Ticket prices at Seattle theaters are nowhere near the ransoms paid for Broadway shows, but if you're a regular theatergoer without a personal trust fund, a theater habit can get pricey in a hurry. Try buying day of show, ushering, or attending preview performances.

The days when artists could bring their work in off the streets and be discovered by a gallery owner have gone the way of the Lana Turner/soda fountain story. Artists say it helps to have a middleman—a socialite, patron, or arts consultant—take your work in for you.

Day of show: If you wait to buy tickets until the day of the show you run the risk of a sellout. **Ticket/Ticket**, a half-price ticket agency in a booth on the upper level of the Broadway Market (401 Broadway E). Unless a show is the talk of the town, chances are they'll have tickets for that night's performance at half price (plus a service charge of about $1.25 per ticket). Ticket/Ticket handles nearly all theaters in town (from the Rep to fringe productions) and sells cut-rate entry to dance and musical events on the day of show. There's validated parking in the garage below the market.

Ticket/Ticket
Broadway Market, Second Level
401 Broadway E
324-2744
Open Tues.–Sun. 10 a.m.–7 p.m.
Cash only.

Ushering: Most theaters welcome volunteer ushers with open arms. Pass out programs for half an hour, see the show for free. The bigger theaters have regular lists of ushers who sign up to work one night for every show in a season, as well as a list of emergency ushers they can call in a pinch. Theaters especially need volunteers during the winter holidays, when big annual productions (ACT's *A Christmas Carol*, Bathhouse's *Big Broadcast*, The Group's *Voices of Christmas*) stretch the regular usher roster.
Previews: All the large theaters hold preview performances the week before a show opens that carry a cheaper ticket price than the regular-run seats. Check on these early, though; at The Rep preview seats go mighty fast. Also note: Double-dipping on the cheap tickets is legal—Ticket/Ticket sells half-price preview tickets on the day of show.

Rush tickets (last-minute sales) and discounts for students, seniors, and actors are available at some theaters—but don't leave home without your ID.

How to break in to Seattle's theatrical arts scene: All the theaters have open call at least once a year. Make phone contacts, especially with the Actors Equity Guild, Contact Seattle, and all theaters to see what auditions are coming up; attend a LOFT meeting; pick up a copy of The Actor's Handbook: Seattle & The Pacific Northwest at a bookstore.

CHEAP-SEAT GUIDE TO LOCAL THEATERS

A Contemporary Theatre (ACT)
Ushering: ACT has a regular roster of volunteer ushers who are scheduled to work one performance of all shows during the season. Over 300 ushers now crowd the list, but the ushering coordinator says she needs emergency ushers who can be called on short notice. Call ACT, 285-3220, and leave a message for Christine Jew, ushering coordinator.
Rush/Previews/Discounts: ACT schedules four preview performances prior to the Thursday-night opening of a show: Saturday, Sunday, Tuesday, and Wednesday. Tickets are $10 advance, $5 day of show.

Alice B. Theatre
Ushering: Alice B. uses volunteer ushers; pass out programs, see the show. Call 32-ALICE and leave a message or call the administrative office at 322-5723.
Rush/Previews/Discounts: Alice B. doesn't offer rush tickets (although Ticket/Ticket usually does). The theater often schedules two previews prior to a show's opening. One is open to the public, one is a subscriber preview, although tickets can usually be found for both; price $5.

The Bathhouse Theatre
Ushering: The Bathhouse has a regular list of ushers but has room for more. Leave a message for Jean Law, volunteer usher coordinator, at the Bathhouse box office (524-9108).
Rush/Previews/Discounts: The theater stages two preview performances on the Tuesday and Wednesday before the Thursday-night opening. Subscribers get first crack at the previews (and sometimes snap up most of the tickets), but everyone else gets a shot at $7 a pop. Student rush tickets are $6.50 for any performance a half hour before showtime, depending on availability.

The Empty Space
Ushering: Empty Space maintains three lists of volunteer ushers. **Usher subscribers** receive a subscription discount in exchange for their service. Ushers work one night of every production, ushering, stuffing programs, and helping clean up after the show. In return they receive a season subscription for $30 ($6 per show). **Esprit de Corps** are volunteers who work on a variety of projects for the theater (call the theater for information, 324-5161). **Single-production volunteers** contact the theater about ushering for just a night or two at a specific performance. Call 587-3737 and ask for the house manager.
Rush/Previews/Discounts: The theater usually runs four preview performances the week of opening night, which sell out fast. A preview ticket is $10, compared with $13–$18 during the regular run. Empty Space offers $2 discounts on tickets purchased in advance for students, actors, and senior citizens. Half-price rush tickets are available 15 minutes before showtime for anyone.

Intiman sponsors a "pay what you can" performance one night during every run —usually the last Saturday matinee for each play. Pay a minimum of $1. Tickets are up for grabs two weeks prior to the performance, must be purchased at the Intiman box office, and go quickly.

Intiman Theatre
Ushering: Intiman keeps a roster of people who pay $7 for the season and usher once per show, as well as a list of emergency ushers who'll show up on a moment's notice. Usually the entire season is taken care of with the first list. Call 626-0775 and ask for the house manager.
Rush/Previews/Discounts: Intiman has four preview performances before opening night; tickets are $11. Students may purchase seats one hour before showtime for half price.

Seattle Group Theatre
Ushering: The Group box office manager keeps an ushering schedule behind the counter. Call 545-4969 and see which dates aren't yet taken; they don't operate any formal assigned series.
Rush/Previews/Discounts: If you're a UW student, The Group is the best buy in town. All tickets at all times for UW students are $5. All other students can purchase tickets on the day of show for $5. Six preview performances run before opening night. Tickets are $8.

Seattle Repertory Theatre
Ushering: The Rep doesn't use volunteer ushers but does offer discounts for preview shows and student rush tickets.
Rush/Previews/Discounts: Three previews run before the Thursday opening night; tickets range from $6.50–$11.50. Student rush tickets at $6 are available 10 minutes before the show if there are empty seats.

AND ABOUT THAT HANDLING FEE

A large percentage of Seattle concert tickets are sold almost exclusively through Ticketmaster. In exchange for the convenience of computerized access to every ticket on sale, customers can expect to pay a service charge (called a "telephone handling fee" or a "convenience charge" or an "outlet fee") of anywhere from $1 to almost $5. Due to differences in sales agreements, the proportion of service charge to ticket price varies.

Ticketmaster
In-person purchases at The Bon (Third Avenue and Pine or Northgate Mall) and Tower Records/Video (4321 University Way NE or 500 Mercer St.); telephone purchases and information, 628-0888.

A LESSON IN THEATER DESIGN

For those who think a rake is what you use for leaves in the yard, and for those of you ready to buy that "best seat" front center, here's a cursory lesson about Seattle's theaters.

Most theaters in Seattle have what is known as a proscenium arch that forms the opening to the stage. The Opera House stage is a classic example.

But you'll also find thrust stages ("theater in the semi-circle," as at ACT). These stages extend out into the audience, with seating arranged on three sides of the stage. The thrust stage is designed to create a sense of intimacy between actors and audience. You may feel a performance is transformed into a tactile, dynamic experience, or you may find your viewing concentration broken by the more obvious presence of the audience surrounding the stage.

Then there's the arena stage, also known as "theater in the round." Seattle has one, UW's Penthouse Theater. Seating completely surrounds the stage and most closely resembles Shakespeare's Globe Theatre. This stage design presents the greatest challenge for designers, choreographers, and directors, who must plan performances with a view from the audience's every angle.

Seattle's older theaters usually have a large middle section of seats separated from smaller seating areas by aisles in the orchestra and balconies. In newer theaters seats tend to be arranged fanlike, spreading back from the stage, broken only by aisles on the far sides. Visibility is usually improved with greater "rake" or slope of the seats.

Keep in mind that good acoustics depend on both the design of the theater and the quality of the amplification/sound system used (if

Ticketmaster fees are not included in tickets' advertised prices. And sometimes superior seats are held for purchasers of expensive package tickets that include dinner, parking, and other extras. But there's virtually no alternative source for many tickets, so concertgoers have to play by Ticketmaster's rules.

any). Some theaters, such as Meany Hall, have been designed for both musical and theatrical performances, and provide very good viewing and acoustics. Other theaters, such as Intiman, are designed only for theatrical performances, and do not provide the best acoustics for the most exquisite chamber music concert. In theatrical spaces you'll find theater design does not lend itself to "mixing"; listeners mainly hear the instruments directly in front of them.

Some theaters designed as vaudeville houses (like the Moore) are generally long and deep and not designed to hold sound in the same way as those designed for the symphony.

Other performance spaces, such as the Kingdome, present tremendous difficulties for shows using either their own or the house sound system. During its construction, sound absorption was dropped out of the Kingdome budget, and without absorption, sound reflects heavily from the domed roof and walls during performances. Only shows like Wings, which used two of their own tremendously powerful systems, are able to overpower the reflection of their own music.

Theater design includes the work of acousticians, who work with the architects to make the most of space and sound. Have you ever gazed in awe at the thousands of lavish sculpted figures adorning the house of the Pantages Theatre in Tacoma? More than a monument to the Goddess of Theater, these ornate interiors break up or absorb sound, resulting in better listening quality.

The best acoustics can be found in the most unexpected places. Check out the rows beneath the lip of balconies, at the back of the house, and theaters where sound is not lost in high, open spaces.

Sources: SSG research; Mac Perkins of Pacific Northwest Theater Association

THE BEST AND WORST SEATS

A Contemporary Theatre (ACT)
100 W Roy St.
Seattle, WA 98119
Box office: 285-5110

ACT sells 10,131 series tickets per year, and 14,000 singles (not including *A Christmas Carol*, which sells about 21,000 tickets per year, or the Flying Karamazov Brothers, which sells about the same). Capacity of the theater is 450. ACT plans to move into its new theater (at Second and Pike) in 1991.

ACT features a thrust stage. Most seats provide excellent viewing, with the exception of the rows on the extreme sides of the house, in sections A and F. These seats are cheaper due to a diminished view and blockage of sound from their closeness to the theater's wall—don't sit there no matter what.

Although visual quality varies from performance to performance, choosing seats on the side of the stage gives you the advantage of "audience watching," or seeing the reaction of fellow viewers as the drama unfolds before you. While James Verdery (ACT production director) admits that this can be "distracting for some people," he says the beauty of theater is that it is a live medium and has a natural interaction between audience and performance....

The new building will feature two theaters—one thrust and one proscenium stage—and improved facilities.

Alice B. Theatre
1535 11th St.
Seattle, WA 98122
Box office: 322-5423
The Alice B. Theatre provides a showcase for gay and lesbian theme material, featuring local artists in a mix of political performance art and musical theater. The small 148-seat house and modified thrust stage offer excellent viewing and acoustics within an atmosphere of intimacy. Sit anywhere.

The Alice B. Theatre Company is often housed in the Theater Off Jackson in the International District (409 Seventh Ave. S).

Bagley Wright Theatre
155 Mercer St.
Seattle, WA 98109
Box office: 443-2222

The newest and most modern of the Seattle theaters, the Bagley Wright Theatre has a proscenium stage with a wide hall and a balcony. This large 850-seat house was designed mainly for speaking voice, so musical performances need a boost from acousticians.

The mezzanine seats can be difficult for tall patrons—the rows are pretty close together. And for short people, the front row of the balcony is a problem since the railing is right at eye level. Occasionally, sightlines aren't as good from the far side seats, though sets are usually designed with that flaw in mind. The balcony can seem steep to older playgoers, who might want to stick with the main-floor seats.

The Bagley Wright is home of the Seattle Repertory Theatre Company, winner of a Tony award 1989 for best regional theater. The building's been shrouded in scandal because of faulty construction, but approximately 23,000 season ticketholders don't seem to mind. Total attendance in a year for the Rep is about 155,900.

Bathhouse Theatre
7312 W. Greenlake Dr. N
Seattle, WA 98103
Box office: 524-9108
Originally built in 1927 as (what else?) a bathhouse, the building served as a dressing room for swimmers at Green Lake before its eventual transformation into a theater in 1969.

Most-sought-after theater jobs: the Seattle Repertory Theatre, which pays the most and has most visibility nationally, and the 5th Avenue Theatre road shows.

Like the ACT Theatre, the Bathhouse is small (143 seats) and has a three-quarters thrust stage. Visually, people say there are no bad seats. They're pretty close together though, so you do get to know your neighbor. Anyway, you don't get much choice; the Bathhouse has no assigned seats and no seating chart.

Broadway Performance Hall
1625 Broadway
Seattle, WA 98122
Box office: 323-2623
The Broadway Performance Hall, or BPH, has excellent sightlines from its 295 seats, which are in steeply raked rows curving back from a proscenium stage. The stage is all that remains of the old Broadway High School auditorium after Seattle Central Community College built on the site in 1979. This is a very versatile theater, with half of all its performances dance, one-fourth music, and one-fourth lectures. BPH has very good acoustics for music and speaking voice.

The Coliseum
First Ave. N and Thomas St.
Seattle Center
Customer service: 684-7200
The Coliseum is a large performance arena with 15,000 seats. The Coliseum features many big-name rock music performers who bring their own sound systems to Seattle for their shows. It is difficult to achieve high-quality sound in such an enormous space, and success at this varies depending on each show's equipment. Stay away or be prepared.

The Empty Space Theatre
107 Occidental Ave. S
Seattle, WA 98104
Box office: 467-6000
The Empty Space Theatre is widely respected for its "cutting edge" material. Located in the Old Pioneer Square Theater, the house has festival seating for its 158 seats. Acoustics here are not fantastic, but the theater is so small it doesn't really matter. Empty Space is working on getting more comfortable seats than the stiff ones here; let's hope they do. Those who don't like crowding won't like the seats against the wall; those who don't like looking up pantlegs and getting saliva from enunciating actors should stay away from the first couple of rows.

The Ethnic Theatre
3940 Brooklyn Ave. NE
Seattle, WA 98105
543-4327
Home of one of Seattle's smaller theaters, the Seattle Group Theatre specializes in African American/ethnic material. The 195-seat house has a modified thrust stage, excellent visibility, and very good acoustics. Try sitting toward the back rows for an eye-level view of the action.

5th Avenue Theatre
1308 Fifth Ave.
Seattle, WA 98101
Box office: 625-1900
Probably the most beautiful theater in Seattle with its lavish elegance, hand-carved ceilings, and black marble and gilded interiors. This proscenium-stage theater has 2,138 seats and a balcony that stretches 200-plus feet up from the stage.

Try to get seats up front on the first level or in the first few rows of the balcony, but if you can't, take binoculars.

Although the 5th Avenue has a very good house sound system, achieving quality sound is difficult due to the high upward reach of the place. Avoid sitting beyond the cross-aisle rows in the balcony because sound sometimes gets lost. Some shows also lose sound beneath the balcony, depending on the sound system used.

Intiman Playhouse
201 Mercer St.
Seattle, WA 98109
Box office: 626-0782
Visibility and acoustics are excellent in the pleasantly raked 424-seat, proscenium-thrust theater, where you'll never be more than 11 seats from the stage. Performances focus on the spoken word. It's also pretty good for chamber music, though not

for anything larger. Intiman has approximately 8,000 subscribers for its five-play season, and another 16,172 single-ticketholders.

Jane Addams Auditorium/Civic Light Opera Company
11051 34th Ave. NE
Seattle, WA 98125
Box office: 363-2809
One of the only theaters in Seattle (besides the 5th Avenue and Paramount) to do large musicals with large orchestras, the Civic Light Opera has an unusual mix of local talent in its professional, semi-professional, volunteer, and community-member company.

The company is housed in the Jane Addams auditorium at The Summit School, a large, nicely graduated house with proscenium-arched stage. Most of the theater's seats provide good viewing, with the exception of the first few rows. Here performers on stage may be obstructed from view by the waving arms of the orchestra director or the heads of musicians. (Without an orchestra pit, musicians are arranged at the base of the stage.)

Beware of the perennial favorites, rows K forward; you'll have trouble getting a broad view of productions and these rows fall within a "cone of silence," a triangular area projecting from front rows A and B, seats 5 and 6 through rows C–H, terminating middle center at about row H. Within this area sound is "muddy" due to the position of speakers at the stairs on either side of the stage.

Best acoustics are just under the lip of the balcony in rows L–S. Here words and music sound clearer after bouncing off the balcony overhang, and you'll find lots of legroom in row L because of the separating aisle. Acoustics are also quite good at the rear of the hall beneath the balcony, but only if your eagle-eyes can make up for being so far from stage. Avoid rows J and K (10 and 11), where sightlines are into the wings, unless you enjoy seeing the stage crew and company rushing around in the wings between scenes. Would be nice if they had padded seats....

Kane Hall
University of Washington, DG-10
Seattle, WA 98195
543-2985
Performances at Kane Hall vary, although the original intention of the place was for academic lectures. There are 708 seats in the auditorium, a stage that's really a lecture platform, and a balcony. Music mixes less here, which means you will tend to hear only the instruments directly in front of you.

Meany Theater
University of Washington
George Washington Lane
at NE 40th St.
Seattle, WA 98195
Box office: 543-4880
An excellent place to hear opera and see dance, the Meany Theater has a wide proscenium stage with a shallow 1,206-seat house. This space was designed more for singing voice, music, and dance performances than for drama and spoken voice.

Its proscenium opening is the widest in Seattle, giving Meany Hall good sightlines for orchestra performances, although occasionally audience members can see into the wings if masking is inadequate. To be on the safe side, avoid seats on the extreme outside aisles of the house. Sit in the first two rows of the balcony only if you are tall enough to see over the edge of the balcony partition.

The Moore Theater
1932 Second Ave.
Seattle, WA 98101
Box Office: 443-1744
Originally a vaudeville house, the Moore seats about 1,400 and has a long, deep, and ornate house, proscenium stage, and two balconies, the second of which has been closed but may be reopened in 1991. Acoustics here vary from good to poor. Deep under the balcony there are dead zones, but up to about 15 rows under the lip of the balcony the seats are OK.

Sightlines tend to be very good, but avoid the steeply raked balcony if you are susceptible to vertigo or nosebleeds.

New City Theatre
1634 11th Ave.
Seattle, WA 98122
323-6800
Avant-garde and new material from local artists and directors is the specialty in the small, 100-seat "multiple configuration" theater. Seating arrangements vary depending on the type of performance. Sightlines and acoustics are excellent; theater is intimate.

Nippon Kan Theater
628 S Washington St.
Seattle, WA 98104
224-0181
Built in 1910, this 400-seat theater is small and intimate—an ideal setting for solo performances. All kinds of musical offerings here.

Paramount Theatre
901 Pine St.
Seattle, WA 98101
Box office: 682-1414
This proscenium-stage theater has 2,832 seats divided between the floor and two balconies. The Paramount's acoustics vary depending on the quality of equipment used by shows. It was maligned last year by experts

Union actors use the Actors Equity Guild Hotline, 284-8269, to find out everything from audition times to possible ushering/clean-up jobs to cheap temporary housing. The hotline is updated every Tuesday.

who said the Seattle Symphony should not move there because of acoustical difficulties and the lack of room on the stage. Rock fans don't seem to care...

For the best musical experience try seats just under the lip of the balcony.

The Penthouse Theatre
University of Washington
Stevens Way
Seattle, WA 98195
543-4880
The first "theater in the round" in the U.S., the Penthouse has 171 seats in its oval-shaped house. Its small size will provide you with clear acoustics, and unusual perspective. Sightlines are very good. It's scheduled to be moved because of UW expansion, but as a historical landmark it will continue to house plays in its new location.

Seattle Opera House
Mercer St. & Third Ave.
Seattle Center
Seattle, WA 98109
Box office: 684-7200
Opera tickets: 443-4711
The Opera House has 3,075 pleasantly raked, comfortable seats. But watch out for the back rows under the balcony—you'll want your money back when you can't hear.

Box seats are best if you can afford them. They cost between $75 and $85 per night for center seats, $65–$71 side seats. No surprise—best ones are center first balcony.

Short people at the Opera House shouldn't sit mid-center main floor where it flattens out or they'll be dodging the head of the tall guy in front all night.

The two balconies offer greater visibility than on the house floor. The opera house gang is made up of the Seattle Opera, Pacific Northwest Ballet, and the Seattle Symphony. They're all crowding in there until a new symphony hall comes along.

The Studio Theater
Meany Theater (see above)
The "Mini Meany," as it is sometimes called, has 229-plus seats. It's a "black box" theater (where seats can be moved into various configurations), but usually plays as a proscenium stage. Acoustics here are very good, with excellent sightlines. The Studio Theater is used by the UW's School of Drama, as is the Glenn Hughes Playhouse on University Way and 41st.

Washington Hall Performance Gallery
153 14th Ave.
Seattle, WA 98122
325-7901
Plan ahead if you want a good seat for a performance at On The Boards. Shows at this 250-seat theater nearly always sell out, and with no reserved seating you'll need to arrive early. Seats in the balcony give the best view for dance performances, but if you want a more comfortable seat, try sitting on the main floor. Due to the small size, acoustics are good.

PLUGGING IN

Since the city's art scene is spread around, plugging into your scene of choice can be problematic. What if you're tired of Jazz Alley and want something a bit more underground? And what if all you know about rock concerts is what's advertised at the Paramount? To find out about the underbelly of Seattle's art world, you have to hang out, watch coffeehouse windows, and do some investigative work.

General info sources

Listings of arts events include:
- *Seattle Best Places*, Sasquatch Books: lists of galleries and their specialties, theater, opera, dance, and music organizations.
- Seattle Center Hotline: listings of what's happening at the center. Call 684-8582 and press 4 for arts info.
- *Seattle Post-Intelligencer*: daily (Fridays—"What's Happening" section).
- *Seattle Times*: daily (Fridays—"Tempo" section).
- *Seattle Weekly*: out Wednesdays (extensive "Goings On" calendar).

More specific sources

Seattle area arts publications:
- *ArtsFocus*, performing arts, 624-6113
- *ArtLife*, gallery guide, 367-6831
- *Earshot Jazz*, local jazz, 547-6763
- *Northwest Ethnic News*, ethnic arts, published by Ethnic Heritage Council, 726-0357.
- *Reflex*, contemporary art and art politics, published in association with 9-1-1 Contemporary Arts Center, 682-7688.
- *The Rocket*, rock music, 728-7625
- *Seattle Alternative Film and Video Calendar*, 682-6552.
- *Seattle Arts*, newsletter of Seattle Arts Commission, 684-7171.
- *Seattle/King County Events*, published by the Seattle King County Convention and Visitors Bureau, 461-5840.
- *Victory Music Review*, folk and ethnic music, 863-6617.

WINDOW SHOPPING

Flyers are the medium of choice for most arts groups. Here are a few places to look for the latest flyers from some of the more avant-garde groups:
AFLN Art Gallery and Cafe (Capitol Hill)
Allegro Espresso Bar (U District)
Art in Form Bookstore (Belltown)
B&O Espresso (Broadway)
Cyclops (Belltown)
Elliott Bay Cafe, First and Main (Pioneer Square)
Espresso Roma (Broadway and U District)
OK Hotel (under the viaduct between Main and Washington)
Still Life in Fremont Coffeehouse (Fremont)
Virginia Inn, art bar (downtown)

Or if you want to talk to people from the literati and avant-garde groups, try the Blue Moon in the University District on 45th. They'll tell you not only what's going on, but what should be going on—and more.

ARTS GROUPS

Allied Arts Foundation
1001 Fourth Ave.
Seattle, WA 98154
624-0432
Provides project sponsorship for a wide variety of individual artists, arts organizations, and coalitions of arts groups.

Allied Arts of Seattle
107 S Main St.
Seattle, WA 98104
624-0432
A membership advocacy organization devoted to various arts, preservation, and urban design issues.

Art In Form
2237 Second Ave.
Seattle, WA 98121
441-0867
A bookstore with museum catalogs, recordings, and periodicals on contemporary art. Also has a mail-order catalog. Research materials on specific contemporary artists or art topics are available.

Artech Inc.
169 Western Ave. W
Seattle, WA 98119
284-8822
Fine arts handling, including exhibition design and installation, packing and crating, shipping, custom fabrication of sculpture stands, art collections management, rental of temporary display walls, storage, restoration, and repair of damaged artworks.

Artist Trust
1331 Third Ave.
Seattle, WA 98101
467-8734
Information, services, and fellowships for artists in the state. Quarterly newsletter.

Artists Equity
284-8269 Hotline
Local chapter of national organization.

Bumbershoot
P.O. Box 21134
Seattle, WA 98111
443-5233
September arts festival at the Seattle Center.

Business Volunteers for the Arts
600 University St., Suite 1200
Seattle, WA 98101
461-7209
Places volunteers from businesses with nonprofit arts and cultural organizations.

Centrum
105 S Main St., Suite 204
Seattle, WA 98104
625-9779
Offers performances, workshops, and temporary residences for writers in Port Townsend.

Fabrication Specialties
527 S Portland St.
Seattle, WA 98108
763-8292
Collaborates with artists on both public and private pieces fabricated in metal, concrete, glass, stone.

Fremont Fine Arts Foundry
154 N 35th St.
Seattle, WA 98103
632-4880
Visual arts facility which includes 10 artist studio-residences, a day studio for classes, workshops, or individual projects, a stone-carving yard, a hot-glass shop, a darkroom, the Fremont Fine Arts Gallery, and a foundry equipped for casting nonferrous metals, mostly bronze and aluminum.

Nine-One-One
Contemporary Arts Media Center
117 Yale Ave. N
Seattle, WA 98109
682-6552
Contemporary arts resource center. Performances, exhibitions, newsletter, and video editing facility. Publishers of *Reflex* magazine.

Pacific Northwest Arts & Crafts Fair
301 Bellevue Square
Bellevue, WA 98004
454-4900
July arts fair.

Seattle Artists Coalition
415 30th Ave.
Seattle, WA 98122
340-0917
Association of artists and arts administrators who meet bimonthly to discuss issues and community actions.

Seattle Women's Caucus for Art (SWCA)
University YWCA
4057 Roosevelt Way NE
Seattle, WA 98105
784-5338
One of 31 chapters of a national organization (WCA) that serves over 3,500 women in the visual arts professions.

Washington Alliance for Arts Education (WAAE)
158 Thomas St.
Seattle, WA 98109
441-4501
Promotes arts education programs.

Washington State Arts Alliance
P.O. Box 9407
Seattle, WA 98109
443-3505
Advocacy for arts at the state, county, and city level.

Washington Volunteer Lawyers for the Arts (WVLA).
600 First Ave.
Seattle, WA 98104
223-0502
Legal assistance and referrals on a sliding-fee scale. Workshops on issues of special interest to artists including contracts and copyrights.

Women Painters of Washington State
Seattle Art Museum
Volunteer Park
Seattle, WA 98112
362-8872 or 363-8863
Statewide group of women painters, sculptors, craftswomen, and printmakers.

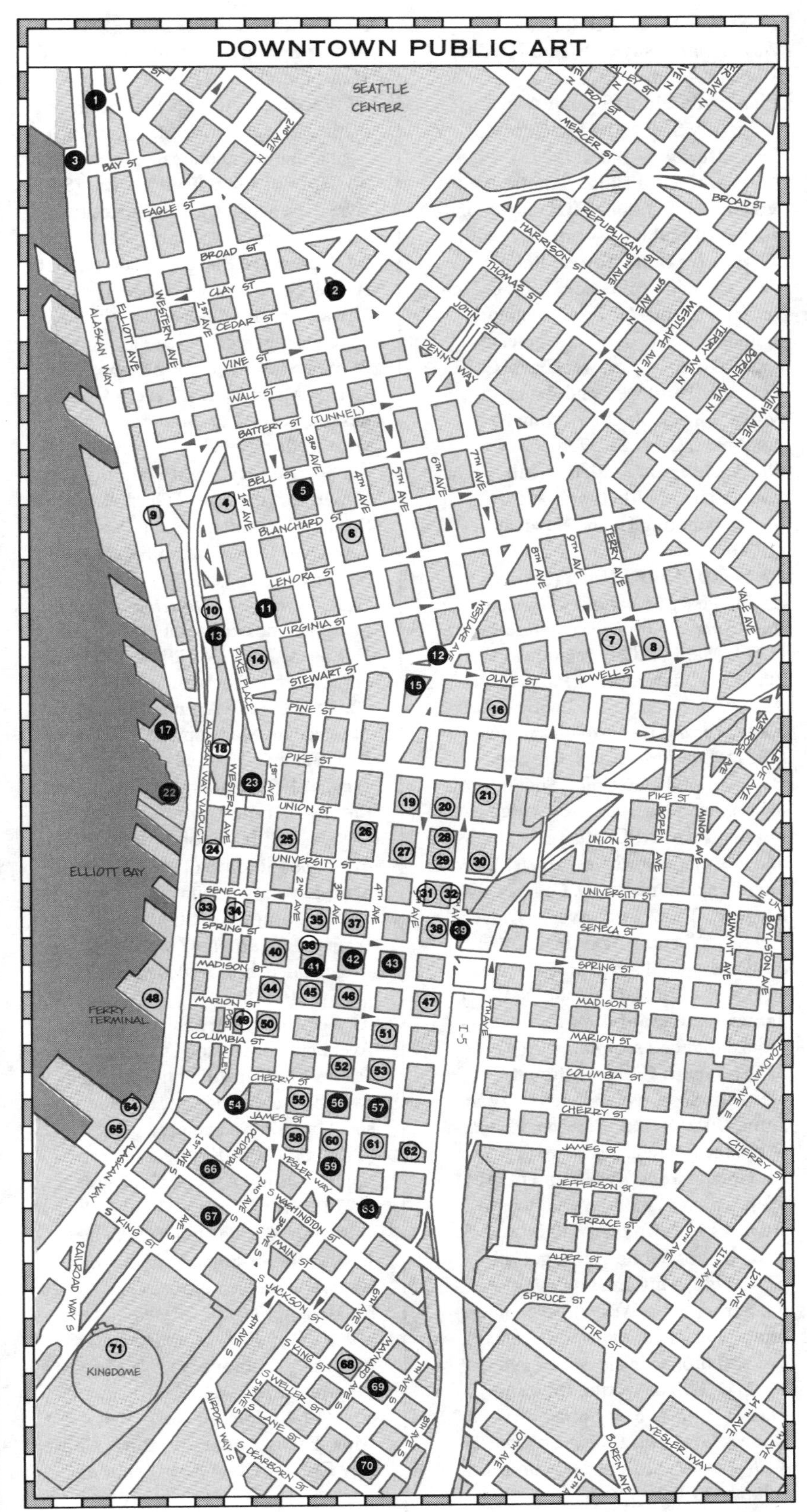

Downtown

1. 3131 Elliott Ave.: David Govadere, *10 Feet into the Future*—aluminum sculpture (1987).

2. Tilikum Place (Fifth Ave. & Denny Way): **Richard Beyer**, fountain basin—granite, boulders (1975); **James A. Wehn**, *Chief Seattle*—bronze statue (in fountain basin) (1908). **Edwards Bldg.** (2615 Fifth Ave., overlooking Tilikum Place): **Arturo Artorez**, *Realm of the Seahawks*—mural (1985).

3. Myrtle Edwards Park (Alaskan Way & Bay St.): **Michael Heizer**, *Adjacent, Against, Upon*—concrete, granite sculpture (1976).

4. First Ave. & Bell St.: **Kathy Fridstein**, photo collage (1980).

5. Regrade Park (Third & Bell)—**Lloyd Hamrol**, *Gyrojack*—concrete sculpture (1979); **Richard Beyer**, *Three Dogs*—sandstone (1978).

6. Fourth & Blanchard Bldg.—**Alexander Calder**, *Grand Crinkly*—metal mobile; **Howard Garnitz**, *He and She*—bronze sculpture, anchored to wooden benches (1978–79).

7. Gethsemane Lutheran Church (Stewart St. & Ninth Ave.): **August Werner**—stone relief.

8. King County Medical Service (Terry Ave. & Howell St.): **Norman Warsinske**, fountain (1964).

9. Bell St. Hillclimb (at Elliott): **Lewis "Buster" Simpson**, *High Rise Birdhouses*—plastic army helmet liners (1983).

10. 2001 Western Ave. (courtyard): **Mike Phiffer**, *Market Green*—tubular steel (1979); **Joe Wheeler**, untitled granite sculpture (1982).

11. First Avenue (Virginia St. to Denny Way): **Lewis "Buster" Simpson, Jack Mackie, Paul and Deborah Rhinehart**, *First Avenue Project*—sidewalk treatment, trees, benches (1986).

12. McGraw Square (Stewart St. & Westlake Ave. N): **Richard Brooks**, *Gov. J. H. McGraw*—bronze (1913).

13. Market Park (north end of Pike Place Market, First Ave. & Pike St.): **Marvin Oliver**, design; **James Bender**, carving—two totem poles, one traditional and one contemporary (1983).

14. Post Alley Stewart House Courtyard: H. Ramsay, *Stewart House Birdhouse* (1980).
15. Westlake Park (Fifth Ave. & Westlake): **Robert Maki, Hanna/Olin Architects**, design team project (1988).
16. Pacific Northwest Bell (Seventh Ave. & Pine St.): **Tony Angell**, *San Juan Otters*—bronze sculpture (plaza) (1976). Inside, a collection of artworks by Northwest artists, available for viewing by appointment.
17. Seattle Aquarium (Pier 59, Alaskan Way at Pike St.): **Jay Kohn,** *Beyond the Reef*—oil on canvas (1982); untitled—acrylic on Plexiglas panels (1978). **Tony Angell**, *Orca Whale* (1977). **Dale Chihuly**, *Sea Forms*—glass (1987).
18. Hillclimb Court at Pike St.: **Michael Fajans,** *Evan, Where's Your Hat?*—mural (1983). **Michael Oren**, untitled—carved stone (1981). **Toby Owen**, *Portrait of Claud LeGouaille*—painted relief (1981). **Wendy Brawer**, *Put & Take*—three-dimensional collage (1979).
19. Washington Mutual Savings (Fifth Ave. & Union St.): **Harold Balazs**, *Northwest Herbal*—enamel (1978).
20. Logan Bldg. (Fifth Ave. & Union St.): **Archie Graber**, *Wild Geese*—bronze sculpture (1959).
21. Sheraton Hotel (Sixth Ave. & Pike St.)—Collection: **Parks Anderson, Susan Backman, Jeffrey Bishop, Colleen Chartier, Carl Chew, Dwight Coburn, Karen Guzak, Stephen Hazel, Paul Heald, William Hoppe, Paul Horiuchi, Diane Katsiaficas, Larry Kirkland, Carolyn Law, Jacob Lawrence, Paul Macapia, Alden Mason, Nancy Mee, Mary Ann Peters, Bill Ritchie, Connie Ritchie, Norie Sato, Robert Sperry, Adrienne Salinger, Dan Smith, Stanley Smith, James Washington Jr.**
22. Waterfront Park (Union St. & Elliott Ave.): **James FitzGerald, Margaret Tomkins**, *Waterfront Fountain*—bronze fountain (1974).
23. Union Substation (Union St. & Post Alley): **Ann Sperry**, *Seattle Garden*—painted steel (1988).
24. Seattle Steam Plant (Alaskan Way & University St.): **Tom Holder**, *Ribbons*—mural (1975).
25. Arcade Bldg. (Second Ave. & University St.): **Miro FitzGerald**, *Cross Member*—mural (1975).
26. Washington Bldg. (Fourth Ave. & Union St.): **James FitzGerald**, untitled wall sculpture—bronze (1960).
27. Rainier Bank Tower: Rainier National Bank collection (Fifth & University). **Rodin**, *La Terre*, sculpture in main lobby (Fourth & University), open 10 a.m.–4 p.m. weekdays. Collection of Northwest and Asian artworks is available for viewing by appointment. Call 621-5736.
28. Washington Athletic Club (Sixth Ave. & Union St.): **James Wehn**, plaque honoring Hanna Newman (1930).
29. Seattle Hilton Hotel (Sixth Ave. & University St.): **James Hansen**, *Rune Singer*—bronze sculpture (1974). **Sam Gilliam**, painting (1973).
30. One Union Square Plaza (Sixth Ave. & University St.): Lobby—**Lee Kelly**, *Torana Gateway*—sculpture (1982). Interior—Jones, Grey and Bayley (3600 One Union Square) Collection includes a complete volume of original **Edward Curtis** photographs and works by Northwest artists. Viewing by appointment only. Call 624-0900.
31. IBM Bldg. (Fifth Ave. & University St.): **Norman Warsinske**, *Wind on Water*—wall sculpture—welded steel with gold leaf (in lobby) (1964). **James FitzGerald**, *IBM Fountain*—bronze fountain sculpture (1964).
32. Plymouth Congregational Church (Sixth Ave. & University St.): **James FitzGerald**, *Pinkham Fountain*—bronze fountain sculpture (1967).
33. Cornerstone Development (1011 Western Ave., #500): A number of artworks in downtown buildings are available for public viewing. Call 623-9374 for information.
34. Spring St. & Western Ave.: **anonymous**, *Duck Feet Imprints*—concrete and cast bronze in sidewalk (1983).
35. 1111 Third Avenue Building Plaza (Third Ave. & Spring St.): **Robert Graham**, *Dance Columns I & II*—bronze sculptures on bronze columns (1982).
36. Rainier National Bank (Second Ave. & Spring St., on alley): **Richard Haas**, mural (1981).
37. Pacific Northwest Bell Bldg. (Third Ave. at Spring St.): **Jan Zach**—aluminum sculptures.
38. Crowne Plaza/Holiday Inn (Sixth Ave. & Seneca St.): **James Rosati**, *Loo Wit*—steel sculpture (1980).
39. Naramore Plaza (SE corner, Sixth Ave. & Seneca St.): **George Tsutakawa**, *Naramore Fountain*—bronze, concrete, aggregate (1967).
40. Warshal's Sporting Goods (First Ave. at Madison St.): **Teresa Goins**, design; **Jerry Lee**, *Mountain Landscape Mural* (1984).
41. Seattle City Light Building Customer Service Area (Third Ave. & Spring St.): **Alden Mason**, *Seattle City Light Promenade*, four acrylic-on-canvas murals (1987). **Jean Cory Beall**, *Water into Electricity*—Venetian glass mosaic mural (1958). **Albert E. Booth, John W. Elliott**, *Evolution of Lighting*—Britannia metal (1935).
42. 1001 Fourth Avenue Plaza (Fourth Ave. betwn. Madison & Spring sts.): **Sam Francis**, untitled—acrylic on canvas (1979). **Henry Moore**, *Three Piece Vertebrae*—bronze sculpture (1968). **Emille Antoine Bourdelle**, *Penelope*—bronze (1968). **George Tsutakawa**, two fountains—bronze (1968). **James Washington Jr.** *Series in Creation, #7, #8, #9, & #10*—stone benches, Andes mountain granite (1968).
43. Seattle Public Library (Fourth Ave. betwn. Madison & Spring sts.): **James FitzGerald**, untitled screen—cast and welded bronze, enamel on sheet brass, fused colored glass (1958–60). **Rita Kepner**, *In Transition Is Unity*—African black granite (1978). **Rita Kepner**, *Negative Round*—African wonder stone (1971). **George Tsutakawa**, *Fountain of Wisdom*—welded bronze (1960). **Glen E. Alps**, *Activity in Growth*—steel (1960). **Ray E. Jensen**, *Pursuit of Knowledge*—bronze (1960). **James Wegner**, *Alice*—California sugar pine (1966). Interior works by **Glen E. Alps, Parks Anderson, Doris Chase, Fay Chong, Everett DuPen, Paul**

Horiuchi, Frank Okada, Susanne Sleek, James Washington Jr., James Wegner.

44. Federal Bldg. (Second Ave. & Marion St.): **Harold Balazs**, *Seattle Project*—sheet copper; bronze sculpture (1976). **Isamu Noguchi**, *Landscape of Time*—pink granite, stone (1975). **Philip McCracken**, *Freedom*—bronze sculpture (1976). *Burke Building remnants*—Terra-cotta remnants of the building formerly standing on the site were incorporated into the plaza by architects Fred Bassetti & Co.

45. First Interstate Center (Third Ave. btwn. Madison & Marion): **Beverly Pepper**, *Moline Markers*—five iron sculptures; also interior work (1984).

46. Bank of California Center (900 Fourth Ave., btwn. Madison & Marion): Bogle & Gates—a private collection concentrating on Northwest artists; call 682-5151. Other interior artwork as well.

47. Madison Hotel (Sixth Ave. & Madison St.): **Dale Chihuly**, *Seaform Series*—blown glass (1983). **Al Held**, *Venetian II*—painting (1980). **Hilda Morris**, *Turning*—bronze sculpture (1980).

48. Ferry Terminal (Pier 52, Alaskan Way & Marion St.): **George Tsutakawa**, *The Joshua Green Fountain*—bronze (1966); interior works.

49. Colman Bldg. (First Ave. btwn. Columbia and Marion): **Dudley Pratt**, *Washington Industries*—cast bronze gates (1929).

50. Norton Bldg. (Second Ave. & Columbia St.): **Philip McCracken**, *Restless Bird*—cast concrete (1959).

51. First United Methodist Church (Fifth Ave. at Marion): **Paul Lewing**—ceramic tiles (1982).

52. Chamber of Commerce Bldg. (Columbia St. & Third Ave.): **Morgan Padelford, Mildren Stumer**—bas-relief (1924).

53. Columbia Center (Fifth Ave. & Columbia St.): **Anthony Caro**, *Rape of the Sabine*—steel.

54. Pioneer Place (Yesler Way & First Ave. S): **James A. Wehn**, *Chief Seattle Fountain*—bronze, cast iron (1909). **Charles Brown and William H. Brown** with **James Starrish, Robert Harris, William Andrews, James Andrews**, *Seattle Totem Pole* (replica)—Alaska red cedar (1939–40); **Julian Everett**, *Pergola*—cast iron, glass (1909).

55. Alaska Bldg. (SE corner, Second Ave. & Cherry St.): **Ernest Norling**, *Alaska's Industries and Resources*—oil on canvas mural (1958).

56. Public Safety Building (Fourth Ave. & James St.): **Dudley Pratt**, *Gold Star Mother*—marble relief (1950). (Third Ave. & Cherry St.): **James Wehn**, *Seattle Insignia*—bronze relief. Washington Memorial Plaza (Fourth & Cherry, formerly Public Safety Bldg. Plaza): **Robert Irwin**, *Nine Spaces, Nine Trees*—plaza design; plum trees, blue mesh fencing (1983).

57. Seattle Municipal Bldg. (Fourth Ave. & Cherry St.): **Everett DuPen**, carved wood screens (1962). **Glen E. Alps**, *Fountain of Waterfalls*—mixed media (1962).

58. Smith Tower (Yesler & Second Ave.), King County Arts Commission Gallery (11th floor): changing exhibits of Portable Collection and Gallery Program artists (1987).

59. Prefontaine Place (Third Ave. btwn. Yesler & Jefferson): **Carl F. Gould Sr.**, fountain with turtles—granite, blue tile (1925).

60. King County Courthouse (Third Ave. & James St.): **William Ivey**, *Abstraction*—oil on canvas (1982). **Norie Sato**, *Images from the Phosphor Coast*—cibachrome prints (1985).

61. King County Admin. Bldg. (Fourth Ave. & James St.): **George Tsutakawa**, *Sandworm*—stainless steel sculpture (1986). **Robert Sperry**, *Untitled #625*—ceramic tile wall in lobby (1985).

62. King County Correctional Facility (Fifth Ave. & Jefferson St.): **Benson Shaw**, *Torus, Torum II*—concrete relief panels (1984). **Martha Schwartz**, *Garden*—ceramic tile plaza (1987).

63. 400 Yesler Bldg. (Fifth Ave. & Yesler): **Michael Fajans**, *Covert Ensemble*—mural (1979).

64. Pier 49 (Alaskan Way & S Washington St.): **John Hagan**, Tlingit totem pole—wood (1975).

65. Pier 48 (Alaskan Way & S Main St.): **Amos Wallace**, *Kahan*—wood panels (1969).

66. Occidental Square (Occidental S & S Washington): **Duane Pasco**, *Sun and Raven, Man Riding a Whale, Tsonqua, Totem Bear*—painted cedar totems (c. 1970–75). (Occidental S & S Main sts.): **Ilze Jones**, *Water Spigot*—cast bronze bolted on concrete gazebo (1971–73).

67. Fire Station 10 (Headquarters) (Second S & S Main): **Tom Askman**, *Firefighter Silhouettes*—brass (1987). **Ellen Ziegler**, *Firefighter's Memorial*—terrazzo and brass (1987).

68. Bush Hotel (Maynard S & S King St., overlooking Hing Hay Park): **John Woo**, *Dragon*—mural (1977).

69. Maynard Ave. & Jackson St.: **George Tsutakawa**, *Street Furniture*—bronze sculpture (1979).

70. International Children's Park (Seventh Ave. S & S Lane): **Gerard Tsutakawa**, *Sand Dragon Play Sculpture*—bronze, steel sculpture (1980).

71. Kingdome (King St. & Occidental): **Harold Balazs**, *untitled*—enamel on steel mural (1977). **Philip McCracken**, *Kingdome Bronzes*—five cast-bronze relief panels (1978). **Jacob Lawrence**, *Games*—vitreous enamel on steel mural (1980). **Michael Spafford**, *Tumbling Figure: 5 Stages*—painted aluminum panels (1980).

Seattle Center

17. Bagley Wright Theatre, exterior: **Stephen Antonakos**, untitled—red neon (1983).

18. Playhouse: James W. Washington Jr., *Barbet*—carved river boulder (1964); **James FitzGerald**, *Fountain of the Northwest*—bronze (1962). Interior works by **Maria Frank Abrams, Kenneth Callahan, Sir Jacob Epstein, William Ivey, Philip McCracken, Frank Okada, Lisel Salzer, Margaret Tomkins, James Washington Jr.** & other Northwest artists. Portable Works Collection.

19. Francois Stahly, *The Lang Fountain*—cast bronze (1962).

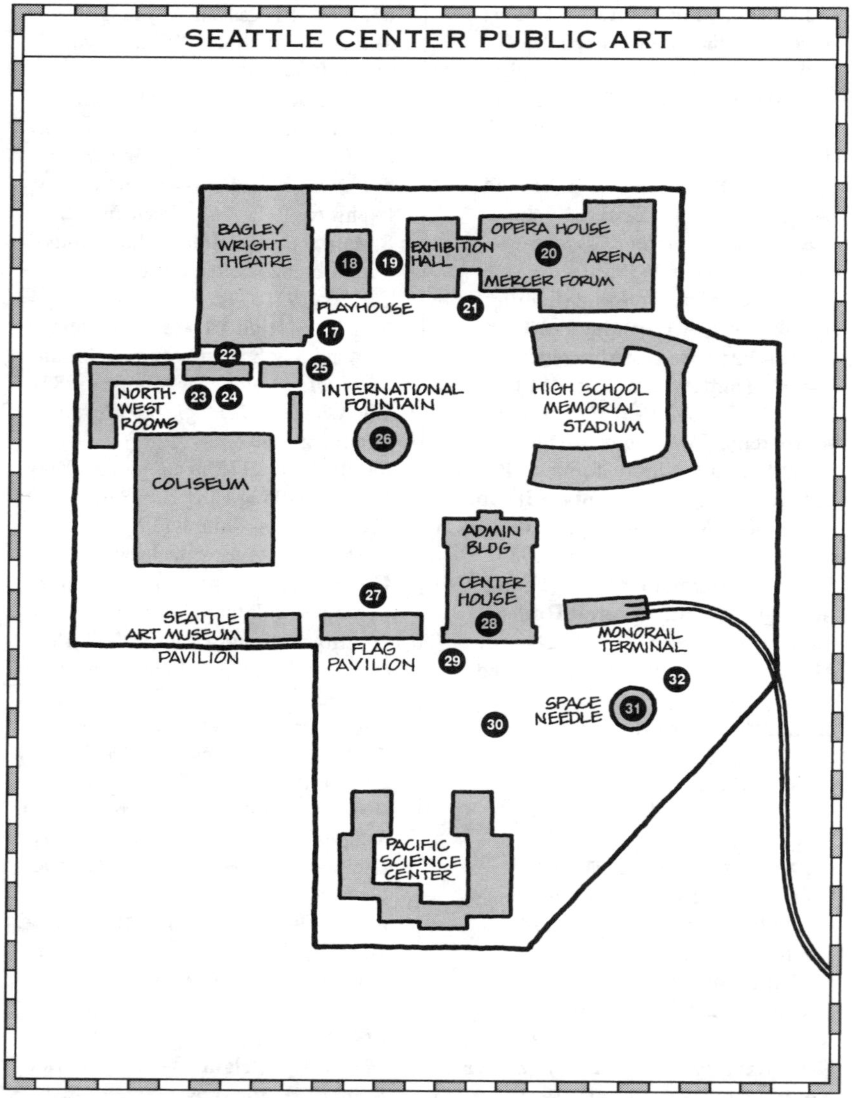

SEATTLE CENTER PUBLIC ART

BAGLEY WRIGHT THEATRE
18
19
EXHIBITION HALL
OPERA HOUSE
20
ARENA
MERCER FORUM
PLAYHOUSE
21
17
22
25
NORTH-WEST ROOMS
23
24
INTERNATIONAL FOUNTAIN
26
HIGH SCHOOL MEMORIAL STADIUM
COLISEUM
ADMIN BLDG
CENTER HOUSE
27
28
SEATTLE ART MUSEUM PAVILION
FLAG PAVILION
29
MONORAIL TERMINAL
32
SPACE NEEDLE
31
30
PACIFIC SCIENCE CENTER

20. Opera House: Interior works by **Guy Anderson, Harold Balazs, Morris Graves, Max Ingrand, Walter F. Isaacs, Ray Jensen, Hilda Morris, Ted Rand, John Robinson, Howard Smith, Mark Tobey, Roger Shimomura, Michael Spafford, Lois Graham, Patti Warashina, Jack Chevalier** and other Northwest artists.

21. Alonzo Victor Lewis, *Doughboy*—cast bronze (1921–32).

22. Tony Smith, *Moses*—steel sculpture (1968/1975).

23. Jack Fletcher, steel and cast concrete fountain (1963).

24. Everett DuPen, *Fountain of Creation*—bronze sculpture in basin (1962).

25. Randy Hayes, *Pool*—oil on marine plywood under Plexiglas (1985).

26. Kazuyuki Matsushita and **Hideki Shimizu**, *International Fountain* (1962).

27. Ronald Bladen, *Black Lightning*—steel sculpture (1980).

28. Center House—(theater, first floor): **Liza von Rosenstiel**, *Setting the Stage*—oil on canvas mural (1987). **William Peter Sildar**, *Queue VI*—wood sculpture (1975). Portable Works Collection throughout the building.

29. Duane Pasco, with **Victor Mowatt** and **Earl Muldon**, *Seattle Center Totem Pole*—carved and painted Western red cedar (1970).

30. Paul Horiuchi, *Seattle Mural*—Venetian glass tile (1962).

31. Alexander Liberman, *Olympic Iliad*—steel sculpture (1984).

32. Lauren Ewing, *The Endless Gate*—steel sculpture (1985).

NOAA public artwork projects

1. Martin Puryear, *Knoll for NOAA*.
2. Scott Burton, *Viewpoint*.
3. Siah Armajani, *NOAA Bridge*.
4. George Trakas, *Berth Haven*.
5. Douglas Hollis, *A Sound Garden*.
6. Siah Armajani, *NOAA Bridge*.

CHAPTER

14

SEATTLE: A CITY IN NEED

POVERTY

HOUSING

CHARITY

VOLUNTEERING

HOMELESS

SHELTERS

DRUGS

ALCOHOL

"In the past five years the city has acquiesced in the rape of the downtown area. This massive destruction of downtown low-income housing and the human scale of our city has been done solely for the sake of private gain." (Source: Church Council

of Greater Seattle, "State of the City Report")

And we thought we were so livable and all. Gentrification of traditional low-income housing areas has resulted in a plethora of emergency service centers, housing activists, and downright angry citizens. Here's another shot across the bow from the same report:

"Since 1983, when City of Seattle made an official commitment to preserving 7,311 units of downtown low-income housing, 1,310 units (additional) have been lost." Ouch! If you want to know what the social problems in Seattle are, start with housing and homelessness and next look at drug abuse.

While you're at it, look at the problem from another perspective: how to gain access to the dizzying array of social programs that are out there to help people in need.

WHEN IN CRISIS...

The social service network in Seattle consists of 600 private and nonprofit organizations as well as hundreds of city, county, state, and federal employees who administer a wealth of services. The churches are picking up more than their share; almost every denomination is heavily involved in services for needy people. Add to these the large numbers of social workers in private practice running small clinics and group therapies, and the network soon takes on the appearance of a maze.

Getting access to that maze can be tough. If you don't know whether a program exists to meet your needs, be persistent in your research. It probably does. And if you can't pay, or can't pay much, speak up. Most agencies operate on a sliding-scale basis.

Here's the first resource you need to know about: the Crisis Clinic. Begun as a crisis intervention hotline in the socially conscious sixties, the Crisis Clinic began keeping a Rolodex file of referral numbers for all kinds of mental health and emergency services. The list was eventually indexed, cross-referenced using a decimal numbering system, and put on a computer.

In addition to 24-hour crisis intervention, the Crisis Clinic is now under contract to provide general information and referral services for all United Way agencies through this databank, and refers clients to non–United Way agencies as well. (Even the telephone directory listing for the King County Human Resources Division mental health services says, "Call the Crisis Clinic.")

The Crisis Clinic will refer you to any one of: 78 organizations that need or will train volunteers; 31 places to find a language interpreter; 106 hotline numbers; 97 places where your donations of goods are welcome and lists of what's needed; 49 places where you can get free clothing, food, and other assistance —in some cases attendance at chapel is required; or 41 listings for low-cost housing or housing referrals.

The clinic provides information not only to its own line, but also to the downtown branch of the Seattle Public Library. The library has the Resource File index, which refers you to a 850-page volume of lists of agencies and services.

Major listings in the index are: education (support, formal, informal); environmental quality (animals, services); health care (community health, health supportive services, human reproduction, inpatient medical care, outpatient medical care).

Be careful when checking the index; the abbreviations can be tricky. For example, the listing "Cult/Spiritual Services for the Disabled" actually is an abbreviation for Cultural/Spiritual Services and lists mostly mainstream churches.

A smattering of the Crisis Clinic's broad, diverse, and unique listings:

Agent Orange Hotline
(800) 562-2308
State Dept. of Veterans Affairs

Crisis Clinic
1515 Dexter Ave. N, Suite 300
Seattle, WA 98109
461-3222

Dial-a-Complaint
(800) 562-6150
Billing disputes with telephone and power companies.

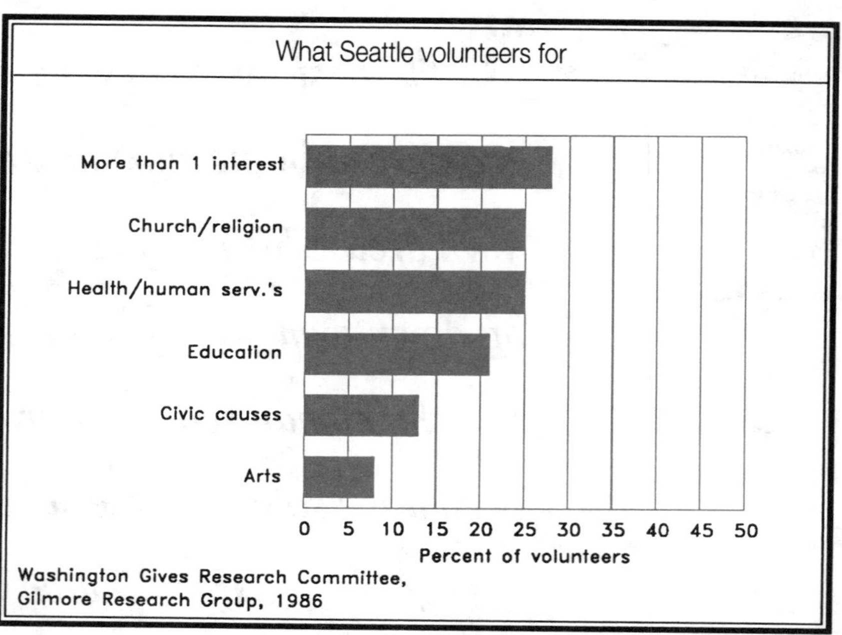

Washington Gives Research Committee, Gilmore Research Group, 1986

Eastern European Refugee Clinic
223-3540
Mental health counseling for Eastern European refugees and immigrants.

Ingersoll Gender Support
329-6651
Counseling, support, referral for transsexuals and transvestites.

Sex and Love Addicts Anonymous
200 W Mercer St., Suite 300
Seattle, WA 98119
(phone number not available)
Support group for addiction to lust and sex; focus on sexual minorities.

National Odd Shoe Exchange
(602) 246-8725
Shoe exchange for people with odd-sized feet.

P.S. My Baby Died
728-0054
Parents of stillborns.

A CHICKEN IN EVERY POT, A ROOF OVERHEAD?

"In 1969, a full-time minimum wage worker was at 109.4% of poverty level. In 1986 (last figure available), a full-time minimum wage job equalled 75% of poverty level."(Church Council of Greater Seattle Report)

It's called being underemployed and there's some—not enough, but some—help out there for those who are considered low income. Low-income housing is available to anyone in one of three categories:

- Involuntarily displaced or homeless (no permanent nighttime address).
- Those living in substandard housing or paying more than 50% of their gross income for rent and utilities (often elderly or handicapped).
- Everyone else whose low level of income makes them eligible (typically includes the mentally ill or those with family dysfunction).

The Seattle Housing Authority waiting list

Unit size	# Families on waiting list	Length of wait
1 bedroom	471	5 months
2 bedroom	326	6 months
3 bedroom	219	18 months
4 bedroom	56	24 months
5 bedroom	8	24 months

Source: Seattle Dept. of Human Resources, 1989

Clients are rated by need: homeless first, then those paying disproportionate amounts of income for housing, then everyone else.

What are the income levels for low-income housing? It depends on which housing authority you're dealing with—there are seven in the Greater Seattle area. What the federal Housing and Urban Development Department (HUD) calls "low income"—which would make someone eligible for low-income housing—is 80% of the median income in the county, or $23,250 per year for one person. Another category, "very low income," is set at 50% of the median income, or $14,550 for one person living in King County.

HOW TO APPLY

The Seattle Housing Authority (SHA) accepts applications and verifies all the information given as well as family status. If the applicant is qualified and homeless, SHA must provide transitional housing until permanent housing becomes available, sometimes in low-cost hotels or motels. Transitional housing is often used from three to four weeks to a couple of months before permanent housing is secured. If qualified and not homeless, the applicant's name is added to the waiting list for the first available housing.

BUT WHERE TO SLEEP?

How much low-income housing is available in Seattle? The answer is difficult to pin down and depends on how much help you need as well as whether you're dealing with one of the seven separate housing authorities in King, Snohomish, and Pierce Counties or with HUD. Each of these agencies has a variety of rental and rent subsidy programs. Keep after them until you get help, if you feel you may qualify. And check around; it could be well worth the time you spend.

No one will help you find rent-subsidized housing—it's up to you. Apartment-house owners don't have to advertise that it's available.

Everett Housing Authority
1401 Poplar St.
Everett, WA 98201
258-9222

King County Housing Authority
15455 65th Ave. S
Seattle, WA 98188
244-7750

Pierce County Housing Authority
603 S Polk St.
Tacoma, WA 98445
535-4400

Renton Housing Authority
P.O. Box 2316
Renton, WA 98056-0316
226-1850

Seattle Housing Authority
120 Sixth Ave. N
Seattle, WA 98109
443-4400

Snohomish County Housing Authority
3425 Broadway
Everett, WA 98201
259-5543

Tacoma Housing Authority
1728 E 44th St.
Tacoma, WA 98404
475-1170

Seattle Housing Authority owns 10,000 units; King County Housing Authority owns 3,500 units (1,700 elderly, 1,800 family); and Renton Housing Authority owns 310 units. Total owned units: 13,810. Turnover rate: 25–30% per year.
Source: Seattle Housing Authority

OTHER TYPES OF HOUSING

Seattle and King County issue rent certificates so that low-income residents can rent private housing at a cost to them of no more than 30% of their total income. The feds pick up the tab for the balance of the private rents. The federal government allocates money to states which allocate it to counties to fund the program.

HEARD ON THE STREET

"Everything has been full for months—people are open to creative suggestions for places to live, they're turning to friends...things seem to be in a downward spiral all over. The situation is becoming chronic rather than acute."

City Survival Services Unit
spokesperson Karen Dawson, 1989

HUD also has a number of subsidy contract programs with private apartment-house owners. These owners have borrowed money from HUD under various loan programs and are under contract to make a certain number of the units (sometimes all of them) available for low-income housing.

The prospective tenant applies directly to the landlord, who "keeps his own waiting list, has the right of tenant selection, processes applications, verifies income, assets, allowances and eligibility and determines rent by completing the Tenant Certification as required by HUD regulations."

But HUD periodically publishes a list of private apartment houses in its program. Get it by calling the HUD office in Seattle, 442-1439. HUD doesn't know which have vacancies; it's up to the prospective tenant to find them, which can pose a problem if you can't afford a phone. The list in 1989 showed 7,800 possible rental units in all areas of King County and includes apartment-building addresses, phone numbers, unit sizes, and programs for which the units are eligible.

WHO ARE SEATTLE'S HOMELESS?

When you think of the homeless, you might be thinking of the lines of men under the viaduct trying to get into the missions on a cold winter night. But the city's homeless are a broad mix of the very young, the very old, families, individuals, disabled, non-disabled, and the mentally ill. The common characteristics are lack of a permanent nighttime address and being flat broke.

Homeless facts

• Conservative estimates show that 1,500 to 3,000 homeless are served by the shelter network on any given day, one-third of whom are children. Other estimates show from 3,000 to 5,000 homeless on Seattle's streets per day.
• The shelters serve 15,000 in a year. Not all the homeless are served by the shelter network, particularly the mentally ill. (Seattle's bushy hillsides, such as those near the Yesler overpass or the Bell Street stairway, are often "home" to indigents who plop down a mat and sometimes even build small campfires.)
• At least 7,000 homeless are single adults: 90% men, 10% women.
• The homeless have high levels of disability which include alcoholism (50–60% of men), drug abuse, mental illness (10% of men), and physical impairment.
• Forty-five percent of the single women homeless are victims of domestic violence or other abuse, 30% of single women shelter clients are mentally ill, and the percentage outside the shelters is considered to be much higher.
• At least 5,000 homeless who come to shelters are families. The majority (54%) are single mothers with children, although the number of two-parent families is increasing.
• Over half of all homeless families are minorities. The average family includes 2.2 children.
• The vast majority of families are public assistance recipients whose grants do not enable them to afford housing, are new to the area and seeking employment, or are fleeing domestic violence.
• Shelters serve 4,000 children under the age of 18, over half of whom are under the age of 6.
• At least 3,000 are street kids—youths not part of any family structure. Some are as young as 11 or 12; most are 15–19.
• There are 165 shelter beds available for youths, but the majority require referrals by the Department of Social and Health Services.
• A total of six [not a typo] shelter beds are available for youths on a drop-in basis.
• Seattle has over 1,500 emergency shelter beds and 28 shelter providers.
Source: Various social service agencies and reports

SEATTLE'S DESERTED: THE MENTALLY ILL

State mental hospital populations dropped from 5,000 in the 1970s to 1,700 in 1989. According to shelter managers in Seattle, many of those released are now among the homeless populations on Seattle streets. No emergency shelters exist specifically for the mentally ill. At any given time, 100 to 120 mentally ill people are in the county jail.
Source: Division of Mental Health, DSHS

The most important thing when confronted by a panhandler is to at least give an answer either way, say shelter operators. Whether you give or not is a decision each person has to make. If you want to give, go ahead—often they really do need the money for food; they aren't all out there for sinister reasons. And if you don't want to give, don't just look away and keep walking. Say no—treat the panhandler as a person. When people ignore them it perpetuates the idea they're not fully human.

A FEW MORE FACTS

Downtown Seattle has lost 15,000 housing units since 1960, and developers have demolished 1,269 low-income units in the past two years. In the next five years, 1,000 low-income units are to be built in Seattle with taxpayers' money.
Source: Seattle Homeless Advocacy Group

The federal contribution to Seattle's housing programs dropped from $40 million in 1981 to $3 million in 1988. Federal block grants, which support shelters and other social services, dropped from $17.2 million in 1980 to $10.4 million in 1990.

From 1980 to 1986, 3,300 persons were displaced from Seattle by high-rise office buildings.

BUDDY, CAN YOU SPARE A DIME?

So should you give that change in your pocket to a panhandler or not? Nothing produces more guilt than passing someone by who wants just a nickel (or $0.13 as the guy nicknamed "Thirteen" down by the Market always asks for). Some panhandlers have dogs and beg for "money for dog food"; some have signs asking for money for the kids left behind; and some have a great song and dance about how they just left home in Bellingham and stupidly wound up in Seattle without a dime and everything would be OK and they could get home if you'd just part with. . . . You get the idea. One guy at least uses humor: "No refunds," his sign says.

What to do? Some people give and some don't. Some try to buy some soup or coffee and give it to the panhandlers—an effort met with mixed results. The big question is, are you destroying their livers with your hard-earned pocket change?

Panhandling in Seattle peaked dramatically a few years ago for

several reasons. First, police drunk checks were phased out when public drunkenness no longer was considered a crime. Second, the Police Crime Prevention Unit at the SPD believes the Pioneer Square and Market areas fostered a "seedy" atmosphere that attracts panhandlers. The third reason involved a federal program to help alcoholics. Attracted by grants of $300 a month, the recipients quickly drank their way through the money and panhandled to make ends meet. The indigents were attracted to this area by the program, making Seattle the Panhandler Capital for a while.

Reports suggest actually less panhandling on Seattle streets now (maybe the rain sent them south, to Sacramento, as one street guy says), but panhandlers work areas where there is lots of foot traffic and so it seems as if they're everywhere.

It's difficult to tell how much a panhandler in Seattle makes, but some street people estimate it's between $20 and $30 a day.

Most panhandlers are not dangerous, most are alcoholics and homeless. Many are mentally ill.

Seattle has an aggressive panhandler law; harassing anyone for money or any other reason is a misdemeanor on Seattle streets. Most panhandlers know this and will leave you alone rather than risk arrest.

EMERGENCY SHELTERS

While giving or not giving to panhandlers may be the source of angst, many emergency shelters have no qualms about accepting donations and/or offers of volunteer time. In fact, most have volunteer coordinators who will tell you how you can best help.

One caution: At Thanksgiving everyone wants to help. One volunteer said she showed up to feed the hungry along with huge crowds of others doing the same thing. They were jostling elbows to get to the needy—who were in the minority—

and under their breath saying, "That's *my* needy person, that's *my* needy person." Volunteers are still needed on holidays, but they're needed throughout the year, too. Many groups have daily soup kitchens and welcome help.

Seattle's shelters

Bethlehem House
4139 42nd SW
Seattle, WA 98116
937-7521
Serves two-parent and single-parent families with children.

Bread of Life Mission
97 S Main St.
Seattle, WA 98104
682-3579
Serves single men.

Broadview Emergency Shelter
P.O. Box 31151
Seattle, WA 98103
622-3108
Women with children and single women.

Catherine Booth House
P.O. Box 20128
Seattle, WA 98102
324-4943
Battered women with children and single women.

Catholic Community Services Emergency Assistance Program
P.O. Box 22608
Seattle, WA 98122
323-6336
Two-parent and single-parent families, couples, and single adults.

Central Area Motivation Program
722 18th Ave.
Seattle, WA 98122
329-4111
Two-parent and single-parent families, couples, and single adults.

Downtown Emergency Service Center
210 Jefferson St.
Seattle, WA 98104
464-1570
24-hour homeless shelter for single men and women.

El Centro de la Raza
2524 16th Ave. S
Seattle, WA 98144
329-3837
Two-parent and single-parent families, couples, and single adults.

Friendly Inn
American Hotel
Second and Fourth floors
520 S King St.
Seattle, WA 98104
628-2008
Two-parent and single-parent families, and married couples.

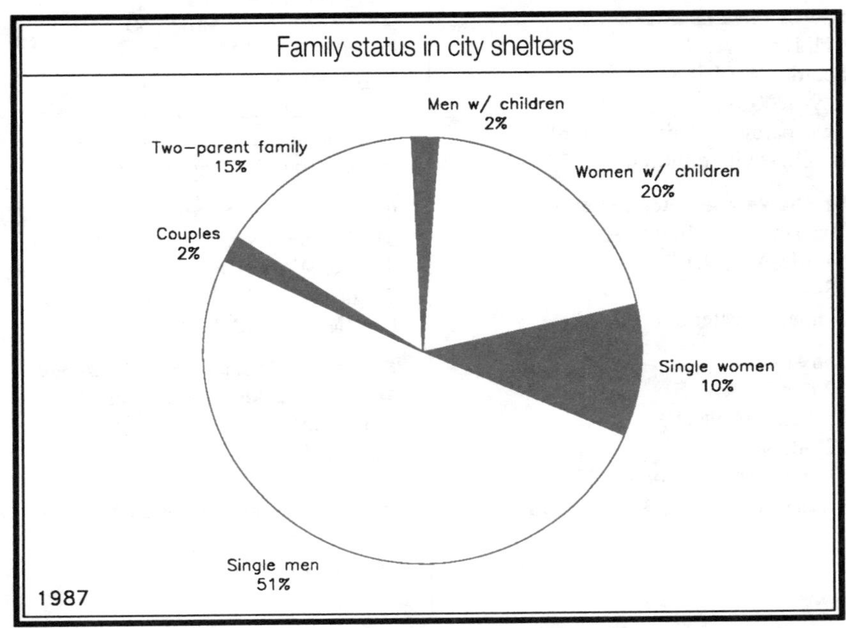

> **HEARD ON THE STREET**
>
> "No way should you give them money. You can't tell the difference between a drug addict and the homeless."
>
> Steve, a sometimes street person working for Strand Helpers

Immanuel Lutheran
1215 Thomas St.
Seattle, WA 98109
622-1930
Single men.

Lutheran Compass Center
Men's and Women's Programs
77 S Washington St.
Seattle, WA 98104
461-7837
Single men and women.

New Beginnings
P.O. Box 75125
Seattle, WA 98125-0125
522-9474
Battered women with children and single women.

Operation Nightwatch
P.O. Box 21181
Seattle, WA 98111
448-8804
Two-parent and single-parent families with children, couples, and single adults. Operation Nightwatch takes referrals and places in shelters people who haven't found a place to stay after 9 p.m. Crisis counseling.

Orion Multi-Service Center
1820 Terry Ave.
Seattle, WA 98101
223-1303
Young men and women, 11–20 years old.

Peniel Mission
2421 First Ave.
Seattle, WA 98121
441-7700
Single men and women.

Providence Hospitality House
914 14th Ave.
Seattle, WA 98122
322-2107
Women with children.

What can middle-class Seattle do about the homeless? Volunteer. Almost every shelter or social service agency maintains a list of volunteers they can call on. With Strand Helpers you can wash dishes and serve meals at the park across from the county courthouse. Also, Strand Helpers (as well as the shelters) accepts donations of blankets and coats.

Or, if washing dishes isn't your style, try giving those odd jobs around the house to someone from the Millionair Club Charity. The charity places casual laborers in temporary jobs on a first-come, first-served basis. So does the Salvation Army.

HEARD ON THE STREET

"I tell kids to go sleep in abandoned buildings and show them where they are. It's kind of weird, but that's all we have."

Shelter operator

Sacred Heart Shelter
232 Warren Ave. N
Seattle, WA 98109
285-7489
Two-parent and single-parent families and single women.

Seattle Emergency Housing Service
905 Spruce St., Suite 111
Seattle, WA 98104
461-3660
Two-parent and single-parent families with children.

Seattle Indian Center
611 12th Ave. S
Seattle, WA 98144
329-8700
Two-parent and single-parent families with children.

Seattle Veterans Action Center
105 14th Ave., Suite 2A
Seattle, WA 98122
684-4708
Homeless veterans.

The Shelter
6201 46th Ave. S
Seattle, WA 98118
725-8888
Young men and women, 11–17 years old.

St. Martin de Porres
1561 Alaskan Way S
Seattle, WA 98134
323-6341
Single men, 50 years and older.

St. Vincent de Paul
1001 Fairview Ave. N
Seattle, WA 98109
623-1695
Two-parent and single-parent families, couples, and single women.

Traveler's Aid Society
909 Fourth Ave., Suite 630
Seatttle, WA 98104
461-3888
Two-parent and single-parent families, couples, and single adults who are new to or leaving the area.

Union Gospel Mission
318 Second Ave.
Seattle, WA 98104
Single men, 622-5177, women and families, 628-2008.

Washington Association of Churches Refugee Housing Project
225 N 70th St.
Seattle, WA 98103
789-7297
Two-parent and single-parent families, couples, and single adults from Central America.

YMCA Downtown—Young Adults in Transition
909 Fourth Ave.
Seattle, WA 98104
382-5018
Young men and women, 18–22 years old.

YWCA Downtown Emergency Shelter
1118 Fifth Ave.
Seattle, WA 98101
461-4876
Women with children and single women.

YWCA—East Cherry Emergency Shelter
2820 E Cherry St.
Seattle, WA 98122
461-8480
Two-parent and single-parent families with children.

And more help

Homeless Donation Service
461-3200
A joint project of the city and Crisis Clinic, this is a referral service for those who want to donate such things as bedding and clothing to the homeless. The Crisis Clinic's Community Information Line has a data bank of 30 shelter programs and their needs. So if you want to donate, for example, blankets, the donation service will tell you which shelter is most in need of them and how to contact shelter operators. In 1989 the service received 1,000 calls and over $100,000 worth of donations.

Millionair Club Charity
2515 Western Ave.
Seattle, WA 98121
728-5600, 441-7835
Breakfast, Mon.–Fri.; dinner, Mon.–Sat. Also employment placement. And here's the answer to the question everyone asks: Why does the Millionair Club spell its name without an "e" on the end? Because it's not associated with any millionaire. It operates on a million dollar budget, which it gets in donations from a variety of sources.

Northwest Harvest
711 Cherry St.
P.O. Box 12272
Seattle, WA 98104
625-0755
Northwest Harvest is a center for food collections and distribution. Food is dispersed through community hunger programs as well as directly to senior citizen centers and relief missions. Needs are assessed weekly. Call Northwest Harvest (or local food banks) if you have food to contribute. Or watch for food drives. Most needed are powdered milk, food staples, packaged goods, and dietetic and baby foods. And, of course, money.

Seattle Department of Human Resources
Survival Services Unit
Alaska Bldg.
618 Second Ave.
Seattle, WA 98104
684-0179
Unit through which food, shelter, and clothing issues are funneled. Handles large and small donations too.

The Sharehouse
Associated Program of Church Council of Greater Seattle
4759 15th Ave. NE
Seattle, WA 98105
684-0179
Central warehouse project where surplus items from manufacturers are stored to be distributed to shelters in Seattle. The Sharehouse specializes in collecting *new* things in its warehouse as opposed to used items, and is targeting local manufacturers for donations.

Strand Helpers
5747 Martin Luther King Way S
Seattle, WA 98118
723-6082
Almost legendary service for street people. Serves food, distributes blankets, provides transportation, does almost anything else needed. Every day from noon on, Strand Helpers serves food to 300–1,000 people at the park across from the county courthouse.

Most welcome donations to homeless shelters: appliances, beddings and linen, clothing, children's items, non-perishable food, furniture, personal hygiene supplies, office equipment, and cash.

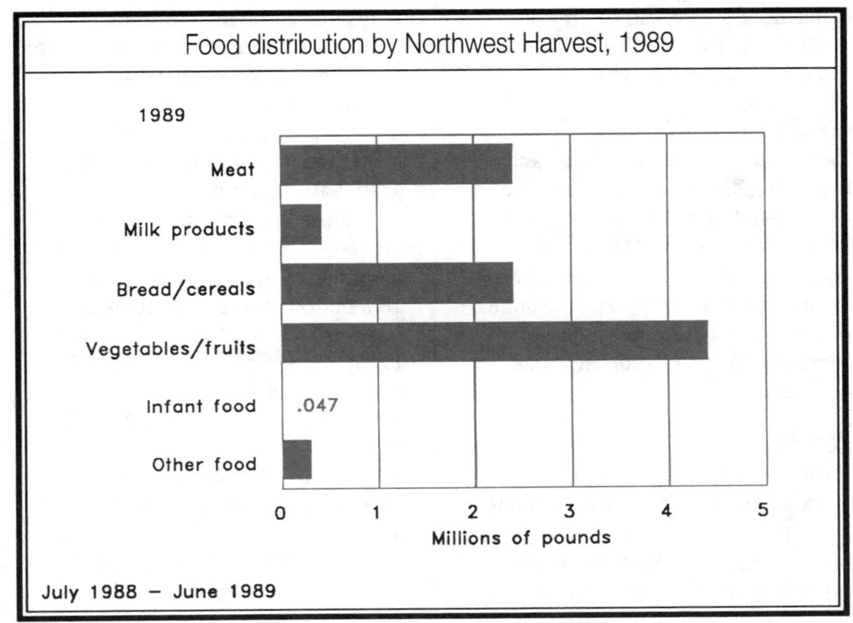

1989 food distribution by Northwest Harvest

Meat: 2.4 million pounds
Milk products: 417,435 pounds
Bread/cereals: 2.4 million pounds
Vegetables/fruit: 4.4 million pounds
Infant food: 47,362 pounds
Other food: 295,108 pounds
Total food: 10 million pounds

Northwest Harvest distributes 651,548 pounds of chicken backs and necks in a year and 806,000 pounds of turkey meat.

The Metropolitan Grill, hangout for stockbrokers, businesspeople, and politicians, sells 196,000 pounds of steak in a year or 98 tons.

Source: Consolidated Restaurants, Northwest Harvest

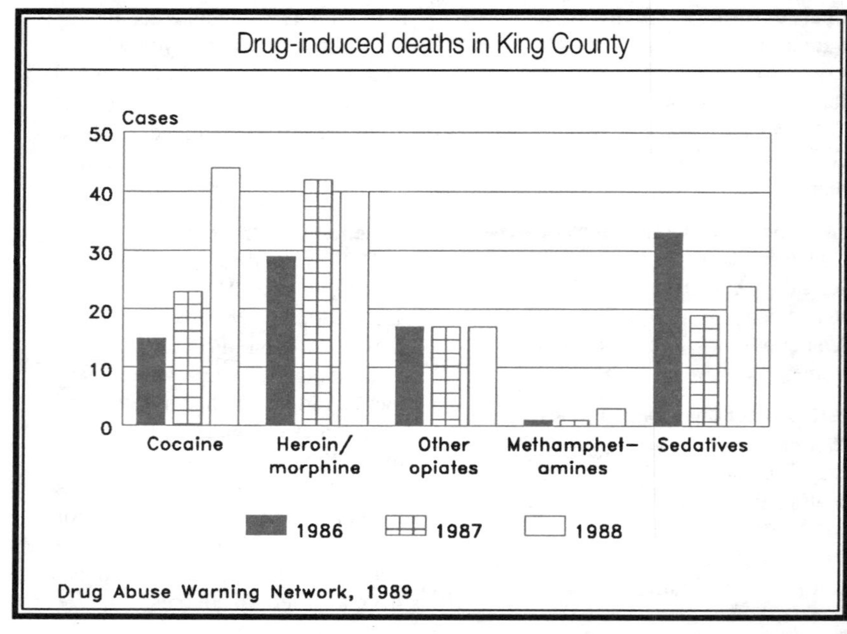

SEATTLE DRUGS OF CHOICE

If drug use in Seattle were a horse race, the past five years would have seen cocaine edging up on heroin as the most-used illegal drug, finally passing it by a nose, as it were.

The coke epidemic

Cocaine use in Seattle/King County is on the rise—in fact, health officials call it a cocaine epidemic. Here's the story from the streets:

Price: Cocaine here sold in early 1989 for $20,000 to $24,000 per kilogram or around $10,000 a pound. Street-level prices stabilized at $800–$1,100 per ounce; one-sixteenth-ounce quantities (called "teeners") are being sold for $120 each. A gram of flake cocaine is priced at $60. Crack cocaine continues to sell for $20 per rock, albeit the size of the rock is dwindling.

Purity: In Seattle, bulk samples of cocaine reveal purity levels at 90%, with street-level samples about 55%. Crack purity ranges from 70% to 95%, with most samples at or above 90%.

Source: The vast majority of Seattle's cocaine trafficking, along with its heroin trade, continues to be orchestrated by an Hispanic organization, according to city officials. Most street dealers get their supply from this organization, but no individual gang or group controls the street-level market.

Distributors: Youth street gangs, primarily from LA, distribute crack, with the resulting "turf wars." Residents around 23rd and Cherry have dubbed the strip "death row" because of the gang activity.

Deadly combos

"Seedballing"—using cocaine and heroin together—as a proportion of all drug-induced deaths increased from 6% in 1985 to 24% in 1988, then decreased to 15% in the first three quarters of 1989. But the annual number of heroin/morphine-related deaths has leveled off at about 40 per year.

Heroin

Virtually all the heroin in this area is black tar from Mexico, with a small amount from Southeast Asia. Prices vary from $250 to $400 per gram, depending on the source. Small quantities of black tar heroin, one-sixteenth of a gram known as "match heads," remain available for $20–$25. Purity levels of black tar are 40% to 70% here.

THE LATEST IN DRUGS

Seattle police and county narcotics officers have recently encountered miniscule amounts of a smokable freebase mixture of black tar heroin and crack cocaine in local street markets, called "chocolate rock." It's the new smokable speedball.

Meanwhile, marijuana farming has hit all-time highs, so to speak, with most Washington farmers selling out-of-state. Emergency-room mentions of marijuana jumped from 18.3 per quarter in 1986 to 54 in 1988 to 76 in the first quarter of 1989. A gram of "bud" can still be purchased for $10; a pound of local marijuana costs between $2,000 and $3,000.

"Ice" and "glass," smokable forms of methamphetamine hydrochloride, are being bought and sold in the Seattle/Tacoma area.

They're expensive, selling for $10,000–$12,000 per kilogram, or $4–$125 per gram on the streets. The drugs are coming from southern California and Hawaii.

And in a repeat performance: Area law enforcement agencies are reporting more encounters with LSD or "blotter acid" in local high schools and among younger college students. (Bellevue narcotics officers seized over 7,000 hits of acid through third-quarter 1989 compared with less than a hundred in each of the previous two years. Local prices are at $2–$3 per hit.)

Source: Seattle-King County Department of Public Health

ALCOHOL, THE OLD STANDBY

Alcoholics Anonymous sponsors 720 meetings each week in King County—and it's only one service out there offering help to those addicted to alcohol. The Crisis Clinic has a long list of facilities and services, and the King County Division of Alcoholism and Substance Abuse has its own 24-hour hotline for drug and alcohol abuse help: 722-3700. That line serves 35,000 people each year seeking help either for themselves or for someone else.

King County supplies more of the abuse services in the Seattle area, though many neighborhoods have their own community alcohol and substance abuse centers. Some operate drug- and alcohol-free houses with low rents.

Some of the services provided by the county

Emergency Service Patrol: The patrol assists downtown Seattle police in picking up, screening, and referring people found inebriated or high on drugs on the streets or while driving.

"Detox" (King County Detoxification Center): 105-bed facility. While public inebriation is no longer a crime in Washington State, it is considered a serious health and safety problem. Detox evaluates about 1,000 people a month. Seventy-five to 80% of those referred are picked up in the Pioneer Square area and are chronic inebriates with a return rate of 75%. Detox also takes people picked up for driving while intoxicated (DWI), traffic violations, and drug addiction.

Detox evaluates those picked up and either accepts them for on-the-spot treatment or refers them to an appropriate county or private treatment facility. AA and Al-Anon are considered to be the best long-term solutions.

North Rehabilitation Facility: A minimum-security county jail facility which provides rehab and education for those convicted of DWI.

Cedar Hills: A 208-bed inpatient residence for long-term and intensive treatment. Counseling and inpatient services cost about $1,000 per month.

Outpatient and Youth Treatment Clinics: Five clinics serve a population of 400 to 900 each. Sliding-scale fees.

Alcohol Involuntary Treatment Services: Provides counselors stationed at Harborview to assess and intervene in cases of alcoholism. Involuntary treatment is handled through the court system, with papers filed to direct the alcoholic to submit to treatment.

Methadone services: Provides methadone and monitoring to rehabilitate heroin addicts.

ADATSA: Assessment and case management services.

Prevention services: Drug and alcohol abuse prevention education.

Some 60 "for profit" organizations provide alcohol and drug treatment services in Seattle.

For information on where to turn for help, consult the following list.

Al-Anon Information Service
625-0000

Crisis Clinic
461-3200

King County Division of Alcoholism and Substance Abuse
296-7615

Mothers Against Drunk Driving (MADD)
624-6903

Washington State Substance Abuse Coalition
14700 Main St.
Bellevue, WA 98007
747-9111

HOME SWEET HOME?

More than 8,000 domestic abuse cases were reported in Seattle in 1988—and the FBI estimates that only 1 in 10 domestic violence assaults is reported to police. In King County more than 16,000 domestic violence calls were made to police that same year.

If you think that's depressing, consider these nuggets from the lives of many of Seattle's women:

- In 1987 Seattle's shelters for battered women turned away an estimated 5,500 victims of domestic violence.
- 25–35% of battered women are pregnant.
- Nearly half the single women and female-headed households in Seattle that are homeless are homeless due to domestic violence.
- Arrests for domestic violence increased from 387 in 1983 to 2,475 in 1985 and have continued at about 2,300 annually.

There are no domestic violence prevention programs in the Seattle schools.

Domestic violence resources

Catherine Booth House
324-4943

City of Seattle Family Violence Project
684-7770

Domestic Violence Hotline
(800) 562-6025

Hickman House
932-5341

Lesbian Resource Center
322-3953

New Beginnings Shelter for Battered Women
522-9472

Planned Parenthood
328-7700

Women in Recovery
722-6117

Accessibility guides and information for the disabled

Access Seattle
Easter Seal Society of Washington
521 Second Ave. W
Seattle, WA 98119
281-5700
Guidebook to handicapped accessible places in Seattle.

American Friends Service Committee
814 NE 40th St.
Seattle, WA 98105
632-0500

Governor's Committee on Disability Issues and Employment
105 14th Ave.
Seattle, WA 98122
684-4532
Resource list of statewide access for disabled tourists.

Senior Services and Centers
1601 Second Ave., Suite 800
Seattle, WA 98101
483-3110

United Way Information and Referral Service
1530 Eastlake Ave. E
Seattle, WA 98102
447-3200

CHAPTER

15

TAKING SEATTLE'S PULSE

AILMENTS

MORTALITY STATS

C-SECTIONS

INSURANCE

COSTS

SMOKERS

HOSPITALS

AIDS

DRINKING WATER

COVERAGE

All right, Seattle. Lie down on the x-ray table and let's examine your state of health. It's true you have a whole hill of hospitals—Pill Hill. And you have one of the largest populations of bicycling commuters in the country, plus a whole bunch of people who swear they know CPR. Despite those huddled knots of smokers puffing away outside downtown office buildings, you have more non-smokers than elsewhere. And, Alar or not, you are the #6 city in the nation in apple consumption, a true believer in the old apple-a-day theory.

But, while on the surface the prognosis seems hopeful, there are threats lurking. A visit to the doctor is in order.

PUFF STUFF

Number of smokers in Washington State: 1.2 million, about 25% of the adult population. National average: about 30–35% of the adult population.

Number of cigarettes the state's smokers consume per day: 30 million (assuming one pack per day consumption). If you were to dump all those cigarettes into the Kingdome, they'd make a pile 21 inches deep.

Source: American Lung Association

American Lung Association of Washington
2625 Third Ave.
Seattle, WA 98121
441-5100
Focuses on asthma, environmental health, and smoking cessation. Summer camps for children with asthma, "lung clubs" for people with chronic lung disease, smoking cessation clinics, and anti-smoking school curricula. Call to get on the mailing list.

Fresh Air for Non-Smokers (FANS)
932-7011
Activists dedicated to the banning of smoking in public places.

Tobacco Addiction Coordinating Council
2625 Third Ave.
Seattle, WA 98121
441-5100
Activists for vending machine legislation and other tobacco-related legislation.

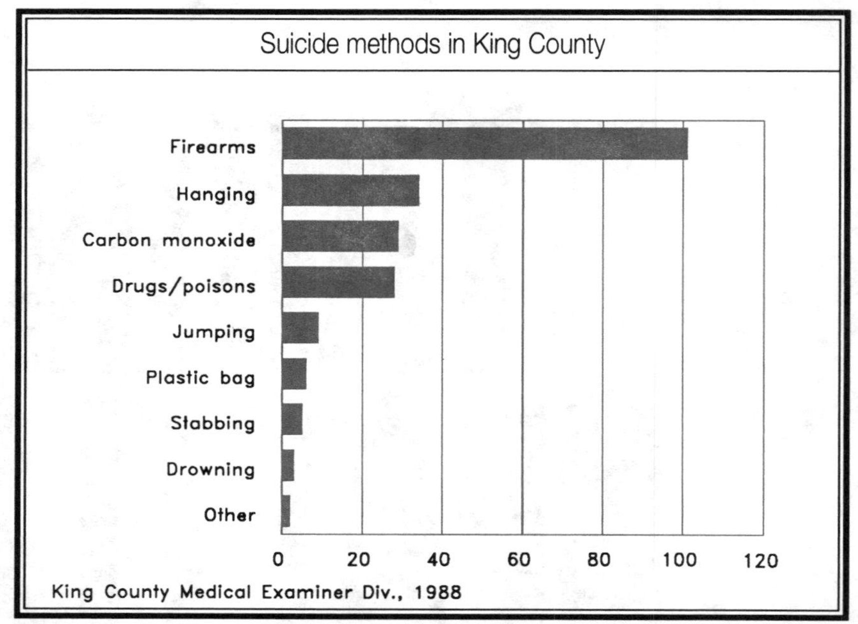

HEART CITY

If you're going to have a heart attack, have it in Seattle, the city where you're most likely to receive cardio-pulmonary resuscitation (CPR), according to an official at the American Heart Association national headquarters in Dallas. The city does have the highest rate of citizens trained in CPR, according to Barbara Breight at the Medic Two program that oversees CPR training in King County. (One in three Seattleites has been trained in CPR, and over 24,000 people are trained—or retrained in a refresher course—in King County every year.)

Medic Two
684-7274
Information on CPR training.

American Heart Association
632-6881
Memorials, gifts, information.

WHAT AILS YOU

Judging by walk-in and call-in complaints at Group Health Cooperative's central hospital, Seattle's top 12 health complaints have to do with:

Stomach aches
Back pain
Congestion
Cough
Ear aches
Headaches
Fever in kids
Rashes
Sore throats
Urinary tract infections
Vaginitis or sexually transmitted disease
Injuries

DEATH AND DYING

In King County, heart disease is the leading cause of death, closely followed by cancer. The statistic that's really startling, however, is that in the 25–44 age group AIDS is now the second leading cause of death. In 1988 alone, 101 young men died of

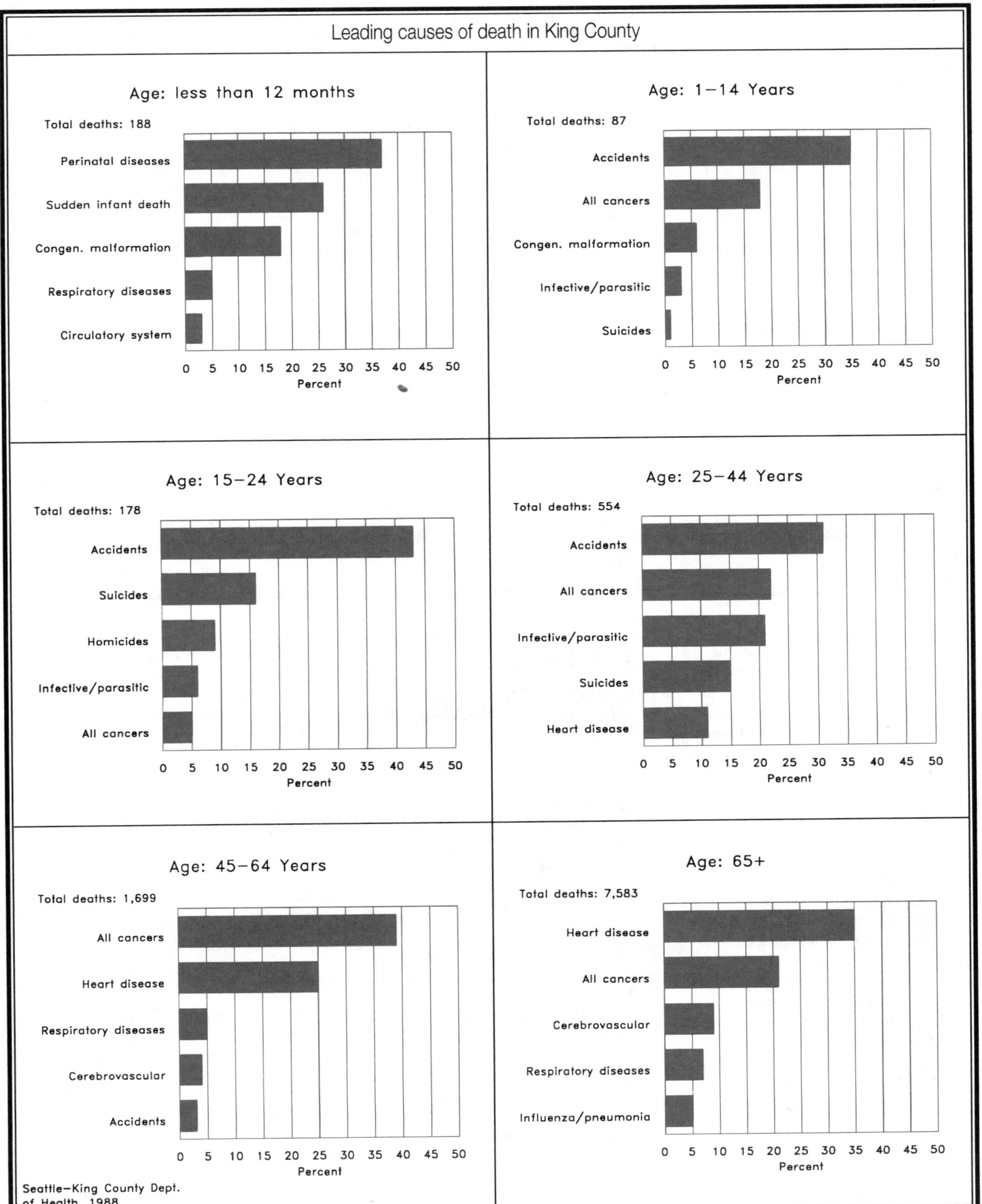
Leading causes of death in King County
Age: less than 12 months
Total deaths: 188
Perinatal diseases
Sudden infant death
Congen. malformation
Respiratory diseases
Circulatory system
0 5 10 15 20 25 30 35 40 45 50
Percent
Age: 1–14 Years
Total deaths: 87
Accidents
All cancers
Congen. malformation
Infective/parasitic
Suicides
0 5 10 15 20 25 30 35 40 45 50
Percent
Age: 15–24 Years
Total deaths: 178
Accidents
Suicides
Homicides
Infective/parasitic
All cancers
0 5 10 15 20 25 30 35 40 45 50
Percent
Age: 25–44 Years
Total deaths: 554
Accidents
All cancers
Infective/parasitic
Suicides
Heart disease
0 5 10 15 20 25 30 35 40 45 50
Percent
Age: 45–64 Years
Total deaths: 1,699
All cancers
Heart disease
Respiratory diseases
Cerebrovascular
Accidents
0 5 10 15 20 25 30 35 40 45 50
Percent
Age: 65+
Total deaths: 7,583
Heart disease
All cancers
Cerebrovascular
Respiratory diseases
Influenza/pneumonia
0 5 10 15 20 25 30 35 40 45 50
Percent
Seattle–King County Dept. of Health, 1988

Birth and death in King County

Rates are per 1,000 population.

Year	County pop.	BIRTHS Number	BIRTHS Rate	DEATHS Number	DEATHS Rate
1980	1.27 million	17,562	13.8	9,664	7.6
1981	1.31	18,388	14.0	9,247	7.1
1982	1.31	18,811	14.3	9,714	7.4
1983	1.32	18,533	14.1	9,749	7.4
1984	1.33	18,974	14.3	10,013	7.5
1985	1.35	19,778	14.7	10,341	7.7
1986	1.36	19,953	14.7	10,211	7.5
1987	1.38	20,423	14.8	10,199	7.4
1988*	1.45	24,049	16.6	11,555	8.0
Other comparisons					
Washington State 1988			14.7		7.8
Nationwide 1988			15.9		8.8

*1988 figures are unofficial, and include non-resident births within King County (other figures are only for resident births).

Source: Seattle-King Co. Dept. of Public Health

AIDS. In the 15–24-year-old category, of the 178 deaths 28 were suicides—another disturbing statistic.

The King County Medical Examiner has the unenviable job of investigating sudden, violent, unexpected, and suspicious deaths. In 1988, for example, he investigated over 1,530 of the 11,556 deaths in the county.

In an annual report, the examiner comments on outstanding factors noted in investigations during the year, primarily the use of alcohol, drugs, and firearms in violent deaths. In 1988 he noted that of all the traffic fatalities in which blood alcohol tests were performed, 40% of drivers tested positive. Firearms accounted for 49% of homicides and 46.5% of suicides. Of drug-caused deaths in 1988, 38% involved cocaine—up from 15% three years previously.

COUNTY MORTALITY STATISTICS

Number of traffic fatalities: 176
- Number of fatalities that tested positive for presence of alcohol: 71
- Number of people who died in an automobile: 155
- Number who died wearing seatbelts: 40
- Number of deaths involving motorcyclists: 35
- Percentage of motorcyclists killed who were not wearing helmets: 70
- Number of murders: 9
- Number of suicides: 217
- Drownings (does not include homicide or suicide): 26
- Number of drug-caused deaths: 119 (Number cocaine or opiate related: 61)

Source: County Medical Examiner 1988 Annual Report

King County Medical Examiner's Office
850 Alder St.
Seattle, WA 98104
223-3232

INFANT MORTALITY RATES

King County's infant mortality rate had dipped from 1985's high of 9.5 for every 1,000 live births, but during 1988 it began to go up again.

FOOD COMPLAINTS

Got a stomach ache? Eight hundred people per year call the Environmental Health Department with complaints about aches and pains they think came from having eaten at

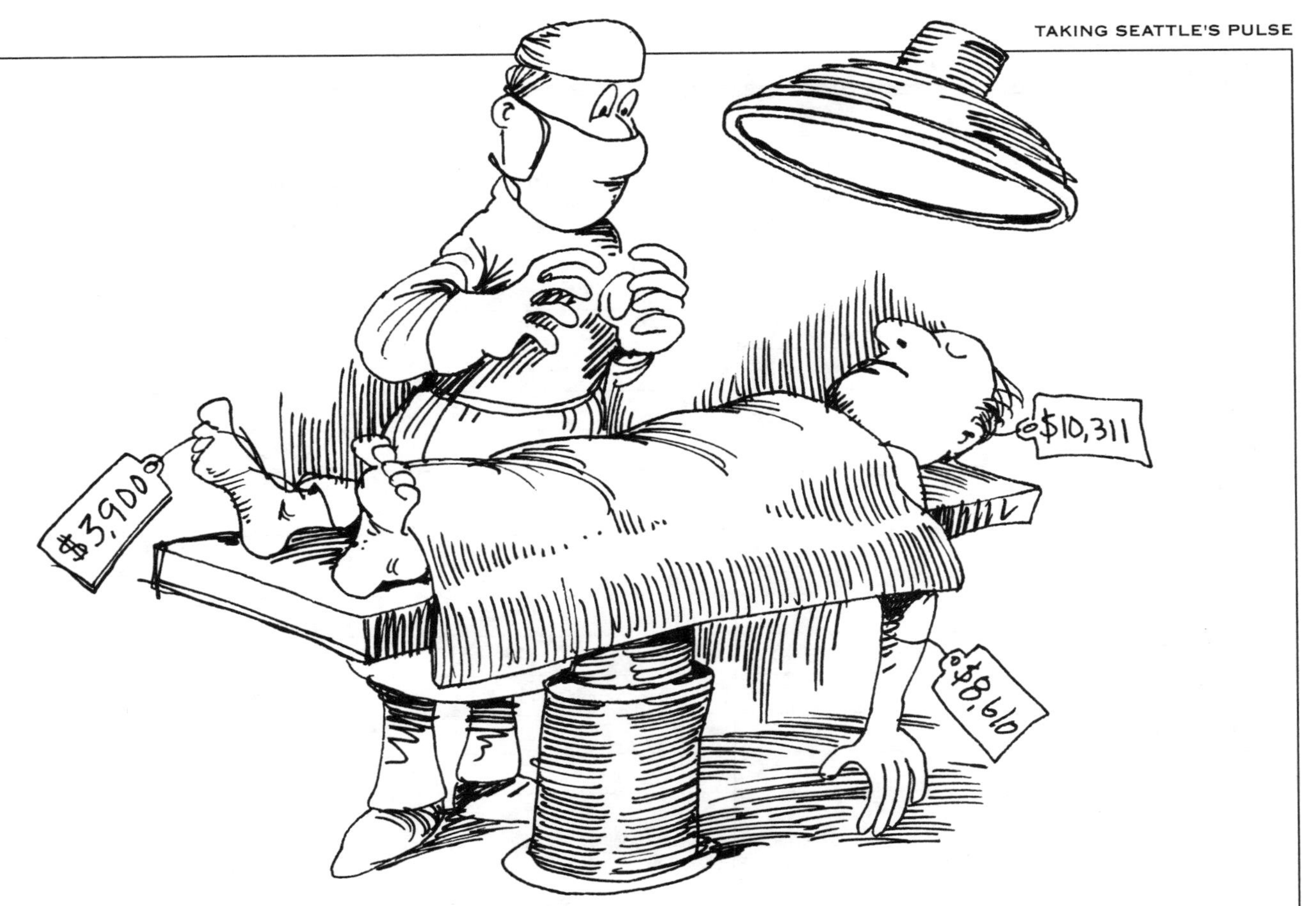

restaurants. Of those, only about 30 of the food-borne illnesses are traced to food establishments. On the other hand, 120 restaurants in the city are closed by the health department every year for health violations.

Environmental Health Dept.
Central office: 296-4632
North office: 296-4838
South office: 296-4666
Eastside: 296-4932
To report food complaints.

GUIDE TO SEATTLE HOSPITALS

The aptly named Pill Hill, located between Ninth Avenue and Broadway, is not the only place to find Seattle's hospitals. In fact, hospitals and clinics are big business in both hills and valleys in the city, and on the Eastside too. In fact, they now compete over bodies to inhabit their beds. That competition results in heavy advertising, but also in more and varied services. For example, many hospitals offer services such as sleep disorder or sports clinics. Many also offer "well-care" seminars and activities, sponsoring such programs as mall walks for senior citizens.

It's best to shop around for a hospital when you're well; office-based doctors are usually connected to one or more hospitals and can recommend an appropriate facility for you. The Washington State Hospital Commission in Olympia notes that there has been a dramatic increase in use and cost of medical care over the past decade in the state. Some of the reasons for the increase are obvious, such as a growing elderly population, but others are worth noting.

Overuse of health care. The commission says many payment systems encourage overuse of the doctor's office, emergency room, and prescriptions.
Defensive medicine. Malpractice suits have increased (as have insurance rates), which can result in physicians ordering unnecessary tests, the commission says.
Technology. Hospitals believe in having the latest in medical technology. But if the hospital doesn't have enough patients to keep the equipment busy, the cost is often passed on to other patients in the hospital.
Medical insurance that hides the true cost of medical care from the consumer.
Little incentive for physicians or hospitals to hold down costs.

And so, on to hospital shopping. Please note that the percentage of

Hospitals

	Ballard Community Hospital	Children's Hospital & Medical Center	Fifth Avenue Hospital at Northgate	Group Health Cooperative General Hospital
Beds	163	208	80	340 central hospital 179 eastside
Occupancy rate	62%	77%	NA	82%
Admissions/year	NA	8576	NA	14,380
Avg.#patients/day	NA	159	NA	204
Avg. stay	7.3 days	6.94 days	4.47 days	NA
Physicians	141	988	NA	197 central 145 eastside
Nurses	123 19 FTE*	354	11	268 central 135 eastside
Medicare mortality rate	(1988) 12.4%	NA	9.5%	9.8%
Predicted mortality rate	6.7%–14.5%	NA	3.3% –13.7%	7.3% –14.5%
Medicare patients	50%	less than 1%	33%	NA
Medicaid patients	5%	31%	8%	NA
Charity care	less than 1%	7%	less than 1%	NA

*Full-Time-Equivalent. Sources: Washington State Hospital Commission, American Hospital Association Guide to Health Care Field, Health Care Financing Administration

Illness Category	Cases	Average charge ($)*	Cases	Average charge ($)*	Cases	Average charge ($)*	Cases	Average charge ($)*
Stroke	99	4,926	14	3,963	5	5,800	—	—
Lung tumors	13	4,681	3	2,068	2	4,560	—	—
Pneumonia	53	5,388	0	0	16	4,902	—	—
Asthma/bronchitis	50	4,202	3	4,190	6	4,573	—	—
Corory bypass	0	0	0	0	0	0		—
Heart failure	127	5,037	23	2,772	0	0	—	—
Appendectomy	18	2,581	43	2,382	3	3,014	—	—
Ulcer	42	3,907	18	2,018	8	4,841	—	—
Digestive disorder	52	3,131	5	1,823	9	3,065	—	—
Gall bladder surgery	28	3,756	0	0	0	0	—	—
Back/neck surgery	81	4,480	10	5,225	7	4,609	—	—
Birth	166	1,747	0	0	9	1,484	—	—
Birth C-section	(25.5%) 57	3,399	0	0	(18.2%) 2	2,119	—	—
Chemotherapy	23	2,209	594	2,109	0	0	—	—
Psychosis	58	7,401	6	4,292	1	2,723	—	—
Substance abuse	31	1,825	2	1,837	13	1,802	—	—

* Does not include fees for attending physician. Source: Washington State Hospital Commission, "Advice to Consumers on Hospital Charges," June, 1989

	Harborview Medical Center	Highline Community Hospital	Northwest Hospital	Providence Medical Center
Beds	330	135	236 (AHA, 1988)	376
Occupancy rate	85.8%	NA	65%	74%
Admissions/year	11,252	NA	10,654	16,741
Avg. #patients/day	277	NA	152	273
Avg. stay	8.94 days	4.07 days	5.3 days	5.93 days
Physicians	157	NA	245	310
Nurses	480	129	341	711 22 FTE*
Medicare mortality rate	19%	14.1%	11.4%	9.4%
Predicted mortality rate	11.3% –19.5%	7.4% –15.2%	7.4% –14.7%	5.7% –13%
Medicare patients	21%	44%	50%	50%
Medicaid patients	44%	5%	4%	11%
Charity care	25%	3%	3%	5%

*Full-Time-Equivalent. Sources: Washington State Hospital Commission, American Hospital Association Guide to Health Care Field, Health Care Financing Administration

Illness Category	Cases	Average charge ($)*	Cases	Average charge ($)*	Cases	Average charge ($)*	Cases	Average charge ($)*
Stroke	97	5,047	94	4,321	180	5,477	195	5,056
Lung tumors	19	4,442	30	5,252	34	3,570	62	4,644
Pneumonia	153	3,526	84	4,998	141	4,881	178	4,738
Asthma/bronchitis	61	2,599	39	3,545	72	3,717	70	3,743
Coronary bypass	0	0	0	0	0	0	661	18,956
Heart failure	108	3,569	153	3,671	189	4,300	254	4,368
Appendectomy	23	2,416	35	2,521	46	2,274	40	2,702
Ulcer	79	3,424	58	3,271	97	3,328	96	3,724
Digestive disorder	89	2,491	91	2,429	167	2,509	169	3,076
Gall bladder surgery	13	3,702	46	3,879	83	3,596	67	3,755
Back/neck surgery	19	5,596	40	3,894	215	4,018	130	4,189
Birth	1	1,089	470	1,314	977	1,850	765	1,607
Birth C-section	0	0	(27.5%) 179	3,229	(23.8%) 305	3,371	(17.5%) 162	3,257
Chemotherapy	7	3,407	49	2,563	256	1,723	175	2,447
Psychosis	1,348	3,990	11	2,658	15	3,449	648	4,003
Substance abuse	46	2,139	18	1,005	4	1,349	10	2,406

* Does not include fees for attending physician. Source: Washington State Hospital Commission, "Advice to Consumers on Hospital Charges," June, 1989

	St. Cabrini Hospital of Seattle	Swedish Hospital Medical Center	University Hospital	Virginia Mason Hospital
Beds	160	697	450	310
Occupancy rate	54.5%	76%	77%	66%
Admissions/year	3,441	27,381	13,174	13,400
Avg. #patients/day	87	434	297	NA
Avg. stay	7.87 days	6.2 days	8.21 days	6.27 days
Physicians	138	487	340	435
Nurses	137	1050 55 FTE*	672 30 FTE*	406 16 FTE*
Medicare mortality rates	9.8%	11.6%	9.1%	8.4%
Predicted mortality rates	5.8% –14.1%	6.7% –13.9%	6.7% –14.4%	7.1% –14.4%
Medicare patients	51%	32%	27%	48%
Medicaid patients	8%	5%	20%	6%
Charity care	1%	3%	3%	3%

*Full-Time-Equivalent. Sources: Washington State Hospital Commission, American Hospital Association Guide to Health Care Field, Health Care Financing Administration

Illness Category	Cases	Average charge ($)*	Cases	Average charge ($)*	Cases	Average charge ($)*	Cases	Average charge ($)*
Stroke	27	5,441	240	4,409	56	5,164	126	4,623
Lung tumors	11	5,211	155	4,025	25	6,121	64	4,007
Pneumonia	32	6,014	227	4,432	67	4,193	101	4,228
Asthma/bronchitis	17	4,385	107	3,765	29	2,961	50	3,099
Coronary bypass	0	0	158	15,392	382	14,463	98	19,097
Heart failure	52	5,051	301	3,659	94	3,212	201	3,872
Appendectomy	1	2,329	51	2,326	24	2,759	36	2,494
Ulcer	18	4,734	153	3,254	38	3,684	60	3,154
Digestive disorder	23	3,331	324	2,323	88	2,890	141	2,830
Gall bladder surgery	3	4,883	142	3,128	15	3,776	125	3,443
Back/neck surgery	3	5,176	770	3,990	57	4,865	234	4,046
Birth	0	0	2,000	1,660	1,047	1,498	756	1,425
Birth C-section	0	0	(21.9%) 560	3,023	(15.4%) 191	3,406	(17.8%) 164	3,130
Chemotherapy	16	3,037	930	1,607	322	2,662	325	2,031
Psychosis	356	4,374	24	2,376	24	2,376	36	3,115
Substance abuse	69	1,597	5	1,733	15	2,483	6	1,883

* Does not include fees for attending physician. Source: Washington State Hospital Commission, "dvice to Consumers on Hospital Charges," June, 1989

Medicare and Medicaid is a percentage of the hospital's total rate-setting revenue, not percentage of patients.

The costs of various operations/services are from a booklet available to the public through the Hospital Commission entitled *Advice to Consumers on Hospital Charges*, published in June 1989. Copies can be ordered from Washington State Hospital Commission, Evergreen Plaza Building, Suite 206, 711 S Capitol Way, Olympia, WA 98504. Cost $1.

The mortality rates given are from the Health Care Financing Administration. The rate represents the percentage of Medicare patients who were discharged in the calendar year and who died within 30 days of their last admission to the hospital. The range for predicted mortality is an estimate based on the patient mix of a particular hospital.

Keep in mind that one hospital might have different death rates than another because of its patient mix. For example, Harborview has more trauma cases than other hospitals and its mortality rate reflects that. The Health Care Financing Administration urges that the mortality information not be used as a direct measure of quality of care, but rather as a screening tool. Consumers should use it to ask questions of physicians.

Ballard Community Hospital
Northwest Market and Barnes
P.O. Box C-70707
Seattle, WA 98107
782-2700
Special services: Remodeled, expanded, and fully computerized intensive care unit (ICU). One-to-one nursing care and private rooms in Family Childbirth Center, Seattle Sleep Disorders Center, mammography in private clinic adjacent to hospital, Health Partners program, 24-hour Nurse (health info 24 hours a day), free van transportation, free parking.

Children's Hospital and Medical Center
4800 Sand Point Way NE
Seattle, WA 98105
526-2000
Special services: Renowned pediatric medical center, Children's Resource Line, Resource Center (library for patient and family education) development programs.

Fifth Avenue Hospital at Northgate
10560 Fifth Ave. NE
Seattle, WA 98125
364-2050
Special services: Coronary care unit, intensive care unit.

Group Health Cooperative General Hospital
201 16th Ave. E
Seattle, WA 98112
326-3000
Group Health is the Northwest's largest health maintenance organization (HMO), providing complete and coordinated care for a fixed, prepaid fee with minimum co-payments and deductions. It's the nation's 11th largest HMO overall, and the third largest nonprofit HMO.
Special services: Maternity, immediate care nursery, pediatrics, neurosurgery, orthopedic surgery, ambulatory surgery program. Group Health is affiliated with UW teaching, research, and patient care programs, and affiliated with Children's Hospital in opening a joint Eastside Adolescent Center.

Cost for individual cases is covered by co-op individual dues which vary by age. For example, dues for ages 21–30 are $95.29/month base rate, or $65.20/month base rate with $500 deductible.

Harborview Medical Center
325 Ninth Ave.
Seattle, WA 98104
223-3000
Special services: Emergency/trauma center, regional epilepsy center, center for anxiety and depression, Northwest Lipid Research Clinic, sexual assault center, injury prevention and research center, Northwest regional burn center, major clinical site for newly designed UW Center for AIDS Research (one of seven such programs in the country).

Highline Community Hospital
16251 Sylvester Road SW
(4 miles west of Sea-Tac Airport)
Seattle, WA 98166
244-9970
Special services: Barney Clark special care unit.

Northwest Hospital
1550 N 115th St.
Seattle, WA 98133
364-0500
Special services: Northwest Tumor Institute, Hospice Northwest, cancer care, rehab center, MED-INFO (medical information and physician referral line).

Providence Medical Center
500 17th Ave.
Seattle, WA 98122
320-2000
Special services: Heart center, respiratory care center, CancerCare, rehabilitation services, mental health, Family Childbirth Center.

Saint Cabrini Hospital of Seattle
920 Terry Ave.
Seattle, WA 98104
682-0500
Number of beds includes 33 beds in nursing-home type unit. Special services: Geriatric assessment, intensive care.

Swedish Hospital Medical Center
747 Summit Ave.
Seattle, WA 98104
386-6000
Special services: Antepartum unit for high-risk pregnancies, neonatology (special care nursery), 24-hour renal transplant service, Tumor Institute, two bone marrow transplant units available in affiliation with Fred Hutchinson Research Center. Also surgical specialties with over 24,000 procedures performed each year, seven laser units, etc.

University Hospital
1959 NE Pacific St.
Seattle, WA 98195
548-3300

Wander through University Hospital and you can't help but be struck by the variety of things going on here. It's most often thought of as a teaching facility for the UW School of Medicine, which it is, but it's also part of the Warren G. Magnuson Health Sciences Center and has 12 major units (through the sciences center) in dentistry, medicine, nursing, pharmacy, public health, community medicine, and social work; four centers (Alcohol and Drug Abuse Institute, Child Development and Mental Retardation Center, Regional Primate Research Center, Research Center in Oral Biology); and two medical centers (University of Washington Medical Center and Harborview Medical Center). The hospital also features a regional clinical referral center and a major research institution.

Special services: Cardiac diagnostic services, cardiac surgery, cancer care services, bone and joint center, neonatal intensive care unit, multidisciplinary pain services, and Northwest Spinal Cord Injury Center.

Virginia Mason Hospital
925 Seneca St.
Seattle, WA 98101
624-1144
Special services: Critical care, diagnostic medicine, immunology research, diabetes, cancer, heart, women's health, specialty medicine, lithotripsy, MRI.

Fred Hutchinson Cancer Research Center
1124 Columbia St. (First Hill)
Seattle, WA 98104
467-5000
Fred Hutchinson is in a class by itself since it's a research center rather than hospital. Fred Hutch is one of 20 comprehensive cancer centers in the nation and the only federally designated center in the Northwest. The only patient service the center offers is bone marrow transplants and it accepts patients from all over the world, performing close to 4,000 transplants—more than at any other location.

More than 200 research projects are under way at the center. They focus on three areas: basic sciences, clinical research, and public health sciences.

The center operates the Cancer Information Service to answer questions from the public about cancer. It also publishes a number of booklets for the public on cancer risks, avoiding cancer, and how to seek the most appropriate diagnosis and treatment. Personnel: 1,500 staff members, including M.D.'s, Ph.D.'s, technicians, and clerical, nursing, clinical, and secretarial staff.

Budget: $76 million, with funding from federal and private grants and contracts, as well as contributions.

History: Named for Fred Hutchinson, a Northwest native and major league baseball player and manager, who died of cancer in 1964 at the age of 45. The center opened in 1975.

Purpose: To eliminate cancer as a human disease problem.

Site: Five buildings on First Hill, with a new center on southeast Lake Union to open in the next five to nine years.

Cancer Information Service
(800) 4-CANCER

HOSPITALS SPECIALIZING IN SUBSTANCE ABUSE

Ballard Community Hospital
NW Market and Barnes
Seattle, WA 98107
789-7209
Head of Substance Abuse Program: Ed Hunt

Riverton General Hospital
12844 Military Road S
Seattle, WA 98168
248-4790
Head of Substance Abuse Program: Dan Nichols

Saint Cabrini Hospital
920 Terry Ave.
Seattle, WA 98104
583-4344
Head of Substance Abuse Program: Brendan Coleman

Seattle hospitals' Cesarean section rates

Hospital	C-rate 1988*	C-rate 1987	Births 1987	Neonatal ICU
Ballard	25.6%	33.3%	6	No
Children's	Does not perform births			
Fifth Avenue	23.1%	32.7%	55	No
Group Health	18.5%	NA	NA	Yes
Harborview	0.0%	0.0%	0	No
Highline	29.7%	28.1%	730	No
Northwest	26.9%	23.7%	2,240	No
Providence	19.3%	17.9%	1,225	No
St. Cabrini	Does not perform births			
Swedish	23.8%	25.1%	3,569	Yes
University	21.3%	23.2%	2,074	Yes
Virginia Mason	16.4%	20.7%	1,123	No

*Latest available 1988 figures are for six months.

Sources: Public Citizen Health Research Group

Schick Shadel Hospital
12101 Ambaum Blvd. SW
Seattle, WA 98146
244-8100

Seattle Indian Health Board
611 12th Ave. S
Seattle, WA 98114
Outpatient clinic: 324-9360
Thunderbird Treatment Center:
722-7152 (inpatient)

CESAREAN SECTION RATES

There is a growing concern in the U.S. about the number of Cesarean deliveries in hospitals. Cesarean sections are the most frequently performed major surgical operations and, according to the Public Citizen's Health Research Group, the most frequently unnecessary.

The ideal ratio of C-sections to total births in any one hospital is not carved in stone, but the Research Group says the appropriate range for C-section rates—"if the operation were used only when medically indicated"—is between 7% and 17%. For a state the figure used is 12%; Washington State's 1988 C-section rate was 21.7% (13,825 C-sections). The group's report says that of the 63,708 total births in Washington in 1988, 6,207 were unnecessary C-sections. The Research Group suggests that pregnant women ask hospital administrators what the rate of C-section births is. If it's a community hospital, the rate should be close to 7%; if it's a referral hospital with a neonatal care unit (which handles more difficult cases), the rate will be closer to 17%.

Doctors keep track of their vaginal birth vs. C-section birth rate too, sometimes pushing prospective C-section births off onto another doctor to keep their record clean.

MARRY A DOCTOR, MY DEAR

Want to know how much your doctor makes? It depends on his or her specialty, of course, and there's a wide range depending on seniority, what the market will bear, and all that. Below is a rough rundown of doctors' salaries in the Seattle area.

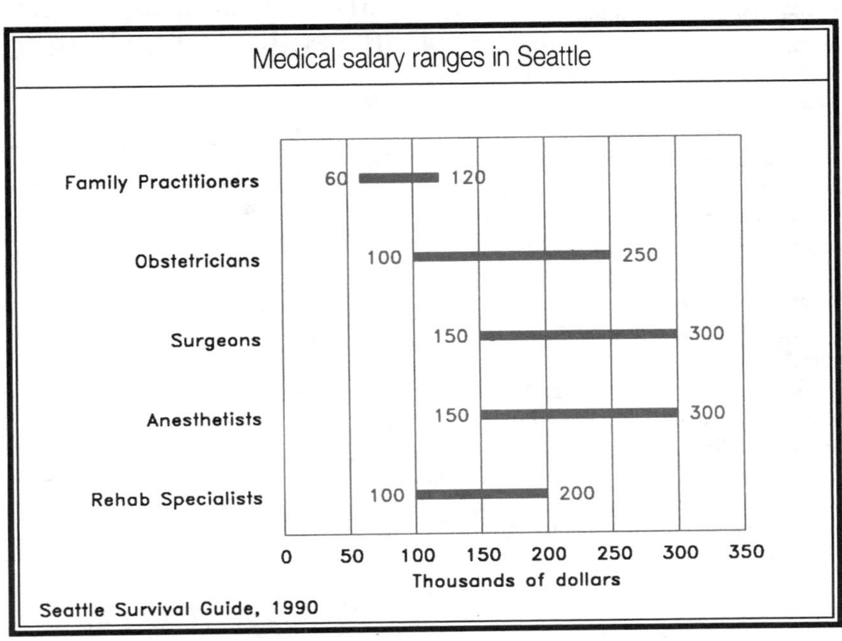

Nurses' salaries

Nationwide	Minimum	Maximum
Staff Nurse	$22,485	$31,144
Head Nurse	28,182	39,189
Supervisor	29,077	40,748
Director of Nursing	39,239	56,141
West Coast		
Staff Nurse	$24,041	$34,360
Head Nurse	30,770	43,279
Supervisor	31,289	44,570
Director of Nursing	45,473	62,975

Source: National Assn. of Health Care Recruiters, June 1988 survey

AIDS: THE STAGGERING FACTS

The figures are earthshaking: One in every 100 people in the Seattle–King County region might be infected with Human Immunodeficiency Virus (HIV).

That statistic from the AIDS Prevention Project of the Seattle–King County Department of Public Health makes a few assumptions, such as that about 15% of the Seattle–King County region is gay, that half of those are male, and that those males who are tested for HIV are representative of the rest of the population. The Project people say the figure is as close to a true number as they can get because doctors are not required to report HIV-positive statistics to any agency (although they must report AIDS cases).

Testing HIV positive means a person has been exposed to the virus at some point. He or she may have slight symptoms or may not even become sick. Researchers think that the average time it takes to develop full-blown AIDS is between 9 and 14 years, and they think a small percentage of people who test positive never develop AIDS symptoms.

Acquired Immune Deficiency Syndrome (AIDS) is actually the end stage of the HIV virus, the point at which a person catches pneumonia or develops cancer or contracts another, fatal, infection.

Those who are HIV positive are infected and able to transmit the virus to other people through sexual contact or transmission of blood.

At mid-1990 there were about 1,280 cases of AIDS in King County. From 1982 to December 1989, 699 persons in King County died from AIDS.

A word on AIDS statistics: Physicians are required to report AIDS cases to the county, but may take up to six months after the initial diagnosis to file their report. Therefore, statistics lag behind reality; the lower figures for the first quarter of 1990 do not represent a reduction in AIDS—it's just that the numbers aren't complete.

Deaths due to AIDS are counted in a unique way. A figure is given for the number of cases diagnosed as AIDS in a quarter, followed by the number of those diagnosed in that quarter who have died. For example, the figure for fourth quarter 1988 means that of the 80 people diagnosed as having AIDS, 25 have died. If more of those 80 die, the statistics for that quarter will change.

AIDS cases and deaths in Seattle–King County

1988 BY QUARTER	1	2	3	4
Cases	74	85	82	80
Deaths	39	38	35	25
1989 BY QUARTER	**1**	**2**	**3**	**4**
Cases	81	85	56	78
Deaths	23	19	11	13
1990 BY QUARTER	**1**			
Cases	48			
Deaths	3			

Source: Northwest AIDS Foundation and AIDS Prevention Project

One more caution: Statistics from the public health system versus those from AIDS foundations differ because the health system counts only deaths from AIDS itself; foundations often count deaths of those with the AIDS virus for any reason, including suicide.

Resources

Most AIDS- and HIV-related resources can be found by contacting the Northwest AIDS Foundation at 329-6923 or the AIDS Prevention Project at 296-4999.

AIDS Prevention Project Hotline
296-4999

U.S. Health Service AIDS Hotline
(800) 342-AIDS

Washington State AIDS Hotline
(800) 272-AIDS

Health Care

Seattle clinics with a focus on HIV and a sliding fee schedule:

Country Doctor Community Clinic
500 19th Ave. E
Seattle, WA
461-4503

Harborview AIDS Clinic
325 Ninth Ave.
Seattle, WA 98104
223-3241
HIV Patient Supervisor: Pam Ryan

Pike Market Community Clinic
1930 Post Alley
Seattle, WA 98101
728-4143

Seattle Gay Clinic
500 19th Ave. E
Seattle, WA
461-4540
Nurse practitioner, limited clinical monitoring, and referrals.

Sea-Mar Community Health Center
8720 14th Ave. E
Seattle, WA 98108
762-3730 (Spanish speaking)

45th St. Community Clinic
1629 N 45th St.
Seattle, WA 98103
633-3350

Swedish Hospital
747 Summit Ave.
Seattle, WA 98104
386-6000

Sexually transmitted diseases in Seattle–King County

Gonorrhea	Cases	Rate per 1,000 pop.
1986	3,991	293
1987	3,812	275
1988	3,443	238*
1989	3,012*	208*
Infectious Syphilis		
1986	59	4.3
1987	70	5.0
1988	87	6.1
1989	170*	11.8*

* Unofficial figures

Sources: Seattle-King Co. Dept. of Public Health 1987 Vital Statistics Report; Barbara Krekeler of the Sexually Transmitted Disease Clinic at Harborview

HIV Patient Supervisor: Margo Bykonen

University of Washington Medical Center AIDS Clinic
1595 NE Pacific St.
Seattle, WA 98159
548-4728
HIV Patient Supervisor: Connie O'Hara

Experimental treatment

AIDS Clinical Trial Unit (ACTU)
223-3184
Sponsored by the University of Washington/Harborview Medical Center. Screening tests, study medications, lab, and clinical monitoring free to HIV-positive persons who participate in ACTU studies.
Support groups: (See also: Chapter 8, page 111, *Manning the Barricades.*)

Health care specialists for women and children

Children's Hospital and Medical Center
Infectious Disease Specialty Clinic
4800 Sand Point Way NE
Seattle, WA 98105
526-2116

Columbia Health Center
4400 37th Ave. S
Seattle, WA 98118
587-4650
Medical/dental for children and adolescents.

Harborview Pediatric Clinic
325 Ninth Ave.
Seattle, WA 98104
223-3335
Medical services for HIV-positive children.

Harborview Women's Clinic
(See address above)
223-3367
Medical and prenatal care for HIV-positive women.

Odessa Brown Children's Clinic
2101 E Yesler Way
Seattle, WA 98104
329-7870
Medical/dental for children and adolescents.

AIDS support groups

ACT UP
(AIDS Coalition to Unleash Power)
726-1678
Activist group committed to ending AIDS crisis through nonviolent protest and putting pressure on those impeding response to epidemic.

AIDS Housing of Washington
623-8292
Develops housing for people living with AIDS.

AIDS Training Project
University of Washington
543-9750
Provides AIDS education and training for health care providers.

American Civil Liberties Union of Washington
624-2180
Legal services for AIDS victims.

Association of People Living with AIDS (APLWA)
329-3382
Education and outreach to gay black males.

Chicken Soup Brigade
328-8979
Meals, transportation, and other services to people with AIDS.

Coordinate Family Services
296-5080
Case management services for HIV-positive women and children, and their families.

Delta Society
226-7357
Information for people with HIV who own pets.

Health Information Network
784-5655
Education and referral.

In Touch
328-2711
Massage therapy for people with AIDS.

National Lawyers Guild, Seattle Chapter
622-5144
Legal aid.

Northwest AIDS Foundation
329-6923
329-6963 (referrals)
Social work, case management, housing issues, education.

Parents and Friends of Lesbians and Gays
325-7724
Support services for gays, lesbians, families, friends, mates, and spouses.

People of Color Against AIDS Network (POCAAN)
322-7061
Education and referral for blacks, Haitians, Latinos, Native Americans, and Asian/Pacific Islanders.

Project Aries
543-7511
Counseling to help men achieve sexual safety.

Rise 'n Shine
628-8949
Emotional support services for children affected by AIDS.

The Rubber Tree (Zero Population Growth Seattle)
633-4750
Low-cost condoms, spermicides, and lubricants; educational materials.

Seattle AIDS Support Group
322-AIDS, 322-2437
Support groups and drop-in center.

Seattle Counseling Service
329-8707
Information and counseling for sexual minorities.

Seattle Gay Clinic
461-4540
Health care and info for gay males.

Seattle Reiki AIDS Project
282-2203
Reiki (massage) treatment for people affected by AIDS.

Seattle Treatment Exchange Project
329-4857
Info on alternative and experimental treatment for people with HIV.

Shanti
322-0279
Emotional support and training for individuals and loved ones facing AIDS.

Problems with health insurance? Contact the State Insurance Commission, 464-6262. That office has information for the consumer, including consumer tips and rights. And it has the ins and outs of a new health care program developed for Washington residents who can't afford health insurance, a pilot project called "Basic Health."

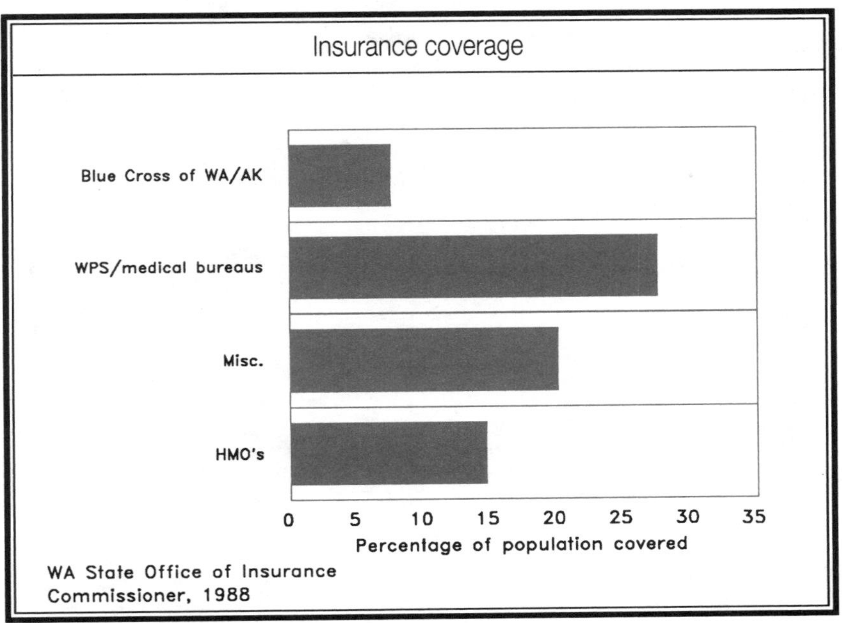

Stonewall Recovery Services
461-4546
Drug and alcohol counseling and education for gays and lesbians.

Tel-Med
621-9450 (recording)
Information on AIDS and HIV.

Washington State Human Rights Commission (Seattle)
464-6500
Investigates complaints of discrimination against persons with AIDS/HIV; information and referral.

Who's covered

Washington state is pretty well covered as far as health insurance goes. In 1988 70% of the residents were covered by some type of insurance. Here's the breakdown:

MORE TO YOUR WATER

There's more to your drinking water than you might think. Seattle has fluoridated its water since 1970 and the dental community says tooth decay has been reduced by as much as 50% to 70%. It's been controversial in some cities for supposed side effects, but fluoride is widely accepted in the U.S. In Washington State, 39.1% of the population uses fluoridated water, which gives the state a national ranking of 36th. The places with the largest percentage of population drinking fluoridated water? Washington, D.C., followed by Illinois.

CHAPTER 16

COPS AND ROBBERS

PRECINCTS

GANGS

THEFT

COURTS

937-CLUE

PATROLS

DRUGS

911

LAWYERS

VICTIMS

The good news: You are less likely to be murdered, raped, robbed, or assaulted in Seattle than a person in 80% of American cities of comparable size. Violent crime here increased 30% between 1983 and 1988, but only three cities near Seattle's size have lower violent crime rates. And the recent trend is hopeful: The rate of serious crime (violent and property offenses) went up 30% between 1984 and 1988, but leveled off in 1988 and went down by 7.2% in 1989.

The bad news: Bolt the doors and lock the windows. The city's main crime problem is people taking things, not hurting each other. Auto theft has increased 150% in the last five years. The city's rate of property crime is so high that when serious property crimes (such as burglary, larceny, and auto theft) are combined with violent crime, the resulting overall crime rate crowns Seattle the crime capital of mid-range metropolises. For that honor we beat out cities such as Boston, Baltimore, and Washington, D.C.

When compared to cities of 250,000–500,000 population, Seattle fares a little better—but not much. Miami has a higher crime rate, as do Atlanta, Tampa, and Fort Worth. The only comparable West Coast city with a higher rate is Portland, which was lately crowned bank robbery capital of the nation.

CAR 54, WHERE ARE YOU?

The Seattle Police Department's (SPD) patrol officers are housed in four precincts, North, South, East, and West. One captain serves as precinct commander, while each shift has a lieutenant who serves as commander of all activity on that shift.

The precincts operate on three shifts. First shift (4 a.m.–12 noon): 89 officers, 12 sergeants. Second shift (12 noon–8 p.m.): 220 officers, 22 sergeants. Third shift (8 p.m.–4 a.m.): 209 officers, 17 sergeants.

Calls received: First shift, 22%; second shift, 41%; third shift, 37%.

Average number of officers per precinct walking or riding (on bicycles) beats during the day: 39.

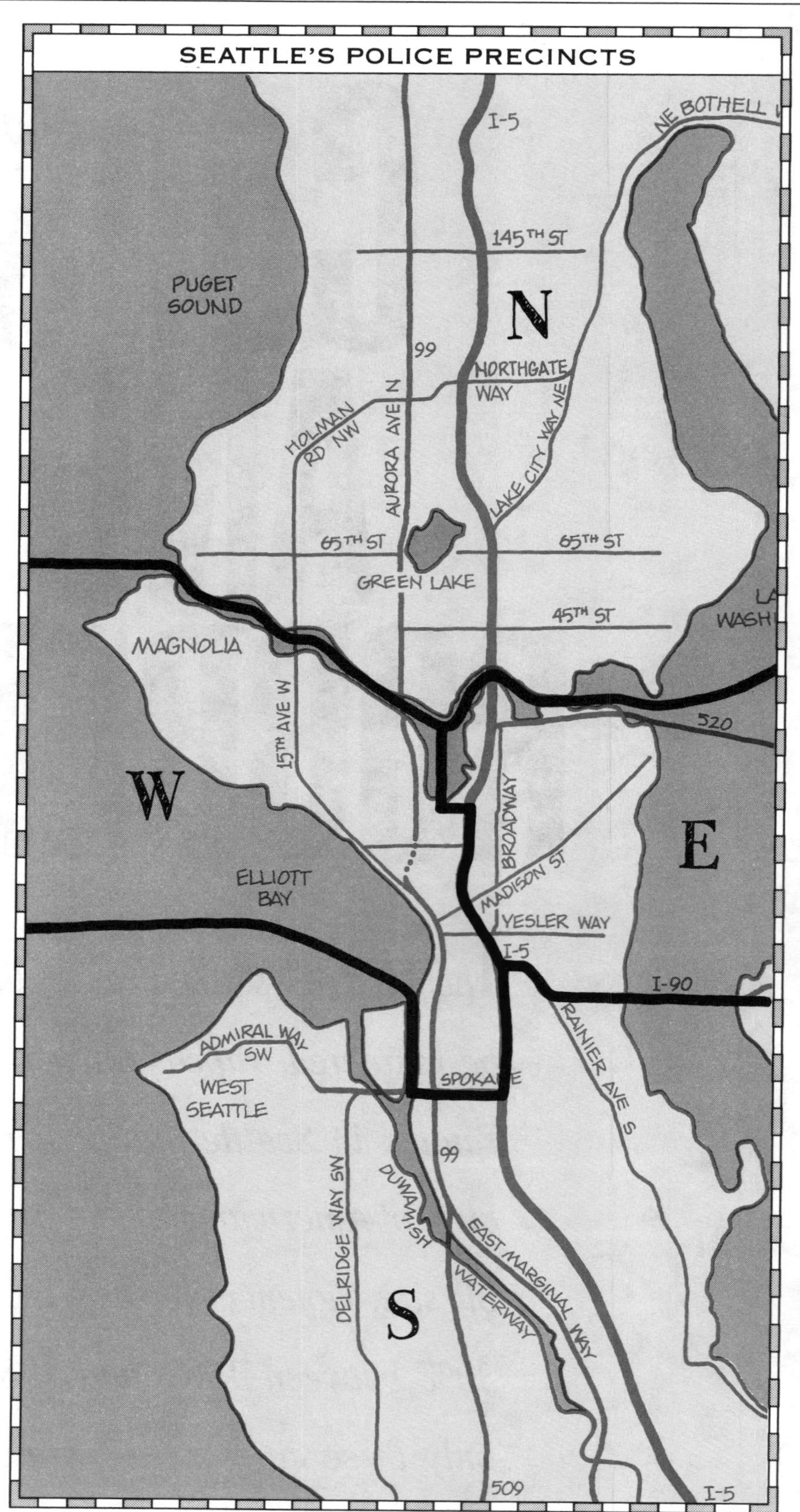

The SPD has 20 officers on pedal patrol (mountain bikes): 8 downtown, 6 on Capitol Hill, 6 in Holly Park and Alki during summer.

North Precinct
10049 College Way N
684-0850
Located across the street from North Seattle Community College, just west of I-5 near the Northgate shopping mall.
North Precinct population: 211,660 (42.6% of city).
Percentage of serious offenses (murder, rape, robbery, burglary, aggravated assault, larceny, auto theft, and arson) committed in North Precinct in 1989: 29.9%
Number of serious crimes, 1989: 19,781
Number of serious crimes, 1988: 21,828
(Change in serious crime, 1988 to 1989: -9.4%)
Number of officers (1988): 152
North Precinct Commander:
Capt. Lawrence Farrar

West Precinct
610 Third Ave.
684-8917
Located on the third floor of the Public Safety Building (SPD headquarters) at Third and James.
West Precinct population: 63,890 (12.9% of city).
Percentage of serious offenses committed in West Precinct: 26.29%
Number of serious crimes, 1989: 17,393
Number of serious crimes, 1988: 17,601
(Change in serious crime, 1988 to 1989: –1.2%)
Number of officers: 173
West Precinct Commander:
Capt. Michael O'Mahony

East Precinct
1519 Twelfth Ave.
684-4300
Located at the corner of 12th and Pine, two blocks east of Broadway.
To report crimes that don't necessarily need immediate police response (e.g., to let the police know there's drug dealing going down on the corner), call the East Precinct Crime Prevention Coalition's Hotline: 325-BUST.
East Precinct population: 88,502 (17.8% of city).
Percentage of serious offenses committed in East Precinct: 23.07%
Number of serious crimes, 1989: 15,264
Number of serious crimes, 1988: 17,635
(Change in serious crime, 1988 to 1989: –1.3%)
Number of officers: 158
East Precinct Commander:
Capt. John Pirak

South Precinct
3001 S Myrtle
386-1850
Located on the opposite side of I-5 from Boeing Field, across the street from the Van Asselt Community Center. Crime in south Seattle dropped over 7% from 1987 to 1988 (while the rest of the city saw a 1.3% average increase), and dropped another

5.5% in 1989, due mainly to the SPD's police/community crime reduction program. The program includes community reporting hotlines, four-officer Anti-Crime Teams that concentrate on specific problem areas within the precinct, and expanded crime prevention and proactive policing programs.
South Precinct population: 133,148 (26.8% of city)
Percentage of serious offenses committed in South Precinct: 20.74%
Number of serious crimes, 1989: 13,719
Number of serious crimes, 1988: 14,524
(Change in serious crime, 1988 to 1989: -5.5%)
Number of officers: 143
South Precinct Commander: Capt. Donald Marquart

SPECIAL OPERATIONS DIVISION

This division contains the Traffic and Metropolitan Sections, which include the Special Patrol Unit, the Harbor Patrol Unit, the Mounted Unit, and the Canine Patrol Unit. It is located in the Public Safety Building.

Special Patrol Unit. The largest of the units in the Metro Section. When dignitaries come to town, this is the unit that protects them; they also work special situations like labor strikes and other demonstrations, and provide backup to patrol units. The primary job of the Special Patrol Unit is serving arrest warrants where the servee is apt to be less than cooperative, and assisting narcotics units in executing search warrants.

Harbor Patrol Unit (684-4071). Responsible for all waters within the city limits. It operates out of a dock and maintenance area at 1717 N Northlake Place on Lake Union.

Number of boats: 8; total staff: 24; citations issued in 1989: 1,298; tons of debris (logs, nets, barrels) cleared annually: 600.

The unit patrols Lake Union, Puget Sound north of the West Point Lighthouse, within the city limits on Lake Washington, and the Ship Canal. In addition to keeping the law on the lakes, the floating policemen shore up a houseboat or two every year when storms threaten to sink them. Call the Harbor Patrol Unit when you're in trouble on Lake Union or around the harbor. Who patrols south of West Point? The Seattle Fire Department which has fire boats on Elliott Bay. But they really only respond to fire calls. In effect, there is no law enforcement in the city waters south of the lighthouse. If you're in real trouble on the Sound, call the Coast Guard.
Channel 16, VHF, for emergencies
Channel 22, VHF, for non-emergencies
24-hour Emergency Line: 442-5886
Coast Guard Information: 442-5295

The speed limit on Lake Union is 7 knots from the beginning of the channel out to the Sound, and 7 knots to Lake Washington. At the north end of the lake there is a small area bounded by yellow buoys where there isn't a speed limit. It's a test course for shipyards to run engines and test out boats. They have to shut down to 7 knots at either end of the course.

Lake Washington doesn't have a speed limit except within 100 yards of the shore or bridges where the limit is 7 knots.

Mounted Patrol Unit (386-4238). Stables at Discovery Park (3801 W Government Way). One sergeant, four officers (eight officers during summer).

Cops on horses—they patrol the Kingdome after Seahawk games and big concerts, and trot through Pioneer Square on a regular basis. As ridiculous as this idea seems in the high-tech age, patrolling on horses is extremely effective in crowd control. Various city agencies say the public use of beaches and parks noticeably increases when the mounted patrols make regular appearances—the cop-and-horse team lowers the fear of crime. Some estimate one officer in the saddle is equal, in terms of crowd control, to four on foot.

Canine Patrol Unit (684-7472).

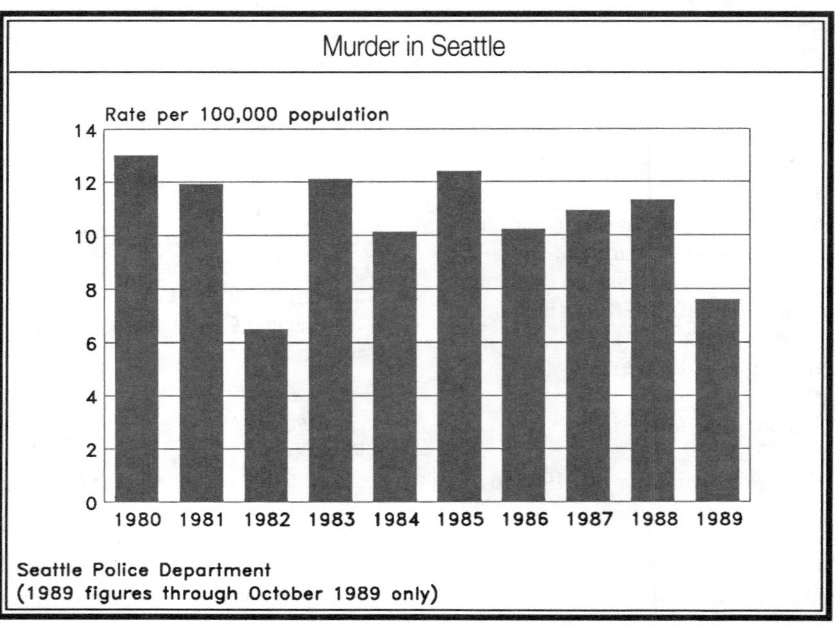

Averaged six officer-and-dog teams during 1985–87. One dog is trained to sniff out explosives, and several can locate narcotics. Unfortunately, six dogs were forced to retire in 1987 and 1988 for medical reasons, so the unit isn't always up to full strength.

VIOLENCE: NOT QUITE A WAY OF LIFE

Murder. Relative to other metropolitan regions, Seattle is not a killing town. The number of murders since 1983 has remained fairly stable at between 50 and 60 per year until 1989, when it dropped to below 40. Most occur in the downtown area and in parts of central and south Seattle.

- Number of murders in 1989: 38
- Number solved (police arrest suspect and turn over to prosecutors): 33
- Murders per 100,000 population: 7.6
- Average murders per 100,000 population in cities over 250,000: 19.8
- Percentage of 1989 murders solved: 87%
- Percentage solved in cities over 250,000: 69%

Rape. The number of reported rapes in Seattle has remained relatively steady over the past 10 years, but is higher than the average for cities of over 250,000 population.

- Number of rape incidents in 1989: 478
- Number per 100,000 population: 96.1
- Number per 100,000 population in cities over 250,000: 74*
- Percentage of Seattle rape cases solved in 1989: 53%*
- Average percentage solved in cities over 250,000: 52%*

The higher incidence of rape in Seattle can be interpreted three ways: Either a woman is at higher risk in Seattle or, as a recent police department management study claimed, the higher rate may be "due to the City's program encouraging

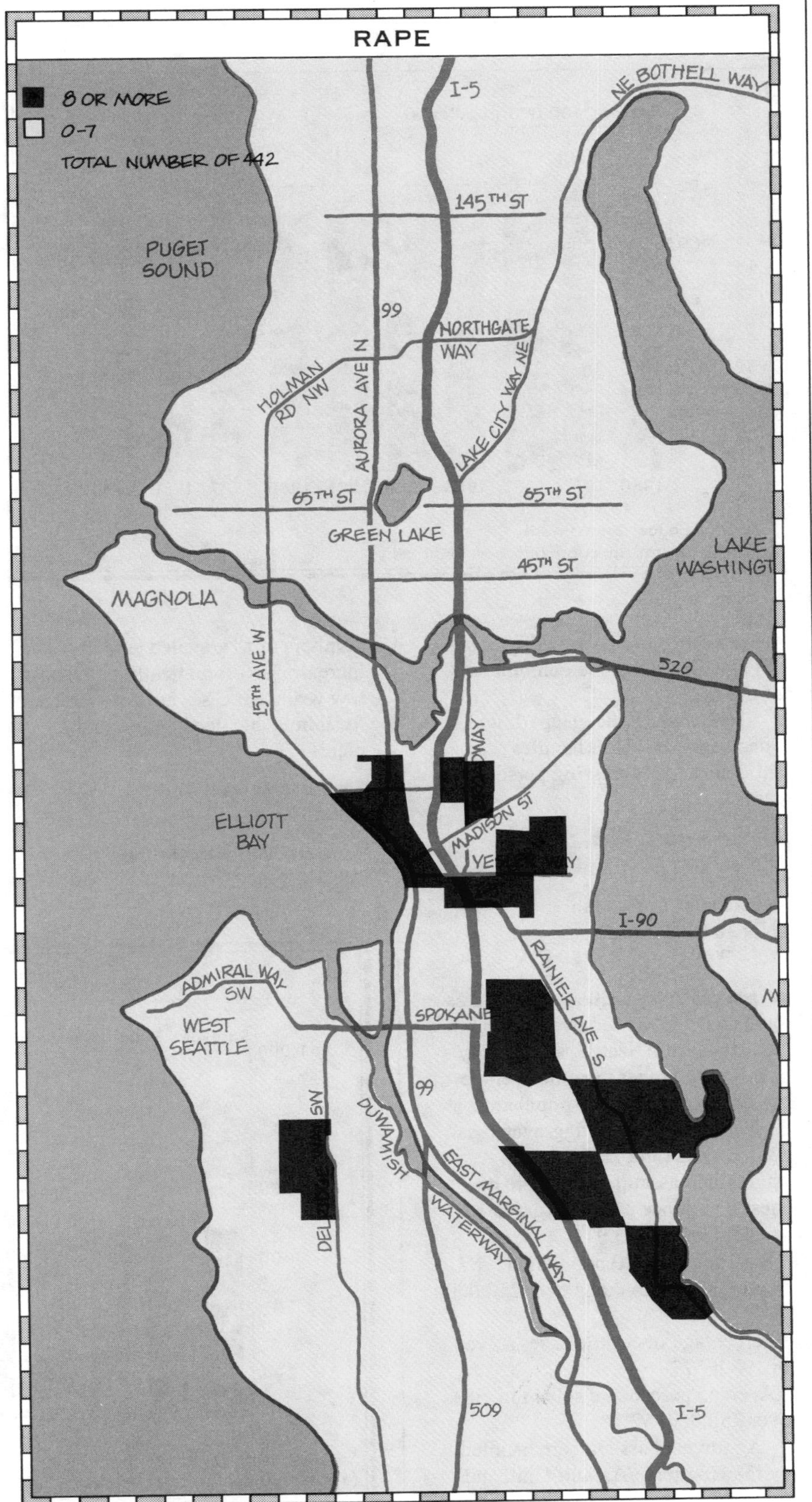

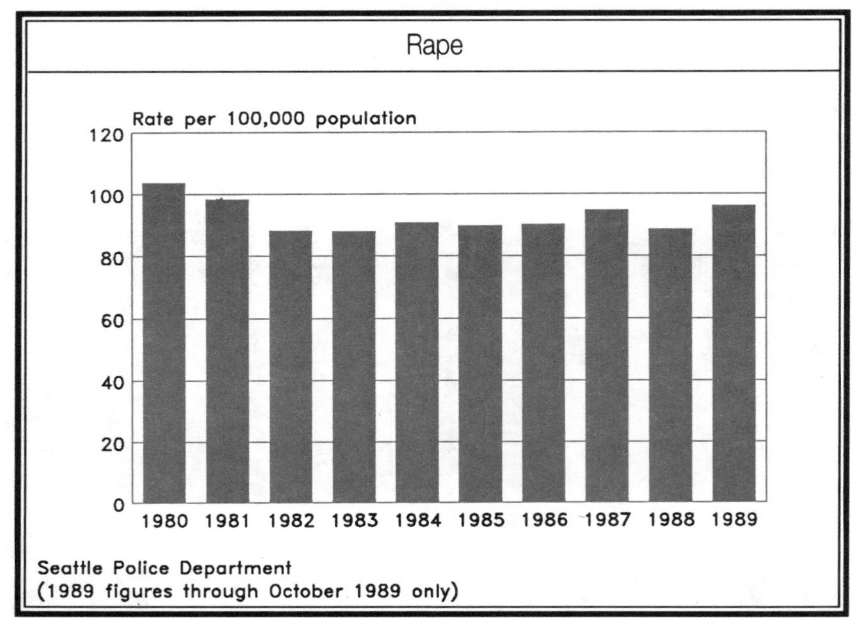

the reporting and prosecuting of sexual assaults," or some combination of the two.

The Seattle Police Department Special Assault Unit handles rape, child abuse, and missing persons cases.

Special Assault Unit
684-5575

Rape Relief Crisis Line
(Not an SPD office)
226-7273

Aggravated assault. Aggravated assaults have increased over 50% in the last 10 years in Seattle, and the city's rate is a bit higher than the average for cities over 250,000 population.

Nearly 60% of all aggravated assault arrests (and 26% of non-aggravated assault arrests) are domestic violence cases. Aggravated assaults in 1989: 3,914

- Rate per 100,000 population: 787
- Average rate in cities over 250,000: 717*
- Percentage of Seattle cases solved in 1989: 57%
- Average percentage solved in cities over 250,000: 57%*

Aggravated assaults are handled by the Homicide/Assault Unit, and numbers of aggravated assaults have increased so dramatically in the past few years that cases are now screened for immediate need before assignment.

Homicide/Assault Unit
684-5550

Domestic Violence Hotline
(800) 562-6025

Shelter for Battered Women Information
461-3200

Seattle Police Dept. Family Violence Unit
684-7770

Robbery. Includes extortions, strong-arm robberies, and purse snatches.

- Number of robberies in 1989: 2,448
- Rate per 100,000 population: 492
Average rate in cities over 250,000: 689*
- Clearance rate (cases solved) for 1989 Seattle robberies: 32%
- Average clearance rate in cities over 250,000: 25%*

*(1987 figure; 1988–89 statistics not available.)

GOODBYE TO THE VCR: PROPERTY CRIMES

Burglary/theft. To get an idea of the chances of the police department catching the thief who has just burglarized your home—let alone return of the swiped VCR, stereo, and

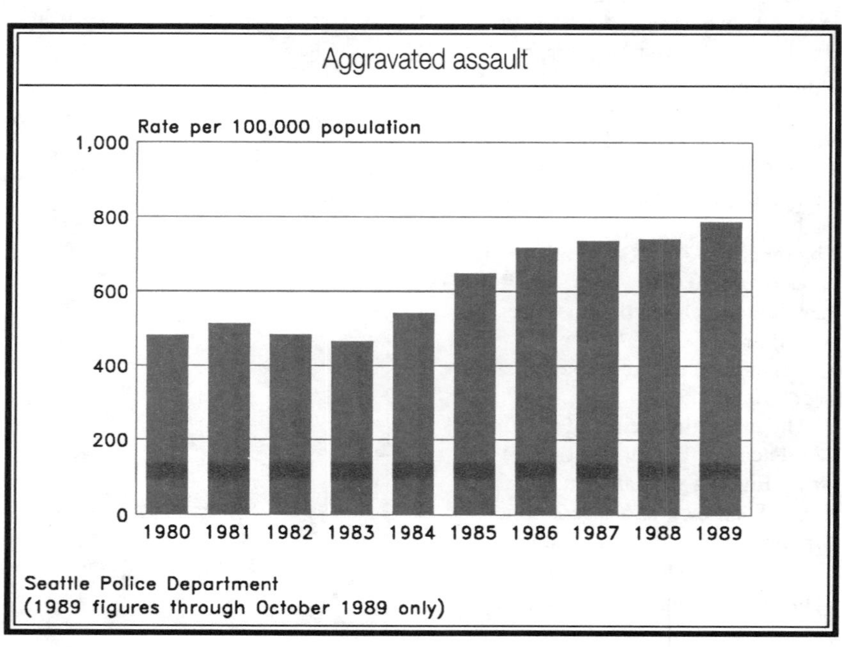

silver—take a look at some numbers.

- Number of burglaries and thefts reported in 1989: 53,702
- Number of detectives responsible for investigating all burglaries and thefts in the city: 23
- Ratio of thefts and burglaries to detectives: 2,335:1
- Number of cases a detective actually investigates, per year: about 175
- Number cleared: 9,250.

In other words, 6% of all burglaries and 21% of all thefts are solved. In 1987, the average burglary clearance rate for cities over 250,000 was not quite double the SPD's—11.6%. Seattle's theft clearance rate is a little higher—21% (compared with the average of 17%).

The only way to increase the chance that your stolen property will be found and returned is by knowing the serial number of the VCR, stereo, etc., or some unique identifying symbol (a scratched-in social security number, for example).

The Seattle Public Library loans engraving tools at each of its 23 branch libraries and in the media department of the downtown library. Call 386-4667. If a thief just ripped off your Toshiba, the police can enter the serial number into a computer file and notify you if it turns up. Otherwise you're out of luck.

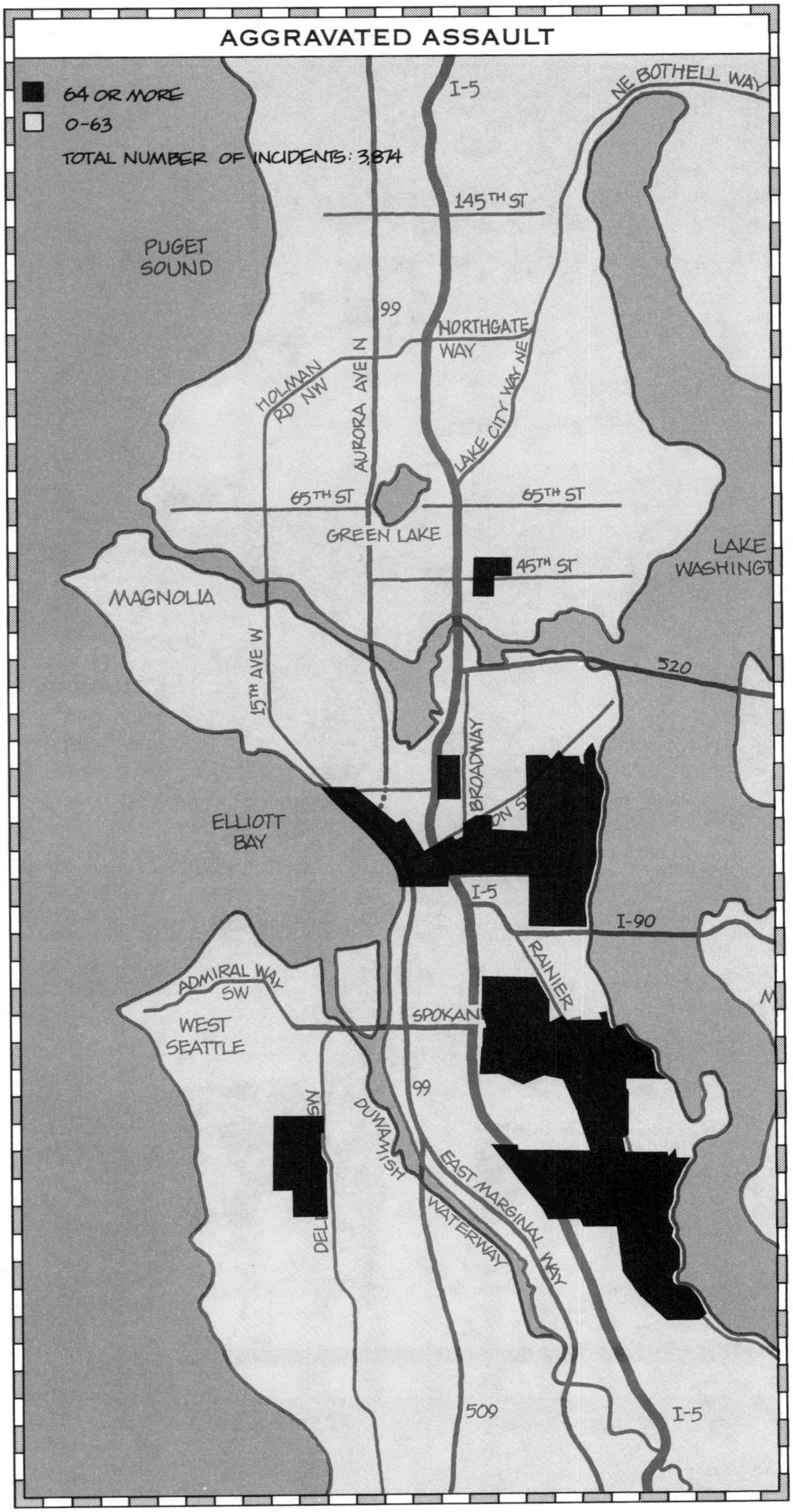

AGGRAVATED ASSAULT

64 OR MORE
0-63
TOTAL NUMBER OF INCIDENTS: 3,874

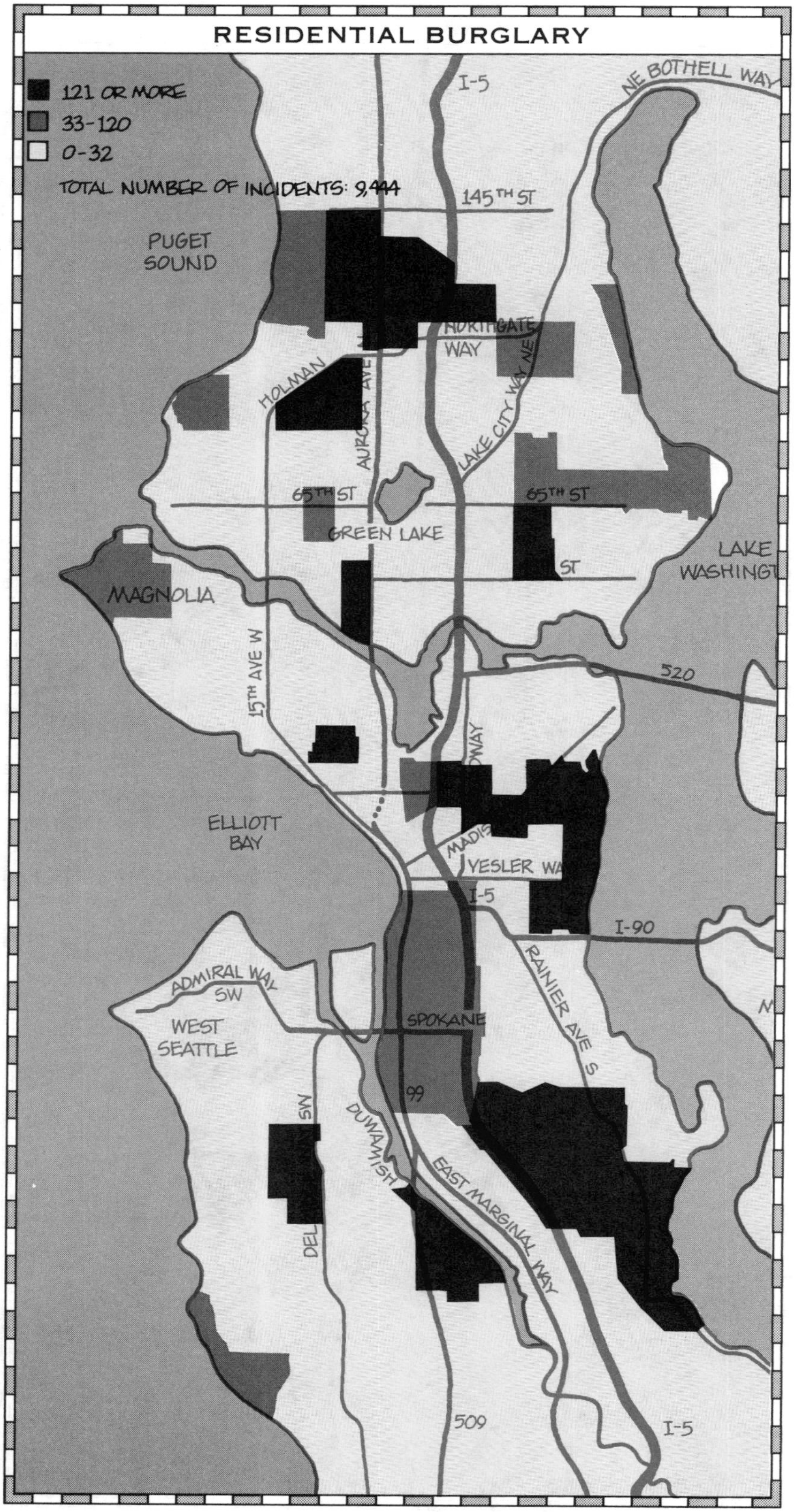

RESIDENTIAL BURGLARY

- 121 OR MORE
- 33-120
- 0-32

TOTAL NUMBER OF INCIDENTS: 9,444

BUT WILL I GET MY VCR BACK?

Not likely—the recovery rate for stolen property, aside from automobiles, is about 6%.

A large percentage of burglaries are connected to narcotics; users steal the stuff, then sell or trade it to support a habit. One cop who regularly busted rock houses (where crack cocaine is sold and used) says it's not uncommon to find the house bare—except for the hot VCRs and stereos stacked in the closet. In a typical *month* in 1989, over $790,000 worth of electronics (stereos, televisions, etc.) was reported stolen. Just under $30,000 worth of the goods was recovered.

The Commercial Anti-Fencing Squad and the Property Recovery Squad are part of the SPD Burglary/Theft Unit. The Anti-Fencing Squad—a sergeant and six detectives—has increasingly focused on drug investigations due to the close association

Because the Seattle Police Department is flooded with theft and burglary cases, each case is handled according to how much information is available to identify the thief. If your case has some good leads and witnesses, it will probably make it to the hands of a detective in the Burglary/Theft Squad. If your case is short on leads, bet the farm that it'll be dispatched to police purgatory, also known as inactive file status.

between fencing and drug sales. The Property Recovery Squad—a sergeant and four detectives—investigates pawn shops and scrap yards in the city, and monitors gun shops.
Amount of value of property stolen in 1989: $41.6 million.
Amount recovered: $12 million.

Property Recovery Squad
684-5737

Burglary/Theft Unit
684-5700

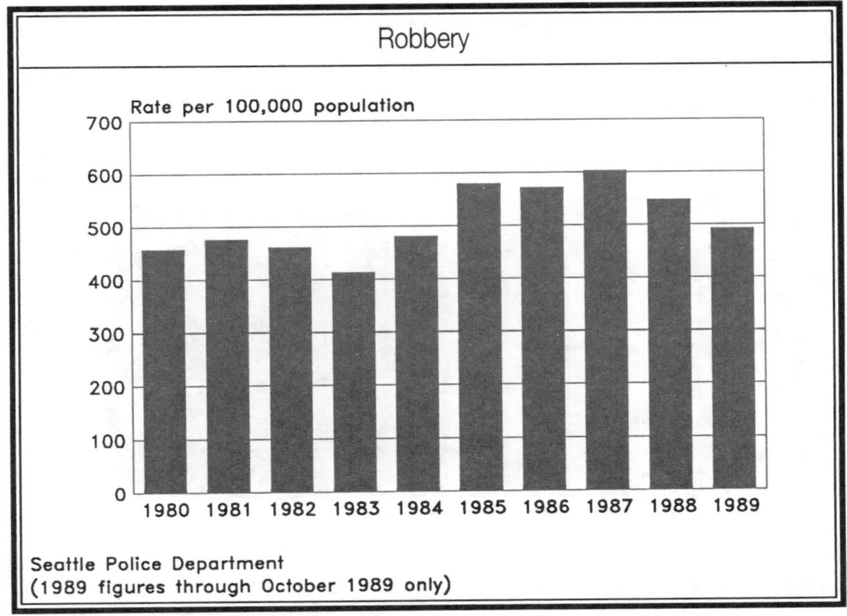

HAPPINESS IS A "BORROWED" CAR

The recovery rate for stolen vehicles is extraordinarily high—the police recover about 96–97% of cars pilfered in the city. The national recovery rate is about 60%. The reason for the high recovery in Seattle is that, for the most part, cars around here are stolen for joy rides; there isn't a big market for hot automobiles. (Any car crook with a nick of sense would ply his trade in LA, anyway).

In a typical month in 1989, $956,000 worth of motor vehicles was stolen; in that same month $919,000 worth of stolen cars was recovered.

But "recovered" doesn't mean your Volvo will come back to the garage untouched. Recovered cars are generally damaged to some extent, and if the stereo was anything more than a factory AM-only system, it's gone. Double ditto for the car phone.

- Number of cars stolen in Seattle, per day (1983): 6
- Number of cars stolen in Seattle, per day (1988): 16
- Number recovered, per day (1988): 15
- Number of cars stolen in Seattle, per day (1989): 20 to 30

What kinds of cars get stolen most often? VW Rabbits are popular with thieves—probably because they're easy to break into. And the discriminating thief likes Datsun 240Zs, 260Zs, and 280Zs—those sporty models are common in auto theft reports. Japanese cars in the pre-1963 vintage get stolen too; locks hadn't been perfected back then.

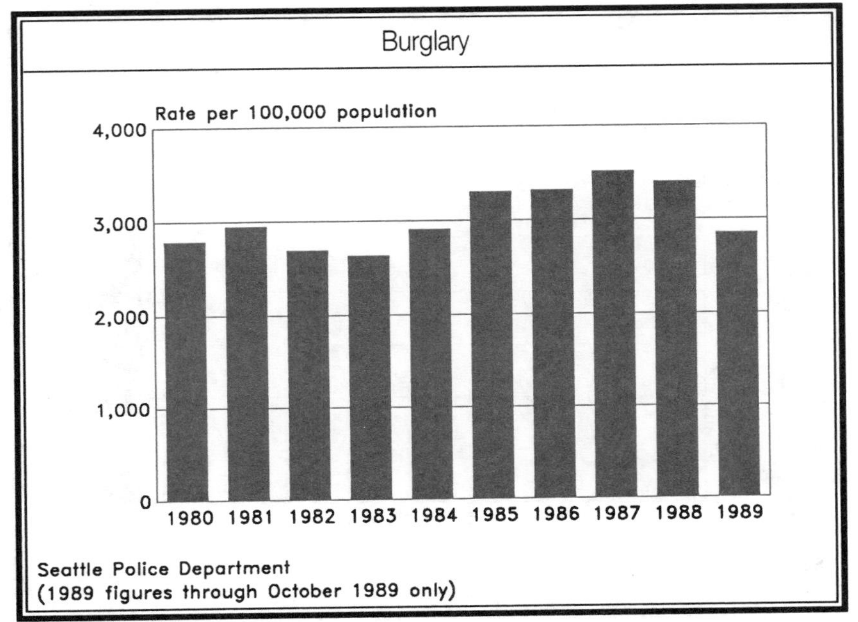

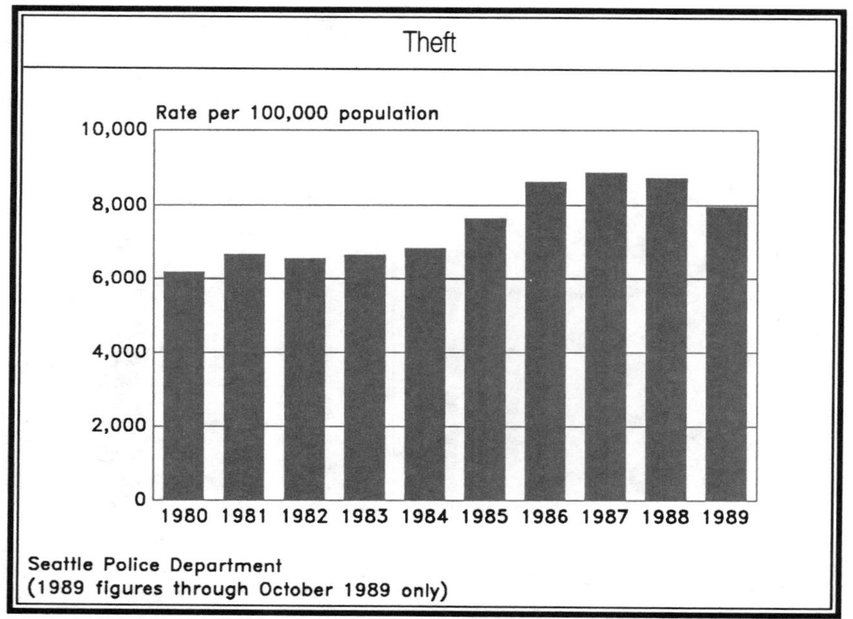

- Dollar amount of cars stolen, (1989): $10,217,792
- Dollar amount recovered (1989): $9,655,637
- Number of auto theft cases cleared, per day (1989): 2

The auto theft rate has increased more than any other crime, more than doubling since 1983. And although police recover most of the cars, they don't necessarily catch many of the thieves.

- Percentage of auto thefts cleared in (1983): 15%
- Percentage cleared (1989): 13%

Auto Theft Squad
684-8940

What can you do to prevent your car from being stolen? Car alarms help—but most thieves know how to disarm them. Park in a garage, says the police department wryly.

DRUG SOCIETY

Narcotics arrests doubled from 1987 to 1990 as Seattleites have come to learn all they ever wanted to know—and more—about crack houses.

There are 35 police personnel assigned to investigate rock houses and drug sales.

Stats:

- Number of felony narcotics arrests in 1986: 1,527; in 1988: 3,663; in 1989: 4,040
- Cocaine seized in 1987: 10.8 kilos
- Cocaine seized in 1989: 25.2 kilos
- Narcotics violation arrests, 1988: 2,887 adults
- Narcotics violation arrests, 1989: 4,428 adults.

Source: Seattle Police Dept. annual reports

Police have identified nearly 600 gang members and hangers-on in the city since the start of 1987. Most of those are Bloods, Crips, or Black Gangster Disciples.

Bloods wear red and are fewer in number than the Crips, who wear blue. Both gangs came from Los Angeles—more than 100 LA gang members have been prosecuted in local courts. The BGDs are a local gang whose members wear black caps and black bandannas, and whose numbers are growing.

GANG ACTIVITY

Police say gangs were responsible for at least 11 murders in the city in 1988. They are also responsible for the increase in drive-by shootings.

- Drive-by shootings in 1987: 3
- Drive-by shootings in 1988: 50
- Drive-by shootings in 1989: 150+

SPD Narcotics Section
684-5797

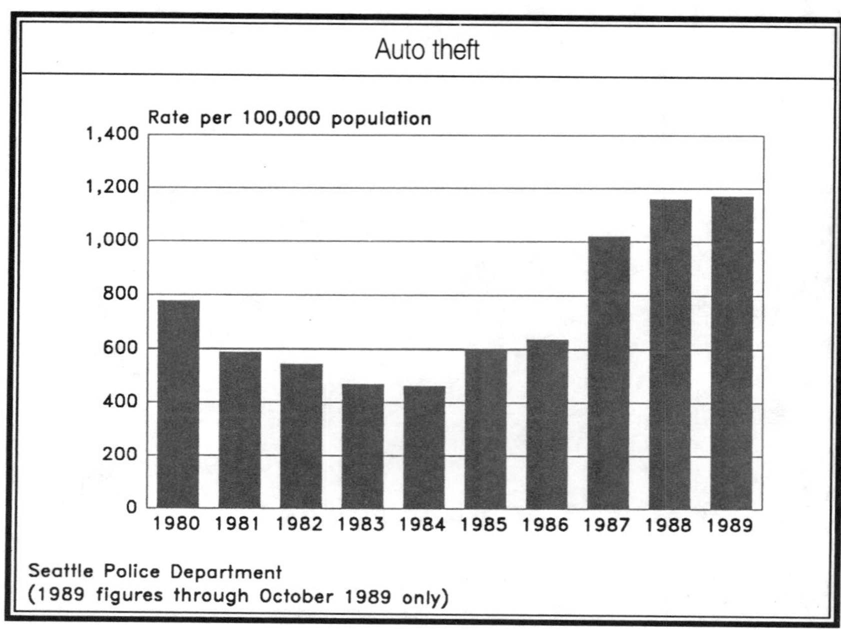

South Seattle Crime Prevention Council
723-CLUE

West Seattle Crime Hotline
937-CLUE

THAT CRACK HOUSE NEXT DOOR

If a crack house is operating in your neighborhood, what can you do? A number of things:

- Call the police, either 911 or the Narcotics Section, and let them know about it.
- Watch the house. Record the makes and license numbers of cars that visit the house, the traffic through the house during any given day, and any names you can get.
- If you're in the southern part of the city, call the info in to the South Seattle Crime Prevention Council. The SSCPC gets about 600 calls a month on problems ranging from graffiti to crack houses. They record the calls and let the South Precinct know where the problem houses and areas are.
- In the West Precinct, call the West Seattle hotline listed above.
- Find out who the owner of the house is. He or she is probably not the person doing the dealing. One place to locate the owner is the King County Tax Assessor's Office on the seventh floor of the King County Administration Building (at Fourth and James). Punch in the address on the public access computer terminals there, and the database will tell you who's paying taxes on the property. If you can locate the owner and let him or her know what's happening and that abatement proceedings (where the city takes over the property) might be in the offing if the house isn't cleaned up, you'll probably see action.
- Learn who the tenant and owner are, then find out if the utility bills—especially the water bill—are in arrears. If the city can shut off water, it can shut the house down.

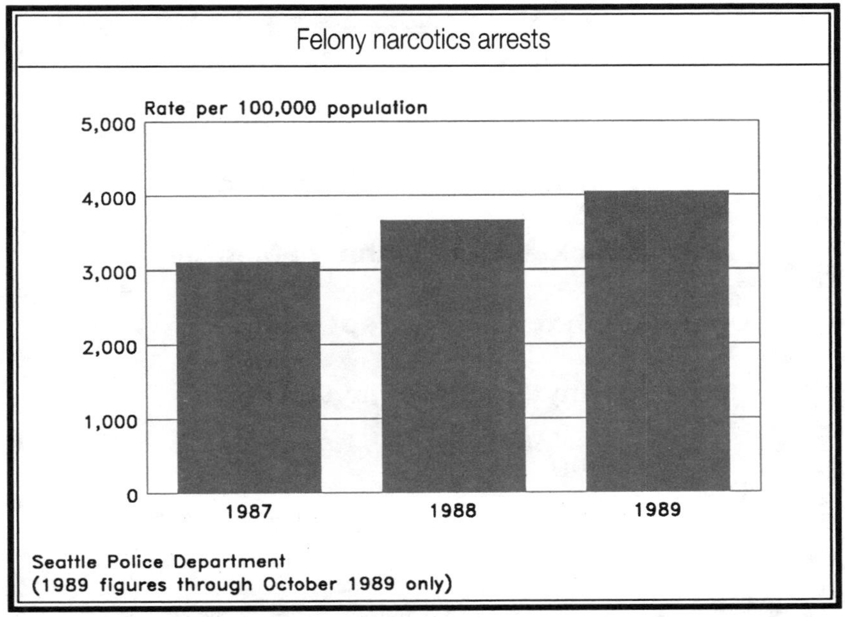

HOW, WHEN, AND WHY THE POLICE RESPOND TO CALLS

About 911. Seattle's 911 service is unusual in that 911 is used for both emergency and non-emergency access to the police. In cities where 911 is reserved exclusively for emergencies, operators will cut off a caller if they determine the situation is not a crisis.

When you call 911, you are routed to one of 19 telephone lines leading to the police department's communications center. A certain number of lines are allocated to different regions of the city, so if it's a particularly busy night in your part of town, you may wait a while before your call is answered. Waiting is rare, however; the average 911 call is picked up within 4 to 5 seconds.

When you call 911 to alert the police of an emergency, your call is given a priority rating, which determines how fast the cops respond to your call. The priorities are:

Critical Dispatch. Acute need for dispatch. The life of a citizen or officer is in obvious danger; this call goes out for crimes-in-progress like shootings and stabbings.

Immediate Dispatch. Dispatch at once; nearly critical. Other crimes-in-progress, or ones that are imminent, or just occurred. Includes major disturbances with weapons, serious injury accidents, most alarms.

Urgent Dispatch. Dispatch nearly immediately. Circumstances where quick police response could nab the suspects; altercations that could really get out of hand if not policed quickly; incidents where there is a threat of violence, injury, or damage to property. Also, unknown injury or minor injury accidents.

Prompt Dispatch. Dispatch as soon as possible. Most noise and traffic complaints are "prompt dispatch." Also used for investigations or minor incident complaints in which response time is not a critical factor.

Dispatch as Available. Self-explanatory. Mischief or nuisance complaints such as snowballing, firecrackers, etc. Lowest priority calls;

HEARD ON THE STREET

"Only a fool pays full price for a traffic ticket. Rare is the magistrate or judge that won't accept your excuse for anything from jaywalking to speeding."

Habitual jaywalker

dispatched after all others are taken care of.

- Number of 911 calls, for police only, in 1988, per hour: 98
- Number of calls dispatched, per hour: 36.

FOLLOW-UP

Cases, like dispatch calls, are assigned on a priority basis starting with the most serious felonies and ranging down to the least serious. After that, a number of factors determine whether your case will be assigned to an investigator—let alone solved. These are:

If the perpetrator has been identified, or can be. If a gun or dangerous weapon was used. If serious injury took place. If there's an unusual, unique *modus operandi* or obvious pattern to the crime. In the case of a residential burglary, if the house was occupied at the time. If the crime took place on a unique premise (church, community institution, etc.). If a large loss occurred. If a gun without a serial number is reported stolen. If the complainant was the victim of a similar crime within the past six months. If there are leads or evidence to follow up. If the crime has the potential for creating unusual community or police interest.

When the case is assigned, the detective takes statements and examines leads (mainly on the phone). The case is then either submitted to the prosecutor for action, referred to the court unit for possible prosecution as a misdemeanor, or filed in records as "Inactive."

The victim is notified of the case status in a letter from the department.

ROCKET DOCKET: SEATTLE MUNICIPAL COURT

It is known as "The Zoo," "a pit," and "Court of the Rocket Docket." If you're unfamiliar with how it works, Seattle Municipal Court can seem like the judicial equivalent of the proverbial Chinese fire drill. Expect to be confused, expect an interminable wait, and you will not be disappointed. As of this writing, the municipal court system is one of the hottest political potatoes in Seattle politics. It is overheated, overcrowded, and most people involved agree that the system has broken down.

The problem, grossly simplified, is this: If you are accused of a misdemeanor you are entitled to a jury trial. You can demand a jury trial for a charge of swiping a six-pack from 7-Eleven. If you are no fool, you realize that if you demand a jury trial your case will be delayed and delayed, prosecutors will have trouble contacting witnesses, and your case may ultimately be dismissed.

The city's municipal court hears all misdemeanors (crimes carrying a maximum sentence of one year in jail and a $5,000 fine) and civil disputes under $10,000. Traffic court is adjudicated by six magistrates (there are no jury trials).

Every week 120 jury trials are scheduled for a court system that was designed to handle 12. Prosecutors have to prioritize their caseload—the more violent and flagrant cases rise above the petty.

If the defendant chooses to disappear—many do—the judge issues a bench warrant (usually $1,000) for the defendant's arrest. Municipal court judges issue, on average, 110 per day. In an early Monday session in Department One, bench warrants are passed out like morning coffee.

Six judges sat on municipal court benches in 1985, when 6,386 trials were requested. Nine judges sat on municipal court benches in 1989, when roughly three times that many were requested.

A typical week works like this: On Friday, a list is made of all the cases set to go to trial the following week; a certain number are set for Monday, some for Tuesday, etc. If you are involved in a case coming to trial and you're not sure when or where it will be heard, call the Calendar and Trial Coordinator (684-5679); calling that number after 3:30 p.m. on Friday will connect you to a recording with the next week's schedule.

Municipal Court General Information
684-5600

Calendar and Trial Coordinator
684-5679

Warrants
610 Third Ave.
Public Safety Bldg. (PSB)
Room 105: 684-5690

Court Administrator
Esther Bauman, PSB 1100:
684-8707

Judges Chambers
PSB 1100: 684-8709

Courtrooms
Known as "Departments": 684-8709
#1 Judge Stephen R. Schaefer, PSB 700: 684-5678
#2 Judge Ron Kessler, 300 Dexter Horton Bldg.: 684-7668
#3 Judge Ron Mamiya, PSB 422: 684-5672
#4 Judge Barbara Yanick, PSB 424: 684-5672
#5 Judge George Holifield, PSB 112: 684-5666
#6 Judge Barbara Madsen, PSB 111: 684-5666
#7 Judge Helen Halpert, Jail Court room—Room 211, King County Jail: 386-1539
#10 Night Court, Judge Nicole K. MacInnes, PSB 424: 684-5672

The Public Defenders Association offers what they call the "Attorney of the Day." Between 12:45 and 1:45 p.m. every weekday, an attorney from PDA will dispense free legal advice over the phone on basic questions. Call 447-3900.

Traffic court is a division of municipal court, and it's not exactly traffic court—the six magistrates who hear cases aren't limited to traffic disputes, although that area does make up 65% of their caseload.

To contest a citation, fill out the back of the ticket and the court will send you a hearing date, which will be about four to six weeks in the future. The magistrates' offices are on the first floor of the Public Safety Building. Expect to wait 10–30 minutes; the actual hearing will take about 5 minutes. If you've got a good excuse and a good driving record, chances are the magistrate will knock down the fine or toss out the violation altogether.

Recorded Parking Citation Information
684-5410

Recorded Info on All Other Citations
684-5400

Magistrate Hearings
Continuances: 684-8704
Hearing Dates: 684-5600

THE SEARCH FOR PERRY MASON

If you find yourself collared by the heavy hand of the law, you'll need a defense attorney. Fortunately (or unfortunately, depending on your point of view), Seattle is full of attorneys. They're not all defense attorneys, but the pickings for a defendant aren't slim.

PUBLIC DEFENDERS

The public defender's office in Seattle is actually made up of four organizations: Associated Counsel for the Accused (ACA), Society of Counsel Representing Accused Persons (SCRAP), Northwest Defenders Association, and the Public Defenders Association (PDA). Seattle and King County contract with these agencies to provide attorneys when you need free legal defense. The King County Office of Public Defense assigns your case to one of the four, and they take it from there.

Associated Counsel for the Accused (ACA)
Alaska Bldg.
624-8105
53 attorneys. Handles felonies (38% of public defense felonies), juveniles, muni court cases, and most (74%) of the public defense cases in district court.

King County Office of Public Defense
321 Smith Tower
506 Second Ave.
296-7662

Northwest Defenders Association
157 Yesler Way, Suite 203
623-5091
14 attorneys. Handles juvenile and municipal court cases, also some district court work. No felony cases.

Public Defenders Association
810 Third Ave.
(8th Floor, Central Bldg.)
447-3900
Largest of the four defense organizations, has 80 attorneys. Handles most felonies (PDA takes 41% of felony public defense cases), juvenile cases, municipal court cases (48%), all involuntary commitment cases (mental health and alcohol), and a few district court cases.

Society of Counsel Representing Accused Persons (SCRAP)
1401 E Jefferson St., Suite 200
322-8400
36 attorneys. Handles felony cases and a large portion (36%) of public defense juvenile cases. SCRAP does not operate in municipal or district court.

OTHER LEGAL SERVICES

Lawyers Referral Service does what its name implies; sponsored by the Washington State Bar Associaton, 623-2551.
Evergreen Legal Services offers free legal advice to low-income citizens, 464-5911.
Free Legal Clinics (call 624-9365 for additional info).

HIRING THE TOP GUNS IN TOWN

If you're really in a fix with a criminal case (and money is no object), these are the defense lawyers to call, according to courthouse sources and the book *The Best Lawyers In America* (1987 edition).

John Henry Browne
811 First Ave., Suite 650
624-7364

Dan Dubitzky
710 Cherry St.
476-6709

Laurence Finegold
Finegold & Zulaf
Tower Bldg., 13th Floor
682-9274

Murray Guterson
Culp Dwyer Guterson & Grader
One Union Square, 27th Floor
624-7141

Darrell Hallett
Chicoine & Hallett
Waterfront Place One, Suite 803
223-0800

Richard Hansen/David Allen
Allen & Hansen
600 First Ave.
447-9681

Good number to know: 723-CLUE, south Seattle Crime Prevention Hotline. Give them info on dealing, rock houses, graffiti, etc. and they'll let the police know about it. Also 937-CLUE in West Seattle.

Peter Mair
Mair Abercrombie Camiel & Rummonds
710 Cherry St.
624-1551

Mark Mestel/John Muenster
Mestel & Muenster
1613 Smith Tower
467-7500

Katrina Pflaumer
2200 Smith Tower
622-5943

Anthony Savage
607 Third Ave.
682-1882

Irwin Schwartz
710 Cherry St.
623-5084

LOWLIFE

The SPD's Vice Squad handles the city's lowlife, everything from the world's oldest profession to gambling and pornography. Prostitutes frequent certain corners of the city, most notably near the Yesler overpass, Broadway, and Sea-Tac.

They used to hang out at Sixth and Pike, but the cops put a stop to that. Second and Pike is popular for all sorts of lowlife after midnight, when it comes alive with drug dealers and kids looking for action. Aurora, once made lively after dark by the prostitutes, has calmed down in recent years after the merchants and residents posted signs asking people to report the license numbers of "johns" stopping along the strip. Most of the signs ended up in teenagers' bedrooms, but increased patrolling of the area helped.

PISTOL PACKIN' CITY

It's not only the police who carry guns in Seattle. And it's not only those with gun permits from the city who carry guns. But those who are

If you are the type who doesn't pay parking tickets, the police will put a hold on your vehicle license. And driving with expired tabs is one sure way to attract the attention of police, who will let you know in haste that you are wanted on an outstanding warrant. If you're curious about your current bill, call the muni court office (684-5600) and give them either your vehicle license or a case number. They'll look up your file on computer and give you a list of individual tickets and a grand total.

conscientious enough to get a permit have been on the increase.

Gun permits issued in recent years

1984: 3,741
1985: 2,756
1986: 436 (The reason for the low number is that the renewal period was changed from every two years to every four.)
1987: 2,361
1988: 3,832

More women are carrying guns than ever before. In Seattle, local gun/sporting goods stores report handgun sales to women have increased 50% since 1985. Most of the buyers are first-time gun owners. Classes for women-only in handgun defense have been taken by more than 400 women at a range in Mountlake Terrace recently.

Agencies serving victims of crime

Seattle Police Department Victim Assistance Section
801 Dexter Horton Bldg.
710 Second Ave.
Seattle, WA 98104
684-7777

King County Prosecutor's Victim's Assistance Unit
King Co. Courthouse, Room E542
516 Third Ave.
Seattle, WA 98104
296-9552

Families and Friends of Missing Persons and Violent Crime Victims
P.O. Box 27529
Seattle, WA 98125
362-1081

Mothers Against Drunk Driving
1511 Third Ave., Suite 911
Seattle, WA 98101
624-6903

Harborview Sexual Assault Center
325 Ninth Ave.
Seattle, WA 98104
223-3047

Seattle Rape Relief
1825 S Jackson St., Suite 102
Seattle, WA 98144
Business: 325-5531 (TTY)
Crisis: 632-7273

Family Violence Project
Seattle City Attorney's Office
1055 Dexter Horton Bldg.
710 Second Ave.
Seattle, WA 98104
684-7770 (TTY)

CHAPTER

A KIDS PLACE OR WHAT?

SERVICES

FOSTER CARE

ADOPTION

CAMPS

FUN

RUNAWAYS

DAY CARE

LIBRARIES

ZOO

DIAPERS

Kids in Seattle are becoming as scarce as cash in Martin Selig's bank account. They have undergone a disappearing act, thanks to the gentrification of the city's neighborhoods and the attractions of the wide open spaces of the suburbs. People think the bitter busing issue that has polarized parents and public schools is at the root of this mass exodus of kids, but the most precipitous decline took place *before* the district began busing students to integrate the schools in 1978.

The seventies were the years when huge layoffs at Boeing, a declining birthrate, and the lure of the suburbs drained Seattle of middle-class families and changed the demographic face of the city, perhaps forever.

In 1990 Seattle's under-18 population is about half the size it was 20 years ago. Since the late 1960s, when Seattle public school enrollment topped 100,000, the number of public school students has dropped by 60%. That trend shows no sign of reversal.

While the population of kids has been dwindling, the city has been hurling services at those remaining 80,000 or so under-18-year olds. As a KidsPlace, the name coined by former Mayor Charles Royer, the city has been scrambling to arrest the departure of children and families, and to turn Seattle into a giant playground.

Has it been successful? Well, Royer got a lot of press out of the KidsPlace program, which was exemplified by media-friendly events such as KidsDay, and the creation of an office at city hall dedicated to issues affecting children and youth. But some critics charged that Royer's actions were inspired political moves of no substance. Royer and his backers bristled at the accusation. Whatever the motives behind Royer's inspiration, they have produced some genuine results.

KidsPlace has functioned outside of city hall since 1987, independent of (and hopefully more permanent than) the political agendas of city council members. The city has made good progress on 20 of the 30 goals set forth in a five-year plan to improve conditions for children citywide, including: expanded health care and child care for low-income families; longer hours at neighborhood recreation centers; restoring many playground programs that had been shut down for budget reasons; developing a bike route network; and making downtown a safer, "friendlier" place for kids.

There have been some setbacks, of course. For example, Metro still charges full fare for children. The campaign to lower fares was thwarted when Metro announced it would institute cheaper kids' fares while raising fares for senior citizens. The resultant outcry from the seniors' lobby killed that idea.

HEARD ON THE STREET

"The census map [of 1980] shows that the neighborhoods that kept their kids tended to be either very rich or very poor."

Dawn Hanson Smart,
City of Seattle Human Services, Strategic Planning Office

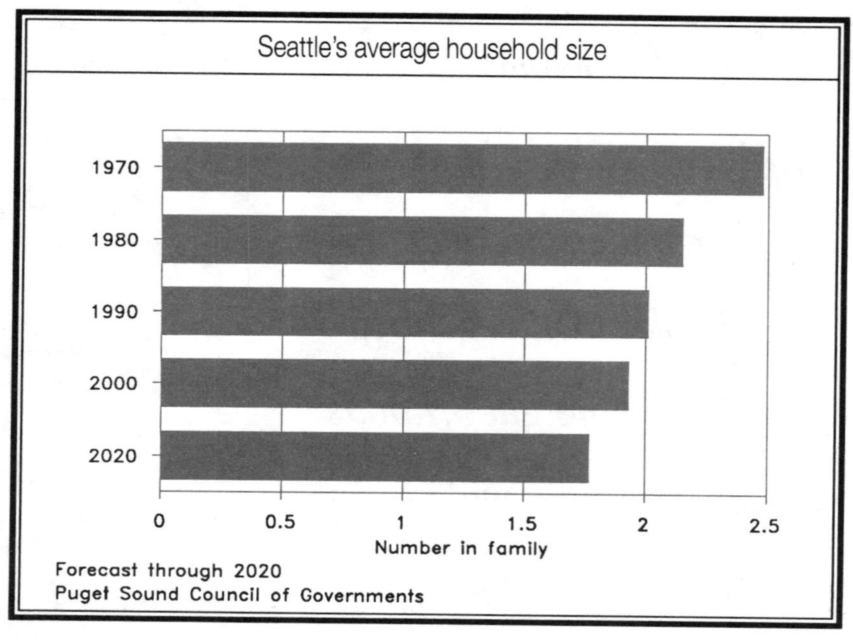

STANDING UP FOR KIDS

KidsPlace was started as a joint project of the Junior League, the YMCA, and the City of Seattle. Forty local corporations and nonprofit groups helped sponsor the program and establish its goals: to put children and families "high on Seattle's economic, cultural and political agenda."

It includes a 75-member KidsBoard, an advisory group of teens who are supposed to be learning leadership skills and influencing city decisions affecting youth. One of their projects is the Teen Hotline, a sort of peer listening program. KidsBoard struck out on requiring teacher competency tests—it was a bit ahead of its time. Two KidsBoard members are on the city's Commission on Children and Youth, a mayor-or-council-appointed body charged with evaluating the city's efforts to take care of its kids.

KidsPlace and its best-known creation, KidsDay, have been widely imitated nationally. Congress even designated the second Sunday in October as national Children's Day. Seattle is changing its KidsDay celebration to conform with that date, but will still observe some KidsDay events in April as usual. The celebration includes free rides on the waterfront trolley, skateboard exhibitions, awards for kids, and more.

KidsPlace
158 Thomas, Suite 14
Seattle, WA 98109
441-0848
Teen Hotline: 382-KIDS

Seattle Commission on Children and Youth
105 Union, Suite 160
Seattle, WA 98101
386-1140

MONEY TALKS

To a degree unique among major U.S. cities, Seattle puts its money where its mouth is, each year channeling nearly $13 million in local tax dollars to programs benefiting children and youth. These include not only the usual health clinics and recreation programs, but also subsidized day care for low-income families and $2 million for various public school activities. Up until the time that community development block grants began to dwindle during the Reagan years, Seattle was among the few cities that used the grants for human services, not just for capital improvements.

The spending has had a good effect on some things in the city. Health and social services are abundant and relatively well-coordinated. Examples: The percentage of pregnant women receiving little or no prenatal care in King County is 27% below the national average; the infant mortality rate (12.4 per 1,000 births in 1989 [preliminary figures] in Seattle; 9 per 1,000 births in King County) has been generally declining since the 1970s.

The teen birth rate in King County went down in the 1980s—from 9.8% of all births in 1980 to 8.3% in 1988. Nationally the rate is 50 births per 1,000 girls.

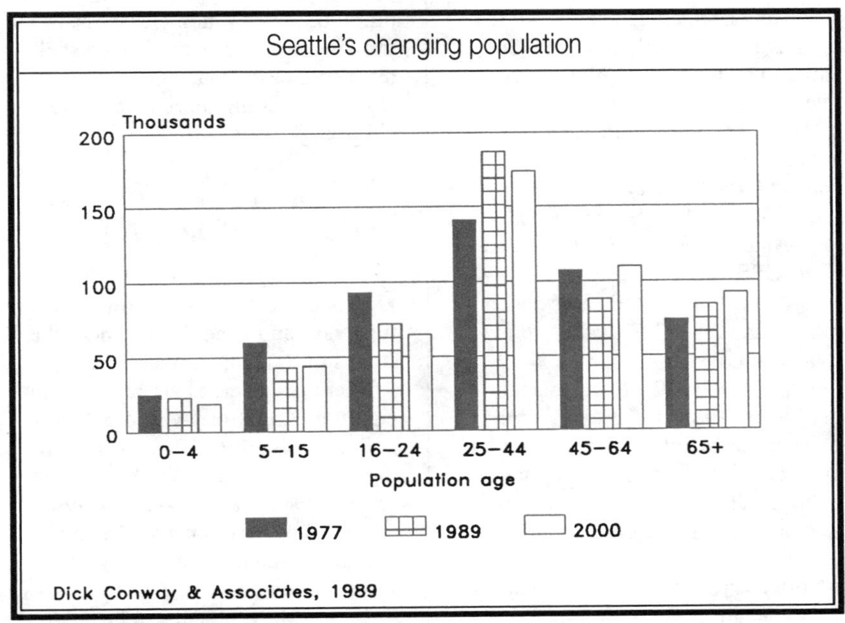

THE FLIP SIDE

KidsPlace or not, Seattle's youth are still victims of both social and familial abuse, and often fare little better than in other big cities. Child

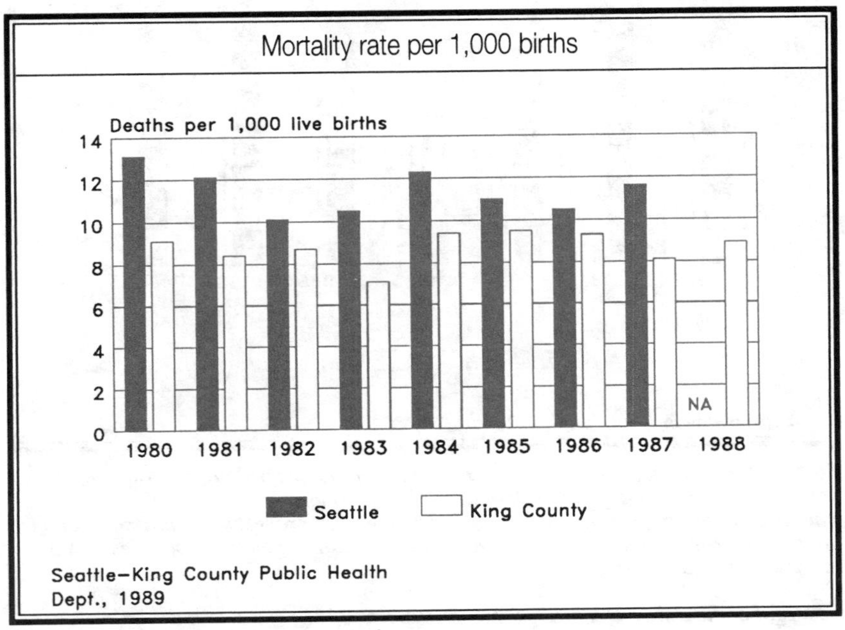

abuse and neglect are at an all-time high. During 1989 there were 9,269 children added to the Child Protective Services (CPS) caseload, up from the 6,675 added in 1988, an increase of 39%.

Seattle CPS Activity
Jan.–Aug., 1989: 6,563 cases added
Jan.–Aug., 1988: 5,237 cases added

Kent CPS
Jan.–Aug., 1989: 3,119 cases added
Jan.–Aug., 1988: 2,570 cases added

Bellevue CPS
Jan.–Aug., 1989: 2,216 cases added
Jan.–Aug., 1988: 1,091 cases added

There were not only more kid victims, but also more kid perpetrators of crime: Juvenile offenses increased from 8,208 in 1982 to 9,390 in 1988. The increase was in so-called "lesser" offenses such as assault, prostitution, vandalism, drug, liquor, and weapons violations.

An estimated 15.8% of all Seattle children under 18 live in poverty—23% higher than the city's adult poverty rate. The most extreme condition of poverty, homelessness, is a growing problem. City-funded shelters serve more than 6,000 family clients, including more than 3,600 children.

ON THE STREET

No one knows for sure how many runaways and street kids wander the streets of Seattle, but more than 5,000 runaway cases are reported annually in King County, and in Seattle police receive 150–200 calls pertaining to runaways per month, or about 2,400 calls a year. Most runaways appear to be between ages 15 and 19, though some are as young as 11 or 12.

Some 800 youths are believed to be on the city's streets on a regular basis, and up to 2,000 involved in street life at some point during a year. The majority of street-involved youth can be found in the downtown area, but the University District, Broadway, and neighborhoods in South Seattle and the Central District are reporting increasing numbers.

According to Ann Rudnicki, program director of Orion Multi-Service Center, 75% of street kids have been physically and/or sexually abused.

With that many kids needing shelter, pitifully few beds are available for them (only about 165) and almost all require referrals through the State Department of Social and Health Services. A large percentage, between 300 and 800 of the street kids, are believed to be involved in juvenile prostitution.

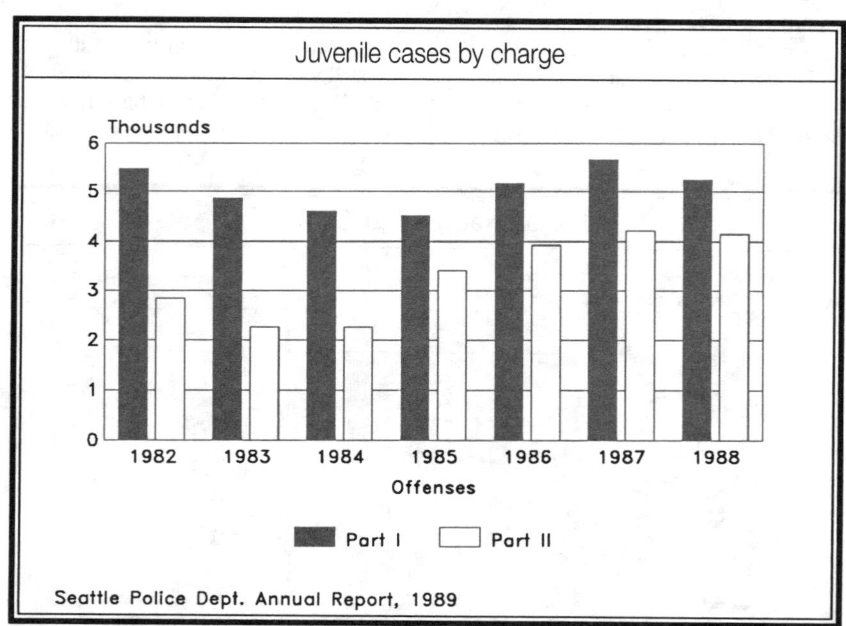

***Part I offenses** include the most serious crimes: murder, manslaughter, rape, robbery, aggravated assault, burglary, theft, auto theft, and arson.*
***Part II offenses** include: assault, forgery, fraud, stolen property, vandalism, weapons violations, prostitution, sex offenses, narcotics violations, gambling offenses, liquor violations, and disorderly conduct.*

Source: Seattle Police Department annual reports, 1988

Organizations that come to the aid of parents or kids in times of crisis:

Child Protective Services (CPS)
Dept. of Social and Health Services
2809 26th Ave. S
Seattle, WA 98144
721-4115
Investigates complaints of child abuse, neglect, and exploitation. Names confidential.

Childhaven
316 Broadway
Seattle, WA 98122
624-6477
Day treatment center for abused children. Free.

Committee for Children
172 20th Ave.
Seattle, WA 98122
322-5050
Started by Dr. Jennifer James, this group provides training, education materials, and curricula on child abuse prevention and personal safety.

Council for Prevention of Child Abuse and Neglect
1305 Fourth Ave., Room 202
Seattle, WA 98101
343-2590
Programs to prevent abuse. Also a Parent Line (support and information service for parents who have questions about parenting). Referral service too, and library open to the public.

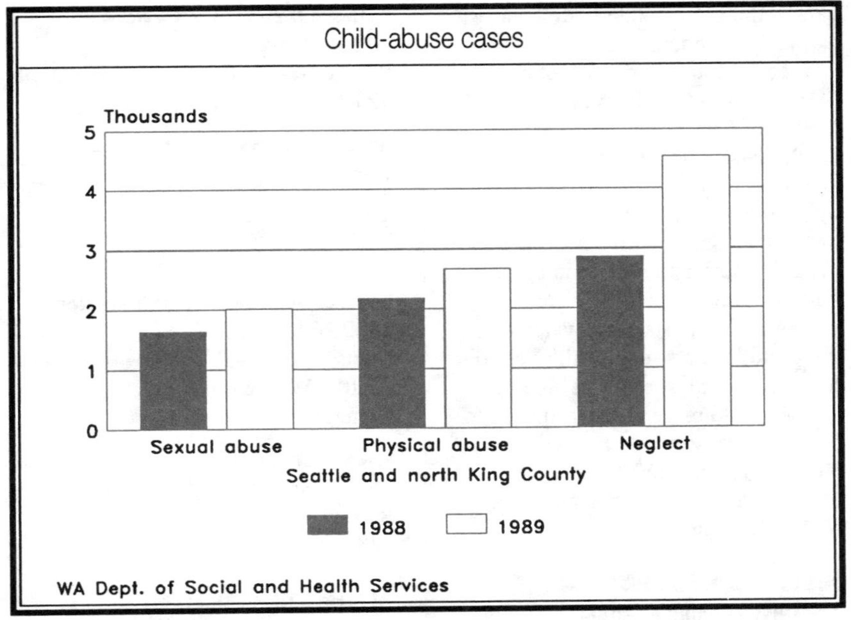

Crisis Clinic
1515 Dexter Ave. N, Suite 300
Seattle, WA 98109
Community Information Line:
461-3200
Clearinghouse for referrals and help for parents and children. 24 hours.

Friends of Youth
P.O. Box 12
Issaquah, WA 98027
392-KIDS
Two shelters for runaways, outpatient counseling, licensing of foster parents, teen mom program. Serves Eastside Renton to Bothell.

KING COUNTY SERVICES

Runaway Crisis, King County
328-0805

Medina Children's Service
P.O. Box 22638
Seattle, WA 98122-0638
324-9470
In cooperation with the City of Seattle, the Seattle/King County Public Health Department, and Seattle School District, Medina administers the Teen Age Pregnancy Project (TAPP), among other services.

Neighborhood House
905 Spruce St.
Seattle, WA 98104
461-8430
Provides social services to the residents of five Seattle-area public housing communities. Services include legal advocacy, food and clothing referrals, and transportation. Also administers a child care program with conveniently located branch centers.

Orion Multi-Service Center (Seattle Youth and Community Services)
The Shelter
6201 46th Ave. S
Seattle, WA 98118
725-8888
Runs an outreach program, with beds, for street kids and homeless youth.

Runaway Hotline
(800) 442-TEEN
Hotline for kids who need a place to stay, run by Friends of Youth.

Runaway Hotline Service
(800) 231-6946
Relays messages between runaway children and parents. Information too.

The Teen Hotline
382-5437 or 382-KIDS
Sponsored by Metro-Center YMCA and staffed by trained teens, Mon.–Thurs. 4–7p.m. They give crisis counseling and references for long-term counselors and shelters..

Youth Advocates
2317 E John St.
Seattle, WA 98112
322-7838

EVERY PARENT'S NIGHTMARE

Your teenager doesn't come home on time, and dawn finds you wringing your hands. Could it be that he or she has run away? What to do? The people at Friends of Youth, an Eastside agency that helps runaways and their families, say there's not a lot you can do. But here's where to start:

- Be your own detective. Check with the child's friends about where he or she might be and when your child was seen last.
- Check with school counselors to see if your child was in school that day. In other words, determine how long he or she has been gone.
- If you do find your child, he or she doesn't have to come home—it's children's legal right to make their own choices.
- If your child refuses to come home and you feel he or she is in a bad or dangerous situation, call Children's Protective Services. They may investigate.
- Call the police if your child has been gone for more than 24 hours. But don't expect much—they will only investigate if there's a specific problem, such as your child hanging out at a crack house.
- Once you have found your child, get outside help. Try the family counseling Friends of Youth and other agencies provide. They try to get your child to talk to you—if the child won't talk, be prepared to wait him or her out.

PROFILE OF A RUNAWAY, KING COUNTY

Average age: Girls, 15.6; Boys, 16.2.
Sex: 54% male; 46% female.
Racial makeup: 58% white; 18% Native American; 9% African American; 4% Samoan; 4% Hispanic; 3% Asian.
Abuse: More than 50% of runaways have a history of sexual or physical abuse.
School: More than 50% have dropped out or been suspended.
Drugs: 63% have been involved with drugs and alcohol.
Involvement in juvenile justice system: 43%.
Reasons for leaving: Abandonment, rejection, boredom, unhappiness, serious family or school problems, conflict over sexual identity.
Source: Seattle Human Services Strategic Planning Office, "Homeless Youth in Seattle"

FOSTER CARE AND ADOPTION

Foster care in Seattle is in good condition—nearly 1,700 kids live with foster parents, and about 164 are in group care. There's no waiting list for kids needing foster parents, but at any one time, about 67 kids are on a waiting list for group care.

The state funds foster care in two ways: direct payment to foster parents, and payment to volunteer agencies like the Children's Home Society that fund group facilities for foster kids.

Adoption is, of course, a different situation. In the Seattle area, as in any city, there's always a need for adoptive parents for older or special-need kids. The only figures on how many kids are available overall for adoption are national estimates. Of the 500,000 children needing foster care in the U.S., 300,000 are legally available for adoption.

One Seattle agency, Adoption Services of WACAP (Western Association of Concerned Adoptive Parents), places 50 to 100 babies per year under the Options for Pregnancy program, a system whereby birth parents choose adoptive parents for their newborn and remain in contact with the child as he or she grows.

WACAP reports a two-year waiting period for a young healthy child. Minority couples might be able to adopt a child more quickly. It used to be that there was a shorter wait for Korean children, but Korea is no longer sending 6,000 babies per year to American homes.

Foster care resource list

The Casey Family Program
7210 Roosevelt Way NE
Seattle, WA 98115
522-4673

Catholic Community Services
100 23rd Ave. S
Seattle, WA 98144
323-6336

Children's Home Society of Washington
3300 NE 65th St.
Seattle, WA 98115
524-6020

Dept. of Social and Health Services
2809 26th Ave. S
Mail Stop N56-1
Seattle, WA 98144
General info: 721-4527

Friends of Youth
2500 Lake Washington Blvd. N
Renton, WA 98056
228-5775
or
P.O. Box 12
Issaquah, WA 98027
392-KIDS

HEARD ON THE STREET

"It's going to get worse before it gets better in Seattle because of the mobility of our society. With the growth we're experiencing, the social institutions...can't handle what neighborhoods and extended familiies used to handle."

Ann Rudnicki, program manager,
Orion Multi-Service Center

Jewish Family Service
1214 Boylston Ave.
Seattle, WA 98101
461-3240

Lutheran Social Services
6920 220th SW
Montlake Terrace, WA 98043
672-6009

Youth Advocates
2317 E John St.
Seattle, WA 98112
322-7838

Adoption resource list

Adoption Center of Washington
2001 Sixth Ave., Suite 2300
Seattle, WA 98121
624-2229

Adoption Information Exchange
P.O. Box 55183
Seattle, WA 98155
325-9500

Adoption Services of WACAP
543 Industry Dr.
Tukwila, WA 98188
575-4550

Catholic Community Services
P.O. Box 22608
100 23rd Ave. S
Seattle, WA 98144
323-6336

Children's Home Society of Washington
3300 NE 65th St.
Seattle, WA 98115
524-6020

Hope Services
424 N 130th St.
Seattle, WA 98133
367-4604

Jewish Family Service
1214 Boylston Ave.
Seattle, WA 98101
461-3240

Medina Children's Service
123 16th Ave.
Seattle, WA 98122
461-4520

Community resources

Adoption Resource Center
Children's Home Society of Washington
3300 NE 65th St.
Seattle, WA 98115
524-6020
Support for those touched by adoption. Includes Adoption Shop (bookstore with materials on adoption).

Advocates of Single Adoptive Parents / Northwest
725-4980

Becoming Adoptive Parents
c/o Childbirth Education Association
14310 Greenwood Ave. N
Seattle, WA 98133
486-9713 (Kathy Kirchnar)
Class for families waiting for arrival of an infant.

One Church One Child of Washington State
723-6224
Recruits African American families to adopt African American children.

Korean Identity Development Society (KIDS)
503 N 190th St.
Seattle, WA 98133
542-8646
Teaches Korean culture to Korean-American children.

Northwest Adoption Exchange
909 NE 43rd St., Suite 208
Seattle, WA 98105
632-1480

THE DAY CARE MAZE

The first thing parents looking for day care should know about is a wonderful publication called *Kids Pages*, put out by The School's Out Consortium hosted by YWCA of Seattle–King County. Although it's aimed at parents of school-age children, it has great information on everything from day care licensing to assistance in paying for child care. It includes facts on 185 child care centers. It also has lists of enrichment programs for youth at museums, employment centers, tutoring services, etc. *Kids Pages* is available at the Seattle Public Library and the Child and Family Resource and Referral Center, 461-3207.

The City of Seattle Department of Human Resources and the state's DSHS put out a booklet called Choosing Child Care: A Consumer Guide for Parents that includes a checklist of what to ask child care providers. Pick it up at the Child and Family Resource and Referral Center, 2410 E Cherry, Seattle, WA 98122.

About 1,600 licensed day care operators have set up shop in the Seattle/King County area; more than half are based in their own homes (up to 6 kids) and the vast majority of the remainder are mini-centers (up to 12 kids). The average monthly cost of day care in Seattle is $395. (Source: Seattle Family and Youth Services Division)

Although there seem to be lots of providers, more are needed.

The real trick is finding *conveniently located* day care. The Department of Social and Health Services (DSHS) does licensing, but doesn't give out lists of day cares in the normal course of business. The Crisis Clinic and the city combined to form the Child and Family Resource and Referral Center (461-3207) which produces a day care newsletter (primarily for child care providers) and a list of day care options in your zip

King County day care need

	1998 Children in need of care	1987 Licensed slots	1998 Gap	Percent to be cared for in licensed slots
North	7,133	911	6,222	13
East	23,552	7,322	16,230	31
South	39,649	7,741	31,908	20
Balance of county total	70,334	15,974	54,360	23
Seattle*	21,472	9,488	11,984	44
King County total	91,806	25,462	66,344	28

* The number of children in child care is expected to decline in Seattle due to decreases in number of residents in age bracket.

Source: King County Child Care Needs Assessment, 1988

code or near your work. The trouble is that the number is only answered from 9 a.m. to 1 p.m. and is often busy. Some people (18,037 in 1988, to be exact) got through because 77,000 referrals were made that year. Added phone lines should make it easier to get through.

Spanking or hitting is not allowed in licensed child care programs. If you want to know if there have been complaints about a child care program, call DSHS Child Care Licensing, at: Family Day Care Homes and In-Home Mini-Centers: Eastside, 455-7219; South King County, 872-2345; or Seattle, 721-4080.

Centers and Out-of-Home Mini-Centers: all of Seattle-King County, 721-4080.

DAY CARE RESOURCES

The Resourceful Parent
MicroPublish Co.
P.O. Box 781
Bellevue, WA 98009
392-4453
Guide to child care (profiles of individual facilities), education, and health care for King County. Sells for $8.95. Published 1989.

Camp Fire's Phone Friend
Seattle/King County Council
8511 15th Ave. NE
Seattle, WA 98115
(800) 543-8255
An after-school helpline for children, Mon.–Fri., 3–6 p.m.

Child and Family Resource and Referral Center
2410 E Cherry St. (next to the old Horace Mann School)
Seattle, WA 98122
461-3207

City of Seattle Dept. of Human Resources
Division of Family and Youth Services
Arcade Plaza Bldg.
105 Union St., Suite 160
Seattle, WA 98101
386-1050

Day Care Referral Service
461-3207
Mon.–Fri., 9 a.m. to 1 p.m.

Dept. of Social and Health Services (DSHS)
P.O. Box 94107
1737 Airport Way S
Seattle, WA 98124
626-5900

Family Child Care Association of King County
1225 Fourth Ave. S, Suite A
Seattle, WA 98134
467-1552
Licensed providers who make referrals for parents.

Gentle Care Program
Auburn General Hospital
20 Second St. NE
Auburn, WA 98002
833-7711, Ext. 350
Takes mildly ill children. Ask for the nurse's office.

Child care licensing requirements

Ages of children	Max. ratio of staff/children	Maximum group size
1–11 months	1/4	8
12–29 months	1/7	14
30 months–5 years	1/10	20
6 years and older	1/15	30

Source: Dept. of Social and Health Services

HEARD ON THE STREET

"Our attitude is, the buck stops here. We will not transfer your call, we'll answer it. It has to be a really bizarre request that we will not try to fill."

Taryn Oestreich, Children's Research Center

Tender Loving Care, Virginia Mason Hospital
1201 Terry St.
Seattle, WA 98111
583-6521
Takes mildly ill children.

University of Washington Child Care Coordinating Office
1410 NE Campus Parkway, PB-10
Seattle, WA 98195
543-1041
Child care subsidies for UW students, faculty, and staff.

SEATTLE'S PRO-KID LIBRARIES

The Seattle Public Library is becoming something of a surrogate parent for latchkey kids, with free after-school activities at four libraries: Beacon Hill, Holly Park, High Point, Madrona–Sally Goldmark. Hours are generally from about 3:30 p.m.–7:00 p.m., but parents need to call each library for exact times. Called S.P.L.A.S.H. (Seattle Public Library After School Happenings), the program provides summer activities for kids. There's a homework program, where volunteers help kids with their school work, at the Douglass-Truth and Rainier Beach branches.

The library is also developing study guides targeted to minority kids who may be shy about asking questions in class. It's also working on a "family literacy" program.

Name to know: Elizabeth Stroup, city librarian and pro-kid activist, who started many of the library's children's programs.

Seattle Public Library Programs for Children
1000 Fourth Ave.
Seattle, WA 98101
386-4636

HOW ABOUT A PARENTSPLACE?

Being a parent sounds easy—until you become one. First parenting means getting up all night, then it's shivering at Little League games, and then adolescents-from-hell take over your life. But there's help out there—in the form of parenting workshops and classes.

The most prolific in terms of services for parents is:

Children's Hospital and Medical Center
4800 Sand Point Way NE
Seattle, WA 98105
526-2000

Here's a partial rundown on what Children's offers:

Children's Resource Center: Fifth Floor, Wing A of the hospital, 526-2201. Open to the public as well as to parents of children at the hospital, the Resource Center has books, brochures, and articles on diverse topics such as preventive health care, child safety, childhood illnesses, parenting, and growth and development.

The Center's library contains 1,000 books and 1,500 pamphlets on everything from how to form a babysitting co-op to dwarfism. If you want information on a medical problem, you can look at the same books the doctors use in the hospital's medical library. There is also information on Seattle area activities.

Children's Resource Line: 526-2500. Staffed seven days a week by a pediatrics-registered nurses: provides parents with information on development and health care issues, and treatment of injuries and illnesses. Will refer you to physicians if needed.

Good Growing: a series of monthly programs focusing on the most requested parenting and child health topics. Designed for adults, teens, and children. Call Resource Center (526-2201) for free series schedule and to pre-register. Also sponsors health fairs and support groups.

Seattle Poison Center: Located at Children's, the Poison Center is staffed 24 hours a day by professionals who answer more than 60,000 calls annually. They identify proper medical treatment for over 400,000 toxic substances. 526-2121, (800) 732-6985.

The Resource Center also puts out a number of publications, including a guide to summer camps for children with special needs, booklets on child's play and developmental delays from birth to age three, and a guide to childhood emergencies and illnesses.

The hospital itself is a 200-bed medical facility serving a four-state region. Eighty percent of its patients are under three years old. It's a big operation, with 59 pediatric subspecialty clinics and the largest auxiliary in the U.S. (15,000 guild members). The board of trustees is all women.

Adolescent pregnancies in King County

	Age 10–14	Age 15–17	Age 18–19
Live births	17	539	934
Fetal deaths	1	1	5
Abortions	65	1,073	1,615
Total pregnancies	83	1,613	2,554

Source: Seattle-King Co. Dept. of Public Health, 1988

MORE PARENTING HELP

In case that isn't enough help, there's more:

Family Life Education Network is a coalition of social service agencies that puts out a brochure of parenting (and youth) classes. The classes are offered by various organizations such as Youth Suicide Prevention Group, Seattle Children's Home, and Ryther Child Center. It includes a Community Information Line, 461-3200, that offers additional resources. For a copy of the brochure call Children's Home Society, 524-6020.

Program for Early Parent Support (PEPS) is a group that trains volunteers to lead support groups for parents of infants throughout King County. 547-8570.

Parents Anonymous is a support group for stressed-out parents to prevent them from taking their frustrations out on their kids. Evening calls are fielded by parent volunteers. 524-5977.

COPCAN (King Co. Council for Prevention of Child Abuse and Neglect), 343-2590, answers calls during regular business hours from parents and others needing information or referral on child-related matters.

Northwest Hospital, 364-2229, offers parenting classes, as do many hospitals in the area. Check with yours.

Central Area Mental Health Center has a parenting group for parents of clients. Meets during the day to discuss roles of parents of children with mental health needs. An evening class is open to the community. Sliding fees, 723-1980.

Ruth Dykeman Center, 242-1698, has a parent training program for parents of emotionally disturbed elementary age children.

Ryther Child Center, 525-5050, has a parenting class for parents of emotionally disturbed children.

Children's Home Society, 524-6020, has a Parent Aid program that matches abusive or potentially abusive parents with volunteers. The program focuses on preventing abuse and neglect. The society also

Activity fees and memberships

Source: SSG research

Destination	Adult daily fee	Child daily fee	Annual membership
Woodland Park Zoo	$4 Seniors: $2	Ages 6–17: $2 Under 6: free	Family: $35 Indiv: $20
Seattle Aquarium	$4.50 Seniors: $2.50	Ages 13–18: $2.50 Ages 6–12: $.75 5 and under: free	Family: $30 Indiv.: $20 Youths and seniors: $15
Pacific Science Center	$5 Seniors: $4	Ages 6–13: $4 Ages 2–5: $3 Under 2: free	$35
Seattle Children's Theatre	$12 (one show)	$7 (one show)	(six shows) Children: $37.50 Adults: $63.00 (three shows) Children: $18.75 Adults: $33.00
Seattle Children's Museum	$3	$3 Under 1: free	$30

offers respite care service to give parents time away from their parenting responsibilities.

FUN STUFF

Fun with kids is always a subjective thing. There was a picture in the paper a while back of a mom helping her three-year-old learn to ski. The little girl was crying—hard—and had been all day. The mother is quoted as saying it was a worthwhile experience anyway. But fun? Well, to each his or her own.

Seattle is renowned for its cultural and recreational opportunities for children, but kids aren't going to stumble upon them themselves. Parental imagination is a necessary ingredient—as, often, is the parental pocketbook. Most of these opportunities cost bucks; for instance, a day at the zoo will cost a family of four $12 in admission fees alone. (And you can hardly go without a stop for hot dogs and peanuts. Beware of the gift shop.) You can get a yearly membership for $35 for the family—a bargain with its unlimited visits and free guest passes for grandma and grandpa.

THE MUST-DO STUFF

The city's Parks and Recreation Department puts out a great summer calendar for kids, listing all kinds of activities. There's a lip sync contest in June for kids (this one's free!) and an all-city high school dance (not free), as well as such artsy-craftsy things as clay-play, cartooning, and art history at community centers. There's even something for kids at that in-between age called "Art for Almost Teens." And then of course there's the group piano lesson. The Department of Parks and Recreation has classes all year round. For information on those classes held near you, call the community center in your neighborhood. For general info, call 684-4075.

Many families do round-robin memberships: the zoo this year, the Pacific Science Center the next, then the Aquarium, and the Seattle Children's Theatre after that.

The Seattle Public Library has summer programs for children too. (Remember those summer reading clubs? Yes, they still exist.) Some are for toddlers, others for kids in grades K–6. And the library has computer workshops for kids 8–12. Register at 386-4675.

Camp Long is another absolute must. Run by the Department of Parks and Recreation, the 68-acre urban park offers all sorts of programs, and even some rustic cabins for getting away from it all without leaving town. The programs for adults and kids include stargazing sessions, introduction to rock climbing (seven-year-olds and up), bat culture classes, astronomy with the camp telescope, and more. There's even an outdoor recreation equipment and clothing exchange in December.

Camp Long
5200 35th Ave. SW
Seattle, WA 98126
684-7434

Woodland Park Zoo offers special activities, although the strolling-around opportunities are grrrr-eat too. Some family things are:
Discovery Room: From 12:30–3:30 p.m. on weekends, visitors can hold a tortoise shell, watch wildlife videos, and use the Zookeeper computer. Discovery Carts are also stationed around the grounds where you can feel the hair of a giraffe's tail and learn more about animal life.
Summer programs: Talks by zookeepers and naturalists are given at several locations. Signs announcing the next talk are posted at the different exhibits. Guess which are most popular? Elephants and raptors, a.k.a. birds of prey.
Other classes: Except in winter, the zoo offers educational classes for children, families, and adults. Some are field trips, some are held at the zoo.
Annual summer concert series: Benefit performances by acoustical recording artists are given Wednesday nights for five weeks during the summer.

For more information on educational programs, call the zoo's education department, 684-4800.

Stroller rental is available at the Woodland Park Zoo Activities and Resources Center (located by West Gate) and the ZooStore (located near the South Gate). Umbrellas are available at no charge for use in the zoo.

Now that the zoo has what it calls bioclimatic zones (natural habitats for the animals), it's sometimes hard to see the lions in the savanna. They can hide in the tall grass and that's that. Our inside sources say the best time to see them is around 10 a.m.—when they're likely to be most active.

DO THE ZOO—KIDSTYLE

Here are some tried and true, proven thrill-makers:
Family Farm. Open Memorial Day to Labor Day. Kids can get up close and pet the animals, not to mention smelling the rabbits and seeing the eggs hatch.
Pony rides. For $1, kids can ride around and around a pony ring astride a tiny steed.
Raptors. The zoo has a Bird of Prey program on weekends all summer long where kids can watch raptors in flight. Check at the entrance gates for times.
Gorillas. Bobo's gone, but his memory (or is it some other essence of gorilla?) lingers on. The gorillas are usually right upfront where kids can get a good look at them. Kids love the orangutans too, although their area is old and depressing. (A new one is on the planning boards.)
The nursery. When there are baby animals that can't stay with their mothers, they are put in the nursery in the Family Farm area. Kids can press their noses right up against the glass and watch.
The hippos. A personal favorite, they are usually wallowing in the mud close at hand on the savanna. Kids love talking about how much they look like Dad.

Woodland Park Zoo
5500 Phinney Ave. N
Seattle, WA 98103-5897
Administration: 684-4800
Admissions: 684-4892
Hours are 10 a.m.–6 p.m., April–Sept.; 10 a.m.–5 p.m., Oct. and March; 10 a.m.–4 p.m., Nov.–Feb.; open daily including Thanksgiving and Christmas.

SEATTLE CHILDREN'S THEATRE

Seattle Children's Theatre (SCT) is another big boon to parents looking for something to do with their kids. It's also a boon to kids who hope their future is on the screen or stage.

SCT has acting classes taught by their faculty for kids ages 3 to 19 from fall through spring. (Your child can *learn* how to be a clown instead of just improvising.) Classes include

Seattle Children's Theatre performances sell out fast, especially for name shows. But a truly Seattle phenomenon is that if it's a nice day, tickets will free up on the day of performance. (People want to be out in the sun, not inside a theater.) Go to the box office and put your name on the waiting list. If you don't get in, go see the bears.

Don't bring babes in arms to SCT—there's no place to take them if they get fussy. Maybe the new theater will have a "crying room."

mime, makeup, comedy, dramatic scenes, playwriting, and more. Cost per quarter runs from $35 to $185, depending on the subject.

There are six professional performances a year given by SCT, which is currently at the Poncho Theatre next to the zoo. (In 1992 SCT plans to move to a new facility behind the Pacific Arts Center building, just south of the Second and Thomas gate entrance to the Seattle Center.) The performances are usually smash hits—with adults as well as kids—and tickets sell out quickly. The new theater's larger seating capacity should help alleviate the problem. After each performance the actors and actresses come out on stage to answer questions from kids in the audience.

Seattle Children's Theatre
Administrative Office
305 Harrison St. (at Seattle Center)
Seattle, WA 98109
443-0807
Ticket Office
The Poncho Theatre
N 50th St. and Fremont Ave. N
633-4567

SEATTLE CENTER

Here's a little challenge for parents: Try going to the Seattle Center Fun Forest and not being sucked into spending money on the arcade galleries. The kids say they just want to go on the rides—honest, really. But once there, they're sure they could hit that tower of bottles with the baseball and those balloons are just sitting ducks for the arrows, not to mention the sitting ducks themselves at the shooting gallery. Ah, well—give them a dollar and see how many they can make it through.

Seattle Center has more than the Fun Forest. Public programs that would interest families with kids include: Whirligig, an indoor winter carnival for families beginning at the end of February; Easter Egg Hunt, an annual event for children ages 2–10; Imagination Celebration/Arts Festival for Kids, which is usually held in April, with hands-on arts activities; KidsDay, usually in April though may switch to October, with lots of free activities; International Children's Theater Festival, in May, with children's theater performances by worldwide renowned entertainers; Artspring / Children's Handicapped Arts Festival, in June, a hands-on arts festival for and by handicapped children; KOMO KidsFair, in August, family day with entertainment, workshops, and sports; Bumbershoot, September, anything-goes entertainment; Winterfest, December, holiday entertainment.

Of course, there's also the Pacific Science Center, which many kids think of as the center itself. There are three or four strollers there available for use on a first-come basis.

And there's Seattle Children's Museum, which has a child-sized neighborhood set up, as well as other activities for the 8-and-under crowd. Adults must accompany children.

Seattle Center numbers
Center House: 684-7200
Fun Forest Amusement Park: 728-1585
Pacific Science Center: 443-2001
Seattle Center Monorail: 684-7183
Seattle Children's Museum: 441-1767
Space Needle: 443-2100

THE SEATTLE AQUARIUM

The Seattle Aquarium is another favorite. It has a touch tank for the kids, and the Underwater Dome is perfect for tracking octopi. In spring and summer the Aquarium offers family classes—some are field trips, such as to Seattle's tidepools, others are held at the Aquarium. Longer "Outdoor Adventures" include canoe and kayak trips, and exploration of tidepools on the Olympic Peninsula.

Seattle Aquarium
Pier 59
Waterfront Park
386-4320 (recording)
386-4300 (live)
Hours: Labor Day–Memorial Day, 10 a.m.–5 p.m. daily; Memorial Day–Labor Day, 10 a.m.–7 p.m. daily.

HAPPY CAMPERS

You don't have to go far to go away to camp. Here are some in-city opportunities.

Boys and Girls Clubs. Day camp and overnight camps, too, for kids ages 6 to 16. Call the Central Seattle Club to get the phone number of the club in your neighborhood, 324-7317.

Camp Fire Day Camps. For boys and girls in grades 1–8, held in Southwest King County on Vashon Island and Camp Long, 854-3676; East King County in Issaquah and Bothell, 453-7020; South King County in Auburn, Enumclaw, and the Kent area, 854-3676; and North King County at Carkeek Park Day Camp, 461-8550.

Central Area Girls Club. For girls ages 5–12. Activities include math and science projects, computer workshops, field trips. Sliding fee. 329-3310 or 722-0822.

Gatzert Kids Club. Summer activities including field trips, sports, clinics, projects, experiments. 329-6424 or 722-0822.
Pacific Science Center Summer Camps. "Ages 9 to 99." Some day camps, some residential (family) camps. These camps examine everything from rocketry, light, and lasers to stones and bones. The residential camps include whale watching in the San Juans and hikes in the Cascades. There are also "Science Celebration" classes for those under 9. For a catalog, call 443-2925.
Totem Girl Scout Day and Resident Camps. The Girl Scouts have two resident camps in the area, for Scout and non-Scout girls, 7–17, and an extensive day camp program, 633-5600.
YMCA Day Camp. Forty locations in the area, with drop-off and pick-up sites in neighborhoods, for kids grades K–9. The YMCA also has two overnight co-ed camps, Camp Orkila and Camp Colman. To register, call downtown, 382-5000; Bellevue, 746-9900; East Madison, 322-6969; Highline, 244-5880; North Seattle, 524-1400; Northshore, 485-9797; Redmond, 881-3067; Southeast Seattle, 322-6969; West Seattle, 935-6000.
YWCA Summer Day Camp. For children entering grades 1–6. Field trips to Seattle's parks and places of interest, and other activities, 461-8489.

QUINTESSENTIAL SEATTLE FUN

Some haunts are just as much a part of a child's life here as, well, chasing squirrels in the pocket parks or avoiding the duck poop at Gasworks.
Kid culture: The Seattle Symphony offers four Discover Music! concerts in the Opera House on Saturday mornings for children and their families. At one hour each, the concerts are specifically designed to hold the attention of children ages 6–10. Favorites are "Peter and the Wolf" (sells out quickly) and "Tubby the Tuba," but the program changes so it's best to call. Tickets for the series are $24 for adults, $18 for children; or $7 and $5 respectively for single concerts. Discover Music! Series, 443-4747.
Tradition: What's childhood in Seattle without memories of the Seafair Torchlight Parade? So it's crowded and there are too many cars with waving dignitaries, and too many trucks with hydroplanes. So you can't park for miles and the curbs are packed eight deep with parade-goers. So it's dog-eat-dog juggling for a place that is suddenly shadowed by teenagers crowding in front of you. It's still the best place to be scared by a Seafair pirate and to see a purely anti-TV, real-life event. Yes, there are still baton twirlers and balloon hawkers; neighborhood communities still decorate floats with aluminum flowers and clowns still make kids laugh.

Get there early, take a blanket to sit on, and let the kids stay up late. They'll remember going until the time they take their own kids.
A fishy lesson: Go to the Hiram Chittenden Locks when the salmon are leaping their way up the fish ladder. Keep a good hold on the kids' hands while crossing the locks themselves and make sure they don't lean too far over the ladder itself to watch

Five theaters in Seattle have soundproof cry rooms available: Crest, Guild 45th, Metro, Northgate, Varsity. Northgate has the best: The whole third balcony is just for mom or dad 'n' babe. The other theaters have smaller rooms. Be sure to check that the movie you want to see is on the scream room screen.
Most theaters, whether they have a cry room or not, offer passes for parents who have to leave a theater with an unhappy baby.

Changing baby

Source: SSG research

Place	Stroller rental	Changing table
Aquarium	No	Yes
Pacific Science Center	Yes (free)	Yes
Seattle Center House	No	Yes
Zoo	Yes	In new restrooms

the salmon from above. The windows below give a closer view, but kids like the challenge of spotting one outside as it takes a grand leap. Best viewing time: Fourth of July weekend.

Where the kids want to go (and you don't): the Space Needle. Despite its being upstaged by elevators in office buildings around town and despite its overabundance of tourists, the Space Needle is a place kids love. Couldn't be the video games galore up top, could it? Leave your quarters at home and take them up to see the view. It's pretty pricey: $3.50 for adults, $1.75 for children 5–12.

Fun for teenagers?: Hmmm. The city does put on a high school dance once a year (see above). There are high school sports and clubs. And there's always cruising Alki—oops, no more since the city passed an anti-cruising ordinance and anti-boombox ordinance. There's no curfew in Seattle, so teens can stay out late, according to the city, if not parental, law. Try the acting classes at SCT, if you can afford it. Or suggest employment—it can be fun.

Youth employment agencies
Youth: 343-2482
Seattle Youth: 386-1050
Junior Helper (9–15): 725-2100

Carousel: Every Christmas season the huge antique carousel comes back to Westlake Center and crowds of children and adults climb aboard the 36 carousel horses and 4 chariots for a musical ride around and around. Rides are free, and donations of either canned food or money are accepted for Northwest Harvest's food bank. In 1989 the public gave nearly $25,000 to the food bank at the carousel site—enough to fill the warehouse for the first quarter of 1990.

The carousel belongs to the Perron family of Perron's Carousels Unlimited in Portland. The project has been underwritten by Great American Bank. In addition to the horses, many of which are original, the 1914 carousel has 800 lights on it. To find out when the carousel is open, call the Downtown Seattle Association, 623-0340, or pick up a holiday brochure around Thanksgiving time at a retail store downtown.

Holiday cheer: The Downtown Seattle Association also sponsors free carriage rides downtown during the season, with a station at Fourth and Pine. And there is brunch with Santa, tree-lighting ceremonies at Pioneer Square and Westlake Center, the Jingle Bell Run, Great Figgy Pudding contest (caroling), strolling minstrels, and more—all are outlined in the holiday brochure available at retail centers during the holidays.

WHERE TO CHANGE

Don't even think about putting that baby on the floor to change the sweet little thing! Most public places have changing tables in the women's restrooms (which says something about expectations that fathers will change diapers). Mall and department store restrooms are generally equipped with high counters; there's a nursery area at Seattle-Tacoma International Airport too. And the larger Washington State Ferries have changing rooms.

Publications for Parents

Discover Seattle with Kids
by Rosanne Cohn
A guide to things to do with kids, including where to take them for a birthday party, tours for groups, activities. $9.95 at bookstores.

Northwest Baby
15417 204th Ave. SE
Renton, WA 98056
235-6826
Published monthly by Baby Diaper Service for parents of babies.

Seattle's Child
733 17th Ave. E
P.O. Box 22578
Seattle, WA 98122
322-2594
The local resource for things to do, children's issues. Also annual reader's poll called Golden Bootie Awards. Published monthly.

The Resourceful Parent
P.O. Box 781
Bellevue, WA 98009
392-4453
Guide to child care, education, and health service in King County and soon to include Snohomish County. $8.95 at bookstores.

CHAPTER

18

BOATS, BALLS AND BEACHES

PARKS

SWIMMING

WATERFRONT

LOCKS

OLMSTED

TENNIS

BOATS

GOLF

It's a source of some irritation to employers that when the sun comes out, all of Seattle goes out to play. And there's plenty to play at: boats and bikes, swimming holes and golf courses, even lawn bowling greens. You can find maps of Seattle's finest

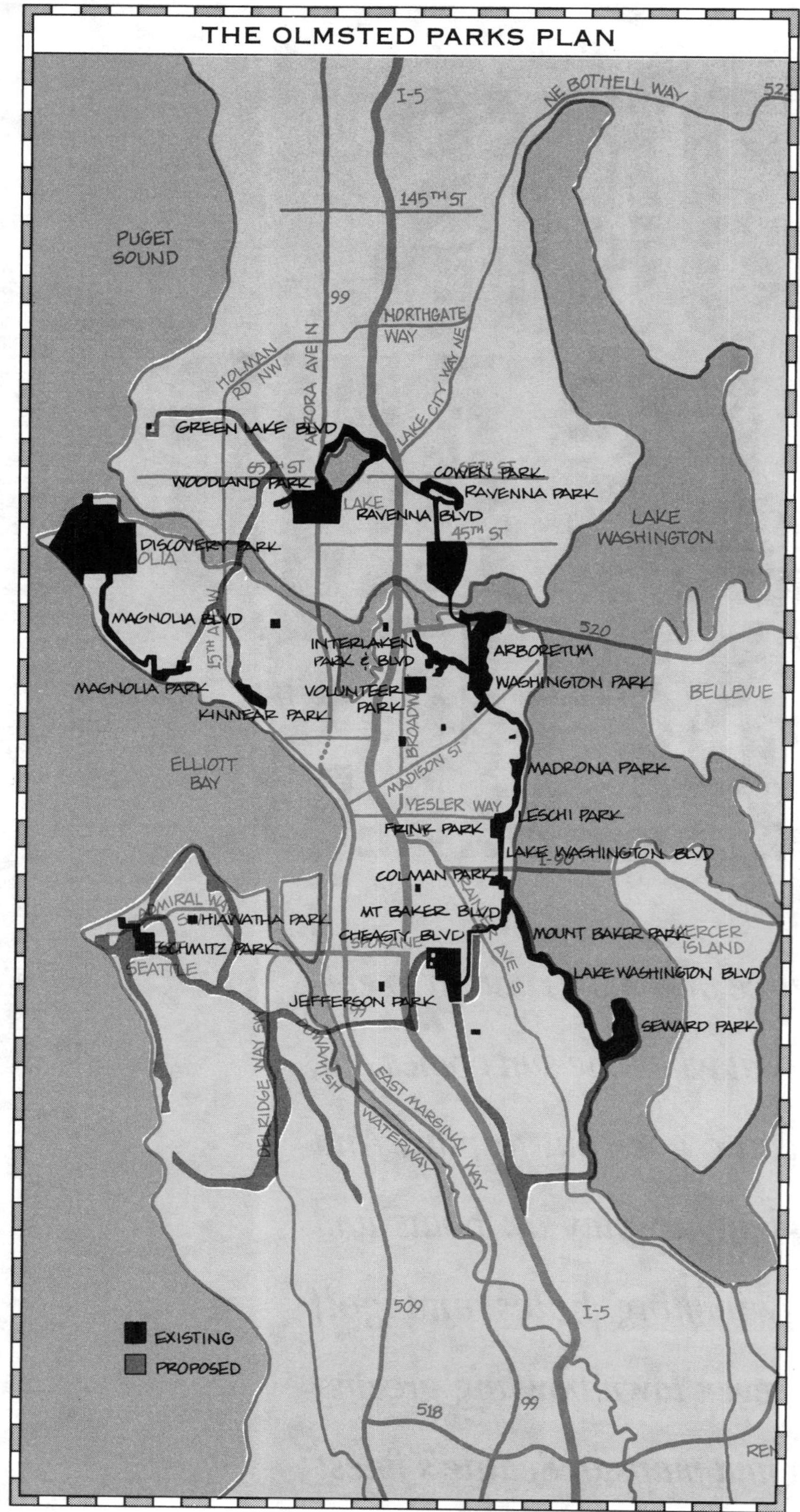

play spots from several different sources, but we're talking survival here. Don't send the kids out to swim on a saltwater beach without you—there aren't any lifeguards. Lifeguards do supervise lakeside beaches, but not all of them.

And then there's the problem of where to moor your boat. You probably don't want to wait for a slip at Shilshole; you'll be setting up a rocking chair on board by the time you get one.

So this is the serious side of play, recreation for the analytical among us—still fun, but fun based on strategy.

A PARK PLACE

Seattle has over 5,000 acres of parkland, comprising more than 300 parks and playgrounds, everything from tiny pocket parks to huge wooded habitats like Discovery Park.

NAMES TO KNOW

Frederick Law Olmsted Jr. and John Charles Olmsted had a profound influence not only on the city of Seattle, but on landscape architecture in general. Here the Olmsted firm designed a parks system connected by boulevards and including Volunteer Park, Lake Washington Boulevard, the Arboretum, and Seward Park. Wherever you go, you'll hear of the Olmsted parks.

PARK POWER

The parks department, formally known as the Department of Parks and Recreation, is under the jurisdiction of the Board of Park Commissioners. So if you *really* want some improvement to the park nearest you, those are the folks to call. Seven

Take the kids out to the Carkeek Park Model Airplane Airport. Actually, the airport is an open-space runway where kids and adults can test out their crafts. If the gate to the park is open, just drive out to the field; if it's closed, you'll have to walk. If you want to plan a birthday party there, call 684-4075 and ask to speak to George Long. And one more thing. The Fairmont Playfield softball diamond is reserved for children.

commissioners serve three-year terms and meet twice a month, usually at the Seattle Art Museum in Volunteer Park.

Parks superintendent: Holly Miller, 684-8022

Board members:

Harvey Boll
Dodd Drue
John Hancock
Puni Hokea
Karen Morgan, chairperson
Meson Morgan
Jane Sylvester

GREAT POCKET PARKS

Everyone has a favorite park, the place where they take the kids to paddle in the water and all.... Sometimes these are marked on the map, sometimes not. In the interest of the public's right to know (but certainly not giving away every secret spot), here are some great pocket parks.

Ten accessible beaches can be found at road ends between Madison Park on the north and Madrona to the south. The beaches are of varying quality, and finding them means you either have to know the area or get a map. You can also ask in the neighborhood—you'll either be pointed in the right direction or sent toward Elliott Bay.

- Swingset just north of Madison Park (sits there all by itself).
- Roanoke Park. Block-long park on 10th Avenue E and Edgar. Oasis of green between 520 and I-5.
- Al Larkins Park. Corner of 34th Avenue and E Pike Street. Winding path for child cyclists, bench, and neighborhood meeting area.
- Madrona Playground, 33rd Avenue and E Spring. Everything you need: tennis, basketball, climbing things, large green field.
- Grand Avenue E and E Pine Street. Wooden observation deck, climbable wooden posts, big wooden steps, looks out over Madrona Drive.
- Denny Blaine Lake Park bus stop, corner of E Denny Way and Madrona Place E. Small shallow pool filled with leaves and lily pads.
- Interlaken Drive E/Interlaken Boulevard, from E Roanoke to Lake Washington Boulevard E. Winding drive through dense forest, great for walking or biking.
- Wallingford Playfield. Wallingford Avenue N and N 43rd Street. Elaborate wooden climbing contraption. Big playfield.
- 15th Avenue E at Garfield. Lake, Cascades, University lookout. Exquisite moon view on the water.

PARK CHARACTERISTICS

Every park has its own character and/or characters. Of course, it's dangerous to label them because things change rapidly, but here's a partial rundown of some characteristics that have stayed pretty much the same.

Freeway Park downtown is perceived as unsafe because there are lots of places to hide. It feels unsafe to be alone there and it has a history of crime.

Burke–Gilman Trail has not had any problems, according to park officials, except for the occasional flasher.

Gay/lesbian hangouts are: Madison Park Beach (north side, gay men; south side, families); Volunteer Park (gay cruising on west side, south of tennis courts, site of gay pride rally; also mixed with families, dog walkers, and everybody else); Denny Blaine Beach (used to be lesbians; now more mixed crowd except on north end where lesbians and gay men hang out); Woodland Park (gay cruising 1 p.m.–3 p.m. weekdays, signs outside bathroom from police and gay community discouraging sexual contact in parks).

Good doggie parks: Marymoor on the Eastside has a dog exercise area and you don't have to leash dogs, though they have to stay within voice range. (Also has fields where dogs aren't allowed.) Volunteer Park informally hosts dogs and owners at about dinnertime, from 5 p.m.–7 p.m., when you'll see lots of dogs being walked. Magnuson Park has big fields with lots of dog people and dog playmates.

Family beaches: Madrona Beach and Mt. Baker Beach are both racially mixed, family beaches. Families also go to Matthews Beach, Green Lake, and Volunteer Park wading pools.

Alki Beach attracts throngs of young people in the summer. A law prohibiting car cruising is enforced.

Camp Long is a great place for weddings.

Discovery Park is a habitat park. (See Chapter 5, page 65, *The Urban Wilderness.*)

Golden Gardens is known for its intoxicating sunsets. It's a very romantic place, great for birthday parties and to enjoy blustery winter weather.

Green Lake hosts the avid exercisers and the Sony Walkman crowd.

TENNIS, ANYONE?

The parks department maintains almost 60 tennis sites—so why are the courts always full? Well, they aren't, they're just full when YOU want them.

Busiest times at park tennis courts: 5:30–9:30 p.m. weekdays (especially in summer), all day Saturday and Sunday.

Moderately busy times: early mornings in summer.

Barren wastelands: dawn and mid-afternoon weekdays (especially in winter).

Selected courts

Ballard
14th Ave. NW and NW 67th St.

Bryant
40th Ave. NE and NE 65th St.

Laurelhurst Community Center
4554 NE 41st St. (lights)

Leschi Park
100 Lakeside S (solitary and secluded)

The Seattle Tennis Center is very busy, but not always full. Best times to get in are between noon and 3 p.m. Also, summer is less busy because most people want to play outside, which frees up the indoor courts—except when the tournaments are on or the rain is falling.

Lincoln Park
Fauntleroy Ave. SW and SW Webster St.

Lower Woodland Park
W Green Lake Way N (lights)

Luther Burbank Park
2040 84th Ave. SE

Madison Park
43rd Ave. E & E Lynn St. (lights)

Magnolia Playfield
34th Ave. W and W Smith St.

Meadowbrook
30th Ave. NE and NE 107th St.

Miller Field
20th Ave. E and E Republic St. (lights)

Montlake Community Center
1618 E Calhoun

Rainier Playfield
Rainier Ave. S and S Alaska St.

Riverview
12th Ave. SW and SW Othello St.

Rodgers Field
Eastlake and E Roanoke (usually pretty empty, but bus fumes can be overwhelming at rush hour)

University of Washington
Montlake Blvd. (14 courts—5 lit—and 6 more up on campus)

Volunteer Park
15th Ave. E and E Prospect St.

Courts you might have a chance at getting onto (no crowds): Madrona Playground Courts (two lit) and 23rd and Cherry courts (three lit). The two courts in Discovery Park are usually open though not particularly well kept. Also, check your local high school.

Parks department courts are used on a first-come, first-served basis or reserved in advance. If you purchase a $10 reservation card, you can make phone reservations (684-4077); otherwise make reservations in person at the office of Seattle Parks and Recreation (5201 Green Lake Way N). Fees are $3 per 1½ hours of court time.

The Seattle Tennis Center (2000 Martin Luther King Jr. Way S, 684-4764) has 10 indoor courts and rates of $9 for singles, $11 for doubles. Fees are for 1 hour and 15 minutes, and in order to make reservations, you need a phone reservation card that costs another $15 per year. You can book up to six days in advance but call at 7:15 a.m. if you want a court during prime hours. The Center also has four outdoor courts (free).

SWIMMERS BEWARE

Seattle has a high incidence of drowning. In general, saltwater beaches do not have lifeguards; freshwater ones do. In 1988, latest figures available, 39 of the 304 accidental deaths in Seattle–King County were caused by drowning. Six of those victims were from 1 to 5 years old, 10 were 20 to 29. Washington State's drowning rate is higher than the national average, at 2.2 deaths per every 100,000 residents in 1986. The national average was 1.8.

Non-lifeguarded saltwater beaches include: Alki Beach Park, Don Armeni Boat Ramp, Carkeek Park, Gas Works Park, Golden Gardens, Lincoln Park, Lowman Beach, Me-Kwa-mooks, North Beach Community, and Washington School Site.

Lifeguarded beaches (mid-June to Labor Day) include: Green Lake Park, Madison Park, Madrona Park, Magnolia Park, Magnuson Park, Mt. Baker Park, Pritchard Island Bathing Beach, and Seward Park.

Many other small beaches on the lake do not have lifeguards.

ON THE WATERFRONT

Want to know what those container ships are doing in Elliott Bay? The Port of Seattle manages several public access areas, and many of them have exhibits designed to teach you about seagoing commerce. Others have piers for fishing, footpaths, and, in one case, an exercise course.

To get a copy of the port's guide to its shoreline parks and viewpoints, call 728-3400. They'll send you a slick brochure detailing exactly what's available.

Interesting port parks

- Terminal 91 Bike Path: This 4,000-foot paved path connects with Elliott Bay and Myrtle Edwards parks, Interbay, and Fishermen's Terminal.
- Elliott Bay Park: At Pier 86 enter from either Pier 70 on the south or Elliott Avenue on the north. The park has 10.5 landscaped acres and 4,100 feet of shoreline, including an exercise course.
- Elliott Bay Fishing Pier: Pier 86, west of the grain elevator, has fish-cleaning stations, bait and tackle concessions, and a 400-foot pier. Whether you should eat what you catch is debatable (see Chapter 5, page 65, *The Urban Wilderness*).
- Terminal 105 Viewpoint: Views of Duwamish River activities, fishing pier, launch for small boats.

Once you find them, the periscopes at the end of Pier 48 are great for viewing trade activities up close at Terminals 46 and 37. Interpretive signs are out here as well. The site is isolated and occasionally transients set up house here.

The very best place to see the port's huge cranes at work is in West Seattle, at the overlook on Admiral Way.

Park resources

Adopt-A-Park
684-8009
Parks department–sponsored program to get community members involved in the city's parks.

Friends of Seattle's Olmsted Parks
P.O. Box 15984
Seattle, WA 98115-0984
The group schedules lectures, tours, and special events. Membership is from $7 to $50+.

King County Division of Natural Resources and Parks
2040 84th Ave. SE
Mercer Island, WA 98040
296-4232
Information on county parks, map, pamphlet.

Outdoor Recreation Information Center
1018 First Ave.
Seattle, WA 98104
442-0170
Guidebooks, TRIS (see below), maps, etc.

Port of Seattle
Pier 66
2201 Alaskan Way
Seattle, WA 98121
P.O. Box 1209
Seattle, WA 98111
728-3000

Seattle Department of Parks and Recreation (SDPR)
710 Second Ave.
Seattle, WA 98104
684-7583
Keyed maps of the system available.

SDPR Recreation Information Office
5201 Green Lake Way N
Seattle, WA 98103
684-4075

Ballfield scheduling: 684-4077 (indiv.), 684-4082 (league)
Evening adult recreation: 684-7095
Maintenance/vandalism reports: 684-4075
Park use permits: 684-4080
Picnic permits: 684-4075
Tennis reservations: 684-4081

TRIS—computerized Trails Information System
Seattle Public Library
1000 Fourth Ave.
Seattle, WA 98104
386-4625
Trail conditions.

U.S. Forest Service
1022 First Ave.
Seattle, WA 98104
442-5400
Maps, computerized trails information system (TRIS), brochures, walk-in help.

Washington State Parks and Recreation Commission
7150 Cleanwater Lane, KY-11
Olympia, WA 98504-5711
753-2027 (Sept.–Apr.)
(800) 562-0990 (May–Aug.)
Information on state parks, map, brochures.

Washington State Trails Directory
Interagency Committee for Outdoor Recreation
4800 Capitol Blvd., KP-11
Tumwater, WA 98504-5611
753-7140
Map of trail resources, statewide.

MESSING ABOUT IN BOATS

Shilshole Bay Marina, one of the few saltwater marinas around, has a waiting list of 800 names—or up to seven years for a 30- to 40-foot slip! The folks at the Port of Seattle raised the rates at Shilshole in 1989, where the rates had been lower than at other marinas, in hopes the waiting list would dwindle.

Map key
1. Shilshole Bay Marina
Located at the end of the fuel dock ("J" dock). Coin operated (24 hours).
2. Fishermen's Terminal
Located at the end of the fuel dock. Coin operated (24 hours).
3. Chandler's Cove
Dock will accommodate vessels up to 65 feet. Coin operated (24 hours).
4. Duke's Yacht Club
Dock will accommodate vessels up to 40 feet. Coin operated (24 hours).
5. Harbor Village (north end of Lake Washington)
Bilge pump-out and holding tank pump-out stations (24 hours).
6. Carillon Point Marina (south of Kirkland)
Located on the southernmost dock. Coin operated (24 hours).
7. Harbor Island Marina
Gain access to the pump-out facility and pay for its use at the Marina office. (Open 9 a.m.–5 p.m., 7 days a week.)
Source: Boaters Task Force

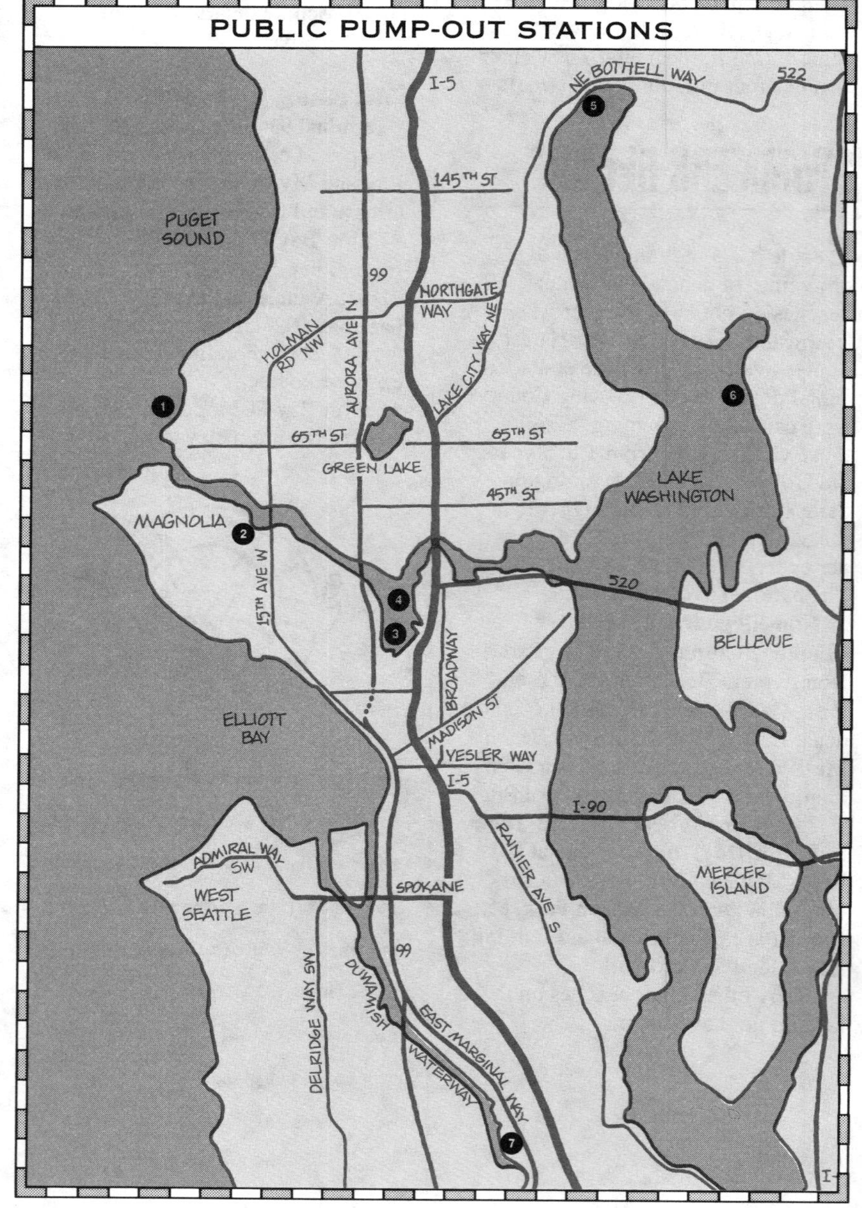

Marina mania

Source: 1990 UW Sea Grant

Marina	Price per foot/month open slip*	Occupancy rate(%)**	Waiting list***
Ballard Mill Marina	$5.25	100/96	40
Cadranell	5.00	100/100	+
CCR Marine-Boatworld	6.90	100/100	+
Chris Berg, Inc.	4.00	100/100	20
Commercial Marine	4.50	98/85	+
Davidson's Marina (covered)	4.50	100/90	+
Duwamish Yacht Club	5.25	90/75	#
Elliott Bay Marina	6.50	100/100	#
Ewing Street	4.50	100/100	+
Fremont Boat Co.	5.00	100/98	#
Gasworks Pk. Marina	7.50	100/98	+
Harbor Is. Marina	5.50	100/90	25
Harbor Village Marina	6.50	100/95	+
2040 Westlake Moorage	4.00(+ $6security)	100/100	20
Lake Union Drydock	5.00	100/100	+
Lake Union Landing	6.00	96/96	+
Lakewood Boat House	3.75	100/100	35
Leschi Yacht Basin	5.50	100/95	30
Leschi Sailboat	3.75	100/100	31
Lockhaven Marina	4.50	96/96	35
McGinnis Marina	4.10	90/90	5
Meydenbauer Bay Marina	5.00	100/100	5
Newport Yacht Basin	5.75	100/100	+
Northlake Marina	4.25	98/98	+
Ole & Charlies (Sea.)	4.00	65/60	0
Parkshore Marina	4.67	100/98	40
Quartermaster Marina	3.84	100/100	35
Seattle Marina ('87)	5.50	99/99	+
Shilshole Bay Marina	5.01	100/100	800
South Park Marina	4.17	98/90	0
Stimson Marina	5.00	96/93	10
St. Vincent de Paul Marina	5.00	90/90	#
Tillicum Marina ('87)	4.50	100/100	10
University Boat Mart	3.25	100/100	125

* Unless otherwise noted, prices are for a 30-foot, open slip at peak season rates.
** Figures are listed for peak season and off season respectively.

*** Notation in this column is:
+ waiting list not kept
# waiting list kept, but no tabulation of how many boaters on it.

The Coast Guard sponsors boating safety classes throughout the year at various locations. Call 442-7355 for the one nearest you. Other boating safety courses are sponsored through the YWCA, YMCA, and local yacht clubs and marinas.

UNLOCKING THE LOCKS

There aren't really regulations for going through Hiram Chittenden Locks, but if you don't want to look like a fool to all the schoolkids and tourists watching, it's nice to have some idea of what you're doing. You don't have to have a motor to go through the locks; kayaks and rowboats go through all the time and just tie up to boats or to the floats there.

Tips for going through the locks

Shortest wait: Weekdays, poor weather days, mid-winter.
Hectic times: Just before three-day weekends, last day of the weekend, opening day of boating season, before and after the Seafair Hydroplane Races.
How long it will take: The locks are open 24 hours a day. Average passage takes about 25 minutes through the large lock (which holds about 100 small boats in one lockage), and 10 minutes through the small one. Ocean-going vessels and log tows require a half-hour.
Most frequent mistakes boaters make in the locks: panicking, running engines full ahead, or letting engines die.
Hints: Go down to the locks and watch the whole process on land before trying it in a boat. If you have a cruiser or sailboat, you need two 50-foot lines on board, bumpers for both sides of the boat, and at least two people on board (one for the bow and one for the stern).

A brochure, "Guidelines for Boaters," is available from the Visitors Center on the main road through the locks, or from the small or large lock-operating house.

Boating resources

Army Corps of Engineers (Seattle District)
4735 E Marginal Way S
Seattle, WA 98134
764-3750

Boat Licensing Hotline
(800) 521-9319

Boaters Task Force
1530 Westlake Ave. N, Suite 400
Seattle, WA 98109
285-8683
Recreational boaters' group formed to educate boaters about how their actions can cause pollution. Under the Department of Ecology and Seattle Office for Long Range Planning.

Coast Guard
915 Second Ave.
Seattle, WA 98104
Emergency line: 286-5400 (24-hour)
Information: 442-5295

Hiram Chittenden Locks
3015 NW 54th St.
Seattle, WA 98107
Locks: 783-7001
Visitor Center: 783-7059

Boat rentals

Center for Wooden Boats
1010 Valley St.
382-2628
Wooden rowboats and sailboats.

Greenlake Boat Rentals
7351 E Green Lake Dr. N
527-0171
Paddle boats, rowboats, canoes.

Northwest Outdoor Center of Lake Union
2100 Westlake Ave. N
281-9694
Kayaks, canoes, and shells.

Pacific Water Sports
16205 Pacific Hwy. S
246-9385
Kayaks and canoes.

Rowing Northwest
3304 Fuhrman Ave. E
324-5800
Rowing shells.

Seacrest Boat House
1660 Harbor Ave. N
932-1050
16-foot aluminum boats.

Smart Bait & Boat Rental, Inc.
6049 Seaview NW
782-8322
14-foot aluminum boats with motor.

Swallows Nest
2308 Sixth Ave. N
633-0408
Rents kayaks, canoes, camping equipment.

Swiftwater
4235 Fremont Ave. N
547-3377
Inflatable river rafts that hold from 1 to 10 people, non-motorized.

UW Waterfront Activities Center
SE corner of Husky Stadium parking lot
543-9433
Canoe rental.

GOLF TEES AND FEES

There are some good public golf courses around and some spectacular private ones. Of course, they all cost, especially if you want to join the private ones for a year.

Par for the course

Golf course	Public/Private	Fee	Rate	Difficulty
Bear Creek Country Club	private	$35,000/yr $145/mo No waiting list	PNGA	72.4
Bellevue Municipal	public	$12	PNGA	66.4
Jackson Park Municipal	public	50-play ticket for price of 40 ($400). Reservations a week in advance recommended	PNGA	68.0
Jefferson Park	public	$15	PNGA	67.9
Tyee Valley	public	$695/yr $13 Reservations recommended	PNGA	67.2
West Seattle	public	$15/$10 for King County residents	PNGA	69.7
Broadmoor	private	$90,000/yr		
Overlake	private	60,000/yr		
Sand Point	private	55,000/yr		
Glendale	private	50,500/yr		
Sahalee	private	45,500/yr		
Seattle	private	40,000/yr		
Inglewood	private	35,000/yr		
Rainier	private	30,000/yr		
Meridian Valley	private	24,000/yr		
Fairwood	private	18,000/yr		
Twin Lakes	private	16,000/yr		
Mill Creek	private	10,000/yr		
Glen Acres	private	3,000/yr		

Source: "Private Golf Fees Soar Like Tee Shots," by Dan Raley, *P-I*, March 14, 1990; Seattle Survival Guide research.

QUINTESSENTIAL SEATTLE: SEAFAIR

Fess up—you love Seafair. Despite its espresso bars and new breweries, Seattle also offers down-home entertainment, just as it has for the last 41 years. Communities save their parades for Seafair, grown men act like clowns (more than usual), and pirates kiss preteens without fear of a sexual harassment suit. What could be more 1950s and still be fun? Over 55 events take place during the three weeks of Seafair, which are mid-July to early August.

The Torchlight Parade is held the Friday before the hydroplane races every year.

Seafair
The Westin Bldg.
2001 Sixth Ave., Suite 2800
Seattle, WA 98121-2574
728-0123

TOP TEN ATTRACTIONS IN KING COUNTY

1. Kingdome: 2.5 million visitors annually
2. Lake Sammamish State Park: 1.7 million
3. Space Needle: 1.2 million
4. Longacres: 1.1 million
5. Woodland Park Zoo: 828,455
6. Pacific Science Center: 828,320
7. Seattle Aquarium: 619,060
8. Dash Point State Park: 382,860

9. Omnidome: 250,000
10. Pioneer Square Underground Tours: 144,148
Source: Downtown Seattle Assn., 1988

PROBLEM PARKS

Seattle has less crime in its parks than other cities, but as the city grows so do problems in the parks. Cruising in cars and boombox racket caused the city to pass laws prohibiting amplified sound and cruising in certain parks, including Alki Beach.

The most persistent crime in parks is car prowls (theft from cars). All parks are patrolled with an overlapping system called "umbrella cars." In the summer, officers patrol all day; the horse patrol unit patrols all year. Downtown parks are patrolled by bikes all year.

The city doesn't have a list of what crimes have been committed at what parks, but gang activity has resulted in some parks being closed nights; in fact, many of the city's parks have special restrictions on them these days and more nighttime closures are being added to the list all the time.

Parks with special restrictions

Alki Beach
Closed 11 p.m.–6 a.m., Apr. 15 to Oct. 1
Reasons: Loud parties, cruising, vandalism and litter, beach parties, loud noise, and beach fires.

Fauntleroy Park
Closed sunset–6 a.m.
"Trespassers will be prosecuted"
No fires
Reasons: Citizen complaints, fire department concerns. Camping, drinking, and drug activity in the wooded area; fires, intimidation, and vandalism of surrounding community.

Flo Ware Park
Closed 10 p.m.–6 a.m.
Reasons: Citizen complaints, police recommendation. Drug activity, rise in crime in neighborhood, noise, drinking, intimidation of park patrons.

Garfield Playground
Closed 11 p.m.–6 a.m.
Reasons: Citizen demands, police requests. Gang activity, drug activity, concerns regarding elevated crime, vandalism, intimidation, and harassment of community.

Lower Kinnear
Closed sunset–6 a.m.
No fires
Reasons: Citizen, fire department concerns. People camp in wooded area, start fires—sparks from fires threaten homes above park, campers intimidate community.

Martha Washington School
Closed sunset–6 a.m.
Reasons: Citizen complaints. Heavy vandalism, and break-ins. Vandals can be injured in building; building set on fire in 1987; guard on duty.

Miller Park
Closed 11 p.m.–6 a.m.
Reasons: Citizen complaints, police recommendation. Drug activity, gang activity, drinking, intimidation of parks' patrons.

Othello Playground
Closed 10 p.m.–6 a.m.
Reasons: Citizen complaints, police request. Heavy gang/drug activity, intimidation of community, rise in crime in neighborhood.

Pratt Playground
Closed sunset–6 a.m.
Reasons: Citizen complaints, police request. Heavy drug/gang activity, intimidation of community, rise of crime in neighborhood.

Pritchard Beach
Closed sunset–6 a.m.
Reasons: Citizen complaints, police concern. Partying, loud noise, vandalism, drug activity; may be reopened with parking restrictions.

Ross Playground
Closed sunset–6 a.m.
Reasons: Citizen concerns. Heavy drug activity, partying, heavy vandalism; rise in crime in neighborhood.

Roxhill Park
Closed 10 p.m.–6 a.m.
Reasons: Citizen complaints, police recommendations. Drug activity, gang activity, drinking, intimidation of park patrons.

Seward Park
Closed 11 p.m.–6 a.m.
Reasons: Citizen concerns, police request. Heavy drug/gang activity, noise, drinking, intimidation of neighborhood; may be re-opened.

University Playground
Closed 10 p.m.–6 a.m.
Reasons: Citizen complaints. Drug/transient activity, rise in crime in neighborhood; intimidation of parks patrons, neighborhood, vandalism, noise, drinking; may be re-opened.

Other nighttime closures include: Arboretum (upper loop road only), Carkeek Park, Discovery Park, Golden Gardens, Laurelhurst Park, Lincoln Park, Magnuson Park, Matthews Beach, Schmitz Park, Stan Sayers Park, Volunteer Park, Westcrest, and Woodland Park.

All parks are closed to unattended vehicles between 2 a.m. and 6 a.m.

The anti-cruising ordinance is in effect at the following parks: Alki Beach, Don Armeni Boat Ramp, and Lake Washington Boulevard.

HEALTH AND PLAYGROUNDS

One night a Seattle police officer found 18 used condoms in Volunteer Park. Parents panic, understandably, when they find condoms and discarded syringes in parks and playgrounds. Used needles aren't exactly compatible with bare feet and little kids, but they are a fact of life in some of the area's parks and on the beaches.

The risk of disease transmission from a condom or discarded syringe is low. But if you have questions, call the city's Hazard Line at 296-4692. If you find hazardous items in a park, call the parks department:

Seattle Department of Parks and Recreation
684-4082

King County Parks Division
296-4232 or 296-8100 after hours

Teach kids not to pick up or play with certain discarded objects that they might find. If the kids are too young to understand about condoms, tell them not to pick up used "balloons."

Used condoms should simply be thrown away in the garbage. Pick them up with a tool or by wrapping them in paper, plastic, etc.

The health department does not come out to pick up discarded syringes. You need to dispose of them yourself. Use gloves or tools to pick up the syringe and needle. Be very careful and handle the syringe only by the plunger or barrel, not the needle. Put syringes with needles in a wide-mouth plastic container or coffee can, and seal it. Then take it to any health department clinic or the needle disposal centers below.

If you are stuck by a discarded needle, wash the injury with soap and water. Contact a doctor if any signs of infection occur, such as redness or fever. It's unlikely that a virus, such as hepatitis or HIV/AIDS, would be transmitted this way.

If needles are a recurring problem in an area, report it to the police.

Public health centers for needle disposal

Central Environmental Health Center
170 20th Ave.
296-4692

Columbia Health Center
3722 S Hudson St.
296-4650

Downtown Public Health Center
Public Safety Bldg., 14th Floor
Third Ave. and James
296-4755

East Public Health Center
2424 156th Ave. NE
Bellevue
296-4920

Federal Way Clinic
1814 S 324th St.
Federal Way
296-8410

North Public Health Center
10501 Meridian Ave. N
296-4765

South Public Health Center
20 Auburn Ave.
Auburn
296-8400

Southeast Public Health Center
3001 NE Fourth St.
Renton
296-4700

Southwest Public Health Clinics
2901 S 128th St.
Burien
296-4718

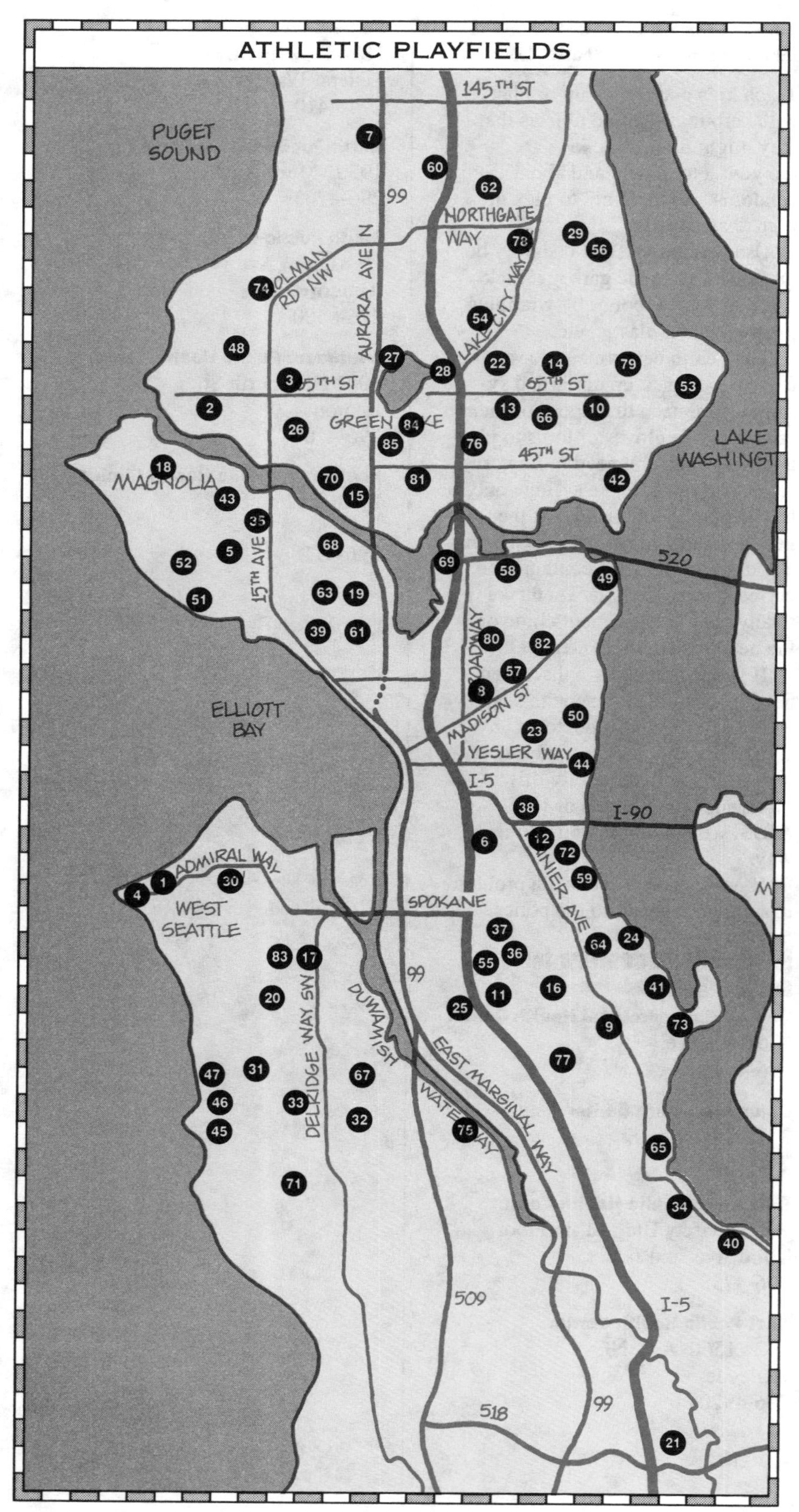

Map key to athletic playfields

1. Alki Playground—58th SW & SW Stevens (1S, 1Sc, 2Tn*)
2. Ballard Playground—NW 60th & 28th NW (2S*, 1Sc*, 2R)
3. Ballard Pool Courts—NW 67th & 14th NW (4Tn*)
4. Bar-S Playground—65th SW & SW Hanford (2L)
5. Bayview Playground—25th W & W Raye (1L, 1Sc)
6. Beacon Hill Playground—14th S & S Holgate (1L, 1S, 2TnR)
7. Bitter Lake Playground—N 130th & Linden N (1S* 1B*, 1C*, 4Tn*)
8. Bobby Morris Playfield—11th E & E Pine (1S* 1B*, 1Sc*, 3Tn*)
9. Brighton Playfield—42nd S & S Juneau (1S 1B*, 1Sc*, 2Tn)
10. Bryant Playground—NE 65th & 40th NE (2)
11. Cleveland Playground—13th S & S Lucile (1ScT)
12. Colman Playground—23rd S & S Grand (1L, 1Sc)
13. Cowen Park—University Way NE & NE Ravenna Blvd. (1L, 3Tn)
14. Dahl Playfield—25th NE & NE 77th (2S 1S* 1B, 1F 1Sc)
15. Day Playground—Fremont N & N 41st (1S, 1S)
16. Dearborn Park—S Brandon & 30th S (2Tn)
17. Delridge Playfield—SW Oregon & Delridge Way SW (1S* 1B*, 1Sc*, 2Tn)
18. Discovery Park—36th W & W Government Way (2Tn)
19. East Queen Anne Playground—Second N & Howe
20. Fairmount Playground—Fauntleroy SW & SW Brandon (1S, 1Sc)
21. Fort Dent Athletic Center—Interurban at Southcenter Pkwy., Tukwila (4S*, 1S* 1S 2F, Cricket)
22. Froula Playground—NE 72nd & 12th NE (2Tn)
23. Garfield Playfield—23rd E & E Cherry (1S* 1S 1B*, 1F*, 3Tn*)
24. Genesee Playfield—46th S & S Genesee (2Sc, 2Tn*)
25. Georgetown Playground—Corson S & S Homer (1Sc*, 1Tn)
26. Gilman Playground—11th NW & NW 54th (2L, 1Sc, 2Tn)

27. Green Lake Park—N 73rd & W Green Lake Dr N (2Tn)
28. Green Lake Playfield—E Green Lake Dr N & Latona NE (2S 1B, 1C, 3Tn)
29. Hale Playfield—35th Ave NE & NE 110th (1ScT)
30. Hiawatha Playfield—California SW & SW Lander (1S* 1S/L 1B, T* 1Sc* 3Tn*)
31. High Point Playfield—34th SW & SW Myrtle (1S 1B, 1Sc*, 2Tn)
32. Highland Park Playground—11th SW & SW Thistle (1S 1B, 1Sc, 1Tn)
33. Hughes Playground—29th SW & SW Holden (2S, 1Sc)
34. Hutchinson Playground—59th S & S Pilgrim (2S, 1Sc, 2Tn)
35. Interbay Athletic Field—17th W & W Dravus (2S*, 1Sc 1C*)
36. Jefferson Park—3801 Beacon Ave. S (2Tn*)
37. Jefferson Playfield—16th S & S Dakota (3S 1B, 1C)
38. Judkins Park & Playfield—22nd S & S Charles (1S 1B, 1Sc 1F)
39. Kinnear Park—Seventh W & W Olympic Pl. (1Tn)
40. Lakeridge Playground—Rainier S btwn. 68th & Cornell (1L, 1Tn)
41. Lakewood Playground—50th S & S Angeline (1S, 1Sc)
42. Laurelhurst Playfield—NE 41st & 48th NE (2S, 1Sc, 4Tn*R)
43. Lawton Park—27th W & W Thurman (1L)
44. Leschi Park—100 Lakeside S (1Tn)
45. Lincoln Park—Fauntleroy Way SW & SW Kenyon (1S/L 2B, 1F, 2Tn)
46. Lincoln Park Annex—Fauntleroy SW & SW Webster (6*R)
47. Lowman Beach Park—48th SW & Beach Dr. SW (1Tn)
48. Loyal Heights Playfield—NW 75th & 22nd NW (1S*1B, 1F*)
49. Madison Park—43rd E & E Lynn (2Tn*)
50. Madrona Playground—34th E & E Spring (1L, 2Tn*)
51. Magnolia Park—31st W & W Garfield (2Tn)
52. Magnolia Playfield—34th W & W Smith (3S 1S* 1B, 2Sc 1Sc* 2* 2Tn)
53. Magnuson Park—Sand Point Way NE & 65th NE (2S, 2Sc, 6)
54. Maple Leaf Playground—NE 82nd & Roosevelt Way NE (1L, 1Sc)
55. Maple Wood Playground—Corson S & S Angeline (2S, 1Sc)
56. Meadowbrook Playfield—30th NE & NE 107th (2S 1B, 6Tn*)
57. Miller Playfield—20th E & E Republican (1S* 1S/B*, 1Sc*, 2Tn*)
58. Montlake Playfield—16th E & E Calhoun (1B, 1ScT, 2Tn)
59. Mt. Baker Park—S McClellan & Lake Park Dr. S (2Tn)
60. Northacres Park—First NE & NE 130th (1L 1S, 1Sc)
61. Observatory Courts—First N & W Lee (2Tn)
62. Pinehurst Playground—14th NE btwn. 120th & NE 123rd (1L)
63. Queen Anne Playfield—First W & W Howe (1B* 1S* 1L, 1Sc)
64. Rainier Playfield—Rainier S & S Alaska (1S* 1B* 1L, 1F*, 4Tn*)
65. Rainier Beach Playfield—Rainier S & S Cloverdale (2S, 1Sc, 4Tn*)
66. Ravenna Park—20th NE & NE 58th (1S, 1Sc, 2Tn)
67. Riverview Playfield—12th SW & SW Othello (4S, 1F 1SC, 2Tn)
68. Rodgers Park/Queen Anne Bowl—Third W & W Fulton (1ScT, 3TnR)
69. Rogers Playground—Eastlake E & E Roanoke (1S/L, 1Sc, 2Tn)
70. Ross Playground—Third NW & NW 43rd (2L)
71. Roxhill Park—29th SW & SW Roxbury (2S, 1Sc)
72. Seattle Tennis Center—2000 M.L. King Jr. Way S (10*4Tn)
73. Seward Park—Lk. Wash. Blvd. S & S Juneau (2Tn)
74. Soundview Playfield—15th NW & NW 90th (2S 1L 1B, 1F 1Sc, 2Tn)
75. South Park Playground—Eighth S & S Sullivan (2S, 1Sc, 2Tn)
76. University Playground—Ninth NE & NE 50th (1S, 1Sc, 2TnR)
77. Van Asselt Playground—32nd S & S Myrtle (2S, 1Sc, 2Tn)
78. Victory Heights Playground—NE 107th & 19th NE (1Tn)
79. View Ridge Playfield—NE 70th & 45th NE (1S 1B, 1C)
80. Volunteer Park—15th E & E Prospect (2* 2Tn)
81. Wallingford Playfield—N 43rd & Wallingford N (1Sc, 2Tn)
82. Washington Park—Lk. Wash. Blvd. E & E Madison (1S* 1S, 1Sc*)
83. West Seattle Stadium—35th SW & SW Snoqualmie (1C* T*)
84. Woodland Park (Lower)—Green Lake Way N btwn. N 50th & N 56th (4S* 1B, T 2Sc*, 10Tn*)
85. Woodland Park N 50th & Midvale N (4Tn)

Key:
S = Softball
B = Baseball
L = Little League
F = Football
Sc = Soccer
C = Combination
T = Track
Tn = Tennis
R = Backboard (Tennis)
* = Lighted

CHAPTER

19

THE SPORTING LIFE

PRO SPORTS

SEAHAWKS

SONICS

HUSKIES

HORSES

TICKET PRICES

MARINERS

HOCKEY

KINGDOME

HYDROS

Is Seattle a sports city? Well, sometimes yes and sometimes no. Spectator sportswise, it's a football city; it's not a baseball city (ask the Mariners). It's a basketball city (well, sort of), but not a soccer city. Participant sports is another subject altogether and in that instance, Seattle is definitely a sports city. In sports as in so many other things, the specter of Seattleites as fit, enthusiastic, and ultimately outdoorsy is raised. Spectator sports, sure we've got 'em. But participant sports—well, scratch a Seattleite and you'll find an amateur soccer team member, an over-the-hill basketballer, a tavern-sponsored softball pitcher, or even someone who belongs to the local armwrestlers' association. And Little League—there are so many men and women out there living vicariously through their 11-year-olds that it's a wonder any business gets done in Seattle after 3:30 p.m. in the spring.

That's not to say that Seattle doesn't stream toward the Kingdome on a Friday night like a flash flood set loose in a canyon. It does.

THE TICKET TICKER

You don't decide at the last minute to go to a Seahawks game, but you could decide at the very last minute to go to a Mariners game (except for opening night). Ticket savvy has become a sport in itself.

THE HOT SEAHAWKS

If ticket temperature is measured in terms of difficulty of acquisition, then the Seattle Seahawks of the National Football League (NFL) are far and away the hottest ticket in town. This despite the fact that the team has never reached the Super

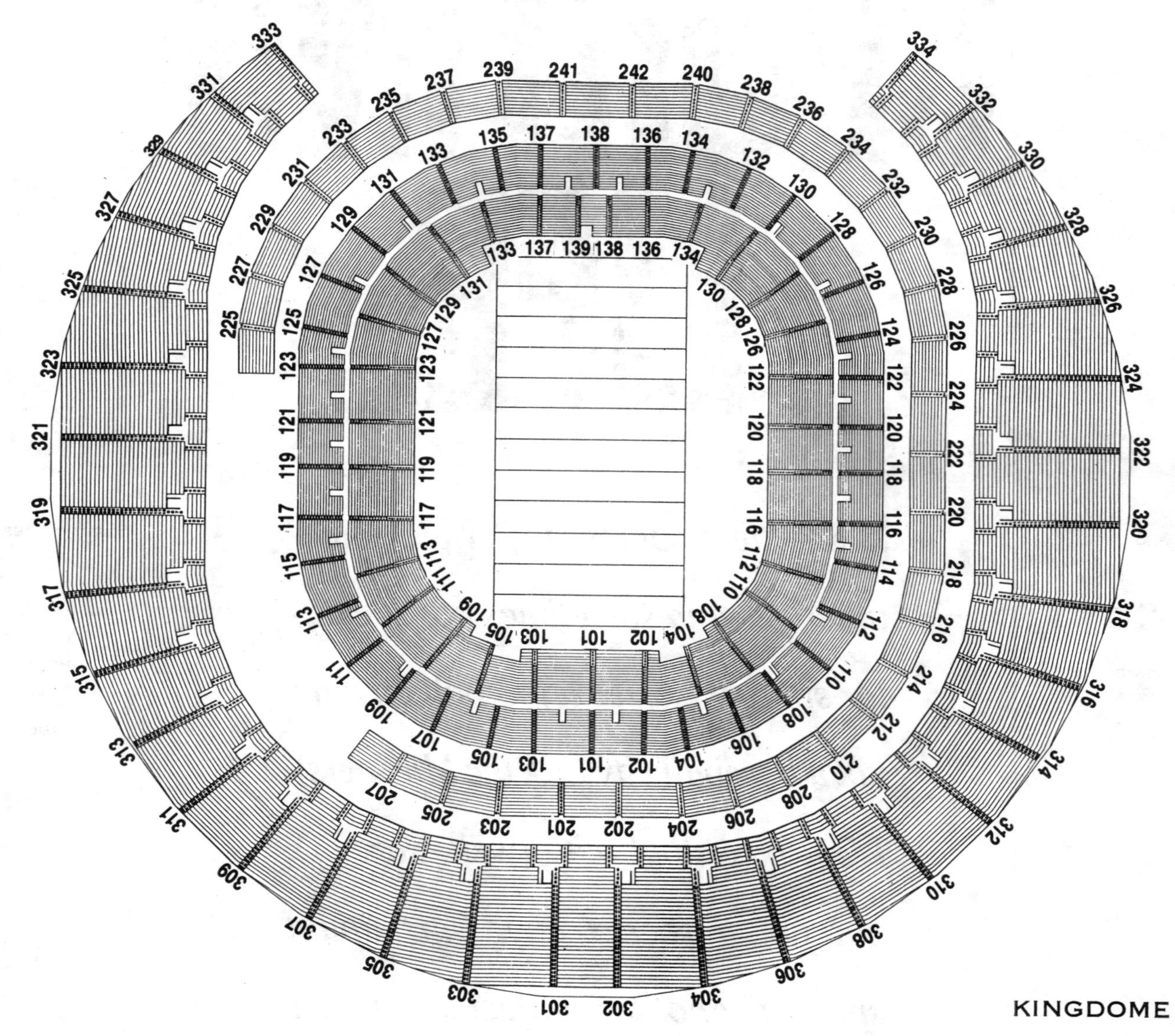

KINGDOME

FOOTBALL SEATING

Bowl, has never won a conference championship, and has won only one division championship.

Seattle plays in the Western Division of the American Football Conference. It plays home games each season against the Los Angeles Raiders, Denver Broncos, Kansas City Chiefs, San Diego Chargers, and four other games each season against different teams from the NFL's other five divisions.

Since the Seahawks' founding in 1976, only one Seahawk home game has not been an official sellout. The waiting list for season tickets is 30,000 names long. In 1988 when 100 season ticketholders cancelled, their lucky replacements were fans who had signed up in 1978.

Seattle Seahawks
11220 NE 53rd St.
Kirkland, WA 98033
827-9777
Home stadium: Kingdome, 64,981 seating capacity
Ticket prices: $35, $29, $25, $19/seat per game; season tickets for eight regular-season home games and two preseason games: $350, $290, $250, $190.

LUKEWARM SONICS

Not so hot are the Seattle SuperSonics of the National Basketball Association (NBA). The Sonics won their one and only NBA championship in the 1978–79 season, and have not returned to anything resembling contention since. Still, having been established in 1967, they are Seattle's oldest professional sports franchise, and thus occupy a special place in the hearts of Northwest sports fans. The NBA is becoming a pricey game, though, and Sonic tickets, at $29, $24, $21, $18, $12, and $5, don't come cheap. And they're going up.

The SuperSonics play in the Pacific Division of the NBA's Western Conference. Few of their home games are sellouts, save for the three each year they play against divisional-rival Los Angeles Lakers.

Occasionally, Seahawks ticketholders who cannot attend certain games donate their tickets to the Children's Home Society, which sells them at face value to fans who call at the right time. Children's Home Society: 524-6020.

The Sonics have played for years in the Seattle Center Coliseum, a moribund structure built for the 1962 World's Fair and intended to be a temporary structure. The roof leaks, the toilets overflow, the building is invariably too cold, and there's no replay screen. When the place is full, there isn't enough of anything: food, drink, ushers, bathrooms, or umbrellas. It's no wonder the Sonics want to move. Let's just hope their games live up to their new arena—now under construction south of the Kingdome.

Seattle SuperSonics
190 Queen Anne Ave. N
P.O. Box 900911
Seattle, WA 98109-9711
281-5800
Home arena: Seattle Center Coliseum (14,250 seats)
41 home games per year

As one sportswriter says, "NEVER pay to get into the Kingdome for a Seahawks game—they always look better on television."

THE TEAM FANS LOVE ANYWAY

At the bottom of the pro sports barrel lurk the Seattle Mariners, the losingest franchise in Major League Baseball history. Founded in 1977, the Mariners have never had a season in which they won more games than they lost. Playing in the seven-team Western Division of the American League, the team has never finished higher than fourth place. They have been the very definition of futility, embarrassment, sad-sackness, ineptitude....

The Mariners play in the Kingdome, which, marvelous as it is for football, used to be abysmal for baseball. But with the advent of M's owner Jeff Smulyan on the scene, the Kingdome positively pulses with marketing know-how, from fireworks inside the dome to a Fan-o-meter that gets the crowd worked into a frenzy.

Rumors persist that once, sometime in the distant past, the M's sold out a game, and so in 1990, the fans decided to try to match that and sold out opening night. The stadium seats 59,438 for baseball. Sometimes as many as 20,000 seats are actually used.

Baseball, in Seattle as elsewhere, is sports' best buy. For $10.50, fans can buy a lower-deck box seat on the infield or along the foul lines; for $8.50, a second-deck infield or foul-line seat; $5.50 buys a third-deck seat; and $4.50 a general admission ticket, with seats in the outfield grandstands. (1990 prices)

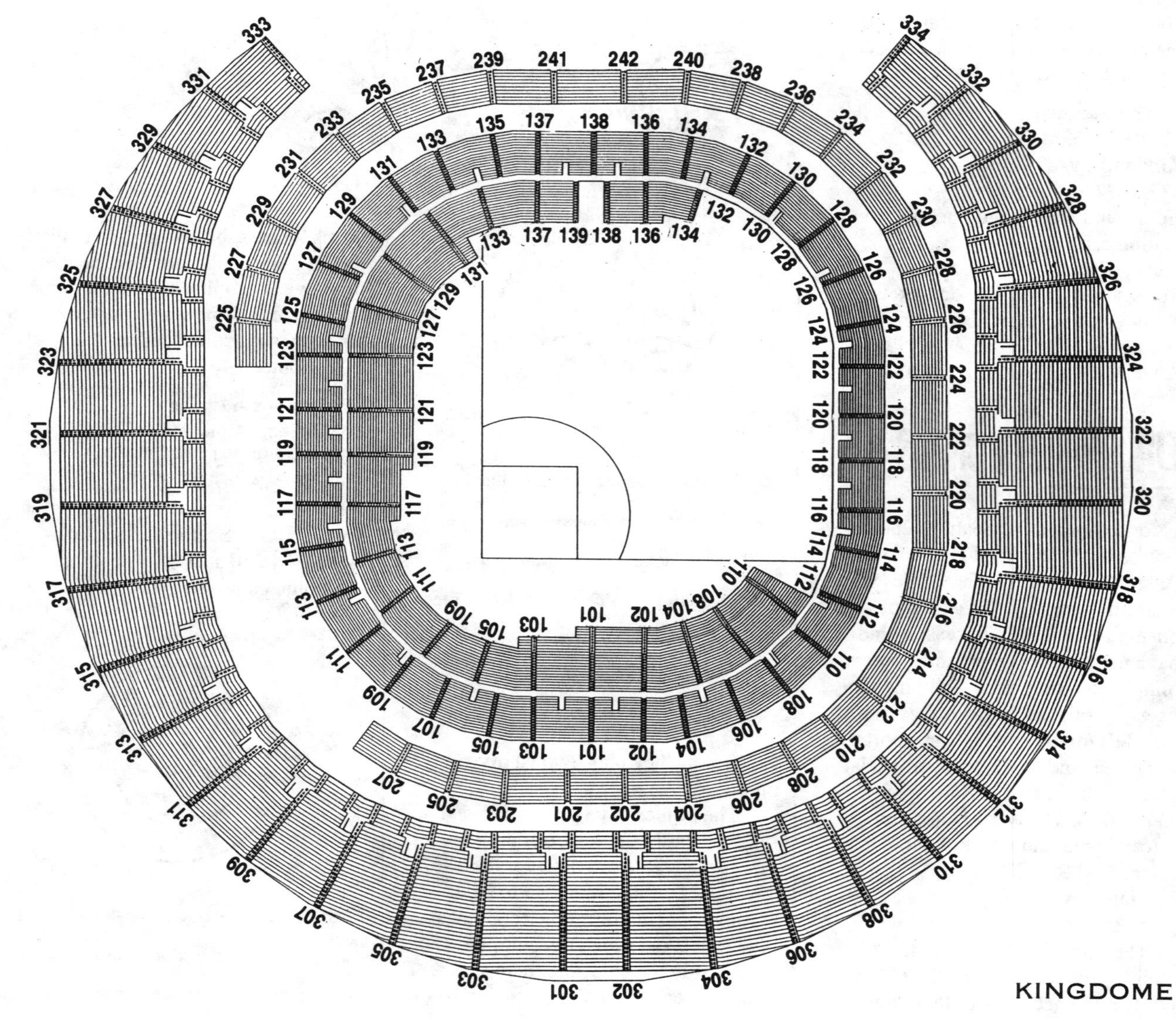

KINGDOME

BASEBALL SEATING

The jury's still out on the new food at the Kingdome. Sure you can get pizza delivered to your seat and sure you can get non-baseball type gourmet-style food. And sure the prices are better than they used to be when Kingdome food was the most expensive in the universe. Try it and see, but our vote for best sporting food: Longacres (while it lasts). Second-best: Everett Memorial Stadium, particularly the pizza, hot dogs, and chili. The Giants also serve garden-variety beer and designer beer in gigantic cups for low, low prices.

Season tickets, as of 1990, are: VIP box seats (best seats in the house): $800 per season; box seats, $750 per season; club (200-level) seats, $610; and view (300-level) seats, $550.

Season tickets, which reserve the seat in question for all 81 home games, save the ticketholder 10%–12% per game.

The Mariners also offer several other ticket-buying options. The 40-game "Weekend Plan": Box $380, Club $315, View $210; the 41-game Business Plan (Monday-through-Thursday games, same prices as Weekend Plan). Groups of 40 to 399 people can buy tickets at a $1 discount, and groups of 400 or more can save $2 off the regular price.

Catered parties: in Kingdome dining rooms with a view of the field.

Seattle plays 81 games each season at home, and—thanks to the stadium's much-maligned roof—there has never been a rainout.

Seattle Mariners
411 First Ave. S
P.O. Box 4100
Seattle, WA 98104
628-3555

CULT HOCKEY

Seattle's minor-league hockey franchise, the Seattle Thunderbirds of the Western Hockey League, has something of a cult following in the Northwest. Taking on such exotic rivals as the Brandon Wheat Kings, the T-birds play raucous, fight-bedecked, enthusiastic hockey in front of rabid fans, many of whom look like extras from the Paul Newman cult classic, *Slap Shot*.

The Thunderbirds play in the Seattle Center Arena, which seats 4,139. Seats are $9.50 for adults, $8.00 for 12-and-unders, senior citizens, or military personnel, in all but the corner seats (which go for $6.50).

Seattle Thunderbirds
P.O. Box 19391
Seattle, WA 98109
728-9124

Kids 14-and-under can buy Mariners 300-level seats for $3.50 and general admission seats for $2.50. A $2.50 ticket for the left-field seats is a terrific buy, if only because it is the best spot from which to catch a home run ball.

KICKIN' ALL THE WAY

The Seattle Storm of the Western Soccer League (WSL) is Seattle's professional soccer franchise.

Pro soccer is slowly rebuilding itself across the country in the wake of the folding, some years ago, of the North American Soccer League. There are 10 teams in the WSL, covering Washington, Oregon, California, Colorado, Utah, Arizona, and New Mexico.

The team plays in Memorial Stadium at the Seattle Center and is arguably part of pro sports' wave of the distant future. There will come a day when soccer is America's biggest game, and this league looks to have the staying power to be around when that day comes. The league is building slowly, keeping salaries in line with revenues, and employing exclusively American-born and -trained players.

Seattle Storm (Football Club Seattle)
2815 Second Ave., Suite 300
Seattle, WA 98121-9990
441-3390

AND DON'T FORGET THE HUSKIES

The University of Washington has 19 intercollegiate sports; it sells tickets for 17 of them.

For 14 of the sports, prices are $4 for adults, $2 for children, high-school students, and senior citizens. The 14 are:
Men's baseball
Men's and women's cross-country
Men's and women's golf
Women's gymnastics
Men's soccer
Men's and women's swimming
Men's and women's tennis
Men's and women's track and field
Women's volleyball

For two sports, men's and women's crew, there is no admission charge—just take a seat along the Montlake Cut.

The three major Husky sports are football (Division IA), and women's and men's basketball (Pacific-10 Conference). For men's basketball, reserved seats are $10 per game, and general admission seats are $5 per game for adults, $4 for children and senior citizens. "Family plan" tickets (two adults and three children, or one adult and four children) cost $13. Season ticket prices depend upon the number of home games. (In 1990, for example, a season ticket for 16 home games cost $160.)

For women's basketball, which currently is far and away the greatest game in town, the UW women are perennial Pac-10 champions or near-champions, and are ranked among the top teams nationally every season. Reserved seats, $6.00; general admission, $5.00 adults, $2.50 children and senior citizens. "Family plan" tickets, $12. Since they are so hot, these tickets are slated to rise in price so check ahead.

The hottest ticket for UW sports is, of course, football, which is played in 72,500-seat Husky Stadium. Besides the game, you get a stunning view of Lake Washington through the open end of the stadium. Football ticket-purchase options for the 1990 season included:

- Season ticket, $108 (6 games).
- Individual seats: $20 for the big games; $17 for others.
- Four-game package, called "Family plan," with seats in west end zone, $80.
- General admission seats, in bleachers behind east end zone, are $10.00 for some games, $8.50 for others (adults), $7.00 (children and senior citizens).

The best seats in Husky Stadium can be had by making contributions of $75, $150, or $250 per seat to the Tyee Club. A contribution entitles you to the right to pay season-ticket price for prime seats. The higher the contribution, the better the seat. Call ticket office for application.

University of Washington Huskies
101 Graves Bldg., 6C-20
Seattle, WA 98195
Ticket office: 543-2200

WHAT GOES ON IN THE ORANGE JUICE SQUEEZER?

The Kingdome, a.k.a. King County Stadium, stages several other sporting events each year, to the delight of the hordes from the dark corners of King, Snohomish, and Kitsap Counties. The most wonderful event each year is the Kingbowl, held the first weekend in December. The Kingbowl is the state high-school football championships in all five divisions: B-8 (8-man football), B-11, A, AA, and AAA. There's nothing quite like watching small-town America compete at football.

And the Kingdome will host the 1991 and 1993 NCAA West regional games for the national college men's basketball championship, and the 1995 Final Four championship

Kingdome behind-the-scene public tours are available mid-April through mid-September. They are at 11 a.m., 1 p.m., and 3 p.m. Monday–Saturday. Cost is $2.50 for adults and teens, $1.25 for seniors and children under 12. Show up at Gate 10. You get a whiff of the locker room (and of the press box), visit the museum and (of course) the gift shop, and maybe even get a player's-eye view from the field.

games. The Kingdome also hosts a 3-on-3 basketball tournament every summer.

For the macho among us, there are three "dirt track" events per year at the dome:

- Supercross (motorcycles on dirt track).
- Mickey Thompson Grand Prix (trucks, tractors, buses, cars, cycles...various pulling and racing events).
- The Thrill Show (weird stuff a la Evel Knieval).

The Kingdome also has shows nonstop during the winter, including the Boat Show in January and the Sportsman's Expo in February.

Kingdome
Office of Promotions
201 S King St.
Seattle, WA 98104
296-3663
For a complete schedule of the shows.

NAMES FOR THE KINGDOME

Another sport in Seattle is thinking up names for the Kingdome roof. A few favorites:
Umbrella
Orange juice squeezer
Big mushroom
Condom
Giant flywheel
Upside down saucer
Flying saucer
Very ugly (not a name, but probably what it gets called the most)

THEY'RE OFF! LONGACRES THOROUGHBRED RACING

The crown jewel in the Seattle sporting kingdom, Longacres is the oldest thoroughbred track on the West Coast. It is far and away the most colorful, character-rich sporting spectacle in the city.

Races are held every Wednesday through Sunday, from April 4 until September 4, with 10 races or so held each day. Admission to the track is $3.25; and seats are $2.50 for the grandstand, $2.50 for the paddock club, and $5.00 for window seats in the paddock club. North end of the grandstand is free. The view is best from the clubhouse boxes. Parking is $1 for general, off-in-the-distance lots, $4 for the "preferred" lot, and $6 for valet service. Go with the general. The more money you can save for betting, the better.

Wednesday through Friday racing begins at 5 p.m. (gates open at 3:30) and on Saturday, Sunday, and holidays at 1 p.m. (gates open at 11:30). On Saturday and Sunday mornings, the track also holds a tour of the backstretch, reservations for which can be had by calling (800) 7-DOO-DAH.

Save this for Seattle trivia contests or as conversation gambit during a slow inning at a Mariners game... Kingdome facts: It opened in 1976; it has the largest single-span concrete roof in the world; there are seven acres of roof; builders used 443 tons of structural steel and 52,800 cubic yards of concrete in the building; the concrete weighs 105,600 tons; and the interior contains 67 million cubic feet of air within the building's perimeter.

The Longacres track is everything a racetrack should be. They have the best concessions in the universe: There are seven restaurants at the track, serving everything from gourmet meals to hot dogs and pizza, along with beer, wine, and cocktails. Buy a *Racing Form*, teach yourself to handicap the races, eat the sandwiches, drink the beer, and revel in the language around you. And when you lose, curse the jockey.

Each season, 1.2 million people come to follow the horses.

Longacres
Exit 1, Interstate 405
West Valley Highway
P.O. Box 60
Renton, WA 98057
226-3131

BASEBALL THE OLD-FASHIONED WAY

A mid-summer night at the Everett Giants' outdoor ballpark is the stuff of which American dreams are made. Every baseball fan should head for Memorial Stadium in Everett to see the Rookie-League Everett Giants in action.

The Giants, who are part of the San Francisco Giants organization, play 38 games, from June 18 to September 3. The stadium is like the

Longacres was sold to The Boeing Company in September 1990. The future of the track is unclear. We hope it survives.

Worst ambience: Seattle Center Coliseum. Second-worst: Kingdome. Best: Longacres, unless you're at a UW women's basketball game against Stanford when the house (Hec Edmundson) is sold out.

major-league teams' spring training parks. It's cozy, seating 3,600, and is beautiful, the owners having a great eye for the aesthetics of ballparks. The grandstands have chair seating with plenty of leg room. The ballplayers, in their first year of pro ball, are enthusiastic, earnest, and hungry. The stands are packed with families, teenage groupies, and small children. The concessions are fabulous—one national magazine rated Everett's ballpark food as the best in the country.

Reserved seats are $5.00 for adults, $3.50 for children under 14; general admission tickets, which buy you bench seats in bleachers along the first- and third-baselines, are $4.00 and $2.50 (children). Parking is free. Sunday games begin at 2 p.m., other days at 7 p.m. The Giants also have a great PA system, a super announcer, and a fabulous selection of rock music. Stick around after the game to watch the groupies at work. Woo woo.

Everett Giants
2118 Broadway (just off I-5, Exit 192)
Everett, WA 98201
258-3673

THE HYDROS

Seattle's most established sporting event is the anachronistic Rainier Cup Hydroplane Race, which is the centerpiece for the city's annual Seafair celebration. Held early every August, the cup is a race among huge hydroplanes—which are sperm-cell-shaped boats that skim along the top of the water, and have engines like those on Indianapolis 500 racers, thus enabling them to travel at speeds well in excess of 150 miles per hour over a two-mile oval course at the south end of Lake Washington.

The first races were held in 1950, making hydroplaning Seattle's oldest professional sport. While most fans watch from their own boats, moored the night before out close to the course, and others watch from homes and beach fronts along the lake, Seafair has its own section of prime viewing beach.

Admission to Seafair's official viewing area is $8 in advance, $10 at the gate. Kids under 12 accompanied by an adult get in free, and seniors 62 years old and older get in for $1. Bleacher seating is $18. Pit passes are $10/day, or four days for $25. Pit tours are an additional $5. More privileged seating includes the "Captain's Club," at $100 per person, $25 for kids under 12; the Sky Box, for $13,000 per box; Hospitality Suites A ($9,000) and B ($8,000); and motorhomes at $2,000 each.

Seafair
The Westin Building
2001 Sixth Ave., Suite 2800
Seattle, WA 98121-2574
728-0123

ATHLETES TO WATCH

Seattle Mariners Ken Griffey, Jr., Harold Reynolds, and Alvin Davis. Seattle SuperSonics Xavier McDaniel, Dana Barros, and Shawn Kemp. Seattle Seahawks Dave Krieg, Brian Blades, Dave Wyman, and Bryan Millard.

CHAPTER

20

THROUGH THE SCHOOL MAZE

HIGH SCHOOLS

ELEMENTARY SCHOOLS

ALTERNATIVE SCHOOLS

CLUSTERS

SCORES

MIDDLE SCHOOLS

MAGNET PROGRAMS

BEST TEACHERS

BUSING

GRADUATES

They call it controlled choice, the process by which students are assigned to schools in the Seattle school system. After the recent years of turmoil, the controlled-choice method is apparently working. Parents are happier (so far). Students are getting the choices they want (usually). As things smooth out, it's fair (if not safe) to predict that eyes will turn to the real problem of the schools: funding.

But for the consumers—parents and students—there's still the problem of choosing a school and, once chosen, getting to know it.

How to tell which is the best school for your student? Here's one way:

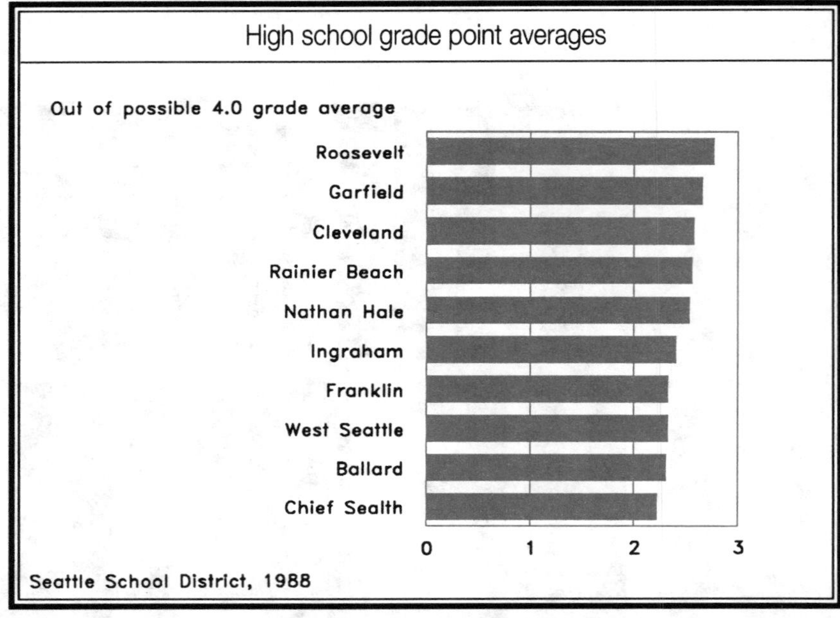

BEYOND THE SNIFF TEST

A friend of ours swears by what he calls "the sniff test." He maintains there's no substitute for personal presence in the classroom and suggests just walking into a school and asking, unannounced, to visit a class. He literally sniffs out what's going on and, more by osmosis than by any real scientific analysis, decides if this is a place he—much less his kids—would want to spend almost a third of the day.

With a nod toward that particular idea, the following guide to Seattle's public schools and some private schools is meant to help parents know what questions to ask—it is not designed to rate schools.

One caution: Public schools are required to report certain things that private schools are not, such as weapons confiscated. (Private schools have only to turn to the next name on the waiting list to solve that problem—a luxury not immediately allowed public schools.)

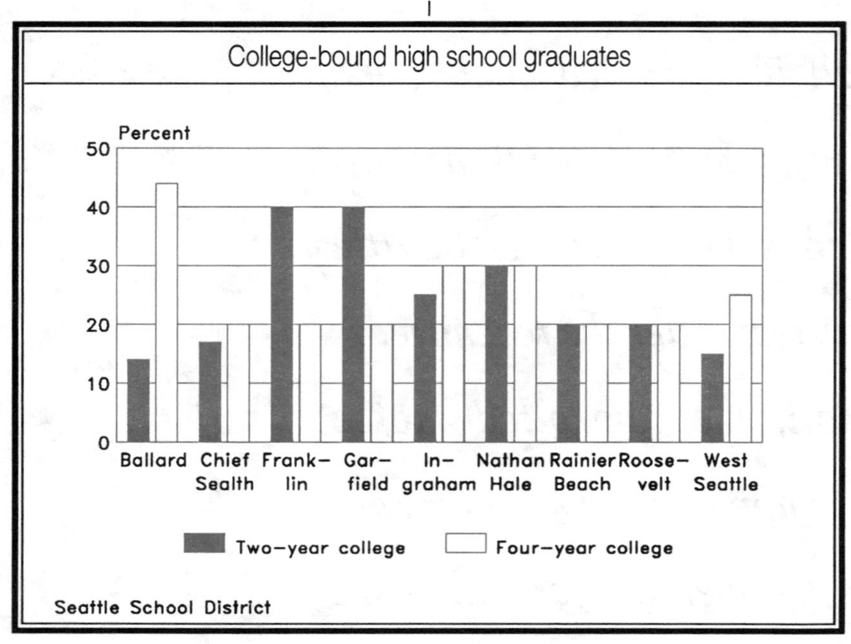

And another: We've attempted to note the strongest programs at schools by asking those who know, the school personnel themselves. In some cases, we obtained a good list of programs, in others, nothing. Again, parents should be asking the same questions.

The purpose of including the number of students in various lunch programs is to let you know if a school includes a cross section of Seattle society. You can see the percentage of low- or lower middle–income families from looking at the number of students who qualify for reduced-cost or free lunch in a particular school. A family of four qualifies for reduced-cost lunch with a monthly income of $1,865; for free lunch, $1,310. A family of three qualifies for reduced-cost lunch with a monthly income of $1,550; for free lunch, $1,090.

The Horizon and the Accelerated Progress Program, or APP, offer special enrichment for high-potential students who qualify based on test scores (top 5% for Horizon, top 1% for APP) and other information. One elementary school in each controlled choice cluster offers a Horizon program; all middle schools and high schools offer some Horizon classes in core subjects. The APP curriculum is available only at Madrona Elementary, Washington Middle School, and Garfield High.

The Seattle schools have struggled toward racial equality, succeeding in some instances more than others. Figures on percentages of minority students in schools are below, too.

With all that in mind, peruse the primer of Seattle schools. Except where noted, figures are for the 1989–90 school year.

PUBLIC HIGH SCHOOLS

In general, there are one principal and two assistant principals per Seattle high school. One counselor per 400 students is available, as is one librarian. Average teacher/student ratio is one teacher to 30 students. The teachers' union stipulates a teacher is not to have more than 150 students per day.

By way of comparison, Bellevue high schools average 27.3 students to each teacher. Edmonds averages 23 students to one teacher.

The test scores given below are one indication of the type and strength of programs offered in a school, but are a bit difficult to understand. They are from the most recent (1989) California Achievement Tests administered in the schools. The scores show how a mid-most student in each school performed in relation to other students across the nation. For example, at Ballard High School, the mid-most student scored better than 55.5 percent of students in the national group in reading. At Chief Sealth, the mid-most student scored better than 59 percent of students in the national group in reading.

Caveat: The state dropout rates for schools given here are controversial, so we've included the school district's too, where available. The district complains that the state

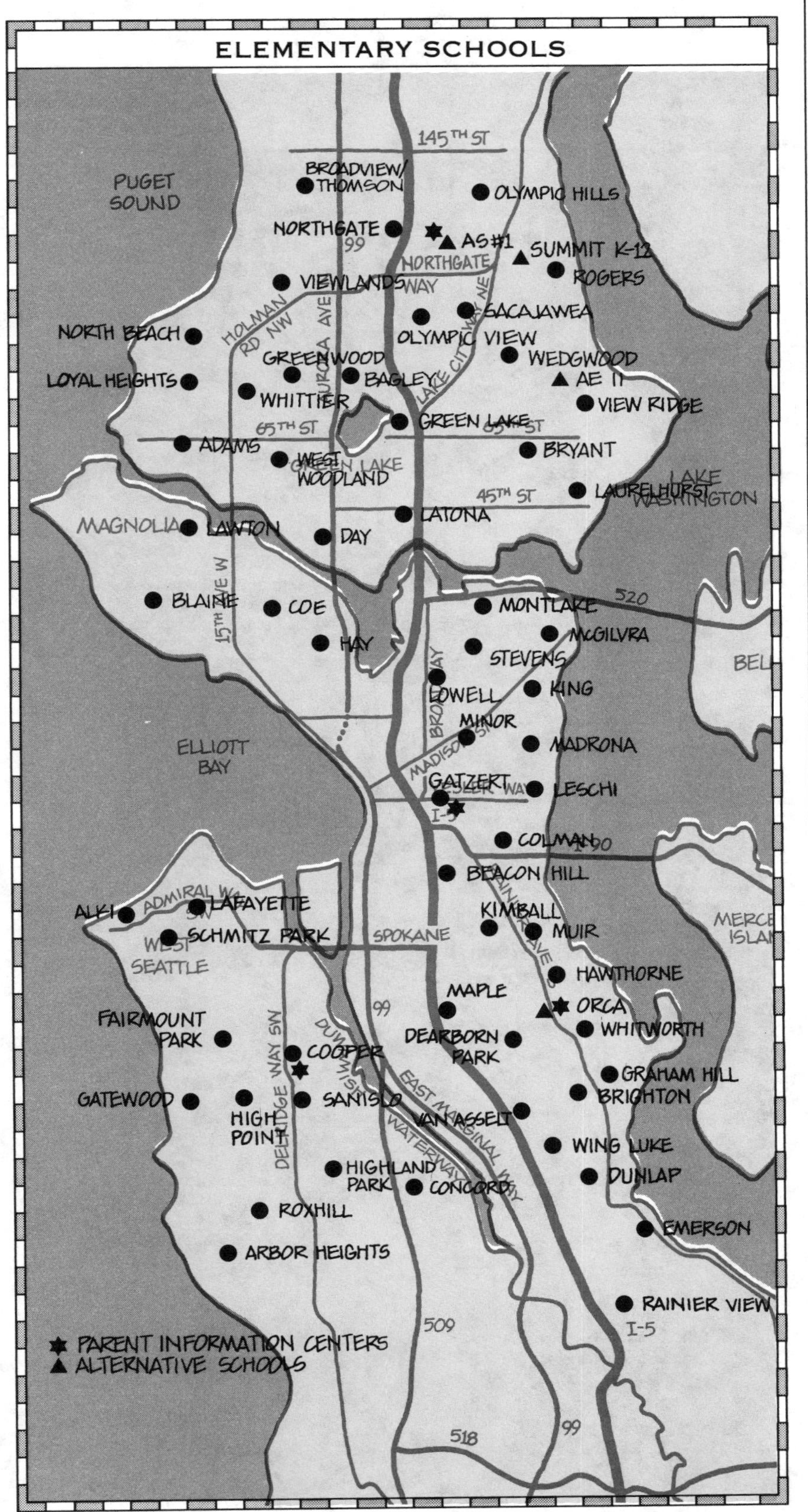

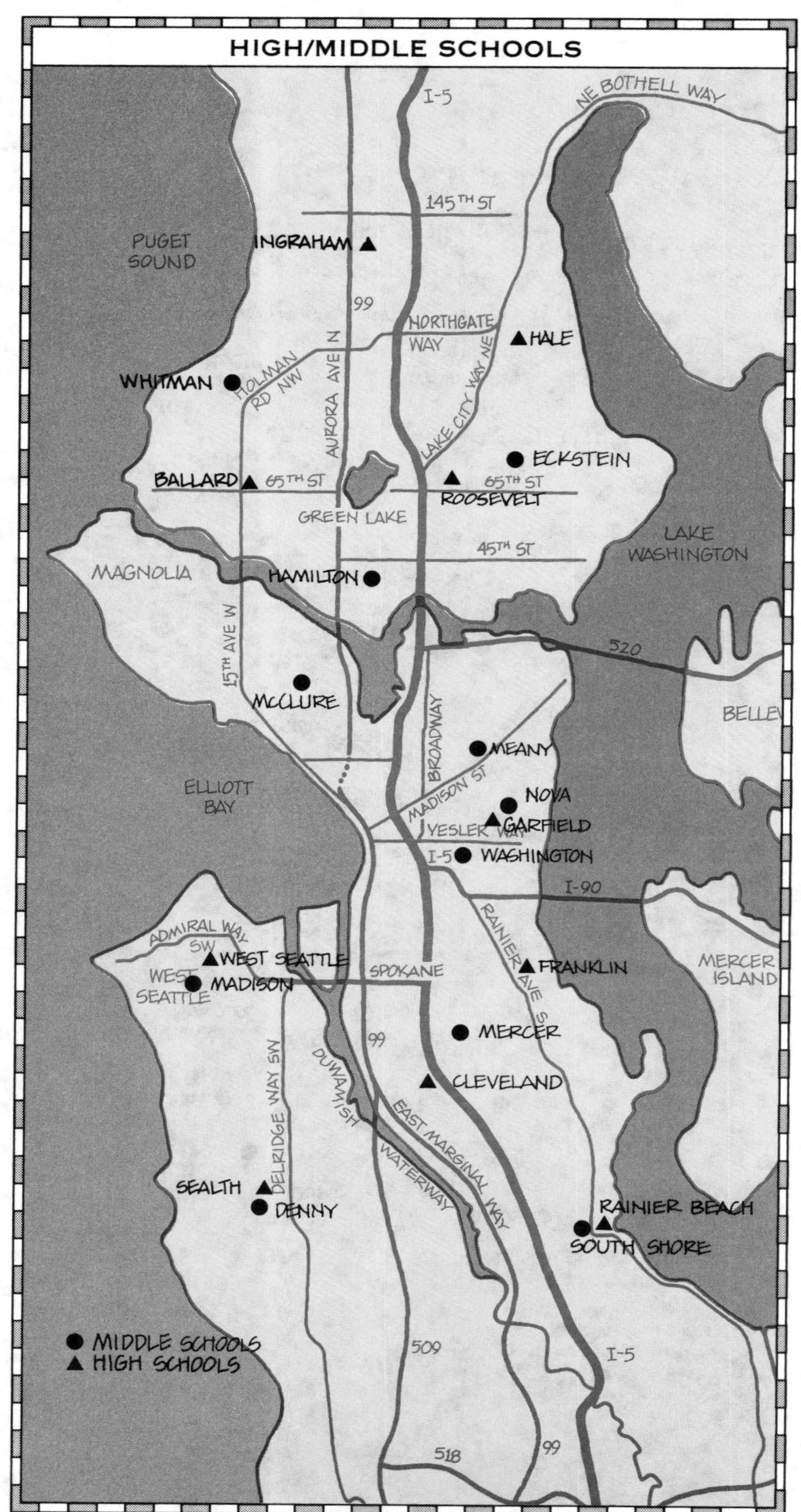

figures are misleading because students transfer to other schools or leave and come back several times, and so are not really dropouts. The school district counts as dropouts students who leave the district without transferring to another school or graduating and who do not return the following fall.

Seattle School District (SSD) says its dropout rate in 1987–88 for high schools was 15.9%; for middle schools, 8.6%; and for elementary schools, 5.8%.

Security incidents include arson, assault, bombs, burglary, disturbances, drugs, harassment, robbery, sex offenses, theft, trespassing, vandalism, and weapons possession.

MIDDLE SCHOOLS

Please refer to the chart on middle schools in this chapter. All the Seattle middle schools now include sixth grade, which until recently was part of elementary school. Average class size is 29.5 students.
Average class size in Bellevue middle schools is 26.2; Edmonds, 23.

ELEMENTARY SCHOOLS

Please refer to the chart on elementary schools in this chapter. Here's a rundown on educational acronyms: CAMPI stands for Central Area Mothers for Peace and Improvement (a preschool program for four-year-olds in Brighton, Muir, Leschi, and Minor schools). DISTAR is the Direct Instructional Teaching of Arithmetic and Reading used in grades K–5 at the schools indicated. A number of elementary schools offer an Early Childhood Model program that provides small group instruction at levels appropriate to the needs of individual students.

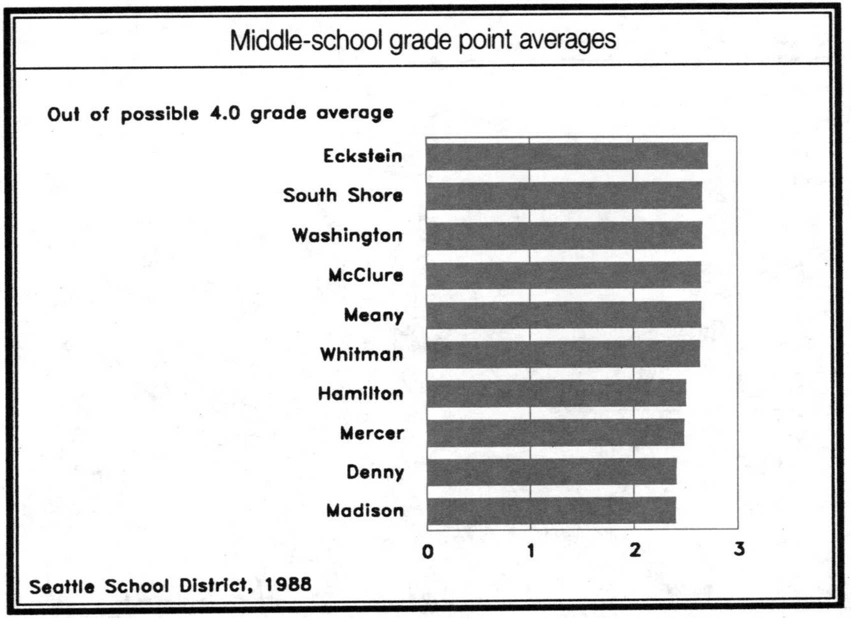

MAGNET PROGRAMS AND THEIR SCHOOLS

Elementary schools. The Academic Academy magnet program enhances basic skills in science/math or writing/speech or both by the use of computers and other advanced materials. Available at Arbor Heights, Bagley, Brighton, Dunlap, Emerson, Lawton, Minor; to be added 1990–91, Gatzert and Van Asselt.

The World Cultures magnet program emphasizes understanding cultural differences through the study of a language other than English, and by looking at international geography, government, art, music, etc. Available at Bryant, Day, Highland Park, and Maple.

The Elementary Demonstration Project brings disadvantaged children up to grade level through individual instruction and by letting students learn at their own speed. Available at Coleman and Hawthorne.

High schools. The Aviation magnet program is a proposed program in aircraft maintenance and avionics to be developed in conjunction with major aviation manufacturers and airlines; expansion of the current hospitality magnet is to include a tourism and airline support component. To be available at Chief Sealth.

The Horti/Floriculture magnet program is an introduction to commercial gardening, landscape architecture, garden center management, and related areas. (Combined with the Radio/TV magnet, this program is now part of a larger Vocational Education magnet in development at Nathan Hale.)

The Hospitality magnet introduces students to employment and training possibilities in the tourism and hospitality industries (to be combined with proposed aviation magnet at Chief Sealth).

The International Education magnet includes an emphasis on world problems and issues within the core curricula, plus an International Core component on specific cultures. Available at Cleveland.

The Marine/Health Sciences magnet program includes enriched courses in science, math, and health, with a focus on computer technology and marine ecology. Available at Garfield.

The Radio/TV Communications magnet program is designed to mix hands-on experience in the school's broadcast facility with regular academic coursework. Available at Nathan Hale, which is also the home of radio station KNHC.

The Teacher Academy is a college prep program at Rainier Beach designed to identify and encourage minority students who have the potential to become teachers.

ALTERNATIVE SCHOOLS

Alternative programs within the Seattle schools differ from the district's typical fare both in teaching philosophies and in techniques. They use methods and materials not usually found in regular programs—open-concept and multigraded classes and experiential approaches, for example. Alternative schools also provide opportunities for children who have special barriers (language, cultural, or social) and needs that can't be met elsewhere in the system (teen-age parent programs with day care, night classes). Some alternative programs are more "alternative" than others in structure and in choices available to students. More than any other segment of the district, these programs require firsthand investigation via talks with principals, teachers, parents, and students before you consider them for your child.

Alternative School 1 (AE-1)
Pinehurst Building
11530 12th Ave. NE
281-6970
Open-concept program for K–8 focusing on "experiential learning for non-linear learners"; parents are involved in program development and in teaching; pre-enrollment interview required; 124 students.

Alternative School 2 (AE-2)
Decatur Elementary
7711 43rd Ave. NE
281-6770

Open-concept school for K–5 emphasizing individual instruction; no letter grades; evaluation via parent conferences; currently serves Zone 1; 265 students.

American Indian Heritage High School
315 22nd Ave. S
286-4590
Emphasis on Native American history, literature, and culture; academic and vocational courses; social-support services; 61 students; open to all races.

Escuela Latona/Alternative School 3 (AE-3)
Latona Elementary
401 NE 42nd St.
281-6530
Structured program emphasizing basic skills and the study of the Spanish language and Latino culture for K–5; currently serves Zone 2; 160 students.

The Gypsy Alternative School
Bagley Elementary
7821 Stone Way N
281-6242
For Gypsy children, K–5, whose parents want them to maintain their cultural identity; single classroom; some use of Romany language; families often accompany children to school; 25 students; only program of its kind in the country.

Other programs

Marshall Alternative High School
520 NE Ravenna Blvd.
281-6115
281-6146 (Evening High School)
Provides special programs for high-risk secondary students who live north of the ship canal: dropouts, underachievers, teen-age parents (day care provided), students re-entering school after suspension or expulsions; also offers GED Focus, Evening High School for those who can't attend school during the day; 400 students.

New Option Middle School
at Washington Middle School
2101 S Jackson St.
286-4581
Open to sixth graders, with more grades to be added in the future, the new school has global citizenship as its central theme, with an initial focus on the Pacific Rim. Students go out into the community and spend time at day care centers and visiting musuems. Exchange programs are planned. Students expected: 150.

NOVA
2410 E Cherry St.
281-6363
Individualized, flexible high school program in which students may earn credits toward a diploma at NOVA or at another Seattle public school or community college, or through tutorials; students sign contracts outlining a plan of instruction and schedule of evaluations; ungraded; 125 students.

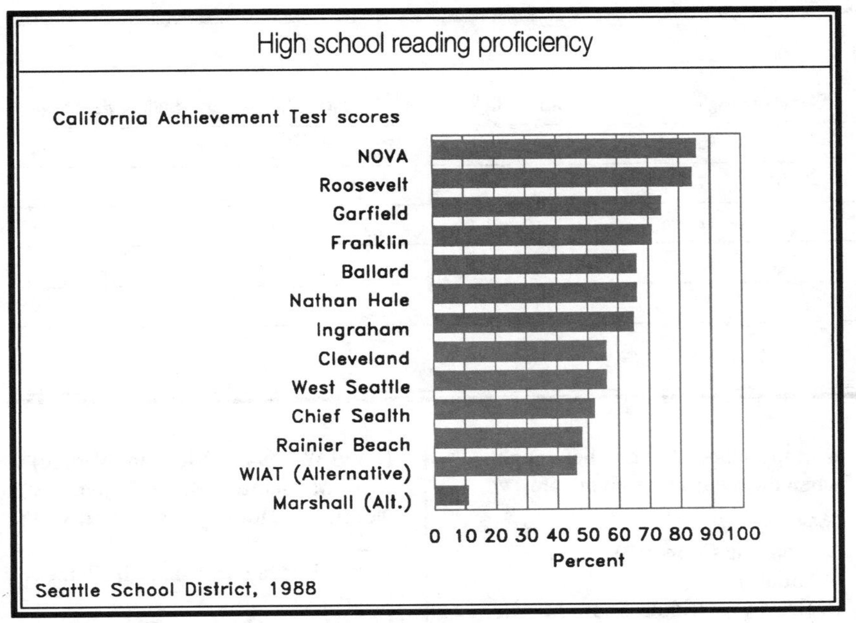

Orca
Columbia Elementary
2528 S Ferdinand St.
281-6310
Basic skills plus special emphasis on arts and environmental sciences for K–5; parental involvement encouraged; currently serves Zones 2 and 3; 200 students.

Proyecto Saber tutoring
(Ballard, Ingraham, Chief Sealth high schools; Denny, Hamilton, and Mercer middle schools; Beacon Hill, Concord, Cooper, Greenwood, High Point, Highland Park, Roxhill, and Sanislo elementaries)
281-6066
Tutoring and support services and a limited number of classes for Latino/Chicano students; bilingual/bicultural staff; Zones 1 and 3; 500 students.

Seattle Alternative High School
315 22nd Ave. S
286-4568
Program similar to Marshall's, for students who live south of the ship canal; 200 students.

Summit K-12
11051 34th Ave. NE
281-6880
The only K–12 alternative in the district, multicultural curriculum; cross-age tutoring; multigrade classrooms; emphasis on arts and physical education; 625 students.

TOPS (The Option Program at Stevens)
Stevens Elementary
1242 18th Ave. E
281-6760
Basic skills emphasis, plus exploration of the urban environment outside of school; currently K–5, next year K–6, pending School Board approval will go to grade 8; waiting list in some grade levels and for racial balance; currently serves Zone 2; 159 students.

IN FRONT OF THE BLACKBOARD

In a survey done by the Seattle Kids-Place advisory committee, the city's teenagers emphatically said one of the things they would like to see for kids is the authority to grade teachers. Obviously, students would love to have that kind of power over their teachers, and just as obviously they don't get it. Probably the best way to judge a teacher is to go into the classroom and watch. Don't be afraid to ask questions afterwards and try to talk to a few of the students for their perspectives.

If students have their favorite teachers, teachers have their favorite schools. We checked with education administrators to come up with this

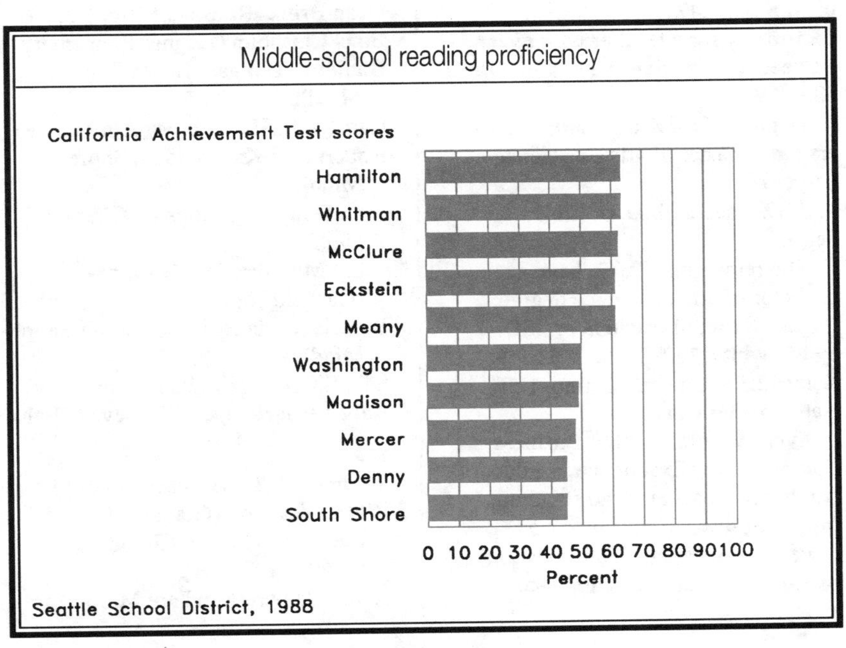

Crime in the high schools

	Ballard High	Cleveland High	Franklin High	Garfield High	Nathan Hale High
Assault	11	13	11	21	12
Drugs	9	4	8	8	5
Vandalism	8	17	3	3	4
Weapons	1	NA	5	5 (1 gun)	3
Total cases	95	90	41	85	39

list of schools considered plums by the city's future teachers:
Garfield High School
Gatzert Elementary
Laurelhurst Elementary
Lawton Elementary
Roosevelt High School
Viewlands Elementary
Wedgwood Elementary
Whitworth Elementary

TEACHER FACTS

Wages: Beginning wage for a Seattle School district teacher with a B.A. or B.S.: $18,304.

A beginning teacher with an M.A. or M.S.: $21,471.

Top pay for a teacher with over 13 years of experience and a Ph.D.: $37,859.

Degrees: 36.2% of Seattle teachers have master of arts or science degrees.

1.5% have a Ph.D. or Ed.D. degree.

The remaining 62.3% have a bachelor of arts or science degree.

Racial mix of teachers in SSD: 69.8% white, 14.5% black, 11.9% Asian, 2.3% Chicano Latino, 1.5% Native American.

Every year the Seattle Business Committee for Excellence in Education honors teachers who stand out from the crowd. Those who've received the Excellence in Education award in the last five years, listed with the schools where they taught when the award was given, are:

1985

Dawnmarie Cooper (Whitman Middle)
Beatrice Cox (South Shore Middle)
Ramona Curtis (Northgate Elementary)
Kay Doces (Decatur Elementary)
Lori Eickelberg (South Shore Middle)
Emmett Kinkade (Cleveland High)
Akiko Kurose (Laurelhurst Elementary)
Vernon Oshiro (McClure Middle)
Loretta Smithburg (Rainier Beach High)
Donald Tredo (Cooper Elementary)

1986

Dean Brink (Roosevelt High)
Ethel Chisholm (Hughes Elementary)
Daniel L. Dungan (South Shore Middle)
Carolyn R. Hall (Gypsy Alternative)
Robert Earl Knatt (South Shore Middle)
John Douglas Livingston (Franklin High)
Craig McIntyre MacGowan (Garfield High)
Rosalie Maria Romano (South Shore Middle)
Saki Shimizu (Kimball Elementary)
Ruben Van Kempen (Roosevelt High)

1987

Yvonne E. Carr (Roosevelt High)
Rita Concannon (Graham Hill Elementary: Early Childhood Education Center)
Helene Down (McClure Middle)
David W. Dwyer (McClure Middle)
Steve M. Hansen (Minor Elementary)
Norman L. Hollingshead (Whitworth Elementary)
Lillian Horita (Graham Hill Elementary)
Marcellea J. Mihailov (Rainier Beach High)
Carole Rindal (AE–2 Decatur Elementary)
Richard W. Thompson (Ingraham High)

1988

Ivan R. Ellis (Nathan Hale High)
Andrew J. Harper (Sacajawea Elementary)
Kathryn M. Jolly (Beacon Hill Elementary)
Lynn Knell-Jones (Franklin High)
John Y. Nakamura (Whitworth Elementary)
Thomas L. Pogreba (Ingraham High)
Nancy I. Scranton, Ph.D. (South Shore Middle)
Terri L. Skjei (Sacajawea Elementary)
Catherine Smullyan (Summit K–12 Alternate School)
Priscilla Ellen Trush (Green Lake Elementary)

1989

Karalyn Gates (Cooper Elementary)
Jane Goetz (Sacajawea Elementary)
Yolanda Gonzalez (B.F. Day Elementary)
Doreen R. Hamilton (Rainier Beach Elementary)
Bettye L.C. Jordan (Olympic View Elementary)

	Ingraham High	Rainier Beach	Roosevelt High	Chief Sealth	West Seattle High
Assault	11	10	7	9	5
Drugs	5	9	8	5	5
Vandalism	12	2	13	2	3
Weapons	4 (2 guns)	6 (1 gun)	3	4 (1 shotgun)	4 (1 gun)
Total cases	120	55	76	35	46

Figures are 88-89, total is total security cases, including arson, theft, trespassing, etc.

Source: Seattle Public School Security Office

Bruce Katka (Summit K–12 Alternative)
Joan Marie Northfield (Nathan Hale High)
Janice Sherwood (Coe Elementary)
William C. Towner (Kimball Elementary)
Sallie Williams (South Shore Middle)

1990
Wanda Breaux (Adams Elementary)
Judy Johnston (Arbor Heights Elementary)
Jenifer Lynne Katahira (Madrona Elementary)
Ken Lee (Ballard High)
Wanda Faye Lofton (Graham Hill Elementary)
Lucretia Robinson (Chief Sealth High)
Jay Sasnett (Washington Middle)
Zoa Marie Shumway (Whitworth Elementary)
Diane Tourville (Rainier Beach High)
Michael Wiater (NOVA Alternative High)

Three tell their stories

In the end, no matter what the system for getting a child into a particular school, it falls upon the parents to get around the system if it doesn't work for them. In the fall of 1989 parents used unique methods to deal with school district bureaucracy.

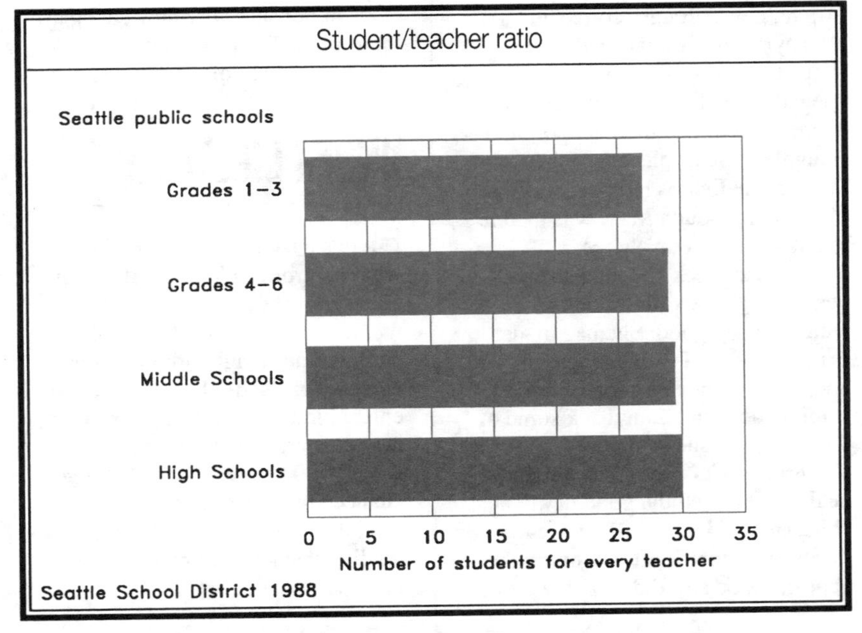

Helen Stevens: Helen Stevens is convinced that only luck has an effect on what happens to families in the Seattle school system.

She stayed up nights until 2 a.m. crying, wondering how she could get her children, a son in kindergarten and a daughter in second grade, to be assigned to the same school. Owen was assigned to Sacajawea and Gabby to Beacon Hill. Stevens wanted them in Olympic View.

She appealed the assignments on the basis that siblings should be able to attend the same school. Appeals were denied, and board members told her they had no power to change the assignment.

After that, she called every school board member often, phoning their homes sometimes as early as 7 a.m. She phoned the governor, appeared on television, and spoke to newspapers to have her case heard. "None of it made a difference," she says. Days before school was going to start she got a commitment from the district to have both children attend Beacon Hill. The next day, the kindergarten teacher from Olympic View called to say another kindergarten was added. Then the principal called to inform Stevens about a combination second/third-grade class with room. In the meantime Sacajawea's principal called to say there was room for Stevens's daughter after all.

But the principals' pleadings with district administrators went unheeded. Principals didn't have the power,

Tips for parents from parents for getting through the maze:

- **Request a hearing.**
- **Turn in applications on time.**
- **To expand your options, have your child tested for special programs.**
- **Talk to more than one person.**
- **Don't take no for an answer.**
- **Don't wait for people to call you back. Keep calling them.**
- **Refuse to leave the office until you get who or what you want.**
- **Get to know a school board member.**
- **Get to know the principal at the school of your choice.**
- **Talk frequently with staff at Parent Information Centers or the student placement office and talk with as many staffers as possible.**
- **Don't whine. It doesn't help to tell employees that your child's needs can't be met anywhere else than that specific classroom or school.**
- **Don't threaten to take your child out of the system. Promise instead to stick around and be a problem.**
- **Understand "tie breaker" rules, i.e., siblings in the same program, distance from school, etc.**
- **Go public. Be visible and loud with your complaints and concerns.**
- **Be persistent.**

Stevens was told, to place students in their schools.

The news from Olympic View was good, though, and the two children ended up, after all, going to school together.

Mary Leloo: A friend of Mary Leloo's, who happened to be a teacher in the Seattle School district, recommended that Leloo shame the administration so the powers that be might change their minds about sending her children to a school that didn't make her list of top five choices.

Leloo called the teacher in tears because the district assigned a whole group of children who had attended Martin Luther King Elementary to Beacon Hill. Leloo wanted her boy and girl, both in first grade, to attend either Sacajawea or Olympic View. That was her decision after visiting 28 different first grades.

"She told me, 'Draw attention to yourself and let people know what these people did to you,'" Leloo recalled. So one Tuesday night she left her dinner guests at home, packed up some sleeping bags and her three children, and set up camp in front of district headquarters.

The TV cameras arrived shortly thereafter, followed by newspaper photographers and reporters. A teacher who saw her story on the 11 p.m. news brought coffee and a little sympathy around midnight. When the administration building opened early the next morning, staff members confided their support and smuggled sweet rolls out to the family. The Leloos left peacefully at 10:30 a.m., though Mary was unable to talk to anyone in charge.

The next week she filed an appeal, though she didn't think it would do any good. She had made her statement. "I wanted them to know this [administration building] is mine too. I'm taking back some of the territory," she said.

Three weeks after filing her appeal she received the good news: her children could attend Sacajawea.

Several months after winning the appeal, Leloo still didn't know the reason the district changed its mind. "I knew several people who had better reasons, really, than I did, and they lost their appeals."

Stephanie Wilson: Stephanie Wilson left careful instructions with her mother to sign up the Wilson twins while she was out of the country during registration. The grandmother listed Hay Elementary, the Wilson's neighborhood school, as the family's first choice, followed by three other schools.

When the Wilsons received their assignment in August it wasn't what they expected or wanted at all: Brighton Elementary was their last choice.

So Stephanie Wilson began a phone campaign. "I called every office every day," she says. She phoned the Parent Information Center, the Student Placement Office, and the Zone II office religiously. The most common responses were "I don't know" and "The computers are down."

In the meantime Wilson put her children on the waiting list at Hay and filed an appeal with the district, which she lost. She kept her children out of school for about three weeks.

Then the phone call came from the Zone II office. Her boy and girl could attend Hay after all.

"I'm not sure why they changed their minds," says Wilson. "I think persistence paid off."

UNDER CONTROL

Here's a short primer explaining what controlled choice is all about:

Clusters: These are groupings of five to eight elementary schools, including your neighborhood school.

Elementary school: As your child enters kindergarten or comes into a new cluster, you can pick which school you desire, and there's a good chance you'll get your first choice; after that, the child is able to keep attending that school until graduation to middle school.

Middle School: Your cluster is expanded to include two middle schools, including the one closest to your home. You can choose which one you want when your child enters sixth grade, with chances of getting your first choice dependent upon racial balance.
High School: Your cluster expands again to include two high schools; the same admissions procedure applies.
Zones: The city is divided into three zones, each of which is run as a somewhat autonomous subdistrict with its own assistant superintendent.
Application deadlines for choosing your school: For elementary schools, February 23; middle schools and high schools, March 30.
More information: The district has three Parent Information Centers, or PICs:

Northwest PIC
11530 12th Ave. NE
281-6989

Southeast PIC
4724 Rainier Ave. S
286-4581

Southwest PIC
5950 Delridge Way SW
281-6998
PIC hours: Monday, Wednesday 12–7 p.m.; Tuesday, Thursday, Friday, 9 a.m.–6 p.m.

SCHOOL DISTRICT RESOURCE LIST

The Seattle School Board of Directors meets two Wednesdays a month, usually in the Administrative and Service Center auditorium, 815 Fourth Avenue N. Call the Board office, 281-6102, for date and time or to contact a board member.

Members of the School Board, who serve four-year terms, are:
Ellen Roe (District 1)
524-2751
Marilyn S. Smith (District 2)
587-6595
Connie Sidles (District 3)
522-7513
Amy Hagopian (District 4)
286-4596
Michael Preston (District 5)
322-6640
Kenneth Eastlack (District 6)
286-4552
Al Sugiyama (District 7)
723-2286
Superintendent: William M. Kendrick
Office, 281-6100

Other school district resources

School District Archives
281-6564
Call for appointment.

Bilingual Ed office
298-7970

Boren School Book Center
5950 Delridge Way SW
762-4984
Free books for low-income students

Dropouts
281-6777
Outreach/intake unit for dropouts.

Drug/alcohol program
298-7060

Gifted students
298-7940
Info on advanced placement.
Free books for low-income students, located at Boren School.

Facilities office
281-6374

Food services
281-6335

Hearing office
281-6645
To appeal district decisions regarding your child.

Homework hotline, 281-MATH
Monday thru Thursday, 6–8 p.m.
Sponsored by the University of Washington MESA (Math, Engineering, Science Achievement) Program and the district. For help with math homework.

Kindergarten info
281-6355

Parent Teacher Student Association
789-4223
Sponsors parenting workshops, fund raising, etc.

Preschool info
298-7894

Transportation office
281-6900

Student records
281-6569

YET MORE RESOURCES

Educational Referral Services
2222 Eastlake Ave. E
323-1838
A private consulting company matching children, ages 2½–18, to local private and public schools and national boarding schools. Yvonne Jones, director, and Carol Robins, early childhood specialist, handle about 40 requests per month. Fees are between $65 and $75 an hour, with an estimated 2–4 hours per child. Boarding school research and match is $525 flat fee.

Seattle's Child/Eastside Parent
P.O. Box 22578
Seattle, WA 98122
322-2594
Prints a free Education Directory supplement annually.

Citizens Education Center Northwest
105 S Main St.
624-9955
Nonprofit organization dedicated to excellence in public education for all children. Members get use of extensive library on schools, legislative updates, discounts on publications, etc.

Seattle Business Committee for Excellence in Education
P.O. Box 9831
Seattle, WA
363-6906
Group established in 1984 to honor outstanding public school teachers. The committee is comprised of corporate contributors and individuals.

SEATTLE'S PRIVATE SCHOOLS

Please refer to the chart on private schools in this chapter. Seattle has 12,600 students attending its 67 private and parochial elementary and secondary schools. What follows is a representative sampling. In the schools listed, enrollments range from a dozen students to more than 700; some schools base their programs on strongly held religious beliefs, while others have designed curricula based on specific academic theories and methods.

Parents considering private schools have another element to consider: tuition. And, often, waiting lists.

Private schools collect records differently than the public schools do—which accounts for the variations in statistics here.

A note on the charts

The test scores are for 1989 California Achievement Tests. Dropout rates are for 1987–88. All other figures are for the 1988–89 school year and come from school district records.

Information on private schools was collected by Seattle Survival Guide research.

Public high schools

	Ballard High School **1418 NW 65th St.** **281-6010**	**Cleveland High School** **5511 15th Ave. S** **281-6020**	**Franklin High School** **3013 S Mt. Baker Blvd.** **281-6030**
Students	1,148	720	1,187
FTE classroom teachers	31.2	24.4	42.8
Full-time classroom teachers	60	53	55
School built/remodeled	1915/1925/1941/1959	1927/1957	1990
Principal	Raymond Christophersen	Dr. Andres Tangalin	Jim McConnell
Foreign languages offered	French, German, Spanish	French, Japanese, Mandarin, Spanish	Four years of French and Spanish, three of Japanese.
College bound	58%	45%	40%
Hot programs	Academy of Finance, a junior-senior program on career options for 30 qualified students. "Most modern computer lab in SSD." Marketing education program with student store and marketing studies. Proyecto Saber tutoring.	All-city International Focus Magnet, with international education courses incorporated into regular curriculum and specialized classes. Bilingual Orientation Center, serving students new to U.S. National computer link with selected schools throughout the nation who are participating in education reform projects.	Strong humanities program for all-city students; Multi-Arts program; science emphasis for ninth graders; commercial arts program; extensive drama program including touring company; BelCanto choir/vocal ensemble, participation in Law and Society competition; Academy of Finance trains students specializing in business and includes a summer intern program.
Minority students	47.5%	69%	64.4%
Test scores	Reading 55.5% Language Arts 46% Math 59%	Reading 46% Language Arts 45% Math 60%	Reading 66% Language Arts 51% Math 63%
Grade point average	2.31 (last semester, 1988)	2.58	2.33
Discipline	short-term suspensions 8.8% long-term suspensions 6.6% expulsions 1.3%	short-term suspensions 9.3% long-term suspensions 7.9% expulsions 1.6%	short-term suspensions 14.3% long-term suspensions 4.1% expulsions 0.7%
Students below grade level	27.7% (1988–89)	26%	21.9%
Dropout rate	44% (state, 1986–87); 15% (district 1987–88)	37.2% (state), 11% (district)	45% (state), 12% (district)
Popular sports	373 participants in 1988–89; football, wrestling, tennis, track.	321 participants; football, soccer, and basketball.	414 participants; football, track, basketball, swimming. Football team AAA Metro Champs for last two years. Women's basketball to state tournament seven times in last eight years.
Free or reduced-cost lunch	360	206	319
Security incidents	95	90	41
Weapons confiscated	1	4	5
Notable			

	Garfield High School **400 23rd Ave.** **281-6040**	**Ingraham High School** **1819 N 135th St.** **281-6080**	**Nathan Hale High School** **10750 30th Ave. NE** **281-6920**
Students	1,188	1,183	926
FTE classroom teachers	40.8	39.4	31.1
Full-time classroom teachers	54 (1 part-time)	61	73
School built/remodeled	1920/1923/1928	1959	1963/1970/1972
Principal	Perry Wilkins	Ammon McWashington	Tom Lord
Foreign languages offered	French, German, Japanese, Spanish	French, German, Japanese, Spanish	French, Spanish
College bound	60%	55%	60%
Hot programs	Magnet Science Program; includes marine and health science with field trips to Papua New Guinea, Kenya, Great Barrier Reef; music department, with award-winning Jazz Band and Chamber Orchestra; Black literature collection; technical education including commercial kitchen.	Only advanced placement program in district in art; bilingual and newcomer programs; Proyecto Saber tutoring.	Four-year humanities program, with language arts and social studies courses in a two-hour sequence; child and family psychology classes; hands-on technology course; satellite telecommunications.
Minority students	53.8%	54.5%	53.6%
Test scores	Reading 78% Language Arts 61% Math 73%	Reading 58% Language Arts 44% Math 57%	Reading 60% Language Arts 48% Math 58%
Grade point average	2.61	2.41	2.54
Discipline	short-term suspensions 10.5% long-term suspensions 1.4% expulsions 1.4%	short-term suspensions 22.2% long-term suspensions 2.2% expulsions 1.1%	short-term suspensions 6.9% long-term suspensions 2.7% expulsions 0.9%
Students below grade level	20%	25.5%	24.4%
Dropout rate	35.15% (state), 11.2% (district)	33.87% (state), (district) not available	34.31% (state), 7.2% (district)
Popular sports	641 participants; track, football, tennis. Bulldog sports program includes intramural pickleball tournaments and state basketball tournaments; fastest track athletes in district.	474 participants; football, basketball, tennis.	489 participants; tennis, basketball, football. Metro wrestling champs last five years; individual champ in women's cross country in 1988; and state champ in women's individual swimming in 1986; only AA school in the last five years to qualify for district in men's basketball; two-time defending champ in Women's Gold.
Free or reduced-cost lunch	173	330	253
Security incidents	85	120	39
Weapons confiscated	5 (1 gun)	4 (2 guns)	3
Notable	Most National Merit Scholars in the state.		Received National Council of Teachers of English Writing Award nine times in 13 years.

	Rainier Beach High School **8815 Seward Park S** **281-6090**	**Roosevelt High School** **1410 NE 66th St.** **281-6050**	**Chief Sealth High School** **2600 SW Thistle St.** **281-6060**	**West Seattle High School** **4075 SW Stevens St.** **281-6070**
Students	760	1,368	958	871
FTE classroom teachers	28	46.4	30.8	28.6
Full-time classroom teachers	48 (includes 5 special ed, 4 bilingual teachers)	62	46 (part-time: 3)	61
School built/remodeled	1960	1922/1927/1960	1956	1917/1924/1954
Principal	Tom Bailey	Joan Roberson	Joan Butterworth	Sharon L. Green
Foreign languages offered	French, Spanish	French, Latin, Spanish	Spanish and French	French, German, Japanese, Latin, Spanish
College bound	40%	60%	37%	40%
Hot programs	Only Teen Health Center in the district and first in the state to offer on-site services from team of medical professionals; College Into High School Program, offers college credit courses in several subjects; Writing Project; automotive technology and maintenance; Principles of Technology, for careers in engineering and technology; gospel choir; largest speech and debate team in district.	Award-winning concert orchestra, chamber orchestra and jazz band; Computer Team; Hearing Impaired Drama (Talking Hands Players and extensive other drama programs); science seminar; extensive honors and advanced placement program.	Integrated Humanities Course with focus on Pacific Rim and Asian culture, economics,and literature; Mentor Law Program; Shakespeare emphasis in English with annual field trips to Ashland; Feast Program emphasizing baking and catering; Proyecto Saber tutoring.	Gemologist-taught jewelry-making course; computer science.
Minority students	76.5%	40.3%	65.5%	53.5%
Test scores	Reading 42% Language Arts 36.5% Math 49%	Reading 82% Language Arts 69% Math 80%	Reading 40.5% Language Arts 40% Math 48.5%	Reading 46% Language Arts 42% Math 49%
Grade point average	2.56	2.77	2.22	2.33
Discipline	short-term suspensions 13.3% long-term suspensions 4.2% expulsions 2.4%	short-term suspensions 11% long-term suspensions 2.3% expulsions 0.9%	short-term suspensions 14.4% long-term suspensions 4.1% expulsions 0.7%	short-term suspensions 12.4% long-term suspensions 6.6% expulsions 0.9%
Students below grade level	29.3%	16.1%	34.2%	33.8%
Dropout rate	33% (state), 9% (district)	23% (state), 6% (district)	44% (state), 15% (district)	48%, highest in city (state); 15% (district)
Popular sports	295 participants; football, basketball, tennis. Champs in basketball, soccer, swimming, and track.	670 participants; football, basketball, track.	326 participants; football, softball, tennis.	314 participants; football, basketball, tennis.
Free or reduced-cost lunch	220	159	353	346
Security incidents	55	76	35	46
Weapons confiscated	6 (1 gun)	3	4	4 (1 gun)
Notable	Winner of 1988 Sea-King County Economic Development Council's Award for Excellence.	Over 100 seniors earn Presidential Academic Fitness Awards every year.		

Public middle schools

	Asa Mercer Middle School 1600 S Columbian Way 281-6170	South Shore Middle School 8825 Rainier Ave. S 281-6180
Students	890	660
FTE classroom teachers	39	26
Full-time classroom teachers	47	35
School built/remodeled	1957	1973
Principal	Dean Sanders	Dr. Robert Gary
Foreign languages offered	French, Spanish, Chinese (Mandarin)	French and Spanish
Hot programs	Music and vocal	Team approach
Minority students	55.2%	64.2%
Test scores	Reading 75% Language Arts 70% Math 74.5%	Reading 55% Language Arts 57% Math 58%
Grade point average	2.48	2.66
Discipline	short-term suspensions 28.9% long-term suspensions 6.1% expulsions 1.8%	short-term suspensions 13.2% long-term suspensions 4.1% expulsions 0.2%
Students below grade level	20.5%	19.1%
Dropout rate	9.4% (district)	10.8% (district)
Free or reduced-cost lunches	435	358
Sports	None	Strong intramural program before and after school
Security incidents	68	22
Weapons confiscated	3 (2 guns)	3

	Denny Middle School 8402 30th Ave. SW 281-6110	Eckstein Middle School 3003 NE 75th St. 281-6120	Hamilton Middle School 1610 N 41st St. 281-6130
Students	884	1,015	760
FTE classroom teachers	32	35	26
Full-time classroom teachers	43	55	35 (Part-time & ESL: 4)
School built/remodeled	1952	1950/1968	1926/1970
Principal	Joan Allen	Lynn Caldwell	Allen Nakano
Foreign languages offered	French, Spanish	French, German, Japanese, Spanish	Spanish and French
Hot programs	Strong math department (teachers use team approach), bilingual program; Proyecto Saber tutoring.	Satellite and cable television in each classroom; orchestra and band; only middle school with TV and radio studio.	TheatreWorks drama program in conjunction with Seattle Children's Theatre; Proyecto Saber tutoring.
Minority students	58.9%	53.2%	47.5%
Test scores	Reading 45% Language Arts 41% Math 44.5%	Reading 65% Language Arts 61% Math 62%	Reading 71% Language Arts 61% Math 62%
Grade point average	2.41	2.72	2.50
Discipline	short-term suspensions 5.7% long-term suspensions 7% expulsions 1.6%	short-term suspensions 10% long-term suspensions 2.5% expulsions 0.7%	short-term suspensions 16.4% long-term suspensions 5% expulsions 2.1%
Students below grade level	26.7% (1988–89)	23.9%	17.7%
Dropout rate	9% (district)	4.1% (district)	7.9% (district)
Free or reduced-cost lunch	493	395	261
Sports	Intramurals before and after school.	Intramurals after school four nights a week.	After school intramurals four nights a week.
Security incidents	22	22	10
Weapons confiscated	4	4	3 (1 gun)

	Madison Middle School **3429 45th Ave. SW** **281-6140**	**McClure Middle School** **1915 First Ave. W** **281-6150**	**Meany Middle School** **301 21st Ave. E** **281-6160**
Students	854	686	650
FTE classroom teachers	30	27	27
Full-time classroom teachers	37 (Special ed, bilingual: 7)	35	40
School built/remodeled	1929/1931/1972	1964	1902/1945/1951/1955/1962
Principal	John DuGay	Ben Nakagawa	Bruce Hunter
Foreign languages offered	French	French, Japanese, Spanish	Japanese, French, Spanish
Hot programs	Bilingual program, Life Skills class for seventh graders.	Math magnet, science	Science emphasis, English as second language
Minority students	57.8%	57.3%	69.8%
Test scores	Reading 35% Language Arts 34% Math 51%	Reading 62% Language Arts 52% Math 55%	Reading 38% Language Arts 37% Math 49%
Grade point average	2.40	2.65	2.65
Discipline	short-term suspensions 1.9% long-term suspensions 4.9% expulsions 0	short-term suspensions 22.1% long-term suspensions 3.5% expulsions 1.0%	short-term suspensions 12.2% long-term suspensions 1.9% expulsions 0.6%
Students below grade level	14.6%	19.3%	26.3%
Dropout rate	8.2% (district)	9.5% (district)	5.3% (district)
Free or reduced-cost lunches	429	247	195
Sports	After-school intramurals	After-school intramurals	NA
Security incidents	28	25	29
Weapons confiscated	3	3	0

	Washington Middle School **2101 S Jackson St.** **281-6190**	**Whitman Middle School** **9201 15th Ave. NW** **281-6930**
Students	786	1,059
FTE classroom teachers	31	39
Full-time classroom teachers	37	56
School built/remodeled	1964	1959
Principal	John Thorp	Bi Hoa Caldwell
Foreign languages offered	Accelerated French and Japanese, Spanish	French , Spanish
Hot programs	Arts and Industrial Design, band, math-science, high tech	QUESTS & It's your Future (skills for adolescents), strong guidance program
Minority students	43.4%	NA
Test scores	Reading 59% Language Arts 54% Math 52%	Reading Language Arts Math
Grade point average	2.66	2.64
Discipline	short-term suspensions 20.1% long-term suspensions 5.0% expulsions 0.2%	short-term suspensions 25% long-term suspensions 7.1% expulsions 2.1%
Students below grade level	17.8%	NA
Dropout rate	4.4% (district)	4.4% (district)
Free or reduced-cost lunches	346	314
Sports	Some after-school programs	Before and after school
Security incidents	80	17
Weapons confiscated	3	0

Public elementary schools

	Adams Elementary School 6222 28th Ave. NW 281-6210	**Alki Elementary 3010 59th Ave. SW 281-6220**	**Arbor Heights Elementary School 3701 SW 104th St. 281-6230**	**Bagley Elementary School 7821 Stone Ave. N 281-6240**
Students	474	304	239	234
FTE classroom teachers	16	9.5	7	9.5
School built/remodeled	1988	1951/1965	1949	1931
Principal	Joanne Franey	Patricia Sander	Bruce Fowler	Ora Franklin
Hot programs	DISTAR in Kindergarten	Academic Achievement; Early Childhood Model	Academic Academy magnet	Academic Academy magnet
Computers available to students	8 Apple IIe	9	22	4
Minority students	43.8%	55.3%	38%	31.7%
Test scores	Reading 64% Language Arts 60% Math 58%	Reading 71% Language Arts 64% Math 71%	Reading 51% Language Arts 50% Math 56%	Reading 71% Language Arts 75% Math 70.5%
Dropout rate	7% (district)	6.5% (district)	9.2% (district)	8.3% (district)
Students below grade level	18.3%	16.9%	22.6%	16.5%
Free or reduced-cost lunches	178	154	91	64
Discipline	short-term suspensions 0 long-term suspensions 0 expulsions 0	short-term suspensions 0.6% long-term suspensions 0 expulsions 0	short-term suspensions 7.1% long-term suspensions 1.6% expulsions 0	short-term suspensions 1.2% long-term suspensions 0 expulsions 0

	Beacon Hill Elementary School 2025 14th Ave. S 281-6250	**Blaine Elementary School 2550 34th Ave. W 281-6260**	**Brighton Elementary School 4425 S Holly St. 281-6270**	**Broadview Elementary School 13052 Greenwood Ave. N 281-6280**
Students	275	430	218	372
FTE classroom teachers	12.5	14.5	8.5	12
School built/remodeled	1971	1962	1922/1945/1953	1961/1981
Principal	Sonja Hampton	Betty Gray	William Lagreid	Norman Smith
Hot programs	Early Childhood Model, Help One Student to Succeed (HOST), Proyecto Saber tutoring	Math and reading labs, instrumental music	CAMPI, DISTAR in K, Academic Academy magnet	Horizon
Computers available to students	19	6	15 (15 more to be added)	15
Minority students	89.8%	39.9%	80%	49.2%
Test scores	Reading 54% Language Arts 54.5% Math 58%	Reading 74% Language Arts 65% Math 74%	Reading 53% Language Arts 48% Math 44%	Reading 59% Language Arts 48% Math 55%
Dropout rate	5.2% (district)	8.3% (district)	6.5% (district)	5.7% (district)
Students below grade level	19%	16%	17.7%	17.4%
Free or reduced-cost lunches	170	106	142	122
Discipline	short-term suspensions 6.3% long-term suspensions 1.4% expulsions 0	short-term suspensions 0.7% long-term suspensions 0 expulsions 0	short-term suspensions 0.3% long-term suspensions 0 expulsions 0	short-term suspensions 1% long-term suspensions 0 expulsions 0

	Bryant Elementary School **3311 NE 60th St.** **281-6290**	**Coe Elementary School** **2433 Sixth Ave. W** **281-6940**	**Colman Elementary School** **2501 S Irving St.** **281-6603**	**Concord Elementary School** **723 S Concord St.** **281-6320**
Students	393	426	134	290
FTE classroom teachers	11.5	13.5	9	9
School built/remodeled	1926	1906/1973	1989	1914/1971
Principal	Terry Acena	Carl Leatherman	Ed Jefferson	Dr. T.M. Gonzales
Hot programs	Early Childhood Model; World Cultures magnet (focus on Asia)	Private Initiative and Public Education (PIPE) partnership with Seattle Center	DISTAR K-2; Academic Achievement Project; Early Childhood Model, Horizon, Elementary Demonstration Project	World Cultures magnet (focus on Latin America); Academic Achievement Project, Early Childhood Model, Proyecto Saber tutoring
Computers available to students	16	8	0	20
Minority students	48.7%	44%	72.2%	58.4%
Test scores	Reading 65% Language Arts 64% Math 67%	Reading 80.5% Language Arts 77% Math 75%	— (new school)	Reading 40% Language Arts 40% Math 48%
Dropout rate	8.5% (district)	6.2% (district)	—	12.9% (district)
Students below grade level	11.4%	14.2%	NA	22.6%
Free or reduced-cost lunches	147	155	74	175
Discipline	short-term suspensions 0 long-term suspensions 0 expulsions 0	short-term suspensions 1.8% long-term suspensions 0 expulsions 0	—	short-term suspensions 1.1% long-term suspensions 0 expulsions 0

	Cooper Elementary School **5950 Delridge Way SW** **281-6330**	**B.F. Day Elementary School** **3921 Linden Ave. N** **281-6340**	**Dearborn Park Elementary School** **2820 S Orcas St.** **281-6350**	**Dunlap Elementary School** **8621 46th Ave. S** **281-6370**
Students	460	281	222	259
FTE classroom teachers	15	7	9	11
School built/remodeled	1964	1895	1971	1924/1953
Principal	Doug Nuetzmann	Carole Williams	Carmen Tsuboi Chan	John Moffitt
Hot programs	Academic Achievement Project; Early Childhood Model; Proyecto Saber tutoring	World Cultures magnet (focus on Africa); Early Childhood Model	Early Childhood Model	Academic Academy magnet; Early Childhood Model
Computers available to students	7	10	10 IBM	10
Minority students	59.8%	65.4%	75.3%	84%
Test scores	Reading 47% Language Arts 56% Math 56%	Reading 50% Language Arts 46% Math 34%	Reading 59% Language Arts 54% Math 52%	Reading 39% Language Arts 42% Math 42%
Dropout rate	4.2% (district)	5.7% (district)	2.9% (district)	8.5% (district)
Students below grade level	20.4%	11.4%	17.7%	17.2%
Free or reduced-cost lunches	281	162	102	163
Discipline	short-term suspensions 4.2% long-term suspensions 0 expulsions 0.6%	short-term suspensions 1.2% long-term suspensions 0 expulsions 0.3%	short-term suspensions 5.1% long-term suspensions 0.4% expulsions 0	short-term suspensions 3.9% long-term suspensions 0.3% expulsions 0.3%

	Emerson Elementary School 9709 60th Ave. S 281-6380	**Fairmount Park 3800 SW Findlay 281-6390**	**Gatewood Elementary School 4320 SW Myrtle St. 281-6950**	**Gatzert Elementary School 1301 E Yesler Way 281-6410**
Students	310	315	215	345
FTE classroom teachers	11	12	6.5	10
School built/remodeled	1909/1930	1963	1910 (new school opens fall, 1991)	1988
Principal	Ed James	Vicki Yee	Theresa Marie Floyd	Robert A. Bass Sr.
Hot programs	Academic Academy magnet; Early Childhood Model	NA	DISTAR in K	Academic Achievement program; Early Childhood Model; will add Academic Academy magnet program for 1990-91 school year.
Computers available to students	30	17	12	12
Minority students	78.7%	40.7%	41.6%	77.2%
Test scores	Reading 41% Language Arts 37% Math 42%	Reading 56% Language Arts 49% Math 54%	Reading 56% Language Arts 55% Math 49%	Reading 41% Language Arts 63% Math 55%
Dropout rate	3.8% (district)	4.6% (district)	7.9% (district)	8.1% (district)
Students below grade level	13.9%	22.6%	25.7%	12.1%
Free or reduced-cost lunches	125	126	87	192
Discipline	short-term suspensions 2.1% long-term suspensions 0 expulsions 0	short-term suspensions 0 long-term suspensions 0 expulsions 0	short-term suspensions 4.2% long-term suspensions 0.4% expulsions 0	short-term suspensions 0 long-term suspensions 0 expulsions 0.4%

	Graham Hill Elementary School 5149 S Graham St. 281-6430	**Green Lake Elementary School 2400 N 65th St. 281-6440**	**Greenwood Elementary School 144 NW 80th St. 281-6450**	**Hawthorne Elementary School 4100 39th S 281-6664**
Students	246	319	318	381
FTE classroom teachers	12.5	11.5	12.5	12.5
School built/remodeled	1960	1970	1909/1921	1989
Principal	Margaret Reeder	Harvey Deutsch	Joanna Cairns	John Morefield
Hot programs	Academic Achievement; Horizon; Early Childhood Model	Artist-in-Residence, Arts specialist	Math Challenge (new); Proyecto Saber tutoring	Early Childhood Model; Elementary Demonstration Project
Computers available to students	28	8	4	25
Minority students	72.2%	43.2%	47.1%	63.6%
Test scores	Reading 51% Language Arts 45% Math 49%	Reading 74% Language Arts 69% Math 70%	Reading 59.5% Language Arts 59% Math 59%	— (new)
Dropout rate	9.5% (district)	3.8% (district)	8.8% (district)	—
Students below grade level	15.1%	6.3%	23.9%	—
Free or reduced-cost lunches	128	117	146	187
Discipline	short-term suspensions 2.6% long-term suspensions 0 expulsions 0	short-term suspensions 3.1% long-term suspensions 0 expulsions 0	short-term suspensions 0 long-term suspensions 0 expulsions 0	—

	Hay Elementary School 201 Garfield St. 281-6460	High Point Elementary School 6760 34th Ave. SW 281-6470	Highland Park Elementary School 1012 SW Trenton St. 281-6480	Kimball Elementary School 3200 23rd Ave. S 281-6870
Students	407	403	441	430
FTE classroom teachers	13.5	12.5	15.5	17.5
School built/remodeled	1989	1988	1921/1926/1936	1971
Principal	Evette Mardesich	Dave Ward	Venus Placer-Barber	Victoria Foreman
Hot programs	Early Childhood Model	Early Childhood Model, Proyecto Saber tutoring	World Cultures magnet (focus on Western Europe), Proyecto Saber tutoring	Open concept class
Computers available to students	18	18	12	8
Minority students	36.7%	66.1%	46.8%	64.4%
Test scores	Reading 64% Language Arts 58% Math 69%	Reading 45.5% Language Arts 56% Math 56%	Reading 53% Language Arts 44% Math 57.5%	Reading 61% Language Arts 54% Math 59.5%
Dropout rate	5.3% (district)	7.7% (district)	8.4% (district)	2.4% (district)
Students below grade level	18.3%	18.2%	13.5%	12.7%
Free or reduced-cost lunches	101	301	190	167
Discipline	short-term suspensions 0.2% long-term suspensions 0 expulsions 0	short-term suspensions 0 long-term suspensions 0 expulsions 0	short-term suspensions 1.1% long-term suspensions 0.4% expulsions 0	short-term suspensions 0.7% long-term suspensions 0.2% expulsions 0

	Martin Luther King Elementary School 3201 E Republican St. 281-6510	Lafayette Elementary School 2645 California Ave. SW 281-6520	Latona Elementary School 401 NE 42nd St. 281-6530	Laurelhurst Elementary School 4530 46th Ave. NE 281-6540
Students	172	431	139	371
FTE classroom teachers	6	15.5	11.5	12.5
School built/remodeled	1913/1958	1950/1953	1906/1918	1929/1950
Principal	Iva (Pat) Tolliver	James Abernethy	Elizabeth Berg	Ken Seno
Hot programs	Early Childhood Model	Horizon	Alternative Elementary 3	MultiArts magnet; bilingual center
Computers available to students	16	7	5	18
Minority students	72.9%	44.6%	38.1%	39.4%
Test scores	Reading 61% Language Arts 63% Math 68%	Reading 57% Language Arts 54% Math 55%	Reading 68% Language Arts 58.5% Math 63%	Reading 81% Language Arts 77% Math 81%
Dropout rate	2.6% (district)	6.4% (district)	2.5% (district)	0.8% (district)
Students below grade level	17.7%	18.7%	14.8%	12.7%
Free or reduced-cost lunches	87	128	42	82
Discipline	short-term suspensions 2.2% long-term suspensions 0.7% expulsions 0	short-term suspensions 0 long-term suspensions 0 expulsions 0	short-term suspensions 1% long-term suspensions 0 expulsions 0	short-term suspensions 0.3% long-term suspensions 0 expulsions 0

	Lawton Elementary School 3901 W Dravus St. 281-6550	**Leschi Elementary School 135 32nd Ave. 281-6560**	**Lowell Elementary School 1058 E Mercer St. 281-6570**	**Loyal Heights Elementary School 2511 NW 80th St. 281-6580**
Students	225	358	315	389
FTE classroom teachers	8	13	8	13.5
School built/remodeled	1990	1988	1911/1960	1931/1946
Principal	William Johnson	Will Roberson	M.C. Simmons	Thomas R. Slawson
Hot programs	Early Childhood Model; Academic Academy magnet	CAMPI, DISTAR in K, Horizon	DISTAR K-5	DISTAR K-2
Computers available to students	18	8	17	21
Minority students	38.7%	74.3%	67.4%	39.4%
Test scores	Reading 52% Language Arts 49.5% Math 49%	Reading 42% Language Arts 40% Math 38.5%	Reading 58.5% Language Arts 55% Math 59%	Reading 76% Language Arts 70% Math 71%
Dropout rate	7.9% (district)	4.6% (district)	11.2% (district)	2.5% (district)
Students below grade level	9.4%	15.8%	17.9%	10%
Free or reduced-cost lunches	66	168	170	98
Discipline	short-term suspensions 1.1% long-term suspensions 0 expulsions 0	short-term suspensions 1.6% long-term suspensions 0 expulsions 0	short-term suspensions 0 long-term suspensions 0 expulsions 0	short-term suspensions 0.6% long-term suspensions 0 expulsions 0

	Madrona Elementary School 1121 33rd Ave. 281-6590	**Maple Elementary School 4925 Corson Ave. S 281-6960**	**McGilvra Elementary School 1617 38th Ave. E 281-6610**	**Minor Elementary School 18th & East Union Streets 281-6620**
Students	447	413	231	312
FTE classroom teachers	19.5	15.5	8	12
School built/remodeled	1917/1961	1971	1910/1942/1972	1890/1941/1960
Principal	Margie Kates	Lynn Fuller	James Oftebro	Dr. Karen Ho'o
Hot programs	Early Childhood Model	World Cultures magnet (funding pending: focus on Latin America)	Music program	CAMPI; Early Childhood Model; Academic Achievement Project; Academic Academy magnet
Computers available to students	35	9	2	55
Minority students	60%	61.9%	58.4%	73.4%
Test scores	Reading 50% Language Arts 43% Math 42%	Reading 59% Language Arts 63% Math 63%	Reading 62% Language Arts 59% Math 55%	Reading 47% Language Arts 49% Math 54%
Dropout rate	7.9% (district)	3.2% (district)	4.7% (district)	5.1% (district)
Students below grade level	21.4%	13.2%	14.1%	14.5%
Free or reduced-cost lunches	139	139	91	184
Discipline	short-term suspensions 1.2% long-term suspensions 0 expulsions 0.2%	short-term suspensions 0 long-term suspensions 0 expulsions 0	short-term suspensions 2.3% long-term suspensions 0.5% expulsions 0	short-term suspensions 0.3% long-term suspensions 0 expulsions 0

	Montlake Elementary School 2409 22nd Ave. E 281-6860	**Muir Elementary School 3301 S Horton St. 281-6630**	**North Beach Elementary School 9018 24th Ave. NW 281-6640**	**Northgate Elementary School 11725 First Ave. NE 281-6650**
Students	251	232	251	176
FTE classroom teachers	8.5	10.5	9	9.5
School built/remodeled	1913	1910/1924/1971	1958	1953/1956
Principal	La Vaun Dennett	Harry Nelson	Kathleen Lindsey	Dorothy Woods
Hot programs	Computer classes, art, special-ed students integrated into regular curriculum, Schools for the 21st Century grantee	CAMPI; DISTAR K-2; Horizon; Early Childhood Model	Chapter 1 for students needing extra help	DISTAR in K
Computers available to students	18	18	14	25
Minority students	44%	60.6%	36.3%	49.1%
Test scores	Reading 60% Language Arts 42.5% Math 62%	Reading 59% Language Arts 46% Math 49%	Reading 76% Language Arts 76.5% Math 79%	Reading 51% Language Arts 51% Math 46%
Dropout rate	3.8% (district)	5.0% (district)	4.8% (district)	6.7% (district)
Students below grade level	7.7%	7.8%	11.2%	16.4%
Free or reduced-cost lunches	61	101	39	114
Discipline	short-term suspensions 0 long-term suspensions 0 expulsions 0	short-term suspensions 0 long-term suspensions 0 expulsions 0	short-term suspensions 0 long-term suspensions 0 expulsions 0	short-term suspensions 1.4% long-term suspensions 0 expulsions 0.9%

	Olympic Hills Elementary School 13018 20th Ave. NE 281-6660	**Olympic View Elementary School 504 NE 95th St. 281-6670**	**Rainier View Elementary School 11650 Beacon Ave. S 281-6680**	**Rogers Elementary School 4030 NE 109th St. 281-6690**
Students	307	408	203	313
FTE classroom teachers	12	16	8	11.5
School built/remodeled	1954	1989	1961	1956
Principal	Nancy Chin	Bob Stone	Lillie Brown	Lyle G. Staley
Hot programs	None	Early Childhood Model	DISTAR in K, Early Childhood Model	Early Childhood Model
Computers available to students	15	21	6	4
Minority students	49.3%	37.2%	82.6%	39.9%
Test scores	Reading 56% Language Arts 53% Math 54%	Reading 70% Language Arts 60% Math 63%	Reading 37% Language Arts 38% Math 44%	Reading 61% Language Arts 56% Math 59%
Dropout rate	2.4% (district)	3.5% (district)	5.1% (district)	4.5% (district)
Students below grade level	12.2%	16.3%	15.6%	13.7%
Free or reduced-cost lunches	98	119	93	110
Discipline	short-term suspensions 5.9% long-term suspensions 0 expulsions 0.3%	short-term suspensions 0.3% long-term suspensions 0 expulsions 0	short-term suspensions 0 long-term suspensions 0 expulsions 0	short-term suspensions 0 long-term suspensions 0 expulsions 0

	Roxhill Elementary School 9430 30th Ave. SW 281-6980	**Sacajawea Elementary School 9501 20th Ave. NE 281-6710**	**Sanislo Elementary School 1812 SW Myrtle St. 281-6730**	**Schmitz Park Elementary School 5000 SW Spokane St. 281-6740**
Students	309	285	331	337
FTE classroom teachers	10.5	11.5	11.5	11.5
School built/remodeled	1959	c. 1950	1970	1962
Principal	Rodrigo L. Barron	Beverly Walker	Don Damon	Joan Armitage
Hot programs	Music, computer lab, developmental preschool and kindergarten, Proyecto Saber tutoring	Early Childhood Model	Open-concept classrooms; SCATS (aerobic and circus acts performing group); Proyecto Saber tutoring	Chapter 1; special education; science and computer teacher
Computers available to students	16	17	6	8
Minority students	46.1%	28.5%	53.8%	39.6%
Test scores	Reading 43% Language Arts 46% Math 44%	Reading 64% Language Arts 59% Math 61%	Reading 55% Language Arts 59% Math 59%	Reading 64% Language Arts 63% Math 74%
Dropout rate	10.4% (district)	2.7% (district)	1.2% (district)	10.1% (district)
Students below grade level	17.3%	21.6%	22.8%	13.6%
Free or reduced-cost lunches	147	64	138	99
Discipline	short-term suspensions 0 long-term suspensions 0 expulsions 0	short-term suspensions 0.4% long-term suspensions 0 expulsions 0	short-term suspensions 0.8% long-term suspensions 0 expulsions 0	short-term suspensions 0 long-term suspensions 0 expulsions 0

	Stevens Elementary School 1242 18th Ave. E 281-6760	**Van Asselt Elementary School 7201 Beacon Ave. S 281-6780**	**View Ridge Elementary School 7047 50th Ave. NE 281-6790**	**Viewlands Elementary School 10525 Third Ave. NW 281-6990**
Students	367	382	505	434
FTE classroom teachers	12.5	12	16	16
School built/remodeled	1906/1928	1862/1907/1951	1948	1953
Principal	Karen Kodama	William Cooke	Teofilo Cadiente	Lois Freeborn
Hot programs	The Option Program at Stevens (TOPS); Excel (marine science)	Early Childhood Model; Academic Academy magnet (1990-91)	Classes for hearing impaired and dyspraxic students	Bilingual; science
Computers available to students	2	27	17	10
Minority students	46.5%	83.4%	49.7%	46%
Test scores	Reading 71% Language Arts 60% Math 65%	Reading 42.5% Language Arts 54% Math 53%	Reading 82% Language Arts 83% Math 82%	Reading 56% Language Arts 56% Math 57%
Dropout rate	3.9% (district)	7.5% (district)	2.5% (district)	2.8% (district)
Students below grade level	11.8%	13.5%	9.4%	12.8%
Free or reduced-cost lunches	92	272	132	190
Discipline	short-term suspensions 3.6% long-term suspensions 0 expulsions 0.3%	short-term suspensions 0.2% long-term suspensions 0 expulsions 0	short-term suspensions 0 long-term suspensions 0 expulsions 0	short-term suspensions 1.7% long-term suspensions 0.4% expulsions 0.4%

	Wedgwood Elementary School 2720 NE 85th St. 281-6810	**West Woodland Monroe Elementary School 1810 NW 65th St. 281-6820**	**Whittier Elementary School 7501 13th Ave. NW 281-6830**	**Whitworth 5215 46th Ave. S 281-6840**	**Wing Luke Elementary School 3701 S Kenyon St. 281-6850**
Students	348	467	285	479	220
FTE classroom teachers	11.5	13.5	10.5	18	9
School built/remodeled	1954	New school, fall 1991	1908/1928	cq	1971
Principal	Cheryl Leeson	James Alexander	Clarence L. Brown	Gary Tubbs	Sybil Brown
Hot programs	Horizon	Early Childhood Model	Horizon	Chapter 1; handicapped program	Early Childhood Model
Computers available to students	16	18	19	25	10
Minority students	42.7%	44.7%	38.6%	67.2%	75.3%
Test scores	Reading 61.5% Language Arts 51% Math 61.5%	Reading 66% Language Arts 65% Math 66.5%	Reading 59% Language Arts 51.5% Math 58.5%	Reading 54% Language Arts 49% Math 59%	Reading 46% Language Arts 49% Math 44%
Dropout rate	4.6% (district)	2% (district)	15.2% (district)	4% (district)	4.6% (district)
Students below grade level	11.4%	13.3%	23%	14.4%	18.1%
Free or reduced-cost lunches	64	216	80	187	122
Discipline	short-term suspensions 0.4% long-term suspensions 0 expulsions 0	short-term suspensions 0.9% long-term suspensions 0 expulsions 0	short-term suspensions 9.6% long-term suspensions 0 expulsions 0	short-term suspensions 1.5% long-term suspensions 0 expulsions 0	short-term suspensions 2.3% long-term suspensions 0 expulsions 0.3%

Source for above: Seattle School District records, school surveys

Private schools

	Bertschi School **2227 10th Ave. E** **Seattle, WA 98102** **324-5476**	**Blanchet High School** **8200 Wallingford Ave. N** **Seattle, WA 98103** **527-7711**	**Bush School** **405 36th Ave. E** **Seattle, WA 98112** **322-7978**
Type	Preschool–5	High school, coed, Roman Catholic	K–12, coed
Enrollment	130	760	535
Class size	14–18 (larger classes in older age groups)	26	Varies
Minority students	16.1%	8.2%	9.6%
Teacher/student ratio	1:14–18	1:26	1:9
Academic emphasis	Strong academic emphasis; children work at own speed in classroom; group work encouraged; "We encourage the kids to takerisks"	College preparatory	College preparatory, experiential learning
Sports	PE teacher; after-school intramural sports (swimming, gymnastics, soccer, basketball, T-ball, baseball) and ballet	All boys and girls sports, Metro AAA League	All interscholastic sports, Sea-Tac B League, all non-public schools
Waiting list	For all grades	None	Some grades in lower school and middle school
Tuition (annual unless noted)	Preschool $4,800; K–5 $5,100	Catholics $2,750; non-Catholics $3,300	$6,204–$8,097
College bound	—	85%	100%
Application procedure	Apply by March 1 for coming year; $40 application fee; preschool and first-grade children visit school, meet with teacher and school director in small class situation. Older children sit in on classroom for a day. No formal testing. Notification by March 30.	Written application at beginning of year or semester breaks	Parent interviews, academic testing, student visit required; administers joint admissions test with four other private schools; applicant is guided by a Bush student, talks with teachers; reactions are solicited from student guides in evaluating prospective students; major entry points, grades K, 6, and 9; looking for students who are responsible, for commitment to the school, sense of personal worth, desire to do well.
Notes		Teachers are mostly lay professionals; religious instruction required of all students.	Students must do a community service, sport, or theater "action module" to graduate; much personal freedom; some students find it difficult to adjust.

	Epiphany School **3710 Howell St.** **Seattle, WA 98122** **323-9011**	**Evergreen School** **for Gifted Children** **15202 Meridian Ave. N** **Seattle, WA 98133** **364-2650**	**Holy Names Academy** **728 21st Ave. E** **Seattle, WA 98112** **323-4272**
Type	Preschool–6	Preschool–8	High school, girls, Roman Catholic
Enrollment	131	260	267
Class size	Preschool, 12 students per class; K–6, 16–18 per class	12–16, depending on age and grade level	Varies
Minority students	14.2%	14.2%	34.3%
Teacher/student ratio	1:12–18	1:12	1:17
Academic emphasis	Traditional nonsectarian elementary school	Individual curriculum for gifted students encouraging self-motivation and problem-solving; writing and computer skills; French, German, and Chinese; global awareness; science; music and drama; enrichment activities.	College preparatory
Sports	PE instructor; new gym	PE for younger students, competitive soccer, tennis, cross-country running, track and field, and baseball for ages 9 and up	Very active program—track, soccer, volleyball, basketball, backpacking, hiking, cross-country skiing; new gym
Waiting list	NA	Nearly all grades	Yes, turned away freshmen in 1989
Tuition (annual unless noted)	NA	Preschool $2,753 plus $130 for supplies; 4- to 8-year-olds $5,321; 9–11 $5,621; 12–13 $5,921	$3,000
College bound	—	A small number (two last year) go on to the University of Washington's Early Entrance Program.	90%
Application procedure	Open house for prospective parents (late January); application, student visit; applicants in grades 1 and up are tested. "With younger grades, the sooner [you apply] the better"; rolling applications begin January; grades 1–3 most competitive for entry.	IQ testing required for ages 4 and above; application due February 28 for fall entrance; student visit; open houses and tours available.	Interview with director, principal, vice principal; testing (twice a year); meet with committee.
Notes	Instruction in French, music, art, and computers; also have 3 full-time tutors for children with language-skills difficulties.	Individual and small-group instruction; non-graded curriculum.	Emphasizes mind, body, and spirit equally.

	Islamic School of Seattle **720 25th Ave.** **Seattle, WA 98112** **329-5735**	**King School** **19531 Dayton Ave. N** **Seattle, WA 98133** **546-7258**	**King School** **19303 Fremont Ave. N** **Seattle, WA 98133** **546-7241**
Type	Elementary	K–6	7–12
Enrollment	12	598	500
Class size	Varies	25	20
Minority students	NA	NA	NA
Teacher/student ratio	1:10	1:25	1:12
Academic emphasis	Bilingual education—teaching in Arabic and English; Koran, Islamic religion, social studies from Islamic point of view; stresses pride in heritage.	Regular elementary curriculum with the addition of Bible and chapel.	College preparatory
Sports	Playground sports	PE program	Football, volleyball (Fall); basketball (Winter); track/field, golf (Spring)
Waiting list	None	None	None
Tuition (annual unless noted)	$160/month	Half-day Kindergarten $2,020; Full day Kindergarten $2,895; 1–3 $3,135; 4–6 $3,370	Varies depending on how many children the family has in grades 7–12; 1 student $4,020; 2 students $3,580; 3 students $3,050
College bound	—	95%	4 year, 80%; 2 year, 15%; 95% total
Application procedure	Call office; testing, placement, referral from last school.	Fill out application; $35 application fee; interview; notified if accepted; $135/family registration fee.	Call the office for an application kit; $35 application fee; admissions test, recommendations; if accepted must pay registration fee ($45 of it goes towards first year tuition).
Notes	Primarily foreign students, though started for American Black Muslim community; not equipped to deal with students with special problems.		

	Lakeside Schools **13510 First NE (Middle)** **14050 First NE (Upper)** **Seattle, WA 98125** **368-3600**	**Morningside Academy** **810 18th Ave.** **Seattle, WA 98122** **329-9412**	**Northwest School** **1415 Summit Ave.** **Seattle, WA 98122** **682-7309**
Type	Middle, 5–8; Upper, 9–12	K–12	High school
Enrollment	673	15	225
Class size	Varies	Varies	12-18
Minority students	22.7%	60%	12%
Teacher/student ratio	1:8	1:5	NA
Academic emphasis	College preparatory	Individuals with learning problems; tutoring	College preparatory
Sports	All interscholastic sports, Metro AA league	Swimming	After-school sports (soccer, rowing, basketball, skiing, volleyball), no emphasis on competitive sports
Waiting list	None	None	At some grade levels
Tuition (annual unless noted)	Grades 5–6, $7,330; grades 7–8, $7,990; grades 9–12, $8,590	$5,000	$5,800–$7,050; student-prepared lunches included; kitchen experience is part of curriculum.
College bound	100%	NA	100%
Application procedure	In November for following fall; administers joint admissions tests with four other private schools; 39.9% acceptance rate, no carry-over.	Interview with director; testing	Extensive application process: recommendations, transcripts, tests.
Notes	Class of 1990 Scholastic Aptitude Test (SAT) scores, verbal 574, math 617	Ungraded school, individual progress.	Core curriculum in humanities, international studies, area studies; exchange programs; arts; environmental program.

	O'Dea High School **802 Terry Ave.** **Seattle, WA 98104** **622-6596**	**Perkins Elementary School** **4649 Sunnyside Ave. N** **Seattle, WA 98103** **632-7154**	**St. Joseph School** **700 18th Ave. E** **Seattle, WA 98112** **329-3260**
Type	High school, boys, Roman Catholic, Christian Brothers	1–5	K–8 (half Catholic, half non–Catholic)
Enrollment	415–435	141	560
Class size	25	15–20	Varies by grade, 20–25
Minority students	28.4%	8.5%	23.5%
Teacher/student ratio	NA	1:18	Varies by grade
Academic emphasis	College preparatory	Strong academic emphasis; French, computers, music, and art are part of the daily curriculum.	Arts and sciences
Sports	All boys' sports, Metro AAA League	PE teacher teaches basketball, tennis, and physical fitness. After-school sports through Wallingford Boys and Girls Clubs.	Catholic Youth Program (all sports except football)
Waiting list	No carry-over	Sometimes for first grade	Yes; best chance of entry at kindergarten; most waiting lists are in higher grades.
Tuition (annual unless noted)	Catholics $2,300; non-Catholics $2,652	$4,100 includes $275 enrollment deposit	$2,868; financial aid and parish subsidies (for parishioners) available
College bound	85–90%	Most Perkins students go on to private secondary schools or enter advanced placement programs in Seattle public schools.	
Application procedure	Call school; entrance exam, transcripts.	Make appointment to tour school; open house February; apply by March for the coming year; $275 deposit required with application; notification within two weeks.	Application and interview; process over by end of February.
Notes	SAT scores above average; five National Merit Scholars last year; religious studies and Latin required; most students come from Catholic elementary schools, though this is not a prerequisite.	Perkins accepts a small proportion of children with slight learning or physical disabilities who can be readily assimilated into the classroom and who can adapt to the building's limitations.	Strong music program; good computer lab and computer program; transporta-tion: school owns two vans, buses in about 60 students; most students go on to private or parochial high schools.

	Seattle Academy of Arts and Sciences 1432 15th Ave. Seattle, WA 98112 323-6600	Seattle Country Day School 2619 Fourth Ave. N Seattle, WA 98109 284-6220	Seattle Hebrew Academy 1617 Interlaken Dr. E Seattle, WA 98112 323-5750
Type	Grades 6–12	K–8	Preschool–8
Enrollment	110	247	240
Class size	14–16 students per class	16	16
Minority students	10.1%	6.2%	NA
Teacher/student ratio	1:14–16	1:16	1:16
Academic emphasis	College preparatory	Special education for high IQ children, especially for the creatively gifted	Dual curriculum—complete secular program plus Judaic studies (approximately half-day in each)
Sports	Member of Sea-Tac League; field soccer, basketball, and tennis teams	PE program, intramural sports grades 3–8	Full PE program, including basketball and soccer
Waiting list	Doesn't maintain one	Yes, K–1 levels; large numbers of applications at 2–3 levels; accepts 1 in 3 applicants; tries to direct rejected applicants to alternatives.	None
Tuition (annual unless noted)	Grades 6–8, $7,190; grades 9–12, $7,490 (does not include books)	$5,450; $375 space reservation fee; 1 out of 5 students on partial scholarship	$4,000
College bound	100%		
Application procedure	Written statement, exam, family interview, school visit; administers joint admissions tests with four other private schools; March 15 deadline for fall admission.	Parental visit, student exam (Wechsler Intelligence Scale for Children); recommendations, transcripts, and achievement tests for older students; begin application process October, end mid-March; most openings at K–1 level; $140 application fee.	Letter of application, application filled out by parents; interview; rolling applications; most apply February–April for coming year.
Notes	Balance between structured program and casual relationship between kids and teachers; extensive performing and visual arts program.	Strict profile for acceptance—top 1–3 percent intellectually, plus creative gifts; stresses challenge to imagination, self-discipline for maximum use of gifts, social and emotional maturity; students often go on to Lakeside, Bush, Seattle Prep, and to public high schools with accelerated programs.	Accepts only Jewish students ("While we're an Orthodox Jewish school, we accept children of any Jewish background"); fairly intense academic program; students generally score one to two grades ahead of national norm; students go on to Jewish (Yeshiva High School) and secular private and public high schools.

	Seattle Preparatory School **2400 11th Ave. E** **Seattle, WA 98102** **324-0400**	**Spruce St. School** **411 Yale Ave. N** **Seattle, WA 98109** **621-9211**	**University Preparatory** **8000 25th Ave. NE** **Seattle, WA 98115** **525-2714**
Type	High school, Roman Catholic, Jesuit	K–3	Grades 6–12
Enrollment	606	64	232
Class size	14	16	16 (maximum)
Minority students	17.7%	12%	13.8%
Teacher/student ratio	1:14	NA	1:10 or less
Academic emphasis	College preparatory, religious	Integrated learning with an emphasis on humanities; literature, drama, publish own works with own press.	College prep; traditional liberal arts and sciences with emphasis on writing skills; sciences are lab-oriented.
Sports	Metro AA League; compete in nearly all sports.	Gymnastics, basketball, ball skills, soccer.	Basketball, soccer, cross-country teams compete in Sea-Tac League.
Waiting list	NA	None	Grades 6 and 8
Tuition (annual unless noted)	$3,600	$5,100	Middle school $6,525; high school $6,800; books $200; incidental fee $400
College bound	99–100%	—	95%
Application procedure	No exam; teacher referral and from standard tests; $175 application fee; accepted 180 applications out of 320 in 1989.	Call for information; morning visit; fill out application, $40 application fee; those accepted will be notified by March 30 with acceptance letters; candidates have until April 10 to send back contract with $510 deposit; revolving registration.	March 1 deadline; administers joint admissions tests with four other private schools; visit, interview, and two teacher recommendations; notification by March 30.
Notes	Open house February 4; scholarship exams and financial aid; average SAT scores: 500 verbal, 550 math; endowed school.		

	Villa Academy **5001 NE 50th St.** **Seattle, WA 98105** **524-8885**	**West Seattle Christian School** **4401 42nd Ave. SW** **Seattle, WA 98116** **938-1414**
Type	K–8, Catholic	Preschool–6
Enrollment	344	238
Class size	20	Varies
Minority students	9.6%	9.1%
Teacher/student ratio	NA	1:15
Academic emphasis	General elementary	Christian elementary
Sports	PE program	None
Waiting list	Varies by grade	Rarely
Tuition (annual unless noted)	K–5 $3,525; 6–8 $3,825	Preschool, $457; 1–6, $1,561
College bound		
Application procedure	January; $50 deposit; parent visit; tour; testing	Register in March; interviews with parent and child.
Notes	Three-fourths of all students go on to Seattle Preparatory.	Run by West Seattle Christian Church since 1969; does not accept children with behavior problems.

	Westside Place **144 NE 54th St.** **Seattle, WA 98105** **522-3476**	**Zion Academy** **620 20th Ave. S** **Seattle, WA 98144** **322-2926**
Type	8 to 18 yrs.	Preschool–8
Enrollment	50	450
Class size	8–10	24–27
Minority students	30%	99.1%
Teacher/student ratio	1:8–10	NA
Academic emphasis	Work with students who have average or above-average abilities who have not had success in traditional school setting. Math, history, science, fine arts, wood shop, language arts.	"Open Court" method—heavy emphasis on phonics and Marva Collins' teachings
Sports	PE program	PE and playground sports
Waiting list	None	All grades; 100 on current list
Tuition (annual unless noted)	$7,700	$155/month
College bound	NA	
Application procedure	Call for application and they will direct you through application process.	Interview older students.
Notes	Most students stay in program for two years; capable of graduating students; main goal is to develop academic and social skills so students will have more choices in terms of school placement.	High expectations; parent involvement mandatory; majority go on to private schools; feed-in program with Bush.

CHAPTER 21

IVY LEAGUE, SEATTLE STYLE

UW

RESEARCH

FRATS

BEST CLASSES

COMMUNITY COLLEGES

BRANCH CAMPUSES

PROFESSORS

SORORITIES

BEST COFFEE

CONTINUING ED

Approximately one-fifth of the city's population dons a backpack and treks off daily to an institute of higher education. The city's community colleges alone attract over 56,000 students. The rest of the students are spread over several private universities and colleges and, of course, that denizen of local learnedness, the University of Washington.

Seattle exists in the shadow of the "U-Dub," one of the nation's foremost research institutions but one that remains a well-kept secret outside the state. About 33,675 students are enrolled at the UW at any one time, enjoying the fruits of the 680-acre tree-lined campus with its Gothic-style buildings that truly do have ivy profusely growing on the walls. By way of contrast, there are the angular contemporary buildings; but it's the stately older ones around the quadrangles that set the character of the campus.

Despite its overbearing presence, the UW isn't the only stalwart institute-of-choice for Seattle's residents. There are over 152 private schools teaching general-interest subjects and another 134 teaching business and vocational skills, as well as art, dance, and music skills ad infinitum. There are even schools that teach parachute jumping, knitting, dog training, and foot reflexology.

Whether you are a student or not, local colleges offer opportunities for you. For example, the UW sponsors lectures and performances, and welcomes the public to browse in its libraries and archives.

Many UW professors are involved locally in various seminars and workshops; most will answer questions on the phone about their field. The UW has a great "tickle file" that lists which professor is studying what and how you can reach him or her.

UNIVERSITY OF WASHINGTON

By far the leading educational institution in the city, the UW is a sedate university, with its students leaning more toward conservatism and business majors than social activism. Occasionally there's a demonstration in Red Square, but the square's more likely to house an art exhibit. The biggest uproar in years involving the University was over a male student who crashed a Women's Studies course and accused the professor of bias. He made it to "Oprah Winfrey" and beyond. So much for radicalism.

UW Facts

- The UW was opened November 4, 1861, in downtown Seattle and was moved to its present location in 1895.
- It's the largest single campus institution of higher education in the West, with more than 100 permanent buildings.
- The UW has a library collection of more than 4.5 million volumes.
- The UW sponsors more than 50 study-abroad programs and exchanges in 20 countries.
- Approximately 19.6% of the student body is made up of minorities, with an average of 4,261 Asians per quarter.
- The student body is 48.5% women and 51.5% men.
- 87% of students are state residents; 75% are undergraduates.
- Average age of students is mid-twenties.
- Washington resident tuition per quarter (1990): undergrad $61/credit or $609 full-time (9–18 credits); law, $948 full-time; medical or dental, $1,535 full-time.
- Degrees offered in 16 schools and colleges, and over 100 academic disciplines.
- Schools: Business, Dentistry, Law, Medicine, Nursing, Pharmacy, Public Affairs, Public Health and Community Medicine, Social Work.
- Colleges: Architecture and Urban Planning, Arts and Sciences, Education, Engineering, Forest Resources, Ocean and Fishery Sciences.
- Graduate degees offered in all areas including Library and Information Science.

UW's popular programs by enrollment

Winter Quarter, 1990

Undergraduate:	Arts and Sciences	18,637
	Business	1,441
	Engineering	1,464
Graduate:		
	Arts and Sciences	2,587
	Engineering	1,022
	Medicine	659
	Law School	425
	Dentistry School	202

NOTHING BUT THE BEST

Trends in what to study are as changeable as fashion trends: one day it's a miniskirt, the next ankle-length; one year it's business school, the next English lit. Currently it's arts and sciences in the lead, followed by engineering and business running neck-and-neck.

From outside the school, the word is that the UW's most highly regarded programs are nursing, international studies, business, medical education, rehabilitation medicine, Scandinavian languages and literature, and atmospheric sciences.

NAMES TO NOTE

A few professors who are considered tops in their field as well as popular with their students:
Jon Bridgman (history)
John Butler (business policy)
Stan Chernikoff (geology)
Hans Dehmelt (physics—Nobel Prize winner, 1989)
John Keating (psychology)
Nancy Kenney (psychology)
Willis Konick (comparative lit.)
Don Pember (communications)
Pepper Schwartz (sociology)
Dennis Willows (zoology)

Many students at the UW have a hard go of it at first. It's true that many professors are experts in their fields, but to the lowly student, they are often only the little dots on the other side of the lectern in a huge lecture hall.

Personal contact is often left to graduate-student teaching assistants, many of whom speak English as a second—or third—language.

So to help new students through the maze, here are some tips gathered from old students:

• "The first thing to do is find a parking place." Parking in the U District is definitely a hassle. Cheapest is the Montlake lot ($0.75, $0.25 for carpools), but it's a long walk uphill to campus. Parking permits are available, but they're expensive ($72/quarter) and restricted to certain lots. To get a permit go to 3917 University Way NE or call 545-1543. Call at the end of the quarter to get a permit for the following quarter. There's also parking at the Odegaard underground lot off 15th NE, but be there before 9 a.m. There's parking in lots north of campus for about $3/day, but they fill up fast. If you can find two friends, you are considered a carpool and you can park on campus for $1. There's parking on 15th, some free spots mixed in with the meters from 45th to 50th, and all free north of 50th. These spaces go fast so be there at 9 a.m. when the west side of the street opens for parking.

• Find a good place to study. South Campus Center: On a Saturday or Sunday morning you can get your own room with a couch and a view

HEARD ON THE STREET

"Somewhere down at the end of a long, long hall, around a maze of corners and behind a little door is someone who can help you."

UW student

of the lake. Odegaard Library couches are comfortable—maybe too comfortable if you want to be productive. The graduate reading room in Suzzallo is lofty, beautiful, and very quiet. The Boiserie in the Burke Museum and several cafes on University Way ("The Ave") will let you sit all day if you buy a cup of coffee.

- Learn to take multiple choice tests. "It's merely a process of elimination, knowledge of the subject is not always a necessity."
- Use the ASUW (Associated Students, University of Washington) for everything. If you are confused, lost, depressed about school, give them a call and they'll find someone you can talk to (543-1780). They have info on a ton of student services such as research interns, study skills seminars, the Writing Center, bike shop, poster shop, publishing, etc.
- Warning: Be careful if you're wearing hard-soled shoes and it's raining. With all the little hills around campus you're guaranteed to slip if you don't watch out. Embarrassing, as well as dangerous.
- Grab the student coupon books distributed at the bookstore the first day of classes before they're gone. The coupons are good at cafes around "The Ave" and can cut your food bill in half. Also good for haircuts, supplies, clothing.
- If you're planning to rush a fraternity or sorority, set up an easy freshman year schedule. You are going to need plenty of time for all those "pledgling" activities.
- Most important tip: Get to know a counselor in your department. At first you'll be shunted off to Arts and Science advisors, but once you get a focus, try to work closely with someone in your department. That person can smooth the way to getting you what you want—and can make or break your educational experience.
- The new (improved?) computerized registration. Demand for classes far outstrips supply, so register early. If you really want to get into a class you have to beat STAR (Student Telephone Assisted Registration). It ostensibly opens at 6 a.m., but start dialing at 5:45—sometimes you can get through early. If you still can't get into a class, go see the professor on the first day to ask about overloading. You'll get an access code if you're lucky (a little brown-nosing never hurts).

FRATS

Over 2,100 young males live in the 31-member fraternity system at the UW. The grade point average requirement is 2.5–3.0 and rush is informal, meaning that prospective candidates can visit any fraternity at any time. There's a formal rush around the second week of September, but fraternities usually have already decided who they will pledge. Costs average $3,100/year depending on the house. There are usually 68 men to a house.

Most prestigious houses: Theta Chi and Delta Chi—generally for the richest, preppiest guys. Party house: Beta.

Interfraternity Council
301-B Hub, FK-30
University of Washington
Seattle, WA 98195
543-1800

SORORITIES

Eighteen sororities participate in a formal rush lasting approximately four days in mid-September. UW housing is available during this time but must be applied for before May. Average cost per quarter at sorority houses is $850 room and board, plus first-time membership fees to be paid during the first year of pledge. Those fees include a $50 pledge fee, $15–$75 badge, $115 initiation fee, and $200 building fund fee.

Most prestigious house: Kappa Alpha Theta. Popular houses: Delta Delta Delta ("Tri-Delts"—known as the dizzy blondes' house); Delta Gamma ("DGs"—the smarter, more likely to succeed types); Alpha Delta Pi ("ADPi's"—the average, all-American types).

Panhellenic Association
301-C Hub, FK-30
University of Washington
Seattle, WA 98195
543-1810

UW—THE LANDLORD

The bulldozers will be active on campus from now through the year 2001 thanks to construction projects that will add 1.7 million square feet of space. Included will be new science and music/liberal arts facilities; a business administration executive center; cultural, housing, and recreational facilities; parking spaces; open space; and a circulation system that incorporates an underpass at Montlake and Pacific streets.

But the UW owns more than the land it uses on campus. In fact, it owns a huge chunk of downtown Seattle, the 10-acre Metropolitan Tract. What the university does not own, though many think it does, is the Arboretum. The grounds of the Arboretum are owned by the City of Seattle, but the UW is responsible for maintenance of the plant collection there.

LAND OWNED BY THE UW OFF-CAMPUS

Big Beef Creek Laboratory (Seabeck, Kitsap County). Studies in the College of Ocean and Fishery Sciences.
- Friday Harbor Laboratories (Friday Harbor, San Juan County). Studies in botany, atmospheric sciences, oceanography, and zoology.
- Lake Lliamna Field Station (Lliamna, Alaska). Research in the College of Ocean and Fishery Sciences.
- Lee Forest (Maltby, King County), Moore Memorial Forest (Salmon le Sac, Kittitas County), Pack Forest (Eatonville, Pierce County). Research in the College of Forest Resources.
- Manastash Ridge Observatory (Kittitas County near Ellensburg). Studies in astronomy.
- Primate Field Station (Medical Lake, Spokane County). Primate breeding facility.
- Ten-acre Metropolitan Tract. Extends from Union to Seneca including the Fourth and Fifth avenue blocks where the Security Pacific Tower (the erstwhile Rainier Tower) and the Four Seasons Olympic are. This is the original site of the University and the land is still owned by the UW.
- Tri-Cities University Center (Richland, Benton County). Graduate programs for professional employees in the Hanford area in science and engineering, along with master's degrees in education and business administration.

Classes guaranteed to increase your GPA and minimize time and effort expended:

- **Psych. 101 (watch out for falling chickens)**
- **Psych. 210 (human sexuality)**
- **Soc. 240 (you can schedule your own exam dates)**
- **English 181**

Classes you shouldn't get through the UW without taking:

- **Comparative literature (Willis Konick)**
- **History (Jon Bridgman)**
- **Business, Government and Society 200 (Steven Hale, part-time lecturer)**
- **English 271 (creative writing)**
- **Chem. Eng. 109 (creative thinking)**

Classes you should avoid like the plague unless they are required:

- **The entire accounting series**

BRANCH CAMPUSES

Recent approval of branch campuses for the UW has resulted in some confusion and political hash-slinging. For example, how much should a professor be paid at a branch campus? As much as at the UW? How much status, or lack thereof, should go along with the job? Is it a training ground? Is the degree offered from the UW or from UW/Bothell? And on and on.

At any rate, there are two upper-division and master's degree branches planned for, one in Tacoma and one in the Bothell area. The initial budget provides for 400 students at each (300 FTE). By 2010 plans are to serve 5,000 upper-division students and 1,000 graduate students at the Tacoma branch, and 4,000 upper-division students and 800 graduate students at the Bothell branch.

A baccalaureate degree program in liberal studies is available at each site, with other degree programs to be added in the future.

RESEARCH KUDOS

UW ranks fourth in the nation in corporate grants received and is among the top five schools receiving federal grants and contracts for scientific research. As a research leader, the UW has made discoveries in kidney dialysis, and liver and pancreas transplants. A major study of Alzheimer's Disease is in progress, and one of the nation's top burn centers has been established at Harborview Medical Center.

Much of the research done on campus is based at the Warren G. Magnuson Health Sciences Center, which features two teaching hospitals, six schools, and five multi-disciplinary research centers. Research is also conducted at the Urban Horticultural Center and the botanical and drug-plant gardens. The UW has ongoing studies in physics, chemistry, cancer therapy, nuclear medicine, and radiation biology—all in the nuclear physics lab that houses a Van de Graf accelerator and cyclotron.

In addition to those oft-touted accomplishments, the UW is noted for the Jackson School of International Studies, whose curriculum includes speakers from around the world.

YOUR TAX DOLLARS AT WORK: PUBLIC ACCESS

You don't have to be a student to take advantage of what's going on at the UW. It is actually fun to rub shoulders with students at the Boiserie—and some of the most innovative theater, dance, opera, etc. can be had just by paying attention to those flyers tacked on telephone poles in the U District. Here's a list of how your tax dollars are at work for the general public through the UW.

PUBLIC PAYOFF

Speaker's Bureau. Seven hundred faculty and staff are available to discuss topics in many fields of general interest. Some speakers require a fee, and offering an honorarium never hurts.

Speaker's Bureau Guide
543-9198

• Resource Tip File. Ever wonder why there's always a UW prof quoted in technical articles in the newspapers? It's because of this useful booklet of experts in 768 subjects. Want to know who's in the know about gambling? How about the Mariners' profit margins and taxes? Moth culture? Bat behavior? They are all listed.

UW Information Services
543-2580

• Lectures at the UW are open to all who want to attend, and there is a senior citizen audit program.

Libraries, including archives, are open to the public for research. The incredible Northwest Collection in Suzzallo has historic photos and publications, and there are boxes of records from local old-time companies and groups to be found in other archives. No material can be taken out of the library, however. There are 20 UW libraries in all.

UW Library information
543-9158

• Meany Hall, Glenn Hughes Playhouse, and Penthouse Theater all have music and dance recitals, concerts, dramas, and lectures given by campus and visiting artists.

For theater mailing list and ticket information, call 543-4880.
Glenn Hughes Playhouse:
543-5646
Meany Hall: 543-2742
Penthouse Theater: 543-5638

• Both campus museums are open to the public and give discounts to students.

Henry Art Gallery
Fifth NE and NE Campus Parkway
543-2280
Open 10 a.m.–5 p.m. Tues.–Fri.; 10 a.m.–7 p.m Thurs.; 11 a.m.–5 p.m. Sat., Sun.; and closed Mon.
General admission $2; students/seniors $1; UW students free.

Burke Memorial Museum
17th NE and NE 45th
543-5590
Museum of natural history and anthropology.
Open 10 a.m.–5 p.m. daily, and until 8 p.m. Thurs. Admission free, except for special exhibits.

COFFEE BREAK

There are some good little coffee shops tucked away at the UW where eavesdropping can be productive. You're likely to find architecture types talking Italian hill towns in the cubbyhole in the Architecture Building, and student artists discussing weighty topics in the Art Building basement shop.

Another favorite is the Boiserie in the Burke Museum where the pastries are delicious. It's best to grab a seat about 10 minutes after the hour: it fills up by 25 minutes past. By George in Red Square has good coffee and a wide variety of food. The Hub, a favorite dormy hangout, has a salad bar and cafeteria-style meals. The food isn't great, being a little too greasy for all but student stomachs. The Art Building coffee shop is dimly lit and slightly grungy, but interesting nonetheless. The menu has natural-ingredient foods as well as the usual bagels with cream cheese. The business school has a sorry excuse for a coffee shop in the basement of Balmer Hall called The PAD, with recycled coffee and donuts by 8 a.m. And they have pencils and exam books just in case. Other little holes in the wall exist around campus in almost every major building, and prices are always cheap.

LANDMARK SITES ON CAMPUS

The Sylvan Theater, near Drumheller Fountain, was the site of early graduation ceremonies and is now the site of weddings, plays, banquets, squirrel watching, sunbathing, and studying. It is a grassy stage set with four white columns that once sat in front of the downtown campus.

Broken Obelisk, a sculpture by Barnett Newman, is on the northwest side of Red Square. It's 26 feet high and weighs two tons.

Denny Hall (1895), the oldest and for some time the only building on campus, is a stately old place. Atop the hall sits the Varsity Bell, originally installed at the downtown campus. Today it rings only for homecoming. Denny Hall clock, an ominous presence that can be your friend or your enemy, rings on the hour. When you're in class it pleasantly reminds you there's only 20 minutes left; but when you're late for class it's tolling your doom.

The Observatory, built in 1895 from sandstone left over from Denny Hall construction, is open to the public Monday through Thursday evenings from 8–10 p.m. in fall and spring and 7–9 p.m. in winter. The vintage 6-inch refracting telescope built in 1891 is still in use today.

The Architecture Hall on Stevens Way was built in 1909 and is the last major building remaining from the Alaska-Yukon-Pacific exposition.

The Medicinal Herb Garden, the largest of its kind in the country, was created in 1911 by the UW Dean of Pharmacy. A portion of the garden has plants native to the Northwest, and the rest holds herbs and plants from all over the world. It's near the botany greenhouse.

THE CITY'S OTHER INSTITUTES OF HIGHER LEARNING

Antioch University
2607 Second Ave.
Seattle, WA 98121
441-5352
Antioch is a satellite university of the main campus in Yellow Springs, Ohio. Locally, it's 75% women, many of them returning to school after a few years in the working world. Psychology is the largest program at Antioch, but adult education in general is the school's thrust.
Average enrollment: 440
Average age of students: 39
Degrees: Bachelor of arts completion (wherein students write their own liberal arts programs), master's in psychology, master's in whole-systems design, master of arts in education.
Tuition: Varies by program but ballpark $2,100 to $2,250/quarter full-time; $1,200 half-time.

City University
16661 Northup Way
Bellevue, WA 98008
643-2000
A four-year, private university accredited by the Northwest Association of Schools and Colleges, City University primarily offers evening and weekend classes. There are branches in Seattle, Bremerton, Everett, Bellingham, Port Angeles, Spokane, Tacoma, Yakima, and Vancouver. Grades are pass/fail for undergraduates.
Average enrollment: 4,500
Average age: 37.5
Degrees: Associate (three programs), bachelor's, and master's.
Tuition: Undergraduate, $595/5 credits; graduate, $486/3 credits. Early payment, $535 undergrads, $438 grads. Plus computer time and lab fees if applicable.

Northwest College
5520 108th Ave. NE
P.O. Box 579
Kirkland, WA 98033
822-8266
Northwest is a four-year and two-year private college affiliated with the Assemblies of God church. It's accredited both by the N.W. Association of Schools and Colleges, and by the American Association of Bible Colleges.
Average enrollment: 675
Average age: 22
Degrees: Associate and bachelor's
Tuition: $2,250 for 12–16 credit hours or $187.50/credit hour.

Pacific Lutheran University
Tacoma, WA 98447
535-7430
PLU is a private, four-year university affiliated with the Lutheran church. PLU is set on a 130-acre campus. Majors with the largest enrollment are business administration, education, math/computer science.
Average enrollment: 4,000
Average age of students: 25
Notable programs: Business administration, computer science
Degrees: Bachelor's, master's
Tuition: $9,360/year

Seattle Pacific University
3307 Third Ave. W
Seattle, WA 98119
281-2000 or (800) 336-3344
A private four-year university, SPU is affiliated with the Free Methodists and located on the north side of Queen Anne. It offers an extensive undergraduate summer curriculum.
Average enrollment: 2,791
Average age: 23
Degrees: Bachelor's, master's
Tuition: Undergrads, $3,000 per quarter for 12–17 credits or $250/credit hour; grads, $135–$235/credit hour.

Seattle University
Broadway and Madison
Seattle, WA 98122
296-6000 or (800) 542-0833
Seattle U. is a four-year private college with a Catholic affiliation. It has a small campus in the middle of Seattle and enjoys an especially good reputation for psychology, rehabilitation, and health service courses. Schools of engineering, education, and business are also strong. The campus was recently enlarged.
Average enrollment: 4,411
Degrees: Bachelor's, master's, and doctorate. Bachelor of arts in business administration and bachelor of public administration can be obtained through evening classes. All master's degrees involve evening programs.
Tuition: For most programs, $199/credit for undergrads, $258 for grad students. In psychology the cost is $216/credit for undergrads and $173 for addiction studies.

University of Puget Sound
1500 N Warner
Tacoma, WA 98416
756-3100
Average enrollment: 2,800
Average age of students: 22
Notable programs: Pacific Rim study and travel, business leadership program, honors program.
Degrees: Bachelor of arts/science, master's
Tuition: $10,180/yr.

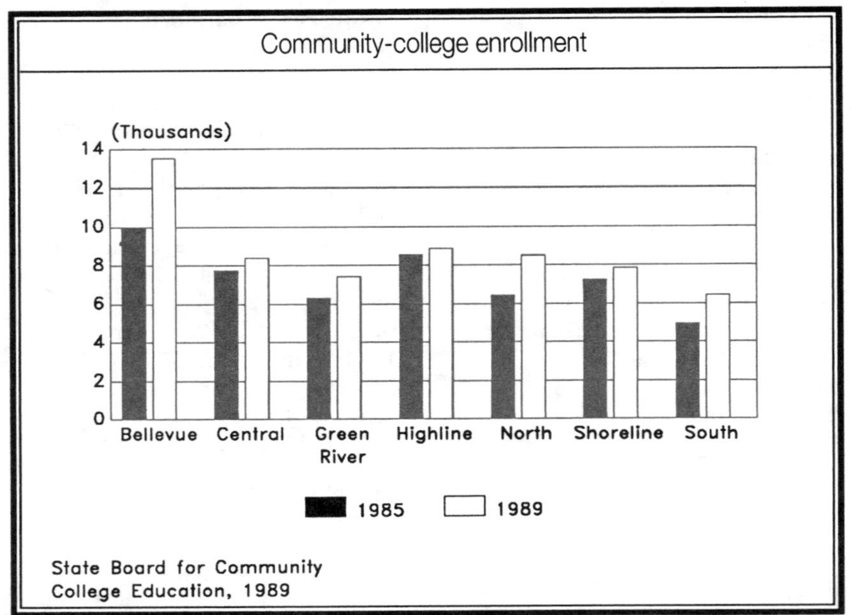

COMMUNITY COLLEGES

Time was that admitting you attended a community college was equivalent to admitting you didn't know where Mt. Rainier was. But community colleges have come into their own and now have an excellent reputation. In Seattle the forerunner of community colleges was Edison Technical School, located in the old Broadway High School and now the site of Seattle Central Community College. The school used to be a great place to get your hair cut for pennies and to eat a few cookies from the pastry class.

Seattle Central and the others have become pretty upscale since those early days, and now offer an expansive array of classes—everything from pilot preparation to coordinated studies (a team-teaching effort of approaching a subject from various perspectives), as well as the two-year associate degree.

Besides the array of classes, the big draw is tuition. Community colleges are half as expensive as the University of Washington.

As with everything else in the city, the community colleges are feeling pinched by growth. Enrollment in all the colleges has increased an average of 16% over the last five years, as the echo boomers of the baby boom generation come of college age. The colleges are attempting to add classes that fill the demands of their particular districts, so it's a good idea to peruse up-to-date catalogs to find what you're looking for.

Community colleges specialize in vocational training, college preparation, basic education, and continuing education. All are under the jurisdiction of the Washington State Board of Community College Education and all have an "open door" policy whereby everyone who applies is accepted, regardless of grade point or other qualifications. Classes are often scheduled to accommodate working students.

Below is a list of the area community colleges along with some of their specialty programs. Enrollment figures are based on fall quarter averages.

Seattle Community College District Office
1500 Harvard Ave.
Seattle, WA 98122
587-4100
Chancellor: Thomas Gonzales
The district office handles administration for the three community colleges: North Seattle, Seattle Central, and South Seattle. In addition to those three campuses, there are three satellite branches: the Maritime Training Center on Lake Washington Ship Canal, the Wood Construction program in Central Seattle, and apprentice training at the Duwamish Industrial Education and Apprentice Center.

Community colleges in Seattle

North Seattle Community College
9600 College Way N
Seattle, WA 98103
527-3600
Average enrollment: 8,500
Average age: 34
Notable programs: Joint agreement with Western Washington University for a bachelor of science degree in electronics technology while taking all coursework at NSCC; training for pharmacy technician, electrical power technician, environmental control technician, instrumentation/watch repair; coordinated studies.
Degrees: Associate (arts, science, fine arts, general studies), vocational certificates.
Tuition: $254 full-time/quarter for residents; $25.40/credit part-time; additional fees for certain classes.

Seattle Central Community College
1701 Broadway
Seattle, WA 98122
587-3800
Average enrollment: 8,409
Average age of students: 30.2
Notable programs: Ophthalmic dispensing, marine training program (non-degree), marine carpentry, wood construction, advertising art, commercial photography, apparel design. One of the first community colleges in the state to offer a coordinated studies program, whereby students pick a subject and learn about its different perspectives from a team of instructors. Also registered nurse program, respiratory therapy, surgical tech training, hospitality, cosmetology, early childhood education.

Degrees: Associate of arts or applied science, vocational certificates.
Tuition: $274/quarter full-time, $27.40/credit part-time.

South Seattle Community College
6000 16th Ave. SW
Seattle, WA 98106
764-5300
Average enrollment: 6,456
Average age of students: 28
Notable programs: Aviation electronics, aviation maintenance, robotics, automotive and diesel technology, hospitality and food science, landscape horticulture, retail floristry, welding and machining. Arboretum open to public with new Chonqing, China, sister-city garden.
Degrees: Associate of arts or applied science, vocational certificates.
Tuition: $274/quarter full-time, $27.40/credit part-time.

Community colleges outside Seattle

Bellevue Community College
3000 Landerholm Circle SE
Bellevue, WA 98007
641-0111
Average enrollment: 14,202
Average age of students: 30.8
Notable programs: Diagnostic ultrasound technician training, radio station, Delta Epsilon Chi (a business/marketing/apparel occupation program working with local businesses), telecourses, radiologic technician.
Degrees: Associate degrees, vocational certificates.
Tuition: $275/quarter full-time for state residents.

Edmonds Community College
20000 68th Ave. W
Lynnwood, WA 98036
771-1500
Average enrollment: 8,200
Average age of students: 30.2 for full-time students
Notable programs: Applied technology training, Japan (Kobe) branch campus, spearheaded Center for Business and Employment Development to aid local businesses, Internet (international education unit for pre-business majors), horticulture, extended learning center, lots of foreign students.
Degrees: Associate (technical arts, arts and sciences, general studies), countless certificate programs.
Tuition: $274 full-time, $27.40/credit.

Green River Community College
12401 SE 320th St.
Auburn, WA 98002
464-6133
Average enrollment: 7,435
Average age of students: 27
Notable programs: Health occupations, water supply/wastewater technology, air traffic control, business, court reporting.
Degrees: Associate in arts, applied arts, or applied science.
Tuition: $274/quarter full-time for residents (1989–90), $27.40/credit hour part-time.

Highline Community College
2400 S 240th St.
P.O. Box 98000
Des Moines, WA 98198-9800
878-3710
Average enrollment: 9,000
Average age of students: 28
Notable programs: Registered nursing, diving technician, air transportation, administration of justice, fashion marketing, dental assisting, auto tech.
Degrees: Associate of arts, general studies, or applied science.
Tuition: $274/full-time (resident), $27.40/credit part-time.

Shoreline Community College
16101 Greenwood Ave. N
Seattle, WA 98133
546-4101
Average enrollment: 7,868
Average age of students: n/a
Notable programs: Environmental technology, international trade, oceanography, biology lab technician, foundation administration, histology, interior merchandising. Speaker's Bureau available to community.
Degrees: Associate degrees, vocational certificates.
Tuition: $273 full-time.

THE ALTERNATIVE APPROACH

General interest schools abound in the city, with the problem being not whether classes in dog grooming, for example, exist, but how to find them. The best way is to follow the advice —just this once—of the phone companies and let your fingers do the walking. The Seattle Telephone Directory has 17 pages of listings on schools that teach the following:

Acting
Art
Baby and child care
Boating
Bowling
Crafts
Dancing
Diving
Dog training
Driving
First aid
Golf
Gymnastics
Karate and martial arts
Knitting
Language
Meditation
Parachute jumping
Public speaking
Reading improvement
Sailing
Sewing
Skiing
Study techniques
Survival
Swimming
Tennis
Yoga

There are 134 schools that teach the following business and vocational subjects and careers:

Accounting and bookkeeping
Aircraft flight training
Airline attendants and agents
Barbers
Bartenders
Beauty
Chiropractic
Computers
Cooking
Court reporting

Data processing
Dental assistants
Dog grooming
Fashion merchandising
Floral arranging and designing
Hypnotism
Insurance
Interior decorating and design
Jewelry design
Management
Massage
Medical assistants
Modeling
Motivation and self-improvement
Music—instrumental
Music—vocal
Navigation
Nurses' aides
Paralegal
Photography
Real estate
Receptionists
Refrigeration
Sales training
Secretarial skills
Security
Stenography
Television and radio broadcasting
Teller training
Theology
Travel
Veterinary medical assistants
Word processing

If your subject still isn't anywhere to be found, call the Seattle Public Library education department, 386-4636.

There are many creditable schools around, but there are some that are less reputable; you'd be advised to ask around, talk to current students and graduates, and sample a few businesses in the field to see if they'd hire someone from a particular school. The following is not a list of recommendations, but rather just a sampling of what's available.

CONTINUING EDUCATION

A selective list of commercial and trade schools.

ASUW Experimental College
307 HUB, FK-30
University of Washington
Seattle, WA 98195
543-4375

This 20-year-old alternative school offers 400 classes per quarter in 30 subject areas. Classes are taught by people with special expertise or training and are held all over the Seattle area. They can vary from a weekend seminar to a full quarter of class meetings. The school offers an astonishing range of classes, varying from the off-beat and wacky (Foot Reflexology or Beginning Past Life Recall) to the mundane but useful (Time Management or A Guide to Life Insurance).

If you're interested in comic book illustration, modern espionage, computer workshops, dog obedience, overcoming procrastination, or a plethora of other subjects, this is the college for you.

The school, sponsored by the Associated Students of UW, is completely self-supporting, and the majority of its operating funds come from student registration fees. Fees are different for each class but start at about $10. UW students pay less than the general public. Many classes are on UW campus.

Great opportunities here for wanna-be teachers.

Leadership Institute of Seattle (LIOS)
1500 Eastlake Ave. E
Seattle, WA 98102
325-5648

Quest—Continuing Education Program
4030 86th Ave. SE
Mercer Island, WA 98040
232-8835

UW Extension
5001 25th Ave. NE
Seattle, WA 98195
543-2320
Some of these courses are taught by UW professors, some by experts from the community at large. Some are for credit, some aren't. The classes are quite serious (The Epic Tradition in Literature, or Latin and Greek in Current Use, for example); some are very practical (consider Corporate Scriptwriting, or DOS and Hard Disk Management). There's also a lecture series offered. Most classes are held on UW campus. Cost varies, but many classes are over $100.

Arts

Art Institute of Seattle
2323 Elliott Ave.
Seattle, WA 98121
448-6600
Accredited programs in design technology, music and video, fashion, photography, etc.

Cornish College of the Arts
710 E Roy St.
Seattle, WA 98102
323-1400
Cornish is a four-year, private fine arts college with a reputation for being less bohemian than other arts institutes. To be admitted students must audition or present a portfolio during an entrance interview. A limited summer curriculum is available. The college offers the option of a letter grade or pass/fail.

Enrollment averages 480 students, most of whom are around 27 to 30 years old. Cornish offers a bachelor of arts degree. Tuition for full-time students taking 12 to 18 hours is $3,430 or $250 per credit hour. Non-credit classes are offered at $165 per hour.

PRATT Fine Art Center
1902 S Main St.
Seattle, WA 98144
328-2200
Classes, workshops, special events, and facilities to rent for members.

School of Visual Concepts
500 Aurora Ave. N
Seattle, WA 98109
623-1560

Beauty

Gene Juarez Academy of Beauty
10715 Eighth Ave. NE
Seattle, WA 98125
365-6900

Metropolitan School of Beauty
13201 Aurora Ave. N
Seattle, WA 98133
364-9090

Mr. Lee's Beauty Colleges
435 E Main St.
Auburn, WA 98002
939-2480

Broadcast

Bailie School of Broadcast
2505 Second Ave.
Seattle, WA 98121
448-1231
The 25-year-old school prepares outgoing types for video, television, and radio.

Business training

Boeing Computer Services Technical School
375 Corporate Drive S
Tukwila, WA 98188
393-0583
Ten-month course on mainframe computers—just like those Boeing uses. Students must go through an entrance interview.

Griffin College, Seattle
2005 Fifth Ave.
Seattle, WA 98101
728-6800
Also in Bellevue and Tacoma.

ITT Technical Institute
12720 Gateway Dr., Suite 100
Seattle, WA 98168
244-3300

Metropolitan Business College
615 Second Ave.
Seattle, WA 98104
624-3773

Flight

ASA Ground School
7277 Perimeter Road S, Suite 218
Seattle, WA 98108
763-1454

Galvin Flying Service, Inc.
7149 Perimeter Road S
Boeing Field
Seattle, WA 98108
763-0350

Languages

Academy of Languages
98 Yesler Way
Seattle, WA 98104
682-4463
University credit is available through the academy, which teaches numerous languages in classes and some in private sessions. Conversation partners include native speakers. There's also a language teacher training program.

Average enrollment is 70–75 day students, 80–100 evening. Maximum class size is 12. There's sometimes a five-week wait to get into classes. Tuition is $190 for a five-week, six-hours-per-week course to get good survival skills in a foreign country. Intensive English as Second Language class costs $650–$700 for 30 hours.

Languages include Japanese, Chinese, German, French, Spanish, Italian, Dutch, Russian. Tamil (India) available by request.

Medical

John Bastyr College of Naturopathic Medicine
144 NE 54th St.
Seattle, WA 98105
523-9585
John Bastyr College teaches the 100-year-old healing art developed by the Germans that tries to integrate physical/herbal/water-cure medicine. The college trains family practitioners in botanical medicine, midwifery, nutrition, physical manipulation, hydrotherapy, and homeopathy.

Average enrollment is 175 students, mostly graduate students. Students must submit a form and letters of recommendation, then have a personal interview before being accepted. There's a 50% acceptance rate.

The college offers a doctorate in naturopathic medicine, and a master's or a bachelor's degree in science. Tuition is $105/credit hour for N.D. students, $96/credit for graduate students, and $84/credit for undergrads.

Brenneke School of Massage and Health Center
160 Roy St.
Seattle, WA 98109
282-1233

Seattle Massage School
7120 Woodlawn Ave. NE
Seattle, WA 98115
527-0807

Seattle Midwifery School
2524 16th Ave. S
Seattle, WA 98144
322-8834

Modeling

Barbizon School of Modeling
1501 Fourth Ave., Suite 305
Seattle, WA 98101
223-1500

Real estate

Mykut Real Estate School
7500 212th Ave. SW, Suite 109
Edmonds, WA 98020
775-6645

Real Estate School
13100 Stone Ave. N
Seattle, WA 98133
363-0600

Technical

Brudvik School of Refrigeration
20926 63rd Ave. W, Suite B
Lynnwood, WA 98036
771-6024

Commercial Driver Training, Inc.
24325 Pacific Hwy. S
Des Moines, WA 98198
824-3970
Truck driver training.

Technical institutes

These offer a wide array of career choice training programs and both full- and part-time classes.

Lake Washington Vocational Technical Institute
11605 132nd Ave. NE
Kirkland, WA 98034
828-5627

Renton Vocational-Technical Institute
3000 NE Fourth St.
Renton, WA 98056
235-2352

Washington Institute of Applied Technology
315 22nd Ave. S
Seattle, WA 98144
587-4800

Miscellaneous

Career Floral Design Institute
13200 Northup Way
Bellevue, WA 98005
746-8340

Charles Tebbetts Hypnotism Training Institute
23607 Hwy. 99
Edmonds, WA 98026
771-8211

Director's Studio of Speech and Drama
1932 Second Ave.
Seattle, WA 98101
441-5080

People's Law School
1809 Seventh Ave., Suite 909
Seattle, WA 98101
464-1011
Local lawyers and judges teach classes that take the mystery out of the legal system. Sessions are one night a week for five to seven weeks at different locations, usually in the fall. Tuition averages $20.

Sales Training Institute, Inc.
1750 112th Ave. NE, Bldg. D
Bellevue, WA 98004
453-8069

Seattle School of Mixology
166 Denny Way
Seattle, WA 98109
441-3838
Bartending school.

CHAPTER

22

Q AND A: THE ACCESS LABYRINTH

INFORMATION

386-INFO

WATER DEPARTMENT

HOTLINES

QUESTIONS

LIBRARIES

PETS ON THE LOOSE

COURT RECORDS

TOLL-FREE

ANSWERS

Reporters and other nosey types follow the 11th commandment: Thou shalt never take "I don't know" for an answer. Information is a wonderful thing simply because there's so much of it out there. Sure, it may take a few dozen phone calls or a trip to somebody's archives and, sure, somebody may tell you rather crudely what you can do with your questions, but the stuff is out there.

Usually the first phone call will lead to the second, the second to the third and on *ad nauseam* until you are screaming "no more info, please." Of course, there are phone wimps out there who cringe at the thought of talking to a complete stranger. The wimps need to know the 12th commandment: Thou shalt not fear; the worst they can do is say no.

Seattle is a great place for information gathering because people very often don't mind taking the time to talk. But be prepared to answer questions yourself; it's still a small enough town that everyone wants to know why you want to know. And pretty soon the whole office will know why you called, and pretty soon the whole building complex and pretty soon—well, maybe those wimps have the right idea.

THE FIRST STOP: THE LIBRARY

Where to make the first phone call? The library, of course. It's part of the family, a third hand, a shoulder to lean on, man's (and woman's) best friend.

The Seattle Public Library has a truly exciting information service. Call and ask anything—from how to spell that suspicious word used by your Scrabble opponent, to who the third vice-president of the U.S. was—and the researchers will come up with an answer. You might have to wait on hold for a while, but the information specialists unfailingly come through with your answer.

The library offers a myriad of other services too. For example, computer equipment is available at these branch libraries: Broadview, Lake City, Rainier Beach, University, and West Seattle. You can reserve one hour of computer time in person or by phone.

There is also a computer with color monitor and Epson printer in the children's department of the downtown library. It operates on a first-come, first-served basis.

A program notebook listing software at each of those libraries is available for use, or you can provide your own. Special software is available for those just learning. Many libraries carry *Computer User*, a free publication containing articles and listings of user groups.

All the Seattle public libraries offer on-line searches, which means they have access to several database services. For example, if you want to see articles on grizzly bears in the Rockies, the librarian will do a search for you and print out the articles—free. You do need to do the search at the appropriate department, depending upon your subject. Sometimes there's a wait.

Two pamphlets list all library services and are available free from the library. They are *Your Seattle Public Library* and *A Guide to Your Downtown Library Resource Center*.

You're eligible for a library card if you live, work, attend school, or pay property taxes in the city of Seattle. Residents of King County may check out materials in any branch if their local library system has an agreement with the Seattle Public Library. For others, there's a yearly fee of $32.

Seattle Public Library fines

Item	Daily fine	Max. fine
Books, audiocassettes, record albums, magazine folders	$ .05	$ 2.00
Videocassettes	1.00	10.00
Reference items	.25	24.00
	1988	**1989**
Borrowers notified of overdue books	118,869	129,893

OVERDUE MATERIALS

Guilt, guilt, guilt. While your library books sit on the table at home, someone else is looking for them in the library. And if that's not enough incentive, here are the fines.

Yes, there is a grace period on overdue books of five days. And yes, if you lose a book you'll have to pay a replacement fee. And the library says there aren't any amnesty days (but we know better!).

WHAT DOES SEATTLE READ

Seattle's a reading city, but exactly where the interests lie is anybody's guess. The library is working on a survey of withdrawn books by Dewey Decimal system and that will give some indication. The heaviest library use seems to be in the media and program services area, followed by art and music.

HOW 386-INFO WORKS

Four librarians answer the information line (two in the evenings), fielding some 76,000 calls a year. They sit in a room at the downtown library, at a round table that has a lazy Susan–type bank of shelves in the center. The shelves are full of resource books, and when you ask your question the librarian spins it around to reach the right book. Voila! The answer.

They get pretty weird calls sometimes: Bar bets are a popular item, Scrabble words another. And in Seattle, unlike some cities, they'll answer homework questions for kids who call. They figure if a kid has taken the time and made the effort to call, they may as well give him or her the answer.

Most popular queries:

- When does the library open/close?
- Do you have this book?
- Questions regarding the Consumer Price Index.
- Questions regarding the Time Zone differences.
- Dates of holidays.
- Resale values of cars.
- Spelling/Grammar.
- Office etiquette (what's the right salutation, how do you type a block style letter, etc.).
- Famous people's birthdays.
- Trivia questions.
- End or beginning of quotations.
- Recipes.
- Homework questions.
- Where to vote.

Some odd ones:

- How do I get a ballpoint pen mark out of a white silk shirt? (Try an ink-removing compound made of cream of tartar and citric powder—sometimes called salts of lemon.)
- Was Nancy Reagan pregnant when she got married? (She was.)
- What was the most popular song of 1957? (It's a toss-up between "Jail House Rock," sung by Elvis, and "Wake Up Li'l Suzie," sung by the Everly Brothers.)

Best times to call: Thursday mornings; or evenings.

Worst times to call: Lunch hours and between 10 a.m. and 4 p.m. (peak hours). No service on Sunday.

Source: Seattle Survival Guide research.

Other services of the Seattle Public Library:

- Dial-a-Story: Recorded folk tales for children, 386-4656.
- Directory service: Phone books and city directories for many cities, 386-4648.
- Genealogy Collection: Resource for tracing family history. For staff schedule, call 386-4636.
- GED exams: Materials for studying for the high school equivalency exam available in the education department, second floor, downtown library.
- Literacy programs around the city for students and tutors.
- Media services: Films, slides, videotapes, and compact discs available; projectors may be borrowed and programs viewed in the library.
- Meeting rooms. (All meetings must be open to the public.)
- Multilingual Collection: Books in over 30 languages as well as newspapers and magazines from other countries.
- Newspapers and magazines: Back issues of Seattle papers and *The New York Times* available on microfilm; current issues of magazines and newspapers, second floor.
- Regional Foundation Center Collection: Help with seeking grants, second floor.
- Securities and Company Information: Stock and bond quotes, information on companies and nonprofit organizations. 386-4650.
- S.P.L.A.S.H. Kids after-school activities at Beacon Hill, High Point, Holly Park, Madrona–Sally Goldmark Library. Monday–Friday, 3–7 p.m.
- Tourist info: Free maps and advice, directions, etc.
- Voter registration is available at branch libraries. Downtown history department has polling places listed too.

Every Seattleite should have the library information number imprinted on the inside of his or her brain: 386-INFO.

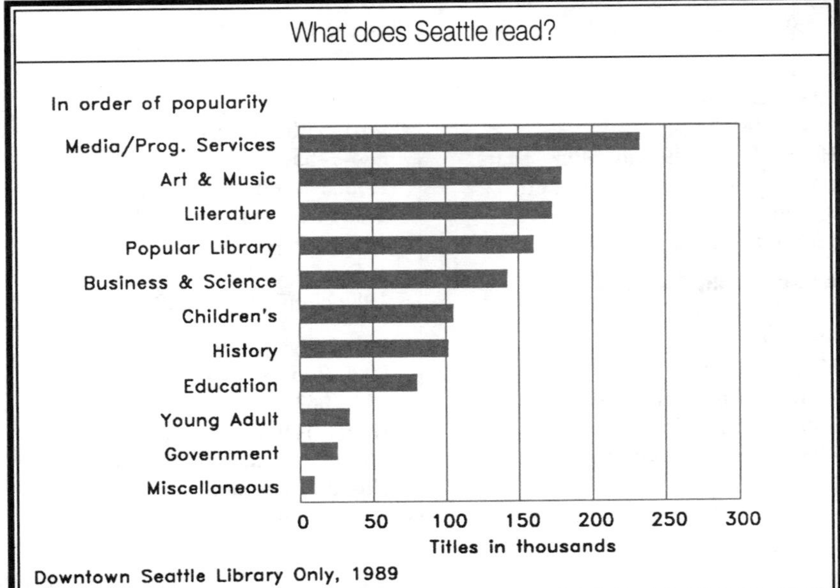

Seattle Public Library branches

Downtown Main Branch
1000 Fourth Ave.
386-4636
Hours: 9 a.m.–9 p.m. weekdays; 9 a.m.–6 p.m. Sat., 1–5 p.m. Sun.
1989 circulation: 1.2 million

Ballard
5711 24th Ave. NW
584-4089
Hours: 10 a.m.–9 p.m. Mon.–Wed.; closed Thurs.; 10 a.m.–6 p.m. Fri. & Sat.; 1–5 p.m. Sun.
1989 circulation: 398,979

Beacon Hill
2519 15th Ave. S
684-4711
Hours: 10 a.m.–7 p.m. Mon. & Wed.; 2–7 p.m. Tues., Thurs. & Fri.; 1–6 p.m. Sat.; closed Sun.
1989 circulation: 63,646

Broadview
12755 Greenwood N
684-7519
Hours: 10 a.m.–9 p.m. Mon.–Thurs.; 10 a.m.–6 p.m. Sat.; closed Fri. & Sun.
1989 circulation: 230,068

Columbia
4721 Rainier Ave. S
386-1908
Hours: 10 a.m.–9 p.m. Mon.–Wed.; 10 a.m.–6 p.m. Fri. & Sat.; closed Thurs. and Sun.
1989 circulation: 140,808

Douglass-Truth
23rd and E Yesler Way
684-4704
Hours: 1–9 p.m. Mon.–Wed.; 10 a.m.–9 p.m. Thurs.; 10 a.m.–6 p.m. Sat.; closed Fri. & Sun.
1989 circulation: 108,918

Fremont
731 N 35th St.
684-4084
Hours: 2–9 p.m. Mon.–Wed.; 2–6 p.m. Thurs.; 11 a.m.–6 p.m. Sat.; closed Fri. & Sun.
1989 circulation: 86,749

Green Lake
7364 Green Lake Drive N
684-7547
Hours: 1–9 p.m. Mon.–Wed.; 10 a.m.–6 p.m. Thurs. & Sat.; closed Fri. & Sun.
1989 circulation: 102,900

Greenwood
8016 Greenwood Ave. N
684-4086
Hours: 1–9 p.m. Mon., Tues. & Thurs.; 10 a.m.–6 p.m. Wed. & Sat.; closed Fri. & Sun.
1989 circulation: 189,453

Henry
425 Harvard Ave. E
684-4715
Hours: 1–9 p.m. Mon. & Tues.; 10 a.m.– 6 p.m. Wed., Thurs. & Sat.; closed Fri. & Sun.
1989 circulation: 155,336

High Point
6338 32nd Ave. SW
684-7454
Hours: 10 a.m.–7 p.m. Mon. & Wed.; 2–7 p.m. Tues., Thurs. & Fri.; 1–6 p.m. Sat.; closed Sun.
1989 circulation: 31,360

Holly Park
6805 32nd Ave. S
386-1905
Hours: 10 a.m.–7 p.m. Mon. & Wed.; 2–7 p.m. Tues., Thurs. & Fri.; 1–6 p.m. Sat.; closed Sun.
1989 circulation: 19,697

Lake City
12501 28th Ave. NE
684-7518
Hours: 10 a.m.–9 p.m. Mon.–Thurs.; 10 a.m.– 6 p.m. Sat.; closed Fri. & Sun.
1989 circulation: 365,792

Madrona-Sally Goldmark
1134 33rd Ave.
684-4705
Hours: 10 a.m.–7 p.m. Mon. & Wed.; 2–7 p.m. Tues., Thurs. & Fri.; 1–6 p.m. Sat.; closed Sun.
1989 circulation: 29,753

Magnolia
2801 34th Ave. W
386-4225
Hours: 1–9 p.m. Mon., Tues. & Thurs.; 10 a.m.–6 p.m. Wed. & Sat.; closed Fri. & Sun.
1989 circulation: 143,951

Montlake
2300 24th Ave. E
684-4720
Hours: Noon–6 p.m. Mon., Thurs. & Sat.; 2–9 p.m. Tues.; closed Wed., Fri. & Sun.
1989 circulation: 42,781

Northeast
6801 35th Ave. NE
684-7539
Hours: 10 a.m.–9 p.m. Mon.–Wed.; 10 a.m.–6 p.m. Fri. & Sat.; 1–5 p.m., Sun.; closed Thurs.
1989 circulation: 481,506

Queen Anne
400 W Garfield St.
386-4227
Hours: 1–9 p.m. Mon., Wed. & Thurs.; 10 a.m.–6 p.m. Tues. & Sat.; closed Fri. & Sun.
1989 circulation: 108,924

Rainier Beach
9125 Rainier Ave. S
386-1906
Hours: 1–9 p.m. Mon., Tues. & Thurs.; 10 a.m.–9 p.m. Wed.; 10 a.m.–6 p.m. Sat.; 1–5 p.m. Sun.; closed Fri.
1989 circulation: 133,593

Southwest
9010 35th Ave. SW
684-7455
Hours: 1–9 p.m. Mon., Tues. & Thurs.; 10 a.m.–9 p.m. Wed.; 10 a.m.–6 p.m. Sat.; closed Fri. & Sun.
1989 circulation: 212,921

University
5009 Roosevelt Way NE
684-4063
Hours: 1–9 p.m. Mon., Tues. & Thurs.; 10 a.m.–6 p.m. Wed. & Sat.; closed Fri. & Sun.
1989 circulation: 185,878

Wallingford-Wilmot
4423 Densmore Ave. N
684-4088
Hours: 5–9 p.m. Mon. & Thurs.; noon–6 p.m. Tues., Fri. & Sat.; closed Wed. & Sun.
1989 circulation: 43,970

West Seattle
2306 42nd Ave. SW
684-7444
Hours: 10 a.m.–9 p.m. Mon.–Wed.; 10 a.m.–6 p.m. Fri. & Sat.; 1–5 p.m. Sun.; closed Thurs.
1989 circulation: 231,124

Mobile Outreach/Bookmobile
425 Harvard Ave. E
684-4713
Hours: 8:30 a.m.–5 p.m. weekdays; closed weekends.
Remember those bookmobiles that visited the schools when you were a kid? They still exist, but not to the same extent they did 20 years ago. Seattle has three bookmobiles and one home service book van that travel to people who do not have access to libraries—the elderly, the homebound, and day care kids. If you'd like to have a bookmobile visit, just call.

OTHER LIBRARIES

Did you know that Microsoft employs 10 librarians and has a special collection of computer literature? Or that your bank probably has a library replete with information on mortgages?

In this information age, libraries exist in almost every major company, hospital, bank, and law firm. Many are either open to the public or accessible upon special request. Call first to ask their hours and to find out if you can wander in—it can be worth it.

We are listing most of the libraries in the Seattle area here, but not all. Hospital libraries with specialties are listed; general health libraries within hospitals aren't. Law firms, most of which have law libraries, aren't listed—look in the phone book and call ahead.

Government libraries

Fort Lewis Library System
Bldg. 2109
Fort Lewis, WA 98433-5000
967-5889
Special collections: Military history.

King County Library System
300 Eighth Ave. N
Seattle, WA 98109
684-9000

Government Research Assistance Library
307 Municipal Bldg.
600 Fourth Ave.
Seattle, WA 98104
684-8031; SCAN 684-8031
Hours: 9 a.m.–5 p.m. weekdays; closed weekends.
Special collections: City and King County information, demographics, environmental impact reports, engineering reports, building code, etc.

Metro Library
821 Second Ave.
Seattle, WA 98104
684-1132
Open to the public 10 a.m.–3 p.m. weekdays.
Special collections: Publications on public transportation, water pollution, toxicants, land use.

Puget Sound Council of Governments
216 First Ave. S
Seattle, WA 98104
464-7532; SCAN 576-7532
Special collections: Regional studies and forecasts, census data. Available for reference or purchase. (Appointment preferred.)

Puget Sound Naval Shipyard Engineering Library
Code 202.5
Puget Sound Naval Shipyard
Bremerton, WA 98314
476-2767
Special collections: Engineering (marine, electrical, electronic, nuclear), naval architecture standards, management, Navy history, industry.

U.S. Army Corps of Engineers Seattle District Library
4735 E Marginal Way S
Seattle, WA 98134
764-3728
Special collections: Technical engineering, law, Army Research Lab, publications, district slide collection, Army and engineering regulations.

U.S. Dept. of Commerce Center
NW and Alaska Fisheries Center
2725 Montlake Blvd.
Seattle, WA 98112
442-7795
Special collections: Fishery biology, management and utilization, oceanography, marine pollution, and food technology.

U.S. Dept. of Commerce
National Oceanic and Atmospheric Administration
Bldg. 3, 7600 Sand Point Way NE
Seattle, WA 98115
526-6241
Special collections: Physical oceanography, marine chemistry, geochemistry, coastal oceanography, ocean engineering, environmental pollution.

U.S. Environmental Protection Agency
Region 10
1200 Sixth Ave.
Seattle, WA 98101
442-1289
Special collections: Air and water pollution, solid waste management, pesticides, environmental law, noise, hazardous wastes, emphasis on states in Region 10.

U.S. National Archives—PNW Region
6125 Sand Point Way NE
Seattle, WA 98115
526-6500
Special collections: 25,000 cu. ft. of Regional office records of federal agencies in Alaska, Idaho, Montana, Oregon, and Washington, 1846 to present. Select microfilm publications from National Archives (50,000 reels).

U.S. National Park Service
Regional Library
83 S King St., Suite 324
Seattle, WA 98104
442-5203
Staff library for Park Service personnel that's open as a reference library to the public. No materials loaned.

Washington Library for the Blind and Physically Handicapped
821 Lenora St.
Seattle, WA 98129
464-6930
Hours: 8:30 a.m.–5 p.m. weekdays; closed weekends.
Special collections: Phonorecords, cassettes, braille, large print, and print reference collection.

Court and law libraries

King County Law Library
W 621 King County Courthouse
Seattle, WA 98104
296-0940

U.S. Courts Library
1018 U.S. Courthouse
1010 Fifth Ave.
Seattle, WA 98104
442-4475
Special collections: Law.

University and college libraries

(Call ahead for addresses and hours)

Bellevue Community College Library Media Center
641-2255; SCAN 334-2255
Special collections: *The New York Times* on microfilm 1851–present; National Union Catalog, 1900–1981.

Cornish Institute of Allied Arts Library
1501 10th Ave. E
Seattle, WA 98102
323-1400

Edmonds Community College Library Media Center
771-1529; SCAN 721-1101
Special collections: Horticulture, law.

Green River Community College Holman Library
833-9111, Ext. 359; SCAN 254-1339
Special collections: ICC reports, 1890–1950; advertising and subliminal persuasion; film and television.

Highline Community College Library
878-3710; SCAN 374-1230
Special collections: Genealogy, law, Federal Depository.

John Bastyr College Library
523-9585
Special collections: Alternative medicine, homeopathy, naturopathic medicine, oriental medicine, nutrition, massage, natural childbirth, botanical medicine, physical therapy.

North Seattle Community College
Instructional Resources Center
527-3607; SCAN 446-3607
Special collections: Electronics, Marxism, Northwest.

Pacific Lutheran University Mortvedt Library
535-7500 (Tacoma)
Special collections: Scandinaviana, religion, and theology.

Seattle Central Community College Library
587-5420

Seattle Pacific University Weter Memorial Library
281-2228
Special collections: Religion, education, nursing.

Seattle University Lemieux Library
296-6230
Special collection: Theology.

Shoreline Community College Ray W. Howard Library Media Center
546-4663
Special collections: Shomberg Collection, 16mm film rental library, regional history.

South Seattle Community College
764-5395; SCAN 628-5395
Special collections: Landscape/horticulture, automotive/diesel mechanics, aviation.

University of Puget Sound Collins Memorial Library
756-3257 (Tacoma), 591-2970, law (Tacoma)
Special collections: Liberal arts, law.

University of Washington Suzzallo Library
543-1760
Staff of 467
Special collections: Pacific Northwest history and culture, historical photography, rare books, Near East, South Asia, Slavic, East Asia, history of medicine; also Humanities and Social Sciences Libraries and Science Libraries. Call individual departments.
Also: Gallagher Law Library, 543-4089; specialty, Anglo-American law, Japanese law.
Health Sciences Library and Information Center, 543-5530
Map Collection Library, 453-9392
Mathematics Research Library, 543-7296
Physics-Astronomy Library, 543-2988

Special interest

(Call ahead for addresses and hours)
As-You-Like-It
329-1794
Special collections: Metaphysics, new age, occult, astrology, Far Eastern thought, rare books on spiritualism, new age music tapes.

Battelle-Seattle Research Center
525-3130
Special collections: Nuclear waste management, human factors in nuclear power plants, and energy policy.

Charles and Emma Frye Art Museum Library
622-9250
Information pertaining to museum's collection.

Genealogy Society of Latter Day Saints
North Seattle Branch
522-1233

Historical Society of Seattle and King Co.
324-1125
Special collections: Seattle, King County, Pacific Northwest, and Alaska history; historical photography, Pacific Northwest maritime history.

Elisabeth C. Miller Horticulture Library
Center for Urban Horticulture Library, UW
543-8616
Special collections: Horticulture, gardening, and garden design; flora of the world, arboreta, and horticulture books and journals.

Mountaineers Library
284-6310
Special collections: Mountaineering, climbing biographies, some rare books on mountaineering and exploration, Mountaineers Foundation Library on conservation and ecology.

Nordic Heritage Museum
W. Johnson Library
789-5707 or 789-5708

Seattle Art Museum Library
Volunteer Park
625-8955

Seattle Genealogical Society Library
682-1410

Sisters of Providence
464-3028
Special collections: Health administration and health planning law.

Washington Library for the Blind and Physically Handicapped
464-6930

Medical libraries

(Call ahead for addresses and hours)
Alcohol and Drug Abuse Institute
543-0937
Special collections: Alcohol abuse, drug abuse.

Children's Hospital and Medical Center Library
526-2118
Special collections: Pediatrics.

Fred Hutchinson Cancer Research Center
467-4314
Special collections: Oncology, biochemistry, molecular biology, genetics, immunology, virology, medicine, pharmacology, hematology.

Group Health Cooperative of Puget Sound Medical Library
326-3393
Special collections: Obstetrics, gynecology, family practice, dermatology, HMOs.

Providence Medical Center
326-5621
Special collections: Clinical medicine, nursing, and cardiovascular medicine.

Business and industry libraries

(Call ahead for addresses and hours)
Advanced Technology Laboratories Library
487-7476
Special collections: Medical ultrasound.

Boeing Archives
655-4756
Special collections: Historical documents of the Boeing Company.

Boeing Company Technical Libraries
237-8311
Special collections: Aerodynamics, aeronautics, artificial intelligence, business, engineering, electronics, computer technology, industrial medicine, International Data Bank, tourism, structures, materials, air transportation.

Brown and Caldwell
281-4000
Special collections: Puget Sound, sanitary engineering.

CH2M Hill Technical Information Center
453-5000
Special collections: Engineering.

Dames and Moore Library
728-0744
Special collections: Marine and aquatic biology, hazardous wastes, geosciences.

Federal Home Loan Bank of Seattle Library
340-8746
Special collections: Savings and loan associations, management, mortgage lending, housing.

Hart Crowser
324-9530
Special collections: Geotechnical engineering, geology/hydrogeology, hazardous waste management and remediation, environmental regulation.

Honeywell, Inc.
356-3645 (Everett)
Special collections: Underwater acoustics, sonar.

John Fluke Mfg. Co.
356-5083 (Everett)
Special collections: Electronics, business, computers.

Microsoft Corp.
936-8239 (Redmond)
Special collections: Computer/microcomputer technical and marketing literature.

Moss Adams Information Center
223-1820
Special collections: Accounting, taxation, estate planning.

The NBBJ Group
223-5124
Special collections: Architecture, planning.

Paccar, Inc.
455-7415
Special collections: Management.

Path
285-3500
Special collections: Tropical diseases, immunizations, primary health care in developing countries.

R.W. Beck and Associates
441-7500
Special collections: Public utilities, civil engineering, solid waste.

Safeco Insurance Co. Library
545-5505
Special collections: Business and insurance, company archives.

Seafirst Bank
358-3292
Special collections: Finance industry, Washington State economy, Northwest industries, economic information on all countries of world, small business.

TRA
682-1133
Special collections: Architecture, airports, building engineering, planning, graphic design.

Newspaper library

(Call ahead for appointment)
Seattle Post-Intelligencer Library
448-8357
Source: Washington State Library System

CITY SOURCES

If you just knew where to call, you could repair your toilet leak, figure out how to read that water meter outside the door, and even report the neighbor who dumped an old washing machine over the edge of the ravine. The city has roomfuls of resourceful people who are waiting breathlessly by the phone for your call.

Let's start with animal queries.

PETS ON THE LOOSE

Seattle has a leash law, one that's heavily enforced. According to city code, the only domestic animals forgiven for wandering without a leash are cats and pigeons—yes, pigeons. Apparently your cat can visit the neighbor's rose garden and thumb (or paw?) its whiskers at the owner. Leashes must be eight feet or shorter, and the animal on the leash must be "in the physical control of a person." In other words, you have to be walking your dog, not the other way around.

Q & A

Q. What should I do with the raccoon that's been eating out of my garbage can?
A. Call the state Game Department to report raccoons and native wildlife, 775-1311. But don't expect them to do your work for you. "Ours is a self-help program," says the receptionist. They'll give you tips on securing your garbage with bungee cords and putting your pet food away. If all else fails, you can borrow a trap and relocate the raccoon

King County Humane Society publishes the Animals and Pets Reference Guide, $2.50, which contains information and directions to resources of all sorts: wild bird clinics, pet poison hotlines, etc. Call 296-7387.

HEARD ON THE STREET

"The Seattle Public Library is one of the few places where everyone is treated in a civilized manner."

A borrower of books

(not to someone else's yard, necessarily). Or, for a fee, the department will send someone out to move the critter for you.

Animal Control Shelter
2061 15th Ave. W
Seattle, WA 98119
386-4254
Animals are kept for three days, then they become available for adoption or are put to sleep. The shelter is open from noon to 6 p.m., seven days a week excluding holidays. It also handles animal complaints.

Animal Nuisance Problems
386-4254

City Municipal Spay/Neuter Clinic
386-4260
Low-cost operations for pets of city residents only. Book ahead—sometimes there's a long waiting list.

County Animal Shelter
(800) 325-6165

Humane Society
641-0080
Taped information.

King County Animal Control
296-7387 or 296-PETS
Complaints, licensing, information outside the city.

King County Rabies Control
296-4880

Lost Pets Hotline
386-7387
Recorded each evening, the hotline describes found animals by age, sex, description, place found, any ID, and whether they are living or dead. If your pet isn't listed, call PAWS, 743-3845 or, on the Eastside, the Bellevue Humane Society, 641-0080.

Seattle Pet Licenses
386-4262
Licenses required for cats and dogs.

State Game Department
775-1311
Report raccoon and other wildlife problems.

CITY ROAD HELP

Need information on the street where you live? The city road maintenance department is divided into two offices, one north of Denny Way and another south of Denny Way.

Road Maintenance Office, North
12555 Ashworth Ave. N
Seattle, WA 98133
684-7508
386-1218 (after 4:30 p.m.)

Road Maintenance Office, South
714 S Charles St.
Seattle, WA 98134
386-1218

Streets and alleys
24-hour line
386-1218
Repair and maintenance, potholes, drainage, surface street flooding.

Asphalt repairs: 386-1225

Signal and sign repair: 386-1206

Sidewalks: 684-5253
Your own responsibility, but the engineering department will assist with questions and complaints.

Sign and signal requests: 684-5086

POWER'S OUT!

Seattle City Light has an information line where you can report problems with your power, trees on the line, or simply the latest outage. Telephone hours are 7:30 a.m.–6 p.m. Mon.–Fri., 8 a.m.–5 p.m. Sat.

Seattle City Light
Info Line: 625-3000
Streetlight repairs: 368-1661
Streetlight complaints: 625-3000
Conservation Information Hotline: 684-3800
Information for those with electrically heated homes and rental properties on conservation and cash discounts and loans for weatherization.
Community relations: 684-3112
Help with problems, billings, services. A trouble-shooting department.

Q & A

Q. My street is so dim I'm afraid to walk the dog after dusk. How can we get better lighting?
A. Call the same folks who light your house, Seattle City Light, at 684-3266, and they'll determine if your street has inadequate lighting. They might do something about it, depending on your neighborhood's clout. Or call the complaint line, 625-3000.

WATERWORKS

Information on your water meter, water efficient gardening, how to find leaks—Seattle's water department is a fount of information, so to speak.

The department puts out several publications you can order by calling 684-5849 and requesting them by number:

Water

#201 How to Locate and Read Your Meter
#202 The Water Supply
#203 Protect Your Pipes In Winter
#205 Detecting Leaks
#206 Fix That Faucet
#207 Repairing Toilet Leaks
#208 Watermain and Water Service Connections
#210 Special Tap Charge
#211 Inspection Requirements for Private Water Line Repair or Construction
#501 Free Water Conservation Kit
#503 Energy Costs Going Through the Roof
#506 Water-Saving Fixtures
#507 Why Conserve Water?
#509 Water Trivia
#510 Are You Wasting Water?
#511 Water Efficient Gardening
#515 Household Water Budget

Sewer

#401 Single-Family Residence Sewer Charge
#402 Duplex Sewer Charge
#403 Commercial Account Sewer Charge and Irrigation Allowances
#404 Drainage Fee

General and Payment Information

#101 Reading Your Combined Utility Bill
#102 Information For Rental Property Owners
#103 When Customers Change at a Property
#104 If the Building on Your Property Is Vacant
#105 Utility Credit Program
#106 Combined Utility Appeal Form
#107 Payment Stations
#108 Unscheduled Estimates of Water Consumption

Other water department numbers

Seattle Water Department
10th Floor, Dexter Horton Bldg.
710 Second Ave.
Seattle, WA 98104
684-5885

The water department offers a free conservation kit to save up to 20% of your water usage.

The first of every year, all customers receive a publication listing water department numbers they might need. Request one by calling 684-5874.

Billing Information: 684-5900
Conservation Office: 684-5879
Credit and Collections: 684-5888
Drainage (general information): 684-7774
Emergency Service: 386-1800 (24 hours)
Service and Inspection: 684-5800
Sewers (backups, permits, and inspection): 684-5253
Surface Street Flooding: 386-1218 (24 hours)
Water Quality Information: 684-7404
Seattle Conservation Corps: 684-0191

The Department of Human Resources has teams that provide neighborhood cleanup, recycling, stream rehabilitation, and waterfront cleanup.

Q & A

Q. I think I have asbestos in my ceiling. What should I do?
A. Call the Hazardous Waste Hotline, 296-4692, a service of the Seattle/King Co. Health Department. The hotline acts as a clearinghouse and will tell you where you can get your ceiling tested and whether it's a problem or not. They can also tell you how and where to dispose of asbestos.

Litter in public areas: 684-5253
Litter on private property: (800) LITTERS or 684-7899
Litter receptacles: 684-5306
Litter around dumpsters: 684-0820
Alley litter: 386-1218
Illegal dumping: 684-5349
Cedar Hills Landfill (accepts hazardous wastes, call ahead): 296-4490

COMPLAINTS, COMPLAINTS

The city has an ombudsman's office where complaints about all kinds of things are directed. This office has consumer books, a city directory, and hotline numbers. If you can't get satisfaction in the departments or you just can't get through the busy signals, call the Citizen Services Bureau, 684-8811. It's a small office, but complaints are taken seriously. Someone will always return your call.

Complaints vary. The bureau doesn't take complaints about the police department or elected officials, but does take everything else. For example, a hot topic for complainers is seaplane noise on Lake Union. The bureau compiles Lake Union seaplane complaints and passes them along to a committee of residents of the area and seaplane companies.

King County Ombudsman: 296-3452

Excessive noise complaints: 296-4632

Seattle Parks and Recreation Department (compliments and concerns): 684-4837

STARRING... THE CITY BIGWIGS

The city of Seattle has its own TV channel, Seattle City Cable 28 (SCC28). The channel provides information about city government services, programs, and meetings. It's coordinated by the Seattle Public Library as part of its information services function.

What's on Channel 28? Full city council meetings (yawn), selected city council committee meetings, and programs produced by or for city departments, among other things. There's also a bulletin board of city events and public service announcements between programs.

Programs are daily at 9 a.m., 1 p.m., 5 p.m., and 9 p.m. To receive a weekly copy of the SCC28 schedule, call 684-8888.

Seattle City Cable
307 Municipal Bldg.
Seattle, WA 98104
684-5384

FROM GAVEL TO MICROFICHE

Very often there is valuable information hidden away in the courts, and accessing court files is not difficult, although it is time consuming. With a few exceptions, court documents are public records. All you need is the names of the parties involved.

ACCESSING COURT RECORDS

At King County Superior Court you can access criminal, civil, probate, and domestic case records for the last 10 years. Go to the sixth floor of the courthouse to the clerk's office, file department. Look up the name of the parties involved on microfiche to find a case number. Take the case number to the clerks and wait until they bring you the records. (For older cases, you can find the records on microfiche filed by name.) It's usually busy and you'll have to wait about 10 minutes. Great spot for attorney watching.

Best time to check court records? First thing in the morning. Hours are 8:30 a.m.–4:30 p.m.

SEATTLE'S COURTS

King County District Court
King County Courthouse
Third and James
Seattle, WA 98104
296-3617
Traffic cases: 296-3565; Civil Department: 296-3550; Small Claims Court: 296-3558.

King County Superior Court
Third and James
Seattle, WA 98104
Clerk: 296-9300; Info: 296-9100; Juvenile Court Clerk: 296-1413. Civil and criminal cases.

Municipal Court
600 Third Ave.
Seattle, WA 98104
684-5600
Court Administrator: 684-8707; parking citations: 684-5410.

State Court of Appeals
Clerk: 464-7750
Cases appealed from superior court decisions, both civil and criminal. Takes two years with approximately 2,000 cases pending now.

U.S. Bankruptcy Court
315 Park Place Bldg., Suite 315
1200 Sixth Ave.
Seattle, WA 98101
442-7545
Only bankruptcy cases (7,000 in 1988 in Seattle).

U.S. Court of Appeals
442-2937
Handles appeals from U.S. District Court, Bankruptcy Court, etc. Second-highest court, under U.S. Supreme Court. The Ninth Circuit Court of Appeals has a branch office in Seattle; headquarters are in San Francisco.

U.S. District Court
1010 Fifth Ave.
Seattle, WA 98104
442-5598
Federal civil cases and criminal felonies.

Consumer affairs/legal referrals

American Civil Liberties Union of Washington
642-2180
General information and referrals.

Better Business Bureau
448-8888
Answers consumers' inquiries about reliability and performance of companies and organizations. Alerts consumers to fraud and misrepresentation, helps clear up misunderstandings. BBB has free booklets on many subjects (after the first free one, they cost 50 cents each). There is a 24-hour information line, 448-8477, and a 24-hour business reporting line, 448-6222.

Free Legal Clinics
624-9365

King County Bar Association Lawyer Referral & Information Service
623-2551
Hours 9 a.m.–4:30 p.m. (closed 12:30–1:30 p.m.). Half hour talk with a $20 fee if referral is made.

State Attorney General
Legal complaints and inquiries, 464-6684 or (800) 551-4636

U.S. Attorneys
442-7970

A HOT LINE ON INFORMATION

There are hotlines for almost everything, from red tide blooms (when you are warned not to eat shellfish from Puget Sound beaches) to information for gay youth. Remember that hotlines, like hot issues, come and go.

Hottest hotlines

Aging and Services for Developmentally Disabled (800) 562-6028
AIDS Hotline: 296-4999 or (800) 678-1595
AIDS Information Hotline: (800) 342-AIDS
AIDS Support Group: 322-2437
AIDS Foundation, Northwest: 329-6923
Air Pollution Control, Puget Sound: 296-7330
Al-Anon: (800) 356-9996
Al-Anon Info Service: 625-0000
Alcohol & Drug Detoxification Center: 296-7650
Alcohol & Drugs: 722-3700 (24 hour)
Alcoholics Anonymous: 587-2838
Alzheimers Assn. of Puget Sound: 365-7488
American Cleft Palate Educ.: (800) 24-CLEFT (24 hours)
American Diabetes Assn.: 632-4576 or (800) 628-8808
American Heart Assn.: 632-6881 or (800) 562-6718
Auto Safety Hotline: (800) 424-9393
Battered Women, New Beginnnings Shelter: 522-9472
Burning Bans: 296-5100
Business Licensing: (800) 562-8203
Cancer Lifeline: 461-4542 (24 hour)
Chemical Manufacturer's Assn., referral center: (800) 262-8200
Child Protective Services, 721-4115 (24 hour)
Child Protective Services, referral: (800) 562-5624
Cocaine Anonymous: 722-6117
Community Info Line, Crisis Clinic: 461-3200
Composting Hotline: 633-0224
Consumer Line: 464-6811
Consumer Price Index Hotline: 442-0645
Cooperative Extension Food Line, King Co.: 296-3443 or (800) 325-6165
Crisis Clinic: 461-3222 (24 hour)
Crisis Line: (800) 244-5767
Disability Insurance Benefits: (800) 562-6074
Divorce Lifeline: 624-2959
Domestic Violence Hotline: (800) 562-6025
Drunk Driving Legal Assistance: 624-8105 (north Seattle), 243-6305 (south Seattle)
Emergency Spill: 867-7000 (24 hour)

Emotional Crisis: 461-3222
Epstein-Barr Hotline (Portland): (503) 684-5261
Family Violence Unit: 684-7770
Fire Permits/Forest Fire Reporting: (800) 527-3305
Fire Prevention: 386-1450
Gamblers Anonymous: 464-9514
Gay Youth Information: 322-0797
Hazard Hotline: 296-4692
Herpes: 223-3272 (Tues.–Thurs., 6:30–9 p.m.)
Homework Hotline (Tues. & Thurs., 6–8:30 p.m.): 281-6744 or 281-6508
Insurance Commissioner Hotline: (800) 562-6900
Insurance Info Hotline: (800) 221-4954
Internal Revenue Hotline: (800) 424-1040
Job Openings, City of Seattle: 684-7999
King Co. Sexual Assault Resource Center: 226-7273 (24 hour)
Language Bank, American Red Cross: 323-2345
Learning Disabilities Info & Referral: 932-5507
Lesbian Resource Center: 322-3953
Literacy Hotline: (800) 323-2550
Lottery Winning Numbers: (800) 545-7510
Lung Line: (800) 222-LUNG
MADD (Mothers Against Drunk Drivers): 624-6903
Marine Information: 526-NOAA
Millionair Club: 728-5600
Missing Children Clearinghouse: (800) 543-5678
Narcotics Anonymous: 329-1618
Noise Complaint Hotline: 382-3760
Nursing Home Patient Abuse and Neglect Reports: (800) 562-6078
Ombudsman, Long Term Care: 838-6810 or (800) 422-1384
Ombudsman, King Co.: 562-6028
Operation Lookout Nat'l Center for Missing Youth: (800) 782-7335
Options for Pregnancy: 575-4559
Planned Parenthood: 328-7711
Poison Center Emergency Info: 526-2121
Rape Relief Crisis Line: 632-7273
Recycling Hotline: (800) 732-9253
Red Tide Hotline: (800) 562-5632
Runaway Hotline: (800) 448-4663
Sexaholics Anonymous: 548-9538
Sexual Assault Center: 223-3047
Sexually Transmitted Diseases: 223-4756
Shelter for Battered Women, Info: 461-3200
Shelter Runaway Center: 725-8888
Speech and Hearing Hotline: (800) 638-TALK
Steelheaders' Hotline: 526-8530
Survivors of Suicide (Crisis Clinic): 461-3210
Turkey Hotline (USDA Meat and Poultry): (800) 535-4555
U-Cut Xmas Tree (Thanksgiving to 12/25): 296-3428 (24 hour)
Victim/Witness Advocacy: 684-7777
Volunteer Bureau of Greater Seattle: 461-3765
Washington State Dairy Council: 632-9335
Welfare Fraud Reports: (800) 562-6906
Whale Hotline: (800) 562-8832
Whitewater Hotline (April–Nov.): 526-8530
Women in Recovery: 722-6117
YMCA Teen Hotline: 382-5437
Youth Suicide Prevention Center: 481-0560

TOLL FREE NUMBERS

Don't you just love that 800 you find in front of some phone numbers? It means it's absolutely free to you, the phone consumer. We called the US West Directories number, (800) 422-8793, and found that you can purchase two AT&T directories that cover the entire U.S. They are *800 Consumer Directory,* $9.95; and *800 Business to Business,* $14.95. They can be ordered by calling (800) 426-8686.

And there's one more directory organized with listings from US West and other sources. It offers more than 2,000 product and service classifications: *The Great 800 Toll Free Directory,* P.O. Box 6944, Jackson, MS 39212, $49.95 plus $4 for handling.

MEDIA RESOURCES

Yes, it's permissible to just call up a reporter and ask what he or she knows about a subject, but be prepared to answer questions about why you care in return. The *Seattle Times* apparently got tired of answering those calls and came up with Info-Line, a free 24-hour recorded telephone service with information on everything from the latest videos in the stores to localized weather forecasts.

The main number for the InfoLine is 464-2000; digits of popular categories are:
Horoscopes: 3000
Mortgage rates, locally: 5000
Northwest ski area operators' report: 9011 or 2443
Northwest weather menu: 9900
Soap opera updates: 6000
Sports report: 9600
Stock market update: 9002
StockQuote hotline: 9805

The *Times* offers other services to its readers too. If you have a problem with articles or ink rubbing off on your hands, call the Ombudsman, 464-8979. If you've been ripped off by a local company, submit problems in writing to Times Troubleshooter, P.O. Box 70, Seattle, WA 98111-0070. The *Times* Home Economist will answer food questions about recipes that have appeared in the *Times*: 464-2300. And major professional and college sports scores are recorded on tape at 464-2290.

The *Post-Intelligencer* has a troubleshooter too, called "Action" column. Submit problems in writing to P.O. Box 1909, Seattle, WA 98111-1909.

For back copies of the *P-I*, call 464-2198.

DATABASES

In this electronic age, it's easier to call up the specific information you need than go pawing through documents. Databases can be financial, statistical, bibliographical, or full text. Vendors are as common as flies on the windowsill in July.

The *Times* and *P-I* libraries use Data Times, a database that includes articles from those papers and 30 or 40 other newspapers. The papers won't do searches for the public, but the public can subscribe to Data Times. Start-up fee for documentation on how to use the system is $85, then there are two options: a monthly fee of $95 with on-line time of $1.59 per minute, or a $15 monthly fee and $2.33 per minute on-line fee.

The University of Washington uses Dialog, a database vendor. UW librarians will do searches on subjects for students, faculty, libraries, businesses, and individuals. The subject database search is $5 per article. Call UW Resources Sharing Program, 543-1878.

LOTTERY INFO

Here you are holding what you're sure is the winning ticket to a $4 million Lotto—but how to find out?

The Washington State Lottery has a hotline, (800) 545-7510, with up-to-date information. Drawings are Wednesdays and Saturdays at 6:59 p.m. and are televised live on KSTW Channel 11. If you miss that and aren't satisfied with the hotline, you can call the Lottery Regional Office, 764-6455 during business hours, or simply go back to the store where you bought your ticket and ask. Outlets have reports.

BEYOND 911: EMERGENCY SERVICES

Call 911 and this is what happens: The city's emergency and crime reporting dispatch center receives the call and routes it to whatever departments need to respond. Your phone number and address appear on the screen as soon as you dial, and emergency information is being passed along as the dispatcher sends out the call. From the time you dial, it takes three seconds to get someone dispatched to help you. Approximately 1.3 million calls are made to 911 in King County per year.

Generally 20% of calls are fire and aid calls and 80% crime. There are 250 dispatchers and call receivers in the system; there's a 20–30% turnover rate due to stress on the job.

But there are emergency services numbers beyond that familiar one:

Civil Defense/Emergency Management
296-3830

Emergency Services Office of Seattle
386-1497

Federal Emergency Management Agency (FEMA)
487-4600

The trouble is that if you wait until you need information from one of these departments, it will most likely be too late. They deal with flooding, earthquakes, hazardous material spills, and natural and man-made disasters.

A few years ago FEMA was laughed out of sight with its recommendations in case of nuclear war, but the agencies do publish booklets on food and water storage, food and water rotation, emergency medical kits, and sanitation. They also put out a basic preparedness checklist.

There are no emergency bomb shelters like the ones we saw in the 1950s. The emergency shelters now are schools and buildings that can house people and store goods. These change according to the disaster so people won't struggle to get to a shelter only to find it was destroyed in the same disaster that demolished their house. The shelter designation is made *after* the emergency.

WHEN IT'S NOT A TEST

Love those annoying beeping "emergency broadcast" tests that interrupt talk shows on the radio? They are more than annoying—they are part of a process that begins as soon as there is a man-made or natural emergency threatening the city or the nation. In Seattle KIRO 710 AM is the designated emergency station. (If for any reason KIRO is unable to broadcast, other stations will take over according to a predetermined ranking.)

An emergency command comes directly from the president, governor, or the city of Seattle (mayor, city executive, emergency management). All commands are sent wireless—no telephones are used. If the message is from the president, it's sent via satellite. Once an emergency is declared and a message received, all radio stations other than the designated one are forbidden to stay on the air. Only the emergency message is allowed on the air. To ensure the message is correct, a sealed envelope is kept at KIRO with a "code of the month." This code is verified as it is sent from either the president, governor, or city emergency officials. Before the message is read, the station transmits the familiar test tone, but the announcer says several times, "This is not a test," followed by the message. The system is tested weekly.

Q & A

Q. When was the emergency broadcast system last used in Seattle?
A. When Mount St. Helens blew.

NOT ONLY CHICKENS

One of the most useful resources in the county is the Cooperative Extension Agency, a program through Washington State University. The extension service started as an agency to give assistance to farmers and their wives and has been expanded to help people with their daily lives. Brochures and tapes are available on money management, food processing and nutrition, and other down-to-earth subjects. But the extension service in King County is most often thought of in connection with gardening.

The public can get a free general catalog of over 200 tapes available by calling 296-DIAL. You can ask for tapes on specific topics: for example, what to do about the black spots on your roses. The service folks are so helpful, you wish they'd just come home with you.

You're not alone in your Northwest gardening problems. The most-often requested tapes at the County Extension Service office are Slugs, Slugs II, Slugs III, Woody Weeds, Blackberries, and Morning Glories.

Several seasonal tapes are available too; in spring and summer, there's a fresh produce hotline and a where-to-cut-trees tape (once requested over 1,000 times on a weekend!).

Other extension services

Master Gardener Program
296-3962 or 296-3440, 10 a.m.–4 p.m., Mon.–Fri.
Twenty-two locations manned by volunteers who love to solve plant problems. Call for locations. Free.

Seattle Food Garden Project
296-3950
Educational gardening project relating to food production in the city. This is usually directed at the low-income population. The group offers a newsletter of information useful to all gardeners in the city.

More key sources

Chautauqua Northwest
1200 Fifth Ave., Suite 510
Seattle, WA 98101
223-1378
Retirees network for community service. Conducts senior market research.

Crisis Clinic
461-3222 or (800) 244-5767
Community Information Line:
461-3200 or (800) 621-INFO
The Crisis Clinic answers hundreds of calls per day. The Crisis Line provides crisis intervention; the Community Information Line helps callers locate appropriate resources. The Crisis Clinic also puts out a list of community groups and resources. The several-inch-thick document is available for browsing at the Seattle Public Library education desk.

Greater Seattle Chamber of Commerce
461-7200
Provides publications for those relocating to Seattle. Sells publications and reports over the counter or with written requests. The chamber has population, economic, and housing information.

Historic Preservation
King County
296-4858

Pike Market Reader Board
624-4500/ext. 2836
Up-to-date information on fresh products at the market.

U.S. Government Printing Office Bookstore
Federal Bldg., Suite 194
915 Second Ave.
Seattle, WA 98174
442-4270
Over 1,000 titles, including the Congressional Directory. Open 8 a.m.–3:30 p.m.

HISTORICAL SOCIETIES

Assn. of King County Historical Organizations
1115 Smith Tower
Seattle, WA 98104
296-8693

Black Heritage Society of Washington State, Inc.
P.O. Box 22565
Seattle, WA 98122
281-6180

Center for Wooden Boats
1010 Valley St.
Seattle, WA 98109
382-2628

Coast Guard Museum/Northwest
1519 Alaskan Way S
Pier 36
Seattle, WA 98134
286-9608

Early Ford V-8 Club of America
P.O. Box 12613
Seattle, WA 98111
821-1283

Electrek: Museum at Georgetown Steam Plant
6607 13th Ave. S
P.O. Box 80322
Seattle, WA 98108
728-1755

Highline School District Museum at Sunnydale
15631 Eighth Ave. S
Seattle, WA 98148
443-2385

Historic Seattle Preservation and Development Authority
207½ First Ave. S
Seattle, WA 98104
622-6952

Historical Society of Seattle and King County
2700 24th Ave. E
Seattle, WA 98112
324-1125

Klondike Gold Rush National Historical Park
117 S Main St.
Seattle, WA 98104
442-7220

Landmarks Magazine
835 Securities Bldg.
Seattle, WA 98101
622-3538

Magic Lantern Society
2902 28th St. SE
Auburn, WA 98002
833-7784

Marymoor Museum
6046 West Sammamish Pkwy. NE
Redmond, WA 98073
885-3684

Morasch House Historical Society
Sea-Tac Museum
(Highline Park Board)
1809 S 140th
Seattle, WA 98168
241-5960

Museum of Flight Foundation
9404 East Marginal Way S
Seattle, WA 98108
764-5700

National Archives/Pacific Northwest
6125 Sand Point Way NE
Seattle, WA 98115
526-6507

Newcastle Historical Society
7331 Lakemont Blvd. SE
Issaquah, WA 98027
255-6996
Private tool museum.

Nordic Heritage Museum
3014 NW 67th St.
Seattle, WA 98117
789-5707

Northwest Seaport
1002 Valley St.
Seattle, WA 98109-4332
447-9800

Pacific Northwest Labor History Assn.
P.O. Box 75048
Seattle, WA 98125

Pioneer Assn. of the State of Washington
Pioneer Hall
1642 43rd Ave. E
Seattle, WA 98112
325-0888

Pioneers of Columbia City and Vicinity
4803 43rd Ave. S
Seattle, WA 98118
723-2775

Puget Sound Railway Historical Assn.
Puget Sound and Snoqualmie Valley RR
P.O. Box 459
Snoqualmie, WA 98065
746-4025 (info on train runs)
888-3030 (Snoqualmie depot)

Roman Catholic Archdiocese of Seattle Archives
910 Marion St.
Seattle, WA 98104
382-4857

Scouting Trail Museum
10021 26th Ave. SW
Seattle, WA 98146
767-6467
Boy and Girl Scout memorabilia.

SCW Publications
620 Fourth and Pike Bldg.
Seattle, WA 98101
622-4256
Publisher of *Little Histories.*

Unlimited Hydroplane Hall of Fame and Museum
P.O. Box 48342
Seattle, WA 98148
243-3816
Museum is soon moving to Tacoma's Waterway.

Virginia V Foundation
911 Western Ave., Suite 405
Seattle, WA 98104
624-9119

Washington State Historical Society
315 N Stadium Way
Tacoma, WA 98403
593-2830

Washington State Jewish Historical Society
2031 Third Ave.
Seattle, WA 98121
443-1903

Washington Trust for Historic Preservation
204 First Ave. S
Seattle, WA 98104
624-7880

Waterfront Awareness
2342 34th Ave. S
Seattle, WA 98144
543-0206

Wing Luke Asian Museum
407 Seventh Ave. S
Seattle, WA 98104
623-5124

About the Author

Theresa Morrow is the quintessential Seattle native. Not only was she born in Seattle, she was raised in a classic box house on Capitol Hill, learned to roller-skate in an alley, swam at Denny Blaine Park, and ate burgers at Dick's. She was kissed by a Seafair pirate when she was 15, attended Holy Names Academy, Seattle University, and the UW, and worked as a reporter for *The Seattle Times.*

Her father was one of the founders of Group Health Cooperative and her brother works for Boeing (doesn't everyone's brother?). Theresa wears REI turtlenecks and ragg wool sweaters to work at her office in Pioneer Square. A regular contributor to regional publications, she wrote the *Seattle Survival Guide* in self-defense.

Future Editions

Please tell us about the groups, organizations, and special features that you feel should be covered in the next edition of *Seattle Survival Guide*. Send your suggestions and best-kept Seattle secrets to:

Seattle Survival Guide
Sasquatch Books
1931 Second Avenue
Seattle, WA 98101